Geoff Harcourt
Source: Tony Jedrej, *Cambridge Evening News*

MARKETS, UNEMPLOYMENT AND ECONOMIC POLICY

Geoff Harcourt has made substantial and wide-ranging contributions to economics in general, and to post-Keynsian economics in particular. In this volume more than forty leading economists pay tribute to and critically evaluate his work.

In particular, contributions focus on:

- the methodological foundations of economic policy-making;
- theoretical and applied analyses of comparative economic systems;
- specific issues in economic policy, including privatization and unemployment.

Contributors are drawn from several countries and represent a wide range of schools in economics.

Philip Arestis is Professor of Economics at the University of East London.

Gabriel Palma is Lecturer in Economics in the Faculty of Economics and Politics, University of Cambridge.

Malcolm Sawyer is Professor of Economics in the School of Business and Economic Studies, University of Leeds.

ROUTLEDGE FRONTIERS OF POLITICAL ECONOMY

MARKETS, UNEMPLOYMENT AND ECONOMIC POLICY

Essays in Honour of Geoff Harcourt
Volume Two

Edited by
Philip Arestis, Gabriel Palma
and Malcolm Sawyer

London and New York

First published 1997
by Routledge
11 New Fetter Lane, London EC4P 4EE

Simultaneously published in the USA and Canada
by Routledge
29 West 35th Street, New York, NY 10001

Typeset in Times by Solidus (Bristol) Limited
Printed and bound in Great Britain by
Mackays of Chatham PLC, Chatham, Kent

British Library Cataloguing in Publication Data
A catalogue record for this book is available from the British Library

Library of Congress Cataloging in Publication Data
A catalogue record for this book has been requested

ISBN 0–415–13390–4

CONTENTS

CONTENTS

CONTENTS

ix

CONTENTS

x

CONTRIBUTORS

Philip Arestis, University of East London, United Kingdom
Tony Atkinson, Nuffield College, University of Oxford, United Kingdom
Samuel Bowles, University of Massachusetts, United States of America
Maurizio Caserta, University of Catania, Italy
Ha-Joon Chang, University of Cambridge, United Kingdom
Victoria Chick, University College London, United Kingdom
John Cornwall, Dalhousie University, Canada
Wendy Cornwall, Mount Saint Vincent University, Halifax, Canada
Andy Cosh, University of Cambridge, United Kingdom
Amitava Krishna Dutt, University of Notre Dame, United States of America
Herbert Gintis, University of Massachusetts, United States of America
Fred Gruen, Australian National University, Australia
Ruth Hancock, King's College, University of London, United Kingdom
Laurence Harris, School of Oriental and African Studies, University of London, United Kingdom
Alan Hughes, University of Cambridge, United Kingdom
Murray C. Kemp, University of New South Wales, Australia
Michael Kitson, University of Cambridge, United Kingdom
Michael A. Landesmann, Johannes Kepler Universität, Linz, Austria
Tony Lawson, University of Cambridge, United Kingdom
Mervyn K. Lewis, University of Nottingham, United Kingdom
Ngo Van Long, McGill University, Canada
John McCombie, University of Cambridge, United Kingdom
Bruce McFarlane, University of Newcastle, Australia
Paul Madden, University of Manchester, United Kingdom
Gay Meeks, University of Cambridge, United Kingdom
Geoff Meeks, University of Cambridge, United Kingdom
J. Stan Metcalfe, University of Manchester, United Kingdom
Jonathan Michie, University of Cambridge, United Kingdom
Edward J. Nell, New School for Social Research, New York, United States of America

Peter Nolan, University of Cambridge, United Kingdom
Ugo Pagano, Università di Siena, Italy
Gabriel Palma, University of Cambridge, United Kingdom
Catherine Waddams Price, University of Warwick, United Kingdom
Peter Riach, De Montfort University, Leicester, United Kingdom
Jochen Runde, University of Cambridge, United Kingdom
Malcolm Sawyer, University of Leeds, United Kingdom
Anwar Shaikh, New School for Social Research, New York, United States
of America
Koji Shimomura, Kobe University, Japan
Ajit Singh, University of Cambridge, United Kingdom
Ian Steedman, Manchester Metropolitan University, United Kingdom
Trevor Stegman, University of New South Wales, Australia
Hugh Stretton, University of Adelaide, Australia
Ferdinando Targetti, Universita degli Studi di Trento, Italy
Antony Thirlwall, University of Kent at Canterbury, United Kingdom
K. Vela Velupillai, Queen's University of Belfast, United Kingdom
John Wells, University of Cambridge, United Kingdom
Geoff Whittington, University of Cambridge, United Kingdom
Frank Wilkinson, University of Cambridge, United Kingdom

FOREWORD

Joe Isaac

A Festschrift which runs into two volumes hardly needs a preface, especially as each volume has an introduction giving a copious account of Geoff Harcourt's life and work. But I could not refuse the honour and pleasure occasioned by the invitation to write the foreword to this volume.

One of the more satisfying rewards of teaching is to encounter students who show the potential of outclassing their teacher in academic ability and achievement. Geoff was one such student in the batch of outstanding students who passed through the University of Melbourne in the early postwar years.

For the younger teachers of economics brought up on *The General Theory*, it was a time of infectious excitement and optimism. There was virtual unanimity on what was to be done: most of us were 'wet' economists at the time; high unemployment, poverty, social and health deprivation were to be relics of the past. 'The Welfare State' was within easy reach, as governments in many countries and of various persuasions, fortified by the community's strong sense of collective responsibility manifest during the still recent Second World War, pledged commitment to it. In retrospect, many of us might have been starry-eyed politically.

This rosy view was sustained for two decades, after which it waned and was overtaken by the philosophy of individualism and the wisdom of allowing the market to operate largely unrestrained by government intervention. Despite a generally high level of chronic unemployment, increased inequality in the distribution of incomes and the creation of a substantial underclass in many countries, economic policy has come to be judged more by the deregulatory processes being adopted and less by the outcomes of the policy. This is now the tenor of mainstream economic thinking.

It will be evident from most of Geoff's writings that he is not in this mainstream; rather, he has been warning, Cassandra-like, against it. For much of his academic life, Geoff has gone against the fashions of contemporary economic thought, at least on matters relating to the efficiency and fairness of the market mechanism and the prevailing phobia about government intervention. This is not surprising. He does not hide his values behind any pretence of positivism, and his policy prescriptions must be considered in the context of his values:

> to make the world a better place for ordinary men and women, to produce a more just and equitable society. In order to do that, you have to understand how particular societies work and where the pockets of power are, and how you can either alter those or work within them and produce desirable results for ordinary people, not just for the people who have power. I see economics as very much a moral as well as a social science and very much the handmaiden of progressive thought.[1]

True to the Cambridge tradition of his mentors he regards the task of the economist to be fruit-bearing, as well as light-bearing.

The large number of contributors to the two volumes of the Festschrift in his honour, is testimony to the fact that his contribution spans a very wide area of economics, in the fields of both theory and policy. Nearly all the papers in this volume deal with some part of his work. This is a remarkable achievement in an age of specialization. It testifies also to the high regard, esteem and affection with which he is held by the international academic community.

Sustaining his academic achievements are his person qualities – integrity, courage, generosity, informality, a sense of humour, and extraordinary energy.

As one who was privileged to have known him and has followed his career from the very threshold of academic life and, perhaps, even to have nudged him slightly in the direction he ultimately took, I bask in his success, and wish him many more years of productivity. Perhaps he might care to tackle econometrics, the one missing item in his extensive repertoire.

NOTE

1   Hamouda, O. (ed.) (1986) *Controversies in Political Economy, Selected Essays of G. C. Harcourt*, New York, New University Press, pp. 4–5.

GEOFF HARCOURT:
A TRIBUTE

For anyone working in the economics faculty at Cambridge, as I used to, Geoff was a central figure. Almost always to be found in his office, he was so genuinely friendly.

With a very broad range of interests in economic analysis, he was willing to provide help and advice to anyone wishing to prepare work for publication. He knew most of the faculty and was always ready to be consulted, ready to provide advice and information about whom to consult about any particular economic issue and about who might be helpful on specific subjects. Though steadily working himself, he was always ready to discuss any aspect of particular issues of economics. I always felt free to drop by his office and discuss with him whatever topic I was interested in working on. He always responded with useful suggestions. He never gave one the feeling that one was interfering with his own interests or projects.

I always felt he constituted a kind of centre to consult about who might be helpful on a wide range of topics. I never felt that I was unduly impinging on his time for work on his own projects. I almost never came to the faculty, for any purpose, without stopping at his office and having a pleasant and often highly informative communication with him on a variety of topics in economics.

Richard Goodwin
University of Siena, Italy

INTRODUCTION

This is one of two volumes published to celebrate the major contributions Geoff Harcourt has made to the discipline of economics and to post-Keynesian economics in particular. During his illustrious career, Geoff has gained enormous respect and admiration from colleagues and friends of varied persuasions, as is amply evidenced by the contributions to these two volumes.

Geoff Harcourt, 'an Australian patriot and a Cambridge economist' in his own words,[1] was born in Melbourne on 27 June 1931. At school he wanted to be a vet – he has always loved birds and other animals – and mostly did science. He took some economics only to 'make up the numbers', as he puts it, but did very well at it, and very badly at physics, so that luckily for us and unluckily for all the animals in the world, he proceeded to do economics at the University of Melbourne. It was Cambridge-oriented economics that he studied there, which he has loved ever since.

It was clear, even at that early stage in Geoff's academic life, that great things were going to happen in the future. His undergraduate dissertation was a clear pointer to the future. Oligopolistic price theory, with firms having as their objective the 'desire for secure profits as much as maximum profits', was integrated with the macroeconomic system of Keynes's *General Theory*, in an attempt to study the behaviour of Australian companies during the Great Depression. Effective demand, especially investment, pricing under conditions of imperfect competition, applied economics and more, were all there. The main ingredients of his undergraduate dissertation were clearly visible in his master's degree dissertation, although its theme was a radically different one, namely a pilot survey of income and saving in Melbourne.

In late July 1955 he and Joan married, 'lived happily ever after', and left Melbourne in mid-August for King's College, Cambridge – where else, indeed? Geoff's Ph.D. turned out to be a study of the economic implications of using historical cost accounting procedures for price formation in a period of inflation, which inevitably entailed implications for measuring income for dividend and tax purposes. It was at this time that Geoff acquainted himself with Robinson's *The Accumulation of Capital*, then newly published. Indeed, he read a paper on the main propositions of the book to three consecutive sessions of the research students seminar, chaired by Robin Marris. Joan Robinson attended the third session. She actually did not think much of that group of students with the exception of 'a chap called Harcourt'. *The*

Accumulation of Capital provided the *core* which has inspired Geoff's contributions to economics, and his teaching. This is not difficult to understand now, perhaps, given the influence on both Joan Robinson and Geoff Harcourt of the writings of Smith, Ricardo, Marx, Marshall, Keynes, Kahn, Kalecki and Sraffa.

Geoff returned to Australia after his Ph.D. at Cambridge, to take up his first lecturing job in the Department of Economics at the University of Adelaide. It was there that he met Eric Russell, his greatest mentor and friend in Australia. On Geoff's own admission he learned a great deal from Eric, including theory, applied economics and policy as it relates to the real world, and how to teach undergraduates economics. He lectured on Kaldor's economics and wrote a critique of Kaldor's theories of distribution and growth as they had been developed by that time. That critique concentrated on the pricing behaviour of the consumption and investment goods sectors, and focused essentially on the full-employment assumption adopted by Kaldor. It essentially argued that the full-employment assumption required strong conditions on pricing behaviour in the two sectors in order for the distributive mechanism to work and for Kaldor's growth models to behave in the intended way. Geoff argued that it was better to drop the un-Keynesian full-employment assumption in favour of keeping the distribution mechanism, a more realistic and relevant aspect of Kaldor's theoretical framework. At about this time he wrote 'The accountant in a golden age', published in 1965 (*Oxford Economic Papers*), which is perhaps his best-known paper after the 1969 *Journal of Economic Literature* survey.

In 1963 Geoff returned to Cambridge on a year's study leave. His interest in oligopolistic industries continued and these aspects of his work were the central focus of the paper published in the *Economic Record* (1965) on the determination of employment and the distribution of income in a two-sector model in the short period. That paper was presented at a seminar the audience of which included, among others, all the famous Cambridge economists of the time. It was in a sense the apotheosis of his enduring concern with, and maturity of his interest in, the idea of oligopoly, which had occupied him since his undergraduate years. This concern is further reflected in his often-quoted paper with Peter Kenyon in *Kyklos* (1976). Not surprisingly, Geoff has come to view the *Economic Record* contribution as his favourite theoretical paper. The seminar must have been a resounding success, for soon after it he was offered a lecturing job in the faculty which he accepted for only three years – he did not wish to let Adelaide University down – and before he knew it, he was elected to a Fellowship in Trinity Hall. The paper he presented at that seminar provided the impetus for a stream of important and influential contributions, with a distinctly strong post-Keynesian thread running through them. These included the choice of technique papers, the best known of which appeared in the *Economic Journal* in March 1968.

Geoff has always been concerned with making the assumptions of the problem in hand explicit and with bringing out the limitations as well as the illuminations of the relevant analysis. An excellent example of this is his *Economic Activity* (with P. H. Karmel and R. H. Wallace, 1967), a book based on a lecture course on Keynesian economics and one that Geoff considers as 'a clear and unpretentious account of the "state of the art" at the time'. The time was the end of 1966 and Geoff was leaving Cambridge for Australia. That was also the era of the Vietnam War and Australia's role in it. Those events and Geoff's political involvement had a profound impact upon him, especially upon his views on the relationship between ideology and analysis. No longer could they be separated in his writings and teaching.

In the midst of all that political fervour, Geoff 'took time off' to write his first piece on the capital controversy for the *Journal of Economic Literature*. The favourable feedback on that paper encouraged Geoff to push on within the area and no fewer than four further papers materialized. The then editor of Cambridge University Press was very impressed by that vast output and asked Geoff to put them together in a book. The first draft was ready, in Geoff's words, 'in two months flat (out!)'. Published in May 1972, under the well-known title *Some Cambridge Controversies in the Theory of Capital* (with subsequent editions in most major languages), the book contained two themes. The first was a critique of the concept of using price as an indication of scarcity in distribution theory, and the second was a methodological critique of utilizing differences to study change. A year's study leave in 1972–3 was spent at Clare Hall as a Visiting Fellow. During that time Geoff gave a number of seminars on the capital debate book, with his afterthoughts being published in *Oxford Economic Papers* in 1976, with the apt title, 'The Cambridge controversies: old ways and new horizons – or dead end?'. It was also then that he formed a close friendship with Tom Asimakopulos (they had already met at Cambridge in the 1950s), which lasted until the latter's premature death in May 1990.

Geoff returned to Adelaide University in 1973. The golden age of capitalism was coming to an end by then, soon followed by the stagflation of the 1970s and the monetarist era. Australia did not stand outside the trend. In 1975 the government there introduced monetarist policies accompanied by confrontationist attitudes between government, capital and labour. Although Geoff had already spent some time drawing out the policy implications of the capital theory debate, the Australian experience gave him a new platform on which to formulate his economic policy views more cogently. At the heart of those ideas was a set of economic policies designed to reduce inflation slowly while maintaining high levels of employment and external balance. Furthermore, redistribution through public-sector policies was seen as the quid pro quo for trade union acceptance of incomes policies. Fiscal and monetary policies were to aim at influencing the level and the rate of growth of economic activity. Nationalization of key industries including financial intermediaries would boost investment, and a fixed exchange rate adjusted from time to time would ensure external balance. When the Australian Labor Party (ALP) was returned to power in 1983, the Accord between trade unions and the government must have owed a great deal to those ideas propounded by Geoff as the economist on the ALP's National Committee of Enquiry in 1978, in the form of background discussion papers. They are still on Geoff's agenda and he has taken them a step further recently in a number of contributions.

In the mid-1970s Geoff developed a new interest in writing intellectual biographies. He has written a steady stream of them, which he has admitted to enjoying enormously – a clear indication of his love of and concern for fellow human beings. Some of this material may very well form the nucleus of the major task he first began when he returned to Cambridge in 1982 (to a teaching post in the Faculty of Economics and Politics and a Fellowship at Jesus). It is to write the intellectual history of Joan Robinson and her circle, and to show the connections between their contributions and those of the classical economists, Marx, and Keynes, as well as of contemporaries whom Joan Robinson and her circle influenced. The project is not finished yet, for good reasons which have to do with Geoff's continuing concern with a number of developments both in economic theory and in economic policy in the real world. But above all, it is A 'Second Edition' of The General Theory, which he is co-editing with Peter Riach and hopes to bring out in 1996, sixty years after the publication of The General Theory, that has taken up much of his time. This is an exciting publication which is intended to tell us what Keynes would have written in the late 1930s had he known what those who succeeded him were to contribute on a number of aspects of The General Theory in the post-war period. 'Putting Keynes back at the forefront of the debate' is the essential purpose of the book. And just to show the world that he has not run out of steam as a surveyor of the passing scene, Geoff published a paper entitled 'Reflections on the developments of economics as a discipline', a piece about the Nobel Prize winners up to Debreu. It was published in the History of Political Economy in 1984.

Since he last returned to Cambridge in 1982, Geoff has been at the centre of the teaching of and research in macroeconomics. He has also been instrumental in the development of the graduate programme in the Faculty of Economics and Politics, and has systematically been the most popular Ph.D. supervisor.

We have tried in this introduction to offer an inevitably short summary of Geoff Harcourt's academic life and work. Just as Mark Perlman has done recently in a preface to a selection of Geoff's essays, we have tried to look into Geoff's four groups of contributions.[2]

1   works analysing contemporary economic theoretical problems;
2   works synthesizing states of debates in economic theory;

3 works having a distinctly biographical flavour and pertaining to various
   contemporary economics; and
4 works pertaining to economic and allied social policies.

Of course this convenient list does not pretend to cover the full range of
material covered in Geoff's massive output of books and papers.

We are delighted, but not surprised, that on 13 June 1994 Geoff was
awarded one of the highest Australian honours of Officer in the General
Division of the Order of Australia (AO), for 'service to economic theory and
to the history of economic thought'. Well done Australia! And yet Geoff still
flourishes as a Reader at Cambridge (he is Reader in the History of Economic
Theory, *ad hominen*), and enjoys himself as ever. Our greatest regret, and his,
we are sure (though he has never shown it at all), is that despite his
achievements, national and international recognition, and his vast contributions to the discipline of economics, he has been denied a full professorship
– although his old university in Adelaide did bestow upon him in 1988 the title
of Professor Emeritus. This, of course, continues the famous Cambridge
tradition of being less than generous in awarding professorships, as, for
example, the failure to so honour Piero Sraffa, Maurice Dobb, Richard
Goodwin, Luigi Pasinetti and others, or the late concessions of professorships
to Joan Robinson and Nicky Kaldor.

The editors of this book are exceptionally grateful for Geoff's help,
encouragement and friendship throughout the years. The speed by which
constructive comments are generously provided on manuscripts and papers,
the breadth and depth of them, his unfailing availability at the other end of the
telephone, his writings and contributions to conferences from which we, and
so many others, have benefited are just some of the ways in which we have
gained through knowing him. We are honoured to have had a long association
with so great a figure as Geoff Harcourt. Many have benefited from his warm
hospitality to visitors to Cambridge. The two volumes we have put together
are intended to mark our enormous respect and admiration for such a great
friend. We are sure that these sentiments are completely shared by all the
contributors to the two volumes, and indeed by many others who would have
liked to have contributed but unfortunately were unable to do so.

There is another aspect of Geoff's skills that makes him almost unique in
academia. He was a player of Australian Rules football in an amateur
capacity. That he was still playing such a physically demanding game at the
age of 47 is no mean feat. As befits an Australian, he was also a keen player
of cricket until a recurring back injury and then his four recent brushes with
death put him out of the game – only temporarily, we are delighted to say.
Undeterred by the back injury, he ran the Cambridge half-marathon in the
mid-1980s, and every day now he goes on a long bike ride. Despite his recent
illness, his resilience is such that he is as sparkling as he has ever been. Geoff
often jokes about those incidents, but then, being intelligently funny is yet

another characteristic of his good nature. This ability adds even more to his humane approach, not just to his economics but also to his fellow human beings, especially his friends.

No introduction of this kind should come to an end without at least a mention of the quiet, and yet dynamic and effective, person who we know has played a central and critical role in supporting what Geoff has managed to achieve in his life. This is, of course, Joan, who has been a reliable and tremendously supportive partner in Geoff's life. She has also been an extremely good and warm friend to all of us, all these years. She, and Wendy, Robert, Timothy, Rebecca, their respective partners and the recent addition of a grandchild (thanks to Wendy and Claudio Sardoni), complete a very happy family indeed.

Nor should we fail to mention Geoff's religious and political convictions, which are central to his economics. It is very pleasing to see how well these three aspects – religion, politics and economics – mesh in his recent paper, 'A "modest proposal" for taming speculators and putting the world on course to prosperity'. They combine with his unfailing compassion for his fellow women and men to give expression to his real feelings about humanity.

Special thanks must go to the contributors for their willingness to respond to our comments and suggestions with forbearance and good humour. Thanks are also extended to the secretaries of the Department of Economics at the University of East London, June Daniels and Christine Nisbet, and the secretary of the School of Business and Economic Studies at the University of Leeds, Eleanor Lynn, for their generous assistance. Finally, Alan Jarvis and his staff, as always, have provided excellent support throughout the period it took to prepare both volumes.

Philip Arestis, Gabriel Palma and Malcolm Sawyer

NOTES

1   All the quotes from Geoff Harcourt in the introduction are from his entry in P. Arestis and M. Sawyer (eds) (1992) *A Biographical Dictionary of Dissenting Economists*, Aldershot: Edward Elgar, pp. 232–41.

2   The four groups are quoted from the preface (written by Mark Perlman) to G. C. Harcourt (1995) *Capitalism, Socialism and Post-Keynesianism*, Cheltenham: Edward Elgar.

1

HORSES FOR COURSES

Tony Lawson

INTRODUCTION

All economists adopt a methodological stance of some kind. These stances are manifest not only in implicit research criteria but also in the advice they offer each other and many of the questions they ask. Familiar examples of the sort of questions and advice that I have in mind include: 'What's your model?'; 'Have you tested it?'; 'Don't think about it, just do it'; 'Avoid discussions about the use of mathematics'; 'Be rigorous'; 'Does it have micro-foundations?'; 'Does it have a (unique) solution (equilibrium)?'; 'Does it support interventionist (*laissez-faire*) policy conclusions?' And while various expressions of this sort are regularly employed by Geoff Harcourt, there is one recommendation that I have heard (or noticed?) him use rather more often than any other. It takes the form of the slogan 'horses for courses'. Its usage in the scientific-methodological context is not unique to Geoff; but, perhaps because I have had the opportunity to interact with him so frequently, I associate it with Geoff before anyone else. In fact, although many who hear this slogan usually give it an immediate nod of approval (which is an interesting phenomenon in itself) I cannot think of any other person who so regularly employs it.[1]

But if the slogan, as a methodological criterion or stipulation, does have a good deal of immediate intuitive appeal, it also requires some unpacking. As far as I am aware there is nowhere this has already been done. My objective here, then, is to suggest a specific interpretation. Once this has been achieved it is obviously of interest to check whether such an apparently general or abstract slogan carries methodological bite. I conclude that it does by examining its implications with regard to an issue which Geoff has himself recently addressed and which is currently as significant as any facing the discipline: the usefulness to economics of mathematical methods.

HORSES FOR COURSES

How then are we to interpret 'horses for courses' in the context of scientific practice? Of course there are many possible translations, and Geoff sometimes interprets the slogan in different ways. The exercise which follows must be seen as rather exploratory. My aim is to provide a translation which at least preserves those aspects which seem both essential to it and likely explanations of its apparent immediate intuitive appeal. This appears to be the minimal requirement of any translation that can be sustained.

In the light of these considerations there are several aspects of the slogan that warrant attention. The first is that it *is* a stipulation. After all, the statement is not of the form "any old horse will do", i.e., whatever the course. It follows that whatever the precise form in which it translates into the scientific context, it does so as a directive or criterion of some sort. This is obviously desirable if repeating the slogan is to make any difference to anything.

A second and fundamental feature is that there is some *matching* going on, and it is a matching of some form of agency or action to its conditions of action. The directive is basically that for a given course, a horse ought to be selected according to its suitability in the light of existing conditions (length of course, firmness of terrain, existence, number and/or height of fences, etc.); or for a given horse, the owner or 'racer' ought to select a course such that the perceived conditions give the horse a comparative advantage. In short, horse is matched to course, or vice versa.

The most obvious way for this feature to be carried over into the scientific context is as the requirement that scientific investigatory practice and the feature of reality to be investigated be in some sense tailored to one another. This clearly necessitates obtaining insights into the nature of the objects of enquiry, as well as an awareness of the metaphysical presuppositions of given methods and procedures. In short, this feature of the stipulation necessitates an attention to ontology, and presupposes a realist orientation.[2] It represents an explicit negation of the epistemic fallacy, i.e. of the erroneous belief that ontology can be reduced to epistemology, that questions about being can be rephrased as questions about knowledge (of being). It distinguishes method from its object.

This second aspect of the 'horses for courses' slogan is, I think, its most essential one. Certainly it is the most essential feature of the interpretation that I am suggesting here. But there is also a (slightly distinct) third feature that warrants emphasis, one which perhaps contributes most to its immediate appeal. This feature is signalled by the apparent ability of the slogan to express much through little – by way of three words, to be precise. This latter result is achieved because the analogy drawn implicitly relates to a (familiar) whole situation: the race course and all that surrounds it. Most obviously, an essential aspect of horse-racing is the goal of winning, which typically means choosing (or riding or owning) the horse which in any given race comes first.[3] In other words, the slogan in question appears to convey, as an additional essential aspect of it, something about the objective or purpose of the event, as well as a method or strategy. And in the scientific context, especially if a realist orientation is implied, this presumably translates to the goal of

2

illuminating (revealing, explaining, understanding) some feature of reality. Object and method of enquiry are 'matched' to one another under the intent of illuminating the former.[4]

Thus, I suspect that Geoff is rather lax and gets it not quite right when sometimes (albeit only sometimes) he suggests that the slogan translates into something like "how you do it depends upon what the purpose is" (e.g. Harcourt 1996: 6). This interpretation (which is barely a stipulation anyway) matches procedures of action to purposes rather than to conditions of action, and thereby neglects that an additional and apparently essential feature of the slogan, and a likely major explanation of its intuitive appeal, is precisely that the purpose is already implicated: to 'pick' the horse which comes first.[5]

In short, I suggest that the most compelling translation of 'horses for courses' in the scientific context pertains to the (usual) situation where the accepted goal is to illuminate (reveal/explain/understand) some feature of reality, and takes the form of the directive that where given methods, techniques or procedures are to be employed, the objects chosen for analysis be of such a nature that the methods appear capable of illuminating them; or where definite aspects of reality are to be illuminated, the methods and procedures followed be fashioned to insights available concerning the nature of such material.

THE USE OF MATHEMATICS IN ECONOMICS

Can this methodological horses for courses (henceforth MHC) directive actually make any difference to anything? This is an important question, because there is obviously no isomorphic relation between a theory of ontology and any set of methods or procedures. Although the noted epistemic fallacy is avoided, the stipulation remains at a high level of generality.[6] Despite this, it is easy enough to provide an initial indication that MHC can bear important implications by considering one of Geoff's own papers. Although many economists express definite, often strongly held, views on the use of mathematics in economics, Geoff is one of the few to have written an entire paper on the topic (Harcourt, 1995 [1993]). In this paper Geoff, amongst other things, surveys a range of prominent assessments on the usefulness of mathematical formalism to economics. The problem, though, is how to choose between them. Towards the end of his paper Geoff acknowledges that he has presented an array of different views, but without making any definite selection. He writes: 'So where does this leave us? Clearly, to take a weighted average of such divergent views would be a cop out.' Geoff, though, does not really take the issue further,[7] other than acknowledging that 'mathematics can be a good servant but, even more, a bad master' (1995: 19). My aim here is to reinforce Geoff's latter intuition by explicitly bringing to bear the version of 'horses for courses' argued for above. Certainly this strategy supports implications that are reasonably clear-cut.

3

CRITERIA OF METHOD SELECTION

Amongst the 'divergent views' explicitly examined and quoted by Geoff,[8] both the assessments of the usefulness of mathematical formalism for economics and the criteria (or implicit stipulations) employed in making these assessments are discernable in statements taken from Marshall, Keynes, Samuelson, Boulding, Debreu, Koopmans, Mirrlees, Chichilinsky, Hahn and Stone. In consequence, it is possible to divide this group into those who do, and those who do not, accept MHC as interpreted here in making such assessments. In fact only three of those listed explicitly and unambiguously emphasize a need to match method to the nature of the object of study in order to illuminate the latter – namely Marshall, Keynes and Boulding. The others draw on criteria or objectives which are either too generally stated to be interpreted here (such as 'scientific advancement'), or rely upon specific criteria and objectives that are noticeably different.

Thus Samuelson makes an unelaborated reference to 'advancing the science' and also invokes the avoidance of 'depraved' types of 'mental gymnastics';[9] Debreu emphasizes procedures which permit sounder judgements of relevance, the ability to give 'ready answers' to new questions through reinterpreting 'primitive concepts', deeper understandings of problems formulated, rigour, the intellectual need of economists for rigour, simplicity and generality, the facilitation of efficient communication and thinking;[10] Koopmans emphasizes the efficiency of establishing logical links between premises and conclusions, explicitness of assumptions, a reasoning process that is not intruded upon by 'associations clinging to words';[11] Mirrlees mentions 'explicitness of assumptions, attention to detail, and rigour' (Mirrlees, 1978: 15–17, quoted in Harcourt, 1995: 15); Chichilinsky singles out clarity, a strong foundation, and 'desired [mathematical] advance in areas which are of great importance for intellectuals and for those whose lives depend on it'[12] (1990: 16); Hahn emphasizes understanding, honesty, modesty, excitement, beauty, the avoidance of being 'enslaved by slogans and shibboleths of practical men and women' (Hahn, 1985: 28, quoted in Harcourt, 1995: 15), a need to establish precise definitions of problems and necessary conditions for definite results; while Stone draws attention to the nature of current practices in a number of social sciences, efficiency in analysing and comparing theories of complex systems, the reduction of generality in models, a need to gain insight into subjects where concepts are vague and information is imprecise, and an interest in understanding reasoning processes behind effective (as opposed to ineffective) decisions.[13]

In all these cases (whatever the accuracy of the claims put forward[14]) the suitability or relevance of methods and procedures to the specific nature of the material that is to be investigated is never explicitly invoked in formulating a criterion. The 'matching' of one with the other is not an issue. Only for Marshall, Keynes and Boulding is this an explicit consideration.

MAKING A SELECTION

But so what? What do we learn from subdividing the contributions referred to by Geoff in this manner? The answer is simply that a systematically different conclusion is reached concerning the relevance of mathematical formalism to economics according to whether or not MHC as interpreted here is invoked. Specifically, while those who fail to question explicitly whether formalistic methods are capable of illuminating social material, infer that the application of mathematical formalism to all areas of economics can only be beneficial, those who employ the criterion draw more or less the opposite conclusion.

Thus, while the former group express only positive views on the use of mathematical methods in economics, Boulding finds, for example, that 'mathematicians themselves set up standards of generality and elegance in their expositions which are a bar to understanding' (Boulding 1948, 1971: 236, quoted in Harcourt 1995: 12); Marshall concludes that 'the application of exact mathematical methods to [the few facts which can be expressed in numbers] is nearly always a waste of time, while in the majority of cases it is positively misleading; ... the world would be further on its way if it had never been done at all' (Pigou 1925: 422, quoted in Harcourt 1995: 6); and Keynes writes of 'symbolic pseudo-mathematical methods of formalising a system of economic analysis' concluding that 'too large a proportion of recent "mathematical" economics are mere concoctions which allow the author to lose sight of the complexities and inter-dependencies of the real world in a maze of pretentious and unhelpful symbols' (Keynes 1936, 1973: 297, 298, quoted in Harcourt 1995: 9).

In short, if we decide to choose between the 'divergent views' brought to our attention by Geoff using his own 'horses for courses' stipulation as a criterion, then the conclusion seems clear. *Ceteris paribus*, support should be given to those who conclude in favour of severely restricting the use of mathematical formalisms of the sort that are regularly found in economics. It is this, is it not, that Geoff is really telling us?

METHODOLOGICAL 'HORSES FOR COURSES' MORE DIRECTLY APPLIED

Even so, it must be admitted that no direct argument for or against mathematical economics has actually been made here. Any conclusion against the use of specific mathematical methods is conditional upon the soundness of MHC as well as the legitimacy of the arguments made by Keynes, Marshall and Boulding in support of their noted conclusions. Of course, I suspect that few would really want to reject the (realist) MHC criterion explicitly, even if many regularly overlook it. Moreover, the observation that 'assessments of leading economists on the validity of extending the use of certain formalisms

5

in economics turn upon whether or not the MHC criterion is invoked' is a partial regularity that *prima facie* suggests that something systematic is going on. A (conjoint) hypothesis which can straightforwardly account for it, certainly, is that (i) the statements selected by Geoff adequately capture the assessments of the various authors; and (ii) these authors have reasoned correctly, so that while the mathematical formalisms in question have numerous attractive aspects, they are not particularly appropriate to the understanding of social reality.

All the same, a direct argument still needs to be made;[15] the case for limiting the use of formalism in economics so far rests merely on the authority of the cited critics. Let me, then, examine more closely at least one of the arguments of one of the 'antagonists'. I focus on Keynes, with whose writings I am more familiar. As Geoff is a major figure in the post-Keynesian tradition, this seems the appropriate example to consider anyway. The question I want to pursue is whether Keynes' reasoning for resisting the encroachment of formalism of the sort found in economics stands up to inspection. For reasons of space I restrict myself to Keynes' assessment of the appropriateness of econometric methods.[16]

METAPHYSICAL PRESUPPOSITIONS

I note, first, that formalistic methods of the sort traditionally used in economics presuppose regularities of the form 'whenever event (type) x then event (type) y'.[17] This formulation can be interpreted generally to include both the probabilistic relationships which characterize econometrics and the deterministic law-like statements ('axioms' or 'assumptions') which are essential to mainstream theorizing. Let me also note that, outside astronomy, most of the event regularities of this sort uncovered in science have been produced in situations of experimental control. At the same time, experimental results are frequently applied outside the experimental situation where event regularities are no longer found. Now the only adequate explanation of this situation of which I am aware interprets reality as structured and open. That is, the confinement of most event regularities, but not of the applications of scientific knowledge, to situations of experimental control can be rendered intelligible if it is acknowledged that the world is (i) structured, in that actual events and states of affairs are produced by equally real underlying structures, mechanisms, powers and tendencies, and (ii) open, in that actual phenomena are typically conjointly determined by numerous often countervailing mechanisms. For, on this conception the noted observations can be explained by seeing the achievement of the well-controlled experiment as the insulation of some fixed or relatively stable causal mechanism from the action of countervailing factors so that the mechanism of interest can be empirically identified. The event regularity so uncovered, in other words, relates the 'triggering' conditions of some mechanism and the way it acts. But the mechanism itself, when triggered, acts inside and outside the experimental conditions, thereby explaining how it is that experimentally determined results can be applied in non-experimental contexts. Thus gravity acts as much on the pen in my hand as on the object falling with constant acceleration in a·vacuum. Laws, on this conception, refer not to event regularities produced in experimental situations but to the causal mechanisms they reveal. In short, event regularities are not the scientific object but a human contrivance which allows underlying causal mechanisms to be revealed.

ATOMISM AND ISOLATIONISM

In the absence of meaningful possibilities of experimental control in the social domain, this analysis bears the consequence that event regularities of relevance to economics can really only be expected if and where sufficiently stable mechanisms spontaneously act in relative isolation. In fact, even the relative isolation of an individual with a constant intrinsic structure does not yet guarantee the production of an event regularity. For the individual may be so structured that, even given an identical set of initial conditions, a range of outcomes remains possible. Restrictions must operate to ensure that but one reaction is possible. In other words, the individuals of analysis must, for all intents and purposes, be atomistic. Certainly, it is a conception of atomistic individuals that is most easily reconciled with these preconditions. Now, the second (sufficiency) requirement for an event regularity, i.e. that of relative isolation, does not necessitate that each individual acts in complete isolation, so long as all other operative factors are either constant in their action, or at least orthogonal to the action of the primary mechanism in question. In other words, if the mechanism or individual of interest cannot be examined in the insulated conditions of experimental control, the hope must be that it acts in a stable environment.

In short, this discussion indicates that a significant reliance upon the formalistic methods of mainstream economics can be rational, accepting MHC, only where there exists something like grounds for supposing that the analysis is concerned with atomistic factors which operate in a homogeneous environment.[18] And, of course, this is far from the typical social situation. It thus follows that use of the sorts of formalistic methods currently dominant in economics must be highly circumscribed.

Now if this argument is most developed in recent realist contributions, the essentials of it are not novel. Indeed, they constitute precisely Keynes' grounds for rejecting the (by now familiar) method of econometrics more than fifty years ago, as set out in his initial response to an invitation from the League of Nations to review Tinbergen's work on business cycles:

There is first of all the central question of methodology, – the logic of applying the method of multiple correlation to unanalysed economic

7

material, which we know to be non-homogeneous through time. If we are dealing with the action of numerically measurable, independent forces, adequately analyzed so that we were dealing with independent atomic factors and between them completely comprehensive, acting with fluctuating relative strength on material constant and homogeneous through time, we might be able to use the method of multiple correlation with some confidence for disentangling the laws of their action ... In fact we know that every one of these conditions is far from being satisfied by the economic material under investigation ...

To proceed to some more detailed comments. The coefficients arrived at are apparently assumed to be constant for 10 years or for a larger period. Yet, surely we know that they are not constant. There is no reason at all why they should not be different every year.

(1973: 285)

These sorts of comments are repeated throughout the late 1930s by Keynes and come to a head in 1939 in the eventual review of Tinbergen's book:

Put broadly, the most important condition is that the environment in all relevant respects, other than the fluctuations in those factors of which we take particular account, should be uniform and homogeneous over a period of time. We cannot be sure that such conditions will persist in the future, even if we find them in the past. But if we find them in the past, we have at any rate some basis for an inductive argument ... [The] main *prima facie* objection to the application of the method of multiple correlation to complex economic problems lies in the apparent lack of any adequate degree of uniformity in the environment.

(1973: 316)

Consider, too, his earlier comment on Edgeworth, which I reproduce from Geoff's paper once more:

Mathematical Psychics has not, as a science or study, fulfilled its early promise ... When the young Edgeworth chose it, he may have looked to find secrets as wonderful as those which the physicists have found since those days. But this has not happened. The atomic hypothesis which has worked so splendidly in physics breaks down in psychics. We are faced at every turn with the problems of organic unity, of discreteness, of discontinuity – the whole is not equal to the sum of the parts, comparisons of quantity fail us, small changes produce large effects, the assumptions of a uniform and homogeneous continuum are not satisfied.

(Keynes, 1993, CW, X 1972: 262, quoted in Harcourt 1995: 9)

In short, conditional upon accepting MHC, the case against the usual types of

8

mathematical formalism found in economics seems forceful, as Keynes realized some time ago.

FINAL COMMENTS AND QUALIFICATIONS

I have indicated one possible, and I think compelling, way in which the slogan 'horses for courses' translates into the scientific context. Certainly I think it is the interpretation of the original slogan that can most easily explain its apparent intuitive appeal to economists, retain features that appear essential, and sustain methodological bite. Nevertheless the interpretation is somewhat tentative. And some may be quite unhappy with it. If so, I hope I might at least succeed in inducing an explicit and reasoned alternative from those who find it objectionable.

I have also indicated how my interpretation of this stipulation can make a difference by applying it to the question of whether or not certain familiar mathematical methods are appropriate in economics. Although the conclusion reached on this is largely negative I have not (of course) suggested that *all* arguments made against the use of formalism in economics are acceptable to anyone who advocates MHC – any more than I have suggested that criteria employed by those advocating mathematical formalism are irrelevant. Certainly bad arguments for or against the use of formalism (arguments from authority, or according to the sorts of policy options that are supported) cannot be endorsed from this (realist) perspective. At the same time, features such as clarity, rigour, and beauty can be accepted as often desirable and/or important. From the point of view in question the latter mostly pragmatic criteria must be seen as mainly insufficient in the social scientific context; the objective includes the illumination of reality.[19]

It is only fitting that I leave the final word on the use of mathematical methods in economics to Geoff. He acknowledges in his 1995 paper that as a 'fledgling economist' he felt the need to know about mathematical economics and like many others was often seduced by it in some form. Where exactly, then, has his 'horses for courses' reasoning on this subject taken his own thinking?

Now that, more and more, we are coming to realise that qualitative as well as quantitative change is the essence of economic processes, it is not clear that traditional mathematical techniques are the appropriate ones to capture this, even in an illustrative manner. Of course, we must continue to try to do so but we must remember that there are other, often more appropriate, languages to be used in economics as well. Keynes sensed, many years ago, that the philosophers had so refined their formal logic that they had cut the umbilical cord that connected their self-contained and consistent systems with the world they were trying to illuminate. Today, we are in danger of doing this too in economics,

9

because of an overemphasis on the use of mathematics, more to the exclusion or at least the down playing of other, more traditional, forms of analysis in economics.

(Harcourt 1995: 22)

ACKNOWLEDGEMENT

For helpful comments on an earlier version I am grateful to John Davis, Aly Fischer, Joëlle Patient, Mark Peacock, Steve Pratten, Pat Northover and Jochen Runde.

NOTES

1 It does on occasion also crop up in Geoff's written contributions. See, for example, Harcourt (1992, 1995, 1996).
2 This characterization seems acceptable, perhaps essential. For Geoff is a key figure in the post-Keynesian tradition, and those in this tradition who have questioned its nature have tended to support an explicitly realist formulation. See, for example, Arestis (1990, 1992) and Dow (1990, 1991).
3 Although a horse considered to have a good chance of winning may only be backed if the 'odds' seem attractive.
4 Of course, certain people sometimes have reasons for going to the race course other than backing a horse which will come first. It is conceivable that a jockey may even purposely avoid winning, as part of a wider attempt to defraud. Sometimes, as annually at Ascot, an apparent objective is to be seen dressed in some outlandish or 'attractive' attire, and so forth. Similarly economists may have their own alternative goals or agenda. These may relate to pleasing those in authority, demonstrating mathematical prowess, arranging data in such a way as to suggest support for some predetermined and preferred result. Some criteria accepted by economists may equally relate to questions of fashion and notions of elegance. But a large part of the appeal of 'horses for courses' is that the *primary* goal is connoted, and so I think this must be recognized as an essential aspect of it, something to carry over in drawing an analogy. Thus I infer the primary scientific goal of illuminating (revealing/understanding/explaining) some feature of reality must be an essential feature of its scientific analogue. Certainly I would expect an acknowledged post-Keynesian such as Geoff to accept this is the essential scientific goal.
5 Horses are used for an array of activities, ranging from ranching to breeding. The horsy slogan to express the weaker interpretation on occasion offered by Geoff would thus have to be something like 'horses according to the objective in question'. If this were the message it would seem to be at least as advantageous to stick with the formulation 'how you do it depends upon what the purpose is'.
6 Of course the 'How you do it depends upon what the purpose is' interpretation is even more general, with significantly less – if any – methodological bite. See below.
7 Perhaps this is one of those occasions on which Geoff implicitly falls back on the weaker interpretation of the slogan, i.e. 'How you do it depends upon what the purpose is'. Indeed, as I have already noted, it is difficult to see how this latter 'stipulation' could really make much difference to anything.
8 Let me emphasize that I am concerned here only with those statements to which

Geoff himself refers. My aim, at this point, is to see if we can get a bit further in choosing amongst them.

9 Samuelson writes: 'The laborious literary working over of essentially simple mathematical concepts such as is characteristic of much of modern economic theory is not only unrewarding from the standpoint of advancing the science, but involves as well mental gymnastics of a peculiarly depraved type' (Samuelson 1948: 6, quoted in Harcourt 1995: 11).

10 Debreu writes:

> the subject of an axiomatic analysis in which primitive concepts are chosen, assumptions concerning them are formulated, and conclusions are derived from those assumptions by means of mathematical reasoning disconnected from any intended interpretation of the primitive concepts. The benefits ... have been numerous. Making the assumptions of a theory entirely explicit permits a sounder judgement about the extent to which it applies to a particular situation. Axiomatization may also give ready answers to new questions when a novel interpretation of primitive concepts is discovered ... Axiomatization, by insisting on mathematical rigor, has repeatedly led economists to a deeper understanding of the problems they were studying, and to the use of mathematical techniques that fitted those problems better. It has established secure bases from which exploration could start in new directions ... Rigor undoubtedly fulfils an intellectual need of many contemporary economic theorists, who therefore seek it for its own sake, but it is also an attribute of a theory that is an effective thinking tool. Two other major attributes of an effective theory are simplicity and generality ... Simplicity makes a theory usable by a greater number of research workers. Generality makes it applicable to a broad class of problems.
>
> The axiomatization of economic theory has helped its practitioners by making available to them the superbly efficient language of mathematics. It has permitted them to communicate with each other, and to think, with a great economy of means. At the same time, the dialogue between economists and mathematicians has become more intense.
>
> (Debreu 1984: 274–5, quoted in Harcourt 1995: 13)

11 Koopmans writes:

> The appropriateness of mathematical reasoning in economics is not dependent upon how firmly or shakily the premises are established. Let us assume for the sake of argument that the attempt to establish premises or at least to explore their implications is worthwhile, that is, economics itself is worthwhile. In that case the justification for mathematical economics depends merely on whether the logical link between the basic premises economists have been led to make and many of their observable and otherwise interesting implications are more efficiently established by mathematical or by verbal reasoning.
>
> (Koopmans 1954: 378, quoted in Harcourt 1995: 13, 14)

And further:

> that the mathematical method when correctly applied forces the investigator to give a complete statement of assuredly non-contradictory assumptions has generally been conceded as far as the relations of the assumptions to the reasoning is [sic] concerned. To this may be added that

the absence of any natural meaning of mathematical symbols, other than the meaning given to them by postulate or by definition, prevents the associations clinging to words from intruding upon the reasoning process.

(Koopmans 1957: 172–3, quoted in Harcourt 1995: 14)

12   In a piece on 'markets and democracy', Chichilinsky writes:

the connection between [the two] is not at all clearly understood . . . [It] has indeed been analyzed by literary means, but it has not been logically or mathematically analyzed in the context of a well-defined model . . .[,] the foundation which is needed. Since both the theory of markets and . . . of social choice have been mathematically formalised . . . not an impossible task . . . we need a logical foundation and a mathematical edifice to build upon these areas which are the daily concern of many people across the world . . . Political economy must build an abstract and general mathematical thinking. It is the only way to assure clarity, a strong foundation and the desired advance in areas which are of great importance for intellectuals and for those whose lives depend upon it.

(Chichilinsky 1990: 27, 39, quoted in Harcourt 1995: 15, 16)

13   Except in a few obstinate pockets of resistence, the use of mathematics in the social sciences is now generally accepted. The reason is not to be found in the outcome of any high-flown philosophical battle but in a number of simple facts. In the first place, many branches of the social sciences are obviously, one might almost say aggressively, quantitative; demography and economics are clear examples of this. In the second place, while theories about the complex systems which are the subject matter of the social sciences can be expressed verbally, their analysis and comparison are greatly helped by formulating them mathematically. In the third place, the application of such theories must remain very general unless the terms in their relationships can be quantified. In the fourth place, mathematics provides a means of obtaining insight even into subjects whose concepts are rather vague and where precise information is hard to come by. Finally, in the social sciences we are interested not only in a description of what happens and of how the different parts of the social system are related, but also in the rational processes that lie behind effective as opposed to ineffective decisions; to a large extent these processes too can be formulated and analyzed mathematically, so that our decisions may eventually come to rest a little more on knowledge and a little less on guess work than they do at present.

(Stone 1996: 1, quoted in Harcourt 1995: 18, 19)

14   And it is easy enough to show that many are not accurate – see, e.g., Dennis (1994, 1995).

15   For I suppose it might be suggested (erroneously) that the phenomenon in question is equally well explained by a conjecture along the lines that good mathematicians by definition advocate ever extending its application in economics; poor ones who find mathematics difficult resist this – with the automatic, if implicit, stipulation that all critics be ignored. There is no doubt that this sort of reasoning is often heard or alluded to. It is of course untenable. Ignoring the obvious circularity in deciding who is able to do mathematics well, it is not even obvious that mathematics is any more difficult than social theory of a critical sort. But more to the point, people who are skilled in the use of something usually recognize its limitations; it is the poor crafts-people who never realize that there

are any. Yet most of those who employ mathematical formalism in economics seem hardly to have an inkling that any formal system is limited in its scope of application. Some, though, have reflected on the matter. Although to quote an 'authority' is not in itself an argument, such is the esteem in which economists seem to hold the mathematical abilities of von Neumann, that the following assessment (quoted by Geoff once more) may prove salutary:

> As a mathematical discipline travels far from its empirical source, or still more, if it is only a second or third generation only indirectly inspired by ideas coming from reality, it is beset with very grave dangers. It becomes more and more purely aestheticising, more and more purely *l'art pour l'art* ... [T]here is a grave danger that the subject will develop along the line of least resistance, that the stream, so far from its course, will separate into a multitude of insignificant branches, and that the discipline will become a disorganised mass of detail and complexities. In other words, at a great distance from its empirical source, or after much 'abstract' inbreeding, a mathematical subject is in danger of degeneration.
>
> (Quoted in Harcourt 1995: 23)

The fact of the matter, however, is that it is not obvious that mathematical economics has *at any stage* been 'inspired by ideas coming from reality'.

16 For a contribution which examines Keynes' assessment of the usefulness to economics of mathematical methods more widely, see O'Donnell (1990). Despite appearances, O'Donnell's and my own interpretations of Keynes on these matters are not so different. O'Donnell is keen to demonstrate that Keynes' opposition to mathematical methods was not *a priori*, but depended on the context. This is precisely my own position. The question that remains fundamental, though, is what is the social context in which the current methods of mathematical economics have relevance?

17 Let me be clear about this. Mathematical economists tend to represent any conditional formulation of the 'whenever this then that' sort in question by a functional one, such as $y = f(x)$. Now functionality and conditionality are not the same thing. Mathematical economists are in error in making a conflation here. The import of this recognition is that there is much more to the claims of mathematical economics than (pure) mathematics (which I take to be the science of operations) and its results. Moreover, it is easy enough to show that contemporary mathematical economists fail to formalize most of what they profess to deal with (for example, intentions, choice, dispositions and beliefs). In short, it can be fairly said that contemporary mathematical economics is logically incoherent and unrigorous (Dennis 1994, 1995). But these failings of the project are not my concern here and do not undermine my assessment of the metaphysical presuppositions of their typical formulations. For whether the formulations of mathematical economists are (as at present) largely incoherent, or even supposing they were rather more rigorously produced, their relevance in either case presupposes that event regularities of the noted form are in evidence. In short, I am concerned here only with the tenability of the metaphysical presuppositions of contemporary mathematical economics. Although logical inadequacies are a further argument against that project, they do not undermine the assessment of the metaphysics of that project that I am making.

18 Of course an event regularity may come about by chance even if these conditions do not hold. Nothing can rule out such a possibility. But while such an eventuality seems *a priori* unlikely, and is certainly not in evidence, economic modellers need more than mere hope in chance occurrences. In order to proceed

13

systematically they need ways of theorizing such sought-after regularities. And for this the assumptions of atomistic individuals acting in isolated or homogeneous environments are obviously compelling.

19　Nor do I wish to suggest that all conceivable mathematical methods must be incapable of aiding the illumination of social phenomena. However, it would seem that methods that are capable of contributing to an understanding of social reality must at a minimum be non-deductivist, and in fact, given the nature of social reality, employ an intentional logic (and so be capable of accommodating dispositions, beliefs and intentions, etc.). I am not aware of such a system being available but I doubt that developments along these lines can be ruled out *a priori*.

REFERENCES

Arestis, P. (1990) 'Post-Keynesianism: a new approach to economics', *Review of Social Economy*, Fall 1990, 48(3): 222–46.

―――― (1992) *The Post-Keynesianism Approach to Economics: An Alternative Analysis of Economic Theory and Policy*, Aldershot: Edward Elgar.

Boulding, K. E. (1948) *Economic Analysis*, revised edition, New York: Harper.

Chichilinsky, G. (1990) 'On the mathematical foundations of political economy', *Contributions to Political Economy*, 9: 25–41.

Debreu, G. (1984) 'Economic theory in the mathematical mode', *American Economic Review*, 74(3): 267–78.

Dennis, K. (1994) 'Formalism in economics', in Hodgson, G., Samuels, W. and Tool, M. (eds) *The Elgar Companion to Institutional and Evolutionary Economics*, Aldershot: Edward Elgar, vol. I: 251–6.

―――― (1995) 'A logical critique of mathematical formalism in economics', *Journal of Methodology*, 2(2): 181–99.

Dow, S. C. (1990) 'Post-Keynesianism as political economy: a methodological discussion', *Review of Political Economy*, 2(3): 345–58.

―――― (1991) 'Post Keynesian school', in Mair, D. and Miller, A. (eds) *Comparative Schools of Economic Thought*, Aldershot: Edward Elgar.

Hahn, F. H. (1985) *Money, Growth and Stability*, Oxford: Basil Blackwell: 10–28.

―――― (1986) 'Living with uncertainty in economics', *Times Literary Supplement*, August: 833–4.

Harcourt, G. C. (1992) 'A Post-Keynesian comment', *Methodus*, 4(1): 30.

―――― (1995) 'On mathematics and economics', *Capitalism, Socialism and Post-Keynesianism: Selected Essays of G. C. Harcourt*, Aldershot: Edward Elgar. (Page references to mimeo, Cambridge, 1993.)

―――― (1996) 'How I do economics', in Medema, S. and Samuels, W. (eds) *How Should Economists do Economics*, Aldershot: Edward Elgar (forthcoming).

Jevons, W. S. (1871) *The Theory of Political Economy*, London: Macmillan.

Keynes, J. M. (1933) *Essays in Biography*, London: Macmillan, CW, X (1972).

―――― (1973) *The General Theory and After. Part II Defence and Development*, (edited by D. Moggridge) London: Macmillan.

Koopmans, T. (1954) 'On the use of mathematics in economics', *Review of Economics and Statistics*, 36: 377–79.

―――― (1957) *Three Essays on the State of Economic Science*, New York: McGraw-Hill.

Mirrlees, J. A. (1978) 'Review of Malinvand (1977): *The Theory of Unemployment Reconsidered*, Economic Journal, 88 (349): 157–9.

O'Donnell, R. M. (1990) 'Keynes on mathematics: philosophical foundations and economic applications', *Cambridge Journal of Economics*, 14: 29–47.

Pigou, A. C. (ed.) (1925) *Memorials of Alfred Marshall*, London: Macmillan.

Samuelson, P. (1948) *Foundations of Economic Analysis*, Cambridge, Mass.: Harvard University Press.

Stone, R. (1966) *Mathematics in the Social Sciences and Other Essays*, London: Chapman & Hall.

2

ABSTRACTION, IDEALIZATION AND ECONOMIC THEORY

Jochen Runde

Geoff Harcourt advocates a pluralist, or what he calls 'horses for courses', approach in his writings on the methodology of economics. I suspect that this attitude is partly one of temperament. For, as everyone knows, Geoff is something of an exception in a discipline not generally noted for the generosity of spirit displayed between its competing factions. Certainly I have never known him but to emphasize the positive aspects of any book, paper, or talk, whatever the methodological or ideological inclinations of its author.

Yet Geoff is clearly no supporter of an 'anything goes' approach to economic analysis. As he sees it, the main methodological alternatives are two:

> One is axiomatic, for example, as Frank Hahn often says, let us see how far the assumption that the world is populated by 'greedy people' will take us. The other starts by observing behaviour, institutions, 'stylized facts' and then constructs simple models incorporating the essence of the observations in order to try to explain the original observations *et al.* Debreu, Arrow, Hahn are outstanding proponents of the first approach, Kaldor, Kalecki, Joan Robinson – also Keynes, Marx and Smith –, of the second.

> (Harcourt 1995)

Geoff is of course well known as a champion of the second, 'stylized facts' approach. The many arguments he has brought to bear in this role, both theoretical and metatheoretical, are more than can be considered here. But one that recurs in his writings, one that is hinted in the passage quoted above, is that the way the world is should condition the way we think about it, where this includes our methods of explanation. As he puts it at the end of a recent paper, '*always* the guiding principle must be the economics of the problem and its importance and relevance, not what economic problem can we fit to any fancy technique that we have come across' (see also Harcourt 1992, 1993). I should like to use the present opportunity to expand on this point by developing a distinction that is often glossed in economics, between abstraction on the one hand and idealization on the other. I shall argue, first, that the highly idealized nature of contemporary economic theory is closely bound up with its commitment to a particular method of explanation and, second, that the viability of this method is not something that can be settled *a priori*, that is, independently of the nature of what is to be explained.

ABSTRACTION AND IDEALIZATION

Although abstraction and idealization are often treated as the same thing in economics, I should like to argue that they are in fact quite different.[1] I shall interpret abstraction as the process of individuating and focusing on an aspect or aspects of some concrete phenomenon of interest, with the aim of concentrating attention on factors that are considered essential to it, for a particular purpose or from a particular point of view, while temporarily relegating factors that are deemed inessential into the background. Idealization in economic theory, in contrast, tends to take the form of postulating limit or ideal types and/or analysing economic phenomena as if they or their component parts exist and operate in isolation from the involvement or interference of aspects of the situation in which they arise.

Abstraction

The notion of abstraction is in many ways a natural and familiar idea. Certainly it is something that we are engaged in all the time. Just as it is impossible for the economist to comprehend the totality of any complex economic phenomenon all in one go, so it is not possible for us to comprehend the totality of whatever situation we are in at any particular moment. Our waking moments are spent constantly shifting and altering our depth of focus on different aspects of the situation we are in. When driving a car, for example, we might focus momentarily on the movements of a pedestrian, abstracting temporarily from the scenery and the conversation of our travelling companion. At other times we focus on the actions of other motorists or the speedometer, driving automatically until our attention is called away again. Yet it is surprisingly difficult to give a precise account of what abstraction consists in, perhaps not least because it seems to be a largely subconscious activity. There nevertheless seem to be three features that are fundamental to it. I shall briefly consider each in turn, bearing in mind that they will tend to be in play concurrently and tend to influence each other.

What is abstracted from, in any situation, is the totality of the given or concrete. But exactly what is abstracted will depend on the questions being asked by the person making the abstraction. The first feature of abstraction, then, is that it is always interest-relative. Take the topic of social rules and conventions – for example, one that has recently been the subject of discussion from a variety of angles in a variety of disciplines.[2] In some places this work focuses on questions such as the ways in which social conventions contribute to social order (or disorder), passing over questions of their emergence and the social and psychological factors that govern their reproduction. In other places it is precisely these factors that are the focus of interest, leaving aside the impact of convention following on the broader social community. While the focus is on different aspects in each case and the abstractions achieved are to this extent interest-relative, then, this does not mean that what is abstracted is subjective in the sense of expressing or corresponding to nothing real.

Second, abstraction never occurs in a vacuum. The mere fact that it is possible to identify and raise questions about some phenomenon already presupposes at least some knowledge about it. So when a researcher asks a question about something, this will already be from the vantage point of accumulated experience and within a framework of existing theories and conceptions (which suggests that the object of scientific research is generally to transform and sharpen existing conceptions of phenomena). By the same token, the process by which some phenomenon of interest is individuated and, if the aim is to understand that phenomenon, the factors that give rise to it, will also depend on existing theories. To continue with the above example, it seems to be widely agreed that conventionality is closely bound up with notions of community and the public nature of conventional behaviour. This suggests that 'picking out' the conventions followed in some community will involve abstracting from what the people do alone in the privacy of their own homes, for example, or when they are asleep. And if the object was to explain how members of that community come to follow conventions, the focus might be on 'focal points' and the force of precedent, the sanctions that non-conformists face or the need people have to 'belong', rather than such factors as local climatic variations or the particular diet followed in the community concerned.

Third, what is abstracted at any particular time also depends on the level of abstraction adopted. For example, if we were interested in why a certain convention is followed in a particular region, we would in all probability have to enquire into highly specific context-dependent features of the community concerned. In contrast, if we were aiming to provide an explanation of social conventions that applies pan-culturally, we would want to be looking at features of convention-following that apply independently of any particular social context. Variations in the level of abstraction may thus help to parse the essential from the non-essential and to determine the space–time extension of the analysis. Abstractions that set spatial limits to the focus taken will limit the factors that can be taken into consideration. Abstractions that set temporal boundaries to the focus taken will set limits on the histories of any particular factors invoked. Finally, it is worth noting that the most general aspects of a phenomenon, those which accompany it most often, need not be the most

18

relevant to its identification and explanation. The apparent fact that conventions are often arbitrary in the sense that they have conventional alternatives, save on bounded rationality and lend stability to social systems may all be general features of conventions, for example, but may well not be relevant when it comes to explaining how it is that people come to follow them without explicitly agreeing to do so.

Idealization

I suggested above that idealization tends to take one of two broad forms in economic theory. The first of these is the use of limit types, 'entities, aspects or situations which are characterised by some feature that is perfect, complete or absolute in some (limiting) sense' (Lawson, forthcoming). Economic theory abounds with examples of limit types: perfect competition, complete preference orderings, perfect foresight, infinitely lived agents, perfectly divisible goods and common knowledge of rationality, to name just a few. Of course it is possible that instances of the kind of limit types postulated in economic theory may be real possibilities. For example, there may be situations in which decision-makers do in fact have completely ordered preferences over some relevant domain, such as when choosing from a simple menu in a restaurant. Typically, however, examples of this kind are the exception rather than the rule. The limit types so characteristic of economic theory might more generally be labelled fictions in the sense that they are the product of a (usually deliberate) transformation or deformation of something real into something that is a mere idea.

The second form of idealization, often flagged with the *ceteris paribus* assumption, is the practice of analysing phenomena as if existing and operating in isolation. I shall follow Mäki (1992, 1994) and call idealizations of this kind theoretical isolations.[3] Theoretical isolations are typically achieved by (or are some combination of) assuming away entirely, assuming away changes in, or assuming away interdependencies between, factors that accompany and may be causally relevant to some phenomenon.[4] Again, contemporary economic theory is replete with examples. Some instances of the first variety include partial equilibrium models and two or three sector 'economies'. Two familiar examples of the practice of assuming away changes in factors that may be causally relevant to some phenomenon of interest are the assumptions of constant tastes and fixed technology. Finally, some examples of the practice of assuming away interdependencies between different aspects of the phenomenon of interest include the separability assumptions on which the subjective expected utility theorem is based (Runde 1995a), perfect competition and, again, the representative agent 'economy'.

The two broad forms of idealization described above are closely related and may well overlap.[5] The assumption of perfect competition, for example, is at once a limit type and an assumption that rules out strategic inter-dependencies between individual agents.

Abstraction versus isolation

One way of thinking about the distinction between abstraction and ideal-ization is that whereas abstraction involves looking at the same real phenomenon from different points of view, idealization typically involves transforming that phenomenon or one or more of its aspects into something that exists only in the realm of ideas. But this way of putting it, while perhaps not overly contentious so far as limit types are concerned, must be qualified in the case of isolations. This issue may be looked at in terms of why particular isolating assumptions are made.

There are two main possibilities. The first is the situation in which isolations are made on ontic grounds, where the phenomenon of interest or its component parts are treated as if acting in isolation because the excluded factors are deemed to be causally irrelevant to the phenomena concerned (or to be acting on them in a constant way).[6] Isolation may here be interpreted as serving to parse the 'greater' causes of some phenomenon from its 'lesser' causes and, to the extent that this is so, there may be no great distance between abstraction on the one hand and isolation in the other. The second possibility is the situation in which isolating assumptions are made on the grounds of analytical convenience in general or mathematical tractability in particular, which, as the above examples suggest, may lead to phenomena being analysed as if acting in isolation from factors that are known to be causally relevant. In this case isolation, no less than the use of limit types, leads to the deformation of the phenomenon of interest into something that exists only in the realm of ideas (such as two-sector or single-agent 'economies'). The difference between abstraction and isolation is again marked here: to abstract an aspect of some phenomenon is not to treat that aspect as if existing and operating in isolation from the context it is abstracted from.[7] Or alternatively, to abstract from specific aspects of some phenomenon is not to treat that which is temporarily out of focus as something that is assumed out of existence.

The distinction between abstraction and isolation is crucial when dealing with phenomena whose system properties do not consist of separable properties of parts of that system. And this will of course often be the case when dealing with social phenomena, the properties of which cannot always be comprehended without reference to their other parts and, often, particular histories. This does not of course mean that features or aspects of an internally related set of structures or processes cannot be considered individually at a moment in time, merely that they cannot be treated as isolated phenomena existing outside of time. It does mean that the comprehension of such structures and processes will generally involve examining them from different

20

levels and planes of abstraction, sometimes focusing on their particular features and passing over the general, sometimes passing over the particulars and focusing on the general. The point is that aspects that characterize some phenomenon at one level or plane of abstraction cannot be dismissed as inconsequential when statements are made about it at other levels or planes of abstraction.

WHY IDEALIZATION?

Given that idealization in economic theory almost always involves the postulation of entities or states of affairs that manifestly do not occur in the world, the question arises as to why economists resort to them at all. This question becomes all the more pressing in view of the fact that economics is routinely criticized on just this point, for making unrealistic assumptions, for concentrating on fictitious 'toy' economies, and so on. The standard response to charges of this kind is to point out that theories and models are necessarily descriptively false, simplifications, exaggerations, isolations, approximations and so forth. We have already noted that it is not possible to make sense of complex social phenomena by attempting to comprehend them in all their aspects in one go. But we have seen that the role of abstraction is precisely to look at phenomena from a particular point of view, focusing on some of their aspects while temporarily leaving others out of focus. Whey then, given that abstraction already does this particular job, does contemporary economic theory put so much weight on idealizations?

I should like to argue that the answer to this question is closely connected with the acceptance of an unwritten and largely unchallenged rule in orthodox economic theory, that the only way to arrive at a precise 'scientific' theorization of some economic phenomenon X is to deduce a statement about that phenomenon (the *explanandum*) from a set of premises that contains statements about initial conditions and at least one law necessary for the deduction (the *explanans*).[8] By 'law' I mean a statement of an association or regularity that always or almost always holds, and which may simply be *a priori* ('agents have preferences' or 'firms maximize profits') or arrived at on an empirical basis. Such laws are not only a precondition for, but also the goal of, deductivist explanations. For if we can 'explain' some phenomenon by showing that it is logically entailed by a set of statements about initial conditions and laws, then that 'explanation' has the same logical form as a statement of a law (namely, 'whenever these conditions, then that outcome'). It turns out, however, that if the deductivist ideal is to be in any way achievable, then at least three strong closure conditions have to be met.[9]

The first condition is that the elementary units referred to in the *explanans* (individual consumers or firms, for example) must be organized or constituted in such a way that they always behave in the same way under the same circumstances. One way of ensuring this is to require that the elementary units

21

exhibit a constant internal structure. The relevant condition is therefore sometimes called the intrinsic condition for closure. Intrinsic constancy of the elementary units of analysis is, however, not sufficient to ensure determinacy at that level (and therefore, in most cases, at the aggregate level). This requires a further reducibility assumption, namely that the individual units of analysis be constituted so as to behave in the same unique way in the same circumstances.

The second condition that has to be met is that the phenomenon of interest must conform to some principle of composition that ensures that the behaviour of the elementary units referred to in *explanans* translates into a determinate outcome (or set or spread of outcomes) at the aggregate level. This is called the aggregational condition for closure and, in general, requires a detailed specification of the rules that govern the interaction of the elementary units of analysis. Again, if the aim is to deduce a unique outcome, this time at the aggregate level, the aggregational condition must be specified in a way that is strong enough to ensure reducibility.[10] Finally, the third fundamental condition that has to be met, the extrinsic condition for closure, is that the *explanandum* phenomenon is effectively isolated from the factors not explicitly taken into account in the analysis itself. The extrinsic condition for closure is met if all extrinsic factors are either physically isolated from the system, or impact on the system in a constant way. In terms of probabilistic formulations the intrinsic condition for closure is met if the extrinsic factors impinge on the system in a way that is constant on average and is not correlated with those explicitly taken into account in the analysis.[11]

In the following section I shall consider some implications of proceeding on the basis of the assumption that these conditions are met. For the moment, I merely want to suggest that the main reason why contemporary economic theory is shot through with fictions of the kind discussed above is that they are necessary to meet the three closure conditions necessary to achieve explanations on deductivist lines.[12] A few examples will suffice to show what I mean. Perhaps the most familiar idealizations used to satisfy the intrinsic condition for closure are the rational utility maximizer and the black-box theory of the firm. In both cases the 'agents' are specified such that they are largely devoid of internal structure and always behave in the same (unique) way in the same circumstances (the utility maximizer is assumed to have fixed tastes, for example, represented by 'well behaved' indifference curves that ensure determinacy). Some familiar examples of the idealizations used to satisfy the aggregational condition for closure include the hypothesis of perfectly competitive equilibrium, the various solution concepts of game theory and the practice of side-stepping the aggregation problem altogether by modelling an economy in terms of the maximization of a representative agent's utility function (see Hoover 1993: 696–8; Kirman 1992). And finally, the extrinsic condition for closure is typically met by the (often unstated) assumption that the phenomenon being explained is operating in isolation from any potentially disturbing factors, that is, that all causally relevant factors have been included in the set of premises from which the phenomenon is being deduced, or that the disturbing factors impact on the system in a constant way.

THE METAPHYSICS OF CLOSURE AND ISOLATION

I have already noted that the use of the deductivist method of explanation is largely unquestioned in the economic theory literature and, consequently, that the assumptions on which it rests are rarely examined. In the previous section I argued that one of the key characteristics of deductivism is its reliance on *a priori* and/or empirical laws, both as a condition for and the goal of (deductivist) explanation. It would therefore seem that proponents of the deductivist method are committed to a particular metaphysics, namely that laws or regularities of the postulated kind exist. Following Lawson, this metaphysical position might be called 'regularity determinism' (that for every event or state of affairs y there exists a set of events or states of affairs x_1, x_2, $\ldots x_n$, such that y and $x_1, x_2, \ldots x_n$ are regularly conjoined under some formulation), or its probabilistic analogue 'regularity stochasticism' (that for every event or state of affairs y there exists a set of events or states of affairs $x_1, x_2, \ldots x_n$, such that y and $x_1, x_2, \ldots x_n$ are regularly conjoined under some set of 'well behaved' probabilistic formulations).

As economists know all too well, however, the problem is that regularities of either of the above kinds are rarely found in the social world. That this is so should not be surprising because the kinds of phenomena that they are interested in – price and interest rate levels, unemployment, the organization of industries and firms, and so on – are typically the product of an ever-changing mix of causal mechanisms that may at different times amplify, impede or override others. Indeed economists are often very good at giving *ex post* rationalizations of predictive failures in terms of the operation of some unanticipated causal mechanism. I gave the formal conditions that have to be met to ensure an event regularity in the preceding section. In practice (and ignoring astronomy) these conditions are typically only met by actively intervening in the world – such as the complex set of isolations that leads to the light turning on (almost) every time I flick the switch. The paradigm case, of course, are situations of experimental control or 'material isolations', where a causal mechanism is 'sealed off' from disturbing phenomena so as to ensure a one-to-one relationship between that mechanism being triggered and some set of its effects. The main alternatives open to defenders of the deductivist approach, from this perspective, seem to be three.

The first is to argue that deductivist economic theory has value despite the paucity of deterministic or 'well-behaved' probabilistic laws in the social world and despite the fact that it does not seem to be well-suited to deriving

23

conclusions that relate in any obvious way to anything to be found 'out there' in the economy. Hahn, for example, turns defence into attack by claiming a virtue of formal theorizing that it

> leaves the practitioner with the suspicion that, what I suppose was once a programme for economics, may be impossible to carry out ... It is not just that there are many variables and complex interactions: it is that the constraints on what is possible seem much weaker than is the case with physical processes ... A theorist then will be surprised if there are 'laws of economies,' in the sense of propositions holding universally, waiting to be discovered.

> (1985: 26–7)

But the whole game then changes. If economic theory is in fact not based on deterministic or 'well-behaved' probabilistic laws, and if the 'explanations' produced, while having the logical form of statements of such laws, are not even expected to have any obvious empirical counterpart, then the bearing of such theory on its subject matter will at best be oblique. In particular, it would then seem necessary to justify it, as Hahn in fact does, on grounds other than its actual or potential success in predicting and/or explaining real economic phenomena (see Runde 1996).

But most economists would probably like to see a firmer empirical connection between their models and the world than Hahn might be prepared to countenance. The second possibility, then, is to attempt to intervene in the social world and make the phenomena under investigation more like that presupposed by the deductivist approach. Recent years have witnessed growing interest in attempts to do just this, to test the predictions of microeconomic models in controlled experimental settings. This approach involves attempting to recreate the conditions specified by the assumptions of a particular model in a laboratory setting, by specifying an 'environment' (tastes and technology), an 'institution' (the language by which agents communicate, the order in which they move and the rules under which messages become contracts and thus allocations) and behaviour (that agents are utility maximizers, choose as if they are risk averters, and so on). Usually it is the assumptions about agent behaviour that are tested, their not being falsified lending to their support given the environment and institution posited. The findings of this literature – for example, that institutions matter, that people often manage to optimize in market interactions without consciously attempting to do so, that less information may be better than more (see, for example, Smith 1991, 1994) – are certainly interesting, often replicable and usually at variance with standard neoclassical theory. But from the perspective of the position developed in the current paper, the value of this work lies not so much in finding regularities but in creating the conditions under which causal mechanisms can be empirically identified. As Elster puts it: 'Laboratory experiments have the great value of isolating and controlling factors so that we can see the mechanisms in their pure form, but they are of limited help in explaining the tug of war between mechanisms that is the rule in social life' (1989a: 216). The point is that the causal mechanisms identified in the laboratory will, if triggered, also exercise their powers outside of it, whether or not the regularities that aided their identification in the laboratory are also manifest outside it (see also Cartwright 1989: chapter 4).

The third and possibly most common argument is that the deductivist models that are currently on offer should be regarded as preliminary steps on the path towards progressively more complex and general models that will in future approach the deductivist ideal. The idea here is that empirical success will eventually be achieved by the method of successive approximation or what Mäki (1994: 151–2) calls 'horizontal deisolation' (the process of adding factors at a particular level of abstraction – sometimes by relaxing the idealizations that helped to neutralize them – to arrive at a 'more comprehensive, more encompassing picture of the causal nexus of the phenomena under consideration'). Again, however, this approach presupposes that the phenomena it is applied to are of a particular kind. It assumes, often without argument, that the phenomena of interest are such that they can be studied as an amalgamation of separable closed systems, in effect that they are decomposable into separable components whose (predictable) effects can then subsequently be aggregated to arrive at an outcome for the system as a whole.[13]

CONCLUDING REMARKS

I have characterized orthodox economic theory in terms of its adherence to the deductivist mode of explanation and argued that the limit types and isolations it employs are typically not abstractions of real social phenomena, but idealizations designed to shore up the closure conditions needed to facilitate deducibility. What, then, if the social world is after all open and highly internally related? If the unspoken assumption that significant aspects of the social world can be comprehended as if they were closed systems were to be rejected, this would seem to call for at least considering the possibility of adopting an alternative model of explanation. This is a subject that would lead beyond the scope of the present paper, although on the basis of the arguments given above, there would seem to be a strong case for an approach that emphasizes abstraction over isolation, as well as the more context-specific 'horses for courses' orientation that Geoff Harcourt favours (see Hamouda and Harcourt 1988: 25). I should merely like to note that there *is* such an alternative, namely the view that to explain some phenomenon is to give information about its causal history, or where a type of phenomenon is being considered, to give information about the types of causal mechanisms that produces it.[14]

ACKNOWLEDGEMENT

I am grateful to Paul Anand, Jörg Bibow, Johan Fedderke, Geoff Hodgson, Eckehard Rosenbaum, Arnis Vilks and Marianna Vintiadis for their helpful comments on earlier drafts of this paper.

NOTES

1 This section draws heavily on the manuscript of Tony Lawson's forthcoming book *Economics and Reality*, particularly on the subject of abstraction. I have not provided detailed references because of the provisional nature of the manuscript when I had access to it.

2 For example, Giddens (1984), Gilbert (1992), Hayek (1973), Lewis (1969) and Orléan (1989).

3 I shall, however, not follow Mäki in using the term 'isolation' to cover what I call abstraction (and what he calls 'vertical isolation').

4 Mäki defines theoretical isolations as occurring where 'a system, relation, process or feature, based on an intellectual operation in constructing a concept, model, or theory, is closed off from the involvement or impact of some other features of the situation' (1992: 325). Theoretical isolations may be thought of as the thought-experiment analogue of material isolations, that is where 'a real system, relation, process, or feature, based on a causal intervention in the processes occurring in the world, is materially isolated from the involvement or causal interference of some other real entities' (p. 325).

5 It may be argued that there is a third form of idealization that is neither a limit type nor an isolation, namely when economists resort to purely fictitious entities such as the Walrasian auctioneer, or Friedman's money-dropping helicopters. I shall pass over idealizations of this kind here.

6 See Simon (1969: 101–3).

7 I am therefore reluctant to follow Cartwright (1989: 187) in interpreting the difference between idealization and abstraction as one between *changing* factors or properties and *subtracting* factors or properties. On the present account, subtracting properties or features is a form of idealization where the phenomenon of interest is internally related with the factors that are 'subtracted' from it.

8 This characterization is easy to confirm by paging through any intermediate or advanced theory text (see Hahn (1985) for an explicit statement). Lawson (forthcoming) regards what he calls deductivism – essentially the deductive-nomological model of explanation (Hempel 1965) – as *the* method of orthodox economic theory. Of course most economic theories do not meet the strict requirements of the model since, amongst other things, they are not based on exceptionless laws. They must therefore be seen as better or worse approximations to full deductive-nomological explanations. It is in recognition of this fact that Hausman (1992) characterizes contemporary microeconomic theory as 'inexact'. But the 'inexactness' of the empirical laws on which a (sound) deductive structure is founded does of course not disturb the logical integrity of that structure. As Hahn puts it: 'It seems of things which are logically true that they are also true. Of course, in economics these are contingent truths – contingent on the truth of axioms' (1984: 6–7). What the recognition of such 'inexactness' does is to qualify such structures as explanations/predictions of real economic phenomena, something Hahn appears to give up on anyway (see below).

9 The present account of these conditions builds on the one given in Lawson (1995a) and supersedes the one given in Runde (1996).

10 This reducibility condition is obviously not met in models with multiple equilibria. But models of this kind are no less in the deductivist paradigm for that: the difference is that they are underdetermined, in the sense that the *explanantia* are insufficient to generate unique outcomes.

11 See Lawson (1995b) for a discussion of probabilistic versions of the deductivist approach.

12 This line of argument is by no means new. See Sen (1986), for example, who discusses how the standard notions of rationality, maximizing and equilibrium are used to circumvent the 'choice problem' (i.e. shoring up the intrinsic condition for closure) and the 'interaction problem' (i.e. shoring up the aggregational condition for closure).

13 Mäki himself recognizes that

> the legitimacy of strong isolations in general can be questioned altogether on the basis of organicist metaphysics. It is possible to hold an organicist view of the constitution of the economy according to which the nature of an element is dependent on its interrelations with other elements. This is the stance adopted by some institutionalist economists who subscribe to what they often call 'holism'. By this they mean the idea that the primary and undistorted object of study in economics should consist of 'organic' social wholes as intertwined sets of institutional structures. Accordingly, the behaviour of separate individuals or markets or even a narrowly conceived 'economy' is not a legitimate object of analysis ... This point relates to a major problem involved in the method of isolation as used in studying social and economic phenomena. This is the question whether the causes of economic phenomena are combined 'mechanically' or 'chemically', to use J.S. Mill's phrases. When causes combine 'mechanically', their effects can be 'added up' like vectors, and the outcome is an additive 'sum' or 'resultant' of the effects of those causes taken singly. On the other hand, when causes are combined 'chemically', some qualitatively novel, emergent outcomes ensue ... It is easier for the method of isolation to deal with the domain of 'mechanics' than that of 'chemistry'. No wonder, therefore, that standard neoclassical economists do their work most of the time as if economics were 'mechanics'. The challenge they are requested to meet concerns the relative adequacy of the 'mechanical' versus the 'chemical' metaphysics and of the methods respectively supported by them in the study of the economy.
>
> (1992: 348–9)

14 For more on this alternative, see Lewis (1986), Lipton (1991), Miller (1987), Elster (1989b), Runde (1995b) and especially Lawson (forthcoming).

REFERENCES

Cartwright, N. (1989) *Nature's Capacities and their Measurement*, Oxford: Oxford University Press.

Elster, J. (1989a) *The Cement of Society: A Study of Social Order*, Cambridge: Cambridge University Press.

—— (1989b) *Nuts and Bolts for the Social Sciences*, Cambridge: Cambridge University Press.

Giddens, A. (1984) *The Constitution of Society. Outline of the Theory of Structuration*, Oxford: Polity Press.

Gilbert, M. (1992) *On Social Facts*, Princeton, N.J.: Princeton University Press.

Hahn, F. (1984) *Equilibrium and Macroeconomics*, Oxford: Basil Blackwell.

—— (1985) *Money, Growth and Stability*, Oxford: Basil Blackwell.

Hamouda, O. F. and Harcourt, G. C. (1988) 'Post Keynesianism: from criticism to coherence?' *Bulletin of Economic Research*, 40: 1–33.

Harcourt, G. C. (1992) 'The legacy of Keynes: theoretical methods and unfinished business', in Sardoni, C. (ed.) *On Political Economists and Modern Political Economy: Selected Essays of G.C. Harcourt*, London: Routledge, 235–49.

—— (1993) 'Mathematics: what should non-mathematicians know? On mathematics and economics'. Paper presented at the Science and the Human Dimension Conference, Jesus College, Cambridge 3–5 September 1993.

—— (1995) 'How I do economics', manuscript, Cambridge University.

Hausman, D. M. (1992) *The Inexact and Separate Science of Economics*, Cambridge: Cambridge University Press.

Hayek, F. (1973) *Law, Legislation and Liberty, vol. 1: Rules and Order*, Chicago, Il.: Chicago University Press.

Hempel, C. (1965) *Aspects of Scientific Explanation*, New York: Free Press.

Hoover, K. D. (1993) 'Causality and temporal order in macroeconomics or why even economists don't know how to get causes from probabilities', *British Journal for the Philosophy of Science*, 44: 693–710.

Kirman, A. P. (1992) 'Whom or what does the representative individual represent?' *Journal of Economic Perspectives*, 6: 117–36.

Lawson, T. (1989) 'Abstraction, tendencies and stylised facts: a realist approach to economic analysis', *Cambridge Journal of Economics*, 13: 59–78.

—— (1995a) 'A realist perspective on contemporary "economic theory"', *Journal of Economic Issues*, 29: 1–32.

—— (1995b) 'The "Lucas Critique": a generalisation', *Cambridge Journal of Economics*, 19: 257–76.

—— (forthcoming). *Economics and Reality*, London: Routledge.

Lewis, D. (1969) *Convention: A Philosophical Study*, Cambridge, Mass.: Harvard University Press.

—— (1986) 'Causal explanation', *Philosophical Papers, Vol. II*, Oxford and New York: Oxford University Press.

Lipton, P. (1991) *Inference to the Best Explanation*, London: Routledge.

Mäki, U. (1992) 'On the method of isolation in economics', *Poznań Studies in the Philosophy of the Sciences and the Humanities*, 26: 317–51.

—— (1994) 'Isolation, idealization and truth in economics', *Poznań Studies in the Philosophy of the Sciences and the Humanities*, 38: 147–68.

Miller, R.W. (1987) *Fact and Method: Explanation, Confirmation and Reality in the Natural and the Social Sciences*, Princeton, N.J.: Princeton University Press.

Orléan, A. (1989) 'Mimetic contagion and speculative bubbles', *Theory and Decision*, 27: 63–92.

Runde, J. (1995a) 'Risk, uncertainty and Bayesian Decision Theory: a Keynesian view', in Dow, S. and Hillard, J. (eds) *Keynes, Knowledge and Uncertainty*, Aldershot: Edward Elgar, 197–210.

—— (1995b) 'Assessing causal explanations', unpublished paper, Cambridge University.

—— (1996) 'Keynesian methodology', in Harcourt, G. C. and Riach, P. (eds) *Keynes's General Theory Second Edition*, London: Routledge.

Sen, A.K. (1986) 'Prediction and economic theory', *Proceedings of the Royal Society*, London, A 407: 3–23.

Simon, H.A. (1969) *The Sciences of the Artificial*, Cambridge, Mass.: MIT Press.

Smith, V. (1991) 'Theory, experiment and economics', in Smith, V. (1991) *Papers in Experimental Economics*, Cambridge: Cambridge University Press: 783–801. Reprinted from the *Journal of Economic Perspectives*, Winter, 1989.

——— (1994) 'Economics in the laboratory', *Journal of Economic Perspectives*, 8: 113–31.

MARKETS, MADNESS AND MANY MIDDLE WAYS

Some reflections on the institutional diversity of capitalism

Ha-Joon Chang

INTRODUCTION

Many of us know and respect Geoff Harcourt for his role in those highbrow theoretical debates of modern economics such as the Capital Controversy, but throughout his career he has always been more than an ivory tower economist and has been constantly engaged in many policy debates. His active engagement in policy debates partially reflects the fundamentally policy-oriented nature of the Keynesian economics that he has studied and taught all his life, but also reflects his concerns, as a dedicated social reformer in the Christian socialist mould, about inequality, injustice, instability, and conflicts that still rule our societies.

In the last few years, Geoff Harcourt has written a number of articles which synthesize his previous works in various areas of economic policy and sketch out what he sees as a more just and rational alternative to the current orthodoxy of neo-liberal free market 'madness' – such as his second Donald Horne lecture, entitled 'Markets, Madness and A Middle Way', delivered in 1992 in Australia, and the 'sequels' to the piece, such as 'Macroeconomic Policy for Australia in the 1990s' and 'A "Modest Proposal" for Taming Speculators and Putting the World on Course to Prosperity'. This essay aims to take his discussions in these papers of a 'middle way' one step further, and argues that recognizing the existence of a number of 'middle ways' and trying to understand each of them better will enable us to think about some interesting theoretical and empirical issues which have received inadequate attention until now.

THE RISE AND FALL OF THE 'MIDDLE WAY'

The notion of the 'middle way', or the 'third way' as it is also known, has been with us since the establishment of the socialist economic system following the 1917 October Revolution in Russia. The challenge posed to the capitalist system by the socialist system was not simply that it claimed to have different objectives – 'fuller' and more 'rational' use of resources, more equitable income distribution, more equal life chances (through universal provision of education, health, etc.), and so on – but it was also that it tried to achieve its objectives on the basis of principles of coordination which were entirely different from those prevailing in the capitalist system. The socialist system denied the role of profit motives in the accumulation of resources and their allocation amongst alternative uses ('production for use value rather than for exchange value'), substituted the 'anarchic' capitalist coordination of the market with a more conscious and more 'orderly' coordination through central planning, and in some cases (notably in the former Yugoslavia) tried to replace the hierarchical management of the capitalist enterprise with a more democratic and participatory form of management.

To the advanced capitalist countries during the interwar period, which were failing in a spectacular way to achieve full capacity utilization, full employment, economic stability and economic growth, such challenge was indeed formidable – especially when combined with the growing strength of labour movements and left-wing political parties in their own societies. One response to this challenge was, of course, the reassertion of the old liberal policy agenda through the adherence to the now defunct *laissez-faire* doctrines (a balanced budget, the Gold Standard, etc.), but there were also various intellectual and political movements that wanted to save capitalism from itself through institutional reforms and the introduction of more centralized coordination (if not outright physical planning) by the government. The group of British economists around John Maynard Keynes, the American New Dealers, and the Swedish social democrats such as Gunnar Myrdal are the well-known representatives of such movements.

These reformers acknowledged, in various degrees, that the increasing importance of large-scale organizations in the modern economy (be they large firms or labour unions) requires a higher degree of conscious centralized coordination than was the norm in the *laissez-faire* phase of capitalism. In this vision of reformed capitalism, an enlightened government works with large organized groups in order to overcome the instability, stagnation, and inequality of the market economy. It is a vision of the world where neither the ruthless competitive struggle between small players, coordinated through the anonymous forces of a free market, nor mechanical bureaucratic management by a planning hierarchy dominates. For these reformers, the fundamental shifts in the political balance of power and the changes in the institutional set-up of capitalism made it necessary to strike a class compromise and to increase centralized coordination, but not to the point of killing off entrepreneurial spirit by abolishing private property and of abolishing the principle of market coordination altogether.

31

Although this vision of the middle way did make some progress in the interwar period, especially with the launch of the New Deal in the USA and the beginning of over half a century's unbroken Social Democratic rule in Sweden, its full realization had to wait until the end of the Second World War. The new economic and political orders established in the advanced capitalist countries after the War emphatically rejected the model of *laissez-faire* capitalism that had failed so spectacularly during the interwar period. The political discrediting of the traditional liberals whose cherished system had failed to deliver prosperity and stability, not to speak of preventing the rise of extremist political forces and then finally the War, allowed the emergence of the so-called 'corporatist' regimes, which allowed a power-sharing between the reform-minded centre-right parties and the non-revolutionary centre-left parties backed by strong organized labour.

Needless to say, there were a number of influential liberal intellectuals, such as Mises (1929), Hayek (1944), Friedman (1962), Buchanan and Tullock (1962), who saw in this new 'collectivist' political and economic order a grave threat to 'free society' (for a fascinating analysis of these arguments from a historical perspective, see Hirschman 1991). They moreover argued that there is no middle way, as, given the interdependence between different policy areas, a government which is serious about achieving the aims of its policies will have to extend the boundaries of its intervention to the point where the economy will become fully planned from the centre in all but name (the so-called slippery-slope argument). These criticisms were to become influential later, but not just yet.

During the first quarter century after the Second World War, the corporatist regimes in the advanced capitalist economies used a wide range of policy tools to change capitalism into what they perceived as something more rational, stable, and 'kind'. Aggregate demand management, the welfare state, public enterprises in strategic industries, indicative planning, and (in some countries) active selective industrial policy through various forms of subsidies and protection were the measures – unknown or unacceptable to the supporters of the old liberal doctrine – but actively used by most advanced capitalist countries during this period. (Shonfield (1965) is a classic work discussing the evolution and the operation of this policy regime.)

This period also saw the rise of interventionist policy regimes in the newly independent developing capitalist countries. In many developing countries, the governments took a very active role in order to pull their economies out of their places in the traditional international division of labour, which condemned their countries to the disadvantageous role of primary product exporters. This structural shift, it was thought, called for industrialization. And for this purpose, these governments used a wide range of measures, in various degrees, such as investment planning, large-scale public investments in infrastructure and heavy industries, tariff protection, quantitative restrictions on trade, controls on foreign investments and technology transfer, and in some cases – notably the East Asian newly industrializing countries (NICs) – export subsidies.

During the following three decades, often dubbed the 'Golden Age of capitalism', the advanced capitalist countries achieved unprecedented levels of economic growth, stability, and equity simultaneously on the basis of such an interventionist policy regime (see Marglin and Schor 1990; Cairncross and Cairncross 1992). Most developing countries also achieved rates of output growth and industrialization which were far beyond what they had ever achieved before, and even in excess of what the developed countries had achieved in their earlier stages of development. Thanks to the success of interventionist policy regimes across the world, the middle way became established as the organizing principle of most capitalist economies during this period. To many, it indeed seemed to provide a happy medium between the suffocating totalitarianism and inefficiency of communism and the systemic instability, stagnation, and inequality of *laissez-faire* capitalism.

However, the notion of the middle way has become distinctly unpopular more recently. Economic performances deteriorated across the world after the 1970s – partly thanks to the very success of the earlier economic developments (e.g., drying up of surplus labour in the advanced countries, saturation of the domestic market for many import substitution industries of developing countries) – and the political consensus that had bolstered the early postwar policy regimes was now seriously challenged. Following this collapse of the Golden Age after the first oil shock, a new politico-economic doctrine known as neoliberalism soon emerged as the dominant economic and political ideology (see essays in Chang and Rowthorn, 1995, for some critical evaluations of neoliberalism).

According to the neoliberals, the existence of what they see as a grossly over-extended state not only threatens personal freedom and introduces arbitrariness in the activities of the government (Mises, Hayek, Buchanan), but also opens the door for the appropriation of the state apparatus by sectional interest groups, including the politicians and the government bureaucrats themselves (Stigler, Niskanen, Olson). Rejecting the corporatist philosophy of the Golden Age, which was based on the notion of 'antagonistic cooperation' between organized groups (capital, labour, farmers, etc.), the neoliberals called for the curtailment and restraint of the state activities and the weakening (if not total disbandment) of those corporate groups, which to them were little more than covert forms of cartels advancing 'special interests'.

Although very few of them actually advocate a full return to the 'nightwatchman state' in the classical mould, the neoliberals emphatically reject the notion of the middle way, the pursuit of which to them has been the source of many current economic and social ills. They argue that the over-extension of the state and the ever-increasing state regulations (often implemented due to the pressures from special interest groups) blunt the economic incentives to work hard and try new things, thus creating inefficiencies and rigidities in the economy that harm its performance. Therefore, in order to revitalise the economy, they argue, it is necessary to restrain the state and liberate individual choices and initiatives from its suffocating grips, through policies such as privatization, deregulation, and budget cuts (for a typical statement of such a policy agenda, see Giersch 1986). Privatization is regarded as necessary in order to restore the profit motive as the motor force behind efficiency and productivity growth. Deregulation, it is argued, would free the entrepreneurs from the straitjacket of government regulations and give them more chances to exercise initiatives and take risk. Tax cuts and a balanced budget (which, together, amounts to budget cuts) are recommended in order to stop the draining away of resources from the productive and efficient private sector to the unproductive and inefficient public sector, to improve the incentives to work hard and invest, and to allow people to exercise more choices in deciding their lifestyles.

IS THERE STILL A MIDDLE WAY?

The neoliberal revolution started in the late 1970s in the advanced capitalist countries which were traditionally more open to liberal ideas, such as the US and the UK – although a few years before them, under General Pinochet, Chile had embarked on the same path, only with more ruthlessness and speed. It then spread to other advanced countries throughout the 1980s – albeit its popularity in these countries was less than that in the US and the UK. Many developing capitalist countries maintained their early postwar policy regime of state-led industrialization (somewhat misleadingly called import-substitution industrialization) until the early 1980s, thanks to the recycled petrodollar, despite deteriorating internal and external economic conditions since the mid-1970s. However, they finally had to succumb to the pressures from inside and outside to restructure their economic policy regimes, when international finance dried up for most of them following the Mexican default in 1982. The spread of neoliberalism reached its peak when the ex-socialist countries of Eastern Europe and the former USSR decided to ditch the 'second way' and fully embrace the neoliberal doctrines in their most radical forms.

As is now becoming clearer, the neoliberal experiments have rarely delivered what they promised. The neoliberal policies in the US and the UK, the advanced capitalist economies which made the most 'progress' in this regard, may have produced some short-term efficiency improvements in some areas, but on the whole have failed to improve the long-term performance of the economy – and all these at the costs of increased inequality in income distribution, higher unemployment, and increased instability of the macroeconomy (at least partly due to the increase in speculative financial activities following financial deregulation). Neoliberal reforms in most developing countries also have failed in general to improve their long-term economic prospects, and have sometimes even led to disastrous results – as seen in the early 1980s economic crisis in Chile or the current Mexican crisis. And what has been happening in many former socialist countries since they embraced the most naive form of neoliberalism testifies to the limitations of the neoliberal policy package, especially in its extreme form – steep decline in the level of activities, rising unemployment, decaying of public services (law and order, health, basic R&D), increasing income inequality, and in some countries, the general disintegration of the basic social fabric.

It is the neoliberal doctrine which created this deplorable state of the world that Geoff Harcourt has recently set himself to criticize. In those papers that we mentioned at the beginning of this article, he delivers some damning criticisms of a doctrine which glorifies individualistic competition at the cost of almost all forms of cooperation, encourages unproductive speculative activities over productive entrepreneurship, is willing to lay idle manpower and capacity in an almost obsessive pursuit of low inflation, and actually damages the long-term growth prospects of the economy by excessive cuts in public spending on education, infrastructural investments and R&D in the name of fiscal prudence and widening of individual choices.

The resulting society resembles increasingly the one which Geoff Harcourt and many of his generation of economists, and before them people like Keynes who were their inspirations, have devoted their professional and personal lives to reform. High unemployment, increasing social and economic inequality, reductions in the long-term growth potential of the economy due to the neglect of investment, research, training and education, and other features of this 'brave new world' are exactly the features of capitalism which these economists wanted to eliminate through the construction and development of the middle way, based on class compromise, social consensus, and commitment to long-term productive investment in human and physical assets.

Geoff Harcourt rightly feels indignant at the current situation, which has created so much unemployment, inequality, and the incentives for unproductive entrepreneurship, in the name of increasing efficiency and growth, both of which frequently have failed to materialize. He outlines a proposal to steer our economies away from what he sees as a madness and back to a sensible middle way. He argues for the restoration of full employment and growth as top policy objectives and the provision of appropriate policy measures. He also calls for the restoration of productive, committed, long-term-oriented entrepreneurship as the driving force behind capitalism. This, according to him, requires macroeconomic measures that will reduce uncertainties which hamper long-term productive investments, on the one

35

hand, and financial incentives which penalize short-term, speculative activities, on the other hand.

NOT JUST ONE, BUT MANY MIDDLE WAYS

Geoff Harcourt's belief in the feasibility of a middle way is amply supported by recent empirical research, which shows that, even after the end of the Golden Age and the alleged end of the middle way, many capitalist economies, developed and developing, have performed well on the basis of policy regimes which were distinctively different from the free market ideal of the neoliberals.

The spectacular industrial and export success of Japan and the East Asian NICs during the postwar period have led to a heated debate on industrial policy. Various studies have revealed that these economies, which were once thought to be paragons of free market economy, succeeded on the basis of active state intervention which aimed to raise productivity and reduce 'excessive' competition. Such findings have led to a debate on whether such intervention, which has little grounding in orthodox economic principles, was indeed feasible and could be beneficial at all (see Johnson 1984; Thompson 1989; World Bank 1993; Chang 1994a). Through the debate, it has become quite widely accepted that conscious coordination and promotion of selected industries by a competent elite bureaucracy can produce productivity growth and structural change much faster than can unrestrained competition.

The superior employment performance in certain 'social corporatist' countries of Europe (especially the Scandinavian countries and Austria) since the mid-1970s (until at least the late 1980s), when all other advanced countries witnessed persistently high levels of unemployment, also attracted the attention of a large number of researchers. It was recognized that such performances were largely due to these countries' tripartite bargaining structure between the centralized union, the employers' organization, and the government, which allowed the maintenance of high employment and sustained investment in return for wage restraints (see Goldthorpe 1984; Schott 1984; Bruno and Sachs 1985; Pekkarinen et al. 1992). Thus, it was concluded that the wage bargaining structure can and does significantly affect the employment and other macroeconomic performances of a country.

The successes of small firms producing for niche markets, in certain parts of the world, such as Emilia-Romagna in Italy, Baden-Württemberg in Germany, and Hong Kong, spawned the literature on 'flexible specialization' and 'industrial districts'. This literature identified the cooperation amongst small firms in areas which are normally subject to competition (e.g., R&D, training, input purchase, marketing) as an important source of industrial dynamism in these regions (Brusco 1982; Piore and Sabel 1984; Portes et al. 1989). It was emphasized that the 'communities' or 'networks' amongst the producers in these regions have provided an important vehicle, which is absent in other economies where 'arm's-length' relations prevail, to overcome the 'collective action' problems in the provision of public goods in a large number setting.

In the studies of the industrial crises and adjustments in the OECD economies during the late 1970s and the early 1980s, it also became increasingly clear that the financial system plays a critical role in determining the ability to restructure their industries (Zysman 1983). In this literature, it was emphasized that the close relationship between the industrial and the financial capitals provided by large banks in countries like Germany, or by the state in countries like France or Japan, gave them superior ability to mobilize 'patient' capital which allowed large-scale, long-term investment that is necessary for major industrial restructuring. Recent debates on 'shareholder vs. stakeholder capitalism' (Dore (1993) provides the best summary; also see Albert 1991 for a more popularized version of the argument) also follows up the similar theme of how different incentive structures for those who supply various inputs to enterprises affect the way in which long-term commitments necessary for productivity growth are generated. In this literature, it is argued that economies such as Germany and Japan, where the enterprises are *not* run purely in the interests of the shareholders, who (due to their ability to 'exit' easily) are more short-term-oriented, but are run in the interests of 'stakeholders' (workers, managers, input suppliers, or even local community), who tend to have longer-term commitments, have better long-term economic performances, because they are better able to encourage long-term investments in various physical and human assets that are necessary for productivity growth.

All these studies show not only that the middle way is feasible and often more desirable in many respects than the free market alternative, but more interestingly that there are not just one, but several middle ways (see also Chang 1994b; Chang and Kozul-Wright 1994). Of course, at one level, we can talk about 'the' middle way, as there clearly is a common thread running through the various types of capitalism that were discussed in the above – namely, that the economies that are able to generate more effective long-term-oriented cooperative arrangements regarding (technological and organizational) learning and investments (in human and physical assets) are likely to outperform the countries that largely rely on classic free market mechanisms, which depend on short-term, individualistic competitive forces. However, at the same time, it is important to recognize the diversity across time and place in the institutional mechanisms that can deliver productive long-term commitment, as this raises questions concerning a number of fundamental neoliberal premises, and more broadly concerning mainstream economics, as we briefly sketch out in the following.

First of all, the recognition of the institutional diversity of capitalism reveals problems with what Hirschman (1981) called the 'monoeconomics' tendency

37

of mainstream economics. This refers to the belief that there is only one set of scientific laws in economics which can, and should, be applied to all economies. However, the above-mentioned researches on different types of capitalism, on the one hand, and the recent theoretical developments in institutional economics (for some examples, see Langlois 1986 and Aoki *et al.* 1990, on the other hand, have shown that the institutional structure of an economy affects the final outcome of a given policy, and therefore that the same policy could produce a wide range of outcomes when applied to countries with different institutional (and other) conditions.

Once this point is recognized, the neoliberal practice of prescribing the same policy package to all countries – with very little regard for their institutional (and indeed other) differences – emerges as an indefensible exercise. As many critiques of the Bretton Woods institutions have pointed out, the prescription of essentially the same policy package to all developing and ex-socialist countries, without due attention to the differences in the institutional and other conditions they each face, has been one of the reasons why their policies have not been very successful in general, and have sometimes produced disastrous results (see Taylor 1987 for developing countries; see Chang and Nolan 1995 on the ex-socialist economies).

Certainly, further research into exactly how different institutional structures affect policy outcome is required before we can fully incorporate institutional factors in our policy design, but recognizing the differences in institutional structure across capitalist economies is the first step towards such a goal.

Secondly, recognizing the institutional diversity of capitalism leads us to question the widespread (and often implicit) belief amongst the neoliberal economists, and many mainstream economists, that markets are somehow more 'natural' institutions and therefore that the free market system is easier to replicate than some other system which requires effective non-market institutions. So whenever we try to propagate some middle ways that have proved successful in certain countries, we encounter criticisms from the neoliberals that they are not relevant to other countries, because they succeeded only because of some peculiar institutions which other countries cannot replicate, such as a competent bureaucracy (say, for East Asian-style industrial policy), strong and well-disciplined trade unions (say, for Scandinavian social corporatism), or strong local community networks (say, for Italian industrial districts). However, the same people never question whether the Anglo-Saxon-style free market system may also suffer from the same 'replicability problem' when it is transplanted, as they implicitly believe effective markets are something that can be easily and quickly, if not instantaneously, created.

However, as Polanyi (1957) so powerfully showed, the supposedly 'natural' evolution of market institutions in the quintessential 'free market' economy of Britain around the Industrial Revolution required wide-ranging and systematic interventions by the government. And the same can be said of the other 'model' free market economy, namely, the US in the earlier phase of its development (see Kozul-Wright 1995). Seen thus, the 'first way' (i.e., free market capitalism) also requires a process of institution-building, and therefore is not necessarily easier to replicate than any of the many middle ways that we talked about – it is just that it requires a different set of institutions. Indeed, if the free market system is as 'natural' and easy to replicate as the neoliberals believe, how is it that very few countries in fact achieved economic development through such a system (say, the UK, the US during certain phases, and Hong Kong), while many more countries have successfully developed through some middle way?

If we wish to make economics more relevant to real-world policy solutions, we need to start by treating the market on an equal footing with other institutions, that is, as an institution that can be (and sometimes has to be) consciously constructed and maintained, and therefore accepting that travelling down the first way will be equally, if not more, difficult than travelling down one of the middle ways.

The third point that arises from the recognition of the institutional diversity of capitalism concerns the hidden 'country biases' in neoliberal economics. The problem is not simply that the neoliberal economists ignore the institutional differences between the real world economies and reduce all of them to a simplified model economy. The problem is also that, in the conceptual construction of the model economy, some country-specific institutions and behavioural patterns – in this case, those of the US and the UK – are uncritically taken as 'universal', thus leading to a fundamentally biased view of the ideal economy against which the real world economies are judged.

For example, the neoliberal arguments about enterprise governance are always based on the premise that the shareholders are, as the owners of enterprises, the ultimate principals in whose interests the enterprises should be run. However, this premise is essentially derived from the institutional configuration of the Anglo-Saxon economies, and therefore does not necessarily hold in other economies. As clearly shown in the shareholder vs. stakeholder debate, in many non-Anglo-Saxon countries, business enterprises are simply not conceptualized, not to mention actually run, as organizations that are there to satisfy the shareholders only, but are run as organizations which serve the interest of everyone who has a stake in them (of course different weights will be given to the interests of different groups).

So even such an apparently innocuous premise like 'enterprises are owned by shareholders and therefore should be run in their interests' turns out to be based on the characteristic institutional configuration of particular (in this case, Anglo-Saxon) economies. By treating this premise as somehow universal, the neoliberals are effectively treating what the non-Anglo-Saxon countries do as 'aberrations' from the model economy, which should, and would, be corrected sooner or later – note, for example, the talks of the 'underdeveloped' stock market of Germany or Japan. But why should, say, the German- or the Japanese-style corporate governance systems be regarded as 'aberrations', when they are much more widespread and often more effective than the Anglo-Saxon-style ones?

Revealing the hidden 'country biases' in certain fundamental premises of neoliberal economics (and more broadly mainstream economics in general), and thus abandoning the (often implicit) assumption that somehow the Anglo-Saxon institutions are 'normal' and those of other countries are (if they are different from the former) aberrations, will be the first step towards the construction of a more balanced and institutionally realistic economic theory.

CONCLUDING REMARKS

In this essay, we have argued that there are significant differences in the ways in which different 'capitalist' countries define the relationship between the economy and the polity, decide the allocation of resources between competing uses, distribute the fruits of growth, provide incentives for people to invest in long-term human and physical assets, encourage people to cooperate with each other, and so on. And, we have argued, only by recognizing such diversity and by developing theories which can accommodate such diversity as an essential part of their theoretical construction, will we be able to make our subject more relevant for the many real-world problems that we face today.

Although the recent revival in institutional economics is an indication that our subject is finally moving that way, we should not delude ourselves into believing that more theoretical advance is all that we need. The fact is that theories have often fallen behind the practice in the area of institutional innovation. Although they often had at their disposal meagre theoretical tools, if any, their desire to improve things enabled the Italian small capitalists, the Japanese bureaucrats, and the Swedish trade unionists, among others, to create novel institutional mechanisms that few professional economists had even thought about. Identifying more varieties of real-life institutions from various capitalist economies (how many of us know, for example, how Swiss industries are organized, or how the Belgian financial system works?) and trying to understand them will be a first step in the intellectual enterprise to construct an economic theory that incorporates the inherent institutional diversity across societies.

As Geoff Harcourt clearly states in one of his recent articles, 'the choice is not between purely command or centrally planned economies, on the one hand, and free market systems, on the other', but 'there is a vital place for a middle way which may contribute to the on-going discussion concerning the creation of just and equitable societies' (Harcourt 1992: 2).

REFERENCES

Albert, M. (1991) *Capitalism vs. Capitalism*, New York: Four Wall Eight Windows.

Aoki, M., Gustafsson, B. and Williamson, O. (eds) (1990) *The Firm as a Nexus of Treaties*, London: Sage Publications.

Bruno, M. and Sachs, J. (1985) *Economics of Worldwide Stagflation*, Cambridge, Mass.: Harvard University Press.

Brusco, M. (1982) 'The Emilian model: productive decentralisation and social integration', *Cambridge Journal of Economics*, 6.

Buchanan, J. and Tullock, G. (1962) *The Calculus of Consent*, Ann Arbor, Mich.: University of Michigan Press.

Cairncross, F. and Cairncross, A. (eds) (1992) *The Legacy of the Golden Age – The 1960s and Their Economic Consequences*, London: Routledge.

Castells, M., Portes, A. and Benton, L. (eds) (1989) *The Informal Economy*, Baltimore, Md.: Johns Hopkins University Press.

Chang, H.-J. (1994a) *The Political Economy of Industrial Policy*, London and Basingstoke: Macmillan.

—— (1994b) 'State, institutions, and structural change', *Structural Change and Economic Dynamics*, 5,2.

—— and Kozul-Wright, R. (1994) 'Organising development: comparing the national systems of entrepreneurship in Sweden and South Korea', *Journal of Development Studies*, 30,4.

—— and Nolan, P. (eds) (1995) *The Transformation of the Communist Economies – Against the Mainstream*, London and Basingstoke: Macmillan.

—— and Rowthorn, B. (eds) (1995) *Role of the State in Economic Change*, Oxford: Oxford University Press.

Dore, R. (1993) 'What makes the Japanese different?', in C. Crouch and D. Marquand (eds), *Ethics and Markets*, Cambridge: Polity Press.

Friedman, M. (1962) *Capitalism and Freedom*, Chicago and London: The University of Chicago Press.

Giersch, H. (1986) 'Liberalisation for faster economic growth', Occasional Paper no. 74, London: Institute of Economic Affairs.

Goldthorpe, J. (ed.) (1984) *Order and Conflict in Contemporary Capitalism*, Oxford: Oxford University Press.

Harcourt, G. (1992) 'Markets, madness and a middle way', The Second Donald Horne Lecture, Sydney, Australia.

Hayek, F. (1944) *The Road to Serfdom*, London: Routledge & Kegan Paul.

Hirschman, A. (1981) 'The rise and decline of development economics', in A. Hirschman, *Essays in Trespassing*, Cambridge: Cambridge University Press.

—— (1991) *The Rhetoric of Reaction*, Cambridge, Mass.: Harvard University Press.

Johnson, C. (ed.) (1984) *The Industrial Policy Debate*, San Francisco, Calif.: Institute for Contemporary Studies.

Kozul-Wright, R. (1995) 'The myth of Anglo-Saxon capitalism: reconstructuring the history of the American state', in H.-J. Chang and B. Rowthorn (eds) *op. cit.*

Langlois, R. (ed.) (1986) *Economics as a Process*, Cambridge: Cambridge University Press.

Marglin, S. and Schor, J. (eds) (1990) *The Golden Age of Capitalism*, Oxford: Oxford University Press.

Mises, L. (1929) 'Interventionism', in L. Mises, *A Critique of Interventionism*, translated by H. Sennholz (1977), New Rochelle, New York: Arlington House.

Pekkarinen, J., Pohjola, M., and Rowthorn, B. (eds) (1992) *Social Corporatism*, Oxford: Oxford University Press.

Piore, M. and Sabel, C. (1984) *The Second Industrial Divide*, New York: Basic Books.

Polanyi, K. (1957) *The Great Transformation*, Boston, Mass.: Beacon Press.

Schott, K. (1984) *Policy, Power and Order*, New Haven and London: Yale University Press.

Taylor, L. (1987) *Varieties of Stabilisation Experiences*, Oxford: Oxford University Press.

Thompson, G. (ed.) (1989) *Industrial Policy: USA and UK Debates*, London: Routledge.

World Bank (1993) *The East Asian Miracle*, New York: Oxford University Press.

Zysman, R. (1983) *Governments, Markets, and Growth*, Oxford: Martin Robertson.

4

EFFICIENT REDISTRIBUTION IN A GLOBALLY COMPETITIVE ECONOMY

Samuel Bowles and Herbert Gintis

INTRODUCTION

In the decades following the Second World War, policy-makers chose from a rich menu of alternative models of egalitarian economic growth. Some advocated nationalization and central planning, to emulate the combination of rapid industrialization and relatively egalitarian distribution experienced by the Soviet Union and China. Others, especially in the developing countries, suggested import substitution policies, promising that both rapid industrial growth and high wages would flow from high tariff barriers. Policy-makers in the advanced capitalist countries largely favoured a Keynesian/social democratic model in which the welfare state and rapid wage growth promoted economic growth by increasing aggregate demand.

The golden age of egalitarian policy is apparently over. Central planning, nationalization, and import substitution models have collapsed, while social democracy has suffered serious political defeats in recent years. In a new environment of heightened international competition, environmental constraints, and other supply-side limits to growth, attention has shifted from equality to productivity and competitiveness.

The growing focus on questions of wages and productivity under this general supply-side rubric has supported a near consensus that wage restraint and the limitation of social expenditures are necessary conditions for adequate economic performance. Society might still opt for egalitarian measures on moral grounds, many now believe, but at the cost of leaving even the poor to suffer in the long run.

While recent attention to issues of productivity is entirely welcome, we believe that abandoning the egalitarian project is ill-founded. The concern with supply-side problems does not preclude egalitarian solutions. There is no simple correspondence between demand-side economics and egalitarian policy on the one hand, and supply-side economics and inegalitarian distributional policies on the other. Figure 1 illustrates a richer menu of choices. Demand-side considerations can as easily justify not only egalitarian

		Distributional aspect of policy	
		Egalitarian	Inegalitarian
Diagnosis of the problem	Demand side	Left Keynesianism	Low-wage export-led growth
	Supply side	Productivity enhancing redistributions	IMF 'structural adjustment' policy

Figure 1 Economic performance and policies

demand-expansion policies, but inegalitarian policies as well, for example in the form of low-wage export-led growth (the 'Demand side' row in Figure 1).[1] Conversely, solving supply-side problems need not involve 'structural adjustments' that increase inequality: students of the social democratic economies of Northern Europe have argued that success in these cases has depended on the long-term productivity effects of such interventions as active labour market policies, human resource development, wage equalization, and high levels of trade union membership[2] (the 'Supply side' row in Figure 1). Our main claim in the pages that follow is that policies of egalitarian redistribution, if designed to be incentive-compatible, can attenuate many of the costly incentive problems facing modern economies and hence can be productivity-enhancing.

EQUITY AND EFFICIENCY: AN OVERVIEW

Inequality fosters conflicts ranging from lack of trust in exchange relationships and incentive problems in the workplace to class conflict and regional clashes. These conflicts are costly to police. Also, they often preclude the cooperation needed for low-cost solutions to coordination problems. Since states in highly unequal societies are often incapable of or have little incentive to solve coordination problems, the result is not only the proliferation of market failures in the private economy, but a reduced capacity to attenuate these failures through public policy.[3]

Economic performance depends on what may be termed the structure of economic governance, namely the institutions, norms, and conventions that regulate the incentives and constraints faced by economic actors, and hence that determine the nature of coordination problems and their solutions. Ideally, a structure of governance is a means of avoiding or attenuating the coordination failures that arise when economic actors' interactions lead to

44

such collectively irrational outcomes as unemployment and environmental degradation.

If the above argument is correct, the structure of economic governance critically influences both the level of productivity and the degree of inequality, and is itself strongly influenced by the degree of inequality. Thus the relationship between inequality and economic performance is mediated by the structure of economic governance: inequality impedes economic performance by obstructing the evolution of productivity-enhancing governance structures. Three arguments may be offered in support of this position.

First, institutional structures supporting high levels of inequality often prove costly to maintain. Solving coordination failures often requires an effective and activist state. But a state so empowered is also capable of redistributing income in response to populist pressures. For this reason wealthy individuals may prefer a weak state in an inefficient economy to a strong state in an efficient economy. Indeed, even under autocratic political regimes, increased inequality heightens the probability that the rich would be unable to contain the populist potential of an activist state. Moreover, states in highly unequal societies often commit a large fraction of the economy's productive potential to enforcing the rules of the game from which the inequalities flow.

Enforcement activities in the private sector may also be counted as costs of reproducing unequal institutions. Enforcement costs of inequality may thus take the form of high levels of expenditure on work supervision, security personnel, police, prison guards and the like. Indeed, one might count unemployment itself as one of the enforcement costs of inequality, since the threat of job loss may be necessary to discipline labour. In less conflictual conditions, unutilized labour might have been allocated to productivity-enhancing activities. In the United States in 1987, for example, the above categories of 'guard labour' constituted over a quarter of the labour force, and the rate of growth of guard labour substantially outstripped that of the labour force in the previous two decades (Bowles, *et al.* 1990). Moreover, in highly inegalitarian societies the abuse of property rights is often widespread, militating against long-term investments by the rich and the poor alike.[4]

A second reason for a positive relationship between efficiency and equality is that more equal societies may be capable of supporting levels of cooperation and trust unavailable in more economically divided societies. Both cooperation and trust are essential to economic performance, particularly where limited or asymmetric information make both state intervention and market allocations inefficient.

Where does cooperation fit into traditional economic theory? A time-honoured prejudice among economists holds that economies may be organized by one of two means: competition or command. Yet neither hierarchical command nor atomistic competition captures the range of

45

economic relationships essential to high levels of economic performance. In any economy, a third type of relationship is ubiquitous and essential: bargaining over the creation and sharing of the results of collaborative efforts.[5] Kenneth Arrow writes:

> It is useful for individuals to have some trust in each other's word. In the absence of trust it would be very costly to arrange for alternative sanctions and guarantees, and many opportunities for mutually beneficial cooperation would have to be forgone ... norms of social behavior, including ethical and moral codes (may be) ... reactions of society to compensate for market failures.
>
> (1969: 22)

One of the possible positive productivity effects of greater equality thus may operate through the political and cultural consequences of redistribution. A well-run welfare state or a relatively equal distribution of property holdings may foster the social solidarity necessary to support cooperation and trust.

These and related sentiments frequently provide the basis for low-cost solutions to coordination problems. A critical example of a coordination problem of this type is, of course, the distribution of income and opportunity. It is perhaps not surprising in this regard that in the more advanced welfare states, and more egalitarian capitalist economies – Sweden, Netherlands, Denmark and Germany, for example – the fraction of workdays lost to strikes in the period 1955–89 averaged less than a third of the level in the United States, Canada, Australia and Italy, countries with less well developed welfare states (US Bureau of Labor Statistics 1990).

By providing the cultural and political preconditions for bargained solutions with sufficient legitimacy to require little enforcement, egalitarian distributions of assets and income may contribute to the solution of complex problems that would otherwise be highly costly to solve.[6]

A third source of equality–productivity complementarity concerns the inefficient incentive structures that arise in economies with highly unequal asset distributions. An example may make this clear. Consider a single owner of a machine who hires a single worker to operate the machine. The worker has little reason to supply a high level of effort, since the owner is the residual claimant on the income associated with the asset and hance receives the profit from the worker's labour. Thus without a high level of monitoring, the level of productivity in the firm will be low. A rental contract in which the worker rents the machine from the owner for a fixed sum and becomes residual claimant on the entire income stream of the firm would avoid this incentive problem, of course.[7] But this solution to the labour effort incentive problem simply displaces the incentive problem to the issue of the maintenance and treatment of the machine – in this case the firm's capital stock itself.

The result of these incentive problems is that the concentrated distribution of capital is in this case inefficient: there exists a more egalitarian distribution, in which the worker becomes the owner of the firm's capital goods which, by more effectively addressing the incentive and monitoring problems involved, allows general improvements in wellbeing (including compensation for the erstwhile owner).

The generic problem here is that behaviours critical to high levels of productivity – hard work and risk-taking, for example – generally are sufficiently difficult to monitor that they cannot be fully specified contractually. As a result, key economic actors – workers and managers, for example – cannot fully capture the productivity effects of their activities, as they would for example if they were the residual claimants on the resulting income stream or asset value. The result is termed an 'incentive incompatibility': the residual claimant has an incentive to enhance productivity, but key actors whose behaviours affect productivity are not residual claimants. Where asset holdings are highly concentrated, those who bear the costs of undertaking productivity-enhancing activities often have little claim on the resulting benefits, the result being costly incentive incompatibilities.

Our small firm example thus supports a more general conclusion, one developed by the modern economic theory of principal–agent relationships. A principal–agent relationship arises when the objectives of A (the principal) are affected by some action of B (the agent) which is costly for B to undertake and costly for A to monitor. An important and uncontroversial proposition in the theory of principal–agent relations is this: where a risk-neutral agent supplies a costly-to-monitor good or service to a principal who is the residual claimant in the transaction, efficiency would be enhanced by transferring residual claimancy from the principal to the agent. This is simply a generalization of the commonsense adage that jobs are better done if the persons doing them own the results, for better or worse, of their own effort. Our argument to follow is in the spirit of this proposition, and demonstrates the possibility of attenuating the resulting incentive incompatibilities through reallocations of residual claimancy accomplished by redistributing assets.

Modern economies, of course, cannot avoid incentive incompatibilities by restoring the simple property ownership structures of the world of small firms with single workers. The economies of scale that characterize all contemporary economies make team production ubiquitous. Thus freeriding and related agency problems will arise under any conceivable set of property distributions and institutional arrangements. Nonetheless, structures of economic governance will differ markedly in the costliness of the incentive incompatibilities to which they give rise.

An example is the democratic firm, in which workers are owners of shares in the firm and residual claimants.[8] While firms of this type have been extensively modelled, most approaches have both abstracted from the problem of endogenous enforcement of effort, and attributed to the worker-owned firm forms of property rights ('collective ownership' for example) which militate against efficient decision-making.[9] The more balanced treatment of the worker-owned firm along the lines of our generic active ownership team supports a more positive evaluation, consistent with recent empirical studies.[10]

While the direct residual claimancy effect is likely to be weak in all but the smallest firms, the mutual monitoring effect in the democratic firm is likely to be powerful. Under passive ownership, workers typically have little incentive to reveal private information concerning the level of effort of fellow team members to the employer, while under active ownership they do have such an incentive, provided only that the cost of revealing information is less than the direct residual claimancy gain from doing so. This is likely to be the case in many circumstances.

An additional reason for the technical efficiency of the democratic firm is that the profit-maximizing labour discipline system adopted by the capitalist firm is inefficient in that it uses too many monitoring resources and not enough wage incentives. This is because the capitalist firm faces two prices in selecting its enforcement structure. One, the price of monitoring (at least under ideal competitive conditions) correctly measures a social marginal cost, for the use of monitoring equipment or personnel consumes resources with valued alternative uses and hence has a social opportunity cost. The payment of a higher wage, by contrast, is simply redistributive, akin to a transfer rather than a claim on resources. As a transfer, the wage corresponds to no social opportunity cost, though it is of course a private cost to the employer. Not surprisingly, then, the capitalist firm uses too little wage incentive and too much monitoring relative to an efficient alternative.

An analogy may make this reasoning clear. Imagine a road haulage company choosing between a shorter route over a toll road and a somewhat longer route without tolls. The two prices in question are the operating cost of the truck and the tolls. The trucking company would rationally treat these two costs as equivalent, perhaps avoiding use of the shorter but costlier toll road. But the toll does not represent a social cost, while the operating costs of the truck (wear and tear, fuel, the driver's time and effort) do. The choice of the longer toll-free route, like the capitalist's choice of lower wages and more intense monitoring, is cost-minimizing but inefficient. Active owners' choice of wage payments and monitoring levels will attenuate this problem: to workers, of course, the wage is not a cost but a payment to themselves, so they would not replicate the inefficient choice of the capitalist.[11]

WEALTH INEQUALITY AND THE IMPEDIMENTS TO ACTIVE OWNERSHIP

In a competitive economy one might expect the ownership of assets (and hence residual claimancy) to accrue to those who can use the assets most efficiently; if workers can make better use of productive assets than capitalist owners, or if resident owners do a better job of housing management than absentee landlords, the relevant assets will, *ceteris paribus*, be worth more to them, and hence one might wonder why they do not purchase the assets and thus acquire the associated control and residual claimancy rights. The result would be to attenuate the market failure associated with the passive ownership of residential housing and productive assets.

But credit markets are afflicted with the same asymmetric information and agency problems that beset the residential housing, wage labour and other markets. Lenders adopt strategies designed to attenuate the conflict of interest between the two sides of the credit market, often requiring borrowers to either post substantial collateral or to invest equity in the project. But equity or collateral requirements either prevent most workers or tenants from borrowing sufficient amounts of funds, or impose prohibitive costs on such transactions. Even when this is not the case, risk-averse agents would not choose to concentrate their wealth in a single asset, and the degree of risk aversion is inversely related to wealth.

Thus, despite the fact that active ownership will be more productive in the delivery of residential services, passive ownership and relatively inefficient delivery of services will dominate in asset-poor communities, because the asset-poor are risk-averse and equity requirements are prevalent as a means of endogenous enforcement in the housing market. Similarly, even when more efficient in regulating work than their capitalist counterparts, worker-owned democratic firms nonetheless operate at a competitive disadvantage and hence do not flourish in a capitalist economy, since wealth constraints inhibit the formation and lower the profitability of such firms.[12] This credit market disability of worker-owned firms obviously has greater force the larger and more transactions-specific is the firm's capital requirement.

Wealth constraints and risk aversion among the asset-poor not only impede the spontaneous formation of active ownership teams; they also imply socially non-optimal decision-making by those teams which do form. Most important of these socially irrational effects is the possibly adverse innovation-reducing effects of a redistribution of residual claimancy and control over assets to the asset-poor. It is socially optimal that risk and innovation be handled in a virtually risk-neutral manner, while economic agents tend to be risk-averse, and more so the larger the portion of their wealth is involved in a particular project. Passive ownership mitigates this problem by vesting control in relatively wealthy, highly diversified and hence less risk-averse individuals and institutions. The internally financed team of active owners can be expected to act in a more risk-avoiding manner, since its members are neither wealthy nor capable of diversifying their asset portfolio. Moreover, in the case of productive teams and residential communities, active owners have an additional reason to shun high-risk high-return projects: since active owners enjoy enforcement rents, they incur bankruptcy costs (the loss of job rents or rents of tenancy) not imposed on their passive owner counterparts.

Such socially non-optimal risk-avoiding behaviour can be attenuated if adequate insurance is available to protect active owners against adverse outcomes. Such insurance may require state provision to avoid an obvious adverse selection problem when participation in an insurance plan is voluntary: active teams with a high probability of loss would want to purchase more insurance. The moral hazard problems associated with such insurance can be handled to the extent that it is possible to distinguish between risks resulting from choices made by agents and those that are independent of their choices, and insuring as fully as possible the risk unassociated with the choice of care. Consistent with this principle is the practice of extending the duration of unemployment insurance in periods of high general unemployment rates. Under reasonable assumptions it can be shown that the reduction in exposure unassociated with the agents' actions induces greater risk-taking on the part of the agent. The contribution to long-run productivity growth of policies based on asset redistribution to active owners may depend strongly on the existence of insurance programmes that approximate this ideal.

Several types of interventions could attenuate the market failures we have identified, including (i) providing publicly funded partial loan insurance to foster the extension of credit to asset-poor borrowers incapable of posting sufficient collateral; (ii) directly subsidizing the asset-poor members of efficient but credit-constrained active ownership teams.[13]

CONCLUSION: THE ECONOMICS AND POLITICS OF REDISTRIBUTION

The notion of productivity-enhancing asset redistribution suggests an approach to public policy: level the playing field by redistributing wealth, while enhancing productivity through a more appropriate alignment of incentives and by fostering competition. Opponents of the inegalitarian outcomes generated in capitalism have sometimes attributed these outcomes to competitive processes, and have sought the attenuation of inequality by suppressing the market. Yet as conservatives have often cogently argued, and as market socialists from Oskar Lange to Pranab Bardhan and John Roemer (1992) have long recognized, in the absence of equivalent new allocational and disciplinary mechanisms, suppressing competition may entail the inefficient production and delivery of goods and services. Egalitarian assignment of control and residual claimancy to active owners, aimed at attenuating incentive incompatibilities arising from the agency problems associated with highly unequal wealth distributions, borrows the traditionally progressive notion of redistributing wealth. But it joins this notion to an endorsement of the disciplining effects of market competition, thus offering the possibility of enjoying the benefits of both.

Thus, while global competition challenges many conventional redistributive policies, it does not preclude a recasting of the egalitarian project consistent with the new economic realities. An economically viable new egalitarianism would rely substantially on the kinds of productivity-enhancing asset-based redistributions that simultaneously promote equality and strengthen the economy's competitive position. The chief impediments to egalitarianism in the globally integrated economy may not be a dearth of economically viable programmes, but rather a surfeit of political obstacles. There are three reasons for this.

First, as we have seen, by enhancing the degree of competition in most markets, international integration reduces the effectiveness of demand expansion policies that once helped secure the support of disparate elements in the egalitarian coalitions. Second, the more highly competitive situation has heightened a divergence of interest between public sector and private sector workers, between the employed and the unemployed, among workers, farmers and those in the informal sector, and between these and other groups whose unified endorsement of egalitarian policies was often critical to their success. Owners of firms in consumer goods industries, for example, may be less likely to join workers in support of wage increases and other domestic demand-enhancing policies, and may look instead to the world market.[14] Finally, to the extent that new policies require asset-based redistributions, they are likely to incur strong opposition by an anti-egalitarian coalition which in many countries can readily unify under the banner of the defence of the existing distribution and definition of property rights.

On the other hand, a broader dispersion of asset holdings in the population and the close association of property holdings with both residence and workplace entailed by the asset-based redistribution strategy would reduce the global mobility of capital and thereby might relax one of the major constraints on egalitarian policy.

NOTES

1 As Bhaduri and Marglin (1989), Rowthorn (1982), Taylor (1985) and others have shown, policies to expand aggregate demand need not be egalitarian.
2 See for instance Moene and Wallerstein (1993), Osmani (1993), and Lim *et al.* (1993).
3 For an analysis of this dynamic, see Birdsall and Sabot (1994).
4 In addition to the works already cited, Eaton and White (1991) develop a model in which inequality reduces productivity by fostering insecurity for property rights, and hence weakens the incentive to invest.
5 A tripartite division of governance structures has been proposed by a number of authors. Ouchi (1981) refers to these as markets, bureaucracies and clans, while Ostrom (1990) analyses centralized, market decentralized and decentralized mutual enforcement systems of governance.
6 Bardhan (1993) and Boyce (1988) argue that the many commons-type

coordination problems are easier to solve where inequality among participants is limited. Singleton and Taylor argue that the failure to solve coordination problems often stems from the lack of community, defined as a set of people with shared beliefs, stable membership, and ongoing, relatively unmediated interaction: 'The more a group resembles a community, the lower are the transactions costs which it must meet in order to solve a given collective action problem' (1992: 319) Putnam (1993) finds that horizontal (egalitarian) networks of civic engagement support forms of cooperation which enhance economic performance while vertical (hierarchical) networks do not.

7   The 'residual claimant' owns whatever remains (the residual) after all fixed claims (in this case the rent paid to the owner) are settled.

8   We have in mind something of the type which, according to Craig and Pencavel (1992), is approximated in practice by the ownership structure of a large number of worker-owned plywood mills in the north-west of the United States. See also Dow (1986) and Fehr (1993). Like the passive owner, the team uses contingent renewal to motivate member effort. Team members who are terminated must sell their share of the asset without penalty (other than the loss of the value of the job).

The decision facing the active ownership firm (abstracting from the problem of the optimal number of members), is to select a level of monitoring m to maximize members' present value v of tenure. Each member receives an income from the team equal to $q(\sum_i e_i)/n - m$, where $q(\cdot)$ is revenue as a function of total team effort. Thus the net payment taking account of the member's forgone interest income, ρk_0 on each member's capital contribution k_0, is $w = q(\sum_i e_i)/n - m, - \rho k_0$. Thus the team must select m according to

$$v = \max_m \frac{u(w, c) - \rho z}{\rho + p(e, m)} + z.$$

Given that each worker's best response function is still of the form $e = e(w, m)$, we interpret the problem as follows: the team collectively selects a level of monitoring and agrees to pay the residual income of the organization to members as a salary equal to w plus the forgone return on assets ρk_0. Each team member j then selects e_j to maximise v_j.

9   Ward (1958), Domar (1966), Vanek (1970), Meade (1972), Furubotn and Pejovich (1974), Jensen and Meckling (1979).

10 Levine and Tyson (1990), for instance, surveyed fourteen studies of worker cooperatives and found positive effects on productivity in thirteen of them, with no negative effects in any. Craig and Pencavel's recent (1992) study of worker-owned plywood firms, however, suggests that labour productivity is lower in the coops than in classical firms. Weitzman and Kruse (1990) surveyed sixteen econometric studies of the effects of profit-sharing on productivity and found that of the total of 226 estimated regression coefficients for variables measuring profit-sharing, 94% were positive and 60% were twice or more than their standard errors, while no negative coefficient estimates were statistically significant by this standard. For related studies supporting this research, see Cable and Fitzroy (1980), Ben-Ner (1988), Ben-Ner and Estrin (1988), Conte and Svejnar (1990). Worker participation in decision-making and residual claimancy status appear to be complementary in that their joint effects exceed the additive effects of each factor separately. For a recent review of the evidence, see Bonin et al. (1993).

11 If the capitalist employer charged workers the non-returnable fee in return for

granting them their employment consistent with workers agreeing to accept employment, it would be in the employer's interest to take account of the workers' preferences in the same manner as the workers would themselves (as the desirability of the job would affect the maximal fee the employer could charge). Thus under what may be termed optimal bonding the capitalist firm and the democratic firm would be identical in this respect. But capitalist firms do not practise optimal bonding.

12 We develop this argument formally in our 1994 paper. Briefly, an active ownership organization is viable only if, in a competitive environment, given the structure of financial markets and the wealth position of potential worker-members, active ownership increases the wealth position of a worker currently enjoying the present value v of tenure in the passive ownership organization.

13 Where they are heterogeneous with respect to risk aversion, members of teams might contract for variable amounts of risk exposure, with voting rights being exercised in proportion to their residual claims. This would allow a Pareto-improving allocation of risk within the team, and would give greater decision-making influence to less risk-averse members.

14 Trade liberalization might enhance the viability of egalitarian coalitions in other respects. Gerschenkron (1944) argues that conflicts over tariff policies obstructed a potentially egalitarian farmer–worker alliance in pre-First World War Germany, for example. A general argument might be made that tariff and other policies that politicize the relative prices of commodities tend to favour within-industry alliances seeking to gain income by altering relative goods prices, rather than cross-industry coalitions seeking to alter income distribution directly. The latter type of coalition may be more viable as a vehicle for egalitarian policy.

REFERENCES

Arrow, K. (1969) 'Political and economic evaluation of social effects and externalities', in M. D. Intriligator (ed.) *Frontiers of Quantitative Economics*, Amsterdam: North Holland.

Bardhan, P. (1993) 'Analytics of the institutions of informal cooperation in rural development', *World Development*, 21(4): 633–9.

—— and Roemer, J. (1992) 'Market socialism: a case for rejuvenation', *Journal of Economic Perspectives*, 6(3) (Summer): 101–16.

Ben-Ner, A. (1988) 'Comparative empirical observations on worker-owned and capitalist firms', *International Journal of Industrial Organization*, 6: 7–31.

—— and Estrin, S. (1988) 'Unions and productivity: unionized firms versus union managed firms', mimeo, University of Minnesota.

Bhaduri, A. and Marglin, S. (1989) 'Profit squeeze, stagnationist models, and Keynesian theory' in Stephen Marglin (ed.) *The Rise and Fall of the Golden Age; Lessons for the 1990s*, Oxford: Oxford University Press.

Birdsall, N. and Sabot, R. (1994) 'Inequality and growth reconsidered', World Bank Working Paper.

Bonin, J. P., Jones, D. C. and Putterman, L. (1993) 'Theoretical and empirical studies of producer cooperatives: will ever the twain meet?', *Journal of Economic Literature*, 33(3) (September): 1290–320.

Bowles, S., Gordon, D. and Weisskopf, T. (1990) *After the Waste Land: A Democratic Alternative for the Year 2000*, New York: Doubleday.

Boyce, J. (1988) 'Technological and institutional alternatives in Asian rice irrigation',

Economic and Political Weekly, March 26.

Cable J. and FitzRoy, F. (1980) 'Co-operation and productivity: some evidence from West German experience', *Economic Analysis and Worker's Management*, 14: 163, 180.

Conte, M.A. and Svejnar, J. (1990) 'The performance effect of employee ownership plans', in Alan Blinder (ed.) *Paying for Productivity: A Look at the Evidence*, Washington, D.C.: Brookings Institution: 143–72.

Craig, B. and Pencavel, J. (1992) 'The behavior of worker cooperatives: the plywood companies of the Pacific Northwest', *American Economic Review*, 82(5): 1083–105.

Domar, E. (1966) 'The Soviet collective farm as a producer cooperative', *American Economic Review*, 56: 743–57.

Dow, G. (1986) 'Control rights, competitive markets, and the labor management debate', *Journal of Comparative Economics*, 10(1): 48–61.

Eaton, B. C. and White, W. B. (1991) 'The distribution of wealth and the efficiency of institutions', *Economic Inquiry*, xxix(2): 336–50.

Fehr, E. (1993) 'The simple analytics of a membership market in a labor-managed economy', in S. Bowles, H. Gintis and B. Gustafsson (eds) *Democracy and Markets: Participation, Accountability, and Efficiency*, Cambridge: Cambridge University Press: 260–76.

Furubotn, E. G. and Pejovich, S. (1974) *The Economics of Property Rights*, Cambridge, Mass.: Ballinger.

Gerschenkron, A. (1944) *Bread and Democracy in Germany*, Berkeley, Calif.: University of California Press.

Jensen, M. C. and Meckling, W. J. (1979) 'Rights and production functions: an application to labor-managed firms and codetermination', *Journal of Business*, 52: 469–506.

Levine, I. and Tyson, L. (1990) 'Participation, productivity, and the firm's environment', in A. Blinder (ed.) *Paying for Productivity: A Look at the Evidence*, Washington, D.C.: Brookings: 183–244.

Lim, L. (1993) 'Singapore' in R. Findlay and S. Wellisz (eds) *The Political Economy of Poverty, Equity, and Growth: Five Small Open Economies*, New York: Oxford University Press for the World Bank.

Moene, K. O. and Wallerstein, M. (1993) 'What is wrong with social democracy?' in P. Bardhan and J. Roemer (eds) *Market Socialism: The Current Debate*, Oxford: Oxford University Press.

Osmani, S. R. (1993) 'Is there a conflict between growth and welfarism? the tale of Sri Lanka', *WIDER*, June.

Ostrom, E. (1990) *Governing the Commons*, Cambridge: Cambridge University Press.

Ouchi, W. (1980) 'Markets, bureaucracies and clans', *Administrative Sciences Quarterly*, 25 (March): 129–41.

Putnam, R. (1993) *Making Democracy Work: Civic Traditions in Modern Italy*, Princeton, N.J.: Princeton University Press.

Rowthorn, B. (1982) 'Demand, real wages, and economic growth', *Theme Papers in Political Economy*, reprinted in *Studii Economici* 18: 3–53.

Singleton S. and Taylor, M. (1992) 'Common property, collective action and community', in *Journal of Theoretical Politics*, 4(3): 309–24.

Taylor, L. (1985) 'A stagnationist model of economic growth', *Cambridge Journal of Economics*, 9(4): 383–403.

US Bureau of Labor Statistics, Office of Productivity and Technology (1990) *Industrial Disputes, Workers Involved, and Worktime Lost, 15 Countries,*

1955–1989, Washington, D.C.
Weitzman, M. and Kruse, D. (1990) 'Profit sharing and productivity', in A. Blinder (ed.) *Paying for Productivity: A Look at the Evidence*, Washington, D.C.: Brookings: 95–142.

5

THE FEARS OF ECONOMISTS

Fred Gruen

INTRODUCTION

Schumpeter, in his massive and erudite *History of Economic Analysis*, assesses economists according to both their analytical competence and their 'vision'. The latter is defined in a number of places, most succinctly in the following terms:

> In every scientific venture, the thing that comes first is vision. . . . before embarking upon analytical work of any kind we must first single out the set of phenomena we wish to investigate and acquire 'intuitively' a preliminary notion of how they hang together . . . in practice we mostly do not start from a vision of our own but from the work of our predecessors or from ideas that float in the public mind.
>
> (Schumpeter 1954: 561–2)[1]

It is useful to give a couple of examples of how Schumpeter uses 'vision' as a method of assessing the work of economists. When looking at the English classical economists (Malthus, West, Ricardo and James Mill) he argues that their vision

> fully justifies their being labelled 'pessimists'. Its well-known features were: pressure of population, present already but still more to be expected: nature's decreasing response to human effort to increase the supply of food: hence falling net returns to industry, more or less constant real wages, and ever-increasing . . . rents of land. . . . The most interesting thing to observe is the complete lack of imagination which that vision reveals. Those writers lived at the threshold of the most spectacular economic developments ever witnessed. Vast possibilities matured into realities under their very eyes. Nevertheless they saw nothing but cramped economies, struggling with ever-decreasing success for their daily bread.
>
> (*Ibid.*: 570–1)

Schumpeter also applied this vision/analysis dichotomy to his assessment of the overall contribution of John Maynard Keynes.

Keynes's work presents an excellent example of our thesis that, in principle, vision of facts and meanings precedes analytical work ... in the beginning of the relevant part of Keynes's work stood his vision of England's aging capitalism and his intuitive diagnosis of it ... : the arteriosclerotic economy whose opportunities for rejuvenating venture decline while the old habits of saving formed in times of plentiful opportunity persist. This vision was clearly formulated in the first pages of the *Economic Consequences of the Peace* (1919) and adumbrated with increasing clearness in successive works, especially in the *Tract on Monetary Reform* (1923) and the *Treatise on Money* (1930) ... This *Treatise* ... failed to express Keynes's vision adequately. Thereupon, with admirable resoluteness, he determined to throw away the impeding pieces of apparatus, and bent to the task of framing an analytic system that would express his fundamental idea *and nothing else*. The result, given to the world in 1936, seems to have satisfied him completely....

(*Ibid.*: 171–2; italics in the original)

In the two cases examined so far the 'visions' have been negative ones. In other words, they have been fears which have impelled these thinkers to construct analytical frameworks which provide intellectual reinforcement for their pessimistic visions. It will be the contention here that economists' visions are much more frequently fears than hopes, though one can of course find the odd example of an optimist among Schumpeter's economic troupe.

Applying Schumpeter's dichotomy to his own work provides another example of a fearsome vision which turned out to be groundless. As a conservative economist who thoroughly approved of the capitalist system, Schumpeter was deeply pessimistic about its future. The obsolescence of the entrepreneurial function, the destruction of the protecting strata (i.e. the monarchy and aristocracy, the army, the church and the bureaucracy), the hostility of intellectuals – and of an organized labour movement – would gradually spell the doom of the capitalist engine of growth which had given us vastly expanded living standards.

In the light of subsequent events, these fears were again hopelessly exaggerated. The quarter century after the Second World War produced the 'Golden Age of Capitalism';[2] a hitherto unprecedented acceleration in the growth of both productivity and living standards in the developed capitalist world – whilst the next quarter century produced the demise of the major alternative form of social organization – i.e. large-scale collective central planning of economic activity.

The aim of this paper will be to examine some other common fears of economists; mostly more recent than those given in Schumpeter's History. We shall start with two fairly clear-cut examples.

PESSIMISM ABOUT THE TERMS OF TRADE AND ABOUT POPULATION CHANGE

Whenever the terms of trade move against a country or group of countries, economists will be found in these countries who will construct an analytical framework as to why these trends will, almost inevitably, continue. The Malthusian theoretical schema can be refined to justify such fears in those countries which specialize in the export of manufactures and in the import of raw materials. It has been reported that W.S. Jevons kept enormous stocks of coal in his basement to guard against the inevitable rise in the price of this scarce, but then essential, raw material.

Early in his career, Keynes was fearful about Britain's terms of trade. 'As early as 1912 Keynes ... pointed to the re-emergence of the "law of diminishing returns for raw products" leading to a shift in the terms of trade against industrial countries ... the nineteenth-century era of cheap food and raw materials was over' (Skidelsky 1992: 149–50). This theme was continued eloquently in chapter 2 of Keynes's *The Economic Consequences of the Peace*.[3]

Beveridge, in his 1923 presidential address to Section F of the British Academy produced statistics which showed that the terms of trade had not turned against the industrial countries and certainly, during the inter-war years, they moved in Britain's favour. On a global level, food production is believed to have outstripped population growth during both the nineteenth and the twentieth centuries. In other words, technical change in food production has outstripped diminishing returns worldwide for some two hundred years now.

But this has not prevented alarmist extrapolations of adverse terms of trade trends for industrial countries whenever such a movement in the terms of trade occurred temporarily. As Maddison put it:

> Although Malthusian fears gradually faded with regard to agricultural land, there has been recurrent concern about other natural resources ... conservationists continued to be gloomy about resource constraints and waste of non-renewable assets ... In the 1950s Colin Clark was worried about exhausting water resources, and the US government set up the Paley Commission because it was concerned about the adequacy of mineral resources.
>
> (1991: 58)

In the 1970s the fear that economic growth was running into constraints because of the exhaustion of fixed natural resources ensured enormous publicity for the Club of Rome's *The Limits to Growth*.

One of the most widely discussed theories concerning the secular terms of trade was the Prebisch–Singer hypothesis published independently by these two economists in 1950 (Prebisch 1950 and Singer 1950). The fears expressed are opposite to those of Malthus, Ricardo, Jevons and Keynes. Based on the lower income elasticity of demand for primary products, and especially for food, Prebisch constructed an analytical framework designed to show that the primary producing countries of 'the periphery' will finish up with a growing income gap, with persistent unemployment and a balance of payments deficit which will impose an important external constraint on economic growth.

There is disagreement as to what the facts show regarding secular movements in the terms of trade.[4] The point made here is that 'visions' are usually negative. In other words, arguments about likely future trends are usually advanced by those who are fearful of the relevant changes (or are addressed to audiences harmed by them). It is rare that 'visions' will be addressed to those who would benefit from some relative price changes.

Negative views also prevail about population change, irrespective of whether authors are concerned about the growth or the decline of populations. As Robin Barlow put it: 'Many of the economists writing on the growth of population, from Malthus to the Club of Rome, are notorious for their bleak view of the future. If population growth is a bad thing, one might be excused for thinking that its decline might be beneficial. But much of the writing on the decline is equally alarmist'.[5]

This does not deny that some fears may have rational bases. As Kissinger is supposed to have said, the mere fact that you are paranoid is no evidence that people aren't after you. But, just as paranoids are likely to exaggerate whether 'people really are after you', so fears are likely to lead to exaggerated judgements about the dangers in store.

ECONOMISTS AND THE STATE

During my professional life, economists have become increasingly fearful about the state. At the time of its publication in 1944, mainstream economists widely regarded Hayek's *Road to Serfdom* as having greatly exaggerated the dangers of too powerful a state.[6] However, with the passage of time, these ideas have become more influential – perhaps associated with the decline of influence of Cambridge (UK) and the rise of Chicago.[7]

No doubt there are many causes for this growing fear of the state. The unspeakable crimes committed by the agents of some states are an obvious candidate. What appeared as an inexorable growth of government expenditure in western democracies (without very clear longer-term benefits) – not to mention the discreditable economic and political performance of the Soviet Union – are other reasons for the eclipse of the earlier, more benign, view of the state.

This earlier benign view was basically that government (and its various constituents, such as legislators and bureaucrats) attempted to further 'the public interest'; however differently this may have been conceived by different people.[8] One should not deny the obvious relevance and validity of the distinguishing assumption of the Public Choice literature – namely that individuals in the political arena, as in the marketplace, are likely to behave in their own self-interest (Mueller 1989: 349). But that self-interest may manifest itself in pursuing 'good' (i.e. public interest) policies – especially if policy-makers can afford to be far-sighted, rather than myopic.

It seems plausible to argue that economists' current dominant emotion towards the state, namely fear, has gone too far. Purely in terms of economic success, the attempt to nobble the state can turn out to be counter-productive. At the level of macroeconomic performance, one of the major themes of the 1970s pursued by Nobel Laureate James Buchanan, the Virginia School (and others) was that inflation is the inevitable outcome of the normal functioning of democratic political institutions and that central aspects of economic policy-making need to be removed from the control of elected representatives.[9]

About this time too, Hayek renewed his suggestion that the government monopoly on the issue of money be discontinued. In spite of the fact that we have not removed most economic policy-making from the control of elected representatives – or turned the issuing of currencies over to private competition – inflation has declined very substantially in most OECD countries since that time.

Furthermore, recent empirical work suggests that there seems to be a clear tendency for deficits to be larger in those democratic countries which are characterized by weaker governments – where weakness is indicated by a short average tenure of government and by the presence of many political parties in the ruling coalition (Roubini and Sachs 1989). Where power is dispersed, either across branches of the government (as in the US), or across many political parties in a coalition government (as is typical in Italy) it has been notoriously difficult to achieve responsible fiscal economic management.

When assessing the economic growth performance of developing countries, it again appears likely that weak governments show up badly. Economists have been intrigued by the 'East Asian miracle', the unparalleled economic growth rates achieved by Japan, Korea, Taiwan and a number of other East Asian economies. That governments have played a major role in this growth is common ground among practically all economists; but some attribute these successes to governments limiting their role solely to making markets function better.[10]

Given the evidence of both the authoritarian and the often interventionist nature of governments in such countries as Japan, Korea, Taiwan, Singapore and China, this latter argument seems difficult to sustain. The World Bank's *The East Asian Miracle. A World Bank Policy Research Report* provides an outline of the different attempts that have been made to identify those policies which have contributed most directly to these economic success stories.

While complete agreement on either the necessary institutional environment or the crucial policies cannot be hoped for, the World Bank stresses three major factors:

> In each High-Performing Asian Economy (HPAE), a technocratic elite insulated to a degree from excessive political pressure supervised macroeconomic management.... All protected essentially conservative macroeconomic policies by limiting the scope for politicians and interest groups to derail those policies ... All of the HPAEs created secure institutional environments for private investment that led to very high levels of private sector-led growth ... The export-push strategy – the use of fundamentals and interventions to encourage rapid export growth – was the HPAEs' most broad based and successful application of selective interventions ... While the changing trading environment will limit the use of highly targeted policies ... the broad pro-export stance characteristics of all eight HPAEs remains viable.
>
> (World Bank 1993: 348–58, *passim*)

In other words, strong governments have the potential to establish good as well as poor environments for their citizens' economic welfare. Attempting to prevent them from doing harm can, at the same time, prevent them from doing good.

At the micro-economic level the liberal revival is mainly concerned with limiting the role of government and maximizing individual freedom (Henderson 1995). Some of its libertarian adherents, including Milton Friedman, take this so far as to oppose such public health measures as governmental anti-smoking campaigns, prohibition of tobacco advertising, and the compulsory installation of seat belts in cars (let alone making it compulsory to wear them).[11] While libertarians argue that economic and personal freedoms are inseparable, that relationship is by no means so clear-cut. Many Asian authoritarian regimes manage to allow a considerable amount of freedom for businesses, which do not rock the boat politically. Again, as Paul Samuelson has pointed out, the outspoken defenders of economic freedoms are not always so outspoken in defence of personal freedom – occasionally leading to the persecution of unpopular minorities by majorities.[12]

A public choice theorist, Barry Weingast, recently argued that there is 'a fundamental political dilemma of an economic system: a government strong enough to protect property rights is also strong enough to confiscate the wealth of its citizens' (1993: 287). Although governments have frequently confiscated wealth in the past, in these days of free capital movements and almost instantaneous transfers of funds, the likelihood of any government in a modern industrial democracy being able to confiscate wealth – without dire short-run electoral consequences – seems an example of one of these far-fetched fears of some observers which we have attempted to document.

THE FEARS OF THE LEFT

The Left has been equally fearful and has detected many 'inevitable' trends which seem, in retrospect, to have been less inevitable. For this the Marxian doctrine of the inevitable contradictions of capitalism laid the basic foundation.

The inevitable contradictions of capitalism

While Schumpeter regarded both the assumptions and techniques of Marx's analytical framework as open to serious objection, he praised it as the only genuinely evolutionary economic theory of its time: 'the grand vision of an immanent evolution of the economic process – that, working through accumulation, somehow destroys the economy as well as the society of competitive capitalism and somehow produces an untenable social situation that will somehow give birth to another type of social organisation – remains' (1954: 441).

It is this basic vision which has remained at the centre of most radical economic thought and has been responsible for repeated forecasts from prominent analysts on the Left of imminent terminal crises about to confront the capitalist world.[13] A perusal of such journals as *The Socialist Register, The New Left Review* and *The Journal of Post Keynesian Economics* over the last two or three decades can produce countless examples.[14]

One of the mechanisms supposedly leading to the collapse of capitalism was 'the fiscal crisis of the state' which – according to O'Connor (1973) – prevents the capitalist state from simultaneously fulfilling two basic and contradictory functions: accumulation (which requires investment to be profitable) and legitimation (which requires greater equality of incomes in the name of achieving more social harmony).

During the 1950s, 1960s and even extending into the 1970s, the Marxist-inspired 'dependency' literature regarded poverty and dependence on the 'periphery' as inevitable under capitalism and under free trade.[15] Since the growth of the Asian 'tiger' economies, however, one has heard less of this supposed inevitability of poverty and dependence of third world countries under global capitalism.

The fear of technology and of de-skilling

While technical change will enable existing products and services to be produced more cheaply and/or allow new commodities to be produced, there are usually winners and losers associated with such changes. That some existing skills can become redundant as a result of technical change was known to both Adam Smith and Karl Marx – though they put very different interpretations on such phenomena.

With the publication of Braverman's *Labor and Monopoly Capital* (1976) Marx's de-skilling hypothesis received a new lease of life. Braverman regarded the reduction of skill in productive jobs as 'the general law of the capitalist division of labor', which he believed to be certainly the most powerful and general force acting upon the organization of work. Countering the obvious evidence of rising levels of formal education, Braverman argues that credentialism explains this rise in educational levels, which are not required for carrying out work in most job categories.

What Braverman's argument does not explain is why employers are prepared to pay more for highly educated workers, if the latter are no more productive – or why economists working with human capital models have been able to show returns to education, even in those situations where credentialism could have no conceivable benefits (e.g. in the productivity of self-employed farmers). Without wishing to deny that technological progress can have all sorts of unsettling effects – effects which can be harmful for individuals whose jobs and livelihoods are threatened – there can be little doubt that the overall effect of technical progress has been to reduce the physical drudgery and the monotony of work and, at the same time, provide many with new and much more interesting and challenging occupations.

Inequality

As Amartya Sen pointed out in his 1972 Radcliffe Lecture on Economic Inequality: 'The idea of inequality is both very simple and very complex. At one level it is the simplest of all ideas and has moved people with an immediate appeal hardly matched by any other concept. At another level it is an exceedingly complex notion which makes statements on inequality highly problematic, and it has been, therefore, the subject of much research, (1973: vii). As a result, one finds careful scholars examining trends in inequalities who are extremely loath to make any definitive statements, while those who are less careful use selected statistics to 'illustrate' general tendencies which turn out to be less general on closer examination.

Growing income inequalities in the majority of OECD countries during the 1980s[16] provides support for the fear of the Left that capitalism inevitably leads to increasing inequalities. However, the 1980s are by no means typical of past trends in the distribution of incomes in the developed world. Looking at the statistics provided by Phelps Brown's *Inequality of Pay* (1977),[17] one obtains a broad impression of declining skill (and professional) differentials for the first six decades of the twentieth century in most of the countries for which these statistics are given. But one also needs to stress that this equalizing tendency is by no means uniform; and that it appears to reverse earlier trends (i.e. during the nineteenth century) – in as far as one can ascertain such earlier trends.

While the growing income inequalities of the 1980s have caught many (non-Marxist) economists by surprise, it is certainly too early to accept this as an inevitable concomitant of free trade and of the unfettered play of private market forces – especially since income inequalities have grown most strongly in those countries, such as Britain and the United States, where conservative governments have greatly assisted it.

SOME CONCLUDING SPECULATIONS

In conclusion it may be interesting to speculate on two issues. First, is there really an asymmetry between fears and hopes among economists; and secondly, are fears typically exaggerated, as they appear to be in this very limited canter through some economists' fears?

I am aware that this collection of examples cannot establish whether fears are more frequent than hopes among economists. It is doubtful how one could establish any such tendency unequivocally. There is perhaps one 'incentive' argument which one can use in favour of the prevalence of fears; namely that they are more 'newsworthy'. As Ross Gittins (Economics editor of the *Sydney Morning Herald*) argued recently: 'bad news is more interesting than good news. Conflict is more newsworthy than co-operation; costs get more attention than benefits; the media tend to highlight problems rather than solutions' (Gittins 1994). If, as Samuelson maintains, scholars' main motivation is the recognition and respect of their peers, it may be that scholars are more attracted to (or are more intrigued by) conflict, problems and disturbing trends – as being inherently more newsworthy and more interesting.

Are there any reasons why one might expect that – in the light of subsequent events – fears turn out to be typically exaggerated? One reason might be that economic actors (or policy-makers) have fears similar to those of economic theorists and – as a result their actions – on occasions, manage to forestall undesirable outcomes. If there is a general belief that the terms of trade of primary products will improve, producers are more likely to make investments in the expectation of such an improvement. Policy-makers certainly react to past trends and try and counter them. In the 1950s they confidently expected a renewal of the depressionary conditions of the 1930s, and in the 1980s a continuation of the inflationary conditions and of negative real interest rates of the 1970s. Hence, what gives rise to fearful extrapolation by scholars, may also give rise to actions by decision-makers which help to counteract such tendencies. Needless to say, this is very speculative – in the tradition of contributions to Festschrifts.

ACKNOWLEDGEMENTS

I thank Heinz Arndt, Bob Gregory, Ann, David and Nicholas Gruen, John Pitchford and John Quiggin for helpful comments on an earlier draft.

NOTES

1 More colloquially, in *Capitalism, Socialism and Democracy*, Schumpeter expressed the opinion that 'people always come to think what they want to think' (240).

2 To quote the title of a recent book on the period (Marglin and Schor 1991).

3 After 1870 there was developed on a large scale an unprecedented situation, and the economic condition of Europe became during the next fifty years unstable and peculiar. The pressure of population on food, which had already been balanced by the accessibility of supplies from America, became for the first time in recorded history reversed. As numbers increased, food was actually easier to secure ... Up to about 1900 a unit of labour applied to industry yielded year by year a purchasing power over an increasing quantity of food. It is possible that about the year 1900 this process began to be reversed, and a diminishing yield of Nature to man's effort was beginning to reassert itself ... Europe's claim on the resources of the New World was becoming precarious; the law of diminishing returns was at last reasserting itself.

(Keynes 1919: 7, 22)

4 See the rival interpretations of Spraos' 1980 *Economic Journal* article in successive contributions on the terms of trade by Ronald Findlay and H. W. Singer respectively in the *New Palgrave*. First Findlay: 'The general consensus on the statistical debate that has arisen on this issue is that there has *not* been any discernible trend for the commodity terms of trade of developing countries to deteriorate'. Singer reads Spraos quite differently: 'the question of transport costs and also the question of improving quality of manufactured goods were used by critical economists to contest the empirical basis of ... Prebisch–Singer hypothesis.... However subsequent analysis has shown that the correction for shipping costs and changing quality would not destroy the empirical basis for the hypothesis'. The most recent work on the subject of which the author is aware is a 1994 study by Robert Lipsey for the World Bank which suggests that the net barter commodity terms of trade have improved, once adjustments are made for quality changes for manufactured products.

5 Robin Barlow's entry on 'declining population' in the *New Palgrave*, p. 758.

6 See, for instance the reviews by A. C. Pigou (*Economic Journal*, June–September 1944), Eric Roll (*American Economic Review*, March 1945), J. J. Spengler (*Southern Economic Journal*, July 1945).

7 Reder, in his excellent intellectual sketch of the Chicago School of Economics, first in the March 1982 issue of the *Journal of Economic Literature* and later in the *New Palgrave*, writes: 'Perhaps the most common characteristic of Chicago economists is distrust of the state. This distrust, together with the belief that, given time, voluntary exchange will usually generate truly desirable reforms, acts as a powerful brake on wayward impulses to improve society through political action'. In his *JEL* paper, Reder speaks of the later (i.e. post-Henry Simons) Chicagoans' fear of government in the following terms:

The state is considered an agent, and one that is exceedingly difficult to monitor or to control. Therefore the state is to be shunned as an inefficient instrument for achieving any given objective – it is better sought privately – and objectives that cannot be achieved except through the state are to be scrutinized carefully and sceptically. Either the political process will frustrate the achievement of the goals altogether, or will drastically alter them in the process of achievement and, in any case waste resources.

(p. 31)

8   In technical, economic jargon, government was regarded as maximizing some sort of social welfare function.

9   Barry (1985) and the references cited there, in particular pp. 280–1.

10 For the most recent examples, see Hughes (1995) and Smith (1995).

11 However, it would not be inconsistent for libertarians to support at least some of these public health measures. The only restriction on economic freedom which libertarians should support are those where such freedoms harm others. It can be argued that there is asymmetry of information in these markets and that the freedom of sellers of cigarettes and of unsafe cars to persuade the public to buy their wares harms others and should therefore not be regarded as an absolute freedom.

12 The McCarthy era, in my judgement, posed a serious threat of American fascism. I knew plenty of people in government and the universities whose civil liberties and careers came into jeopardy ... How did free-market advocates among the economists score as defenders of personal freedoms and civil liberties? ... over several years I kept a quiet tally of the behaviour and private utterances of the leading American and continental libertarians ... The results surprised and distressed me. Worshippers of laissez faire a la Bastiat and Spencer were insensitive and on the whole unsympathetic towards the rights and personal freedoms of scholars. Alone among the members of the Mt. Pelerin Society the name of Fritz Machlup stood out as one willing to incur the personal costs to speak up for John Stuart Mill values ... [I found] a sad lack of genuine concern for human values.

(*The Collected Scientific Papers of Paul Samuelson*, vol. 5: 790)

13 As John Palmer pointed out: 'The word "crisis" is one of the most overworked in the socialist dictionary. It has come to convey less and less with the passing of the years' (1980: 25) – though he then goes on to use exactly this expression as apt for the British economy of the time!

14 For instance, Ernest Mandel argued that a socialist revolution within the USA 'is on the agenda of the next decade or two' (*NLR*, March–April 1969), while Cornwall argued (in *JPKE* of Spring 1979) that 'continuous stagflation with no end in sight can do little but call into question the ability of capitalism to successfully organise economic activities'.

15 The two most important publications were perhaps Baran (1957) and Frank (1967).

16 For evidence see, for instance, chapter 5 on Earnings Inequality in the OECD's 1993 *Employment Outlook*.

17 See in particular, chapter 3, 'The course of change in the pay structure'.

REFERENCES

Baran, P. (1957) *The Political Economy of Growth*, New York: Monthly Review Press.

Barry, B. (1985) 'Does democracy cause inflation? Political ideas of some economists', in Leon N. Lindberg and Charles S. Mayer (eds), *The Politics of Inflation and Economic Stagnation*, Washington, D.C.: Brookings.

Braverman, H. (1976) *Labor and Monopoly Capital*, New York: Monthly Review Press.

Frank, A. G. (1967) *Capitalism and Underdevelopment in Latin America. Historical Studies of Chile and Brazil*, New York: Monthly Press.

Gittins, G. (1994) 'The role of the media in the formulation of economic policy', Research Paper No. 424, Department of Economics, University of Melbourne, August.

Henderson, D. (1995) 'The revival of economic liberalism', *The Australian Economic Review*, 1.

Hughes, H. (1995) 'Why have East Asian countries led economic development?', *The Economic Record*, March: 88–104.

Keynes, J. M. (1919) *The Economic Consequences of the Peace*, London: Macmillan.

Lipsey, R. (1994) *Global Economic Prospects and the Developing Countries*, Washington, D.C.: World Bank.

Maddison, A. (1991) *Dynamic Forces in Capitalist Development*, Oxford: Oxford University Press.

Marglin, S. and Schor, J. B. (1991) *The Golden Age of Capitalism*, Oxford: Clarendon Press.

Mueller, D. (1989) *Public Choice II*, Cambridge: Cambridge University Press.

O'Connor, J. (1973) *The Fiscal Crisis of the State*, New York: St. Martin's Press.

Palmer, J. (1980) 'Economic Crisis', *The Socialist Register*: 25–43.

Phelps Brown, H. (1977) *The Inequality of Pay*, Oxford: Oxford University Press.

Prebisch, R. (1950) *The Economic Development of Latin America and its Principal Problems*, New York: UN Economic Commission for Latin America.

Roubini, N. and Sachs, J. D. (1989) *European Economic Review*, 33: 903–33.

Schumpeter, J.A. (1954) *The History of Economic Analysis* (edited from manuscript by E. B. Schumpeter), London: George Allen & Unwin.

Sen, A. (1973) *On Economic Inequality*, Oxford: Oxford University Press.

Singer, H. W. (1950) 'The distribution of gains between investing and borrowing countries', *American Economic Review*, May.

Skidelsky, R. (1992) *John Maynard Keynes, The Economist as Saviour 1920–1937*, London: Macmillan.

Smith, H. (1995) 'Industry policy in East Asia', *Asian-Pacific Economic Literature*, May: 17–39.

Weingast, B. R. (1993) 'Constitutions as governance structures: the political foundations of secure markets', *Journal of Institutional and Theoretical Economics*, 149(1): 286–311.

World Bank (1993) *The East Asian Miracle. A World Bank Policy Research Report*, Oxford: Oxford University Press.

6

UK PRIVATIZATION
Effects on households
Catherine Waddams Price and Ruth Hancock

THE BRITISH PRIVATIZATION PROGRAMME

The Conservative government privatized many state-owned industries in the 1980s and early 1990s, including all the main public utilities: telephones, gas, water and electricity. This paper considers the distributional effects of these changes on the domestic market, using Family Expenditure Survey (FES) data to identify the economic characteristics (and vulnerability) of those who have gained and lost most from these changes.

The privatization programme effected considerable redistribution between different groups. The government gained the financial value of the firms in exchange for their assets, which were transferred to the private sector. The most fundamental change was in the transfer of ownership from the government to private owners, and the introduction of a regulatory regime which enabled the new owners to keep residual profits. This provided considerable incentives to reduce costs for managers (who were also given shares or options as part of the privatization process), and resulted in substantial efficiency improvements in many industries.

But private ownership also introduced the incentive for monopoly exploitation in industries which had hitherto followed broadly an average cost pricing policy. Such exploitation was curbed by caps on average prices in markets where competition did not seem feasible. Firms responded to these various incentives by reducing costs dramatically, mainly labour costs, and by undertaking some rebalancing between different elements within their price caps.

It is this rebalancing which is the subject of this chapter. In most cases such rebalancing has reflected costs more closely than the previously averaged prices, so there is a gain in terms of efficiency, since consumers now respond to more accurate information about their costs of supply in making consumption decisions. But there are also distributional effects. Consumers gained or lost according to the pattern of their own expenditure and this has not been spread evenly across the different groups of consumers. This is particularly significant for poor consumers who are dependent on pensions or benefits which are adjusted according to the retail price index, since this reflects the average change in price, and not necessarily that for their particular consumption pattern.

CHANGES IN TARIFFS SINCE PRIVATIZATION

The industries which concern us here are the utilities – telecommunications, gas, electricity and water. They share the characteristic of a fixed link to carry the supply of the product or service, and this has a number of consequences for both economic and distributional characteristics. They are all, as a result of this, natural monopolies, so the marginal cost of supply is less than the average cost. The nature of their supply networks also entails considerable joint costs between different groups of consumers, making it difficult to allocate a substantial portion of costs precisely to any one group. Moreover they constitute an 'essential service' for domestic consumers, who require access to the network in order to receive the commodities and services provided; in the case of energy and water these are crucial to health and comfort, while the telephone may be an essential lifeline for older and disabled people.

The industries also have other characteristics in common. All are subject to considerable seasonal and/or time of day variation in demand. So the fixed network, to which all consumers require access, is more or less heavily used at different times of the year or day. The energy industries and water are also subject to uncertainty in demand, where climatic factors which vary considerably between years affect the demand for (and, in the case of water, the supply of) the product. All these aspects have affected both the traditions and the more recent changes in these industries. Technological and other changes in the telecommunications industry mean that though it shares many of the characteristics we have described, the degree to which this is so is often rather less than for the other utilities.

For this study we are interested in the effects of changes on households, and particularly on vulnerable households. We define these as being in the lowest income quintile, those in receipt of income support, those on disability allowances, and households which consist exclusively of one or two pensioners. These categories do not of course *define* hardship or poverty, but they may provide some indication of vulnerability. Moreover the regulators of these industries are often given a special responsibility for the interests of two of these groups: disabled and elderly people. They are therefore particularly germane to our study.

COSTS OF SUPPLY

The fixed networks impose a common cost pattern on the four utilities mentioned. All have expenses of providing and maintaining a network which depend primarily on the number and location of consumers supplied, and the peak throughput; at off-peak times the use of the system will be virtually cost-less, though there may of course be commodity costs involved. Expense is also likely to vary with the geographical area, since the length of the network depends on its geographical coverage, as well as the type of terrain and the distribution of consumers within it. (Rural supply tends to be expensive because the consumers are widely distributed, and urban supply because of the problems of maintaining the infrastructure, and its age.) In particular, gas, electricity and water are more expensive to supply if they have to be carried a long distance from their source. In some cases this also means that these costs have implications for where there should be investment in the source of supply, e.g. in electricity generation plants. In other cases (gas and water) the supply location is determined primarily by nature.

TARIFFS

The tariff structure charged by the industries reflects broadly the costs outlined above, but with considerable variations between industries, regions and over time. In general the nationalized utilities tended to practise cross-subsidies between consumers, charging a much 'flatter' price structure than costs alone would suggest, even allowing for the expense of differentiating between different types of consumer, location and time of year or day. Perhaps the attitude is best indicated by the nationalized British Gas Corporation which, in 1985, just before privatization, replied to a Select Committee question on peak load pricing in the following way: 'if you made it much more expensive to buy gas at peak then you are discouraging people from taking heat at the very moment they need it, when the weather is cold' (Rooke 1985).

The source of such averaging lies in the industries' own perceptions of their duties. They largely followed a policy of average cost pricing in terms of the *level* of their prices under nationalization (thus avoiding both the criticism that they were inefficient when making losses, and the opprobrium of exploitation when profitable). It is easy to see how this philosophy, and a public service ethos, extended to averaging costs between consumers. There was a feeling that it was 'unfair' to charge consumers who happened to be expensive to supply more than those whose costs of supply were lower. Despite the official enthusiasm for marginal cost pricing in the 1960s (White Paper 1967), this view of public service was well entrenched when the privatization programme commenced in the 1980s.

Changes in tariffs, both in level and structure, resulted from a number of pressures associated with privatization. The first, change of ownership, changed the incentives by giving managers a much more direct stake in the profitability of the company. This came in a variety of forms. Many managers had a direct interest through share ownership and options; and the change to private ownership meant that they were exposed to the usual threats of takeover and bankruptcy if they did not maximize profits for the benefit of shareholders as a whole, though the capital markets were far from perfect in this respect. Nevertheless, it is clear that some pressure from investors supported the move towards profit maximization.

However, firms were not free to maximize profits unrestrictedly: they were subject to price caps, administered by individual industry regulators. Monopoly exploitation was curbed by requiring the company to keep its average prices below a certain level, determined relative to the growth in the retail price index. So long as the company adhered to this constraint, residual profits accrued to the company. This clearly gave considerable incentives to the companies to lower costs, but also the freedom to rebalance prices so as to increase profits.

Such rebalancing was possible, since it was an *average* of prices which was capped. So long as the average of these prices stayed below the cap, the firm was free to rebalance within it. The incentives for how prices were rebalanced varied according to the precise form of price cap, British Telecom being subject to a different kind (tariff basket) than gas and electricity (average revenue). Water is difficult to categorize, since most payments for supply are unrelated to consumption, but the regulator made clear his preference for a tariff basket cap (Byatt 1995), which generally produces more efficient incentives for the firm's rebalancing (Bradley and Price 1988). Some additional constraints were applied; for example a separate limit on the standing charge for gas and telecommunications, reflecting the government's or regulator's expectations that there might be considerable rebalancing by raising such standing charges. However some freedom for these firms in rebalancing remained, and indeed was acted upon, as we shall see.

Perhaps even more important than the change of ownership and the new explicit price cap regulation was the increase in competitive pressure. In gas, where for some years it looked as if there would be little competition, this is particularly obvious. In the domestic market, which is the focus of this chapter, there was some rebalancing between standing charge and running rate, but no significant change in the tariff until it became established that competition would be introduced, whereupon the supplier immediately differentiated between consumer types according to their costliness to supply (specifically in terms of speed and method of payment). It is an interesting question why they failed to take advantage of this profit-increasing opportunity in the nine years of private ownership until this point, but it does serve to emphasize the importance of competition as well as ownership and regulation in pricing decisions.

CHANGES IN TARIFF STRUCTURES

Of the four utilities, all except water have reduced the real value of domestic charges since their privatization. In some respects the incentives provided by private ownership and price cap regulation have proved immensely success- ful, and the high profits, increased share values and payments to directors which have caused such a political furore are the result of cost savings which are much higher than anticipated. However, a number of other factors are involved. The most obvious is the low initial share price and light regulation imposed at privatization to ensure successful flotations: all price caps were tightened at their first review, when the government had little to gain from a share price whose value was inflated by light regulation. Moreover, much of the political debate reflects concern not about the size of the benefits, but the distribution of the gains. Expenses have been reduced by drastic reductions in labour costs, both through redundancy and by worsening the conditions of employment for those who remain (an enforced transfer to contract employ- ment often entails loss of sickness and pension benefits).

The focus of this chapter is on which consumers have gained the lion's share of these falls in average price, or borne the brunt of the increases, in the case of water. The savings for most consumers depend on the level of their consumption, because all the industries levy a fixed standing charge, independent of the level of consumption, and a running rate charged per unit consumed (or several, depending on consumption level and time of day). Where the industry has rebalanced its charges between the different elements, different consumers will have gained (or lost) according to their consumption characteristics. In particular, if the standing charge is raised more than the charge per unit consumed (or decreased less), consumers of small quantities will suffer more (or benefit less) in percentage terms than those with large consumption. Since small users may well be poor, this raises issues of equity. This study uses Family Expenditure Survey data to link these consumption characteristics and gains and losses with measures of 'vulnerability'. Of course changes are not necessarily due entirely, or even mainly, to privatiza- tion. In the fuel industries, for example, the fall in world oil prices has lowered raw material costs, so that some fall in prices would have been expected over this period. But since our interest is in how prices have been rebalanced, the cause of the changes is less interesting than how they have affected different groups.

METHODOLOGY

The impact of price changes in two industries is examined in detail, by seeing how they would have affected the households whose expenditure is recorded in the Family Expenditure Survey. This exercise includes one industry where average prices have fallen – gas – and one where they have risen – water –

and examines particularly the effects on disabled and elderly people, for whom the regulators have special responsibility, and groups in receipt of income support and amongst the poorest fifth of households. Of the group for which regulators have special responsibility, the telecommunications regulator estimates there are about six million people with one or more disabilities, and about ten million elderly people in the UK (Oftel 1995). The complexity of the tariffs in telecommunications, and the different tariffs charged by different electricity distributors, made it difficult to extend the analysis to these industries, though there are some indicative conclusions which can be drawn.

To identify the effects of rebalancing, we examined the bills which families would have paid in April 1995, and compared them with those which that family would have paid, with the same level of consumption, at the time of privatization of each industry. Since they were privatized at different times this meant that different periods of time are involved. To make the comparison, we used the latest available Family Expenditure Survey (for 1993), calculating the consumption of the households (in the case of gas) from the expenditure and tariffs in that year. We could then apply the tariffs at privatization and in 1995. We assumed that a similar household would have had similar consumption, i.e. we have made no adjustment for any demand change in response to the changes in tariffs. This enabled us to calculate gains and losses and to attribute them to households according to other characteristics.

GAS

Gas was privatized in 1986, the second utility to be sold, and was generally thought to be lightly regulated, especially since it was left as a vertically integrated industry. In the first five-year period British Gas was required to reduce average prices by 2% in real terms each year, but was allowed to pass through the full extent of its gas purchase costs (about 50% of its total supply costs). From 1991, the price cap (on average revenue) was tightened to 5% below the rate of inflation, and the cost pass-through was amended, with some improvement expected here also. (Since then, market definitions have been amended so that the price cap applied to the domestic market is 4% per annum, but this is equivalent to the previous 5%.) A separate cap applies to the standing charge, which must not be raised in any year by more than the rate of inflation.

The average price per unit of gas has fallen by 33% in real terms since privatization, partly because of falling costs of purchasing from the North Sea. Within this overall average, standing charges have decreased most, especially for consumers who use prepayment meters and are on a different tariff. The separate cap on standing charges has clearly not been binding over the period as a whole, although there was one occasion (1990) when

Table 1 Mean reductions in gas bills since privatization, £ p.a., April 1995 prices, UK

	Total savings £ per annum	% of income	Sample sizes
Poorest 20%	114	5.3	1,002
Second quintile	103	1.8	1,037
Third quintile	117	1.2	1,075
Fourth quintile	120	0.9	1,093
Fifth quintile	139	0.6	1,120
On income support	110	3.3	867
On disability benefit	117	1.5	600
One or two pensioners	96	1.7	1,191
All	119	1.8	5,327

the increase in standing charge for that year was very close to the rate of inflation. Change in the structure of gas charges was speeded by the confirmation (in November 1994) that competition would be introduced to the domestic market from 1996. In January 1995 British Gas introduced lower tariffs for those who paid by direct debit. Our analysis incorporates these changes, taking into account consumers' method of payment, as well as others made since privatization.[1]

Table 1 shows the savings which were made in gas bills between 1986 and 1995. We see from Table 1 that the average savings have been £119 per annum, representing 1.8% of income (after housing costs). The richest have gained most, £139, since they use most gas, and in absolute terms the most vulnerable groups have gained less. In particular the two groups for which the regulator has special responsibility under the 1986 Gas Act, elderly and disabled people, have gained less than average, both in absolute terms and as a proportion of their incomes.

WATER

Water is more complicated than gas, because, like electricity, it is supplied by a number of firms throughout the country. Most domestic water is unmeasured and is charged as a fixed element, plus some element related to the rateable value of the house supplied. Average bills for unmeasured water supply have risen by 31% in real terms since privatization in 1989 (about 5% a year), but the increases in individual water bills vary from 19% to 50%. The average (real) increases for each component part are 28% for the fixed element and 35% for the variable part, but this average contains considerable rebalancing, in both directions, by individual water companies.

Because different water companies have different charges, it was more complex to calculate changes in expenditure; the analysis had to be restricted

Table 2 Mean increases in water bills since privatization, £ p.a., April 1995 prices, England and Wales

	Total increase £ per annum	% of income	Sample sizes
Poorest 20%	56	4.0	295
Second quintile	54	0.9	334
Third quintile	57	0.6	406
Fourth quintile	57	0.3	537
Fifth quintile	65	0.3	585
On income support	54	2.1	66
On disability benefit	56	0.6	70
One or two pensioners	58	0.9	513
All	58	0.9	2,237

to households living in areas where we could identify their suppliers, i.e. there were at most only one water and sewerage company and one separate water supplier in the standard region reported in the FES. Since there is no competition for domestic consumers in water this should not have introduced any bias, but it means that only about a third of households could be included (since we also had to exclude those who paid for their water and sewerage as part of rates or rent). We ignored the possibility that some of the households might be metered (less than 3% of our sample), and restricted the analysis to England and Wales, since the Scottish water industry is still publicly owned. The losses for each household since 1989 were calculated, and the results are shown in Table 2.

Here we see fairly flat levels of increased cost across all groups. It is perhaps surprising that there is not a more marked rise in the cost for those in higher income groups, who might be expected to own more expensive houses with higher rateable values. However the increase is a much higher proportion of income for the poor and for those on income support. The proportional increase is slightly higher for pensioners, but lower for those in receipt of disability pensions. The increase for our sample is higher than the overall average, probably because those customers whose water and sewerage rates were included with rates or rents (and are excluded from our study) typically had low water bills.[2] Nevertheless the comparisons give some idea of the distribution of losses in the water industry. Again, the increases are not necessarily the result of privatization, but this is likely to have affected the way the water companies have chosen to distribute the price increases.

TELECOMMUNICATIONS

BT was the first utility to be privatized, in 1984, and it is the one which has exhibited the most marked rebalancing. Users are charged a fixed sum for connection, and a variety of rates per call depending on the distance and time at which the call is made. Over the eleven years since privatization the price cap has brought down the average charges by 37% in real terms, and every call-related charge has fallen in real terms (by between 18% and 71%), though some have increased in money terms. However the standing charge has increased by 9.4% in real terms, though this is below the 2% per annum increase which was allowed under the separate price cap. This separate cap was removed in 1996.

The distributional consequences of such rebalancing are not clear. The poor may use the phone less and make fewer long distance and peak calls, which have seen the biggest drops in charges. For so-called 'light users' BT has a special tariff which provides connection at half the usual standing charge, and the first few units cheap, with subsequent units at much higher prices. This will help some who might otherwise find the increase in standing charge difficult to pay, and there are efficiency arguments for encouraging additional subscribers to join the system because of network externalities, the benefits which existing customers gain from being able to contact new members. Nevertheless it is unlikely that this adequately encompasses the needs of all the vulnerable groups. In particular some disabled people, especially the deaf who operate telephones manually rather than by voice, may use the phone for long periods and be more dependent on it.

Table 3 Proportionate changes in domestic telephone charges, 1984–April 1995

	Money terms %	Real terms %
Average permitted		−38.7
Average		−37.4
Domestic line rental	+74	+9.4
Local: peak	+3.4	−35.3
standard	+26	−32
cheap	+31	−18
National a: peak	−19.2	−49
standard	−53.1	−71
cheap	+12.3	−30
National b1: peak	−53.1	−71
standard	−38.7	−62
cheap	+12	−30
National b2: peak	−53.5	−71
standard	−50.3	−69
cheap	−8.6	−43

ELECTRICITY

Like water, electricity is supplied by several (twelve) different companies in England and Wales, but since their boundaries do not coincide with standard regions it is impossible to identify the suppliers (and hence the tariff) for participants in the Family Expenditure Survey. Since privatization in 1990 real prices have fallen by about 8%, with the average fall in standing charge being somewhat greater than for the per unit rate. However there are considerable variations between companies, even though they all had a similar price cap at privatization. These caps applied separately to their distribution and supply functions, which contribute different proportions to the costs of each regional electricity company. The table of tariffs and changes is shown in Table 4.

Table 4 Real changes in electricity charges, England and Wales

	% change, 1989–95	
	Standing charge	*p/kWh*
Regional co.		
London	−8.9	−12.0
Seeboard	−29.8	−10.0
Southern	−5.5	−9.1
South Western	−19.4	−6.9
Eastern	−26.8	−3.4
East Midlands	−12.2	−8.1
Midlands	−5.5	−12.2
South Wales	−8.0	−2.4
Manweb	6.4	−9.8
Yorkshire	−3.4	−15.4
Northern	−8.1	−9.1
Norweb	−12.5	−16.1
England and Wales simple average	−13.3	−9.5

Immediately before privatization there was some fall in average running rate, but none in the real value of the standing charge. We suspect the impact of changed electricity prices is similar overall for different income groups, though in areas served by Manweb, where standing charges have risen in real terms, they are likely to be regressive, since poor consumers generally use less fuel and pay a higher proportion of their bill in standing charge.

CONCLUSIONS

Privatization has brought benefits and costs to broad groups of people. Shareholders have gained from increased values of shares sold at a discount at flotation, while employees as a whole have lost through redundancy and deteriorating terms of employment (O'Conell Davidson 1994). Consumers overall have probably gained from their share of the increased productive efficiency which the incentives of privatization have generated, enforced by the price cap regime administered by the regulators. However, not all consumers have gained equally – and some have lost. For households receiving RPI-adjusted benefits, it is the ratio between their gain/loss and the average which is most crucial, since it is the average which determines the adjustment of benefit level. Where we have been able to undertake detailed investigation we see that in both the gas and water industries the changes have tended to be regressive, benefiting the rich more than the poor. For gas the savings per year are below the average level for the poorest 20%, those on income support, disabled and elderly people. In water the increased costs are broadly similar for all groups, representing a higher proportion of the income of the poor, those on income support and disabled people. In both industries it is not clear how the regulators are discharging their special responsibilities with respect to disabled people and those of pensionable age.

Moreover the effect of changes in the gas industry in anticipation of competition in the domestic market is even more worrying. Consumers who do not have access to bank accounts find it difficult to take advantage of lower tariffs, and it looks as though groups who are likely to be categorized as 'bad customers' may find themselves increasingly disadvantaged as competition develops for more attractive households. Though this may be efficient, in the sense of eroding the cross-subsidies which have previously supported those who have difficulty in paying their bills promptly, it will increase the pressure on such families at a time when the state is decreasing other forms of support for them. There is a danger that the utilities, under the pressure of privatization and competition, may contribute to the formation of a disinherited underclass who have increasing difficulties in purchasing the essentials of life. The problem is that it is unclear who should take responsibility for such groups – the industries, their regulators or the government. We suggest that the government should give much clearer guidelines to the regulators about the nature and extent of their responsibilities for groups in special need, including elderly and disabled people who are already nominally part of their responsibility.

NOTES

1   The 1995 changes are analysed in more detail in Hancock and Waddams Price, 1995.
2   We see from the sample sizes in each quintile reported in Table 2 that our sample is, indeed, richer than average.

REFERENCES

Bradley, I. and C. Price (1988) 'The economic regulation of private industries by price constraints', *Journal of Industrial Economics*, XXXVII (1): 99–106.

Byatt, I. (1995) open letter to Ofgas.

Hancock, R. and C. Waddams Price (1995) 'Competition in the British domestic gas market: efficiency and equity', *Fiscal Studies*, August.

O'Connell Davidson, J. (1994) 'Metamorphosis? Privatisation and the restructuring of management and labour', in P. Jackson and C. Price (eds) *Privatisation and Regulation: a Review of the Issues*, Harlow: Longman.

Oftel (1995) *Annual Report 1994*.

Rooke, D. (1985) in 7th report from the Energy Committee, *The Development and Depletion of the UK's Gas Resources*, HCP 76.

White Paper (1967) *Nationalised industries: a Review of Economic and Financial Objectives*, Command paper 3437, London: HMSO.

7

INEQUITY AND ACCESS TO PRIVATE EDUCATION
An overlapping generations model with altruism

Paul Madden

I think the purpose of economics is ... to make the world a better place
for ordinary men and women, to produce a more just and equitable
society. In order to do that you have to understand how particular
societies work and where the pockets of power are, and how you can
either alter those or work within them and produce desirable results.

(Geoff Harcourt, quoted in Hamouda 1986: 5)

INTRODUCTION

We consider an economy in which an indivisible private education good is in
limited supply. We are thinking of a private, secondary education which we
assume would benefit children of all abilities by enhancing their lifetime
incomes, in varying amounts. We also assume that children's abilities can be
completely independent of parental income and ability, and are known by the
time entry to secondary education is to be decided. Parental funding is a
prerequisite for a child to access the private education; capital markets are of
no help as children cannot engage in loan contracts as minors, and parents
cannot take a loan on the child's behalf, committing the children to
repayments after reaching the age of majority. These features are embedded
in a very simple overlapping generations model with parent-to-child altruism
of the 'warm glow' variety (Andreoni 1989) – parents care about their own
consumption and the human capital that they endow on their child as a result
of providing education, following exactly the specification of some recent
models (Banerjee and Newman 1991; Becker 1991: chapter 6; Eckstein and
Zilcha 1994; Galor and Zeira 1990; Saint-Paul and Verdier 1993). It is shown
how a *laissez-faire* policy can lead to a self-perpetuating elite of privately
educated families – children are privately educated if and only if parents are,
irrespective of abilities. Our main result is that this *laissez-faire* outcome is
efficient, but inequitable in a precise and strong sense, for roughly the
following reasons.

In the *laissez-faire* outcome, a switch of the private education from some less able children (who must have rich and therefore privately educated parents) to some more able children (who must have poor parents who were not privately educated) must allow all these children and their descendants to be better off in the Pareto sense, since the switch increases aggregate income accruing to these children as adults. However the (rich) parents of the children who are no longer privately educated lose 'altruistic utility' because of the switch. It may not be possible to compensate these rich parents for this loss by an income transfer from the poor parents of the more able children who are now to be privately educated, leaving these poor parents as well off as under *laissez-faire*, because the poor parents have a higher marginal utility of income. Thus the outcome is Pareto efficient. However, it will be possible to transfer income from the rich to the poor parents so as to make the poor parents better off than the rich were (because of the greater altruistic utility from their more able child), and the rich parents better off than the poor were. The *laissez-faire* outcome is now Pareto efficient but violates Suppes-Sen optimality (equivalent to first-degree stochastic dominance) because it is possible to dominate a permutation of the *laissez-faire* utility levels, thus generating a strong inequity.

In presenting these results, we hope to provide a simple formal model to show how private secondary education could lead to a 'pocket of power' in a self-perpetuating elite of privately educated families, and how this outcome could be inequitable. We also wish to suggest, as in Madden (1995) and following Kolm (1971) and recently Kolm (1989), that the use of the Suppes-Sen criterion has much potential in allowing precise identification and discussion of a powerful inequity concept in economic models – note that Kolm (1971, 1989) uses 'fundamentally dominated' for this inequity, distinguishing different concepts of 'inequity' and 'inadequacy'. Indeed the model here can be viewed as a dynamic variation on the static education model in Madden (1995) which also brings into the picture the important role of parental altruism. In the earlier paper the focus was tertiary education, and inequity was associated with a consumption benefit of this education, 'psychic income' in Becker (1964); pursuit of this benefit could lead to richer, less able students gaining access at the expense of poorer, more able students. Here, instead, there is no consumption benefit; the inequity emerges when poor parents find it too difficult to pay for the private education of their children whilst richer parents are willing to pay for their perhaps less able child. Our focus on inequity as Suppes-Sen suboptimality differentiates the model from previous literature on education and intertemporal resource allocation (e.g. Becker 1991; Creedy 1995; Eckstein and Zilcha 1994; Fernandez and Rogerson 1995; Galor and Zeira 1993; Hare and Ulph 1981; Loury 1981; Saint-Paul and Verdier 1993). The closest results are in Loury (1981) and Eckstein and Zilcha (1994) who study the inegalitarian nature of various education allocations based on second-degree stochastic dominance rather than our first-degree concept.

We note finally the widespread use of private secondary education, especially in developing economies. For instance, using 1975 data Psacharopoulos (1986: 52) reports seventeen LDCs in which over 40% of the total secondary enrolment was in private schools. Of course a much lower fraction of the public education budget goes to secondary education in developing countries than in the developed economies (Psacharopoulos 1986: 54), and the private secondary sector no doubt receives greater support partly as a result of this. What we aim for in this paper is the initial, precise articulation of some of the routes whereby such private secondary education may generate inequity in the long run.

THE OVERLAPPING GENERATIONS MODEL

In each period $t = 0,1,2,\ldots$ a continuum $[0,1]$ of agents is born, and each individual lives for two periods, first as a child and then as an adult; in addition there is a pre-existing continuum $[0,1]$ of adults in period 0. As is common in these models we ignore biology, and assume that for every period t, adult $i \in [0,1]$ is the (sole) parent of child $i \in [0,1]$; where necessary this pair of individuals is referred to as the adult (i,t) and the child (i,t) and together they form the family (i,t).

In each period t, the economy can provide an indivisible education good (we drop the private label, for brevity) to a fraction $\theta \in (0,1)$ of children, at a cost of k per child. We assume that education provision for more than θ children is prohibitively costly, so as to ensure that the access constraint eventually binds. The only economically relevant childhood activity is consumption (or not) of the education good, and $E_t \subset [0,1]$, $t = 0,1,\ldots$ denotes the set of children in t who do receive this education; E_{-1} denotes the given subset of adults in period 0 who have already received the education. We assume throughout that $0 < \mu\ (E_{-1}) \le \theta$ where $\mu(S)$ denotes the Lebesgue measure of $S \subset [0,1]$; subsets and functions on $[0,1]$ are taken to be Lebesgue measurable where required in the sequel.

Children are of one of two types: those who are relatively more able to benefit from the education good, and those who are not so able; we refer to a more able adult to mean that this adult was a more able child, and similarly for less able. The type of a child is common knowledge once the child is born, and $A_t \subset [0,1]$ denotes the set of more able children in period t ($\bar{A}_t \subset [0,1]$ being the less able); A_{-1} is the given subset of more able adults in period 0; $A_t \cap A_{t-1}$ is the set of more able families in t; and so on. We make only a minimal assumption about the relationship between the ability of children and parents, as follows.

Assumption 1

For every $S \subset [0,1]$ where $\mu(S) > 0$ and $\mu(\bar{S}) > 0$, there exists a period $t \geq 0$ in which $\mu(S \cap A_{t-1} \cap A_t) > 0$ and $\mu(\bar{S} \cap \bar{A}_{t-1} \cap \bar{A}_t) > 0$.

This means that the descendants of any set of individuals (S) will eventually (in some period t) include some more able families and, at the same time, the descendants of the complement of S will include some less able families. This offers no role for parental income in determining children's ability and rules out perfect correlation between parent and child abilities, but is consistent with many stochastic and deterministic specifications which do not entail these features. For instance, suppose $p \in (0,1)$ is the *ex ante* stationary probability that a new-born child will be of the more able type and suppose also that p is independent within each generation and independent of parental income and type. Assuming that the realization of a continuum $(S \subset [0,1], 1 > \mu(S) > 0)$ of iid random variables inherits the distribution of each individual random variable (see Judd (1995) on the technical difficulties with this 'law of large numbers'), then a fraction p of the children of S will be more able and so p^2 of the families of these children will be more able families; similarly a fraction $(1-p)^2$ of the families of $\bar{S}$ will be less able. Assumption 1 is then satisfied with any $t \geq 1$. Since *ex ante* uncertainty about children's abilities has no influence in the model, we need not be specific and merely make assumption 1.

The human capital of the adult (i,t), developed during childhood, is denoted $h_t(i)$ and is assumed to satisfy the following for any $t = 1,2,\ldots$ where $\lambda \in (0,1)$ and $y, s > 0$;

$$h_t(i) = \begin{cases} y + s & \text{if } i \in A_{t-1} \cap E_{t-1} \\ y + \lambda s & \text{if } i \in \bar{A}_{t-1} \cap E_{t-1} \\ y & \text{if } i \in \bar{E}_{t-1} \end{cases} \tag{1}$$

Thus all individuals develop at least the same base level of human capital (y), even if uneducated $(i \in \bar{E}_{t-1})$; those children who receive the education good develop an extra amount of s if they are more able $(i \in A_{t-1} \cap E_{t-1})$ and $\lambda s < s$ if they are less able $(i \in \bar{A}_{t-1} \cap E_{t-1})$.

The adult (i,t) earns a gross income of $h_t(i)$ in period t, and ends up with a final consumption to be denoted $c_t(i)$. The lifetime utility of the adult (i,t) is denoted $u_t(i)$ and is assumed to have the following form where $\alpha > \beta > \gamma > 0$:

$$u_t(i) = \alpha \min(c_t(i), d) + \beta \max(c_t(i) - d, 0) + \gamma h_{t+1}(i) \tag{2}$$

Here $\gamma > 0$ indicates the altruism of parent to child, $\beta > \gamma$ places an upper bound on this altruism and $\alpha > \beta$ indicates a diminishing marginal utility of income; the piecewise linear utility function is chosen for simplicity of exposition, and could be replaced by more general specifications without invalidating the broad message of this paper. We refer to the third term on the right-hand side of equation (2) as 'altruistic utility' where convenient.

A feasible allocation given A_{-1}, E_{-1}, is $(E_t, c_t)_0^\infty$, where $E_t \subset [0,1]$ and c_t : $[0,1] \to R_+$ satisfy the following for $t = 0,1,\ldots$:

(a) $\mu(E_t) \leq \theta$

(b) $\int_0^1 c_t(i)\ di \leq (y + s)\ \mu\ (A_{t-1} \cap E_{t-1}) + (y + \lambda s)\ \mu\ (\bar{A}_{t-1} \cap E_{t-1})$
$+ y\mu(\bar{E}_{t-1}) - k\mu(E_t)$.

For a given A_{-1}, E_{-1}. the feasible allocation $(E_t, c_t)_0^\infty$, $t = 0,1,\ldots$, is *Pareto optimal* if there is no other feasible allocation $(\hat{E}_t, \hat{c}_t)_0^\infty$ such that:

(a) for every $t = 0,1,\ldots$, $\hat{u}_t(i) \geq u_t(i)$, for almost everywhere (a.e.) $i \in [0,1]$
(b) for some $t = 0,1,\ldots$, $\hat{u}_t(i) > u_t(i)$, for a.e. $i \in S$, for some $S \subset [0,1]$ where $\mu(S) > 0$,

where $u_t(i)$ and $\hat{u}_t(i)$ are defined in the obvious way from equation (2).

Pareto optimality will be referred to interchangeably as 'efficiency' as is usual. The equity concept we use is very weak and not much more demanding than the Pareto criterion. It is based on the Suppes principle, a basic principle of distributive justice (Suppes 1966; Sen 1970), and has been applied to resource allocation models by Kolm (1989), Madden (1995) and Saposnik (1983). It is equivalently based on first-degree stochastic dominance, and has been used to compare empirical income distributions by Bishop *et al.* (1991). Following the terminology of Saposnik we define as follows.

For a given A_{-1}, E_{-1}, the feasible allocation $(E_t, c_t)_0^\infty$ is Suppes-Sen optimal (SS optimal) if there is no other feasible allocation $(\hat{E}_t, \hat{c}_t)_0^\infty$ and one-to-one function $\sigma : [0,1] \to [0,1]$ such that:

(c) for every $t = 0,1,\ldots$, $\hat{u}_t\ (\sigma(i)) \geq u_t(i)$ for a.e. $i \in [0,1]$
(d) for some $t = 0,1,\ldots$, $\hat{u}_t\ (\sigma(i)) > u_t(i)$ for a.e. $i \in S$ where $S \subset [0,1]$ with $\mu(S) > 0$.

Suppes-Sen optimality presumes ordinal interpersonal comparability of utilities and requires that 'permutations' of an SS optimal utility 'vector' cannot be Pareto dominated. Clearly SS optimality requires Pareto optimality but is 'not much more than that' in requiring only that utility vectors may be permutated prior to the Pareto comparison, thus adding a mild anonymity criterion to that of Pareto. As such SS optimality entails no 'preference for equality'. Optimality based on second-degree stochastic dominance would embody such a preference – see Eckstein and Zilcha (1994) and Loury (1981) who make 'egalitarian' comparisons in education models based on second-degree stochastic dominance, following the earlier literature of Kolm (1968, 1971), Atkinson (1970) and Shorrocks (1983), referred to in Madden (1995) as generalized Lorenz dominance. Here we concentrate exclusively on the weak first-degree, SS optimality concept, violation of this concept signalling a strong 'inequity'. In the next section we describe a particular resource allocation mechanism (*'laissez-faire'*) and study its Pareto and SS optimality.

LAISSEZ-FAIRE: INEFFICIENCY AND INEQUITY

In the *laissez-faire* mechanism there are no taxes or subsidies, and a child will apply for the education if and only if the child's parent is prepared to provide the required funding k. We think of children as being unable to enter into legal contracts, as in reality, so the availability of educational loans on perfect capital markets would be no help. What would be needed is for parents to take out loans to fund the child's education, the loan to be repaid by the child; clearly there are many problems with such an arrangement, and we ignore this possibility.

Let $u_t^F(i)$ (resp., $u_t^{NF}(i)$) denote the lifetime utility of the adult (i,t) if she provides funding (resp. no funding) for her child's education. Then, using equation (2):

$$u_t^F(i) = \alpha \min(h_t(i) - k,d) + \beta \max(h_t(i) - k - d,0) + \gamma h_{t+1}^F(i) \qquad (3)$$

$$u_t^{NF}(i) = \alpha \min(h_t(i),d) + \beta \max(h_t(i) - d,0) + \gamma h_{t+1}^{NF}(i) \qquad (4)$$

where $h_{t+1}^F(i) = \left\{ \begin{array}{ll} y + s & \text{if} \quad i \in A_t \\ y + \lambda s & \text{if} \quad i \in \bar{A}_t \end{array} \right.$ and $h_{t+1}^{NF}(i) = y$

The funding decision depends on comparison of $u_t^F(i)$ and $u_t^{NF}(i)$. The features of interest emerge under the following assumptions about the parameters of the model.

Assumption 2

(a) $y + \lambda s - k > d > y$

(b) $\dfrac{\alpha}{\gamma} k > s > \lambda s > \dfrac{\beta}{\gamma} k$

Here (a) locates the onset of lower marginal utility of income, and this aspect of (a) is innocuous, given the simplifying piecewise linear specification in equation (2); (a) implies that $\lambda s > k$, so that an adult of either type would have been prepared to take out an education loan as a child if she had the facility to do so. Part (b) assumes that the (utility) cost for an uneducated parent to pay for the education of a child (αk) exceeds the benefit even if the child is more able (γs); conversely the (utility) cost for an educated parent to pay for the education of a child (βk) is less than the benefit even if the child is less able ($\gamma \lambda s$). Not surprisingly, a self-perpetuating educated elite now emerges.

Theorem 1

Suppose assumption 2 is satisfied. Then under *laissez-faire*, $E_t = E_{t-1}$ for all $t \geq 0$.

Proof

If $i \in A_{t-1} \cap E_{t-1}$, $t = 0,1 \dots$ then from (1), (3) and (4) and using assumption 2(a):

$$u_t^F(i) = \alpha d + \beta(y + s - k - d) + \gamma h_{t+1}^F(i) \text{ where } h_{t+1}^F(i) \geq y + \lambda$$

$$\text{and } u_t^{NF}(i) = \alpha d + \beta(y + s - d) + \gamma y$$

Hence $u_t^F(i) - u_t^{NF}(i) \geq \gamma \lambda s - \beta k > 0$ from assumption 2(b); moreover this inequality is the same for $i \in \bar{A}_{t-1} \cap E_{t-1}$. So an adult will wish to fund her child's education if the adult herself was educated. On the other hand, if $i \in \bar{E}_{t-1}$, $t = 0,1 \dots$ then, again using assumption 2(a); $u_t^F(i) = \alpha(y - k) + \gamma h_{t+1}^F(i)$ where $h_{t+1}^F(i) \leq y + s$ and $u_t^{NF}(i) = \alpha y + \gamma y$. So $u_t^F(i) - u_t^{NF}(i) \leq \gamma s - \alpha k < 0$ from assumption 2(b). Thus an adult will wish to fund her child's education if and only if the adult was educated herself. Since $\mu(E_{-1}) \leq \theta$, all applicants for education in period 0 can be accommodated. Thus $E_0 = E_{-1}$, and repeating the argument gives $E_t = E_{t-1}$ for any $t = 0,1 \dots$ ∎

The social mobility here is minimal. To be more precise, if one thinks of private education as providing the passport to 'skilled' occupations which earn $y + s$ or $y + \lambda s$ depending on the individual's ability, and if 'unskilled' jobs earn y, then the social mobility transition matrix for transition between these two occupations coincides with the identity matrix, indicating complete occupational immobility. (See Atkinson (1981) for references on occupational mobility and evidence on mobility between income classes, and Shorrocks (1978) for discussion of measures of mobility derived from transition matrices.) There is here a self-perpetuating educated elite whose children maintain the lineage, although some may be of lower ability than children outside the elite. The feel of inefficiency associated with the last sentence is misleading, however, because of the parental altruism involved, as the following result shows.

Theorem 2

Under assumptions 1 and 2 the *laissez-faire* allocation is Pareto optimal.

Proof

Let $(E_t, c_t)_0^\infty$ denote the *laissez-faire* allocation and suppose it is not Pareto optimal, so that there is a feasible alternative $(\hat{E}_t, \hat{c}_t)_0^\infty$ satisfying (a) and (b);

clearly this is impossible if $E_t \cap \hat{E}_t = \hat{E}_t$,a.e for all $t = 0,1\ldots$ since altruistic utilities can then only go down and also in each period the total consumption available for redistribution can only go down, certainly precluding (a) and (b) in any period. Suppose for some t it is not true that $E_t \cap \hat{E}_t = \hat{E}_t$,a.e and let T be the first period in which this happens. Write $S_1 = \bar{E}_T \cap \hat{E}_T$, $\mu_1 = \mu(S_1)$ > 0 and $S_2 = E_T \cap \bar{E}_T$, $\mu_2 = \mu(S_2)$. For $i \in S_1$, the adult (i,T) receives an extra altruistic utility of at most γs in the alternative to *laissez-faire*. Under *laissez-faire* from Theorem 1, i's utility was $\alpha y + y$; in order for the alternative to improve i's position, i could give up consumption of at most z_1, where

$$\alpha(y - z_1) + \gamma(y + s) = \alpha y + \gamma y, \text{ so } z_1 = \frac{\gamma}{\alpha} s.$$ For $i \in S_2$, altruistic utility goes

down by at least $\gamma \lambda s$. Under *laissez-faire* (again from Theorem 1) such an i's consumption was in excess of d, and for the alternative to improve i's position requires an extra consumption of at least z_2 where $\beta z_2 = \gamma \lambda s$, so $z_2 = \gamma \lambda s/\beta$. Adults (i,T) where $i \notin S_1 \cup S_2$ endure no change in altruistic utility and so need no change in consumption to stay as well off as under *laissez-faire*. Consumption of $k(\mu_1 - \mu_2)$ must also be made available in the alternative to *laissez-faire* in order to meet the (possibly) changed numbers of children educated in T. It follows that a necessary condition for (a) and (b) to be true in T is $\mu_2 z_2$

$+ k(\mu_1 - \mu_2) \leq \mu_1 z_1$ which becomes $\mu_2 \left(\dfrac{\gamma \lambda s}{\beta} - k \right) \leq \mu_1 \left(\dfrac{\gamma s}{\alpha} - k \right)$, which is

impossible under assumption 2. The desired conclusion follows therefore. ∎

Thus the self-perpetuating elite may well be Pareto optimal, even if assumption 1 is satisfied and some more able children do not gain access to the education in some period t, whilst some of lesser ability do so. The reason is as follows. It is possible to rearrange the education distribution in period t, along meritocratic lines, switching education from less to more able; the children in t, and all future generations can be made better off in the Pareto sense, since aggregate income in $t+1$ will increase. However the change will cause some rich, elite parents to lose altruistic utility in period t as their children will no longer receive the education after the redistribution; moreover the non-elite parents who gain altruistic utility by the switch are poor in terms of disposable income and cannot compensate the elite losers, thus producing Pareto optimality of *laissez-faire*. On the other hand, if one took instead disposable income away from the elite losers, it may well be possible to make the non-elite parents better off than the elite losers were, and vice versa, since the non-elite parents gain more altruistic utility than the elite lose as their children are more able.

Theorem 3

Under assumptions 1 and 2, the *laissez-faire* allocation is Suppes-Sen dominated.

Proof

From assumption 1, and since $\mu\,(E_{-1}) > 0$, there is a period t in which the following sets have positive measure under *laissez-faire*: $T_1 = \bar{A}_{t-1} \cap \bar{A}_t \cap E_{-1}$ and $T_2 = A_{t-1} \cap A_t \cap \bar{E}_{-1}$. Let $\mu = \min(\mu(T_1),\mu(T_2)) > 0$ and choose $S_1 \subset T_1$, $S_2 \subset T_2$ with $\mu(S_1) = \mu(S_2) = \mu$. We construct an alternative to the *laissez-faire* allocation, first by switching education in t from the children (i,t) where $i \in S_1$ to the children where $i \in S_2$. The switch increases the aggregate consumption available in $t + 1$ (since $s > \lambda s$); keeping fixed at their *laissez-faire* values the allocations of all individuals born in and after $t + 1$ allows (d) to be satisfied for period $t + 1$ (with $\sigma(i) = i$, i.e. (b)) and (c) to be trivially satisfied (as (a)) for all later periods. However, *per se*, the education switch in t changes the lifetime utility of adults in t as follows, because of its altruistic effects. For $i \in S_1, u_t(i)$ changes from $u_t^1(i)$ to $\hat{u}_t^1(i)$ where:

$$u_t^1(i) = \alpha d + \beta(y + \lambda s - k - d) + \gamma(y + \lambda s)$$

$$\hat{u}_t^1(i) = \alpha d + \beta(y + \lambda s - k - d) + \gamma y$$

Now transferring consumption of $\lambda s - k(> 0)$ from each member of S_1 to a member of S_2 is feasible and produces the following utilities where $u_t^2(i)$ is the *laissez-faire* utility for $i \in S_2$:

For $i \in S_1$, $\hat{u}_t^1(i) = \alpha y + \gamma y = u_t^2(i)$

For $i \in S_2$, $\hat{u}_t^2(i) = \alpha d + \beta(y + \lambda s - k - d) + \gamma(y + s) > u_t^1(i)$

Leaving consumption allocations unchanged in t for $i \notin (S_1 \cap S_2)$, and leaving consumption and education allocations unchanged in every period prior to t allows (c) and (d) to be satisfied for every such period. Thus (d) can be satisfied for periods $t, t + 1$ and (c) for every other period, and the *laissez-faire* allocation is SS-dominated. ∎

CONCLUDING REMARKS

This paper studies a much simplified overlapping generations model with parent-to-child altruism. Under a *laissez-faire* mechanism whereby parental funding is the only source of support for children to access private education, we show how a self-perpetuating elite may emerge – children are privately educated if and only if their parents are – and we show how this outcome may be efficient and strongly inequitable. It would be of interest to see how democracy might deal with this outcome and the underlying inequity, by studying alternative mechanisms (e.g. public provision with taxation and scholarships) and by introducing voting over alternative mechanisms, as in the recent literature on the political economy of education (Creedy 1995; Eckstein and Zilcha 1994; Fernandez and Rogerson 1995; Galor and Zeira 1993; Saint-Paul and Verdier 1993). Such an extension will have to address explicitly whether the assumed high quality of private education continues under public provision. It is planned to pursue these extensions of the model in the future. In the mean time we hope to have provided here some useful vocabulary for the precise discussion of inequity and social immobility potentially associated with private education, and some initial indications as to how such adverse features might be propagated.

ACKNOWLEDGEMENT

It is a pleasure to acknowledge Geoff Harcourt's influence over the last 20 years as a much respected colleague. I am also grateful to Geoff, and to Henry Chiu, Len Gill, Serge Kolm and Marco Mariotti for helpful comments on this paper, whose shortcomings remain entirely the author's responsibility.

REFERENCES

Andreoni, J. (1989) 'Giving with impure altruism: applications to charity and Ricardian equivalence', *Journal of Political Economy*, 97: 1447–58.

Atkinson, A. B. (1970) 'On the measurement of inequality', *Journal of Economic Theory*, 2: 244–63.

—— (1981) 'On intergenerational income mobility in Britain', *Journal of Post-Keynesian Economics*, 3(2): 194–218.

Banerjee, A. and Newman, A. (1991) 'Risk-bearing and the theory of income distribution', *Review of Economic Studies*, 58: 211–35.

Becker, G. S. (1964) *Human Capital*, New York: Columbia University Press.

—— (1991) *A Treatise on the Family*, Cambridge, Mass.: Harvard University Press.

Bishop, J. A., Formby, J. P. and Thistle, P. D. (1991) 'Rank dominance and international comparisons of income distributions', *European Economic Review*, 35: 1399–409.

Creedy, J. (1995) *The Economics of Higher Education; an Analysis of Taxes versus Fees*, Aldershot: Edward Elgar.

Eckstein, Z. and Zilcha, I. (1994) 'The effects of compulsory schooling on growth, income distribution and welfare', *Journal of Public Economics*, 54: 339–59.

Fernandez, R. and Rogerson, R. (1995) 'On the political economy of education subsidies', *Review of Economic Studies*, 62(2): 249–62.

Galor, O. and Zeira, J. (1993) 'Income distribution and macroeconomics', *Review of Economic Studies*, 60: 35–52.

Hamouda, O. (ed.) (1986) *Controversies in Political Economy: Selected Essays by G.C. Harcourt*, Brighton: Wheatsheaf Books.

Hare, P. G. and Ulph, D. J. (1981) 'Imperfect capital markets and the public provision of education', *Public Choice*, 36: 481–507.

Judd, K.L. (1985) 'The law of large numbers with a continuum of iid random variables', *Journal of Economic Theory*, 35: 19–25.

Kolm, S.-C. (1968) 'The optimal production of social justice', in H. Guitton and J. Margolis (eds), *Economie Publique*, Paris: CNRS, and *Public Economics*, London: Macmillan.

—— (1971) *Justice et Equité*, Paris: CEPREMAP.

—— (1989) 'Adequacy, equity and fundamental dominance: unanimous and comparable allocations in rational social choice, with applications to marriage and wages', in K. J. Arrow (ed.), *Issues in Contemporary Economics: Volume 1 (Markets and Welfare)*, London: Macmillan.

Loury, G. (1981) 'Intergenerational transfers and the distribution of earnings', *Econometrica*, 49: 843–67.

Madden, P. (1995) 'Suppes-Sen dominance, generalised Lorenz dominance and the welfare economics of competitive equilibrium: some examples', *Journal of Public Economics*.

Psacharopoulos, G. (1986) *Financing Education in Developing Countries*, Washington, D.C.: World Bank.

Saint-Paul, G. and Verdier, T. (1993) 'Education, democracy and growth', *Journal of Development Economics*, 42: 399–407.

Saposnik, R. (1983) 'On evaluating income distributions: rank dominance, the Suppes-Sen grading principle of justice and Pareto optimality', *Public Choice*, 40: 329–36.

Sen, A. K. (1970) *Collective Choice and Social Welfare*, San Francisco, Calif.: Holden-Day.

Shorrocks, A. (1978) 'The measure of mobility', *Econometrica* 46(5): 1013–24.

—— (1983) 'Ranking income distributions', *Economica* 50: 3–18.

Suppes, P. (1966) 'Some formal models of grading principles', *Synthèse*, 6: 284–306.

8

THE ACCOUNTANT IN A TURBULENT AGE

Accounting conventions and the failure of healthy companies

Geoff Meeks and Gay Meeks

This chapter relates to a recurrent theme in Geoff Harcourt's work: the relationship between the numbers conventionally produced in company accounts and the numbers which would be required from accounts to inform rational economic decisions. Geoff's interest dates from his doctoral research on the relationship between historic and current cost accounting – one of the first systematic analyses of the company accounts databank established by the National Institute (Harcourt 1958). Perhaps his best known work in the area is his 1965 OEP paper, 'The accountant in a Golden Age' – a path-breaking critique of the (mis-)use of the accounting rate of return to compare the profitability of different investments, a critique re-invented many years later in the AER by Fisher and McGowan (1983).

We develop a related idea for a 'turbulent age' – exploring ways in which the incomplete information provided in conventional accounts may lead to the failure of economically efficient companies. The role of company failure in the orthodox theory of economic natural selection needs little elaboration: inefficient companies are forced out of business (see Winter (1964) for a discussion and critique). But a literature is developing on ways in which the actual mechanisms of failure may lead to sub-optimal results: either some efficient firms are eliminated or some inefficient ones are allowed to survive (e.g. Webb 1991; White 1989). This chapter pursues the first of these problems, focusing on the use of conventional accounts in the legal contracts which trigger failure. We argue that this can lead to the premature death of efficient companies.

FAILURE IN LAW AND EXIT IN ECONOMICS

Any discussion of the legal conditions for failure has to be tied to a specific legal system, and here we use the British system as an example. Many similar characteristics will, however, be found in other systems (Franks and Torous 1992). Britain's 1986 Insolvency Act may be invoked by the creditor of a company if that company has failed to pay its debts as they have fallen due. And under section 123(2), inability to pay is ultimately shown if the court is satisfied that the value of the company's assets (A) is less than the value of its liabilities (L) (Campbell and Underdown 1991).[1] Thus the insolvency condition is:

$$L > A \qquad (1)$$

However, financial crisis which can lead to failure may be precipitated before this insolvency condition is met if some of the company's liabilities (L) have loan covenants attached. These covenants give the lender the right to accelerate payment of the loan if the borrower has violated certain conditions. The conditions are often specified in terms of accounting variables (Citron 1992), which in turn are defined by Generally Accepted Accounting Practice (GAAP – see e.g. Davies et al. (1989)).[2] A common condition is expressed in terms of net worth: there is a lower limit (W^*) on the difference between assets and liabilities:

$$A - L \geq W^* \qquad (2)$$

If ($A - L$) falls below W^* the creditor may demand accelerated repayment of his loan. This is more stringent than the insolvency condition (1): certain rights pass to the creditor while ($A - L$) is still positive, rather than when it is zero.[3]

Failing to meet conditions such as (2) can in practice lead to insolvency (1) through a process of circular and cumulative causation. If the creditor protected by the loan covenant exercises his right to accelerated payment from a company, the company's initial financial difficulties will obviously be compounded. If the company then fails to pay suppliers on time, normal trade credit is likely to be withdrawn by these suppliers. This further worsening of financial pressures could be sufficient to call into question the company's ability to survive: the auditors might well express this doubt through a 'going concern' qualification. Such an audit qualification might prompt a downward re-evaluation of asset values – from cost to the lower value realizable in a distress or 'fire' sale (Shleifer and Vishny 1992). And ($A - L$) might consequently fall below zero: an initially solvent company becomes insolvent.[4]

Either process can lead to insolvency, then. The question this paper focuses on is: when they do, will the insolvency condition secure the death of the appropriate companies in terms of orthodox natural selection theory? The exit condition prescribed by economics may be written:

$$PV < NRV \qquad (3)$$

Present value (PV), the discounted value of the company's expected net future revenues, should be less than the net realizable value (*NRV*) of the company's assets. In that case the assets can with advantage be redeployed to their best alternative use.

Will the companies becoming insolvent ($A < L$) or breaching loan covenants ($(A - L) < W^*$) overlap perfectly with those which are not economically efficient ($PV < A$)? We explore some cases where this is not so – where economically efficient companies ($PV > A$) actually fail.

RISKY OUTCOMES UNFOLD IN *EX POST* COMPANY ACCOUNTS

Consider as a simple illustration a conventional two-period model with risk. In period 1 a company invests in a project which yields its pay-off in period 2. It decides its investment strategy by computing V_s, the present value (*V*) from the investment contingent on state of the world (*s*). The company proceeds with the investment if:

$$\sum_s p^s V_s > 0 \tag{4}$$

where p^s is the *ex ante* probability of state of the world s ($\sum_s p^s = 1$).

Even though the *sum* of net present values weighted by their respective *ex ante* probabilities (4) is positive, however, net present values for some *individual* states of the world can still be negative. And if for a particular s, V_s is negative, then a company which is entirely debt-financed fails ($A < L$) if that unfavourable s turns out to be the actual state of the world in period 2. It has invested borrowed funds in a project which, in the event, has lost money, even though on a conventionally rational *ex ante* assessment of risk the project was worthwhile.[5]

In period 2, then, even if the company has viable future projects and should survive on economic grounds ($PV > A$), it will find itself insolvent ($A < L$) on the basis of the *ex post* accounts which will be used by the courts. This happens even if management is operating at the peak of efficiency, single-mindedly pursues shareholders' interests, somehow knows the prospective outcomes in every state of the world, etc.

But need the company then fail? Or will creditors not recognize that, as $PV > A$, their collective interests are best served by continuation (then they will recover more of their money)? Problems arise in practice of course because, with asymmetric information, outsiders such as creditors have difficulty disentangling two effects on the company's *ex post* accounts: on the one hand, the effects, traced above, of risky investments rationally and efficiently undertaken but inappropriate to the state of the world which emerged; and, on the other, the effects of managerial incompetence or dishonesty; and this difficulty may make creditors reluctant to give the company 'more rope'. But even if this difficulty is ignored, Webb (1991) has shown that where the creditors' collective interests (as well as the share-holders') *are* served by the survival of the company, still the company may be forced to liquidate.

Webb analyses the first-mover advantages to be gained under the traditional (pre-1986) UK receivership system. If a company with two creditors is technically insolvent ($A < L$) but on economic grounds should survive ($PV > A$), it may pay one of the creditors to make a pre-emptive move to appoint a receiver and force a liquidation. This is because if the insolvent company *is* to be liquidated, the first-mover creditor gains a disproportionate share of its assets. A race on a company's assets is destructive: there is a familiar prisoner's dilemma here – a cooperative solution of continuation of the business would serve both creditors best; but if there is a race, the first mover gains the advantage by appointing a receiver who in law gives priority to that creditor's interests.

The 1986 Insolvency Act was designed to mitigate these problems through the new device of administration. The administrator represents all creditors' claims (he is appointed by the court, not by one creditor, as in the case of the receiver) and some potentially destructive conflicts among creditors can therefore be avoided. However, the appointment of an administrator can be pre-empted by a creditor with a floating charge on the company's assets: such a creditor is entitled to appoint a receiver instead (Franks and Torous 1992). And since the 1986 Act receiverships have vastly outnumbered the appointments of administrators.

THE INCENTIVE TO DEMAND EARLY REPAYMENT UNDER LOAN COVENANTS

The violation of a loan covenant does not give a creditor the right afforded by insolvency to force a company into liquidation; but, as explained earlier, it does give the right to demand accelerated repayment which, in practice, may drive a company into insolvency and out of business. Would it ever be rational for a creditor to make this demand for a company which satisfied the economic condition for survival ($PV > A$)?

One case where this would be in the creditor's interest can be analysed in a conventional two-period framework with risk, similar to the one introduced earlier. Consider an example where in period 1 it pays on an economic calculation to retain the assets in the business and operate them in period 2 ($PV > A$). But PV has been calculated by weighting two equiprobable outcomes in period 2: net revenues of $2R$ in state of the world 1 and net revenues of $-R$ in state 2. If state 1 emerges in period 2, the company will have very healthy *ex post* accounts. But consider the case where state 2 emerges and $-R$ is sufficient to make the company insolvent ($L > A$).

Looking forward from period 1, what choices face a creditor whose loan covenant the company has just violated ($(A - L) < W^*$ in period 1)? Should the creditor exercise his rights to accelerated repayment of L, even if that drives the company out of business? The possibilities are to demand repayment in period 1 and recover the whole of L, or to wait until period 2. If he waits, then if state 1 emerges in period 2, the creditor will still be able to recover the whole of L; but if (equiprobable) state 2 emerges, there will be insufficient assets left in the business to meet in full the company's obligation to the creditor $(A < L)$. The rational creditor should therefore play safe and demand repayment in period 1. This is of course because the creditor has no equity stake in the company; he therefore gets no share of the upside benefits in period 2, but he does suffer from the downside.[6]

DOES 'PREMATURE' DEATH MATTER?

We have concentrated on the role of conventional accounts in legal contracts which trigger the failure of companies which on economic criteria should, and on orthodox natural selection theory would, survive. But do such premature deaths matter? Does liquidation not simply redeploy assets by cancelling the 'nexus of contracts' which constituted the original firm?

At first sight this appears to be the case: if a project is viable on economic grounds $(PV > A)$ then, with perfect capital markets, someone can be expected to buy the assets and operate them profitably. In practice, however, the legal processes of company failure do not just redeploy assets: they also lead to the destruction of assets. The processes impose costs. Most obvious are transaction costs (professional fees, etc.) (Baxter 1967). Probably more substantial still, though less easily quantified, is the loss of intangible assets (reputation, etc.) once a failure is announced (Altman 1984). Important in some cases, but even harder to quantify, is the irreversible loss of 'organizational capital' (Matthews 1985).

The failure process is not, therefore, costless: it is not a matter of indifference if it selects the 'wrong' companies according to economic criteria.

ACKNOWLEDGEMENT

We are grateful to the Institute of Chartered Accountants in England and Wales for support and to Geoffrey Whittington for helpful suggestions.

NOTES

1   Failure to pay debts as they fall due will not always coincide with $(A < L)$: failure to pay can occur when $(A > L)$, or ability to pay when $(A < L)$, if the repayment schedules for debtors and creditors do not coincide.
2   The use of GAAP means, *inter alia*, that the valuation of assets (A) will generally be based on cost. In this paper we assume for the sake of simplicity that cost is equal to net realizable value – but not that cost equals present value. If (as often

happens) net realizable value also diverges from cost, the problems we outline below are compounded.

3 Another common covenant sets a minimum gearing ratio (G^*):

$$A/L > G^*$$

This has a similar effect to condition (2).

4 Comparable processes are easy to find in the financial sector (see Kindleberger (1989)).

5 We assume zero initial equity only to keep the central argument simple.

6 These are issues explored (in different contexts), for example, by Stiglitz (1972) and White (1989).

REFERENCES

Altman, E. I. (1984) 'A further empirical investigation of the bankruptcy cost question', *Journal of Finance*, 39: 1067–90.

Baxter, N. D. (1967) 'Leverage, risk of ruin and the cost of capital', *Journal of Finance*, 22: 395–404.

Campbell, C. and Underdown, B. (1991) *Corporate Insolvency in Practice*, London: Chapman.

Citron, D. B. (1992) 'Financial ratio covenants in UK bank loan contracts and accounting policy choice', *Accounting and Business Research*, 322–35.

Davies, M., Paterson, R. and Wilson, A. (1989) *UK GAAP: Generally Accepted Accounting Practice in the United Kingdom*, London: Longman.

Fisher, F. M. and McGowan, J. J. (1983) 'On the misuse of accounting rates of return to infer monopoly profits', *American Economic Review*, 73: 82–97.

Franks, J. R. and Torous, W. N. (1992) 'Lessons from a comparison of US and UK Insolvency Codes', *Oxford Review of Economic Policy*, 8: 70–82.

Harcourt, G.C. (1958) 'Company taxation and replacement costs', *Accounting and Business Research*, 9(1): 1–16.

—— (1965) 'The accountant in a Golden Age', *Oxford Economic Papers*, 17: 66–80.

Kindleberger, C. P. (1989) *Manias, Panics and Crashes: A History of Financial Crises*, revised edition, London: Macmillan.

Matthews, R. C. O. (1985) 'Darwinism and economic change', in Collard, D. A., Helm, D. R., Scott, M. Fg. and Sen, A. K. (eds), *Economic Theory and Hicksian Themes*, Oxford: Oxford University Press.

Shleifer, A. and Vishny, R. W. (1992) 'Liquidation values and debt capacity: a market equilibrium approach', *Journal of Finance*, 47: 1343–66.

Stiglitz, J. E. (1972) 'Some aspects of the pure theory of corporate finance: bankruptcies and takeovers', *Bell Journal*, 3: 458–82.

Webb, D. C. (1991) 'An economic evaluation of insolvency procedures in the United Kingdom', *Oxford Economic Papers*, 43: 139–57.

White, M. J. (1989) 'The corporate bankruptcy decision', *Journal of Economic Perspectives*, 3: 125–51.

Winter, S. G. (1964) 'Economic "natural selection" and the theory of the firm', *Yale Economic Essays*.

9

THE ECONOMIC RATE OF RETURN AND THE ACCOUNTANT

Geoff Whittington

INTRODUCTION

The economist is most likely to associate Geoff Harcourt's name with the capital theory controversies and the development of post-Keynesian economics. The contents of the present volumes provide ample evidence of his contributions in these fields. However, he has also made an extremely important contribution to bridging the gap between economists and accountants in the related areas of income measurement and the measurement of the rate of return.

In the area of income measurement, Geoff Harcourt's contribution most cited in the accounting literature is *Readings in the Concept and Measurement of Income*, edited jointly with an accountant, Bob Parker (1969). Unlike many collections of readings, this served a really creative purpose by introducing accountants to some of the key economic writings relevant to their own discipline (the reverse flow, from accounting to economics, has, unfortunately, been less strongly apparent). Moreover, the editors' jointly written Introduction provided a synthesis of economic and accounting perspectives which became a standard source of reference in the accounting literature for many years after it was written: for this reason, it was reproduced without amendment in the successor volume (Parker, Harcourt and Whittington 1986).

With regard to the measurement of the rate of return, Geoff Harcourt made a seminal contribution through his paper 'The accountant in a Golden Age' (1965). This explored the relationship between the internal rate of return (IRR) measure favoured by economists, and the accounting rate of return (ARR) produced by accountants and often used in empirical work by economists. The conclusions, based upon a much more thorough and systematic study than had previously appeared in the literature, were extremely pessimistic. As is so often the case, similar work was conducted at the same time on an entirely independent basis (by Ezra Solomon in the USA) and its results were published shortly after the Harcourt paper (Solomon

1966), whose results they confirmed. The papers by Harcourt (1965) and Solomon (1966) are now the standard original references in a literature on the significance of accounting rates of return, which has flourished during the three decades following their publication.

The purpose of the present paper is to trace the course of that debate. In view of Geoff Harcourt's contributions to the history of ideas, it is hoped that it is a fitting tribute to him to trace the history of one of his own ideas.[1]

THE ACCOUNTANT IN A GOLDEN AGE

Harcourt (1965) proposed

> to examine how accurate is the accountant's measure of the rate of profit under Golden Age conditions where uncertainty is absent, expectations are fulfilled, and the rate of profit has an unambiguous meaning. The following question is asked: would the answer obtained by using the accountant's rate of profit correspond with what is known, under the assumed conditions, to be the right answer, namely, that the *ex post* rate of return equals the *ex ante* one.
>
> (*Ibid.*: 66)

In other words, the accountant's calculation of the rate of return (ARR) was to be compared to the economist's measure of the internal rate of return on investment (IRR), using identical raw data.

The method used to assess the correspondence between the ARR and the IRR was computer simulation. Two basic cases were considered: a balanced stock of machines and a steadily growing stock of machines. In each case, there was a variant which allowed for the accumulation of financial assets, making four cases in all. For each of these cases, four different time patterns of cash flows (quasi-rents) from machines were assumed: constant (a 'one hoss shay'pattern), falling, rising, and rising followed by falling. For each of the resulting sub-cases, two different accounting depreciation methods were tested: straight line and reducing balance. For each of the resulting sub-cases, the IRR was compared with the ARR, assuming various different rates of profit (IRR), lengths of life of machines and (where relevant) rates of growth of investment.

The results of the simulations, which were summarized in both tabular and diagrammatic form, showed, in many cases, large divergences between the ARR and the IRR. It had been hoped to identify rules of thumb to adjust for the main errors arising from such factors as quasi-rent pattern or growth rate, but 'it is obvious from the calculations that the relationships involved are too complicated to allow this' (*ibid.*: 80). The paper concluded

> that, as an indication of the realized rate of return the accountant's rate of profit is greatly influenced by irrelevant factors, even under ideal

conditions. Any 'man of words' (or 'deeds' for that matter) who compares rates of profit of different industries, or of the same industry in different countries, and draws inferences from their magnitudes as to the relative profitability of investments in different uses or countries, does so at his peril.

(*Ibid.*: 80)

SOLOMON, VATTER AND THE EARLY AMERICAN DEBATE

Ezra Solomon's paper, 'Return on Investment: the Relation of Book-Yield to True Yield' was published in an American Accounting Association (AAA) volume in 1966. Solomon had given a paper on the subject as early as 1963 (see footnote to Solomon 1966: 232), so that it is clear that Solomon and Harcourt had worked simultaneously in time, but entirely independently, on the same topic. Solomon's paper also followed the method of simulation, but it used a narrower range of alternative assumptions, e.g. a true yield (IRR) of 10% per annum was always assumed. However, four key parameters were varied in the examples: length of project life, cash flow pattern, accounting depreciation policy, and growth rate of the company. The principal conclusion of the study was the same as that of the Harcourt study: 'the ratio of net income to net book assets is not a reliable measure of the return on investment' (*ibid.*: 243). However, Solomon was a little more positive in his view that adjusted ARRs might be useful: 'while we have as yet no precise basis for making these necessary adjustments, the use of models does provide an approximate basis for doing so' (*ibid.*: 243–4). A degree of optimism about the possibility of developing such adjustments was expressed also in Zeff's 'Discussion Comments' on the Solomon paper.

One distinctive feature of the Solomon paper is that he demonstrated analytically that there is a precise correspondence between the ARR and the IRR for a company in balanced growth (i.e. adding similar investments at a steady rate) where the growth rate is equal to the IRR (*ibid.*: 242).

Solomon's paper was published by an academic accounting body (the AAA) and it evoked an early response for an eminent accounting academic, Vatter (1966). The essence of Vatter's critique was to question the validity of the IRR as a standard of comparison for the ARR: 'a mere comparison of two calculations does not establish the inaccuracy or incompetency of one of them' (Vatter 1966: 684). Vatter pointed out that the IRR is essentially an *average* yield over the life of a project, not the yield over a sub-period of the project's life. 'The rate is an annual rate only because we choose to state it that way; it really applies to the entire term' (*ibid.*: 685). He also demonstrated that book yields (ARRs) could be forced, on an annual basis, to be always equal to the IRR if annuity depreciation (based on discounting) were used, but he also pointed out that variable annual ARRs could also be interpreted as (annually variable) discount rates which, like the IRR, would produce zero initial present value of cash flows received over the full life of an investment (*ibid.*: 689–90). This observation provided the essential insight upon which Kay's 1976 analysis (discussed in the next section of this paper) was based. Vatter also questioned the validity of the IRR as a standard for comparison, on the ground that it did not necessarily reflect the opportunity cost of capital (the so-called 'reinvestment' issue). Thus, by questioning the appropriateness of the IRR as a standard, Vatter provided a critique which was to play an important part in the subsequent literature.

Vatter's critique did not, however, have an immediate impact. In 1970 Solomon published a paper which substantially reiterated his 1966 analysis, and in the same year Livingstone and Salamon published the results of a simulation study which was very much in the spirit of Harcourt (1965), but extending the range of assumptions beyond those considered by Harcourt or by Solomon (Livingstone and Salamon 1970: 202). Their results broadly confirmed those of the earlier studies and failed to detect any simple adjustments which would enable ARR to be reconciled with IRR, apart from the special case in which the growth rate is equal to the IRR (which implies that IRR = ARR, so that no adjustment is required).

Stauffer (1971) adopted a more analytical approach to the problem, using mathematical analysis rather than computer simulation, and he extended the range of variables considered, particularly by introducing taxation. However, his conclusions were essentially consistent with those of Solomon, whose work he cited, and Harcourt, whose work he did not cite, and the final sentence of this paper summarizes the predominant view in the academic literature of the time: 'It is clear that further theoretical and empirical research is needed before rates of return can be computed reliably, and interpreted with certainty' (Stauffer 1971: 468).

KAY'S RIPOSTE (1976)

The further work which Stauffer called for was not long in coming, although it came in a British journal, *Oxford Economic Papers*, as a follow-up to Harcourt's paper which had been published in the same journal.

The title of Kay's 1976 paper – 'Accountants, too, could be happy in a Golden Age' – suggests its theme: that there is an underlying analytical relationship between the ARR[2] and the IRR. Kay defined this relationship mathematically and suggested an empirical method for reconciling computed ARRs with IRR. He was thus carrying forward the task which earlier authors had set.

Kay's analysis builds upon the observation by Vatter (1966) that the IRR is really an average return calculated over the full life of an investment project. He demonstrated precisely that the IRR can be derived as a weighted average of (variable) annual ARRs over the lifetime of a project, irrespective of the accounting conventions used to calculate ARR. This strikingly general result arises from the 'cash to cash' nature of a single investment project: over the project's lifetime the difference between the total of cash outlays and cash inflows will determine total accounting profit, irrespective of the accounting measurement methods employed, with the one proviso that the accounts should be articulated, i.e. all gains and losses affecting the balance sheet should flow through the profit and loss account.[3]

The crucial weakness of Kay's analysis was that the formal results hold with complete accuracy only for a full 'cash to cash' situation, i.e. when the full lifetime cash flows of the reporting entity are known. This is plausible for a single investment project, but much less so for a whole firm, which may be viewed as a collection of investment projects of different maturity dates which will be replaced by other investments when they mature, if the business is a 'going concern'. The accountant's typical task is to report periodic profits for a continuing business, so that he has available neither the opening cash outlays nor the terminal cash flows which would be necessary to compile a full accounting history of the firm and obtain the precise estimates of IRR from the accounts which could be derived using the Kay formulae. Kay advocated two means of alleviating this difficulty. First, estimates should be made over as long a period as possible: 'The accountant's rate of profit, measured over a period of years, will be an acceptable measure of the true rate of return: it is over a single year that it may prove seriously misleading' (Kay 1976: 459). Second, the problem of the initial and terminal positions is assumed away by using the accountant's book values as proxies for the economic (discounted cash flow) values which are strictly required: 'The discussion above assumes that the economist accepts the accountant's estimate of the initial and terminal capital stock' (*ibid*.: 453–4).

These assumptions were criticized by Wright (1978), in a robust defence of the Harcourt analysis: 'Alas, we have not escaped from Harcourt's discouraging conclusion' (Wright 1978: 467–8). Kay's (1978) response was that the differences were ones of emphasis rather than logical or factual accuracy: he was concerned to dispel the belief that accounting data had no relevance to economic returns. His later work (Kay and Mayer (1986) and Edwards, Kay and Mayer (1987)), was a much more positive response to Wright's critique.

THE FISHER AND McGOWAN DEBATE IN THE USA

In 1983, in apparent ignorance of the work of both Harcourt (1965) and Kay (1976), Franklin Fisher and John McGowan published an important paper on the subject in the *American Economic Review*. The importance of the paper derived not from the originality of its results (most of which had appeared in the earlier literature), but from its appearance in a leading world economics journal (which guaranteed a series of comments published over the next five years) and its specific orientation towards the assessment of monopoly profits.

The paper arose from Fisher's testimony for IBM in the *US v. IBM* monopoly case (Fisher and McGowan 1983: 82). The title – 'On the misuse of accounting rates of return to infer monopoly profits' – summarizes the theme admirably. The authors' reason for reaching the conclusion that accounting rates of return cannot be used to infer monopoly profits was that 'accounting rates of return, even if properly and consistently measured, provide almost no information about economic rates of return' (Fisher and McGowan 1983: 82). This assertion was supported, in an appendix, by mathematical proofs which confirmed the earlier US studies of Solomon (1966 and 1970), Livingstone and Salamon (1970), and Stauffer (1971). The text contained numerical illustrations. In a later comment, Fisher (1984: 510) remarked that the failure of Fisher and McGowan to cite Harcourt (1965) 'was particularly unfortunate because of all the literature, Harcourt's valuable article is perhaps the one most closely related to our own work'. Fisher was less charitable to Kay (1976), dismissing his contribution by citing Wright (1978).

The debate in the *American Economic Review*, following Fisher and McGowan's paper, comprised nine notes and comments published between 1984 and 1989. Many were concerned with points of detail or with the measurement of monopoly power, rather than with the relationship between the ARR and the IRR. Two issues which did emerge concerning the latter relationship, and which are still live research issues, are the correlation between the ARR and the IRR and the cash recovery rate approach to measuring the IRR.

The correlation between ARR and IRR was discussed by Long and Ravenscraft (1984) in the Fisher and McGowan debate. It had been discussed earlier by Whittington (1979) in a UK accounting journal, but this, like the other papers in the UK literature, does not seem to have reached the USA. The essential point is that, if ARR is correlated with IRR, albeit subject to error, it can be used in statistical analysis as a proxy for IRR, provided the error is unbiased or any bias can be eliminated by the use of control variables. Empirical tests of the correlation between IRR and ARR and the potential bias arising in empirical studies of concentration and profits are provided by Salamon (1988) and Connolly and Hirschey (1988).

The cash recovery rate (CRR) approach owes its origins to Ijiri (1978). The idea is, essentially, to estimate the IRR from the firm's ability to generate cash, given certain assumptions about project life and the cash flow pattern of projects. This concept was introduced into the Fisher and McGowan debate by Salamon (1985 and 1989) and Buijink and Jegers (1989). A summary of the development of the concept is given by Stark (1987), and a new definition of CRR is proposed by Griner and Stark (1988 and 1991). Brief (1985) provides a critique of the earlier literature, and Hubbard and Jensen (1991) a more recent critique. The essential difficulty facing this approach is that it requires assumptions which are strong enough to infer future cash flows.

The CRR proposal and the other literature reviewed hitherto was all set in the context of the original problem set by Harcourt (1965) and Solomon (1966), which was to infer the value of IRR as the ideal economic rate of return. The next significant contribution to the debate, by Edwards, Kay and Mayer (1987) was to question this assumption.

EDWARDS, KAY AND MAYER

In 1987, Edwards, Kay and Mayer (EKM) published their book, *The Economic Analysis of Accounting Profitability*. This took the earlier debate, starting with Harcourt (1965) as background and repeated the analysis of Kay (1976). It then provided a radical alternative to Kay's earlier analysis. The theoretical framework of this new approach had already been published in a short paper by Kay and Mayer (1986).

At the heart of the new approach were two concepts not previously developed (although they had been suggested) in the literature:

1   that the IRR might not be the ideal economic measure it had previously been assumed to be (this had, as we have already seen, been raised by Vatter as early as 1966); and
2   that the ARR might be a better measure of economic performance if the opening and closing values were measured on current cost ('value to the business') principles, which might produce a better proxy for economic values than depreciated historical cost (this idea was implicit in much of the long debate on price change accounting, but was proposed in the ARR/IRR debate by Whittington (1979: 206)).

The first of these new concepts led EKM to consider explicitly the rate of return over a *segment* of a firm's life, thus acknowledging explicitly the accountant's typical problem of measuring returns in a continuing business. They were also accepting Vatter's interpretation of the IRR as an average rate of return over the full (flotation to liquidation) life of a business which would have no particular relevance to performance over a segment (such as an individual) of a firm's life. They therefore re-defined their ideal economic standard as the cost of capital of the firm, ρ, over the segment for which performance was being assessed, which could be as short as an individual year. They then assessed the validity of a specific accounting measure of the rate of return α (which they described as ARR, although, as already noted, it was not the ARR concept used in the earlier literature) by comparing it with the cost of capital. They demonstrated, in both *ex ante* and *ex post* situations, that the comparison of α with ρ gave the correct signals (in terms of the discounted cash flow capital budgeting model) as to the economic profitability of the firm over the segment. EKM's interpretation concentrated on applications to competition policy (presumably as a response to the Fisher and McGowan debate), but the significance of their analysis is wider, e.g. it could equally well be applied to shareholders' assessments of performance.

The second of the new concepts, the use of 'value to the business' (VTB) as a valuation method for accounting, was a crucial component of EKM's new proposal for the accounting rate of return (which, to avoid confusion with the broader traditional ARR concept, will be denoted by α). Value to the business is based on the following algorithm for valuing assets and liabilities:

$V_t = \min [RC_t, RA_t]$
where $RA_t = \max [PV_t, NRV_t]$
and
  V = value to the business
  RC = replacement cost
  RA = recoverable amount
  NRV = net realizable value (from sale)
  PV = present value of future cash flows (from continued ownership)
  t is a point in time.

Thus, in a typical 'going concern' business, assets will be valued at replacement cost, unless replacement would not be justified, in which case recoverable amount is the relevant value. This method of valuation has a long history in the accounting literature (see, for example, the review of the subject in Whittington (1983)), and can be regarded as the current cost equivalent of the accountant's traditional rule 'cost or market value, whichever is the lower'.

EKM's new α measure of the accounting rate of return over a segment of a firm's life was calculated as the return arising from comparing the value of net assets on a VTB basis at the end of the segment, plus net cash outflows to providers of capital during the segment, with the VTB value of net assets at the start of the segment. The validity of α as an economic performance measure was assessed not, as in the previous literature, by its conformity with a measure of IRR, but by the correctness of the decisions which could be reached by comparing α with the cost of capital ρ, on the assumption that $\alpha > \rho$ implied good performance (or, in the *ex ante* case, prospects) and $\alpha < \rho$ implied bad performance (or prospects). In other words, α was used as a *substitute* for IRR in the appraisal process and was not being assessed for exact correspondence with IRR. The resulting analysis demonstrated that, with minor exceptions, α performed well in giving appropriate signals, consistent with the capital budgeting model.

DEVELOPMENTS FOLLOWING EDWARDS, KAY AND MAYER

The Edwards, Kay and Mayer analysis was an important contribution to the continuing debate on the economic interpretation of accounting numbers. Unlike the Fisher and McGowan paper, it was not followed by a spate of critical comments, and it seems virtually to have been ignored in the USA. The only comment of any substance (apart from book reviews) which followed its publication was by Grinyer and Walker (1990), and this was essentially supportive: it demonstrated that the EKM results could be extended to a world of uncertainty by using certainty equivalents.

The main reason why EKM did not evoke a wider response was probably the decline of interest in current cost accounting as the inflation rate slackened during the 1980s. EKM's system depended crucially on the VTB valuation principle, and this was the basis of current cost accounting. There were some theoretical issues surrounding VTB which posed problems, notably the aggregation problem: the sum of the VTBs of individual assets would not necessarily equal the sum of the VTBs of the assets assessed on a more aggregative basis (e.g. at the level of the whole productive unit rather than the individual machine) and this in turn would not necessarily equal the VTB of all of the assets valued together (at the level of the whole business), so that VTB was not an unambiguous concept. However, the main objections were practical: VTB involved comparison of no less than three alternative values (RC, NRV and PV) and each of these was potentially subjective and costly to estimate. In the 1970s, at a time when prices had been changing rapidly, business had been interested in current valuation methods in accounts, because they offered clear benefits of more accurate reporting of economic realities, and less clear, but possibly more important, benefits of relief from taxation and price controls. In the 1980s, lower rates of price change made the benefits less obvious, and experience of applying VTB methods in the USA (from 1979 onwards) and in the UK (from 1980 onwards) made the costs and difficulties more obvious. Thus, by the time EKM published their proposals (1987), the practical prospect of their solution (VTB) being applied was already receding rapidly.

APPLICATION IN THE PUBLIC SECTOR AND UTILITY REGULATION

There was one exception to this general rule: this was the public sector. In 1986, the Byatt Report, addressed to the UK Treasury, advocated a VTB-based accounting system very similar to that of EKM. The recommendation was directed specifically at nationalized industries, but it was claimed that the arguments in favour of it (which were consistent with those of EKM) could also be applied in the private sector. This report was influential not only in encouraging nationalized industries to adopt current cost accounting but also, subsequently, in encouraging regulators of the privatized utilities to adopt it for the purpose of setting price caps. These included British Gas, British Airports (BAA plc), the regional electricity companies and the water companies (of which Mr Byatt became the regulator).

In the privatized utilities, the use of VTB-based accounts to determine economic rates of return for setting regulatory price caps is currently standard practice and therefore an important policy issue. Unfortunately, there are some serious problems in the process (which are reviewed in Whittington (1994)), not least of which is the potential circularity of the PV element in VTB: if PV is the value to emerge from the algorithm as VTB, this cannot be used as a basis for price setting because it will be determined *by* price (through the effect on future cash flows). Another serious difficulty in the case of utilities, which have large, long-lived fixed investment, is the problem of determining replacement costs when technology is changing.

AN OVERVIEW

It should be apparent that the debate initiated by Harcourt (1965) has been substantial and continues to be important. It is far from being resolved, but it has led to important insights into the relationship between accounting numbers and economic decisions. The issues are of considerable intellectual interest, but they are also of great practical importance for the functioning of market economies in general, and for the work of regulators in particular.

An interesting insight provided by the history of this debate is that, although it is often believed that there is a lack of communication between economists and accountants, this gap was spanned in this particular instance. A less obvious gap, which was not always spanned, is that between the USA and the UK literature. An example of this is Fisher and McGowan's initial (1983) failure to cite Harcourt (1965) or Kay (1976). The subsequent neglect in the USA of Edwards, Kay and Mayer is another illustration of the fact that the USA and the UK are divided, not only by a common language, but also by a separate literature.

NOTES

1   A useful supplement to this is the collection of papers edited by Brief (1986) which contains the most important papers published on the subject before 1983. It does not, however, cover the Fisher and McGowan or Edwards, Kay and Mayer debates.

2   Kay adopted the term accounting rate of profit (ARP) for what had been previously known in the literature as ARR. He later compounded this change by using ARR for a different concept (Kay and Mayer 1986).

3   Another contribution in a similar vein was by Peasnell (1982). This uses discrete, rather than continuous, mathematics and uses examples more attuned to the

language of accountants, to whom it is addressed, but it uses a similar theoretical framework to that of Kay and derives some of the same results.

BIBLIOGRAPHY

Brief, R. P. (1985) 'Limitations of using the cash recovery rate to estimate the IRR: a note', *Journal of Business Finance & Accounting*, Autumn: 473–5.

—— (ed.) (1986) *Estimating the Economic Rate of Return from Accounting Data*, New York and London: Garland.

Buijink, W. and Jegers, M. (1989) 'Accounting rates of return: comment', *The American Economic Review*, March: 287–89.

Byatt, I. C. R. (Chairman) (1986) *Accounting for Economic Costs and Changing Prices: A Report to HM Treasury by an Advisory Group* (The Byatt Report), 2 vols., London: HMSO.

Connolly, R. A. and Hirschey, M. (1988) 'Concentration and profits: a test of the accounting bias hypothesis', *Journal of Accounting and Public Policy*, Winter: 313–34.

Edwards, J. S. S., Kay, J. A. and Mayer, C. P. (1987) *The Economic Analysis of Accounting Profitability*, Oxford: Clarendon Press.

Fisher, F. M. (1984) 'The misuse of accounting rates of return: reply', *The American Economic Review*, June: 509–17.

—— and McGowan, J. J. (1983) 'On the misuse of accounting rates of return to infer monopoly profits', *The American Economic Review*, March: 82–97.

Griner, E. H. and Stark, A. W. (1988) 'Cash recovery rates, accounting rates of return, and the estimation of economic performance', *Journal of Accounting and Public Policy*, Winter: 293–311.

—— (1991) 'On the properties of measurement error in cash-recovery-rate-based-estimates of economic performance', *Journal of Accounting and Public Policy*, Fall: 207–23.

Grinyer, J. R. and Walker, M. (1990) 'Deprival value-based accounting rates of return under uncertainty: a note', *The Economic Journal*, September: 918–22.

Harcourt, G. C. (1965) 'The accountant in a golden age', *Oxford Economic Papers*, March: 66–80.

Hubbard, C. M. and Jensen, R. E. (1991) 'Lack of robustness and systematic bias in cash recovery rate methods of deriving internal (economic) rates of return for Business Firms', *Journal of Accounting and Public Policy*, Fall: 225–42.

Ijiri, Y. (1978) 'Cash-flow accounting and its structure', *Journal of Accounting, Auditing and Finance*, Summer: 331–48.

Kay, J. A. (1976) 'Accountants, too, could be happy in a Golden Age: the accountant's rate of profit and the internal rate of return', *Oxford Economic Papers*, November: 447–60.

—— (1978) 'Accounting rate of profit and internal rate of return: a reply', *Oxford Economic Papers*, May: 469–70.

—— and Mayer, C. P. (1986) 'On the application of accounting rates of return', *The Economic Journal*, March: 199–207.

Livingstone, J. L. and Salamon, G. L. (1970) 'Relationship between the accounting and the internal rate of return measures: a synthesis and an analysis', *Journal of Accounting Research*, Autumn: 199–216.

Long, W. F. and Ravenscraft, D. J. (1984) 'The misuse of accounting rates of return: a comment', *The American Economic Review*, June: 494–500.

Parker, R. H. and Harcourt, G. C. (eds) (1969) *Readings in the Concept and Measurement of Income*, London: Cambridge University Press.

—— and Whittington, G. (eds) (1986) *Readings in the Concept and Measurement of Income*, 2nd edn, Deddington, Oxford: Philip Allan.

Peasnell, K.V. (1982) 'Some formal connections between economic values and yields and accounting numbers', *Journal of Business Finance & Accounting*, Autumn: 361–81.

Salamon, G.L. (1985) 'Accounting rates of return', *The American Economic Review*, June: 494–504.

—— (1988) 'On the validity of accounting rates of return in cross-sectional analysis: theory, evidence and implications', *Journal of Accounting and Public Policy*, Winter: 267–92.

—— (1989) 'Accounting rates of return: reply', *The American Economic Review*, March: 290–3.

Solomon, E. (1966) 'Return on investment: the relation of book-yield to true yield', in R. K. Jaedicke, Y. Ijiri, and O. Nielsen (eds) *Research in Accounting Measurement*, Evanston: American Accounting Association: 232–44.

—— (1970) 'Alternative rate of return concepts and their implications for utility regulation', *The Bell Journal of Economics and Management Science*, Spring: 65–81.

Stark, A. W. (1987) 'The cash recovery rate approach to the estimation of economic performance', The Fifth Tom Robertson Memorial Lecture, Edinburgh: Department of Accounting and Business Method, University of Edinburgh.

Stauffer, T. R. (1971) 'The measurement of corporate rates of return: a generalized formulation', *The Bell Journal of Economics and Management Science*, Autumn: 434–69.

Vatter, W. J. (1966) 'Income models, book yield, and the rate of return', *The Accounting Review*, October: 681–98.

Whittington, G. (1979) 'On the use of the accounting rate of return in empirical research', *Accounting and Business Research*, Summer: 201–8.

—— (1983) *Inflation Accounting: An Introduction to the Debate*, Cambridge: Cambridge University Press.

—— (1994) 'Current cost accounting: its role in regulated utilities', *Fiscal Studies*, October: 88–101.

Wright, F. K. (1978) 'Accounting rate of profit and internal rate of return', *Oxford Economic Papers*, May: 464–8.

Zeff, S. A. (1966) 'Discussion comments' on Solomon's 1966 paper, *op. cit.*: 251–4.

10

CORPORATE FINANCE AND CAPITAL ACCUMULATION

Laurence Harris

THE ROLE OF FINANCE

To any enquiry 'what is economics?', many students of Geoff Harcourt's would give the reply that has a tradition going back to Smith, and, more pertinently, Ricardo: 'it is the study of the accumulation of capital'. Many would add that one of the greatest puzzles is the link with effective demand and, within that, the role of the rate of interest in accumulation, thereby reflecting their debt to the Keynesian tradition Geoff Harcourt has carried forward at Cambridge.

In this paper I am concerned with the relationship between the rate of interest, other financial variables, and accumulation. One difficulty in understanding the role of interest has been that our standard models ask the interest rate to carry too much of a burden. An A+ student on Intermediate Macro knows that in the Hicks and Tobin versions of Keynesian models, the rate of interest both links real saving and investment and is the variable linking real investment ('accumulation') to financial conditions, described by liquidity preference in portfolio allocation; at least, they know the *IS* and *LM* curves intersect, which is a graphic representation of that linkage. We have long understood that interest alone cannot account for the link between real saving and investment, so that effective demand, however conceived, has to be a fundamental category. But in a high proportion of macroeconomic models, the interest rate remains the only channel through which financial conditions relate to investment, and that is a simplification that prevents us from understanding fully the role of finance in accumulation.

In the mid-1970s Geoff Harcourt chaired a conference of the International Economics Association, in some ways a defining moment in debates over the foundations of macroeconomics that preceded the rational expectations revolution. His Introduction to the conference volume is a perfect statement of his commitment to letting a hundred flowers bloom, for, while the Introduction makes his own views clear,[1] it surveys the field with scrupulous fairness and ends: 'After all, not to expect too much from any one line of enquiry and to have an open mind that is tolerant of all lines of enquiry is not a bad working rule for social scientists' (Harcourt 1977: 22). One line of enquiry Geoff Harcourt encouraged then, as always, was the Kaleckian, represented by Askimopulos's contribution to the conference, taking the firm as the fundamental microeconomic unit, the actions of which link accumulation to pricing and output and, above all, to finance, which, in the Kaleckian tradition, hinges on the availability of retained profits (*ibid.*: 16–17).

There are ample grounds for believing that accumulation depends upon many aspects of finance apart from the rate of interest and they cannot be proxied by the interest rate. Quantity constraints on the availability of finance; the institutional balance between banks and markets in the financial system; the relative availability of long-term and short-term finance; and the capital structure of corporations, including the degrees of leverage they choose and experience, affect firms' accumulation of capital. This paper is principally concerned with the last-mentioned; I argue that to understand the relation between interest and accumulation, we must address the question of capital structure.

I start with Lavoie's model of capital structure and accumulation in a Steindl–Minsky framework as a benchmark. I then argue that one of the underlying questions it leaves unanswered – what determines the firm's choice of capital structure? – is dealt with in valuable ways by neoclassical corporate finance theory. Although modern corporate finance theory has its roots in choice theoretic behaviour, it has roots traceable to Marx and, mindful of Geoff Harcourt's injunction to be 'tolerant of all lines of enquiry', I go on to discuss some connections between Marx's writings and the arguments of modern corporate finance theory.

CAPITAL STRUCTURE, ACCUMULATION, AND INSTABILITY

In the textbook, neoclassical versions of Keynesian models, investment, I, is a function of the interest rate alone, or, expressed as the rate of accumulation, $I/K = g^i = f(r)$. Given expectations of future profits, changes in the interest rate cause a change in desired capital stock and planned investment as profit-maximizing firms equate the marginal product of capital to the marginal cost of capital over a determinate adjustment period (Jorgensen 1963). Why, then, cannot macroeconomic policy simply and directly manipulate aggregate investment through interest rate policy? Keynes' powerful explanation, in the context of uncertainty, rests on 'animal spirits' (Harris 1979).[2] Another explanation is that investment behaviour relates to firms' leverage, which needs to be included in any model of how financial policy affects investment. The two non-neoclassical writers who have done most to demonstrate the effect corporate leverage ratios can have on the instability of a late capitalist economy, the United States, are Steindl and Minsky. An investment function capturing some of their ideas is proposed by Lavoie. If g^i is the rate of capital accumulation firms choose, $g^i = I/K\, f(\gamma,\ r,\ i\lambda)$ where γ is expected rate of growth of sales, r is the rate of profit, λ the leverage ratio L/K where L represents the stock of debt, and $i\lambda$ is the ratio of interest payments to capital stock. The linearized form is:

$$g^i = \gamma + g_r r - g_i(i\lambda).$$

Arguably the bare bones of Minsky's financial fragility hypothesis and Steindl's views are captured by $g_r r$ and $g_i(i\lambda)$. A higher rate of profit leads to higher accumulation by firms, while increased interest payments generated by rises in the real interest rate or by expansion of the leverage ratio increase firms' 'financial fragility', leading to a slowdown of firms' planned accumulation (Lavoie 1995: 166).[3] The model Lavoie develops rests on two assumptions which warrant further examination. One is that firms do have a desired leverage ratio. But, if they do, what determines it? The second is that there is a direct link between leverage ratios and accumulation: Lavoie follows Steindl in assuming that if firms' actual leverage ratio rises about their target, their response will be to reduce physical investment, in an attempt (possibly unsuccessful) to reduce leverage by reducing new borrowing. In fact, other courses of action are open to firms, in particular the substitution of shares for debt. That follows from the sources and uses of funds constraint facing firms:

$$Y + \Delta S + \Delta D - Div = I$$

where Y is net operating income, ΔS is the value of new share issues, ΔD is the value of new debt, Div is dividend payments, and I is physical investment. Adjustment of the leverage ratio by reducing ΔD in any period can be attempted by increasing share issues instead of cutting investment. Therefore, a second question that should be addressed is: what are the relative costs of equity and debt finance to the firm? In the next section I consider both of those questions.

CAPITAL STRUCTURE IN CORPORATE FINANCE THEORY

Firms' desired leverage ratios and the costs of different forms of finance have been addressed by writers within a Kaleckian and Keynesian framework, most notably Kalecki's own discussion of the choice between internal and external finance (Kalecki 1937), and Minsky's analysis of cyclical fluctuations in desired leverage ratios. But the puzzles left unanswered in Lavoie's model are the central questions of the microeconomics subdiscipline of corporate finance theory, and in these paragraphs I outline some aspects of its answers.

The Modigliani and Miller (1958) model shows that under certain conditions there is no optimum leverage ratio – each is as good as another. Their Proposition 1 is that the firm's debt–equity ratio has no effect on the market value of the firm, therefore shareholders should be indifferent between leverage ratios. The proof is in terms of the arbitrage available to individual investors in perfect capital markets, but the conclusion is more fundamentally a statement of a proposition on the conservation of value. Given the firm's investment in assets and the probability distribution of the income stream they produce, the distribution of that income stream between shareholders and creditors does not affect the value of the firm; the latter is determined wholly by the value of its assets.

Since it appears that actual firms do choose a desired leverage ratio, the importance of the Modigliani–Miller model is that it sets the framework for identifying which of its assumptions is inapplicable in reality. Market imperfections in the form of differential tax treatment of interest and other disbursements of company profits may create a target leverage ratio, but the precise outcome depends partly upon the differences between personal and corporate tax regimes. In the simplest tax system, allowing interest costs against corporate profits tax creates a tax shield which is a positive function of the debt–equity ratio, and the present value of which adds to the firm's value. On the other hand, the higher the leverage ratio, the higher is the probability of financial distress, or, *in extremis*, bankruptcy. Since bankruptcy involves default costs, higher leverage ratios are associated with a higher capitalized expected value of bankruptcy costs. On plausible assumptions, the present value of tax shield minus expected value of bankruptcy costs is a non-linear continuous function of the debt–equity ratio with a negative second derivative, which gives a rationale for firms to choose the leverage ratio which maximizes it.

Although tax shields and bankruptcy costs are well established in the traditional literature as explanations of firms' target leverage ratios, they are to a large extent contingent, as the debate over Miller's 'Debt and taxes' (1977) shows. More fundamental explanations of firms' decisions on capital structure and other variables have been provided by agency-cost theories since Jensen and Meckling (1976) set out some of the major conclusions derivable from them. In their model, the selection of a desired leverage ratio results from minimizing the total agency costs attributable, separately, to equity finance and debt finance.

The agency approach represents a direct challenge to the Modigliani–Miller approach because the assumption of the invariance model which it overturns is one of its most basic. The agency approach employs a concept of the form which is quite different from the traditional one, for it postulates a radical separation between ownership and control. Control is in the hands of managers (the board) while legal ownership belongs to the shareholders, although creditors may effectively take over ownership when the firm faces financial distress. While, in the traditional neoclassical theory of the firm, managers' decisions conform wholly with the shareholders' interest of maximizing the value of the firm, in the agency approach shareholders and

112

managers have conflicting interest. Other stakeholders – whether workers, customers, bondholders, or other creditors – also have conflicting interests.

The seminal agency theory statement of the choice of leverage ratio is organized around two types of conflict: the conflict of interest between shareholders and managers, and that between shareholders and bondholders. Various contracting and monitoring arrangements address those conflicts of interest, but they are costly. The agency costs of equity finance decrease with decreases in the debt–equity ratio; the agency costs of debt finance increase with increases in the debt–equity ratio; the sum of the two gives the total agency costs of finance at each debt–equity ratio, and there exists an optimum debt–equity ratio E^*, where that total cost is at a minimum. Why do the agency costs of outside equity rise as the debt–equity ratio falls? Note that the argument concerns *outside* equity; that is, the proportion of equity not owned by the managers of the firm, and that makes it easy to compare a firm managed by its owner (an owner-manager) with a firm whose owners are separate from the manager. Jensen and Meckling reasoned by starting from a firm where all the equity is owned by the manager – a typical family-owned firm. If the owner-manager then issues equity to outside shareholders, their interests will be different from his or her own. Such managers have an incentive to spend company money on 'perquisites' which benefit them but do not assist the company; standard examples being private jets, luxury travel, or excessive salaries in non-competitive markets.[4]

As a result, outside shareholders have to spend money on monitoring the activities of managers, and those monitoring costs are higher the higher is the proportion of outside shareholding (the lower is the proportion of shares owned by the managers). It is assumed the outside shareholders know that agency costs, the monitoring costs the outside shareholders have to pay in order to monitor their agent, the manager, increase as the leverage ratio declines, or the proportion of outside shareholdings ($S_0/[B_0 + S_0]$) rises. Therefore the price they are willing to pay for the shares is reduced by an amount equal to the present value of those costs. For the original owner-manager, selling shares to outsiders in order to obtain finance, that reduction in the sale price represents a cost of obtaining equity finance, the agency costs of equity.

Why do the agency costs of debt rise as the debt–equity ratio rises? They exist because shareholders' actions can damage the interests of bondholders. For example, shareholders may obtain credit from bondholders supposedly to finance a particular set of physical assets, but they then have an incentive to invest the funds in different, more risky projects. Such asset substitution represents a cost to the bondholders, inducing them to spend money on monitoring arrangements to prevent substitution, but those costs are borne by the shareholders since the bondholders require higher yields to compensate them for those agency costs.

Those agency costs of equity and debt finance, costs incurred because of principal–agent conflicts,[5] can explain firms' leverage ratios as the outcome of cost-minimizing choices. Different formulations of the principal–agent problem have also been used to demonstrate that minimization of agency costs can explain several aspects of firms' financial behaviour: the existence of bond covenants (Smith and Warner 1979; Kalay 1982), the leveraged buyouts used in the takeover boom of the 1980s, and various policies regarding the payment of dividends.

MARX ON FINANCIAL MARKETS AND THE CORPORATION

I have argued that some core theorems of the corporate finance literature can enhance our understanding of the relation between finance and accumulation. That literature is widely considered to belong to a different paradigm from the accumulation models which owe their origins to a tradition associated with Marx, Kalecki, and some Keynesian writings; scholars working in one tradition rarely work in the other. Surprisingly, however, Marx was one of the first to examine the problems which are the subject of today's corporate finance theory and there are parallels, as well as divergencies, between his concerns and modern finance theory.[6] In chapter 27 of *Capital* volume III Marx, and Engels, engage with phenomena that were to become characteristic of capitalism: industrial joint stock companies and stock exchanges. Marx's own views were being formed at a time when those structures were in their infancy. As Engels reflected thirty years later: 'In 1865 the stock exchange was still a *secondary* element in the capitalist system' (Engels 1981: 1045). And the main thrust was the broad argument that, in line with historical laws of capitalism, joint stock companies represent a new form presaging the (apparently not far distant) socialization of production. But however wrong Marx's views on the imminent suppression of capitalism, his commentary on joint stock companies, the stock exchange, and the credit system included observations on the system's specific features which mark him as the first to consider questions which are the core of modern corporate finance theory.

Which propositions of Marx may be seen as precursors of corporate finance theory? The most fundamental theorem of corporate finance is the Fisher Separation Theorem, developed by Irving Fisher in his *Theory of Interest* (1930), and directly underpinning the central role of the maximization of net present value as an operating rule in corporate finance and capital budgeting. In a neoclassical framework Fisher's theorem demonstrates the optimality of separating investment in physical capital from saving (consumption) decisions; in perfect capital markets, the firm should invest in all projects with positive net present value when discounted at the market rate, and the owners' preferred consumption (saving) plans should then, separately, be achieved by borrowing or lending at that rate.

The strong implication of the Fisher Separation Theorem is that investment in physical capital is not determined by the agent's saving propensity.[7] When the financial system studied by Fisher was in its infancy, Marx reached similar conclusions. His concept of capital repudiated the abstinence theorems – that accumulation of capital resulted from capitalists abstaining from consumption in favour of saving – which, in economics, echoed the ethics of protestantism; and Marx's study of the credit system led him to formulate the critique of abstinence theories in terms of the capitalist's ability to borrow the savings of others,[8] as did Fisher.

For Marx, the primacy of production and real accumulation over all aspects of exchange, distribution and finance, is axiomatic. Modigliani and Miller's invariance theorem, which is the foundation of modern corporate finance's theory of capital structure (corporations' financial structure), has a similar strong corollary. Its implication is that wealth cannot be created by financial engineering – in perfect capital markets without taxation or bankruptcy costs, changes in the leverage ratio have no effect on the 'value' of the firm – but, instead, derives only from firms' real operations.

But although the primacy Marx accords to production is paralleled by Modigliani and Miller's, the latter's is an extension of the neoclassical principle of the neutrality of money and is derived from a model in which the firm is a black box located in financial markets, in contrast to Marx's conception of the labour process controlled hierarchically within the firm. Marx and Engels were among the first to note that in the joint stock company the control of the labour process is in the hands of managers who are separate from the owners.[9] In this century, corporate finance theory developed the implications of that separation[10] in two different directions.

The first is an implication of Fisher's Separation Theorem. A corollary of the irrelevance of agents' abstinence is that it does not matter that managers and owners may have different preferences for present over future consumption; as long as managers follow the instruction to invest in any project with positive present value, they maximize shareholders' interests. In other words, assuming managers follow the net present value rule they are obedient agents of the owners. The second, which lies at the heart of the agency cost approach, is the assumption that managers' interests diverge from owners' so that, unless agency costs are incurred to monitor managers or provide incentives or security, they will take actions which reduce shareholders' benefits. In previous paragraphs these actions were described as unwarranted expenditure on managers' own benefits in kind, but more generally they can be conceived as the internal use of resources over and above those investable in positive net present value projects (free cash flow).

The two ways by which corporate finance theory deals with the separation between ownership and control – identification of managers' decisions with the owners' rules, and a principal–agent conflict requiring measures to resolve it – have parallels in Marx's own understanding of the problem. On one hand Marx treats the managers as the 'actual functioning capitalist . . . in charge of other people's capital', but on the other hand the manager is simply skilled labour 'really active in production' like 'the lowest day labourer' (Marx 1981: 567–8). In other words, since Marx identified workers and capitalists as having an inherent conflict of interest, managers were here identified as being on the opposite side of the fence from the firm's owners. In Marxian terms managers hold a 'contradictory class position', generating a principal–agent problem which requires monitoring or other costs to solve.[11]

Interestingly, the parallel between agency cost theories and Marx's observations goes beyond the agency cost to shareholders of controlling managers. In the modern literature a typical example of the agency problems faced by creditors – treating creditors as principals and shareholders as agents – is the possibility of asset substitution, referred to above, under which shareholders have an interest in using funds for higher-risk projects than desired by creditors. Marx, similarly, saw the credit system as providing funds for capitalists who would use them differently from the lenders (and differently from unleveraged investors): 'the great part of the social capital is applied by those who are not its owners, and who therefore proceed quite unlike owners who, when they function themselves, anxiously weigh the limits of their private capital' (*ibid*.: 572).

One of Marx's observations to have resonated through twentieth-century debates on the corporation is his view that the stock market acts as a vehicle for takeovers and the concentration of capital;[12] while Adam Smith had early identified capitalism's proclivity for cartels and monopoly power, Marx was the first to foresee the growth of giant corporations and treat it as a key tendency of capitalism. He argued that stock exchange acquisitions would play a significant role in the process, and Engels added that the three decades between Marx's work and its publication had shown that the stock exchange, together with subsequent innovations such as extensive limited liability, did facilitate the growth of large corporations and trusts, such as the United Alkali Trust (Marx 1981: 568–9, 1046–7).

Whether or not Marx's view that capitalism tends to produce increasingly concentrated ownership of capital is correct, mergers and acquisitions are a major feature of US and British stock markets, occurring in major waves such as the leveraged buyouts of the 1980s, and their analysis is one objective of corporate finance theory. The theory which gained greatest currency in the 1980s was Michael Jensen's, a version of agency cost theory providing a rationale for leveraged buyouts in terms of the conflict of interest between shareholders and managers (Jensen 1986). Free cash flow, internal funds greater than the opportunities for profitable investment in the firm's product lines, enable managers to expand the firm in ways which are not in shareholders' interests. Consequently, they may use them for non-profitable diversification but, at the same time, outsiders have an incentive to take over the firm, using newly issued debt which binds the managers to disburse cash in interest payments instead of controlling it as free cash flow usable for unprofitable ends. In that theory the latter type of takeover is seen as economically beneficial, although the empirical evidence supporting that judgement is based on studies of the gains to shareholders in the target and the acquiring company which, as Crotty and Goldstein (1993) argue, rests on maintained hypotheses which are questionable.

The agency cost approach to mergers and acquisitions illustrates both the threat connecting modern corporate finance to the ideas of Marx and its radical difference. One thread is the central role played by the conflict of interest between managers and owners, suggested by the 'contradictory class position' of the former in Marx's work. One main difference is that corporate finance theory is concerned with the finance of the individual corporation, or sub-groups of corporations, or the financial markets as a whole, while Marx believed the operations of firms and financial markets were ultimately reflections of the general dynamic of capitalist production. Another is that the main Marxian problem of control within the corporation is control of the worker, with the problem of control of managers having a different significance; control of the worker, in order to control the labour process, was seen by Marx as the source of surplus value and, hence, profit. Indeed, while the agency cost model of free cash flow relates takeovers to control over managers, the gains shareholders made in the 1980s takeover boom coincided with reductions in labour rolls, and tighter wage policies in companies which had been taken over (Crotty and Goldstein 1993; Schleifer and Summers 1988; Rossett 1990; Bhagat *et al.* 1990). A fundamental issue in the comparison between Marx's observations on the stock exchange and its status in corporate finance theory concerns the valuation of shares. Despite the empirical evidence that today's stock markets exhibit excess volatility and other phenomena which contravene the efficient markets hypothesis, the latter remains the foundation for corporate finance theory's assumption that share pricing is rational. For Marx the stock market was not a market in which information on corporate fundamentals was efficiently processed and reflec-ted fully in prices, but instead, a market prone to bubbles and, extrapolating from his views on the credit system, a device for swindlers. But it should not be forgotten that the stock market was in its infancy when he wrote. As Engels noted: 'In 1865 the stock market was still a *secondary* element in the capitalist system. At that time, then, the stock exchange was still just a place where the capitalists plundered one another of their accumulated capitals' (Marx 1981: 1046). Nevertheless, it is arguable that after 130 years the jury is still out; it may still be too early to say what the role of stock markets is in the accumulation of capital.

CONCLUSION

To understand the role of finance in capital accumulation we have to go beyond the role of interest as a measure of the cost of capital, and examine both quantity constraints on the availability of internal funds (Croasdale and Harris 1988) and firms' balance sheet choices which determine their target leverage ratios. In other words, the microeconomics of finance and the corporation is a necessary foundation for the macroeconomic models. Modern corporate finance theory has provided valuable new perspectives on those microeconomic choices, most notably in analysing principal–agent problems. The fact that some parallels can be found between those writings and Marx's epigrammatic observations on the financial system, a century earlier, bears testimony to the Harcourt 'working rule': in economics as elsewhere it is desirable to have an open mind, tolerant of different lines of enquiry.

NOTES

1   He said of his essay: 'Of necessity this introduction must be personal and uneven' (Harcourt 1977: 1).

2   For an institutionalist perspective on Keynesian uncertainty, see Crotty (1994).

3   In a short-run model, Lavoie uses the ratios of r and $i\lambda$ to the normal rate of profit in his heuristic explanation of their link with Minsky's concepts. Placing that investment function in a macroeconomic model, Lavoie explores the behaviour of the leverage ratio and the conditions under which instability is generated.

4   They have that incentive because otherwise any extra profits they make for the firm accrue partly to the outside shareholders, rather than as higher rewards to themselves. Moreover, their incentive to increase spending on their perquisites increases as the proportion of outside shareholdings rises, for that reduces the proportion they receive of any increased share value that results from resisting expenditure on perquisites.

5   The principal–agent pairings being shareholder–managers, and bondholders–shareholders respectively.

6   While beginning to formulate my thoughts on this subject, I was fortunate to attend an SOAS seminar addressed by Costas Lapavitsas who made the point, more articulately than I could, that modern finance theory, including the theory of optimal contract design, echoes some of Marx's conclusions. I am grateful to him for helping to clarify my thoughts.

7   Fisher (1930); Fama and Miller (1972); Hirschleifer (1970).

8   'The actual capital that someone possesses ... now becomes simply the basis for a superstructure of credit. ... Equally absurd now is the saying that the origin of capital is saving, since what this speculator demands is precisely that *others* should save for him' (Marx 1981: 570).

9   'Formation of joint-stock companies ... involves ... [t]ransformation of the actual functioning capitalist into a mere manager, in charge of other people's capital, and of the capital owner into a mere owner, a mere money capitalist' (Marx 1981: 567).

10 As did writers in a different, radical, tradition such as Berle and Means.

11 A debate over that 'contradictory class position' holds a famous place in Marxian sociology, the main positions being represented by Miliband (1973); Poulantzas (1973) and Carchedi (1977). One way an economist may interpret Miliband's view that managers (directors and top managers) are identified with the interests of capital is that, although they are not intrinsically identified with shareholders' interests, they, too, have large shareholdings and other stakes as a result of incentive mechanisms being set up to reduce principal–agent conflicts, as the

modern literature on corporate finance and optimal contracting would suggest.

12 Since ownership now exists in the form of shares, its movement and transfer become simply the result of stock exchange dealings, where little fishes are gobbled up by the sharks, and sheep by the stock-exchange wolves' (Marx 1981: 571). Marx's law of concentration and centralization of capitals was predicated upon what he identified as fundamental forces in the sphere of production, but the stock market provided a new and powerful mechanism for effecting it. Note that in the text I use concentration in a modern sense, while Marx would use centralization to refer to takeovers.

REFERENCES

Bhagat, S., Schleifer, A. and Vishny, R. (1990) 'Hostile takeovers in the 1980s: the return to corporate specialization', *Brookings Papers on Economic Activity, Microeconomics*: 1–72.

Carchedi, G. (1977) *On the Economic Identification of Social Classes*, London: Routledge & Kegan Paul.

Croasdale, M. and Harris, L. (1988) 'Internal funds and investment' in L. Harris, J. Coakley, M. Croasdale and T. Evans (eds), *New Perspectives on the Financial System*, London: Croom Helm.

Crotty, J. (1994) 'Are Keynesian uncertainty and macrotheory compatible? Conventional decision making, institutional structures, and conditional stability in Keynesian macromodels' in G. Dymski and R. Pollin (eds) *New Perspectives in Monetary Macroeconomics: Explorations in the Tradition of Hyman P Minsky*, Ann Arbor, Mich.: University of Michigan Press.

——— and Goldstein, D. (1993) 'Do US financial markets allocate credit efficiently? The case of corporate restructuring in the 1980s' in G. Dymski, G. Epstein, R. Pollin (eds) *Transforming the US Financial System: Equity and Efficiency for the 21st Century*, Armonk, N.Y.: ME Sharpe.

Engels, F. (1981) 'Supplement and addendum to Volume 3 of Capital' drafted as two articles for *Neue Zeit* in May 1895, the second of which was unfinished. The quotation in the text is from the version published in K. Marx, *Capital*, vol. 3, Harmondsworth: Penguin.

Fama, E. F. and Miller, M. H. (1972) *The Theory of Finance*, New York: Holt, Reinhart and Winston.

Fisher, I (1930) *The Theory of Interest*, New York: Macmillan.

Harcourt, G. C. (ed.) (1977) *The Microeconomic Foundations of Macroeconomics*, Basingstoke: Macmillan.

Harris, L. (1979) 'Catastrophe theory, utility theory and animal spirit expectations', *Australian Economic Papers*, 18 December.

———, Croakley, J., Croasdale, M. and Evans, T. (1988) *New Perspectives on the Financial System*, London: Croom Helm.

Hirschleifer, J. (1970) *Investment, Interest and Capital*, Englewood Cliffs, N.J.: Prentice-Hall.

Jensen, M. C. (1986) 'Agency costs of free cash flow, corporate finance and takeovers', *American Economic Review*, 76(2): 323–9.

——— and Meckling, W. (1976) 'Theory of the firm: managerial behaviour, agency costs and capital structure', *Journal of Financial Economics*, 3: 305–60.

Jorgensen, D. W. (1963) 'Capital theory and investment behavior', *American Economic Review*, 53: 247–59.

Kalay, A. (1982) 'Stockholder–bondholder conflict and dividend constraints', *Journal of Financial Economics*, 10: 211–33.

Kalecki, M. (1937) 'The principle of increasing risk', *Economica*, 4: 441–7.

Lavoie, M. (1995) 'Interest rates in post-Keynesian models of growth and distribution', *Metroeconomica*, 46(2): 146–77.

Marx, K. (1981) *Capital*, volume 3, Harmondsworth: Penguin.

Miliband, R. (1973) *The State in Capitalist Society*, London: Weidenfeld & Nicolson.

Miller, M. H. (1977) 'Debt and taxes', *Journal of Finance*, 32: 261–76.

Modigliani, F. and Miller, M. H. (1958) 'The cost of capital, corporate finance and the theory of investment', *American Economic Review*, 48: 261–97.

Poulantzas, N. (1973) *Political Power and Social Classes*, London: New Left Books.

Rossett, J. (1990) 'Do union wealth concessions explain takeover premiums?', *Journal of Financial Economics*, 27: 263–82.

Schleifer, A. and Summers, L. (1988) 'Breach of trust in hostile takeovers' in A. Auerbach (ed.) *Takeovers: Causes and Consequences*, Chicago Il.: Chicago University Press, 19–33.

Smith, C. W. Jr. and Warner, J. B. (1979) 'On financial contracting: an analysis of bond covenants', *Journal of Financial Economics*, 7: 117–61.

11

HOW FREE SHOULD TRADE BE NOW?

Hugh Stretton

'The principal economic problem' of the developed industrial nations, Geoff said in his 1993 *Harcourt Plan to Save the World*, 'is sustained mass unemployment with which is associated the need of many of them to restructure in order to solve persistent balance of payments problems'. Discussing *Macroeconomic Policy for Australia* he proposed (among other things) equitable fiscal means of restraining consumption; selective credit rationing; and learning from the NICs 'that we should leave tariff levels where they are, at least in the medium term'. That paper's conclusion reflected Keynes' theory and MITI's practice:

> On the side of real investment the government should take the lead in designing investment incentives which persuade business people to invest in those areas which, overall, the government has decided most need to be developed. Provided those areas are defined broadly enough, the chances of corruption will be lessened, yet neither the government nor its public servants will be able to dodge the responsibility for giving leadership in what should be a partnership between the public and private sectors.
>
> (1995: 31)

What trade and exchange policies might accord with the strategy in countries with persistent exchange deficits?

Some countries do well to trade freely. Others do better to discriminate. Besides old reasons for discriminating there are now some new reasons. They arise from financial deregulation, the change from fractional reserve banking to risk-rated capital adequacy, the failure of market mechanisms which were expected to balance international trade and payments, the reversal of the long trend to greater equality within western countries, and some changing implications of consumer sovereignty in conditions of affluence. But old beliefs persist, and deficit-trading countries bow to international pressure to dismantle what protection they have, without noticing the new risks for deficit traders in a global economy with no national trade controls but with scores of national fiat currencies, and with government-guaranteed private banks free to lend, borrow, exchange and gamble with those currencies as they please.

I think the classical theories of free trade were flawed in the first place. Except perhaps for that heresy, there is nothing new in what follows. It merely brings the new reasons together with the old reasons for some discriminate protection by some countries in some circumstances, to see how the whole case for it looks now.

OLD REASONS FOR FREE TRADE

Two assumptions of the classical theories have been upset by modern developments.

Adam Smith (in *The Wealth of Nations* IV, II, II) thought it was safe to finance a trade deficit by cumulative foreign borrowing as long as output grew faster than the debt did. He offered no comfort to a country such as Australia, whose output now grows at a trend rate of 2% or 3% of GDP per year, while its net foreign debt grows by 6% of GDP per year.

Ricardo's theory of comparative advantage assumes full employment, natural rather than acquired advantages, readily switchable resources, and (it seems to me) English importers gullible enough to pay English rather than Portuguese prices for Portuguese products. Things have changed since 1817.

OLD REASONS FOR PROTECTION

A list of orthodox reasons – free traders' reasons – for allowing some protection can begin with Adam Smith's reasons. Defence industries may be protected. Matching tariffs are proper where equivalent home produce is taxed. Retaliatory tariffs may be justified. Tariff changes should be introduced slowly enough to allow any disemployed workers to find work in other industries.

Next are reasons which got into print in the nineteenth century. Infant industries may usefully be protected until they achieve the scale at which they ought to be able to survive unprotected. That includes industries whose advantages are acquired rather than natural: any lawful means of establishing them may be justified by their mature competitive success. And there is a case for continuing protection of key industries if they enable other industries to survive without protection, and if the gains from the surrounding industries in the cluster are greater than the cost of protecting the key industry. (There is an excellent analysis of the benign externalities of protected Australian carmaking in Chapman (1992)).

There are twentieth-century arguments about rates of change. New industrial competitors keep entering the world market, and so do technical advances. Equipment is outmoded before it is outworn or has repaid its investors. Levels of frictional and transitional unemployment may be permanently higher than they were. Even if markets respond to such shocks in ways which would in due course re-employ the disemployed resources, there is no guarantee that the adjustments will come before the next dislocations do. When dislocations become endemic their costs may be greater than the cost of enough protection to see out the useful life of vintages, achieve deliberate rather than catastrophic technical development, and avoid the short horizons and high mark-ups and prices that go with such uncertainties.

MANAGING THE BALANCE OF PAYMENTS

Countries with advanced economies, to whom foreigners are willing to lend money, may find themselves deficit-trading and in debt for a variety of reasons. It may happen as terms of trade change, as competitive advantages change, as transnational corporations shift production of tradeable goods from country to country. Imports may increase when governments reduce tariffs or other barriers. And they may increase dramatically if the importers' banks are suddenly allowed to finance them by borrowing rather than buying foreign currency to pay for them, and if the exporters' banks are suddenly allowed to create credit for the importers' governments without any additional reserve requirements.

Governments of deficit-trading countries currently hope to balance their trade and payments by one or more of six means: free trade, devaluation or market depreciation of their currencies, financial deregulation, asset sales, unemployment, and import or exchange controls. With rare and temporary exceptions the first five don't work. The sixth is the most economical, efficient and effective method, but there are now powerful intellectual and business pressures, and GATT and WTO pressures, to ban it.

Free trade

Free trade has not recently rescued a deficit-trading country from unbalanced trade or accumulating debt. There is no reason why it should. Even if the theory of comparative advantage were valid, there is no reason to expect that all countries will develop such complementary patterns of comparative advantage that unaided market forces will balance their trade. Trade and exchange are freer now than ever before in this century, and the main deficit traders of twenty years ago are deficit trading still, and deeper in debt than they were.

Devaluation or depreciation

Devaluation or depreciation of deficit traders' currencies was once expected to expand demand for their exports and depress demand for their imports until their trade and payments balanced and their exchange rates consequently stabilized. In practice the opposite more often happens. The theory had necessary assumptions about the price elasticity of demand for exports and imports, the income elasticity of demand for imports, and the price elasticity of supply of exports. Neither in theory nor in practice is there reason to expect that any or all of their elasticities will always be above unity, and for many products in many circumstances they are not. Since market rates of exchange replaced fixed rates in the 1970s all surplus trading countries' currencies have appreciated and their surpluses have increased, and all deficit traders' currencies have depreciated and their deficits have increased. (Figures, and theoretical debates about them, are provided in McCombie and Thirlwall (1994).)

Financial deregulation

Financial deregulation has opened national financial systems to the world money market. Deficit countries borrow foreign capital funds to finance their current exchange deficits. Why do the lenders lend so freely?

First, because they are allowed to. Private international borrowing of capital funds was restricted to a few approved purposes by most OECD countries until it was freed, step by step, through the last twenty years.

Second, western banks have lender of last resort arrangements which effectively guarantee their debts if they are solvent; and if they are not, governments still bail them out because letting them fail is too scary altogether. So private western banks can now borrow abroad with government guarantees to the lenders, but scarcely any public regulation of the borrowers or the uses of borrowed funds.

Third, the change from fractional reserve requirements to risk-rated capital adequacy, completed throughout the OECD in 1988, had the effect of increasing the amount of credit many banks were allowed to create, provided that their additional lending was to OECD governments. With no addition to their capital they could create money to spend on buying their own or foreign bonds.

Those and other effects of the general deregulation converge to keep interest rates high, and to allow unlimited foreign borrowing, public and private, by OECD countries with current exchange deficits. And in most cases those deficits have rising components of debt service.

Internal deregulation has removed some public restraints on all countries' interest rates. The capital-borrowing demands of a number of deficit countries push international rates higher than they would otherwise be. The high interest increases their deficits and accelerates the increase of their debts. Year by year that increases the positive balance of trade – the excess of export earnings over import spending – that it would now take to balance the deficit countries' payments. Meanwhile within debtor and creditor countries, high interest depresses the quantity and quality of new investment, slows growth and helps to maintain substantial unemployment.

But the unemployment is no longer an *unwanted* effect of the high interest rates. Maintaining it is now one purpose of the high rates in a number of debtor countries. After a note on asset sales by debtor countries, we will return to the use of unemployment as a last and worst defence against the further growth of debt.

Asset sales

Some countries finance some of their exchange deficit by selling assets to foreign buyers. Directly or indirectly, by sales of both public and private assets, the vendor countries spend capital to maintain current consumption, and increase their future need for foreign exchange to pay rent or dividends to foreign owners. (The objection does not necessarily apply to direct foreign investment which creates new productive capital in debtor countries.)

Unemployment

Unemployment is currently as high in some exchange-surplus countries as in deficit countries. Its use to restrain demand for imports is obviously only one among its causes. But some governments now treat the balance of payments as the main constraint on their macroeconomic policies; and of those, some restrain demand chiefly by financial means which restrain investment and employment, rather than by fiscal means which ration everyone's spending. Australia may currently offer an extreme example of that approach, but it is the one I know best.

Before the final deregulation of its financial system in 1983, Australia's net foreign debt was about A$5 billion, or A$340 per head of population. It is now about A$160 billion, nearly A$10,000 per head. It grows by more than A$25 billion a year. Remember Adam Smith's warning about consuming more than you produce? Australia's foreign debt grows by about 6% of GDP a year, while the trend rate of growth of the economy is below 3%. Debt-subsidized consumption is growing faster than output – Smith's prescription for decline. And new policy constraints make it hard for output to catch up: for forty years to 1983 the base rate of real interest averaged below 1%; since deregulation it has averaged above 6%. Public saving in the form of infrastructure and other public investment has declined by nearly half through the same years.

The exchange deficit is not yielding to freer trade, to an export boom or to depreciation of the currency. The government won't introduce any new import controls and is committed to dismantling the few that remain. It won't control the foreign borrowing that finances the excess of imports and foreign debt service. So its main defence against inflation and against the increase of foreign debt is to restrain aggregate demand, chiefly by means which reduce poor rather than rich incomes and spending. That's a clumsy approach to the balance of payments: to reduce demand for the 20% or so of goods that they import, Australians must also produce and consume less of the 80% of goods and services which they produce for themselves.

The two main methods of restraining demand are to cut public investment and services (prudent investment and valuable services, in many cases) and to maintain the highest real interest rates in the developed world. Together those methods reduce investment, employment and growth below the levels which would be practicable with appropriate control of imports and foreign borrowing. The high interest does double duty, and three kinds of harm. It restrains investment (and employment, income and demand). It attracts the foreign funds which finance the excess of foreign payments over foreign earnings. And it greatly reduces the efficiency with which resources can be allocated within the national economy.

Australian taxation is among the lowest in the OECD and neither political party any longer dares use it as a means of demand management. So it is fair to say that induced unemployment is now both parties' preferred weapon against inflation, and their preferred means of restraining the growth of foreign debt. To be effective for that second purpose, the reduction of demand would need to be three or more times the desired reduction of demand for imports. (Imports represent about 20% of all demand, but nearer 30% of marginal demand.) With 8% or 9% unemployed now, foreign debt is growing at 15% a year. To bring the demand for imports plus foreign debt service into balance with the country's current foreign earnings would now take a disastrous level of unemployment.

Import or exchange controls

Compared with those ineffective approaches to balancing national payments, trade or exchange controls are more promising. The best approach in some circumstances may be trade control by means of exchange control, as practised by many countries under the Bretton Woods regime, and by Japan through much of the century and a half of her modernization. Rationing the uses of the available exchange allows effective restraint of the growth of foreign debt. It allows a preference for more productive over less productive imports. It allows import controls to operate without necessarily raising import prices. And the regulation of foreign lending and borrowing allows national interest rates to be insulated from world rates (which was one of Keynes' main purposes in the Bretton Woods negotiations). National economies which use that opportunity to run on low rates, with some quantitative control of credit when necessary, can accordingly be more efficient.

Protection

There are finally the traditional uses of protection which most classical and neoclassical economists don't support, usually because they expect them to do more harm than good: to establish and maintain an advanced economy including a range of high-value-added industries; to allow confident long-term investment, and low pricing for long pay-back periods, in those industries; to protect valued local culture, and diverse intellectual and artistic training and job opportunities, for the nation's people; to allow a more egalitarian wage structure than would otherwise prevail; to make full employment easier to achieve and maintain; and to develop and maintain a structure of industries which can balance its trade and payments with the rest of the world.

And there are two old purposes of protection which gain new force from modern productivity, and from the development of a unified free-trading world economy: to weaken consumer sovereignty, and to strengthen national sovereignty or (some would say) citizen sovereignty.

CONSUMER SOVEREIGNTY

Fred Hirsch in *Social Limits to Growth* (1976) and Tibor Scitovsky in *The Joyless Economy* (1976) were among those who began to doubt the value of the further growth of consumption in the advanced economies. Fifteen years later, in *The Market Experience* (1991), Robert Lane reviewed more than a thousand investigations, in a dozen disciplines of social and medical science, into the effects of modern economic activity on human learning, personal development and happiness. He drew four conclusions.

1   Affluent societies have minorities who suffer severely from the direct and indirect effects of poverty and unemployment. A return to full employment could bring large rewards of human development and happiness. While people are poor in rich societies their economic condition can be a powerful determinant of their whole experience of life.
2   But for the large majority who now have a comfortable standard of living, income and consumption contribute much less to personal development and happiness than do family life, friendship, intellectual growth, self-reliance and self-esteem.
3   In the effects which the market economy does have on human development and happiness, it has a mixed record. It does a lot to develop people's intellectual skill and complexity, self-reliance, self-esteem and happiness. But it also generates a good deal of anxiety, competitiveness

and (in some occupations) dependence and subjection. It is wrong to think, as many economists do, that most of those ill effects are necessary conditions of efficiency; for example, insecurity, anxiety, competitiveness and close supervision motivate more bad work than good work. Firms compete – but industries vary. Wherever complex organization and dependable skill and quality control are needed, the firms which compete most successfully tend to be those whose workers are most cooperative rather than competitive, and secure in their jobs. Where irregular hours of low-skilled, low-paid, insecure labour can produce at lowest cost, regulation can often do a good deal to improve the balance of benefits between the producers and the consumers.

4   Except for the poorest, people's personal development and happiness are affected more by their experience at work than by their wealth, income or consumption.

For most of the current shift to more anxious, competitive, insecure and unsatisfying work, Lane does not blame the employers. He blames consumer sovereignty. What happens in the degrading occupations is that 'market forces systematically undermine worker satisfactions and learning in order to advance the interest not so much of owners but of consumers. Consumers may not represent a ruling class, but they are sovereign and those who work are their subjects.' But sovereign and subjects are the same people. As consumers the market allows them to choose between products. As workers it allows them some (usually much narrower) choice between available jobs. But it does not offer them choices between a consumer-dominant economy and a worker-dominant economy – 'there is no market wherein individuals may choose between, say, anxiety over cyclical unemployment and the benefits of more consumer durables. People do not buy economic systems or work cultures, they inherit them.' There is no way for individual choices to reorient the market economy to deliver more work benefits, at the cost where necessary of less consumer benefits.

The market cannot solve that problem. Too many market economists cannot see it is there. They attract Lane's most biting criticism, backed by a formidable accumulation of evidence. He is strongly on the side of retaining, and developing a social capacity to make deliberate choices and trade-offs 'between consumer values and producer values, or more drastically, between the pleasures of consumer wealth and producer happiness'.

If Lane's working life had been at (say) Melbourne rather than Yale he might be more optimistic about developing that capacity, though perhaps not about developing it in the US. From 1907 to about 1985 it was the heart of Australia's 'New Protection' strategy. Tariff protection, central wage-fixing and generous public infrastructure and economic services combined to produce egalitarian wage structures, regulated working conditions, generous and well-distributed household capital, and for a small economy, an unusually wide range of industrial development and occupational choice. The strategy is caricatured by those who are now dismantling it. It was misused at times by some firms and some unions, and mismanaged by some governments. But those were passing troubles. Through most of the century industry and unions cooperated quite well with the strategy. Both were unusually well disciplined by the Hawke government's early tariff and income policies. Through the long postwar boom the strategy delivered steady growth, the world's lowest unemployment and its fastest expansion of home ownership. Labour productivity is still higher per hour than Japan's, and material standards of living are much higher. (Doubters should read Ian Castles' statistical chapter in Sheridan (1991)). That traditional direction of Australian policy – to improve the experience of work, to make full employment the primary source of welfare, and to furnish family life generously with capital aids to productivity rather than passive consumption – was what Lane now wants, and what his evidence suggests that most people want if they have the option.

But that option depends, among other things, on collective uses of sovereignty, including in many circumstances some regulation of trade in goods and money, and some influence on the structure of the national economy.

NATIONAL SOVEREIGNTY

This theme is so familiar that the briefest reminder will do. 'Financial markets', often led by a country's own bankers, now operate with such freedom and scale that they easily intimidate governments whose policies they don't like. So do some press barons. Transnational manufacturers locate production wherever it will do best. In practice that is often in well-off, well-educated, well-governed countries with well-organized and well-paid workers. But there are exceptions, and even where there are not, the local rich often do their best to bully the voters by loudly fearing that capitalists won't come, won't stay, won't invest, won't employ anyone, unless the government abolishes unions, minimum wage laws, industrial and environmental safety requirements, business taxes, progressive taxes. It is true that within the US some firms shop around the states for the 'best', meaning the worst, industrial and environmental and tax regimes, and some state governments bid for their favours accordingly. Critics cite that interstate behaviour as a model of international behaviour in a global economy. But it need only be so if national governments surrender the sovereignty that the American states surrendered in 1789. Until they do, they can still when necessary negotiate from strength and offer foreign investors double incentives: 'If you want to sell it here you must make it here, and if you make it here we'll protect you from competitors who make it elsewhere.'

But governments are currently urging each other to sign away those powers, and not only over trade. In the Uruguay round and now in the WTO there is insistent pressure, especially from the US, to end nations' rights to regulate foreign lending, borrowing, investment and ownership within their territories. With a majority of Congressmen now lawfully on corporate payrolls – including bank and transnational payrolls – the pressure is not likely to ease.

Besides the opportunities they make for corporate misbehaviour, those freedoms do away with the most effective macroeconomic means, and a number of useful microeconomic means, to full employment and balanced payments. National governments may always do well to leave trade and investment as free as they safely can. But that should continue to be a choice, changeable if conditions or national purposes change; not an irrevocable surrender of sovereignty.

It is reasonable to require national governments to use such powers fairly, under rules. But the rules must not condemn deficit-trading countries whether they like it or not to go on spending more than they earn and to run even further into foreign debt and ownership. The rules should be negotiated on the assumption that international trade and exchange are not automatically self-balancing, and would not be so if entirely free. They often need some management. And they should be managed by means which do not rule out (as the present WTO regime threatens to rule out) balanced payments, full employment, or low interest rates and efficient allocation of resources within the countries concerned.

GOVERNMENT FAILURE

Some free traders and most public choice theorists argue that however bad the effects of free trade and exchange may be, the effects of regulated trade and exchange are likely to be worse because of government's usual corruption and incompetence. They expect trade policy to be especially bad because rent-seekers who want tariff protection bring concentrated pressure to bear on politicians, while the masses who will suffer from higher prices are unorganized and inattentive because they are busier with other concerns. Much of this argument originates in the US where the behaviour it describes may be encouraged by the division of powers, and the lobbying by which the legislators allow themselves to earn. But the criticism is heavily biased. Public choice theorists report and generalize from selected cases of misbehaviour. But as far as I know they have not reported, or tried to explain, the radical reduction of most US tariffs through the last fifty years.

Other countries have also had bad cases, or bad phases, of trade policy. But there have been plenty of quite well-reasoned and disciplined uses of trade and exchange controls by most western countries and NICs through this half-century, until some imprudent deregulation in recent years. Economists' criticism of the performance can't be trusted if – as too often happens – it measures the effects of government against the perfectly free, fully employed and self-equilibrating alternative of their imagination – a fiction that is open to most of the familiar objections collected in this paper.

Corporate powers (of joint stock, limited liability and corporate identity) are government creations, and it has long been understood that they are open to such misuse that government has a duty to regulate their use in great detail: hence thousand-page manuals of company and commercial law. The same *was* true of the powers to expand and to gamble with the world's money that governments create when they license and guarantee private banks. The fourteen years' history from the first Mexican default through the US Savings and Loans collapse and the diverse financial scandals of the 1980s to the fall of Barings should be sufficient evidence that banking powers need as strict public discipline as do corporate powers. And the quiet, often unnoticed harm from the loss of long-term low-interest credit for productive industry, especially for young and small firms, is worse than the damage from the reportable disasters.

CONCLUSIONS

If valid, and linked to each other, the bits of reasoning collected in this paper may together support the following, among other conclusions.

- Unhindered trade in goods and money is not reliably self-equilibrating, and can get some national economies into serious trouble.
- National regulation of trade, credit and exchange transactions, tailored economically to each country's situation, is the best way to balance international payments without improvident levels of involuntary debt. That's true whether or not desirable international rules are developed by the World Trade Organization and a successor to the Bretton Woods regime.
- Unlike current approaches to the balance of payments, the necessary regulations can be designed to allow policies of low interest, efficient allocation of capital resources, and full employment, within each national economy.
- Generally speaking, the freer a country wants its trade to be, the more strictly it may need to control its financial system.

Those conclusions don't depend on the remaining, more contentious, three.

- Conditions in the emerging world economy make it reasonable for each country to judge for itself, in the light of its situation and resources and collective purposes, how much or how little trade dependence is likely to serve its people best.
- As a policy consideration, the further growth of consumption in developed countries should rank below, rather than above, full employment, secure and satisfying conditions of work, environmental care, the

equitable distribution of income, and the widest practicable distribution of the household and public capital and services which enable active people to make the most of their family and social life.

- An efficient mixed economy needs pervasive government and performs worse without it. Instead of trying to do without them we should work to make the necessary government and public industries and services as good as we possibly can.

REFERENCES

Castles, I. (1991) 'Living standards in Sydney and Japanese cities: a comparison' in Sheridan, K. (ed.) *The Australian Economy in the Japanese Mirror*, Brisbane: University of Queensland Press.

Chapman, P. (1992) 'Towards an industrial policy' in Carroll, J. and Manne, R. (eds), *Shutdown*, Melbourne: Text.

Harcourt, G. C. (1993) 'The Harcourt plan to save the world', *At the Margin, a Journal of Economic and Social Issues* 1.

—— (1995) 'Macroeconomic policy for Australia in the 1990s' reprinted in G. C. Harcourt, *Capitalism, Socialism and post-Keynesianism*, Aldershot: Edward Elgar.

Hirsch, F. (1976) *Social Limits to Growth*, Cambridge, Mass: Harvard University Press.

Lane, R. (1991) *The Market Experience*, Cambridge: Cambridge University Press.

McCombie, J. S. L. and Thirlwall, A. P. (1994) *Economic Growth and the Balance of Payments Constraint*, London: Macmillan.

Scitovsky, T. (1992) *The Joyless Economy*, Oxford: Oxford University Press.

12

THE COMPETITIVE WEAKNESSES OF THE UK ECONOMY

Michael Kitson

INTRODUCTION

To have destroyed full employment as a goal, let alone the norm it had become; to have greatly increased the inequality of the distribution of income and of property; to have created an underclass and destroyed the dignity, self-respect and hope of a large number of citizens, to have substituted ridiculous rewards for paper shuffling for just rewards for making real and useful things; none of these are achievements of which any society could be proud.

(Harcourt 1992: 1–2)

Despite moderate economic growth during the past twenty years, the policies of the major capitalist economies have done much to damage the social fabric of those countries. There has been misplaced belief that economic growth requires improved incentives (a.k.a. increased inequality) and labour market flexibility (a.k.a. increased unemployment, lower wages and the casualization of the workforce). In his 1992 Donald Horne address, Geoff Harcourt discussed the limitations of this approach in addressing the performance and prospects of the Australian economy.[1] This chapter adopts a similar perspective in assessing the performance of the UK economy. The first part of the paper considers the UK's relatively poor growth performance. The second section argues that the growth process is best understood through a cumulative causation approach. This is followed by a discussion of the issue of competitiveness, and the fourth section considers the competitive weaknesses prevailing in the UK economy.

UK ECONOMIC PERFORMANCE

The UK has been in relative economic decline since the latter part of the nineteenth century. Table 1 shows that in all three major periods (pre-First World War, inter-war and post-Second World War), the UK growth rate has been consistently less than that achieved by the other major capitalist countries. The norm has been for the UK growth rate to be approximately two-thirds of that achieved by the 'world' group. Only during the inter-war sub-periods was this norm disrupted. During the trans-First World War period (1913–29), UK growth performance deteriorated markedly, only to recover significantly during the 1930s. Much of this relative improvement can be ascribed to the UK's positive policy response to the Great Depression (see Kitson and Solomou 1990; Kitson and Michie 1994). The UK's fastest period of sustained growth was during the post-Second World War era. Yet, even during the 'Golden Age', from 1950–73, the UK's growth rate of 3.0% compares with an average growth rate of 4.6% achieved by the other leading capitalist countries.

Table 1 Output growth of the world capitalist countries (Maddison's 16) and the UK, 1870–1989 (annual % growth rates)

		(1) World	(2) UK	(3) UK relative growth rate performance (1/2)
Pre-First World War	1870–1913	2.7	1.9	0.70
Inter-war	1913–37	1.8	1.1	0.61
	1913–29	2.3	0.7	0.30
	1920–37	0.8	2.0	2.50
Post-Second World	1950–89	3.8	2.6	0.68
War	1950–73	4.6	3.0	0.65
	1973–89	2.8	2.0	0.71

Source: Author's calculations from Maddison (1991)

An assessment of the UK's relatively poor growth rate performance must be tempered by consideration of different levels of income. It may be expected that growth rates will differ, as countries have different per capita income levels. As discussed below, countries with relatively low income levels may have relatively higher growth rates as they have the potential to appropriate technologies and organizational techniques from the leading countries. This process, even allowing for the fact that it may be both erratic and confined to countries at broadly similar stages of industrialization, cannot explain Britain's inferior growth performance. The UK's poor growth rate has not just been associated with other industrialized countries catching up with the UK's GDP level, but with those countries overtaking that level. For the past 170 years the UK has been slipping down the GDP league table. In 1820 the UK was the richest of Maddison's sixteen capitalist countries (see Maddison 1991), measured according to GDP per head; by 1870, the UK was second;

by 1913, third; by 1950, fifth; by 1973, tenth; and by 1989, twelfth. Between 1820 and 1989 UK per capita income increased eight-fold – a welcome achievement – yet the average increase, for the sixteen countries, was a fourteen-fold increase.

Table 2 GDP per person, 1950, 1973, and 1992 (1990 $)

		GDP per person (ranks in parentheses)			GDP per person, annual % growth rate (ranks in parentheses)	
1950 Rank		1950	1973	1992	1950–73	1973–92
1	Switzerland	8,939	17,953 (1)	21,036 (1)	3.1 (12)	0.8 (16)
2	UK	6,847	11,932 (7)	15,738 (11)	2.4 (16)	1.5 (12)
3	Sweden	6,738	13,494 (2)	16,927 (8)	3.1 (12)	1.2 (15)
4	Denmark	6,683	13,416 (3)	18,293 (3)	3.1 (12)	1.6 (10)
5	Netherlands	5,850	12,763 (6)	16,898 (9)	3.4 (10)	1.5 (12)
6	Belgium	5,346	11,905 (8)	17,165 (6)	3.5 (9)	1.9 (7)
7	France	5,221	12,940 (5)	17,959 (4)	4.0 (8)	1.7 (9)
8	Norway	4,969	10,229 (12)	17,543 (5)	3.2 (11)	2.9 (1)
9	W. Germany	4,281	13,152 (4)	19,351 (2)	5.0 (4)	2.1 (5)
10	Finland	4,131	10,768 (10)	14,646 (12)	4.3 (7)	1.6 (10)
11	Austria	3,731	11,308 (9)	17,160 (7)	4.9 (6)	2.2 (3)
12	Ireland	3,518	7,023 (15)	10,711 (15)	3.1 (12)	2.2 (3)
13	Italy	3,425	10,409 (11)	16,229 (10)	5.0 (4)	2.4 (2)
14	Spain	2,397	8,739 (13)	12,500 (13)	5.8 (2)	1.9 (7)
15	Portugal	2,132	7,568 (14)	11,130 (14)	5.7 (3)	2.1 (5)
16	Greece	1,558	6,229 (16)	8,238 (16)	6.2 (1)	1.5 (12)

Sources: Maddison (1995) and Crafts (1995)

Further evidence of the UK's relative decline is shown in Table 2, which provides comparative data on the economic performance of the European economies during the post-Second World War period. Although for the whole group there is some evidence of catch-up, with a narrowing of GDP per capita differentials, for the UK the path of relative decline is evident. In 1950 the UK was the second richest European economy, by 1973 it was seventh, and by 1992 it was eleventh. During the period 1950–73, the UK had the lowest growth rate of the sixteen European economies. During the period 1973–92, when all growth rates slowed, its growth rate ranked joint twelfth, with only two European countries having an inferior growth performance.

EXPLANATIONS OF THE GROWTH PROCESS

Neoclassical perspectives

Analysing the growth process, which is essential to the formulation of appropriate policies, has recently occupied much of the efforts of academic economists. Much research has come to the startling conclusion that investment in people and machinery may improve economic growth. Yet this conclusion, although intuitively obvious, flies in the face of traditional neoclassical growth economics, which assumes that capital accumulation is subject to diminishing returns, such that in the long-run the rate of growth is independent of the rate of investment. In traditional neoclassical models the long-run growth of per capita income is dependent on exogenous improvements in technology.

The implication of the traditional neoclassical approach is that economies with similar savings rates and population growth rates will converge to the same level of income per person. Thus, if for whatever reason, countries' initial conditions are such that per capita income levels differ, then subsequent growth rates will be inversely related to the level of output per person, with the scope for catching up being dependent on the extent of the productivity gap.

The evidence in Table 2 suggests that there has been some convergence[2] amongst the Western European economies since 1950. In 1950 the per capita income of the leading European economy (Switzerland) was 5.7 times greater than the lagging economy (Greece); by 1973 the gap had fallen, with Swiss per capita GDP being 2.9 times greater than that of Greece; and by 1992 there had been a further modest reduction in the lead, with Swiss per capita GDP being 2.6 times greater than that of Greece. These results are consistent with Abramovitz's (1986) view that the post-Second World War was one of rapid growth by catching-up. The processes of catching-up and convergence, however, are erratic across time and space. Crafts (1992, 1993) shows that traditional neoclassical models fail to accurately predict postwar convergence and he suggests that convergence rates differ substantially. Furthermore, the pattern of worldwide economic growth during the postwar period suggests that although there has been some convergence *within* groups of countries (such as Europe), there has been widening disparities *between* groups (Dorwick 1992). Simply, the rich have been getting richer, and the poor, relatively poorer.

Overall there is limited evidence of 'conditional' convergence, with catch-up processes being one of many forces that drive the growth process.[3] This, however, is certainly not evident of a Solow-type growth process whereby technical progress, the engine of growth, 'was an exogenously determined, fortuitous and costless occurrence – descending like manna from the heavens' (Shaw 1992: 611). Increased globalization of the world economy, itself an uneven and variable process, has created the potential for follower countries to borrow and adopt new technologies and management techniques from leading countries. Yet, the ability to exploit this potential is dependent on domestic economic conditions, which in turn will reflect the historical legacy, the policy regime and the investment record.

The existence of persistent differences in growth rates, and in some cases, evidence of divergences in growth rates, cannot be easily accommodated within traditional neoclassical growth theories. New neoclassical growth theories, such as Romer (1986) and Lucas (1988), have attempted to resolve this deficiency by incorporating increasing (or non-decreasing) returns to capital. The major contrast between 'new' and traditional neoclassical models is that the former treat technical progress as an endogenous element of the economic system – an element that can be influenced by corporate investment behaviour and public policies. Thus policies which promote investment, or at least certain kinds of investment (such as R&D expenditure and investment in education), may be able to influence the long-term growth rate.

Although the new growth theories provide a more useful insight into the growth process than traditional neoclassical theories, they retain the usual restrictive neoclassical methodology based on the principle of constrained maximization. The models assume full employment and the competitive process is reduced to alternative specifications of market structure – monopolistic competition, oligopoly and so on. Furthermore, as noted by Skott and Auerbach (1995), the new theories largely ignore the importance of historical and institutional structures.

A Kaldorian view

Although increasing returns have only recently been incorporated into neoclassical models of growth, they have been integral to many alternative approaches to growth, stretching back through the work of Kaldor, Myrdal, Young and Marx to Adam Smith. These approaches, however, do not depend on the assumptions and excessive formalization of the neoclassical approach. Full employment is not normally assumed and economic growth is not determined by exogenously given factor endowments.

For Kaldor (1972), manufacturing acts as an engine of growth as it exhibits increasing returns, while services are characterized by constant returns. This proposition may be too simplistic, as increasing returns are likely to exist in services (although there are problems of measurement). The existence of economies of scale means that a nation that is successfully competing in foreign trade can expect that the advantage of an expanding market will increase its competitiveness – including cost competitiveness and other non-price factors, such as product quality, customer service and technological development. Growing economies, for instance, will be able to invest in capital and skills, enabling them to improve processes and products.

Conversely, a nation with poor performance in international trade can expect a trend of deteriorating competitiveness and declining markets – with a lack of investment and a dwindling skill base likely to constrain future growth. Thus, while not explaining initial imbalances, the existence of economies of scale indicates why such imbalances may generate virtuous or vicious circles of growth.

In a neoclassical approach, divergences from 'equilibrium' can be rectified through price adjustment and/or the correction of market failures. A Kaldorian approach indicates that economies do not behave like this. Firstly, history is important (as recognized in recent path dependent models) such that the quantity and quality of factors of production accumulated from the past determine what can be produced in the immediate future. This is inconsistent with conventional equilibrium theory, which asserts that an economy is constrained by exogenous variables (with the exception of technology in the new growth theories). Additionally, it implies that it is difficult and expensive to reverse many economic decisions. If a factory is closed, or if a market is lost, it is difficult to regain the *status quo ante*. Secondly, the impact of economic shocks may not have only a once-and-for-all impact on long-run capacity, but may lead to cumulative changes.

A cumulative causation approach may be taken to suggest that economies may be permanently locked-in to a slow or a fast growth path. This would be misleading as well as inconsistent with the 'stylized facts' of growth. Although cumulative processes may generate forces that encourage divergences in growth, other forces may temper or ameliorate such effects. As noted above, the international transfer of technology may allow the adoption of new techniques – improving the performance of weak economies. Furthermore, successful countries and regions may find that they are 'locked-in' to certain techniques of production or have become overcommitted in certain sectors (Setterfield 1992); factors which will constrain their future growth performance. Additionally, a change in policy regime may improve the growth path of a relatively weak economy, and if particularly successful may create the conditions for a virtuous cycle of growth. Thus, although a cumulative causation approach indicates the forces that generate divergences in growth, such divergences will be affected, and probably bounded, by the institutional, policy and technological regime.

GROWTH AND COMPETITIVENESS

Many orthodox economists have argued vehemently that individual nations do not have a competitiveness problem. Krugman believes that 'the whole concept of competitiveness is at best elusive, at worst meaningless (1994: 280).[4] He goes on to argue:

So, if you hear someone say something along the lines of America needs higher productivity so that it can compete in today's global economy, never mind who he is, or how plausible he sounds. He might as well be wearing a flashing neon sign that reads: 'I DON'T KNOW WHAT I'M TALKING ABOUT'.

(*Ibid.*: 280, capitals in original; one wonders if 'he' could be Laura Tyson.)

In a similarly arrogant, as well as bad-tempered, attack on those who argue that there is a competitiveness problem in Europe, Baldwin argues that:

Intoxicating their audiences with powerful metaphors and provocative buzzwords, the purveyors of 'the competitiveness problem' have won the attention of political leaders throughout the world.

(1995: 75)

The problem with the arguments of Krugman and Baldwin is that much of their rhetoric illustrates that there *is* a competitiveness problem. Their real target is those economists who believe that nations are engaged in a global economic battle and who argue for more interventionist trade and industrial policy (such as Thurow 1993). Krugman accepts, of course, that productivity growth is necessary to increase the standard of living. Thus, policies that improve productivity, which could be termed competitiveness policies, would improve economic welfare. The issue here is one of semantics.

What Krugman does take exception to is the argument that productivity growth is essential to maintain competitiveness in international trade. The substance of his argument is that it is the productivity growth of the whole economy that is important, not just that of the tradeable sector. And, to the extent that there is differential productivity growth between countries, this will be offset by exchange rate changes. Moreover, as the American economy is relatively closed, the tradeable sector is relatively unimportant.

The first problem with the Krugman (1994) approach[5] is that he assumes that increased trade will benefit all trading nations. The benefits of international trade are well known, with emphasis on increased specialization improving the allocation of resources. The potential impacts of increased trade are, however, not universally positive. Increased dependence on trade can make countries more vulnerable in general to external shocks – shocks which may be initiated by national or international factors, but whose impact is transmitted through trade (Kitson and Michie 1995b). More specifically, the distributional impact of exchange rate movements increases as economies become more open on capital and current account, with any given exchange rate movement causing a greater redistribution of income within the domestic economy. Additionally, increased international integration may constrain the growth and weaken the economic structure of some trading nations. Whereas exports are an injection into the foreign trade multiplier, imports are a leakage. Thus, a high dependence on imports – a high import propensity –

may constrain the growth of a domestic economy. Moreover, variations in trade performance in an increasingly integrated world economy may lead to persistent divergences in growth through cumulative causation processes. Increased demand for net exports allows strong countries (or more specifically, the firms and industries within them) to exploit economies of scale, improving their competitiveness and leading to further improvements in their trade performance. Conversely, weaker trading nations may fail to maintain balance of payments equilibrium at a high level of economic activity, with deflationary policies then pursued in an attempt to maintain external balance. The combined impact of poor trade performance and domestic deflation is likely to lead to a cumulative deterioration in relative economic growth as countries fail to exploit the increasing returns associated with a high level of economic activity.

The argument that differential productivity growth between nations can be accommodated by exchange rate changes assumes power of adjustment, which in practice is rather unlikely. The historical record of exchange rate management (see Kitson and Michie 1995a) illustrates that exchange rate adjustment is insufficient to ensure internal and external balance. In the presence of differential productivity performance between nations, the most likely outcome will be differential growth rates in both exports and import penetration, with subsequent implications for economic growth.

Krugman points out that the US is a relatively closed economy; although this reduces the impact of international competitiveness on domestic incomes, it does not negate it completely. As noted above, trade performance can have a large impact on domestic output through the foreign trade multiplier. Furthermore, although the US is relatively closed, the trend is for it to become more open – suggesting that international competitiveness will become a more important factor in the future.

The European economies are highly dependent on international trade, yet Baldwin argues:

> Europe has many economic problems but it does not have a competitiveness problem. It has a problem with the notion of competitiveness. Europe's economic malaise is due to deep structural problems and solving them would be difficult. Drinking the snake oil offered by competitiveness gurus will not help and it might do a good deal of harm.
>
> (1995: 90)

Baldwin is ploughing the same furrow as Krugman. International competitiveness is not important[6] (despite the openness of the European economies); domestic competitiveness, however, is important. For Baldwin, Europe's problem stems from inappropriate labour market institutions and restrictive tax regimes. Thus, despite his protestations, Baldwin is identifying

140

a European competitiveness problem, albeit one that he believes is not transmitted through trade.

So the essence of the debate is concerned with the issue of 'international competitiveness'. The Krugman–Baldwin thesis that this does not matter is not credible. Theoretically, the Harrod foreign trade multiplier (Harrod 1933) shows the dependence of growth on trade. Additionally, the importance of economies of scale means that a nation that is successfully competing in foreign trade can expect that the advantage of an expanding market will increase its competitiveness, and a nation with poor performance in international trade can expect a trend of deteriorating competitiveness and declining markets. Thus, for countries locked into a condition of slow growth and deteriorating trade performance, policies to improve international competitiveness are required. Moreover, such policies need not be beggar-thy-neighbour – the concern of many 'anti-competitiveness' gurus – as an underperforming economy will also be a depressed export market for its trading partners. Policies that improve international competitiveness can, and should, improve both domestic and world income.

ASPECTS OF BRITAIN'S COMPETITIVE FAILURE

The 1995 study of the international competitiveness of forty-nine major countries by the World Economic Forum placed the UK eighteenth, a fall of four places from the previous year's study. The report identified the UK's weakness in manufacturing (35th), investment (45th), infrastructure (16th), education (35th) and management (20th). The causes of the UK's competitive failure can be traced back to long-term factors that have been exacerbated by more recent developments.

Long-term factors: the historical legacy

The historical legacy of the UK being the first industrial nation may have created problems which have accelerated economic decline. The idiosyncratic industrialization process may have hampered subsequent growth and structural adjustment; the UK economy becoming locked-in to an inflexible industrial structure and finding it difficult to respond to the challenge of new markets and new competition.

As shown in Table 3, the UK's export share has been declining since 1870. In part, this can be explained by increased competition as more countries became industrialized. Thus, from the late nineteenth century the export shares of the US and Germany increased markedly, although in 1913 the UK remained the largest exporter. After the Second World War, increased competition came from other European economies and, more recently, Japan. Although it would be expected that, with a growing world economy, the UK's export share would decline, the extent and pace of the decline, coupled with

Table 3 Export shares of four major capitalist countries (%, benchmark years)

	UK	US	Germany	Japan
1870	37.2	11.0	16.6	0.2
1913	27.0	19.1	21.1	1.2
1950	20.5	32.7	5.6	1.9
1973	8.8	23.5	14.5	9.1
1987	8.4	20.1	14.4	13.4

Source: Kitson and Michie (1995a)
Notes: The denominator is total exports of Maddison's sixteen capitalist countries measured in 1985 prices and exchange rates.

rising import penetration, is indicative of major structural weaknesses. Most pertinently, deteriorating trade performance has been associated with relatively poor economic growth.

Medium-term factors: the tarnished 'Golden Age'

A number of factors have contributed to the UK's relatively slow growth during the post-Second World War period. Of central importance has been the interaction between sluggish growth of demand and poor investment. Output failed to grow because demand for British products was low and investment was poor. Poor investment reduces competitiveness, which in turn depresses demand, which in turn reduces the incentive to invest. In addition, investment remained depressed because of the distorted structure of the British economy, combined with bad or non-existent macroeconomic and industrial policies.

As shown in Figure 1, the growth of the capital stock has been declining continuously since 1960 and at the same time unemployment has been rising.[7] During the past forty years there has been a worldwide slowdown in investment amongst the industrialized countries, which may reflect the impact of globalized bond markets on real rates of interest. The retardation of the growth of the UK capital stock, however, has been greater than that experienced in the other major industrialized countries. Since the mid-1960s the growth of the UK capital stock has been inferior to the growth achieved by other major industrialized countries, and during the worldwide slowdown of 1979–89 the UK manufacturing capital stock remained stagnant, whereas that of the other major industrialized economies showed a moderate increase (Kitson and Michie 1966a, 1996b).

The legacy of this poor investment performance has been to leave the UK economy with an inadequate capital stock. This has been a major cause of Britain's indifferent growth performance, constraining technological progress and the expansion of demand. The cumulative effect of this record has resulted in British workers lacking the quantity and quality of capital equipment used by their main competitors.

Apart from international factors, the failure to invest can be traced to structural weaknesses in the domestic economy. First, short-termism in financial markets and biases against the industrial sector have created problems for long-term investment (Hutton 1995). Secondly, macroeconomic instability has dampened 'animal spirits' – it has reduced business confidence, increased uncertainty and contaminated the climate for investment. UK macroeconomic policy during the past thirty years has lurched from one crisis to another. There have been periodic balance of payments crises and politically inspired business cycles leading to exchange rate, and monetary and fiscal, instability. Such macroeconomic volatility has led to the third major problem for investment – the lack of a coherent industrial policy. An attempt was made in the early 1960s to improve long-term growth by establishing the Department of Economic Affairs (DEA) to coordinate economic policy and plan the use of resources. The credibility of the DEA was, however, destroyed by a sterling crisis, and since then there has been no serious attempt to introduce indicative planning, for reasons of political expediency or, more recently, economic dogma.

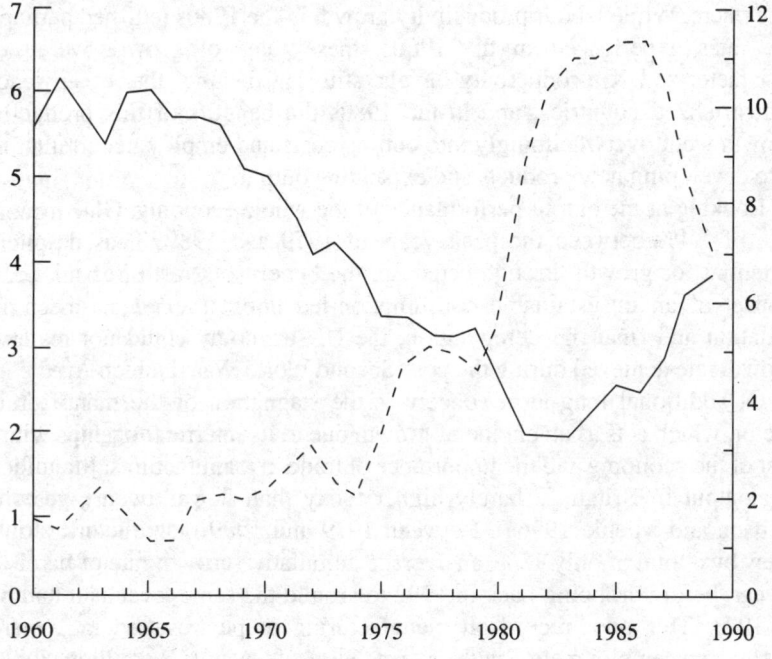

——— Gross capital stock (% change, left-hand scale)
– – – Unemployment (% of civilian labour force (Eurostat definition, right-hand scale)

Figure 1 Investment and unemployment, 1960–89
Sources: O'Mahony (1993) and European Commission (1995)

Short-term factors: Thatcherism and Majorism

For some economists and commentators, the process of Britain's relative economic decline has been halted and reversed by the free market policies implemented during the Thatcher years. Crafts, for example, has argued that Thatcher's 'get tough' approach to trade unions had yielded significant benefits for the economy and that these might endure 'if the bargaining power of workers over manning levels remains weak' (Crafts 1991). Metcalf (1989) argued that there was a decisive improvement in productivity in the 1980s which was due, in part, to a weakening of trade unions.

The improvement in productivity is the key piece of evidence presented in support of the Thatcher Shock (see Crafts (1996) and Eltis (1996), and for an opposing view, Kitson and Michie (1996a)). Certainly, labour productivity in manufacturing grew in the 1980s, although the published figures tend to overestimate the extent of the increase,[8] but this growth was largely due to job cuts rather than increased output, and these jobs were not being lost in a period of full employment when labour would be taken up productively elsewhere. While labour productivity growth in the 1980s returned perhaps to the rates experienced in the 1960s, these rates of growth were never satisfactory; UK productivity levels still lag behind the other leading industrialized countries; and in the 1980s the benefits of this productivity growth went overwhelmingly into cutting costs and employment, rather than into developing new products and expanding output.

Looking at the output performance of the whole economy, GDP grew at a rate of 2.4% between the peak years of 1979 and 1989. Thus despite the potential for growth through catch-up, the benefit of North Sea oil and the impact of an unsustainable consumption-led boom fuelled by asset price inflation and financial deregulation, the UK economy could not match the growth rate achieved during the post-Second World War 'Golden Age'.

Of additional long-term concern is the stagnation of the manufacturing sector, which acts as an engine of growth due to its interrelationships with the rest of the economy and the importance of trade in manufactures. Manufacturing output in Britain is barely higher today than it was twenty years ago (Kitson and Michie 1996a). Between 1979 and 1989 manufacturing output grew by a total of only 15%, an average cumulative growth rate of barely 1% a year, before dropping back in 1992 to around the same level as it had been in 1973. This poor record on manufacturing output resulted in a marked decline in employment, with a net loss of over 1.7 million jobs in manufacturing between 1979 and 1989.

The continued relative decline of the UK economy and the moribundity of manufacturing have been exacerbated by UK macroeconomic policy since the late 1970s. Exchange rate and monetary policy has been directed at 'the overriding priority' of controlling inflation. This has led to periodic over-valuation of the exchange rate, which was particularly damaging during the

Thatcher government's initial monetarist policies in 1979–80 and, more recently, during the UK's membership of the Exchange Rate Mechanism. Additionally, the overreliance on interest rates, a coarse and crude policy instrument, has discouraged investment and business confidence. High and volatile interest rates have been singled out by British businesses as the main impediment to their growth (Small Business Research Centre 1992). Furthermore, the prosperity of the private sector has been hindered by the retrenchment of the public sector. The government's attempts to reduce the size of the public sector and public borrowing in response to quasi-monetarist and supply-side doctrines have not only depressed demand but reduced investment in infrastructure and education.

The UK government's desire since 1979 to target nominal variables (a.k.a. inflation and interest rates) rather than real variables (a.k.a. jobs and output) has led to shifts in policy, which have, in turn, resulted in an increase in the already high level of macroeconomic instability. This has undermined the productive potential of the economy. In addition, privatization and deregulation, the twin pillars of industrial and labour market policy, have reduced incentives to invest in capital and people (Kitson and Michie 1996b). In order to create and sustain a competitive economy, firms require a steadily growing economy which will foster inter-firm cooperation, encourage innovation and product development and the upgrading of the skill base of the economy. UK policy during the 1980s and 1990s has manifestly failed to meet these requirements.

CONCLUSIONS

The UK economy is in the grip of a low-growth low-investment cycle – this reflects its historical legacy, institutional rigidities and inappropriate macroeconomic policy. These problems have been exacerbated by the policy shifts of the 1980s and 1990s which have increased economic instability, generated shocks which have harmed long-run growth potential, and created a productive environment based on threat and uncertainty rather than cooperation and trust.

To ensure future prosperity, policies must be directed at improving competitiveness so as to ensure that economic growth is not constrained by balance of payments problems. The immediate priority is for investment-led growth which will require, first, a sustained growth in demand, and secondly, reform of the financial system. Currently, the composition of aggregate demand is skewed away from investment towards consumption. As growth of the former depends in part on growth of the latter, any attempt to depress consumption would not stimulate investment but would further accentuate the low growth cycle. Fiscal, monetary and exchange rate policies should aim to ensure a continuous and sustainable expansion of aggregate demand, and if there are external shocks, such instruments should be deployed to ameliorate adverse impacts on investment, output and employment.

For the longer term, the major requirement is the creation of a new institutional framework. Fukuyama (1995) has argued that trust, which is embedded in a nation's institutions and culture, provides the 'social capital' necessary for capitalism to prosper. In the UK, however, the dominant institutions, which have evolved from and are embedded in a divisive class system, have created obstacles to growth (Olson 1982). Change is necessary, requiring not only reform of existing institutions but the creation of new institutions that will foster investment in skills and technology, inter-firm cooperation and better relations between employers and employees. This constitutes a major agenda for change, the implementation of which will be difficult and protracted. The first requirements are to discard economic policies based on unrealistic theories and to accept that, in advanced industrialized economies, economic efficiency and growth will improve in a society based on fairness and equity.

ACKNOWLEDGEMENTS

I am grateful to Geoff Harcourt and Jonathan Michie for helpful comments on an earlier version of this chapter.

NOTES

1   These issues are developed in Harcourt (1993, 1994).
2   Gordon (1992) makes a distinction (which he attributes to Abramovitz) between convergence and catch-up. Convergence relates to a reduction in the variance of productivity amongst a group of countries, whereas catch-up concerns a reduction in the gap between a leader and its followers.
3   Empirical evaluations of the convergence hypothesis provide a range of contrasting results (see Baumol 1986, De Long 1988, Dorwick 1992, Dorwick and Nguyen 1989 and Barro 1991). Recent work by Mankiw (1995) has attempted to re-establish support for a Solow-type model by arguing that the empirical limitations of the traditional neoclassical approach were due a failure to correctly estimate human capital.
4   Krugman also argues that 'real economists don't talk about competitiveness' (quoted in *The Economist*, 1995).
5   Although the Krugman (1994) approach does differ from the Krugman (1981) approach and that of Krugman and Venables (1994), where trade can lead to uneven development.
6   This is illustrated by Baldwin's assessment of the EU White Paper: *Growth, Competitiveness and Employment*:

> The White paper tells us that global competitiveness of the European Union is a 'must' for employment creation. This is just plain nonsense, theoretically. Trade has absolutely nothing to do with employment or unemployment in the medium-term. Trade gives rise to market forces that affect the allocation of a nation's resources among sectors. The level of unemployment depends upon national supplies and demands for labour,

national labour market policies and national labour market institutions. Another way to say this is that trade effects which jobs-workers have, not whether they have jobs or not. You don't believe me?

(1995: 85–6)

Well, actually I don't!
And as for exports:

But, you might say, everyone knows that there is a link between employment and trade. After all, exports create jobs. From a theoretical point of view this is dead wrong. From an empirical point of view, it is also wrong.

(*Ibid.*: 86)

7 For a further discussion of the relationship between investment and unemployment, see Rowthorn (1995).
8 See Kitson and Michie (1996b) for a discussion of alternative measures of productivity growth during the 1980s.

REFERENCES

Abramovitz, M. (1986) 'Catching up, forging ahead and falling behind', *Journal of Economic History*, XLIV: 385–406.
Baldwin, R. E. (1995) 'The problem with competitiveness', in Emil Ems (ed.), *35 Years of Free Trade in Europe: Messages for the Future*, Proceedings of EFTA's 35th Anniversary Workshop, Geneva: European Free Trade Association.
Barro, R. J. (1991) 'Economic growth in a cross section of countries', *Quarterly Journal of Economics*, 106: 407–44.
Baumol, W. J. (1976). 'Productivity growth, convergence and welfare', *American Economic Review*, 76: 1072–85.
Crafts, N. (1991) 'Reversing relative economic decline? The 1980s in historical perspective', *Oxford Review of Economic Policy*, 7(3): 81–98.
—— (1992) 'Productivity growth reconsidered', *Economic Policy*, 15 (October): 387–426.
—— (1993) *Can Deindustrialisation Seriously Damage Your Wealth?*, London: Institute of Economic Affairs.
—— (1995) 'The golden age of economic growth in Western Europe', *Economic History Review*, XLVIII (3): 429–47.
—— (1996) 'Deindustrialization and economic growth', *Economic Journal*, 106 (January): 172–83.
De Long, J. B. (1988) 'Productivity growth, convergence, and welfare', *American Economic Review*, 78: 1138–54.
Dorwick, S. (1992) 'Technological catch up and diverging incomes: patterns of economic growth 1960–88', *Economic Journal*, 102 (May): 600–10.
—— and Nguyen, D. T. (1989) 'OECD comparative economic growth, 1950–1985, *American Economic Review*, 79: 1010–30.
The Economist (1995) 'The "C" word', September 9: 104.
Eltis, W. (1996) 'How low profitability and weak innovativeness undermined UK industrial growth', *Economic Journal*, 106 (January): 184–95.
European Commission (1995) *European Economy*, Annual Economic Report for 1995, Brussels and Luxembourg: Directorate-General for Economic and Financial Affairs.

Fukuyama, F. (1995) *Trust: The Social Virtues and the Creation of Prosperity*, London: Hamish Hamilton.

Gordon, R. J. (1992) 'Discussion of crafts', *Economic Policy*, 15 (October): 414–21.

Harcourt, G. C. (1992) *Markets, Madness and a Middle Way*, The Second Donald Horne Address, National Centre for Australian Studies, Monash University, Victoria, Australia; reprinted in Harcourt (1995).

—— (1993) 'Macroeconomic policy for Australia in the 1990s', *Economic and Labour Relations Review*, 4: 167–75; reprinted in Harcourt (1995).

—— (1994) 'A "modest proposal" for taming speculators and putting the world on course to prosperity', *Economic and Political Weekly*, XXIX: 2490–2; reprinted in Harcourt (1995).

—— (1995) *Capitalism, Socialism and Post-Keynesianism: Selected Essays of G. C. Harcourt*, Aldershot: Edward Elgar.

Harrod, R. (1933) *International Economics*, Cambridge: Cambridge University Press.

Hutton, W. (1995) *The State We're In*, London: Jonathan Cape.

Kitson, M. and Michie, J. (1994) 'Depression and recovery: lessons from the interwar period', in J. Michie and J. Grieve Smith (eds), *Unemployment in Europe*, London: Academic Press.

—— (1995a), 'Trade and growth: a historical perspective', in J. Michie and J. Grieve Smith (eds), *Managing The Global Economy*, Oxford: Oxford University Press.

—— (1995b) 'Conflict, cooperation and change: the political economy of trade and trade policy', *Review of International Political Economy*, 2(4): 632–57.

—— (1996a) 'Britain's industrial performance since 1960: underinvestment and relative decline', *Economic Journal*, 106 (January): 196–212.

—— (1996b) 'Manufacturing capacity, investment and employment', in J. Michie and J. Grieve Smith (eds), *Creating Industrial Capacity: Towards Full Employment*, Oxford: Oxford University Press.

Kitson, M. and Solomou, S. (1990) *Protectionism and Economic Revival: The British Interwar Economy*, Cambridge: Cambridge University Press.

Krugman, P. (1981) 'Trade, accumulation and uneven development', *Journal of Development Economics*, 8: 149–61.

—— (1994) *Peddling Prosperity*, London: W. W. Norton.

—— and Venables, A. J. (1994) 'Globalization and the inequality of nations', Centre for Economic Research, Discussion Paper No.1015, September.

Lucas, R. E. (1988) 'On the mechanics of economic development', *Journal of Monetary Economics*, 22.

Maddison, A. (1991) *Dynamic Forces in Capitalist Development: A Long-run Comparative View*, Oxford: Oxford University Press.

—— (1995) *Monitoring the World Economy 1820–1992*, Paris: OECD.

Mankiw, N. G. (1995) 'The growth of nations', *Brookings Papers on Economic Activity*, 1: 275–326.

Metcalf, D. (1989) 'Trade unions and economic performance', *London School of Economics Quarterly*, Spring.

Olson, M. (1982) *The Rise and Decline of Nations*, New Haven, Conn.: Yale University Press.

O'Mahony, M. (1993) 'International measures of fixed capital stocks: a five-country study', National Institute of Economic and Social Research, Discussion Paper no. 51.

Romer, P. (1986) 'Increasing returns and long-run growth', *Journal of Political Economy*, 94: 1002–37.

Rowthorn, R. (1995) 'Capital formation and unemployment', *Oxford Review of Economic Policy*, 11: 26–39.

Setterfield, M. (1992) 'A long run theory of effective demand: modelling macro-economic systems with hysteresis', PhD thesis, Dalhousie University, Canada.

Shaw, G. K. (1992) 'Policy indications of endogenous growth theory', *Economic Journal*, 102 (May): 611–21.

Skott, P. and Auerbach P. (1995) 'Cumulative causation and the "new" theories of economic growth', *Journal of Post Keynesian Economics*, 17(3): 381–402.

Small Business Research Centre (1992) *The State of British Enterprise: Growth, Innovation and Competitive Advantage in Small and Medium Sized Enterprises*, Cambridge: University of Cambridge, Small Business Research Centre.

Thurow, L. (1993) *Head to Head: the Coming Economic Battle Among Japan, Europe and America*, London: Nicholas Brealey.

13

POST-STALINIST SYSTEM REFORM IN CHINA AND RUSSIA

Contrasts and implications

Peter Nolan

INTRODUCTION

I have had the privilege to be Geoff's colleague for the past fifteen years at Jesus College, Cambridge. I have had the benefit of many discussions with him upon the issues touched upon in this short paper. His own work has been consistently characterized by an attempt to affect the 'real world'. This applies not just to writing both 'applied economics' as well as 'economic theory', but also to his lifelong involvement in the real world outside academia, including the struggle against the Vietnam War, working for the Howard League for Penal Reform, advising the Australian Labor Party and tirelessly giving public speeches and broadcasting (I first heard him speaking on the radio in Australia in 1976 in 'Notes from the News'). I am delighted to be able to offer this small token of appreciation of all that he has done through his work to attempt to make the world a better place for everyone to live in.

The contrast in reform paths taken in China and Russia is well known. China conducted cautious, experimental economic reform in a setting of continued authoritarian politics. In every aspect of its reform policies, China defied the western 'transition orthodoxy' of how to reform a communist system of political economy. In the 1980s its half-way house of the socialist market economy was widely perceived to have failed to reform the system successfully. This in turn fed into the creation of the 'transition orthodoxy', which reached a crescendo of confidence among reformers immediately before and after the Tiananmen massacre. The USSR followed this 'transition orthodoxy'. Gorbachev's policy of *perestroika* destroyed the old communist political system. For this 'achievement' Janos Kornai, foremost of the 'transition orthodoxy's' exponents, believed that Gorbachev would 'earn undying merit' (Kornai 1992: 574). Then, under Yeltsin the Russian Federation implemented a programme of massive privatization, frequently referred to as Russia's 'primitive capitalist accumulation'.

The contrast in outcomes from system reform in the former USSR (after 1986) and in China (since 1978) is one of the most important phenomena of the age. This article first outlines some key aspects of this contrast.[1] There will never again be a 'transition' from communism, so policy 'lessons' cannot be drawn from China about other 'transitions'. However, the drastically different ways in which the two giants of the communist world went about this process provides a rich area of research for investigating the practical value of different approaches to social science analysis. The article goes on to explore some areas that might be affected by this dramatic contrast.

ECONOMIC PERFORMANCE DURING THE REFORM PERIOD IN CHINA AND RUSSIA

Output growth

China's record under reform policies placed it in the front rank of international growth performances during the period, with an average annual growth rate of GDP of over 10% from 1980 to 1991 (World Bank 1993). Behind the growth of output there was a massive accumulation process, with huge additions to the stock of capital goods. Large parts of Chinese industry were modernized rapidly with imports of high technology products and with the capital goods produced by modernizing domestic factories.

Soviet economic performance under Gorbachev was poor. National income is estimated to have fallen by 34% from 1989 to 1991 (Khanin 1993b: 7). After the collapse of the communist government, a poor performance turned into a disaster: net material product in 1994 stood at just one-half of the level of 1990 (Government of the Russian Federation 1995). Capital investment in Russia collapsed in the early 1990s, falling by 1994 to just one-third of the level of 1990 (Government of the Russian Federation 1995). Due to the disastrous foreign trade performance and Russia's unattractiveness as a recipient of foreign direct investment, the capital stock was unable to modernize quickly through the import of foreign technology.

Consumption

The improvement in economic performance in China was accompanied by an extraordinary surge in living standards. The level and structure of food intake greatly improved. Huge new consumer durables industries sprang up in the 1980s, with a 'first wave' of goods such as bicycles, watches, TV sets, fridges and washing machines, followed by a more complex array of goods in the 'second wave', including products such as motor cars, motor cycles and video recorders. A massive housebuilding boom took place over the reform years, with space per person more than doubling.

For a large part of the Russian population real incomes fell significantly in the late 1980s and drastically in the early 1990s. In 1992 alone, personal consumption fell by over 30% (Khanin 1993a: 17). Every variety of foreign luxury suddenly was available in the shops; nor did one need to queue for most of these products.[2] However, simultaneously large falls were taking place in the production and consumption of most foodstuffs. Consumption of basic non-food items fell even further: output of textiles and shoes fell by around one-half or more between 1991 and 1993, and in the first half of 1994 their output fell by a further one-third to one-half.

Welfare indicators

In the reform period China did well at raising the incomes of the poorest 40% of the population. This was reflected in the improvement in already extremely favourable 'basic needs' indictors : between 1981 and 1990, there were 'real improvements in mortality ... especially for females above infancy and for children of both sexes' (Banister 1992: 12).

One of the most important consequences of Russia's economic collapse was the disintegration of the health service. This, together with the sharp rise in poverty, caused an 'explosion of morbidity' (Murray Feshbach, quoted in Ellman (1994)). Moreover, the breakdown of government was accompanied by a very large increase in crime. Russia's murder rate for the first half of 1993 stood at 25/100,000 people, placing it firmly in the category of 'high homicide' countries (Ellman 1994).

Poverty

In China a variety of factors combined to produce a remarkable reduction in poverty in the reform period. These included trickle-down from rich regions, explicit government policy to assist poor regions, rapid growth of non-farm employment, and fast income growth in the countryside at large. The number estimated to be in poverty fell from around 270 million in the late 1970s to around 100 million only one decade later (World Bank 1992). After the late 1980s a large fraction of the Russian population experienced a serious deterioration in living standards. The World Bank concluded that Russia's reforms had been accompanied by 'a sharp increase in the incidence and severity of poverty', with the proportion in poverty rising from around one-tenth to 32% by 1993, alongside a 44% increase in the severity of poverty (i.e. the distribution of poverty weighted to reflect the lower welfare of the poorest) (World Bank 1995: i). An important aspect of the impoverishment was the deterioration in diet, reflected in the sharp fall in food production and consumption,[3] despite a substantial rise in the share of food in household budgets.[4]

Inequality

The growth of market forces produced large new inequalities in China during the reform period, especially a rapid widening in the absolute gap between regions. However, China's impoverished rural population achieved faster growth of income than did the urban population. In the early 1980s there occurred a massive, egalitarian land reform. Moreover, the vast bulk of national assets remained in some form of public ownership, with ownership rights residing in the hands of either the central state, the city, the county, or the village community, thereby severely limiting the possibility for wealth accumulation by private individuals. The government at different levels maintained a relatively effective tax systems.

When massive collapse of output occurs in wartime, the hardship is often shared relatively equally, through state controls over production to ensure that basic needs are met for the poorest members of society. In the early 1990s in Russia the reverse happened. In the chaotic economy of the early 1990s Soviet citizens had vastly different capacities, related to age, political position and connections, and initial capital endowments, to benefit from the 'privatization' of assets: in just two years, the bulk of state assets was 'privatized' under lawless conditions. This was the process of 'primitive capital accumulation', which in the West took place over centuries, being conducted at the highest possible speed. A new 'aristocracy' was created, rapidly accumulating a large share of the newly 'privatized' assets. Income distribution shifted at high speed. Alongside the mass privatization of state assets in 1993–4 there was a 'dramatic increase in the purchasing capacity of the wealthier strata of the population', alongside 'even further decline' in that of the poorer segments of the population. The ratio of the income of the top decile to the bottom decile rose from 1:5.4 in 1991 (Weir 1993: 2813) to 1:13.0 in the second quarter of 1994 (*Transition*, July–August 1994).

Psychology

China experienced around one hundred years of national humiliation, beginning in the 1840s with the Opium Wars, extending through to the chaotic period of the warlords from 1911 to 1917. After 1949, despite large achievements, the policies of the Chinese Communist Party produced the disaster of the Great Leap Forward in which as many as 30 million people died from starvation and related illness. The Cultural Revolution in the late 1960s and early 1970s brought anarchy to much of the country, damaged the economy and caused great suffering. The massive success of the economic reforms brought a renewed sense of national pride. The fact that the reform programme was carried out under the Communist Party, with only gradual change in ideology, produced only a limited sense of mass psychological disorientation.

153

Russia's collapse caused national humilation. The sharpest change in social values occurred in a short time, away from collectivism and egalitarianism to rampant individualism. For most Russians the sense of 'social coherence' was smashed. A nationwide condition of 'anomie' was brought into existence with a complete absence of reference points for the individual psyche. The sense of personal uncertainty greatly increased, especially because the changes since the mid-1980s occurred against a background of previously high levels of security in respect to employment, personal safety, education, health and housing.

Human rights

Throughout the reform period China remained a one-party authoritarian state, with several thousand executions in an average year (Amnesty International 1987). However, the reform years saw an explosion in the provision of a wide range of 'human rights', including improved health, education, freedom to migrate, huge increases in employment opportunities, better food, clothing housing and a greatly increased range of cultural products. The decade of economic reform in China saw no trend deterioration in China's exceptionally low death rates. Death rates fell for all age groups beyond the age of one,[5] a remarkable achievement for a country with such low death rates as China (Banister 1992). Life expectancy rose from 67 years in 1981, an already exceptionally high level for a poor country, to 69 years in 1991 (World Bank 1993).

In the late 1980s Soviet citizens gained the right to vote and to speak freely. However, thereafter for most people there was a huge deterioration in other 'human rights', including the right to live safely, to employment, to decent food, to a decent education, housing and health service. Moreover, there was a hugely unequal capacity to benefit from the new 'negative' freedoms (e.g., freedom of speech, freedom to accumulate capital). In the early 1960s the USSR had one of the world's lowest death rates. By the late 1980s, Russia's death rate had risen above the level for middle income countries, standing at 11.4/1000 in 1991, and by 1993 the death rate had risen to 16.2/1000 (Ellman 1994), on a par with that of such countries as Bangladesh, Nigeria, Sudan and Togo. The right to employment was eroded rapidly. By July 1994 the number of unemployed was estimated at around 10 million, or 13% of the economically active population (*Transition*, July–August 1994). However, even the concept of 'unemployment' rapidly lost meaning. There was a rapidly rising 'informal' sector in which a large proportion of the 'self-employed' worked at any kind of 'business', however low the returns per hour. The explosion of these forms of informal sector 'service' activities to a large degree reflected rapidly growing poverty and drastic shrinkage of full-time employment opportunities in the formal sector. The rapid growth of the service sector, from 31% of total employment in 1989 to over 50% (World

Bank 1995: 1) is widely viewed as a reflection of the new vibrancy of the post-reform economy. A more accurate way to view it is to regard it as the consequence of catastrophic deindustrialization.

IMPLICATIONS FOR ECONOMIC THEORY AND POLICY

Evolution verses revolution

Attempting to achieve a comprehensive revolution in all the parameters of socio-economic life is a risky method of trying to improve the performance of economic systems. The Popperian principle of experimentation is much sounder (Popper 1957). Paradoxically, the move out of communism in Russia parallels the move into communism in the same country in 1917. Both were massive, revolutionary, 'historicist' experiments, stimulated by a desire to leap into a better future at a single bound. It is hard to imagine that reflection upon the contrast in outcomes from the different reform paths in China and the former USSR will not reinforce the position of those, who, like Popper, argue for the evolutionary, experimental approach towards economic policy.

Political economy

Economists have improved somewhat their understanding of relatively small problems by modelling and statistically investigating them, while taking the broad parameters of economic life as given. However, when it came to thinking about the huge question of how the communist countries might best make the transition towards a system that would provide a better life for their long-suffering citizens, most economists forgot how little their analysis had taught them about large issues. Instead they plunged into advising about how best to reform the communist systems with great confidence. They leapt from the complexities of their own special fields into grand simplistic general-izations in areas for the analysis of which their training had poorly prepared them. 'Transition theory' was built around such propositions as 'more pain, more gain'; 'system reform is like crossing a chasm: the only way is to leap', and 'reform is like a surgical operation: it is better to quickly cut off the whole limb rather than do so slice by slice'. The deep questions about the way in which the parameters of economic life impact upon economic performance are outside the syllabus of most economics courses. They involve attempting to understand the way in which culture, politics, psychology, and social structure interact with the economy. This branch of the subject has been steadily squeezed out of economics.[6] It is the stuff of political economy in the sense in which the term was understood by the classical economists. If ever an issue called out for real political economy it was the transition from communism.

Plans, commands and markets

'Planning' became progressively more unfashionable from the 1960s onwards. Much of the blame for this derived from a misidentification of 'planning' with the economic methods of the communist countries. The communist economy was not planned. It was a command economy, at least as anarchic in its own way as capitalism. It was precisely during the transition that the communist countries urgently needed good planning. These necessary planning functions had some elements common to most of the reforming communist countries. They included a need for the state carefully to conduct reform experiments; to coordinate the interrelationship between different parts of the reform programme; to maintain social stability by cushioning the impact of the growth of market forces upon different social groups; to protect domestic industry while market forces were being introduced; to support the growth of powerful new firms that could compete internationally; to raise resources (either directly or indirectly) for necessary investment in transport, health, education and power generation; to supervise the reorganization of the use of public assets so as to prevent the emergence of a deeply unequal distribution of asset ownership; and to sustain public involvement in, and understanding of, the complex tasks of the transition. Many of the requisite planning functions in the transition were country-specific, such as the necessity in China for the state to control population growth and to undertake large investments in farm infrastructure.

The reforming government of the USSR misidentified planning with commands. It destroyed the command economy and failed to put into place a planned transition away from that system. The Chinese government realized that in the transition from a command to a more market-oriented economy, a great deal of planning was needed. China's transition from the communist economy is an example of outstandingly good 'planning', in the classic sense in which the word 'planning' was used by Tinbergen (1964), Chakravarty (1987) and Lowe (1965).

Turning points and cumulative causation

Correct and incorrect policy choices at key points can set in motion large processes of either positive or negative cumulative causation that may take a long time to reverse. The reform process in the China and Russia can now be seen to have been a knife-edge situation. It was perfectly possible, if different policies had been chosen, for the results to have been the reverse of those which actually came to pass. The wrong policies could have sent China spinning backwards for an indefinite period. The experience of China before 1949 and in the Great Leap and the Cultural Revolution testified to the real possibility of this happening. Conversely, the correct policies could have liberated the latent productive capacities in the Soviet economy, and ushered in a period of accelerated growth. Once each country set out on its distinctive path away from the command economy, a whole sequence of virtuous and vicious circles of politics and economics was initiated.

In China, initial success in releasing latent productive potentialities in turn encouraged demand growth, which stimulated new investment, both domestic and foreign. This in turn provided increased employment opportunities and permitted technical progress, which in turn allowed further productivity and income growth, all of which in turn contributed to greater social stability, which in turn encouraged further investment. In Russia initial failure to implement policies which released latent productive capacities, but instead destroyed the old system while failing to replace it with a functioning new system, caused a severe recession. The resulting demand downturn greatly discouraged new investment, which in turn damaged opportunities in regular wage employment, thrusting those thereby made unemployed for the regular wage sector into low productivity 'informal' sector employment, and prevented technical progress. This in turn stopped productivity and income growth, all of which in turn contributed to greater social instability, which in turn discouraged further investment.

Role of demand

The generation of economists brought up during or soon after the inter-war depression was, naturally, preoccupied with the demand side of the economy. In the postwar period economics became increasingly preoccupied with the supply side. The transitional orthodoxy gave no thought at all to the role of demand. It assumed that the reforming economies faced an unlimited world demand and that domestic demand had no special function. The contrast between the Chinese and the Russian reform processes emphasizes the importance of the demand side in general and, under certain circumstances, of domestic demand in particular.

The Chinese-style economic reform strategy created a rapidly growing internal demand which made it possible to adjust out of planning through growth ('growing out of the plan'). Improved productivity was achieved through demand-induced investment in new, higher productivity activities, while old ones were allowed to atrophy, rather than being ruthlessly shut down as part of a 'surgical operation'. The growth-oriented 'Chinese path' transitional process contributed to improved productivity by quickly expanding the share of the total capital stock that operated with new techniques. The Russian approach produced a sharp contraction of demand which in turn caused a rapidly shrinking total capital stock towards a small core of currently profitable activities ('collapsing into efficiency').

Infant industry protection

Countries need to protect infant industries. However, the question of what constitutes an 'infant' industry is complex, especially in the reforming socialist economies. An 'infant' industry does not just include an industry which did not exist in any form at some prior point. An 'old' industry which is out-of-date and uncompetitive on international markets, but which is in the process of being modernized and re-structured, can be considered to be an 'infant' industry. It is rational that an industry, or a section of it, which today is uncompetitive and would be bankrupted in open international competition, but which is thought likely to become competitive, be given protection. The increased competitiveness might come about through the industry's own response to changed conditions of competition within the domestic economy and/or through measures undertaken by the government. The measures through which the industry's competitiveness might be increased include foreign investment, outlays on new technology, changed management practices, improvements in product design, changes in the size structure of industry and in the spatial location of industry. All of these things can occur in a reforming socialist economy without its being comprehensively opened up to international competition. This is, indeed, what occurred in Chinese industry in the 1980s. Industries which are today viable and becoming increasing internationally competitive would not exist if the Chinese economy had been opened up at a single stroke to international competitions in the late 1970s.

After decades of complete protection from both domestic and international competition, the socialist countries which opened themselves up to unrestricted international competition saw a large part of their industry devastated. Yet in the long run, given the requisite changes in the economic environment, many of these industries could have become competitive behind protective barriers. One of the key functions of planning in the transition was to identify sectors that were likely to become internationally competitive in the long run and assist them to become so.

Property rights and economic performance

Transferring ownership of a vast array of state assets is hugely time-consuming, and is unlikely to be accomplished equitably if it is done hastily before a market economy has been established. Moreover, it may result in a structure of asset ownership which impedes investment. However, in the transitional economy moving out of the command system, large improvement in performance did not require privatization. Greatly improved performance in the operation of publicly owned assets can be obtained by devising incentives to use property effectively via contracts governing use rights. For almost two decades China has obtained sustained improvements in economic performance in all sectors, based on a system of primarily public ownership of assets, whether that be the nation or the local state.[7] This calls for deep reflection on the relationship between private property and economic incentives.

On reflection, this is unsurprising. A large part of the capitalist system generates strong incentives to effective use of resources without the immediate stimulus of private ownership. The essence of modern capitalism is much more the existence of contracts that encourage effective use of resources by the autonomous manager of those resources, than it is the direct interest of the manager of resources being stimulated by the fact that they own those resources. A wide variety of property rights regimes can now be seen to be compatible with effective economic performance. In between 'all-people' and the individual private ownership of early capitalism is a great variety of property rights arrangements, which may be more or less compatible with strong incentives for managers of those assets to use them effectively to earn income and expand the value of the resources under their disposition.

Distribution of wealth

The myth of individual 'freedom to choose' is central to the ideology of free market capitalism. Daily reality continually confounds this naive view of the way in which life chances are structured, to say nothing of the profound differences in life chances between people in different nations. The origins of class differences in life chances and capacities to benefit from economic opportunities are conveniently forgotten in much of the work that economists undertake. The clarity with which the new, hugely unequal class structure of Russia was created in the early 1990s, that is to say the process of primitive capitalist accumulation, brings home vividly the importance in all societies of class-based differences in the distribution of wealth and income in determining the differences in people's life chances. People's 'freedom to choose' is comprehensively constrained by their class position.

Income growth and basic needs provision

A consistent 'leftist' view in development economics and in the study of the economic history of the advanced capitalist countries has been that 'trickle down' doesn't work. In this perspective, the main path through which to improve the condition of poor people is through redistribution. On the other hand, a consistent theme of much 'free market' analysis has been that growth is the best guarantor of 'basic needs'.

Badly designed redistributive policies, such as many of those in Maoist China, damage the incentives necessary for growth, and in the long run prevent the mass of the population from increasing their income beyond a certain level. China's reforms since the late 1970s show that fast growth independently creates through the market large opportunities for improvement in the welfare of the poorest people. However, it shows also that it is possible to devise policies for redistribution which generate faster improvements in popular welfare than would come from the free market, while simultaneously maintaining incentives for sustained growth. However, China's Maoist past, especially the disaster of the Great Leap Forward, demonstrates that even the most egalitarian of redistributive systems cannot avoid a huge decline in popular welfare if output falls to a sufficiently large degree.

Under Russia's reform programme, there occurred a massive redistribution of income away from the bottom deciles of the population. The top decile or so of the income distribution grew richer in absolute terms at a rapid rate and rapidly increased their share of income and wealth, alongside a disastrous deterioration in output and average income. This was the reverse of 'trickle down', with both output decline and redistribution away from the bottom deciles of the distribution. A fairer sharing of the burden of the economic collapse, such as occurred during the Second World War in Britain, could have reduced greatly the extent of suffering for the bottom deciles of the population. However, it is hard to avoid a large fall in basic needs, however well-intentioned the state might be, if there is a fall in output and income of the order experienced in Russia since the late 1980s. In other words, distributional policies are only part of the way in which to affect the provision of basic needs.

Good government and economic performance

In recent years 'good government' increasingly has been considered to be important in determining economic performance (Reynolds 1985). There was a strong tendency to equate 'good government' with democratic government. This was most explicit in the case of conditionality from western governments in their aid to African states. However, the contrast between the reform process in China and Russia vividly illustrates the inadequacy of such a perspective. China's government under Deng Xiaoping was widely thought to be 'bad', oppressing its people under continued communist political dictatorship, and stubbornly refusing to let go of the planning system. On the other hand, Gorbachev's government was widely thought to be outstandingly 'good' for promoting welfare-enhancing destruction of the Communist Party and trying to push forward with large reform of the 'planned' economy.

It is now obvious that this view was wrong. China's communist dictatorship was vastly 'better' at governing China than the Gorbachev or Yeltsin governments were at governing the USSR and Russia respectively. The reforming Chinese government was vastly better than its Russian counterpart at selecting and implementing 'good' policies that would release

160

the system's productive potentialities and enhance the welfare of the vast bulk of the population.

Human rights, political choice and economic policy

Prior to the end of communism, promotion of narrowly political rights, especially the ending of one-party totalitarian dictatorship, was given high weight as a policy goal both inside and outside the communist countries. Some regarded the overthrow of communism as the primary policy goal, whatever the consequences this might have for the welfare of the citizens of the communist countries. These 'capitalist triumphalists' regarded this as the successful conclusion of the seventy-year struggle between communism and capitalism. For some of these this was a great moral victory and for others a moment simply of sweet revenge. Others thought that the overthrow of communism was in itself a massive improvement in welfare for the citizens of the communist countries. Many people thought that the overthrow would lead to large improvements in economic performance and mass incomes.

'Human rights' include a wide range of rights other than the right to vote in elections and to air opinions freely. They include the rights to food, housing, security of employment, access to health services, and personal security. It can now be seen with much greater clarity than before the reforms, that at certain juncture there may be a trade-off, at least over a reasonably long period, between the achievement of narrowly political rights and the achievement of other human rights.

The relationship between choice of economic policy by a government and voters' rights is complex. The wider were the choices offered to the electorate of a reforming communist country, the more unpredictable were the outcomes for voters. It was impossible for voters to calculate the full effects of revolutionary programmes of system transformation either upon the country or upon themselves individually. Moreover, the more revolutionary was the reforming programme, the less reversible would be the policies by the time the next election occurred. Therefore the electorate was deprived of meaningful choice, and simply voted in the dark, with vague sentiments governing the choices they made. Whether this amounted to more 'democracy' is debatable. Before the overthrow of communism, under circumstances of guaranteed employment, low rents, low or zero-price education and health provision, subsidized food, and effective law and order, many citizens would have given relatively high weight, in their welfare functions, to political liberty. However, after a period of falling incomes, employment insecurity, and collapsing social order, their preferences can be expected to be greatly altered. If they had known before the overthrow of communism that it would lead to an economic and social disaster for a large part of the population, then their support for the change might be expected to have been a great deal less.

CONCLUSION

After the late 1970s China slowly moved away from totalitarian, command economy communism towards a nationalistic, state-guided, bureaucratic market economy, with a high emphasis on harnessing individual entrepreneurial energies within a collectivist framework. The reforms harnessed the potential latent in the old system and set in motion a virtuous circle of growth out of the command economy. China became ever more powerful internationally. In Russia, the reforms quickly destroyed the old state apparatus, but failed to construct an effective successor state. They allowed the creation of a highly unequal and deeply disorienting process of primitive capitalist accumulation. The resulting inequalities in asset ownership will fix the parameters for economic life for many decades to come. The reforms caused a disastrous decline in investment and industrial output, setting in motion a vicious circle of economic collapse. Russia became ever weaker internationally, to the point that its policies were constructed at the direct instruction of the major international capitalist institutions. In the brief space of just a few years it has been humiliated and broken as a great power.

This article contains two implicit counter-factual propositions. First, the selection of different policies in Russia could have produced rapid growth of output and a large improvement in popular living standards. Secondly, the selection of a different set of policies in China could easily have produced a political and economic disaster, with a large decline in popular living standards.

NOTES

1   Systematic comparison of this experience is still in its infancy. See, e.g. Nolan (1995); Sachs and Woo (1994).
2   Instead of queuing for long periods to buy state-rationed products, large numbers of people now stand for hours in flea markets and outside railway and metro station to sell tiny amounts of products over long periods of time.
3   From 1990 to 1994, output of meat fell by 31%, of milk by 23%, of eggs by 21% (Government of Russia 1995: 143), and in 1995, grain output was predicted to reach just 56% of the level of 1990 (*Financial Times*, 5 October 1995). Not only was there a large fall in domestic production, but food imports also fell sharply, from $17 billion in 1990 to $5.3 billion in 1993 (Government of Russia 1995: 151).
4   For blue- and white-collar workers, the share rose from 34% in December 1991 to 45% in March 1994 (Government of Russia 1995: 149).
5   Infant mortality rates rose for females, for special reasons associated with the 'One Child Family' campaign.
6   This was acknowledged even by the mainstream Report by the US Commission on Education in Economics (Report 1991).
7   It is wholly misleading to consider the property rights regime of China's 'township and village enterprises' (TVEs) as 'cooperative'. The owner of local publicly owned assets is the whole community, while the workers in the TVEs typically comprise only a minor share of the workforce and a very small share

of the total population. Serious scholars of the subject now realize more and more that the TVEs are, indeed, a species of state ownership. It is of some interest for property rights theory that one of the most dynamic sectors in the world economy, massively penetrating the markets of the advanced capitalist economies, employing perhaps 60 million workers, is a species of state ownership.

REFERENCES

Amnesty International (1987) *China : Torture and Ill-treatment of Prisoners*, London: Amnesty International Publications.

Aslund, A. (1990) 'Gorbachev, perestroika, and economic crisis,' *Problems of Communism*, January–April: 13–41.

—— (1991) *Gorbachev's Struggle for Economic Reform*, London: Pinter.

Banister, J. (1992) 'Demographic aspects of poverty in China', World Bank, Working Paper.

Bergson, A. and Levine, D. (eds) (1983) *The Soviet Economy: Towards the Year 2000*, London: Allen & Unwin.

Blanchard, O., Dornbusch, R., Krugman, P., Lanyard, R. and Summers, L. (1991) *Reform in Eastern Europe*, Cambridge, Mass.: MIT Press.

Chakravarty, S. (1987) *Development Planning: The Indian Experience*, Oxford: Oxford University Press.

Clague, C. and Rausser, G.C. (1992) *The Emergence of Market Economies in Eastern Europe*, Oxford: Blackwell.

Ellman, M. (1994) 'The increase in death and disease under *katastroika*', *Cambridge Journal of Economics*, 18(4): 329–56.

Galbraith, J. K. (1990) 'The rush to capitalism', *New York Review of Books*, October 25.

Gomulka, S. (1989) 'Shock needed for the Polish economy', *The Guardian*, 19 August.

Government of the Russian Federation (1995) *Russian Economic Trends*, Moscow: Centre for Economic Reform, 4(1).

Hicks, G., (ed.) (1990) *The Broken Mirror: China after Tianamen*, Harlow: Longman.

IMF (1993) 'Russian Federation', *Economic Review*, no. 8, Washington, D.C.: International Monetary Fund.

——, World Bank, OECD and EBRD (1990) *The Economy of the USSR: Summary and Recommendations*, Washington, D.C.: World Bank.

Johnson, C. (1990) 'Foreword', in Hicks (1990), *op. cit.*

Kennet, D. and Lieberman, M. (eds) (1992) *The Road to Capitalism*, Orlando, Fl.: Dryden Press.

Khanin, G. I. (1993a) 'The economic crisis in Russia: possible ways out', *Problems of Economic Transition*, 36(2): 23–7.

—— (1993b) 'Russia's economic situation in 1992', *Problems of Economic Transition*, 36(7): 6–24.

Kornai, J. (1986) 'The Hungarian reform process: visions, hopes, and realities', *Journal of Economic Literature*, 24: 1687–737.

—— (1990) *The Road to a Free Economy*, New York: Norton.

Lipton, D., and Sachs, J. (1990a) 'Creating a market economy in Eastern Europe : the case of Poland', *Brookings Papers on Economic Activity*, vol. 1, reprinted in Kennett and Lieberman (1992).

—— (1990b) 'Privatization in Eastern Europe', *Brookings Papers on Economic Activity*, no. 2, reprinted in Kennett and Lieberman (1992).

Lowe, A. (1965) *On Economic Knowledge*, New York: Harper Row.

Lyons, B. (1992) *China's War on Poverty: A Case Study of Fujian Province, 1985–1990*, Chinese University of Hong Kong, Institute of Asia–Pacific Studies.

Macmillan, J. and Naughton, B. (1991) 'How to reform a planned economy', *Oxford Review of Economic Policy*, 8(1): 130–43.

Nolan, P. (1994) 'Democratisation, human rights and economic reform: the case of China and Russia', *Democratisation*, 1(1): 73–9.

—— (1995) *China's Rise Russia's Fall: Politics, Economics and Planning in the Transition from Stalinism*, London: Macmillan.

Popper, K. (1957) *The Poverty of Historicism*, London: Routledge & Kegan Paul.

Prybyla, J. (1990) 'A broken system', in G. Hicks (ed.) *The Broken Mirror: China after Tiananmen*, London: Longman.

—— (1991) 'The road from socialism: why, where, what and how', *Problems of Communism*, XL (January–April).

Report of the Commission on Graduate Education in Economics (1991) *Journal of Economic Literature*, 29 (September): 1035–53.

Reynolds, L. G. (1985) *Economic Growth in the Third World, 1850–1980*, New Haven, Conn.: Yale University Press.

Sachs, J. and Woo, W. T. (1994) 'Structural factors in the economic reforms of China, Eastern Europe, and the former Soviet Union, *Economic Policy*, 9(18).

Singh, I. (1991) 'Is there schizophrenia about socialist reform?', *Transition*, July–August.

State Statistical Bureau (SSB) (ZGTJNJ) (1984–93) *Chinese Economic Yearbook* (*Zhongguo tongji nianjian*), Beijing: Zhongguo tongji chubanshe.

—— (ZGTJZY) (1984–94) *Statistical Survey of China* (*Zhongguo tongji zhaiyao*), Beijing: Zhongguo tongji chubanshe.

Tinbergen, J. (1964) *Central Planning*, London: Yale University Press.

Transition, various issues, World Bank, Washington D.C.

United Nations, Economic Commission for Europe (1993) *Economic Survey for Europe, 1992–3*, New York: United Nations.

Walters, A. (1991) 'Misapprehensions on privatisation', *International Economic Insights*, 2(1), reprinted in Kennet and Lieberman (1992).

—— (1992) 'The transition to a market economy', in Clague and Rausser (1992), *op. cit.*

Wang Xiaoqiang (1993) 'Groping for stones to cross the river: Chinese price reform against the "Big Bang"', Cambridge University, Department of Applied Economics, Discussion Paper, No. DPET 9305.

Weir, F. (1993) 'Russia's descent into Latin America', *Economic and Political Weekly*, 28(51).

World Bank (1979–94) *World Development Report* (WDR), Washington D.C.: Oxford University Press.

—— (1992) *China: Strategies for Reducing Poverty in the 1990s*, Washington D.C.: World Bank.

—— (1995) *Poverty in Russia : An Assessment*, Washington, D.C.: World Bank.

14

SOCIALISM
Goals and efficiency
Bruce McFarlane

HARCOURT THE SOCIALIST

Since 1958 Harcourt has been a strong advocate of a democratic, collectivist-based society. However, as a serious economic theorist he has necessarily had to engage in discussion about efficiency in such a system: he has tempered his enthusiasm for a socialist pattern of society (he calls it his utopianism) with an awareness that people's assets could be wasted by bad investment strategies, imposing unacceptably high opportunity cost and levels of forced savings on the masses.

Kalecki, in particular had reached the same conclusion (Kalecki 1969: chapters 4–6), and besides his theoretical attempts to work out coefficients of investment effectiveness (Kalecki and Rakowski, in Nove and Nuti (1972)), he tried to put into the hands of Polish managers a set of sensible rules for investment decision-making. There are two or three articles written by Harcourt in the same spirit, in particular Harcourt (1982: 59–64).

Among the many factors behind the demise of that particular form of economic system constructed by Stalinists, the glaring inefficiency of the 'model' in delivering a sensible list of investment projects, as well as an adequate supply of consumer-goods and services, is surely prominent.

The 'list of projects' is important in socialist planning. If there are too many items on the list, the scope for steady increases in personal consumption for citizens will be greatly reduced. If each item on the list is placed there without feasibility testing, there will be trouble. Such items are likely to be carried out badly; the ensuing waste of resources can only further harm productivity, consumption and public morale. It is well known that if people in the socialist countries faced stagnation in personal consumption, they tried to take two jobs, and inevitably worked half-pace at each.

Clearly in all economies, and especially in socialist ones, an efficient mechanism has to be found to devolve decisions about investment to lower levels, while ensuring that the rest of the economic integument is favourable to making such investments 'effective'.

Soviet, Chinese and East European planners resisted ideas and methods geared to putting efficiency nearer the top of the socio-political agenda. True, the voices of reason and reform – Kalecki, Lange, Sik, Kornai – have been present and exerted some influence. But they were not strong enough to obtain the necessary changes in time.

Part of the problem was that officialdom could not draw the clear links which exist between socio-economic goals, on the one hand, and a planning methodology which incorporates 'effectiveness', on the other. As a socialist economist living in the West, G.C. Harcourt nevertheless was able to say and write things that would have had great applicability in the East, and he suggested what such links might be in the context of socialism.

Harcourt, then, finds a place for socio-political goals. He does not want a socialist economy modelled on neoclassical economic theorems, in the manner of Barone or Heal. He is quite firm that collectivist socio-political goals are important (Harcourt in Harcourt and Hamouda (1986: 269); also remarks in his second D. Horne lecture (Harcourt 1992)).

In the second place, Harcourt saw the problems of time-horizons and investment strategies to be part and parcel of socialist economic strategy. He wrote:

> If we are considering bringing nationalisation back for key industries in our economies ... managers would have to be given instructions about the time horizon that they were to bear in mind and also about the overall pattern of development of the economy that the government explicitly has set out.
>
> (Harcourt in Harcourt and Hamouda (1986: 268))

To give 'teeth' to these broader considerations, Harcourt wrote three important articles on the effectiveness of investment: 'The measurement of the rate of profit and the bonus scheme for managers in the Soviet Union', 'The accountant in a golden age' and 'Pricing and the investment decision' (Harcourt and Kerr 1986). These pieces will be referred to below in the context of the wider debate among economists studying the transition from planned to deregulated economies on the issues of economic reform and the 'effectiveness of investment'. I still find his work refreshing and relevant. It is not weighed down with prejudice or by an excessive respect for marginalist principles, given that there is a context of the need to accelerate economic growth.

Goals

This is not the place to write about the various meanings that have been given to 'socialism' since at least Thomas More and the Utopians. But in considering Harcourt's interest in a 'vision' of a collectivist society, it is necessary to recall that a 'socialist' system is one in which productive property (i.e. mainly land and capital) is owned by collective, cooperative or state bodies. Each of these will have 'their' own *modus operandi*, with the first two bound to adopt more decentralized methods of operation, since the economic agents involved in the first two cases will have different objectives functions to that of the state as such.

This coexistence of ownership forms in the one socialist system is not without its problems. Harcourt has remarked on a number of occasions that managers of socialist and nationalized industries are not free from Professor Pigou's faulty 'telescopic' faculty – they do not take the longer view, suggested by traditional-socialist references to 'production according to need'.

Goals and instruments react on each other; this is also true of wrong instruments. For example, the goal is 'higher consumption per head' for the masses; the instrument is accelerated growth of GNP through raising the annual national rate of investment. But should the rate of investment be raised to an excess level (say, 40% of GDP), then the severe trade-off that would ensue between 'growth' and 'consumption' (Kalecki 1969: chapters 4–6) would in all probability bring growth down again through its demoralizing effects on consumption and welfare standard and, ultimately, disincentive to effort would become widespread. This is the key point that Harcourt made in his review of Osiatyński's book on Kalecki (Harcourt and McFarlane 1990) pleading for a modest but sure annual increase in consumption for the workers.

Investment effectiveness

In the 1960s, Harcourt became interested in the problems of investment efficiency at plant level in socialist countries. He wrote a path-breaking article, 'The measurement of the rate of profit and the bonus scheme for managers in the Soviet Union'.

The background to this excursion into difficult territory was the intense debate that followed Professor Liberman's proposals for economic reform in the USSR – proposals that he put forward as early as 1956 and again in 1962. At this time Igor Gordijev and myself were trying to make sense of 'Libermanist' principles (Liberman 1962 in Nove and Nuti 1972), and to introduce them to Australian readers (McFarlane and Gordijev 1964, 1965). Essentially the scheme of the Kharkov professor was to make *rentabilnost*, or profitability, an organic single indicator of plan-fulfilment or enterprise performance. The second prong of his strategy was to set up a bonus scheme within the factory for managers and for workers, which would be built up from payments into it from profits, on a sliding scale. The hope was that material incentives would work their magic and there would be rising real product per man-hour from improved workers' efforts and from a change in managerial behaviour. In particular, Liberman looked forward to a situation in which management would no longer order excessive stocks or unnecessary deliveries of machinery merely because of uncertainty, and that they would 'lift their game' in relation to the choice between investment projects (Liberman 1962 in Nove and Nuti (1972)).

The immediate stimulus to the writing of the Harcourt piece, however, was an article by Merrett in 1964 on the implications of linking bonuses for managers to profits under Soviet conditions. Harcourt started from the position that a manager in the Soviet-type economy might become biased and arbitrary in his selection of investment variants for achieving a given plan output (or bill of goods) because of the sort of profit measurement used in Soviet planning.

Harcourt's very early contributions in this field are of an importance which is, perhaps, better known among specialists on the Soviet Union and Eastern Europe than to the general economist. One reason for this is that discussion about efficient investment selection in a planned socialist economy had hitherto been dominated by two, equally unsatisfactory standpoints.

The first of these, which may be described as the 'official line', held that uniform cross-sectoral coefficients of effectiveness (or their rough reciprocal, the period of recoupment) would be inappropriate in a planned economy anxious to push on, for example, with steel rather than bicycles. (In this example, the superior rate of return on bicycles would always get the 'nod' over steel (McFarlane 1962)).

The second view, associated with such writers as Montias and Grossman, insisted that a uniform marginal coefficient of effectiveness should decide (a) the choice between alternative techniques of production in achieving a given bill of goods and (b) the cut-off point in the list of national investment projects.

What Harcourt's calculations and formulas allow us to do is to issue the socialist manager (or, at least, the manager of socialist projects), with sound investment rules or guiding principles while allowing enough flexibility to adjust the composition of the capital stock without inflicting losses or labour shortages on other parts of the economy.

As mentioned, a lot was written about reform of Soviet enterprise planning thirty years ago in the wake of the 'Liberman scheme' (McFarlane and Gordijev 1964, 1965) but few, apart from Merrett and Harcourt, picked up the point that a *combination* of adherence to a bonus scheme in which managers (and to a certain extent, workers) have a major stake and commitment may result in an inefficient age-composition of the capital stock being chosen or held by managers.

The technical manner in which this comes about, according to Harcourt's reasoning, is as follows. In the work of both Merrett (Harcourt and Kerr 1982: 59) and of Liberman (Liberman 1962 in Nove and Nuti 1972; McFarlane and Gordijev 1964) profitability of the firm (on which bonuses were paid on a sliding scale) may be seen to consist of price minus average variable costs, multiplied by output and expressed as a percentage of total fixed and working capital. Leaving aside minor technical problems concerning the measurement of depreciation and the inherent Soviet practice of under-pricing capital goods, bonuses are calculated on the estimate of the accountant's rate of profit. This is an *ex ante* concept of profit, but Harcourt, showing sharp intuition, picked it as a faulty measure. He demonstrates that even in the Golden Age model of a balanced stock of machines (each with constant expected annual quasi-rent), the accountant's rate of profit will be much more than the internal rate of return. Moreover, the more long-lived the machines in stock, the greater the divergence between the two measures of performance.

The result of a series of remarkable calculations (Harcourt 1982: Table c) indicated that managers in charge of Soviet longer-lived machines got greater benefits from the bonus scheme, in relation to the capital invested.

The practical consequences, warned Harcourt (at a time when Liberman was uncritically supported in the West for his bonus scheme), would be that managers would try to influence the choice of investment projects directly, and also indirectly since higher authorities deciding investment choices will use cost figures reflecting an input–output mix served up by managers.

Finally, in a most useful proposition for its time, Harcourt concluded (given under-pricing of Soviet capital-goods) that if managers have high rates of time discount, the Liberman-style profit bonus scheme would encourage them to choose wrongly.

It is obvious that Harcourt had identified and worked on a problem that is of the utmost significance in socialist planning (McFarlane 1962; Ellman 1979: 119). Effectiveness of investment choice had always fascinated Soviet engineers and planners. In the 1920s, engineer-economists had been careful to base choice of investment projects on economic considerations – as did those in the 1930s who were able to escape Stalin's attention. The 1920s' engineers took into the calculations the costs imposed elsewhere on the economy – the opportunity cost of locking capital resources up in construction projects with long gestation lags. They tried to conceptually penalize an investment programme that would imply more capital costs than its rival, even if it involved lower running costs than other variants. The usual method chosen was the period of recoupment, or a 'shadow' rate of interest that would have to be earned from the savings in running costs.

There were many problems in the application of this formula. These were already obvious by the late 1950s (McFarlane 1962) and it is now clear more thought should have been given, in the socialist countries, to some of the points made in Harcourt's 'Pricing and the investment decision' (in Harcourt and Kerr 1982: 117–19) concerning the role of the pay-off period: that when the pay-off period is considered for the choice of techniques in the investment plans of a firm, the price of output and the money wage rate (as well as labour requirements per unit of output and investment expenditure per unit of output) must be brought into the picture. Here Harcourt had in mind a theorem from

Salter (Harcourt 1962) that, using the recoupment period, if the price of output is increased, the capital intensity of the technique chosen increases, but at a decreasing rate. This means that an engineer-economist using an accounting rate of profit will almost certainly be guided towards a less labour-intensive technique of investment if there is also a desire to expand the internal accumulation of the firm. Here the analysis can be switched from the 'Pricing and investment decision' to the Harcourt 'Soviet bonuses' article where the pitfalls of profit and shadow interest rate calculations are made explicit and necessary adjustments to investment formulas are examined to correct an inbuilt bias towards capital intensity in choice of techniques and/or investment variants.

Growth rates of the whole economy and the problem of effectiveness

Imagine a plan is being constructed to reach political-social goals. To achieve these goals the overall growth rate of the economy needs to be accelerated. Two separate problems now arise:

1   a strategy of economic growth needs to be selected in which the capital–output ratio does not rise to the point where it becomes a drag on the growth rate;
2   a target growth rate of GDP should be chosen which does not imply too big a trade-off between consumption standards and the rate of investment.

Kalecki illustrated vividly what would happen if these conditions were not fulfilled. He shows (1969: chapter 4) that the slope of the $\frac{1}{m}$ curve, if unfavourable as a result of a rising capital–output ratio, will yield little growth for large increases (involving substantial sacrifices) in investment rates. The stiffening resistance of the population will bring about a change in the position and shape of the 'government decision function' which Kalecki used as a locus of points of trade-off, to link high investment rates and unfavourable capital–output ratios with pressure on consumption and consumer resistance.

On this issue of scope for rising consumption, neoclassical economists have written of a 'golden rule'. According to this proposition, the rate of growth of the economy is the discount rate, while a government should encourage firms and sectors to choose techniques of production which actually *maximize* consumption per head. Harcourt demurs. Taking his cue from Kalecki and his own observations of Eastern Europe, Harcourt argues that a gently rising but perpetually increasing level of consumption per head will yield more economic benefit to the masses, a better investment strategy and more political credibility to a socialist regime than any rule incorporating maximum consumption per head targets (Harcourt and McFarlane 1990). Apart from this, the golden rule is mainly relevant in a steady-state, full employment case in a capitalist economy, while conditions in a socialist economy are quite different. There is non-equilibrium, non-steady-state growth because of shortages of capacity and the political factors associated with the socialist investment cycle. What is wanted, then, is something quite different to the policies which flow from a golden rule policy. This surely would be an investment plan that will get a balance between stocks and investment and the demands on these from increased employment in the economy generally. A plan must be able, in a realistic way, to carve out of the national income (in conjunction with some instrumental mechanism) a programme of technical choice that allows such a balance, allows reasonable full employment (though not acute labour shortage) and allows a gradual rise in personal consumption.

Such a policy can be read into the Harcourt articles. What a pity these approaches (and those of Kalecki earlier) were not acted upon before the great socialist malaise of the 1980s led to complete collapse of (flawed) socialist systems.

Investment cycles under socialism

A number of authors (e.g. Bunce 1980) have pointed to the occurrence of investment cycles in Eastern Europe, while Shimakura (1982) speculated on the nature and implications of the Chinese investment cycle (McFarlane 1984). At first, emphasis was on various manifestations of sectoral imbalance rather than (as in capitalism) an overall supply capacity in excess of effective demand. Later work suggested that investment cycles were linked to waves in the import of western capital equipment. Shimakura (1982), for example, used the share of equipment and machinery in China's imports from Japan and found five-year cycles peaking in 1965, 1970, 1975 and 1980.

Whether or not socialist investment cycles are linked to technical factors like this or to 'bunching' due to gestation lags and the age composition of the capital stock (which generates replacement needs), the political aspects are even more important. It is the essence of Kornai's work, for example, that socialist economies are *shortage* economies. This feature lies at the heart of the investment cycle issue. It means that the cycle is inherent in a process that is part-economic, part-political. Suppose the Party is in an expansive, optimistic mood. It will impose high targets. Inevitable shortages of raw materials emerge, accentuated by hoarding. Investment rates soar but are brought crashing down when, under pressure from consumers and managers, the targets are reduced to ease the situation. Overlaying all of this may be a 'socialist political trade cycle' (McFarlane 1984) which, while different from that analysed by Michael Kalecki for capitalist conditions (Kalecki 1972), plays an analogous role. Unlike the shorter-term Kaleckian political trade cycle, the socialist ones have a medium-term character.

What kind of political cycle is involved? Perhaps the simplest explanation is that a cycle of centralism–decentralization is occurring in the political realm. This is because the Party must relax controls (as well as targets and high rates of accumulation) when consumer dissatisfaction rises to levels that threaten (or since 1989 overturn) political legitimacy. The zigzag occurs when Party conservatives and over-ambitious planners again seize control of the commanding heights of the economy and began to 'tighten the screws'. The zig-zag seems to have overlain the technically induced and even the shortage-induced investment cycle and become an important determinant of peaks, length of trough, etc.

A more complex analysis of the interaction between the political and economic aspects is also possible: fixed investment, carried too far, creates imbalances between light and heavy industries. As these imbalances reach excessive proportions, political disputes tend to break out concerning the management of economic crisis and the focus of responsibilities. Serious economic stagnation is reinforced by political instability. Here in the USSR and East European systems we had a recurrent politico-economic 'dynamic' of socialist society – the process of economic contradictions linked to inefficient investment planning and excessive capital construction rates leads to political confrontation and a perpetuation of economic stagnation.

There have been a number of responses to the above 'dynamic'. Cambridge don Suzanne Paine responded by arguing that, since socialist investment cycles have a damaging effect on the personal consumption of the masses (and on the political legitimacy of socialist regimes), planned economy should be abandoned – one might as well seek a mixed economy. Others such as Dobb, saw the dynamic instability arising from too much decentralized decision-making over investment and called for more realistic, yet essentially centralized plans. In the event, many in East Europe have indeed opted for the mixed economy.

While Harcourt did not explicitly discuss the issues raised by socialist investment cycles, he has made a number of remarks about the age composition and differing dynamic quasi-rents of machines parked at different points along aged capital stock and on the instability for a socialist regime that follows from excessive and fluctuating rates of construction investment. That is why, in a review of Osiatyński (Harcourt 1991), he supports a policy of limiting the annual national rate of investment and seeking to deliver at all times a steady and remorseless (even if small) rise in per capita personal consumption of the Soviet citizen. This would not only improve morale (it would make it less necessary, for example, for workers to take two jobs to maintain their standard of living) but it would hit at the diabolical mechanics of the 'shortage economy', a main source of the investment cycle of socialist Eastern Europe.

And to hark back to Harcourt's 'Socialism in your own country' lecture

(1992): he strongly believes that care has to be taken with adjusting the time horizon used in planning and that the politicians' preferences and time horizons are always likely to be the wrong ones for a suffering citizenry, in Australia as well as in Eastern Europe (Harcourt and Hamouda 1986: 268).

Again, writing about rates of investment relative to labour as an influence on the choice of technique, he made the Joan Robinson-style point that the choice of technique will be much more influenced by fluctuations in the rate of investment relative to labour than by the price of factor supplies; hence the efficiency of choice of techniques will be at risk from erratic movements of the investment rates.

SOCIALIST ECONOMIC POLICY

Harcourt notes that he endorses Joseph Steindl's view that 'economic policy is the main inspiration of economic theory' (Harcourt 1994: 460). This is also true of socialist economic policy.

In an article written with Prue Kerr, and in his D. Horne lecture, Harcourt also raised the issue of the limitations of socialist planning in the present era of capitalism, and the necessary acceptance of a mixed economy with an active social market and generous welfare provision for the underprivileged.

According to his article (Harcourt and Kerr 1986) on the 'mixed economy', Harcourt thinks a main characteristic of a so-called mixed economy is that 'the public sector plays a central role in determining the overall level of activity and the composition of national output'.

Having decided that capitalism is, after all, unstable and poses the constant danger of delivering mass unemployment, he says it is not enough to adjust fiscal and monetary policy to smooth out cyclical fluctuation: effort must also be directed towards 'a smooth transition to a predominantly socialist economy'.

Harcourt's remarks in his public lectures (e.g. the Horne lecture) about socialist economic policy cover such areas as incomes policy, monetary policy, fiscal policy and tariffs (on which he remained agnostic for many years). This hardly adds up to what could be termed a *socialist* economic policy in any traditional sense. But what he has tried to do is what Kalecki recommended: lacking a revolutionary 'wave' or prospects of a sudden change in a social system, it is necessary to do what one can for the poorer sectors of society within the existing social and political integument.

One might disagree with Harcourt's assessment that an incomes policy was the *sine qua non* for the recovery of the Australian economy, and a necessary part of the armoury of economic policy during the transition of the Australian economy to export orientation with manufactured items and the integration with the economies of Asia and the Pacific Rim that is occurring with ever more rapid speed. One could hardly disagree, however, that the socialist people had to say something about this transition. It was left to Hugh Stretton and Harcourt to oppose the hegemony of the 'market forces' people in Australia between 1970 and 1980. I believe one could add that his 1992 Donald Horne lecture hints pretty firmly at the need for a strongly interventionist line in relation to both industry policy and the allocation of loanable funds for new productive investments.

MARX, SOCIALISM, HARCOURT

Does Harcourt like Marx – I think yes.[1] But, not of course those 'odious regimes' of Eastern Europe, nor the 'centralistic Marx' over the 'libertarian' Marx. Marx he treats mainly as an insightful commentator on capitalist economy, rather than a socialist prophet (so, ultimately, did Schumpeter).

However, it is also true to say that Harcourt's version of Marx is rather a Robinsonian one, although Harcourt is clearly aware of Maurice Dobb's interpretation too (Dobb 1937). One of the problems of Joan Robinson's *Essay on Marxian Economics* (which was rather a quick read in 1941 anyway) is that it is not very deep. In a worthy attempt to make Marx more unreadable to western economists, categories like 'profit/wage fall', rather than 'rate of exploitation', appeared, robbing Marxist economics of its important philosophical and sociological dimensions. The constant harping on Marx's alleged 'confusion between a stock and a flow' (the clouds disappear if the turnover period of capital is assumed to be one year) and the cheap shots abusing the labour theory of value as an 'incantation', actually show a great ignorance of Marx's relationship to Hegel as a very profound thinker about society, and especially about dynamic movement of ideas, institutions and society at large. While a case could be made for linking Marx directly to Diderot, and studying him from that sort of 'prism', it is hard for anyone who has seriously absorbed Lenin's *Three Sources and Three Components of Marxism* to accept Joan Robinson's protest: 'What is Hegel doing putting his nose between me and Marx?' (Robinson 1959). With the exception of Sibree and McTaggart, Hegelian 'Visions' have falllen on totally stony ground in countries like Britain and Australia. While this has saved people time in not probing some of the less accessible parts of the Hegelian dialectics, it has also stopped economists from seeing that Marx's political economy cannot be split off from his writings in political theory, history and philosophy. To adopt the Joan Robinson approach is to miss many insights relevant to the modern world. This was a point not lost on Kalecki, although it is implicit, rather than explicit in his work. (An exception is his 'Historical materialism and econometric model'.)

It remains true, of course, that by treating Marx as the true heir of Ricardo, Harcourt well understands:

1   the significance of looking at contradictions in the necessary workings of the capitalist system – stagflation, growth without jobs, etc;

2   capitalism is an inherently unstable system, never in equilibrium;
3   that, in the manner of the classical school and Marx he teaches us to
     concentrate firmly on the interaction of capital accumulation, labour
     force growth and technical progress. In the Marxian model, this
     interaction is called 'expanded reproduction';
4   the Marxian notion that critique and exposure of contradictions is equally
     important in the realm of ideas, especially of orthodox ruling ideas,
     refined by Sraffa is something Harcourt took on board in his classical
     book on capital theory, but also in other pieces (Harcourt and Kerr 1982;
     Hamouda and Harcourt 1986). It is not yet clear to me quite where his
     (non-journalistic) essays in biography are leading, but it is suggestive that
     Keynes also wrote detailed analytical biographical essays on Marshall,
     Jevons and others.

Presumably an analytical biography forms part of a more general critique
of ideas that are held for a certain period before being attacked and/or
collapsing. Analytical biography, like critique, is an important part of the
sorting out of ideas. In the case of critique of neoclassical economies, as
Harcourt well recognizes, it is not correct to treat the school of neoclassicism
as one homogeneous reactionary mass, but he positively identified an
orthodoxy that can be used to promote social goals. Walras was far from J.B.
Clark in his personal political outlook. Hence one finds in Harcourt's review
of Nobel laureates in economics, and in his particular biographies, a lively
interest in the rational kernel from such theories.

Harcourt sees Marx as continuing the analysis, which was incorporated
into the 'classical' school, and draws on the conflict in perspective between
this school and the post-1870 marginalists. This drawing out of the
differences and stress on the 'individualistic basis' of neoclassicism echoes
one of Marx's own comments: 'to the prophets of the eighteenth century, on
whose shoulders Smith and Ricardo are still standing, the eighteenth century
individual appears as an ideal' (Marx, quoted in Howard and King (1976:
p. 81)).

This quotation of Marx may be compared with Harcourt's conclusion that
'the great truths associated with Adam Smith's concept of the invisible hand
... became formalised beyond recognition into the virtues of the perfectly
competitive general equilibrium model' (Harcourt 1975: 3).

Harcourt's positive alternative construction to avoid the neoclassical way
of seeing economics is (i) to retain sociological aspects, not treat them as
incidental data – hence he follows Steindl (Harcourt 1994); (ii) to support
Joan Robinson's call for an integration of Sraffa on value and distribution
with Kalecki on 'realization' (i.e. effective demand and the determination of
output). He still finds this synthesis useful. To this he has added (with P.
Kenyon) a theory of finance in relation to output expansion plans of firms that
nicely develops Kalecki. Only the American Minsky can match Harcourt in

this area of economics. Yet it is important to see that this significant technical work is not undertaken for itself but to get a better handle on the way that capitalism not only operates, but necessarily operates.

A PERSONAL NOTE

Professor Harcourt often writes about the late Professor Eric Russell with justifiable enthusiasm and warmth. He sees Russell as the ideal role-model – scholarly, fair and helpful and with left-of-centre views. This is also an accurate description of Harcourt himself. Some years ago I made an intemperate attack on someone's views, and I could see that my tone and stance had distressed Harcourt. This was his Christian socialist morality displaying itself. From that day I ceased such tactics and have ever since, asymptotically approached Geoff's position on both economic principles and the notion that one must work with and through people touched by the spirit, if we are to get at least some way along the road of achieving 'the Kingdom of God on Earth'.

NOTE

1   Cf. his acknowledgement that Prue Kerr got him to see the value of Marx's insight into the necessary workings of capitalist dynamics; he might have added that Prue showed him the Marxian foundations of Kalecki – something Kalecki's ex-pupils (notably in Poland) are at pains to minimize.

REFERENCES

Bunce, V. (1980) 'The political consumption cycle: a comparative analysis', *Soviet Studies* 12.
Dobb, M. H. (1937) *Political Economy and Capitalism*, London: Routledge.
Ellman, M. (1979) *Socialist Planning*, Cambridge: Cambridge University Press.
Harcourt, G. (1962) Review of Salter's *Productivity and Technical Change, The Economic Record* 38(3).
—— (1972) *Some Cambridge Controversies in the Theory of Capital*, Cambridge: Cambridge University Press.
—— (1975) 'Capital theory: much ado about something', *Thames Papers in Political Economy*, Autumn.
—— (1992) 'Markets, madness and a middle way' (Second Donald Horne Lecture), *Australian Quarterly* 64(1).
—— (1994) 'What Joseph Steindl means to my generation', *Review of Political Economy* 6(4).
Harcourt, G. and Hamouda, O. (1986) *Controversies in Political Economy*, Brighton: Harvester Wheatsheaf.
Harcourt, G. and Kenyon, P. (1976) 'Pricing and the investment decision', *Kyklos* 29(3).
Harcourt, G. and Kerr, P. (1982) *The Social Science Imperialists*, London: Routledge.
—— (1986) 'The mixed economy', reprinted in Harcourt and Hamouda (1986).
Harcourt G. and McFarlane, B. (1990) 'Economic planning and democracy',

Australian Journal of Political Science 25(2).

Howard, M. C. and King, J. E. (eds) (1976) *The Economics of Marx*, Harmondsworth: Penguin.

Kalecki, M. (1943) 'Political aspects of full employment', reprinted in Kalecki (1972).

—— (1965) 'Econometric model and historical materialism' in Kowalik (1965).

—— (1969) 'Introduction' to *The Theory of Growth in a Socialist Economy*, Oxford: Blackwell.

—— (1972) *The Last Phase in the Transformation of Capitalism*, New York: Monthly Review Press.

Kalecki, M. and Rakowski, M. (1959) 'The generalized formula for the efficiency of investment', reprinted in Nove and Nuti (1972).

Kowalik, T. (ed.) (1965) *Essays in Honour of Oscar Lange*, Warsaw: Polish Scientific Publishers.

Lewis, P. (1984) *Eastern Europe: Political Crisis and Legitimation*, London: Croom Helm.

Liberman, E. (1962) 'The plan, profits and bonuses', *Pravda* 9 September, in Nove and Nuti (1972).

McFarlane, B. (1962) 'Soviet investment policy', *The Economic Record* 38(2).

—— (1984) 'Political crisis and East European economic reform', in Lewis (1984).

McFarlane, B. and Gordijev, I. (1964) 'Profitability and the Soviet firm', *The Economic Record* 40(4).

—— (1965) 'Profitability and the Soviet firm: a note on the 1964 discussion', *The Economic Record* 41(4).

Marx, K. (1859) Excerpts from *Grundrisse*, in Howard and King (1976).

Nove, A. and Nuti, D. M. (eds) (1972) *Socialist Economics*, Harmondsworth: Penguin.

Robinson, J. (1941) *An Essay on Marxian Economics*, London: Macmillan.

—— (1959) 'Marx, Marshall and Keynes', in *Robinson, Joan: Collected Economic Papers*, volume 1, Oxford: Blackwell.

Shimakura, T. (1982) 'Cycles in the Chinese economy and their political-economic implications', *The Developing Economies* XX(4).

Steindl, J. (1952) *Maturity and Stagnation in the American Economy*, Oxford: Blackwell.

15

UNDERSTANDING EFFECTIVE DEMAND

Capitalism versus socialism

Edward J. Nell

That the economy is demand-driven is perhaps the basic Keynesian insight. That it is a part of the social order, reflecting the class structure, underlies the Marxian approach. Moreover, since the social order develops historically, the Marxian approach implies that the economy likewise develops and changes. Further, uniting this with the Keynesian insight, suggests that development, or important aspects of it, will be demand-driven. Geoff has always emphasized the importance of both Marx and Keynes, and in his work he has tried to unite them. This paper follows in the tradition he has worked so hard to establish.

To see what 'demand-driven' means, however, we need to contrast it with its opposite. So we will first compare two 'modes of operation' of mass production economies, one in which demand is perpetually in short supply, the other in which there is always excess demand. (Very loosely, the first can be identified with 'capitalism', the second, with 'socialism'.) We will also see that the dividing line between them is what Harrod and Domar took to be the 'warranted rate of growth'. However this can be shown to be neither warranted nor a rate of growth. Further, the instability property attributed to the 'warranted rate' turns out to be the *stability* of the mode of operation, the force which prevents the system from crossing the barrier to the other mode.

Harrod–Domar has been taken to be the extension of Keynesian thinking to the long run. This has been a mistake; the so-called 'warranted rate' simply balances aggregate demand against productive capacity. It has no inherent connection with growth. A demand-based theory of growth has to explain why markets can be expected to expand. Such trends are based on innovation and changes in the structure of the economy.

INCENTIVES AND THE MODE OF OPERATION

The working of the market generates pressures for the development and diffusion of technical innovations. It has been argued that uncertainty and the possibility of shortfalls in sales – the presence of excess capacity – will intensify these pressures. On the other hand, it has also been noted that increases in demand lead to faster growth of productivity. So it appears that excess capacity and increases in demand both stimulate technical progress! Is there a contradiction here?

To explore what is at issue, we need to examine the way the market creates pressures to innovate and to sell. One way of doing this is to contrast a market-driven system – one with 'demand shortage' – with a system operating under chronic excess demand – a 'shortage' economy. Capitalism is market-driven; socialism means many things to many people, but in practice, real-world socialist systems have always been shortage economies. We will explore the differences, especially in market incentives, but this is *not* an essay in comparative systems. What actually happened in Eastern Europe and the Soviet Union is not the issue (Nell 1992: 1991).

The two economic systems – capitalism and socialism – will be considered as abstract, idealized forms. Our aim is to understand the role of excess capacity – unemployment – in capitalism. Shortage economies will only be brought in by way of contrast. A capitalist economy will be understood as we have already presented it: some (families? institutions? individuals?) own the means of production, while others do not; capitalist production generates a surplus through the employment of wage labour, and competition establishes a common ratio of surplus to the value of the means of production used. This is the rate of profit, and every capitalist system is characterized by a 'normal' rate of profit, (expressed in the rate of interest on money) which makes it possible to calculate the 'amount of capital' in any sector or industry by capitalizing its net income stream. On this basis, therefore, economic activities can be bought and sold. Capitalist enterprises compete with one another; and liquid capital, funds conferring ownership of or claims against such enterprises, will actively seek out those with the highest rates of return. Hence there is constant pressure to increase the surplus, i.e. to raise productivity.

Under capitalism the ownership and distribution of wealth is given, and the system generates pressure to operate the means of production most efficiently (productively). By contrast, under socialism the efficiency and productivity of the means of production are assumed, but private ownership is abolished and the system seeks to distribute the gains most fairly, taking account of both the general interest and the interests of all. Ownership is vested in bureaucracies supposedly representing the general interest,[1] run in accordance with an overall plan, and income is distributed in proportion to productive contribution, modified by subsidies to those with special needs. Investment is planned to bring about balanced growth at the highest rate consistent with planned consumption. Job security and a basic standard of living are guaranteed to all. Capitalism is regulated by prices and the rate of profits, socialism by quantities and the rate of growth.

Modern economies are essentially monetary systems: capitalist profits do not count until they are realized in money (and socialist incomes must be both paid and spent, before any judgement of fairness can be rendered). Since prices are realized in money, in neither system, therefore, does the money wage – fixed by the wage bargain in the labour market – determine the real wage. Production and distribution are carried out at least partly through market processes – wages are paid and spent, accounts are kept of purchases and sales – although the markets work differently, and the socialist markets are not competitive. Further, in both systems production is largely concentrated in the hands of giant bureaucratic organizations, with easy access to funds and well-placed to lobby the government. And in each a privileged class or stratum can be identified.

Long-term prices are designed, ideally, to recover costs and provide the wherewithal for expansion. (Socialist prices are 'distorted' by social policies abetted by entrenched interests; capitalist prices are distorted by monopoly power and special interests.) An equation for prices that would provide the profits that would underwrite growth can be defined, which, in each case, must be modified by a vector expressing the influences causing deviations from the ideal prices.

Each system employs mass production technologies, but one mode of operation is capitalist, the other socialist. Products and productive equipment are standardized. Worker skills are required, though jobs are also standardized, and the pace of work is set by the machinery; costs are kept down and economies of scale are realized by large plants and long production runs. Prices in both systems have to cover current production costs and contribute to meeting the fixed monetary costs incurred in setting up the mass production plant. In both systems normal or long-run prices of manufactured goods will be inflexible, determined by reproduction costs and a mark-up. The differences will lie in the way the mark-up is set, and the extent to which cost overruns are permitted. Costs and outputs of primary goods (non-produced means of production and basic consumption – farm and fish products, minerals, raw materials, oil, etc.) will fluctuate in both systems, leading to temporary market price changes in capitalism and variations in subsidies in socialism. In neither system, however, do prices reflect relative scarcities.

Prices serve the same function in both systems. At their normal levels they reflect the requirements of reproduction and distribution; when exchanges take place at the correct long-term prices, distribution will be accomplished and reproduction will be made possible. Prices do not reflect relative scarcities – they cannot in capitalism, because with excess capacity and unemployment, factors are not scarce, and they do not in socialism, because planning must ensure that exchanges will accomplish the desired reproduction and expansion.[2]

Prices cover costs and earn normal profits from the operation of presently existing equipment. Choice of technique is therefore irrelevant; a new technique may indeed be more profitable, but it will take time to build new factories, and in the meantime demand will have to be served by current, less efficient plants. Normal prices will be based on normal levels of operation, reflecting normal costs. These will not generally be affected by aggregate shortages or excesses; indeed, within a wide range, variations in demand will tend to have little effect on prices. 'Benchmarks' for normal prices will be established at the time investment decisions are made, based on the prevailing levels of the wage and other costs, on the one hand, and expected market growth on the other. Market prices can be expected to vary around these norms, but in manufacturing sectors even considerable swings in demand may have comparatively little impact. (Kalecki 1954; Eichner 1976; Nell 1991: chapters 16 and 17. For a different route to a similar conclusion, *cf.* Blinder 1988 and Gordon 1990.) Nor would variations in prices tend to correct aggregate imbalances between demand and capacity (Nell 1991: chap. 20; Tobin 1984).[3]

MODES OF OPERATION

Capitalism and socialism have traditionally been defined as modes of production, meaning ways of organizing and controlling the means and processes of production, so as to appropriate the resulting surpluses. This traditional approach does not explain either capitalism's combination of wasted capacity and unnecessary products with innovative dynamism, or the corresponding mix of high capital construction, shortages and frustration apparent in socialism. To understand these problems we shall examine the characteristic modes of operation of the two systems which, following Kornai and Kalecki, may be called 'demand-constrained' and 'resource-constrained', respectively.

The characteristic mode of operation pervades the economic sphere and colours all aspects of it – and much beyond as well. Expectations of enterprises as to prices, quantities, revenues, and capital values, all will be formed on the assumption of normal demand scarcity or normal shortage. Households will likewise plan careers and education of children with an eye to the normal state of the labour market. Public bodies will shape their expenditure and capital construction plans on the basis of the normal conditions of operation. Even the agenda of public policy and the issues in political debate may be shaped more by the mode of operation than by the mode of production.

CHARACTERISTIC INCENTIVE PATTERNS

Each system's mode of operation sets up characteristic incentive patterns, which fit together into a definite style. Under capitalism, the presence of near-universal excess capacity dampens the inducement to invest, in the absence

181

of technological improvements. Capitalist economies tend to build capacity sluggishly, punctuated by strong bursts of expansion, usually stimulated by innovation. Weak and/or uncertain investment, in turn, tends to keep capacity utilization low and to create a shortage of jobs. By contrast, under socialism, near-universal shortages of goods, engendered by the attempt to run all productive processes at full potential, strengthen the inducement to invest, which in turn further intensifies the pressure of demand on capacity. Socialist economies build capacity rapidly and regularly, but fail to innovate or to produce high quality. Output growth in capitalism chiefly comes from technical progress; in socialism, from adding capacity.

A shortage of demand in relation to capacity tends to intensify competition; sales are uncertain – a firm's market could always be lost to competitors. Hence cost-cutting and quality enhancement will be important, perhaps competitively necessary, to attract and keep a share of the limited market. Technical progress in regard to both products and processes is therefore stimulated by the characteristic situation of capitalism, and accounts for a large part of the growth of output.

Such technical development will be of the kind analysed by Adam Smith and Charles Babbage – separation of function and division of labour. Tasks and designs are simplified, clarified, broken down and made more precise, so that tasks and skills are carefully matched and products fit proposed uses. Expensive skilled labour/equipment will not be used for tasks that unskilled workers can perform.

By contrast, chronic excess demand means that neither product improvement nor cost-cutting are necessary to make sales; indeed, sometimes good quality is not even required. When shortages are severe enough, practically anything will be absorbed by the market. But generalized shortage sets up pressure for innovations that can meet several needs or perform several functions at the same time – two birds with one stone. In the face of chronic shortages, jobs must be accomplished without the proper tools or materials, which provides an incentive for redesigning products and equipment, and redefining jobs; equipment and work teams must be adapted to multiple functions. So technical progress takes the form associated with the US Pentagon:[4] functions are combined, rather than separated, and tasks are multiplied instead of divided. These innovations are often admirable – Swiss army knives, for example – but they seldom reduce costs in the long run, for a breakdown in any one function usually incapacitates the whole, so that all functions must be scrapped or shut down for repairs. Thus as functions are added, breakdown/repair costs are multiplied.

Similarly, since a shortage of demand means competition for sales, costs must be kept down by driving hard bargains. Companies will therefore try to drive down money wages; for the same reasons they will try to keep other material and input costs down. Moreover, they will insist on quality for money, since sloppy work or poor quality inputs can mean uncompetitive, unsaleable products. Socialist enterprises, on the other hand, are under no such pressures to keep costs down and quality high. Even with declining quality they can sell their products, and rising costs, though a nuisance, will seldom interfere with the enterprise's plans for expansion. Given the widespread shortages, virtually any reasonable expansion plan will be approved; neither prospective nor realized profitability governs or constrains investment. Capitalism hands out harsh penalties – too liberally, for they fall on many who do not deserve them; socialism hands out easy rewards, also too liberally, for they accrue to many who have done nothing to deserve reward.

These arguments must be treated carefully; it does not follow that capitalism will generate progress and turn out high-quality goods, while socialism will stagnate, drowning in junk. Producing high-quality goods is one important way of competing; introducing marketable innovations is another. But producing cheap goods with hard-to-detect flaws is also a good strategy, as is covering up dangerous defects, pandering to unhealthy desires, building in obsolescence and distributing advantageous misinformation through advertising. Socialist enterprises must meet plan requirements and deadlines, but are under no competitive pressures to sell. Hence, although they may let quality decline and costs rise, for example, socialist publishers can concentrate on culturally significant works, rather than best-sellers. Socialist medical care can be delivered to those who need it, rather than those who can pay for it – although it might arrive too late. The contrast may be less between high versus poor quality goods than between, say, classics that fall apart and are delivered late, and swiftly produced, elegantly marketed trash.

At the risk of generalizing too easily, the argument can be put schematically: under capitalism, waste is generated by 'commission', by actions deliberately undertaken – to produce unnecessary or harmful goods, to add unnecessary features to products, to take expensive but socially wasteful actions to sell, market or promote. By contrast under socialism, waste is generated by 'omission', by actions deliberately left undone or overlooked or neglected – failing to control costs, keep discipline in production, keep a check on quality, distribute effectively, inform the market adequately, and so on. Socially wasteful goods that sell, or activities that promote sales, are not penalized under capitalism – but failure to sell is; omitting to control costs and quality is not penalized under socialism – but failing to meet the production quota is.

Market and bureaucracy are seen as two opposed and incompatible forms of organizing economic activity. Nothing could be further from the truth; modern capitalism is highly bureaucratic, and contemporary socialism is equally obviously a market economy, though a market operated with *excess demand*. The production units of all mass production economies so far have been run by bureaucracies; no alternatives have yet proven workable on a large scale. *Both* systems are bureaucratic and *both* are planned through state agencies, although the scope, nature and objectives of the planning are

183

different. Moreover, all modern economies are market economies; the market may be planned by the state or administered privately or through some mixture of state and private, but it is still a market – goods are produced for sale; ownership changes hands through monetary transactions; monetary income, arising from property or from work, confers the power to consume. But the mode of operation of a market system can be demand-constrained or resource-constrained, and that, we shall argue, makes more difference than whether production is run by bureaucracies professing to represent the citizenry as collective owners or representing shareholders as collective owners.[5]

The 'mode of operation' thus refers to the system as a whole; it determines the character of the system and, in particular, the incentives which govern market behaviour. It follows that a system must be one or the other; demand scarcity and supply shortage cannot easily be mixed without losing the distinctive virtues of each. Capitalism is demand-constrained, i.e. productive capacity will normally exceed aggregate demand; whereas socialism is resource-constrained, meaning that aggregate demand will normally exceed productive capacity. Capitalist firms face a buyer's market, socialist enterprises, a seller's market.

MULTIPLIER ANALYSIS

In a capitalist industrial economy, additional investment spending increases employment in the capital goods sector, leading to an increased wage bill, the proceeds of which are then spent on consumer goods, leading to increased activity in that sector. Investment spending thus causes consumption spending to move in the same direction. (But the reverse does not hold; a decline in consumption spending need not always have the same, or indeed, any general effect on investment.) It also causes energy and materials production to vary directly in the same proportion, and it stimulates replacement activity. Each of these in turn leads to increased activity among its suppliers, as expressed in the matrix multiplier.

In a socialist industrial economy additional investment spending means intensifying the excess demand for capital goods. Since in general changes in the intensity of excess demand lead to attempts to change output in the same direction, when excess demand for capital goods increases, overtime work will rise, equipment will be overworked more, breakdowns and accidents will rise, etc. Any of these effects may result in additional wage income, the spending of which will further increase the demand pressure on consumer goods. Changes in excess investment demand thus generally cause changes in the same direction in excess consumer demand, and may cause further pressure on suppliers of materials and replacements. But as in capitalism, a decrease in excess consumer demand need have no effect on excess investment demand. Suppose, for example, that a rise in consumer prices relative to fixed money wages caused excess consumer demand to fall to zero; no productive capacity would thereby be released which could be transferred to the capital goods sector. (This point will be important when we come to the question of reform in socialism.)

In both capitalist and socialist economies the multiplier reflects the turnover of funds, which passes along the stimulus to activity. 'Injections' set off activity, and variable costs are passed along in the current period, transmitting the stimulus to further industries or sectors. Funds representing capital charges, depreciation and fixed costs are withdrawn, or turn over more slowly. In simplified form, then, the multiplier rests on the ratio of variable costs to total revenue, modified, if necessary to take account of worker saving. (The secondary effects on produced means of production follow from the matrix multiplier – if $\mathbf{i}$ is a vector of injections, and $\mathbf{y}$ one of outputs, then $\mathbf{y} = \mathbf{i}(\mathbf{I} - \mathbf{A})^{-1}$, where $\mathbf{A}$ is the input–output matrix – but will be neglected here to concentrate on the aggregate relationship between demand and capacity.)

The principal injections into aggregate demand are gross investment, I, current business spending (energy, consumption by overhead labour, office expenses), B, government spending, G, and exports, E. To get total demand, these injections (measured in normal prices) must be multiplied by an expression which takes account of taxes, imports, saving out of wages, the wage rate and the productivity of labour (Nell 1988: chap. 5, appendix). Let the coefficients be $t = t(w)$, $m = m(w)$, and $s = s(w)$, where these show the additional taxes, imports and savings that take place when aggregate income (output) increases as the result of additional employment, prompted by additional demand. Hence they are each positive functions of the real wage; even if the marginal tax (import, saving) ratio to individual income were constant, a higher income would mean higher taxes (imports, savings) when an individual changes from unemployed to employed. Moreover, there are good reasons to think that all three may be progressive in both systems. Hence aggregate demand can be written (Nell 1991: IV):

$$[I + B + G + E].\ 1/\{1 + t + m - (1 - s)wn\},$$

where t, m, and s are all increasing functions of the real wage, w.

Aggregate productive capacity is given by the capital stock measured at the given normal prices, multiplied by the productivity of the system. This last depends on the normal average ratio of capital stock to the labour force, and on the number of workers required per unit of output, on average. Aggregate capacity can therefore be written very simply:

$$K.\ 1/(k.n),$$

where K is the total capital stock, k is required capital per worker, and n is labour force per unit of output. Both these coefficients must be measured at established or normal prices.

Now consider these expressions in the light of the earlier discussion.

Characteristically, capitalism will find itself with excess capacity, socialism with excess demand (Nell 1988: chapters 5, 8). Hence, for capitalism:

$$[I + B + G + E].1/\{1 + t + m - (1 - s)wn\} < K.1/(k.n).$$

for socialism:

$$[I + B + G + E].1/\{1 + t + m - (1 - s)wn\} > K.1/(k.n).$$

However, care must be taken interpreting these, for they are not the same. When demand exceeds capacity, the multiplier cannot work properly because additional workers can't so readily be hired; however, existing workers can work overtime and sometimes additional shifts can be added. So the rate at which wages are paid and respent is likely to change as output rises above capacity. An increase in demand pressure will tend to raise w and n, thereby increasing the multiplier, intensifying the pressure, even though employment may not have risen. With this in mind, let's compare the two.

Under capitalism, the existence of excess capacity requires firms to compete for the scarce demand, by cutting costs and improving products. Hence n will tend to decline, increasing the expression for aggregate capacity, while reducing the multiplier. Thus the gap between capacity and demand tends to widen. However, competition may force firms to increase w in proportion to the decline in n, offsetting the impact of increased productivity on the multiplier. But t, m, and s are all increasing functions of w; hence the multiplier will still tend to decline and the gap widen. In any case, however, if overall productivity increases by $x\%$, the new level of income is $(1 + x)Y$; if wages rise in proportion and are wholly spent on consumption, its new level will be $(1 + x)C$. So the new level of demand will be $I + (1 + x)C < (1 + x)Y$; excess capacity increases.

The competitive pressures arising from demand scarcity will tend to reduce normal investment and business spending, or at least increase their variability. Rising productivity increases capacity under conditions in which excess capacity already exists; this will dampen I. Increased efficiency in the use of energy, labour and materials will cut into B, and as superior or more cost-effective equipment designs become available, so that k falls, the reductions will affect I and G as well. Only exports are affected in the reverse way; if product or equipment designs improve, and costs are cut, then exports become more competitive and may increase. Otherwise, the pressures tend to reduce each of the major injections, intensifying stagnation.

This pattern is reversed under socialism. Excess demand – a state of generalized shortage – creates incentives to push production to the extreme. The basic ambitions of the system require pushing production to the limit, and there are in-built tendencies leading to further excess. Demand pressure can arise from the attempt to establish fair levels of pay and appropriate differentials, especially between different ranks in both enterprise and state hierarchies. Fairness requires granting regular pay increases when productivity permanently improves as a result of worker efforts. But if a certain kind of blue-collar pay increases in pace with productivity growth, relativities and hierarchical differentials will be eroded; to preserve them the pay of other workers, including management and white collar pay, must rise. Thus localized increases in productivity can give rise to generalized increases in pay, and consequently in consumer demand.

This can take other forms. New capital goods are normally more productive than old. Thus productivity rises as a function of investment; however, workers using the new and more productive goods are normally exercising the same skills, often in the same jobs, as workers in the old. Fairness therefore demands that they be paid the same. If pay rises with productivity for workers using the new goods, and then, out of concern for fairness, rises for workers using the old, demand will increase more than productivity.

As a consequence of demand pressure, bottlenecks develop, older and outmoded facilities are utilized, workers put in longer hours and make more mistakes, so that productivity falls, i.e. n rises. Moreover, demand pressure will tend to call forth basic productive inputs of poor quality, which often only become available in the wrong proportions or at the wrong times. As facilities are pushed harder, previously retired equipment will be brought back into production, and inappropriate equipment will be adapted, all of which will tend to raise capital used per worker, k. (This is very much in line with the traditional view that costs rise as production facilities are pushed beyond a certain limit.) Hence, as k and n rise, even though K rises, the addition to capacity will be less than is needed, and the general downward pressure on productivity in all facilities may even reduce aggregate capacity, while the increases in n and w will raise the multiplier, expanding aggregate demand; both effects tend to widen the gap.

Scarcity of demand in capitalism promotes product improvement; a better mousetrap attracts the market. Excess demand – generalized shortage – on the other hand, implies a seller's market; leading, after a time, to product deterioration and to delays and inefficiency in services. Product improvement/deterioration is often represented as an increase/decrease in the productivity of inputs, which here would be a further decline/rise in k and n, compounding the effects already noted.

As in the capitalist case, both the presence of the gap and the tendency for it to widen, due to its effects on productivity, will lead to pressures on the spending plans of enterprises. Shortages of capacity in relation to demand are a signal to increase the pace of investment spending, to try to bring new capacity on line as fast as possible. Shortages of inputs will lead enterprises to stockpile inventory. Inefficient operation will lead to larger than necessary business expenses. Hence both I and B will increase. The same will hold for G; in the face of generalized shortages and inefficient operation, the government will have to increase its activities, expand its facilities and stockpile scarce items. Again, the impact on exports will be different. If costs rise and the quality of goods declines, exports will tend to fall. By the same token the propensity to import is likely to rise. Moreover, if selling is easy in the domestic market, but competitive internationally, enterprises will prefer to focus on the domestic scene.

For closed economies, then, in capitalism the tendency to stagnation is reinforced by competition, while socialist markets tend to intensify shortages. Capitalist pressures tend to stimulate technical progress in the form of cost-cutting and product improvement; socialist pressures tend to foster inefficiency, cost-overruns and quality deterioration. Capitalist economies deliver services to those with money – which tends to be a buyer's market; socialist economies to those with need – a seller's market. So again the quality is better under capitalism.

For open economies, these conclusions must be modified by noting that the effect on exports (and perhaps imports) will tend to run in the opposite direction in each case; capitalist incentives stimulate exports, socialist ones weaken them.[6] Neither capitalist nor socialist systems are *radically* unstable; capitalism tends to stagnate, socialism to run shortages, but both tendencies meet countervailing pressures and stay within limits. One source of such pressures is external trade, but others can be found within the domestic economy itself.[7]

PROBLEMS OF GROWTH

When excess capacity exists, whether in a particular sector or in general, changes in demand can be met simply by changing the degree of capacity utilization, which will usually require corresponding changes in employment. When the level of activity is very near the rated maximum, reorganization may be required, for shortages may develop in specific inputs or labour skills, and unit costs may rise – but if the demand pressure is regarded as likely to persist, these temporary shortages can often be overcome by a once-for-all effort, so that costs will fall back to normal. An important implication of this is that changes in the proportions of demand can easily be met, so long as the changes remain within the bounds set by existing capacity. This is extremely important for capitalism, since the incentives to innovation and productivity growth mean that different sectors will be growing at different rates.

By contrast, in an economy in which every sector is operating at full blast, getting the proportions of output correct is both important and difficult.[8] The difficulties are obvious – if there is no reserve capacity, neither aggregate output nor the proportions of output can be adjusted with any ease. There is no room to correct mistakes. It is important because if the proportions are not correct, investment cannot be carried out as planned, with the results not only that growth will be slower than expected, but that some output will be wasted – it may even happen, paradoxically, that excess capacity may emerge!

Growth depends on the structure of the economy. A certain group of industries can be identified which form a special sector – Lowe termed it 'machine tools'; for Sraffa it would be the basics. This sector produces its own means of production, as well as producing basic capital goods for use in other sectors which produce capital goods for use in sectors producing final output. The capacity of this sector not only forms an upper limit to growth, but to increase the growth rate it will be necessary first to increase the capacity of the machine tool sector, which means reducing its sales to other sectors and thus lowering the growth rates of those it supplies. If there is constant pressure on machine tools to deliver, it can never augment its own capacity.

For growth to take place at the maximum rate the output of the basics – machine tools – has to be balanced. If basic output is produced in any other proportions the system will have to grow more slowly; some goods will be in short supply, others in excess. For each basic good a ratio can be formed, the numerator being its total production minus the amount of it used as input in all the various industries, the denominator being the amount used as input by the various industries. These ratios can be called the 'own-rates of surplus'; when they are all equal, then outputs are produced in the proportions that will enable investment of the surplus to reach the maximum rate of growth consistent with the given consumption/wage level. But when the own-rates are not equal, some will be higher and some lower, meaning that some goods will be in surplus and others in deficit, compared to what is needed for investment. The investment which can actually be carried out will therefore be limited by the amounts available, i.e. the limit will be set by the good most in deficit. The surplus goods are simply excess. So the sustainable rate of growth for an economy operating in given proportions will be set by the *smallest* of the physical own-rates of surplus of the basic commodities generated by production in those proportions. In other words, if growth has become unbalanced, in an economy with no excess capacity, the lowest of the 'own-rates' sets the sustainable rate of growth. The more unbalanced growth becomes, the slower it becomes.

RELATION TO THE 'WARRANTED' RATE OF GROWTH

This provides a new insight into the famous Harrod–Domar definition of the warranted rate of growth. That rate just balances aggregate demand and aggregate capacity: aggregate demand, in simplified form, is investment times the multiplier, while total capacity is the capital stock times its productivity. Equating the two gives us the rate of growth (investment divided by total capital) that will keep entrepreneurs just satisfied, namely a rate equal to the productivity of capital times the ratio of withdrawals to income.

But a small deviation from this rate in either direction will be self-augmenting. For a rate that is too low will imply that aggregate demand is less

189

than total capacity – which gives business the signal to cut back investment spending, thereby reducing demand even further. Too high a rate in turn signals a shortage of capacity, and thus the need for speeding up investment. In each case, responding to the market signal worsens the initial imbalance, apparently showing that capitalist growth is seriously unstable (Morishima 1975; Kregel 1980).[9]

The warranted rate is only incidentally a rate of growth; it is actually defined as a level of full utilization. This degree of utilization is brought about by a certain level of investment, which, divided by the capital stock, identifies a growth rate. But exactly the same argument could be made with respect to government spending, G, in a stationary system. Suppose higher levels of G increase the productivity of capital, both private and public (as in fact they do: Aschauer 1989). Then

$$G/z = K/v \text{ which implies } G/K = z/v.$$

This is our version of the multiplier, where $z = 1 - wn = P/Y$. The formula states that the ratio of government spending to total capital must equal the ratio of profit's share to the productivity of total capital, in order for capacity to be fully utilized. This would appear to suggest a policy goal, rather than a growth target. Moreover, if $G/z > K/v$, capacity appears to be too small; hence productivity should be increased. Since productivity is an increasing function of G, the state of the market calls for more government spending. Similarly, if there were excess capacity, the market signal would call for reducing G. There is no growth here at all, yet we find both the Harrod–Domar formula and its instability property!

Nor is the warranted rate a potential, satisfactory balanced growth path for an actual economic system. No capitalist system has ever grown for any time at the warranted rate. Capitalism *always* operates with a margin of excess, not just reserve, capacity. (The Second World War is the exception that proves the rule: the Allied economies were planned, and developed shortages.) Socialist economies, that is the economies of the former Eastern bloc, always tended to operate with a level of aggregate demand above full capacity. In short, the warranted rate is not an achievable target (although it may be approachable, as a matter of policy); instead, it is a dividing line, separating two contrasting modes of operation. The same economic system cannot cycle around the warranted rate, first below, then at, then above it, and so on. Below the balancing point, the system operates one way, generating one pattern of incentives and results; above, an altogether different pattern holds. The original problem was misstated.

NOTES

1   Of course, in practice socialist bureaucrats will develop interests of their own, sometimes conflicting with the plan, just as capitalist managers develop interests

separate from, and sometimes opposed to, those of the firms they manage. (And in either system the interests of the firm, as a particular institution, may clash with more general interests, as embodied in the shareholders, or the plan.) These are important questions, but are not central to the issues here.

2   The price model here will be a simplified version of well-known equations developed elsewhere. Let $\mathbf{A}$ be the input–output matrix showing the average coefficients implied in the existing equipment of present industries, $\mathbf{L}$ the vector of average labour requirements per unit of output (expressed in terms of the consumer goods that support labour), $\mathbf{p}$, the price vector, r, the rate of profit and w the real wage, considered as a percentage mark-up on the basic basket of goods supporting labour. Then, if $\mathbf{A}$ has certain properties,

$$\mathbf{p} = (1 + r)\mathbf{Ap} + w\mathbf{Lp} => \mathbf{p}[\mathbf{I} - (1 + r)\mathbf{A} - w\mathbf{L}] = 0$$

will give the prices and the rate of profit, if the normal or long-run real wage is determined by bargaining, custom and social pressures.

3   This leads to an important conclusion in regard to the debate over 'socialist reforms': if prices reflect the requirements for reproduction and distribution, and if pricing benchmarks are set in connection with investment decisions, the claim that aggregate demand imbalances are due to price or wage 'rigidities', and can be corrected by restoring 'free markets', cannot even be entertained. (*Cf.* Eichner 1976; Wood 1976; and Nell 1991: chap. 17; Nell 1997: chap. 10, for the relationships between pricing and investment.)

4   Perhaps the most familiar and striking examples of such baroque technological innovation are to be found in the US military, *cf.* the Multi Role Combat Aircraft, or nuclear submarines. But the American space programme also provides fine examples – not least the Shuttle – and a study of Soviet military and space technology will also provide specimens, to say nothing of Soviet tractors – two models to do everything. Incidentally, this illustrates the point that actual systems have usually been a mixture of corporate planning and competitive markets. The US military industrial complex is a planning system embedded in market arrangements, just as Soviet agriculture embedded a limited market system in a planning regime (Mary Kaldor).

5   That economies characteristically operate either as demand- or as resource-constrained, runs counter to most current economic thinking. On the one hand it is assumed that aggregate demand in capitalist societies can and often does reach or surpass the level of full employment. This never happens except in wartime, and seldom then. 'Full employment' has been redefined – as an upward-drifting 'natural rate'. In the Second World War, the only time the US ever exceeded full capacity, it began to behave as a shortage economy. On the other hand, shortages in socialism are widely held to be due to systemic inefficiency and slackness in production – 'soft budget constraints', in Kornai's phrase (Kornai 1986; Davis and Charemza 1989). The argument is made that for political and administrative reasons, lazy workers cannot be fired, and inefficient firms cannot be shut down, so bureaucratic socialism is unable to enforce budget constraints. Consequently, enterprises feel no compulsion to cut costs or produce efficiently; so long as they meet their quotas, they will suffer no penalty for being unprofitable or for making costly and unwise investments. But managers and bureaucrats will regularly try to expand their territory; hence, careless of costs, they will bring about inefficiency and general shortages. (An extension of the argument holds that markets and private property, bureaucracy and public property, are strongly linked; efficiency is not, in general, consistent with public ownership (Kornai 1990).)

The facts are correct, but the causality is exactly backwards. Shortages *result* from excess demand, which in turn leads to inefficiency, since everything produced can easily be sold. Budget constraints are soft *because* the incentives to expand are strong; not the other way around. Costs are ignored because of the intensity of demand. (As for the idea that soft budget constraints in themselves engender inefficiency, what could be 'softer' than the budget constraint of a large American corporation? Perhaps only the budget constraint of a Savings and Loan Corporation! Many US government-owned firms, such as TVA, have long been models of efficient operation.) It is competition for scarce demand, not restrictions on current or capital spending, that stimulates cost-cutting.

6   The respective systems of international trade work the same way. The western system puts the burden of adjustment on the weaker nations that run deficits; surplus nations do not have to adjust. To restore balance of payments equilibrium basically requires austerity and unemployment, thereby lowering imports. Thus demand will be lowered throughout the system, until the deficit nations are all either in balance, or at an acceptable level of imbalance. The Comecon system financed deficits; planners tried to achieve balance, but if an imbalance arose the Soviet Union would finance it. No austerity measures were required. Hence the system tended to augment domestic demand pressure.

7   Both systems have built-in tendencies to exacerbate their characteristic condition – stagnation and shortage, respectively. The interaction between demand pressure and the building of capacity, which determines the extent of excess capacity or shortage, itself tends to preserve the gap between demand and capacity, allowing it to fluctuate, but keeping it within limits. (Both also tend to generate offsetting influences in international trade and in the informal sector.) This can be shown by examining simple interactions between two variables – investment and excess capacity for capitalism, investment and shortage for socialism. In each case we will find a cyclical pattern, confining the variation within limits, but always remaining on the same side of the 'warranted' or balanced position, which must therefore be considered a dividing line, rather than a target for practical policy. (Admittedly, these models are too simple and abstract to be realistic, but the forces portrayed are present in each system) (Nell 1991, 1996, 1997.)

8   The maximum rate of growth of the system (with given technique, assumed to be embodied in its plant and equipment), will equal the maximum rate of profit, but will only be attainable if outputs are in the proportions that will produce a physical net surplus consisting of the same goods in the same proportions as the aggregate means of production (Pasinetti 1977: 208–12; Abraham-Frois and Berrebi 1979). For any wage rate above the basic standard of living, there will be a corresponding rate of profit lying below the maximum, according to the inverse wage rate–rate of profit function. If wages are consumed and profits invested, there will be a maximum balanced growth rate corresponding to each level of the wage – but this growth rate can only be attained if the outputs are in the correct proportions. Thus we have the quantity-growth equations, dual to the price-profit system:

$$q = (1 + g)A'q + cL'q => q[I - (1 + g)A' - cL'] = 0$$

which gives the relative quantities, q, associated with the growth rate, g, for a given rate of average per capita consumption, c. If $w = c$, then $r = g$, and q and p will be the corresponding left- and right-hand characteristic vectors (cf. fn.2).

9   This, of course, has led to an enormous literature. Two problems are usually identified. First, there appear to be no market forces to bring the warranted rate into line with the natural rate. Second, the warranted rate is unstable. To rectify

the first, the neoclassical model makes v variable drawing on an aggregate production function. However, investment is assumed to be governed by savings. This approach is undermined by the 'capital theory controversies' (Harcourt 1972; Garegnani 1970; Laibman and Nell 1977; other references in Steedman 1988). The neo-Keynesian model makes s variable, through the pressures of demand on the distribution of income. But it is easily shown that these forces are not in general stabilizing (Nell 1982, 1992). In any case, none of the models proposed in this literature explains the *growth of demand*, in the sense of giving reasons that would lead firms to expect that their markets would *expand* in the foreseeable future at a certain rate.

REFERENCES

Abraham-Frois, G. and Berrebi, E. (1979) *Theory of Value, Prices and Accumulation*, Cambridge: Cambridge University Press.

Aschauer, D. (1989) 'Is public expenditure productive?', *Journal of Monetary Economics*, 23: 177–200.

Blinder, A. (1988) 'The fall and rise of Keynesian economics', *Economic Record*, 64: 278–94.

Davis, C. and Charemza, W. (eds) (1989) *Models of Disequilibrium and Shortage in Centrally Planned Economies*, London: Chapman & Hall.

Domar, E. (1957) *Essays in the Theory of Economic Growth*, New York: Oxford University Press.

Eichner, A. (1976) *The Megacorp and Oligopoly*, Cambridge: Cambridge University Press.

Garegnani, P. (1970) 'Heterogeneous capital, the production function and the theory of distribution', *Review of Economic Studies*, 37: 407–36. Reprinted in Steedman 1988.

Goodwin, R. (1966) 'A growth cycle', in C. H. Feinstein (ed.), *Socialism, Capitalism and Economic Growth*, Cambridge: Cambridge University Press.

Gordon, R. (1990) 'What is New-Keynesian economics', *Journal of Economic Literature*, 28: 1115–71.

Harcourt, G. (1972) *Some Cambridge Controversies in the Theory of Capital*, Cambridge: Cambridge University Press.

—— (1995) *Capitalism, Socialism and Post-Keynesianism*, Aldershot: Edward Elgar.

Kaldor, N. (1985) *Economics Without Equilibrium*, Armonk, N.Y.: M.E. Sharpe.

Kalecki, M. (1954) *Theory of Economic Dynamics*, London: Allen & Unwin.

—— (1986) *Selected Essays on Economic Planning*, Cambridge: Cambridge University Press.

Kornai, J. (1986) *Contradictions and Dilemmas: Studies on the Socialist Economy and Society*, Cambridge, Mass.: MIT Press.

—— (1990) *The Road to a Free Economy*, New York: W.W. Norton.

Kregel, J. (1987) 'Natural and warranted rates of growth', in Eatwell *et al.* (eds), *The New Palgrave*, London: Macmillan.

Laibman, D. and Nell, E. J. (1977) 'Reswitching, Wicksell effects and the neoclassical production function', *American Economic Review*, 67: 878–88. Reprinted in Steedman 1988.

Lowe, A. (1976) *The Path of Economic Growth*, Cambridge: Cambridge University Press.

Morishima, M. (1975) *Theory of Economic Growth*, Oxford: Oxford University Press.

Nell, E. J. (1982) 'Growth, distribution and inflation', *Journal of Post Keynesian Economics*, 5(1), Fall: 104–13. Reprinted in Nell (1992) *Transformational Growth and Effective Demand*, London: Macmillan; New York: New York University Press.

—— (1988) *Prosperity and Public Spending*, London: Unwin Hyman.

—— (1991) 'Capitalism, socialism and effective demand', in E. J. Nell and W. Semmler (eds), *Nicholas Kaldor and Mainstream Economics*, London: Macmillan.

—— (1992) *Transformational Growth and Effective Demand*, London: Macmillan.

—— (1996) *Making Sense of a Changing Economy*, London: Routledge.

—— (1997) *The General Theory of Transformational Growth: Keynes after Sraffa*, Cambridge: Cambridge University Press.

Pasinetti, L. (1977) *Lectures on the Theory of Production*, New York: Columbia University Press.

Steedman, I. (ed.) (1988) *Sraffian Economics*, Vol. I, London: Edward Elgar.

Tobin, J. (1984) *Asset Accumulation and Economic Activity*, Oxford: Blackwell.

16

THE EFFECTS OF CHANGES IN AGGREGATE INCOME SHARES ON AGGREGATE DEMAND

Trevor Stegman

The aim of this paper is to provide some analysis of the effect of changes in the functional distribution of aggregate income (between profit share and wage share) on the level of aggregate demand expenditure.

The functional distribution of aggregate income has been an area of controversy in the development of economic analysis for at least two hundred years. The central issue has remained the process by which relative shares are determined and theoretical debate has concentrated on functional distribution as a resultant – as a 'basic end of economic enquiry' (Ranadive 1978; see also Davidson (1959), and King and Regan (1976) for surveys of the development of differing schools of thought). Although there has been much interest in the effects of changes in wage and profit rates, and changes in relative income shares do play an important part in post-Keynesian long-run growth theory, there has been less interest in the short-run effects of autonomous changes in relative income shares. Perhaps this has been because of a once generally held view that there was an apparent constancy in relative income shares.[1]

Rather than the process by which relative income shares are determined, the question addressed here is concerned with how changes in the way the national income cake is carved up affect the size of the cake. Specifically, this analysis is concerned with the short-run effect of changes in functional distribution on the components of domestic private demand, consumption and investment.

This paper aims first to provide a justification for the approach taken; it then presents a simple model to identify the crucial behavioural assumptions. There then follows a brief summary of the results of a number of attempts to empirically test these assumptions against Australian data; finally the paper presents some implications for policy.

THE EFFECTS OF CHANGES IN FUNCTIONAL DISTRIBUTION

While functional distribution was a central issue in classical theory, with the development of orthodox neoclassical distribution theory (following Hicks 1932) the determination of aggregate income shares became just 'a special case of Price Theory' (Lipsey 1966: 407), with the wage share–profit share distribution being determined by the technical conditions of production in terms of the marginal productivity of aggregate labour and capital. As Dobb (1972) points out, the marginal productivity theory of distribution requires the acceptance of a well-behaved aggregate production function, for an aggregate economy behaving as if it is a profit-maximizing competitive firm. The theoretical flaws in these neoclassical concepts, which were identified in the 'Capital Controversy', provide the basis for post-Keynesian distribution theory (see Kaldor 1955–6; Robinson 1956; Harcourt and Kenyon 1976; Harris 1974; and Wood 1975), although the origins of this approach lie in the writings of Kalecki (1939, 1954).

The common theme in post-Keynesian theories of income distribution is that investment demand determines not only the level of aggregate employment (via the Keynesian multiplier), but also the distribution of income through the pricing decisions of oligopolistic firms (as a mark-up on their variable costs of production). In the more recent developments of post-Keynesian theory the causal mechanism for the second effect is based on capital market imperfections and the non-perfect substitutability of external and internal finance. Because of the need for retained profits to make a required contribution to the financing of any given level of investment, oligopolistic firms set the mark-up to generate the required profitability, and this determines the wage share–profit share division of the national income cake.

In these theories the direction of causation runs from the 'autonomous' investment decision to the resultant factor share distribution. The research reported on in this paper is based on the question of causation running in the opposite direction. For in open economies, in which both cost conditions and pricing decisions are subject to government policy influences, domestic oligopolistic firms cannot be viewed as being completely free to set required mark-ups. Rather than profit margins adjusting to autonomous investment decisions, the issue of investment levels adjusting to firms' exogenously determined profitability circumstances is the question of interest. Harcourt raises this issue in criticizing Kaldor's distribution model as being inapplicable when firms are 'frustrated in the short run by rigidities in profit margins' (1982: 72).

This interest was stimulated by the economic experience of the Australian economy over the 1970s and early 1980s, and the accompanying policy debates. In 1975, and again in 1981, an investment-led recession in activity

196

and employment had closely followed an autonomous real wage rise (relative to productivity) and a consequent squeeze on the profit share of aggregate income. The circumstantial evidence was strong for a causal link, where the reduction in current profitability results in a fall in investment and, via the multiplier effect, a resultant fall in activity and employment.

In the policy debates that accompanied these recessions, a crucial objective of policy (which included a centralized wages and incomes policy) was seen as the restoration of the profit share of aggregate income so as to induce a recovery in real investment demand. There was in fact some policy-induced recovery in the profit share of Australian national income over the second half of the 1970s – unfortunately, investment levels, and consequently the economy and employment growth, remained depressed. The relationship between changes in aggregate income shares and aggregate investment appeared to be asymmetric: a fall in the profit share results in a fall in investment, but a subsequent recovery in the profit share does not result in a recovery in investment.

This asymmetry in the relationship between investment and profitability has also been evidenced in Australia (and elsewhere) for financial variables other than cash flow. Tight monetary policy and high interest rates, after lags which confound policy-makers, eventually result in a reduction in investment. But monetary policy easing and lower interest rates do not seem to automatically lead to an improved investment performance. (Keynes commented on this phenomenon in his 'pushing on a string' analogy.)

In regard to recent experience with regard to wage and profit shares in Australia, it seemed that a useful basic question was: how does an exogenous (policy-induced, say) shift in relative factor shares affect the level of effective demand?

An additional reason for considering the effects of exogenous changes in the wage share–profit share distribution is that scope is provided for analysing the effects of changes in the level of 'real wages' – a variable of great interest to economists and policy-makers, but one with serious conceptual and measurement problems at the aggregate level. If we take output per worker as exogenous in the short run, then changes in the wage share represent changes in the general level of real wages relative to average labour productivity (i.e. changes in real unit labour costs). The effect of a change in real wages (given productivity) on aggregate demand, and hence in a Keynesian model on employment, can be analysed via the effect on demand of the consequent change in relative income shares. (Such an approach is of course inconsistent with neoclassical theory, in which diminishing marginal productivity of labour and capital–labour substitution in response to wage changes are essential elements.)

A SIMPLE MODEL

In this section a simple two-sector (firms and households) model is used to analyse the mechanism by which changes in the functional distribution of income affect the level of aggregate demand.[2] The model has a standard Keynesian framework, in which (below full-employment capacity) output adjusts to match the sum of effective consumption and investment demands, through producer reaction to unintended inventory changes, and 'equilibrium' requires the equality of planned saving and planned investment.

The national accounting identity is:

$$S = I_p + X \tag{1}$$

where X = supply − demand (a measure of deficient aggregate demand); S is planned (= realized) saving; and I_p is planned investment; $I_p + X$ is realized investment.

The model has three distinctive elements:

1 The distribution of aggregate income between wage share and profit share is exogenous – i.e. the profit share $\dfrac{\pi}{Y}$ is exogenous.

$$\frac{\pi}{Y} = V \tag{2}$$

2 The aggregate average propensity to save from a given level of income depends upon the distribution of that income, because of the difference between the marginal propensity to save from profits ($0 < S_\pi < 1$) and the marginal propensity to save from wages ($0 < s_w < 1$) with $s_\pi > s_w$ – following Kaldor (1955–6).[3]

$$\frac{S}{Y} = s_w + (s_\pi - s_w)\frac{\pi}{Y} \tag{3}$$

If the household propensity to save is the same for all types of household income, then s_π is greater than s_w since saving out of profits takes place twice – once as company undistributed income and again as household saving from distributed profits.

With $s_\pi - s_w$ greater than zero, a redistribution of a given level of income from wages to profits will lead to a fall in the level of consumption expenditure generated by that income. Conversely, a rise in the wage share at the expense of the profit share will raise the level of consumption expenditure generated by a given level of aggregate income.

The resultant effect of such distributional shifts on total demand, however, will depend upon the relationship between profitability and investment.

198

3   The third distinctive element of the model is the nature of the investment function. The investment hypothesis proposes that the incentive for investment is related to aggregate activity (via an accelerator mechanism). However, current profitability provides the financial capacity for investment (via the requirement for a minimum proportion of firms' investment expenditure to be undertaken with retained earnings). Therefore current profitability provides a financial constraint on the ability of the corporate sector to undertake desired investment expenditure:

$$I_p = g(\Delta Y) \text{ subject to } I_p \leq k\pi \qquad (4)$$

The financial constraint on investment is derived from the corporate retention ratio, and from minimum target liquidity ratios (the proportion of liquid financial assets in total asset acquisition), and maximum target gearing ratios (of external debt incurrence to total asset acquisition), for firms in the sources and uses of their funds – following Wood (1975). Firms may operate inside the constraint by holding more financial assets than their required minimum, or by issuing less debt than their desired maximum.

The value of k will thus depend upon firms' liquidity preferences and degree of risk aversion, and the availability of credit and the level of interest rates. Restrictive monetary policy for example, would imply less willingness to rely on external finance, a lower value of k, and a higher minimum level of profitability required to contribute to the financing of a given level of investment.

The effect of changes in the profit share on investment demand depends upon whether the financial constraint is binding or not binding. If the constraint is binding, a fall in the profit share of a given income will reduce the level of planned investment. However, if the financial constraint is not binding (or becomes so because the incentive to invest falls), then a rise in profitability does not necessarily lead to increased investment demand – without an increase in the incentive to invest firms use their 'excess' profitability to acquire more financial assets or reduce debt.

In combining equations (1)–(4) to analyse the effect of a change in distribution on aggregate demand, the initial impact of an exogenous change in the profit share V can be determined by using $I_p = \bar{I}$ for the initially given incentive to invest.[4] Solving for X yields the relationship between changes in the profit share and the impact on aggregate demand, and the critical level of the profit share below which the financial constraint provides a continuing depressing effect on investment and output.

In the unconstrained case

$$X = (A + BV)Y - \bar{I} \qquad (5)$$

where $A = s_\pi$ and $B = s_\pi - s_w > 0$.

In the constrained case

$$X = (A - (k{-}B)V)Y \text{ with } k - B > 0^5 \qquad (6)$$

and the critical level of the profit share for which $X = 0$ is $V = \dfrac{A}{k - B}$.

Thus, the direction of the effect on aggregate demand of distributional changes depends upon the financial position of the corporate sector with respect to self-imposed limits on firms' liquidity and debt positions. If the corporate sector in general remains within these financial limits (i.e. if corporate profitability remains sufficient to allow firms to finance their investment plans without violating constraints on their liquidity and debt positions) then a redistribution towards wages of a given income level will raise aggregate demand (by raising consumption demand) and a redistribution towards profits will lower aggregate demand (since there is no incentive or increased investment to offset lower consumption expenditure).

If the profit share falls below the critical level where financial constraints are binding – this critical level is determined by the state of business confidence, the level of interest rates and availability of credit, and the propensities to save – then aggregate demand will fall as the reduction in investment expenditure more than offsets the stimulus to consumption (since $k > s_\pi - s_w$).

Therefore a redistribution towards the wage share will only raise aggregate demand if firms have 'excess' profitability (in the above sense). As long as the profit share is maintained below the critical level the multiplier process will maintain downward pressure on aggregate output. In such a situation a higher profit share is a necessary but not sufficient condition for a recovery in activity – some autonomous stimulus to demand is also required. A higher profit share is necessary to halt the slide but will not in itself reverse it.

This analysis has been presented in the simplest of models – a closed two-sector economy. In an open economy, foreign prices and the ratio of foreign to domestic prices are themselves a source of fluctuations in domestic income shares (for example, when import prices are rising, the maintenance of real wages implies a fall in the domestic profit share of domestic income); capital inflow and outflow provide additional sources and uses of funds for domestic firms; and export demand (as with government demand) provides a potential source of increased activity (and incentive for domestic investment) which is independent of the profit share–wage share ratio. (Expenditure on imports and taxation of course provide additional leakages.) The simple model, however, suffices to identify the crucial determinants of the effect of distributional change on aggregate demand – the difference in saving propensities and the asymmetry in the relationship between investment and current profitability.

SOME EMPIRICAL ANALYSES

This section summarizes the results of some attempts to address the two empirical issues:

1   The difference between the saving propensities from wages and from profits, $s_\pi - s_w$; and
2   whether there is evidence of asymmetry in the relationship between investment demand and current profitability.

With regard to the first issue, in the simple model

$$s_\pi - s_w = r + (1 - r)s_d - s_w \tag{7}$$

where r is the corporate retention ratio ($0 < r < 1$) and s_d is the household marginal propensity to save from distributed profits ($0 < s_d < 1$).

If $s_d = s_w$, then $s_\pi - s_w > 0$ and a redistribution from wages to profits will reduce the level of consumption demand generated from a given level of income.

If $s_d \neq s_w$, then the sign and magnitude of $s_\pi - s_w$ depends on the relative magnitudes of r, s_d and s_w. In particular, if the household marginal propensity to save from distributed profit income is sufficiently smaller than that from wages (that is, if households are substantially more profligate with their property income than with their wage income), then the dampening effect on consumption of a distributive shift from wages to corporate profits may be offset. However, if the corporate retention ratio is large relative to the propensity to save from wages, then $s_\pi - s_w > 0$ even if $s_d < s_w$.

With these conditions in mind, a number of analyses were undertaken of Australian data on household income and corporate dividend and retention behaviour. (Detail on these analyses, the results of which are summarized here, is provided in Stegman (1985).)

Data on household incomes were decomposed by source of income to test whether property income (dividends, interest and rent) was more variable over time than wage income, and whether property income receipts were identified with particular income-level classes. If property income is more variable over time (with a higher 'transitory' component) it might be inferred that it has the higher propensity to save (Friedman 1957). If property income is concentrated in the hands of high-income households with relatively high marginal propensities to save, this also implies that the aggregate marginal propensity to save from distributed profits is higher than that from wages (Klein and Goldberger 1955).

From Box-Jenkins analysis of the respective time series, it was concluded that property income has evidenced more variability about trend than has wage income. However, cross-section data suggested that for Australian households property income was *less* unequally distributed than wage income, due to the significant share of property income received by low

201

income (but asset-rich) retirees (who have low propensities to save).

Although the estimation of an aggregate consumption function using time series regression techniques is notoriously problematic, this procedure was attempted for some Australian data, in order to test for evidence of any significant difference between the household marginal propensities to consume from wage and property incomes.

The procedure followed was to estimate a household consumption function in which the principal explanatory variable, household disposable income, was decomposed by source of income, and to test whether the coefficient on property income was significantly different from that on wage income. The exercise yielded estimates of the annual and long-run marginal propensity to consume from property income (0.655 and 0.774) which were higher than the estimates for wage income (0.514 and 0.607), but the estimates for property income were relatively inefficient (due to multicollinearity in the various income components), and the difference between the two was not statistically significant.

More confidence can be placed in the analysis of Australian corporate sector retention and dividend behaviour over the last two decades (see Chapman *et al.* 1994 and Stegman 1985). The ratio of dividends to annual corporate disposable income evidenced remarkable stability over the 1970s (averaging 0.23). Although there was more variability in the dividend ratio in the 1980s, it never rose above 0.30. With a relatively constant dividend ratio, the retention ratio has borne the burden of rising net interest payments over the 1980s, but has remained high. For the decade of the 1970s (the period on which the consumption function estimates were based), the annual retention ratio averaged 0.54.

On the basis of these Australian studies, it seems reasonable to conclude that the proportion of profit income not distributed to households is sufficiently large, and the probability of the household marginal propensity to consume from distributed profits being significantly greater than that from wages is so low, as to leave little doubt that a redistribution of a given level of aggregate income from wages to profits does have the effect of reducing consumption demand. While the direction of the effect of distributive shifts on consumption may be clear, its magnitude cannot be estimated with any reliability.

The investment hypothesis, in which current profitability is seen as providing the financial constraint on investment expenditure, whereas the incentive to invest is related to aggregate activity via an accelerator process, is the crucial behavioural assumption of the model examined earlier. Two empirical studies have been undertaken to see whether this hypothesis received any empirical support from recent Australian experience.

The first study used aggregate time series data on corporate investment in plant and equipment to test whether the use of current profitability as a constraint rather than as an additional argument improved the statistical performance of a standard accelerator investment function. The detail of the methodology is reported in Stegman (1982).

In summary, the econometric specification of the investment function took the form:

$$I = g_2(\tilde{Y}) \text{ subject to } I \leq g_1(\tilde{\pi})$$

where $\tilde{Y}$ is the vector of accelerator variables, $\tilde{\pi}$ is a vector of profitability variables, and g_1 and g_2 are each functions assumed to satisfy the requirements for linear regression.[6] For estimation this can be respecified as a two-regime switching regression model.

Regime 1 (constrained) : $I = g_1(\tilde{\pi}) \text{ if } g_1(\tilde{\pi}) < g_2(\tilde{Y})$

Regime 2 (unconstrained): $I = g_2(\tilde{Y}) \text{ if } g_1(\tilde{\pi}) \geq g_2(\tilde{Y})$

Maximum likelihood methods can then be employed to estimate both the regression coefficients and the allocation of observations between regimes.

For the 1970s, the composite investment function fitted the data well, caught the turning points, the time periods identified as 'constrained' coincided with *a priori* expectations (periods of squeezed profits and tight monetary policy), and on standard statistical tests the model outperformed alternative specifications with conventional regressors or with profitability added as an additional argument (see Stegman (1982) for the detailed results). The econometric model performed less well for the 1980s – a period in which financial deregulation and interest rate volatility have no doubt generated instability in firms' financial constraint criteria.

The second attempt at seeking empirical support for the investment hypothesis involved the use of cross-section data for a large sample of Australian corporations for the period 1975–90. Balance sheet and flow of funds data for each company for each year were used to classify an observation on a firm's investment behaviour as either 'constrained' or 'unconstrained', and this division was used to run two separate 'pooled' regressions (combining the cross-section and time series data) of an investment function. The investment function regressors included incentive variables (sales growth and Tobin's Q) and a profitability variable ('free cash flow' – defined as profits less dividends, interest and tax payments). A firm was defined as 'unconstrained' in a particular period if 'free cash flow' exceeded investment expenditure. That is, if a firm has more than adequate profitability, after meeting their interest, tax and dividend commitments, to finance all desired investment, and then uses the excess to reduce debt or acquire financial assets, the firm is unconstrained for that period.

The hypothesis the exercise aimed to test was that the 'constrained' regression should evidence significantly different coefficients on both incentive and profitability variables compared to the coefficients of the 'unconstrained' regression. Detail on the methodology and the results are reported in Chapman *et al.* (1994). In summary, the coefficient estimates obtained were consistent with the hypothesis. Sales growth and Q were not significant variables in the constrained equation, although both were significant in the unconstrained equation. While 'free cash flow' was statistically significant in both equations, the estimated coefficient was significantly higher in the constrained equation. These results imply that, on average, the level of cash flow matters more in the determination of firms' investment when they are constrained than when they are unconstrained, and when they are constrained incentive variables have no role. When firms are unconstrained, cash flow matters less, and incentive variables are important determinants of investment. Therefore this second empirical analysis of investment can also be seen as providing some support for the investment hypothesis of equation (4).

POLICY IMPLICATIONS

The mechanisms by which changes in the functional distribution of income affect aggregate demand, as interpreted in the model presented above, have two important implications for macroeconomic policy.

The first is the old Keynesian lesson concerning the ineffectiveness of real-wage cuts alone as a cure for unemployment. While an increase in real wages (relative to productivity) may depress investment and hence output and employment, a fall in real wages and a consequent increase in the profit share is a necessary condition for recovery from recession only in circumstances where too low a profit share is acting to continually depress desired investment through the financing constraint. Even in these conditions a fall in real wages is not sufficient for recovery. In conditions of recession and excess capacity, an increase in output requires an increase in effective demand. A fall in real wages may be necessary, but only as an accompaniment to some direct stimulus to aggregate demand. In the absence of such a stimulus, cuts in real wages make matters worse by reducing consumption demand.

The second implication relates to the damaging effects of over-reliance on monetary policy for short-term stabilization policy. Restrictive monetary policy, imposed to address inflationary or balance of payments pressures, impacts most heavily on real investment demand. In the model presented here the effect is via a tightening of the financial constraint and reduced cash flow for firms. When, in the face of falling investment and hence employment, policy-makers eventually yield to the cries for a loosening of monetary policy, the easing of the financial constraint and increased cash flow provide the financial wherewithal for an investment-led recovery. However, without any incentive from final product demand to increase productive capacity, real investment remains stagnant. Firms use increased liquidity to restore balance sheet positions and 'invest' in existing and financial assets. The resulting inflationary boom in these asset prices inevitably brings a reimposition of tight monetary policy. This cycle provides a downward-ratcheting effect on the level of investment in real productive capital accumulation with consequent detrimental effects on the long-term productive capacity of the economy.

ACKNOWLEDGEMENT

The writings of Geoff Harcourt provided the initial stimulus for the research reported on in this paper and his assistance and advice provided encouragement. For this, and much else, I am extremely grateful to him.

NOTES

1   Constant factor shares are a feature of Cobb's and Douglas's famous function, based on their interpretation of US data (1928: 163). Later, Keynes was also to remark on the alleged constancy of income shares (1939: 48).
2   A more detailed version of this model is presented in Stegman (1980).
3   For simplicity, marginal and average propensities to save are assumed equal. This makes no difference to the model's implications.
4   A more expansive and rigorous derivation of model results is presented in Stegman (1980).
5   As long as household saving is positive (and firms therefore are net borrowers) the coefficient on the investment constraint, k, will be greater than the difference between the marginal propensities to save, B. For a rigorous proof, see Stegman (1980). Put simply, this condition means that the transfer of $1 from a given level of income from profits to wages will reduce investment (when the constraint is binding) by more than it will reduce aggregate saving.
6   The actual functions estimated (from quarterly observations) were:

$$g_1 : I_t = b_0 + \sum_{k=1}^{2} b_k \, \pi_{t-k}$$

$$g_2 : I_t = \beta_0 + \sum_{k=1}^{8} \beta_K^{\Delta} Y_{t-k} + \beta_9 K_{t-1}$$

where:
π_t =   gross operating surplus of trading enterprises deflated by the implicit deflator for expenditure on plant and equipment;
K_t =   capital stock at constant prices;
ΔY_t =   quarterly change in non-farm GDP at constant prices;
I_t =   gross fixed capital expenditure on plant and equipment at constant prices.

REFERENCES

Chapman, D. R., Junor, C. W. and Stegman, T. (1994) 'Cash flow constraints and firms' investment behaviour', School of Economics Discussion Paper No. 94/14 July, University of New South Wales.

Cobb, C. and Douglas, P. (1928) 'A theory of production', *American Economic Review: Papers and Proceedings*, 18(1).

Davidson, P. (1959) *Theories of Income Distribution*, New Brunswick, N.J.: Rutgers University Press.

Dobb, M. (1972) 'The Sraffa system and critique of the neoclassical theory of distribution' in Hunt, E. and Schwartz, J. (eds) *A Critique of Economic Theory*, Harmondsworth: Penguin.

Friedman, M. (1957) *A Theory of the Consumption Function*, Princeton, N.J.: Princeton University Press.

Harcourt, G. (1972) *Some Cambridge Controversies in the Theory of Capital*, Cambridge: Cambridge University Press.

——— (1982) 'A critique of Mr Kaldor's model of income distribution and economic growth' in Harcourt, G. *The Social Science Imperialists*, London: Routledge & Kegan Paul.

——— and Kenyon, P. (1976) 'Pricing and the investment decision', *Kyklos*, 29.

Harris, D. (1974) 'The price policy of firms, the level of employment and the distribution of income in the short run', *Australian Economic Papers*, 13.

Hicks, J. (1932) *The Theory of Wages*, London: Macmillan.

Kaldor, N. (1955–6) 'Alternative theories of distribution', *Review of Economic Studies*, 23.

Kalecki, M. (1939) *Essays in the Theory of Economic Fluctuations*, London: Allen & Unwin.

——— (1954) *The Theory of Economic Dynamics*, London: Allen & Unwin.

Keynes, J. M. (1939) 'Relative movements of real wages and output', *Economic Journal*, 49.

King, J. and Regan, P. (1976) *Relative Income Shares*, London: Macmillan.

Klein, L. and Goldberger, A. (1955) *An Econometric Model of the United States, 1929–1952*, Amsterdam: North Holland.

Lipsey, R. (1966) *Positive Economics*, London: Weidenfeld & Nicolson.

Ranadive, K. (1978) *Income Distribution: The Unsolved Puzzle*, Bombay: Oxford University Press.

Robinson, J. (1956) *The Accumulation of Capital*, London: Macmillan.

Stegman, T. (1980) 'Changes in factor shares and aggregate demand: a simple model with application to Australia', *Australian Economic Papers*, 19.

——— (1982) 'The estimation of an accelerator-type investment function with a profitability constraint by the technique of switching regressions', *Australian Economic Papers*, 21.

——— (1985) 'The effects of real wage changes on the average propensity to consume', U.N.S.W. School of Economics Discussion Paper No. 71, October, University of New South Wales.

Wood, A. (1975) *A Theory of Profits*, Cambridge: Cambridge University Press.

17

MACROECONOMICS AND THE DISTRIBUTION OF INCOME[1]

Tony Atkinson

Geoff Harcourt as an economist has spent much of his life thinking about, and teaching us about, macroeconomics; Geoff as a citizen has been much concerned about the personal distribution of incomes. The subject of this chapter is the relation between these two subjects – or, more accurately, the lack of relation. I must confess to being puzzled, as an outsider to macroeconomics, as to why the factor distribution of income has ceased to be central to macroeconomics, and why there has ceased to be any direct connection between modern macroeconomics and my own particular field of interest – the distribution of personal income.

TODAY'S NEGLECT OF FACTOR SHARES

The subject of the macroeconomics of income distribution – that is, the distribution of national income between wages, profits and rent – seems now to be little discussed. The share of wages, and whether it is constant or rising or falling, was once a central topic in macroeconomics. As a student in the early 1960s, I listened to debates about different theories of distribution, debates in which Geoff took a vigorous part. In fact the macroeconomic theory of distribution seemed to dominate the field of income distribution.

Now, thirty years later, things seem to have changed, and factor shares are not essential to macroeconomics. For instance, the widely used textbook, *Macroeconomics*, by Mankiw (1994) includes in its inside covers eight graphs of key statistics on the United States' economy from 1900 to the present, but these do not include the share of wages or profits in national income. The share of labour income is given later in the text (1994: 75), but the factor share figures are not regarded as of central importance.

Factor shares are typically introduced in connection with the Cobb–Douglas production function; and the main information which students of macroeconomics appear to be given on factor shares is that they are constant over time. According to Mankiw, 'Labor income has remained about 0.7 of total income over a long period of time. This approximate constancy of factor shares is evidence for the Cobb–Douglas production function' (1994: 75).

Hall and Taylor, in their text with the same title, similarly state of factor shares that 'These relative shares are fairly stable from year to year' (1993: 48).

The theme of stability appears in a number of other texts, a United Kingdom example being that of Begg *et al.* (1994), who note there is little change in the share in the United Kingdom between the 1960s and the present. In their European textbook, Burda and Wyplosz (1993) cite Kaldor's stylized facts about the growth of advanced economies and say that

> Remarkably, despite the secular growth of wages and the constancy of the real rate of interest, the distribution of income between capital and labour has been relatively stable. The shares of capital and labour incomes in national product . . . fluctuate about a horizontal trend.
>
> (*Ibid.*: 125)

If we turn to the more advanced of the current textbooks, then the subject is rarely treated. To take two of the best known of such texts, one finds virtually nothing in Sargent's *Macroeconomic Theory* (1987), nor in Blanchard and Fischer's *Lectures on Macroeconomics* (1989). The same is true of contributions to professional journals. At the beginning of 1991, the *Journal of Economic Literature* (*JEL*) introduced a new classification system, including 'aggregate factor income distribution' as category E25. The *JEL* need hardly have bothered. In the next three years (1991–3), there were only twenty-four articles listed, and in some issues of the *JEL* the category was blank. Nine of the twenty-four articles were in the *Review of Radical Political Economics*, and the subject appears to have been largely neglected in the mainstream journals.

MACROECONOMICS OF THE LONG-RUN: GROWTH THEORY OLD AND NEW

The fact that factor shares are relatively little discussed does not mean that nothing is implied about the factor distribution; the action may not be centre stage, but it is certainly taking place. We have therefore to ask what is implicit in macro-theories about the distribution by factor shares. Clearly, I cannot review all areas of macroeconomics here, and I want to focus on the *long-run* behaviour of factor shares. That is, I am concerned with the trend movements rather than short-term fluctuations.

The macroeconomics of the long run is essentially growth theory, and I want to set the scene by reviewing the essential elements of the mainstream theory. First, there is the standard Solow (1956) neoclassical model of aggregate growth, shown in Figure 1. Output is determined by an aggregate production function, with arguments capital and effective labour, where effective labour refers to the fact that there is assumed to be labour-augmenting technical progress at a fixed rate α:

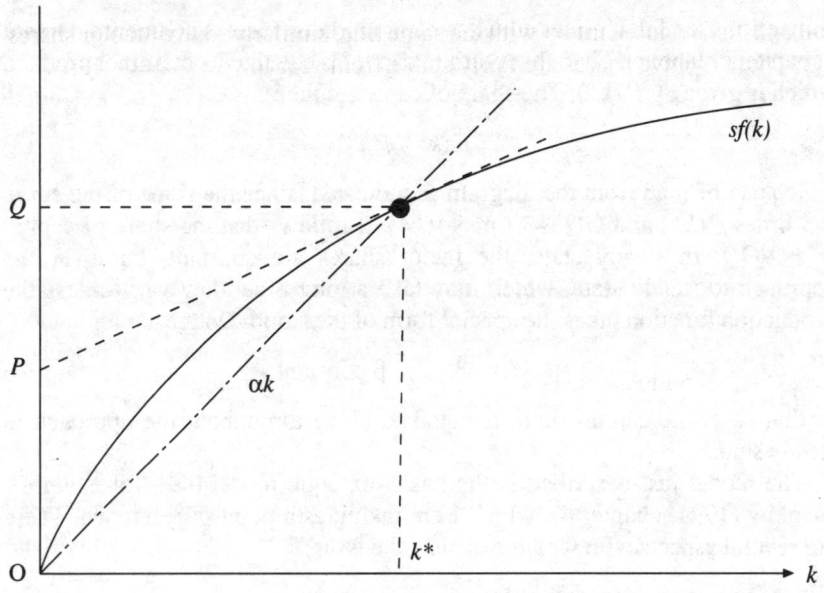

Figure 1 Solow model

$$Y = F(K, L\, e^{\alpha t}) \equiv L\, e^{\alpha t} f(k). \qquad (1)$$

There are constant returns to labour and capital, so that we can (second step in equation (1)) write output as the product of total effective labour and a function $f(k)$ where k is the ratio of capital to effective labour. For simplicity there is assumed to be no population growth, an assumption which is commonly made in the new growth theory to which I come in a moment.

The dynamics of this economy are governed by the savings relationship, which is here taken to be a simple proportional savings function. It then follows that capital per effective unit of labour, k, evolves according to the differential equation:

$$dk/dt = sf(k) - \alpha k. \qquad (2)$$

The term $(-\alpha k)$ comes from the fact that capital needs to increase absolutely to keep pace with the rise in the effectiveness of labour (there is no depreciation). If the production function satisfies certain conditions, then there is a steady state solution, as shown by k^*, and the economy converges towards this level. In steady state, capital is growing at rate α, as is output per worker.

This is a story about the evolution of the aggregate economy, but what about the factor distribution? Suppose that we assume that there is perfect competition, and that prices adjust to clear markets (there is no unemployment of capital or labour). Then the return to capital is equal to its marginal product, which is given by $f'(k^*)$. The share of capital is then

$$k^* f'(k^*)/f(k^*) \tag{3}$$

which can be read from the diagram as indicated, since the slope of the curve is s times $f'(k^*)$ and OQ is s times $f(k^*)$. It follows that the share of capital is PQ/OQ. In steady state, the factor shares are constant, but over the approach to steady state, which may take a long time, they vary unless the production function takes the special form of the Cobb–Douglas:

$$f(k) = k^{1-\beta}, \qquad \beta \text{ constant.} \tag{4}$$

In that case, the capital share is equal to $(1-\beta)$ throughout the approach to steady state.

The model just described is the basic textbook model (see, for example, Mankiw (1994: chapter 4), which I am taking as a point of reference. There are several aspects with which one can take issue:

- the use of an aggregate production function;
- the assumption of perfect competition and market clearing;
- the treatment of savings and the absence of any explicit role for investment;
- the exogeneity of the growth rate.

All of these are serious, but I am going to concentrate here on the last criticism.

NEW GROWTH THEORY

The exogeneity of the growth rate has been one of the major concerns of the 'new growth theory' which emerged in the 1980s. This literature contains a number of strands. Some of these are interesting *and* new (such as the introduction of monopolistic competition into growth theory); some are interesting but not new; some are new but not interesting. In the last of these categories, I put the modelling of aggregate savings as though it were undertaken by a representative, infinite-lived household with perfect knowledge of all future factor and product prices. Savings are assumed to be governed by maximizing the integral of discounted utility from consumption taken from now to infinity. Whatever the attractions of the life-cycle theory, this seems to me to carry it to an absurd extreme. I was rather relieved to open the Winter 1994 *Journal of Economic Perspectives* and find the following statement by Robert Solow:

> Maybe I reveal myself as merely old-fashioned, but I see no redeeming social value in using this construction, which Ramsey intended as a

representation of the decision-making of an idealized policy-maker, as if it were a descriptive model of an industrial capitalist economy.

(1994: 29)

While the functional savings relationships to which this assumption leads may turn out to be quite reasonable, I do not believe that the Ramsey formulation has a particular claim on our attention as an explanation of savings behaviour. If highly calculated intertemporal behaviour is going on, then it seems much more likely to be about investment than about savings. I therefore retain below the simple proportional savings function.

One of the contributions of the new growth theory has been the elaboration of the idea of endogenous technical progress. Suppose again that there is labour-augmenting technical progress:

$$Y = F(K, AL) = A\,Lf(K/AL) \tag{5}$$

but that it is generated by learning by doing, as developed by Arrow (1962). Where the productivity of labour, A, increases with past experience, and past experience is measured by the integral of past gross investment, and there is no depreciation of capital, then A is equal to K, and the production function becomes:

$$Y = K\,Lf(1/L) \equiv K/v. \tag{6}$$

The production function for society, not the individual firm, becomes one in which there are constant returns to scale in K, and I have written the capital–output ratio as v. The fragility of the model's behaviour with respect to this assumption of constant returns to scale in K should be stressed (see Solow (1994)).

In this model, a constant savings rate, s, generates a constant rate of growth of output and capital, equal to

$$dK/dt/K = s\,Y/K = s/v. \tag{7}$$

This is deliberately written to be reminiscent of the Harrodian warranted growth rate. In the Harrod model, there was perceived to be a tension between the warranted rate, determined by savings behaviour, and the rate of growth of the labour force (here zero). What this simple endogenous growth model offers is a resolution of the Harrodian tension through the fact that adding to capital also makes labour more productive through learning by doing.

The model implies that, starting from any arbitrary initial capital stock and labour force, the economy enters immediately into steady state growth. This is shown in Figure 2, which is similar to that in the Solow model, although the causality is different. Rather than the exogenous growth rate determining the steady state capital–labour ratio, now the initial factor endowment determines the capital–output ratio and hence the rate of growth. But in both cases the factor shares are determined. The only point that we have to note

211

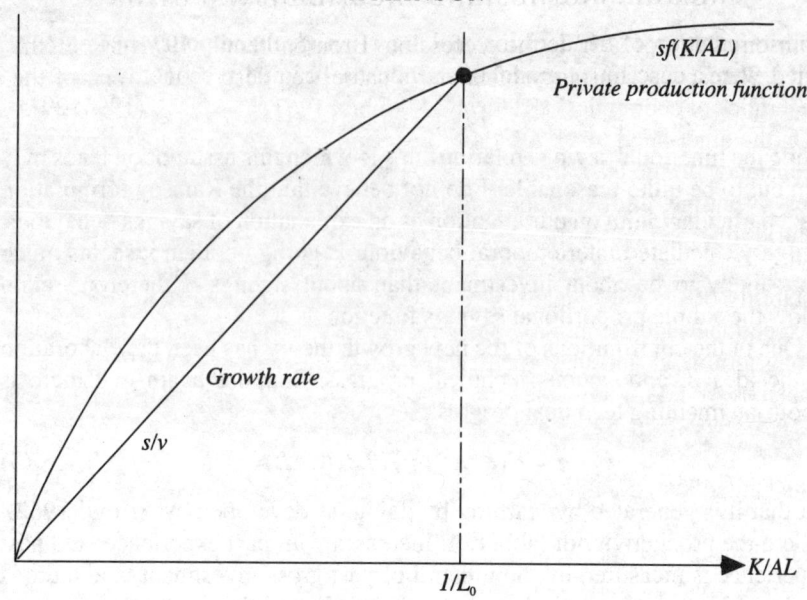

Figure 2 Endogenous growth model

is that the return to capital is the *private* return. The wage is equal to the marginal product of labour, and the shares depend on the production function. In the case of Cobb–Douglas, the share of profit is again $(1 - \beta)$. There is, however, a difference, in that the economy is immediately in steady state, so that it is not just with the Cobb–Douglas that the shares are constant over time. If factor shares are changing over time, then this cannot be explained within the context of the immediate steady growth model.

STYLIZED FACTS

What of the empirical evidence? I referred earlier to the 'stylized fact' of the constancy over time of factor shares. Such facts are notoriously brittle. In the United Kingdom, Bowley's Law of the constancy of relative shares was espoused enthusiastically by Keynes in a well-known quotation:

> The stability of the proportion of the national dividend accruing to labour is one of the most surprising yet best-established facts in the whole range of economic statistics. It is the stability of this ratio for each country which is chiefly remarkable, and this appears to be a long-run, and not merely a short-run phenomenon.

> (1939: 48)

The constancy later formed one of the celebrated stylized facts of Kaldor (1961), and the failure to explain Bowley's Law was described by Joan

212

Robinson as a 'reproach' to the profession (Bronfenbrenner 1971: 81). In the United States, the constancy of labour's share was described as one of the 'great ratios of economics' (Klein and Kosobud 1961).

On the other hand, there are those who have cast doubt on the hypothesis of constancy. In the US, Kravis suggested that the share of labour was slowly rising over time, and Kuznets concluded from examination of a number of countries that

> stability of the wage share in the United Kingdom, if present, was an exceptional and temporary phenomenon ... [in the US there was] a long-term rise; and that long-term stability of the wage share has not been observed for any other country.

(1959: 56)

In the United Kingdom, Matthews *et al.* reached yet another conclusion:

> Over the whole period 1856–1973 there was a significant shift of income from property to labour.... The whole of this substantial rise is accounted for by two abrupt jumps during and immediately after each of the two world wars.... In general, movements within peacetime periods were much less important.

(1982: 163–5)

It is not my intention here to get into the details of the statistics. Part of the disagreements, for example, stem from the fact that some authors, such as Keynes, were referring to the share of 'wages', rather than 'wages and salaries', which I take here. Another difference is in the treatment of the income of the self-employed. Here I simply assume that self-employment income is divided between labour and capital in the same way as other income. There is also the issue of the appropriate adjustment for inflation, for which no correction is made in these figures.

The share of labour on this basis is shown in Figure 3 for the United Kingdom (the labour share is measured on the left-hand axis). It covers the postwar period, so that the large changes referred to by Matthews *et al.* (1982) do not enter the picture. It is not my intention here to attempt to test for the constancy, or otherwise, of the factor shares, but it is apparent from simple inspection of the graph that there are going to be problems in drawing definite conclusions about the long-run behaviour. One could note that the share was the same in 1992 as in 1971 and 1952, and tell a story according to which the share is constant, but rose abnormally in the mid-1970s and fell abnormally in the mid-1980s. On the other hand, taking the last eighteen years on their own, one could tell a story of the share cycling about a downward trend from the peak in 1975, with a fall and then a rise in the 1980s. Even with forty-four years of data, the next few observations could change the way in which we view the world.

213

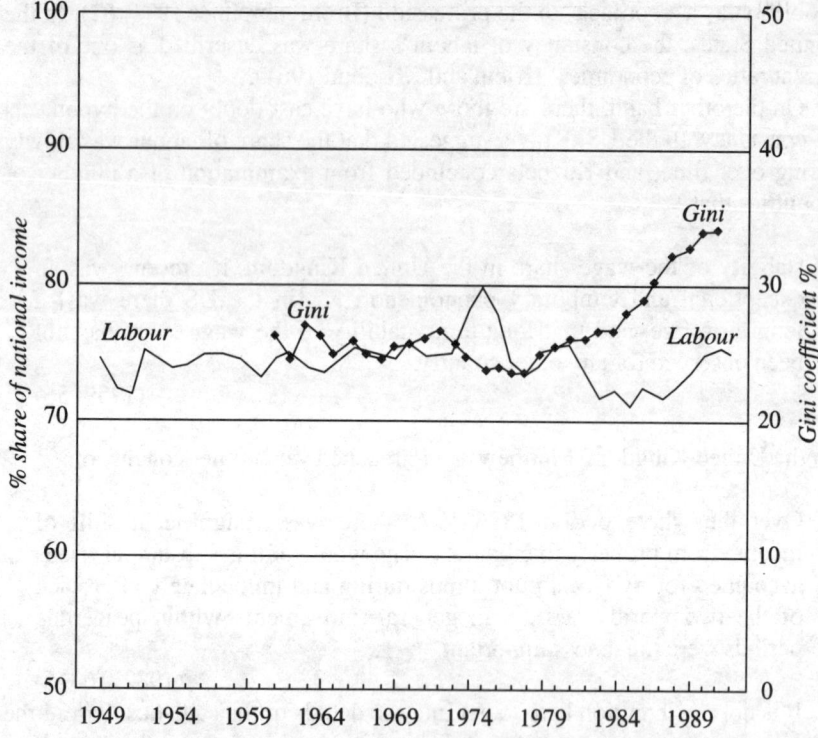

Figure 3 Labour share and Gini coefficient in the United Kingdom
Sources: Labour share calculated as the ratio of income from employment to (gross domestic product minus income from self-employment); incomes are calculated after providing for stock appreciation but before depreciation; gross domestic product is before adjustment for statistical discrepancy:

  1971–1992 from Central Statistical Office (1993: Table 1.4)
  1967–1970 from Central Statistical Office (1989: Table 1.3)
  1962–1966 from Central Statistical Office (1984: Table 1.3)
  1956–1961 from Central Statistical Office (1978: Table 1.2)
  1949–1955 from Central Statistical Office (1971: Table 1).

Figures for 1949–1955 *before* providing for stock appreciation, linked to later series using the figures for 1956 on both bases.
Gini coefficient: 1961–1991 for equivalent household disposable income, with person weights, from Goodman and Webb (1994: A2 (BHC)).

A STATISTICAL NON-FACT

Rather than applying the more rigorous statistical tests of constancy of factor shares which are necessary, I want here instead to draw attention to the absence of any apparent relationship between factor shares and the personal distribution of income. In Figure 3 is also plotted (on the right-hand axis) the movements in the Gini coefficient for the inequality of the distribution of disposable income (indicated by symbols). There was an

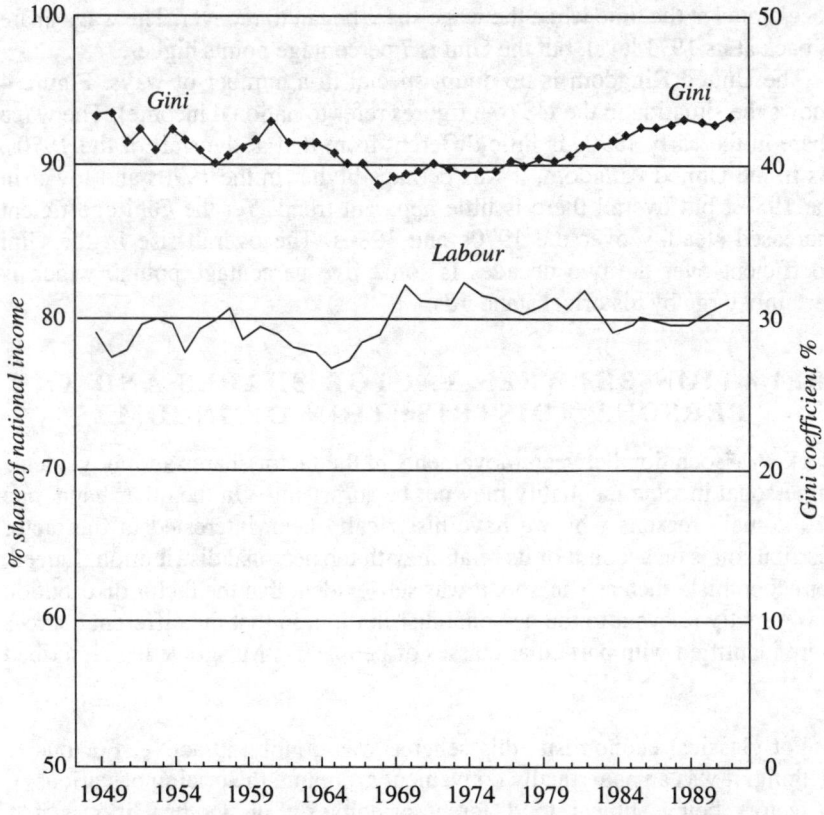

Figure 4 Labour share and Gini coefficient in the United States
Sources: Labour share calculated as ratio of compensation of employees to (national income –
proprietors' income); incomes are calculated with inventory valuation and capital consumption
adjustments,
    1959–1992 from US Government (1994: Table B-25)
    1949–1958 from US Government (1991: Table B-24)
Gini coefficient: 1947–1967 for family (excluding unrelated individuals) gross income,
unadjusted for family size, with family weights, from Nelson (1994: Table 2.1). 1967–1992 for
household gross income, unadjusted for household size, with household weights, from US
Department of Commerce (1993: Table B-3).
Earlier series linked to later series by multiplying by ratio of values for 1967.

episode of declining inequality in the 1970s, when the labour share first
rose and then fell. Over the 1980s, when the labour share first fell then
rose, inequality increased, with a particularly sharp rise post-1985. The
Gini coefficient is only one index of inequality, but other indicators, such
as the decile shares, show a similar pattern (Goodman and Webb 1994).

What is striking is the lack of apparent relation between these two series.
One might naively expect a rise in the share of wages to be associated with
a fall in the Gini coefficient. But, although the wage share fell in the early
1980s when inequality began to rise, the worsening of the Gini coefficient

215

accelerated at the time when the wage share began to recover. The wage share is back at its 1971 level, but the Gini is 7 percentage points higher.

The United Kingdom is no doubt special in a number of ways. Figure 4 shows the situation in the US (the figures refer to national income). The wage share in the early 1990s is little different from that at the start of the 1970s. As in the United Kingdom, it was perhaps higher in the 1970s and lower in the 1980s, but overall there is little apparent trend. Yet the Gini coefficient increased steadily over the 1970s and 1980s. The overall rise in the Gini coefficient over the two decades is some five percentage points, which is certainly large by historical standards.

RELATION BETWEEN FACTOR SHARES AND THE PERSONAL DISTRIBUTION OF INCOME

Lack of association between movements in the factor shares and movements in personal income inequality may not be surprising. On the other hand, one of the main reasons why we have historically been interested in the factor distribution is on account of its relation with the personal distribution. Indeed, for economists such as Ricardo, it was self-evident that the factor distribution was directly relevant to the personal distribution, in that the different sources were identified with particular classes of people. As Musgrave has described it,

> For classical economists, this scheme was doubly attractive. For one thing, it was an analytically convenient grouping, the pricing of various factors being subject to different principles. For another, it was a socially relevant grouping, as the division of society into capitalists, landlords, and workers gave a fair picture of social stratification in the England of the early nineteenth century.
>
> (1959: 223)

Today, however, this schema is scarcely adequate. There are six major reasons why a theory of factor income distribution does not in itself provide a theory of personal distribution.

Heterogeneity of incomes

The first reason is the need to explain the distribution of factor incomes *within* classes, such as the size distribution of wages. This is particularly relevant in seeking to explain the recent trend in income inequality. In the United Kingdom, there is plain evidence of widening differentials in the distribution of wage income: for men, the real earnings of the bottom decile grew by 11% between 1983 and 1992, compared with 29% for the median, and 51% for the top decile (OECD 1993: 164). The same is true in the United States (Levy and

Murnane 1992), although it is not universal, since there are countries in which one finds little evidence of widening dispersion.

Human capital

Part of the explanation of changes in the earnings distribution is to be found in human capital. The production function considered so far incorporates physical capital, but not human capital, that is the investment which people make in themselves in the form of education, training or other activities which raise their productivity. Human capital has been a leading feature of the new growth theory, which has drawn attention to the fact that part of the share of wages represents a return to this form of investment. The empirical work of Mankiw *et al.* (1992), for example, leads them to conclude that L^β should be replaced in the Cobb–Douglas production function by $(HL)^{\beta/2}$, so that half the share of wages is attributable to human capital.

Diversity of sources

Rather than people being identified with a single source of income, they now receive income from a range of sources, so that one individual may be in receipt of wages, interest income, and rent (for example through owning a house). A worker is not simply reliant on wages. This diversity of sources is in part associated with different stages of the individual life-cycle. In the early stages of adulthood, people may largely depend on wage income, and may borrow to finance housing and other capital purchases, but as they get older acquire savings which provide an increasing source of income, especially after retirement. The diversity of sources means that we cannot draw any direct implications for the personal distribution from observations of changes in factor prices. It is tempting to assume that a rise in the wage share benefits the lower part of the income distribution. This was the thinking underlying Figures 4 and 5. But a rise in the wage share may benefit those currently in work at the expense, in part, of those who are retired. If pensioners are to be found at the bottom of the personal income distribution, then the poorest may lose in relative terms. Capital income may accrue particularly to the elderly, whose total current income may be below-average – a far remove from the capitalist or *rentier* envisaged by classical economists. The net impact on the current distribution is unclear, to say nothing of the difficulty of calculating the effect in terms of lifetime incomes.

Intervening institutions

The production model referred to above does not explicitly allow for the existence of institutions such as corporations, financial intermediaries or pension funds, which stand between the production side of the economy and the receipt of household incomes. Corporations modify the links between returns to factors and the incomes received. The company receives profits, part of which are paid out in dividends, but part is retained for further investment. Personal incomes are not equal to profits but to dividends plus capital gains, which may be a different amount. A second class of intermediaries consists of pension funds. They own shares, real property, and other assets, receiving the income from these assets and paying it out, or accumulating it, on behalf of the members of the pension schemes. The importance of such intermediaries is illustrated by the pattern of ownership of company shares. In the United Kingdom there has been a long-term decline in the proportion of shares belonging directly to individuals. In 1963 individuals owned 54% of United Kingdom ordinary shares; by 1992 this had declined to 21.3% (Hofmann and Lambert 1993: Table 1), with 34.7% of United Kingdom ordinary shares owned by pension funds, and 16.5% by insurance companies (the next largest holding – 12.8% – was by overseas residents). The existence of this kind of intervening institution means that we have to allow for private transfers as a source of personal income which has no counterpart in national income.

Income from abroad

Individuals and companies receive income from abroad, and make payments abroad. This applies to individual earnings and self-employment, but is particularly important for the corporate sector, where companies operate in many countries and receive profit income from subsidiaries, and for the ownership of foreign securities, whether bonds or equities. In the United Kingdom corporate sector, income from abroad net of profits due abroad rose from 6.5% of domestic income in 1979 to 13.8% in 1989 (Central Statistical Office 1993: Table 3.2). The flows are both ways: as we have just seen, overseas residents own a sizeable fraction of United Kingdom ordinary shares.

Impact of the state budget

Taxes, transfers, interest on the national debt, the financing of nationalized industries, and their privatization, all influence the personal distribution of income. The gross incomes generated by production are typically modified by taxation, used to finance public spending, including transfers which constitute a fifth source of personal incomes. The state may in part finance spending through borrowing, and the national debt adds to the range of assets which may be held by the personal sector. Interest on the national debt is a source of income which again has no counterpart on the production side.

The elements outlined above are illustrated in Figure 5, which sets out

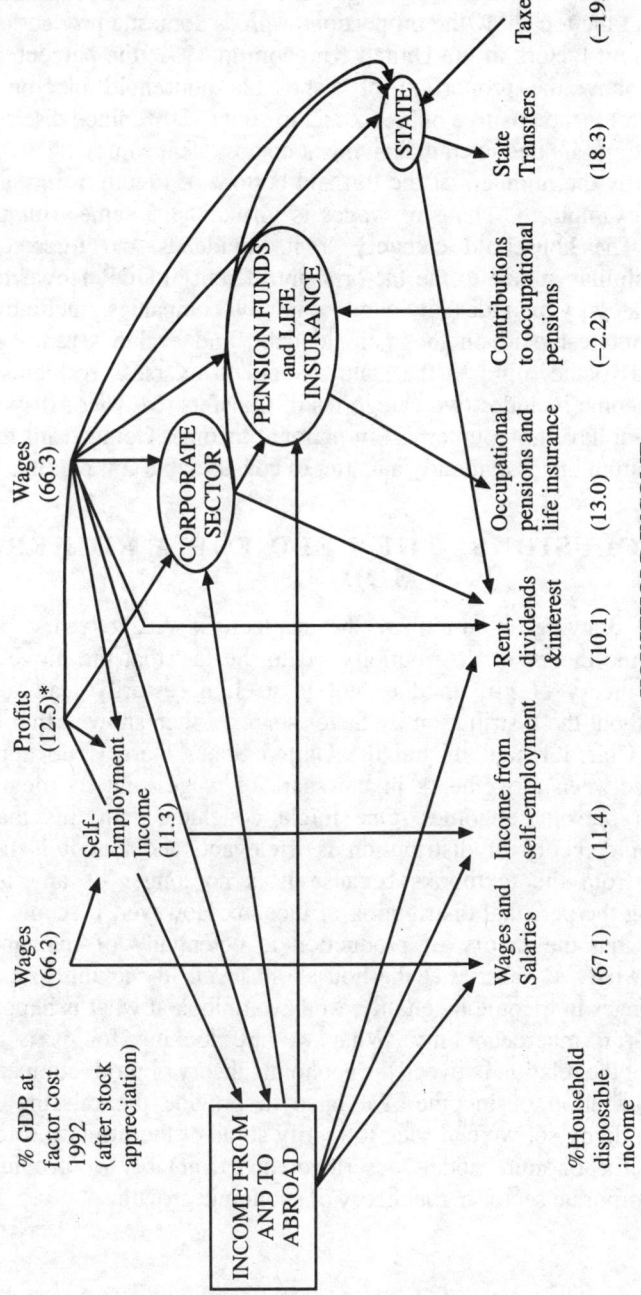

PRODUCTION

HOUSEHOLD INCOME

Figure 5 Links between factor and personal distributions of income

Sources (a) %GDP from Central Statistical Office (1993), Table 1.4. Omitted category is imputed charge for consumption of non-trading capital.
(b) % household income from Central Statistical Office (1993), Table 4.9. Omitted category (1.8%) is income in kind.

Note: *Excluding part accruing to self-employed.

schematically the links between the factor and personal distributions of income (although it does not distinguish explicitly human capital). The percentages at the top show the proportion of gross domestic product (GDP) paid to different factors in the United Kingdom in 1992; the percentages at the bottom show the proportion of disposable household income from different sources (the positive numbers add to some 120%, since direct taxes and contributions are deducted in arriving at disposable income).

Superficially the numbers at the top and bottom of Figure 5 may appear similar: for example the share of wages is virtually the same. But this is misleading. The household category 'rent, dividends and interest', for instance, is similar in size to the factor share of rent in GDP. However, the household category includes dividends paid by companies, income from abroad and interest paid on the national debt, and excludes rent paid to pension funds or accruing to the state or paid to overseas residents. The household income includes two categories of transfers (31.3% of disposable income) which have no counterpart in national income. Going from the top line to the bottom line is evidently a matter of considerable complexity.

CONCLUSIONS: THE NEED FOR A RICHER MODEL

I began by drawing attention to the neglect in recent years of the macroeconomic theory of distribution, and to the fact that the move to an endogenous theory of growth does not in itself necessarily lead to new predictions about the distribution by factor shares. I then showed that in the case of the United Kingdom and the United States there is no apparent association between movements in the share of wages and the degree of inequality of personal incomes. One might conclude from this that the macroeconomic theory of distribution is irrelevant, and that it is largely disappeared from the textbooks because it is no longer of any use in understanding the personal distribution of income. However, it seems to me indisputable that the theory of production is potentially of relevance in interpreting what we observe at the household level. In seeking to explain long-run changes in income inequality, we have to look at what is happening to the long-run macroeconomy. What we are looking for is a richer explanation of the relation between the economic theory of production and the personal distribution of income. We have to provide the missing links. Moreover, in doing so, we can seek to rectify some of the limitations of the long-run macroeconomic models described earlier, notably by providing a role for the corporate sector in the theory of economic growth.

NOTE

1 This chapter draws on material developed at greater length in my Caffè Lectures given in Rome, April 1994 (Atkinson, forthcoming).

REFERENCES

Atkinson, A. B. (forthcoming) *Caffè Lectures*, Cambridge: Cambridge University Press.

Begg, D., Fischer, S. and Dornbusch, R. (1994) *Principles of Economics*, Maidenhead: McGraw-Hill.

Blanchard, O. J. and Fischer, S. (1989) *Lectures on Macroeconomics*, Cambridge, Mass.: MIT Press.

Bronfenbrenner, M. (1971) *Income Distribution Theory*, London: Macmillan.

Burda, M. and Wyplosz, C. (1993) *Macroeconomics*, Oxford: Oxford University Press.

Central Statistical Office (1971) *National Income and Expenditure 1971*, London: HMSO.

——— (1978) *National Income and Expenditure 1967–77*, London: HMSO.

——— (1984) *United Kingdom National Accounts 1984*, London: HMSO.

——— (1989) *United Kingdom National Accounts 1989*, London: HMSO.

——— (1993a) *Family Spending 1992*, London: HMSO.

——— (1993b) *United Kingdom National Accounts 1993*, London: HMSO.

Goodman, A. and Webb, S. (1994) 'For richer, for poorer,' Institute for Fiscal Studies, Commentary No. 42, London.

Hall, R. E. and Taylor, J. B. (1993) *Macroeconomics*, fourth edn, New York: W.W. Norton.

Hofmann, E. and Lambert, S. (1993) 'The 1993 share register survey', *Economic Trends*, 480: 124–9.

Kaldor, N. (1957) 'A model of economic growth', *Economic Journal*, 67: 591–624.

——— (1961) 'Capital accumulation and economic growth', in Lutz, F. A. and Hague, D. C. (eds) *The Theory of Capital*, London: Macmillan.

Klein, L. R. and Kosobud, R. F. (1961) 'Some econometrics of growth: great ratios of economics', *Quarterly Journal of Economics*, 75: 173–98.

Kuznets, S. (1955) 'Economic growth and income inequality', *American Economic Review*, 45: 1–28.

——— (1959) 'Quantitative aspects of the economic growth of nations: IV. Distribution of national income by factor shares', *Economic Development and Cultural Change*, 7 (April): Part II, 1–100.

Levy, F. and Murnane, R. J. (1992) 'U.S. earnings levels and earnings inequality: a review of recent trends and proposed explanations', *Journal of Economic Literature*, 30: 1333–81.

Mankiw, N. G. (1994) *Macroeconomics*, New York: Worth.

———, Romer, D. and Weil, D. (1992) 'A contribution to the empirics of economic growth', *Quarterly Journal of Economics*, 107: 407–37.

Matthews, R. C. O., Feinstein, C. H. and Odling-Smee, J. C. (1982) *British Economic Growth 1856–1973*, Oxford: Clarendon Press.

Musgrave, R. A. (1959) *The Theory of Public Finance*, New York: McGraw-Hill.

Nelson, C. T. (1994) 'Levels and changes in the distribution of U.S. income', in J. H. Bergstrand *et al.* (eds), *The Changing Distribution of Income in an Open U.S. Economy*, Amsterdam: Elsevier Science.

OECD (1993) 'Earnings inequality: changes in the 1980s', Chapter 5, *Employment Outlook, 1993*.

Ricardo, D. (1951) *The Works and Correspondence of David Ricardo*, ed. P. Sraffa, Cambridge: Cambridge University Press, Vol. VIII.

Sargent, T.J. (1987) *Macroeconomic Theory*, New York: Academic Press.

Solow, R. M. (1956) 'A contribution to the theory of economic growth', *Quarterly Journal of Economics*, 70: 65–94.

—— (1994) 'Perspectives on growth theory', *Journal of Economic Perspectives*, 8: 45–54.

US Department of Commerce (1993) *Money Income of Households, Families, and Persons in the United States: 1992*, Current Population Reports, Series P-60, No. 184, Washington D.C.

US Government (1991) *Economic Report of the President*, Washington, D.C.: United States Government Printing Office.

—— (1994) *Economic Report of the President*, Washington D.C.: United States Government Printing Office.

18

PROVISIONAL EQUILIBRIUM AND MACROECONOMIC THEORY

Victoria Chick and Maurizio Caserta

It hardly needs saying that a concept so central to economics as equilibrium would be a subject to which Geoff Harcourt would have devoted much deep thought. It is therefore with some trepidation that we offer this paper in his honour. It can be seen as a contribution to the way of doing economics known in Cambridge, perhaps because Newmarket is so close by, as 'horses for courses'.

INTRODUCTION

Despite calls to abolish the use of equilibrium in economic theorizing (Kaldor 1972, 1985; Kornai 1971), it remains a central organizing principle in economics. Yet equilibrium is defined by the establishment of a variety of conditions: the equality of supply and demand, the coordination of choice, the self-enforcement of agreements, the meeting of expectations (rational or otherwise), constancy of variables or of their rate of change, equality of profits, confirmation of theory. It is hardly surprising to find that these different meanings can give rise to substantial misunderstandings.[1] Corresponding to these meanings are diverse contexts: the theory of exchange, non-cooperative games, the theory of production, employment, capacity utilization, capital accumulation, portfolio balance.

For the purpose of the present paper we group equilibria into two sets, which we shall call final equilibria and provisional equilibria. We argue that the latter class should be the norm in economics, on the grounds that the economy is an open system, constantly evolving, and that the equilibria which we label provisional are consistent with the modelling of such processes, while final equilibria are not.[2]

The paper's not-very-hidden agendum is to alter the perception that provisional equilibria are in some way imperfect, not *really* equilibria at all, and that only final equilibria should be taken seriously. Our view, *per contra*, is that finding final equilibria is a challenging but ultimately futile intellectual game and only provisional equilibria are suitable for use in economic models.

The class of provisional equilibria is already known to all of us, as you will see from the examples which will constitute the body of the paper, but it has not been identified as a class, or given a name, still less a robust justification. Most of the paper is devoted to putting familiar concepts into the present context. We first characterize the two classes of equilibria. Before illustrating our distinction with the work of Marshall, Keynes, Harrod and post-Keynesian growth theory, there is a need to make another distinction, between theory which only considers equilibrium and theory which can comprehend disequilibrium states, although organized around an equilibrium concept. Under post-Keynesian growth theory the new concept of the medium term is introduced. It develops, further than the other examples, the notion that change can be endogenous to theory without being entirely co-opted into an equilibrium framework.

It should be noted that it is not our purpose to give an exhaustive account. There are many types of equilibrium which others know better than we do and which they may wish to place in this framework for themselves.

TWO TYPES OF EQUILIBRIA

Final equilibria are those after which the economy may replicate its activities, but there are no further changes. It is a class of teleological positions, toward which the economy is either portrayed as 'tending', or for the discovery of which it is waiting,[3] while all activity is suspended. The classic example of the former is the neo-Ricardian concept of equi-profit equilibrium, which has been called 'the economists' equivalent of the physicists' concept of universal heat death' (Chick 1996): that position implies that all capital has found its 'right place', no firms will grow or decline, no new industries will be founded, competition is over because there are no further gains from it. There is nowhere to go, nothing to learn, no scope for innovation or further evolution. The only saving grace is that this is only a position towards which the economy is supposed to be moving; there is no necessity ever to arrive.

The same dismal prospect characterizes neo-Walrasian equilibrium; in fact it is worse, for here there is no travelling, only arrival: it is equilibrium or nothing. Until the equilibrium price vector is found, no trades or production take place; we must wait for equilibrium before we are 'permitted' to do anything. But once equilibrium is found, all trades, including insurance for dated contingencies in the future, are settled.[4] Again, there is nowhere to go, nothing to do. There are no experiments, no leaps into the unknown; no tears, but no joy either.

The second category of equilibria we call provisional equilibrium. Both the characterization of the equilibrium itself and the position of equilibrium in theorizing is much more pragmatic in this category. These are equilibria which serve a particular, limited theoretical purpose. There are examples of this approach in the physical sciences: the equilibrium of a pendulum is a local concept which does not require that the whole of the rest of the world has come to an end – a final equilibrium if ever there was one. If the pendulum is in equilibrium while the rest of the world continues to be in flux we have (local) equilibrium within (global) disequilibrium. The pendulum's equilibrium is provisional. It can easily be appreciated that literally all the problems which exercise human interest and attention have to do with less-than-final states of equilibrium, or with disequilibrium.

The difference between the pendulum and the provisional equilibrium we wish to discuss is that once the pendulum reaches equilibrium it will stay there unless disturbed by an exogenous shock, whereas the constructions for which provisional equilibrium provides a reference point model situations which may eventually be transformed, but the very decisions which bring about a provisional equilibrium, into something else, with a new provisional equilibrium. In other words, the shock may be endogenous. It is the reference to a system which contains in it the seeds of its own development and change that is the force of the word provisional. Thus provisional equilibrium is consistent with innovation, learning and evolution.

EQUILIBRIUM AND CHANGE

Equilibrium implies a stable position of rest, or constant motion. Change is a particularly difficult matter in the context of final equilibrium. It has been handled in one of two different ways. It can either be exogenous, disrupting the equilibrium, or entirely expected and thus absorbed within the logic of equilibrium. When it is exogenous, which implies that it is unknown, a sharp discontinuity is introduced; all activities are suspended until a new equilibrium is found. This is the world of comparative statics. Comparative static analysis, however, does not offer any indication as to how the system moves from one equilibrium to another, or whether the system can make that transition at all.

At the other extreme, change confined to what is known and predictable can also be associated with the notion of final equilibrium. It becomes part of the equilibrium itself. The concept of equilibrium may shift from being a point of rest to a steady rate of change (Dore 1984–85). We know this as comparative dynamics, in which, one cannot fail to notice, change has been deprived of its novelty.

Clearly, an external shock could equally disrupt a moving equilibrium. Therefore, conditions for equilibrium, both in its static and in its dynamic version, are either perfectly realized or non-existent.

By contrast, we argue, in the context of which provisional equilibrium is a part, change does not have to conform to one of the two extremes where it is either entirely unknown and unexpected, or entirely known and expected. Between these two extremes lie a number of possibilities where change

225

preserves its novelty but at the same time is not entirely unexpected. These possibilities introduce a measure of continuity in the evolution of the economic system, without ruling out different responses to the emergence of change.

Thus provisional equilibrium is compatible with evolution, that is, with endogenous change. However, there will always be a tension between equilibrium and change, which arises because equilibrium by definition describes a position of rest or a steady path of change, yet there are dynamic forces propelling the system to deviate from this position, or path-forces which disrupt the equilibrium. The forces for change may be exogenous or endogenous; they may be generated by learning or may simply result from the passage of time. Yet it takes time to learn, and even the effects of the passage of time may themselves take time to become significant. Change is not necessarily continuous, and it certainly need not be modelled as if it were continuous. Change may be forestalled by the costs of implementation or by the sheer force of inertia, which in terms of human decision-making is usefully described as the maintenance of conventions. Yet conventions change, and the causes of a change in conventions (what we characterize later as rupture) can be the object of theory.

THEORY WITH AN EQUILIBRIUM AND EQUILIBRIUM THEORY

At the outset an important distinction must be made between theories which have an equilibrium result and theories whose only purpose is to identify and characterize an equilibrium. The second we call equilibrium theory. The two types of final equilibrium discussed above are the product of theory of this type. So is the microeconomic, partial-equilibrium theory of supply and demand: as Joan Robinson was so fond of telling us, only the equilibrium point, where supply equals demand, 'exists', and there is no way to get into equilibrium; one has to be in it from the Fall of Adam or not at all (Robinson 1978a; see also Robinson 1974).

Some economists are quite content to make only equilibrium statements: for example, neo-Ricardians are fond of saying that if one is not analysing the 'long run', one is not doing theory at all. By long run they mean the final equilibrium toward which the economy is supposed to be tending. To them, nothing else is worth the intellectual effort. Despite this, in neo-Ricardian theory there is a plausible story about the approach to equilibrium. This is true even though this long run has nothing to do with time; they say that the long run exists 'now' and at all times. It is a reference point 'located' out of time. Yet all the imagery is 'timeful': quasi-rents will be equalized by the process of competition, and a process necessarily operates through time.

The same combination of static theory and timeful verbal argument is found wherever comparative statics are used. The purpose is to suggest applicability of a static technique to the real world, where the past is given and the future is unknown. Yet we have it on high authority (Samuelson 1947) that the dynamics attaching to static theory must be 'added on'; this is the correspondence principle. It is another way of saying that statics are equilibrium theory – that no disequilibrium 'exists'.

Some theory is, of course, dynamic. But here too there are important distinctions to be made. First, there is the dynamic theory in which the entire path, from initial conditions to (equilibrium) conclusion, is given by the theory. If the limit of that process is defined as the equilibrium, then the fact that the path of, say, the accelerator or the Harrod model may be studied takes these theories outside equilibrium theory, even though each of these theories has an equilibrium. By contrast, Joan Robinson's (1956) 'ages' (Golden, Leaden, etc.), are (ironically) pure equilibrium theory.

This type of dynamics is often called mechanical, though it applies equally well to the seed giving rise to the plant. What is meant is that there is no room for learning. A second class of dynamic theories allows for learning. The rules for learning may be included in the theory, so that questions of convergence to equilibrium (where equilibrium is defined as a steady state or limit cycle) can be asked. When the problem of convergence is considered, at one level we have left the realm of equilibrium theory.

However, as Loasby (1991) has brought out, there is another level, a way of defining equilibrium, suggested by Hahn (1973), which takes us back into the realm of equilibrium theory. Hahn proposes to define equilibrium as the situation in which 'the economy' is giving agents signals which do not cause agents to alter their theory (Hahn 1973: 59). The theory encompasses rules for learning: Hahn specifies Bayesian updating rules for agents' forecasts. This kind of learning, the rules for which are predetermined, is thus consistent with his concept of equilibrium. Whether we have equilibrium theory or not is thus a question of the level at which we specify equilibrium.

Hahn's framework cannot encompass what Shackle (1949) calls the crucial decision, that which irreversibly changes the situation in which the decision was originally made, and changes it not toward something predetermined about which the subject 'learns' but into something new and perhaps quite unexpected. *A fortiori*, learning which is creative is excluded, since by definition it does not conform to rules.

The crucial decision need not require the creative choice, however: a decision made according to rule may still be crucial. An investment decision made by formula and simply expanding capacity using existing technique is, in a world without free disposal, just as much a crucial decision, as irreversible and environment-altering, as something involving more interesting thought processes and risks. The creative act and the crucial decision are fundamental to economic evolution. By reason of their intractability, they are the areas least attended to in economic theory.

227

PROVISIONAL EQUILIBRIUM ELABORATED

Nested equilibria

We have seen that the same theory can be regarded as equilibrium theory or not, depending on the level at which equilibrium is defined. Equilibrium as market clearing is nested within the concept of equilibrium as a position of rest. Similarly, equilibrium as a stationary state is a subset of equilibrium as steady state. Both of these are defined at the level of the variables, the results of economic decisions. They are contained, along with other possibilities, by what we shall refer to as a Hahn equilibrium, while a Hahn equilibrium would be destroyed by creative action. Thus, short of final equilibrium there are some outcomes which we describe as equilibrium at one level and dis-equilibrium at another. Since whether or not we are entitled to call something equilibrium depends on where in these nested sets of concepts we decide to locate, any definition short of final equilibrium can be regarded as provisional.

In economics, equilibrium is a concept which is constructed for a theoretical purpose. Economic theory is faced with enormous complexity, especially, but not exclusively, to do with time and openness. Complexity is made manageable by imposing constraints on what adjustments are allowed and what can reasonably be kept constant. A familiar example is Marshallian periods.

Marshallian periods

Marshallian periods are a method of dealing with continuous economic processes by discontinuous means, with processes which occur in time by static means which are out of time. Each period, and its associated equilibrium, is defined with respect to constraints which are appropriate to the study of a particular problem. The market period is appropriate to the study of exchange, the short period to production, and the long period to capital accumulation.

Periods are the construct of the theorist, though they bear some relationship to reality – particularly the reality of the passage of time. The market period is constrained by the assumption of a fixed output. Equilibrium is defined as market clearing and adjustment is through variations in prices.

The period being at the choice of the theorist, it can be changed at will. However, there is a timeful connection between these periods. A market day is one of a succession of days, over which, depending on market outcomes or other forecasts, agents may decide to vary their output or even the capital devoted to producing the output. Changing capital takes even more time and more confidence than changing output, by reason of both the cost and the irreversibility of capital decisions.

When output is allowed to change, we are in the short period, with a new equilibrium, achieved by adjustment of price and new output. The market equilibrium was provisional on the constraints imposed by the theorist. It is overturned when the constraints of the market period are released. The short period is itself constrained, this time by the assumption of a fixed capital stock. When the capital stock is allowed to change, we are in the long period. Long-period industry equilibrium is characterized by a continual growth and decay of firms while maintaining normal profits throughout.[5]

The General Theory

As is well known, *The General Theory* (Keynes 1936) also uses the Marshallian device of periods. The bulk of the book, concerned as it is with output and employment, takes place in the short period. (One always produces with the capital already in one's possession, for even if new capital is coming on stream, it is not yet productive.) Yet Keynes's short-period equilibrium, which adopts this assumption, was criticized (Leontief, Tobin) as not *really* being an equilibrium, for if investment is taking place, the capital stock is changing, and if a variable is changing, we are not in equilibrium. Most recently Rogers (1989) has adopted this view, arguing that if *The General Theory* is not a long-period story, it counts for little, since short-period equilibrium is temporary. This is a confusion of 'period' with 'run' – a distinction Geoff Harcourt has gone to great pains to insist upon. If the argument of this paper is accepted, Rogers's criticism is also misplaced as a search for a (the?) final equilibrium, where nothing less is acceptable.

In the hands of Keynes, the nearest equivalent of the market period[6] has been called by some interpreters (Chick 1983, Amadeo 1989) the production period. This is the period for which demand is forecast and the decision to produce is made; once made, it is irrevocable for the period. Both flows of new output and stocks of finished goods are available for sale; in this it differs from Marshall's market period.

If at the end of this period expectations are met, there is encouragement to make the same decision next period. But if demand is subject to fluctuation – as it surely is in Keynes (and in the world) – one observation will never be sufficient to confirm the status of the observation. Expectations could be met by a fluke, and disappointment of expectation is not necessarily a signal to change either output or price next period. Neither is there any cut-and-dried rule about the number of observations one would need; surely that would depend on the characteristics of the industry's demand, the costs of changing output, and the temperament of the producer.[7]

The short-period equilibrium is defined variously, but equivalently, by expectations of demand, sales or profits being met or by saving being equal to investment. The short period encompasses an indeterminate number of production periods. Keynes's short-period equilibrium has been identified as a type of temporary equilibrium (e.g. Bliss 1975). Hicks (1939) defined temporary equilibrium contingent on unaltered expectations, which in the *General Theory* context means both long-term expectations, so that the level of investment is constant, and short-period expectations, which govern the production decision. Temporary equilibrium is clearly a type of provisional equilibrium.[8]

Cost, investment and periods

Notice that we have introduced at least four reasons for provisional equilibrium: subjective inertia, cost, signal extraction and analytical convenience. We propose now to explore further the role of inertia based on cost. Let us return for a moment to Marshallian partial analysis, this time of short-run and long-run costs. At any time, even when a firm is maximizing short-period profits, it is supposed that there exist other possibilities of production, either larger scale or better technology, which would cut the costs of production and increase profits (the book of blueprints). In what sense, therefore, can we talk of short-period equilibrium, when opportunities remain unexploited?

Opportunities remain unexploited because investment is costly. Entrepreneurs have to be confident of the persistence of current levels of demand or expect rising demand for a period of time long enough to justify the extra expense. Whereas in Marshall, what is putting off the investment decision is left unexplained, in *The General Theory* the balance between unexpected benefits and costs is represented by long-term expectations and the rate of interest, respectively.[9]

Long-period equilibrium is not analysed by Keynes, except to ask whether the likely outcome of accumulation will result in saturation of the capital stock at or before the full-employment rate of saving (to which his answer was 'most likely, before'). We can reasonably infer that he considered the question of whether entrepreneurs' expectations of long-term profits would be realized (the long-period equivalent of his short-period equilibrium) to be irrelevant. The result would not guide entrepreneurs' future action, as the circumstances surrounding the investment decision would have changed. Thus 'progress' toward the neo-Ricardian final equilibrium depends, if it is to happen at all, on continual recalculation and the repeated exercise of animal spirits, in new and always uncertain circumstances. Convergence is far from guaranteed.

The *General Theory* system, therefore, utilizes a provisional short-period equilibrium to reach the key conclusion that unemployment can persist. The long-period analysis is also solely devoted to this question, concluding that unemployment is unlikely to be solved by further capital accumulation either. The path to long-period equilibrium is not sketched out in terms of producers' behaviour, and the purpose of the long-period analysis is focused on a single issue.

As just mentioned, in Keynes's analysis long-period expectations are exogenous and realized results offer no guide as to how long-period expectations should be determined or revised. Although in the shifting equilibrium model (Kregel 1976) long-period expectations are no longer fixed, there is still no assumption as to how long-period expectations might change following a disappointment in short-period expectations. In any case, much depends on subjective and capricious animal spirits – the exogenous element in Keynes's story. A theory of capital accumulation cannot be based on exogenous shocks, however important they may be in practice. One needs to have some means of evaluating investment projects incorporated into the model. This is the task of growth theory.

Post-Keynesian growth theory

Post-Keynesian growth theory shows that a theory of accumulation can be built on Keynesian foundations, not only in the sense that entrepreneurial propensities and expectations are given due consideration, but also in the sense that the provisional nature of equilibrium is brought to light.

Unlike Keynes, variations in actual, observed demand or capacity utilization as a means of evaluating investment projects play a major role in Harrod's knife-edge story.[10] There, decisions about the amount of investment depend heavily on the current level of output or degree of capacity utilization. However, no equilibrium rate of growth can be restored once the previous equilibrium is lost. Thus despite the explicit consideration of a mechanism whereby investment decisions can be revised, Harrod's model does not seem very satisfactory either, because the theory predicts an instability which is out of keeping with reality: 'it is an outstanding characteristic of the economic system in which we live that ... it is not violently unstable' (Keynes 1936: 249).

Keynes and Harrod represent therefore two extreme examples in the treatment of the relation between investment and demand: in Keynes's treatment investment is independent of current demand, while in Harrod's, investment depends too strongly on current demand, as is clear from the explosive path the economy can take after warranted equilibrium is lost. It is interesting to ask, then, given the inadequacy of both approaches, whether somewhere in between, a growth model based on the relation between investment and demand cannot be devised. This model should have an equilibrium where the demand generated by current investment is precisely at the level which warrants that investment.

Since we are dealing with growth, this theory would normally belong to the long period. But there are other associations with the long period, especially normal profits, which inhibited the search for this relationship (Caserta 1993). To free the analysis from these associations, it was decided to call the resulting equilibrium 'medium-term'. The advantage of the medium term lies in the possibility of separating long-term from medium-term motivations for investment. While long-term investment is related to the sustainable expected *rate* of growth of demand over time, medium-term investment is designed to create the correct initial conditions, that is, to alter the scale of capacity when it is still inappropriate to the current *level* of demand.

In order to make sense of this distinction one can think of capacity as made up of a certain number of units ('firms' or 'plants'). Each unit will grow at a particular rate, depending on various circumstances, but it is not necessarily true that the existing number of units is the correct one given the appropriate scale of the system as a whole. So at any given time the existing capacity will have to provide not only for the new capital equipment warranted by the growth potential of the economy, but also for the need to alter the number of capacity units in the economy.

To each of these two notions, long-term and medium-term motivations for investment, would be associated the two corresponding notions of long-term and medium-term profits and expectations. Long-term expectations concern the profitability of investment in conditions of normality, i.e. once capacity has completely adjusted to demand. Medium-term expectations concern the profitability of investment as a signal that current capacity is inappropriate to the level of demand. When capacity is adjusted to demand, these profits will be obviously equal to zero,[11] but since demand is, on post-Keynesian principles, a constraint, this medium-term equilibrium does not necessarily imply traditional long-period zero-profit equilibrium. If there is a shortage of capacity, supernormal profits will signal that more capacity is required; if there is excess capacity, lower than normal profits will signal that some capacity must be phased out.

Long-period normal profits, on the other hand, reflect the profits that can be gained once the correct initial conditions have been established. Higher normal profits will induce each individual capacity-unit to grow faster, but no additional unit will be considered necessary at any point in time. Similarly, lower normal profits will bring about slower growth, but no removal of excess capacity will be taken into consideration.

The first result of this separation is that now investment depends only partly on current demand: variations in demand affect only medium-term investment. The worst effects of the knife-edge would thus be avoided. The second result comes from the application of Keynes's procedure, as reconstructed by Kregel (1976), to a situation where the long-term–medium-term dichotomy is adopted. By assuming constant long-term expectations, an equilibrium rate of growth can be found, where only medium-term expectations have to be fulfilled. We obtain a model then where investment is made to depend in some specified way on current demand or capacity utilization and where, also, a mechanism exists for evaluating investment projects. An equilibrium rate of growth is shown to be compatible with a Keynesian investment demand, where it is investment which determines saving, and not the other way round.

That such an equilibrium is possible is shown in a body of literature on growth and capacity utilization which builds on Steindl's central theme,[12] i.e. the tendency of capitalist economies to stagnate at low levels of growth and a low degree of capacity utilization. With an investment function which depends on capacity utilization, and a saving function which depends on income and, hence, capacity utilization, an equilibrium is shown to exist where saving equals investment. Only by a fluke could this equilibrium imply a degree of capacity utilization equal to long-term normal capacity.

But can an equilibrium rate of growth be compatible with unadjusted capacity? The answer to this question, which was left unanswered in that body of literature, depends on what notion of equilibrium one has in mind. If what is referred to is final equilibrium, implying that all conflicts have been resolved and that what was there to be learned has been learned, the answer must be in the negative. Medium-term equilibrium implies that no checks are being carried out for long-term investment. The rate of profit which justifies long-term investment is not known yet. If, on the other hand, the preferred notion is that of provisional equilibrium, the answer is certainly in the positive. Such a notion of equilibrium does not confine change and evolution to the occurrence of exogenous events. On the contrary, change might develop from within as a result of the passage of time or of a process of learning, or as a result of the resolution of a previously contained conflict. This means that an equilibrium rate of growth with a constant other-than-normal degree of capacity utilization is a perfectly legitimate construct.

Provisional equilibria originate from the compatibility of some economic relations, while some parameters are kept constant. Equilibrium, therefore, is not presented as a state of perfect harmony: emphasis is placed on some crucial relation which helps explain the current state of order in the economic relations. When it comes to medium-term equilibrium, the crucial relations are those between investment and demand: the investment function and the multiplier effect. Equilibrium results from the coordination of these two relations: the current level of demand as reflected in the degree of capacity utilization turns out to be precisely that required by current investment. Investors realize that they have invested exactly the correct amount required by the current situation of excess capacity.

The preservation of this state of affairs hinges on the provisional suspension of the power of attraction of normal profits and normal utilization which guide long-term investment. It is not inconceivable that while capacity is being adjusted, generating an independent growth dynamics, judgement on the long-term investment plan is provisionally suspended, while investment is carried out according to some previous pattern. It is precisely this suspended judgement which makes this equilibrium possible and at the same time provisional.

While this equilibrium is being preserved, a process of learning is being carried out, concerning that part of investment appropriate to the long-term growth of the system. However, there can be nothing permanent in an equilibrium established on these foundations, for there must come a time when that process of learning is formalized and tested against reality. In the meantime, action is decided on a conventional basis, while attention is concentrated elsewhere: long-term investment is given and constant, while an equilibrium is established by making compatible a part of investment with the overall outcome of the system, as reflected in the degree of capacity utilization.

CONCLUSION

When equilibrium is conceived as provisional in nature it is easy to see that change need not be the result of an exogenous shock, but rather may emerge quite naturally from within the system. The idea that a system could be in equilibrium at one level and disequilibrium at another and contain contradictions which are the source of change is not, in fact, new: it was well expressed by Joan Robinson in 1962. The systems she had in mind were historical and causal, open systems:

> An economy may be in equilibrium from a short-period point of view and yet contain within itself incompatibilities that are soon going to knock it out of equilibrium ... Or it may be in equilibrium also from a long-period point of view so that the position will reproduce itself, or expand or contract in a smooth, regular manner, over the future, provided that no external disturbance occurs. The path that the model then follows appears exactly like the equilibrium path, but it is still an historical, causal story that has to be told – the economy follows the path because the expectations and behaviour reactions of its inhabitants are causing it to do so.
>
> (Robinson 1962: 26)

Change can be seen as the manifestation of what was previously hidden or 'locked in the pound of *ceteris paribus*'. It is as if something eventually comes to the surface after having travelled under water for some time. In fact one could argue that change is *always* the manifestation of what was previously under water. As Loasby put it, 'The distinction between incremental and discontinuous change is an imposed distinction. All change involves at least one discontinuity; no change obliterates the past' (1991: 19).

If this is the case, there is always some preparation for change going on. One can conveniently ignore it for the sake of analysis, but it would be unwise to forget it, or to assume that everybody else has forgotten it. This paper has provided a few examples of equilibria which allow for the possibility that some preparation for change is being made while equilibrium is preserved. These examples range from Marshall's market equilibrium to a non-traditional growth equilibrium, and include Keynes's short period. It has been

234

argued that what in all these examples is kept constant for the purpose of theory is not constant in actual fact. The fact that the implications of some changes are not admitted when constructing the model should not lead one to believe that these changes are exogenous. Provisional equilibria are analytical constructions which can handle change which is neither entirely exogenous nor entirely absorbed within the established equilibrium.

The use of equilibrium in economics has been attacked, often with great sophistication and power (Kornai, Kaldor, Loasby). But we submit that these attacks have been, quite properly, against final equilibrium and equilibrium theory. We hope that the distinctions drawn in this paper, between final and provisional equilibrium and between equilibrium theory and the uses of equilibrium in theories which can deal also with disequilibrium, will focus critical attention on the two legitimate targets, while not wasting energy in (to our mind misplaced) attacks on *all* equilibrium concepts indiscriminately. To our understanding, provisional equilibrium is entirely compatible with the study of evolution and with the post-Keynesian project.

ACKNOWLEDGEMENTS

We are indebted to Giovanni Caravale, Roy Rotheim and Claudio Sardoni; we alone are responsible for errors and omissions which remain.

NOTES

1 For an example relating to Keynes's unemployment equilibrium, see Chick (1978).
2 There is a point of view which argues that equilibrium need not be related to anything resembling an underlying process (Hahn 1973). We simply dissent from this view. See the section on equilibrium theory below.
3 The question of convergence to these equilibria (stability) is at best handled as a separate issue (Samuelson's correspondence principle); at worst the problem is ignored (of which Hahn (1984: 9) complains).
4 Walras himself did not see his system in this way. Although he went to some trouble to suspend action prior to equilibrium (by means of 'fictive tickets') he saw his system as the outcome of a process (tatonnement). It has, however, proved logically impossible to be out of, and therefore groping for, equilibria of this type (Robinson 1978a).
5 It is widely believed that if there is perfect (or, better, atomistic) competition, there can never be supernormal profits. But to eliminate supernormal profits requires entry and exit of firms, which in turn requires change in the capital stock; we are in the long period.
6 There is no pure exchange model in *The General Theory*.
7 See the literature on signal extraction for treatment of the purely mathematical aspects of the problem.
8 Curiously, although 'temporary' implies a contrast with 'permanent', no definition of permanent equilibrium was offered by Hicks or has been proposed since, apart from the final equilibria we discuss, which are not commensurate.

9 Of course we are only dealing here with the results of 'cold calculation', not with
   the all-important animal spirits.
10 While we find Kregel's (1980) argument about Harrod's intentions compelling,
   what Harrod actually achieved was undeniably the knife-edge model.
11 Assuming there is no labour constraint.
12 See Dutt (1990) for references.

REFERENCES

Amadeo, E. J. (1989) *Keynes's Principle of Effective Demand*, Aldershot: Edward
   Elgar.
Bliss, C. J. (1975) 'The reappraisal of Keynes' economics: an appraisal', in M. Parkin
   and A. R., Nobay (eds), *Current Economic Problems*, Cambridge: Cambridge
   University Press.
Caserta, M. (1993) 'Capacity utilisation, effective demand and unsteady growth',
   Ph.D. dissertation, University of London.
Chick, V. (1978) 'The nature of the Keynesian revolution: a reassessment', *Australian
   Economic Papers*, 17 (June): 1–20.
────── (1983) *Macroeconomics after Keynes: A Reconsideration of The General
   Theory*, Boston, Mass.: MIT Press.
────── (1996) 'Order out of chaos in economics? Some lessons from the philosophy
   of science', in S. C. Dow and J. Hillard (eds), *Keynes, Uncertainty and Knowledge*,
   Aldershot: Edward Elgar.
Dore, M. H. I. (1984–85) 'On the concept of equilibrium', *Journal of Post Keynesian
   Economics*, 7(2): 193–206.
Dutt, A. K. (1990) *Growth, Distribution and Uneven Development*, Cambridge:
   Cambridge University Press.
Hahn, F. H. (1973) 'On the notion of equilibrium in economics', in Hahn (1984) *op.
   cit.*.
────── (1984) *Equilibrium and Macroeconomics*, Oxford: Basil Blackwell.
Harrod, R. F. (1936) 'An essay in dynamic theory', *Economic Journal*, 49.
Hicks, J. R. (1939) *Value and Capital*, Oxford: The Clarendon Press.
Kaldor, N. (1972) 'The irrelevance of equilibrium economics', *Economic Journal*,
   82.
────── (1985) *Economics without Equilibrium*, Cardiff: University College Cardiff
   Press.
Keynes, J. M. (1936) *The General Theory of Employment, Interest and Money*,
   London: Macmillan.
Kornai, J. (1971) *Anti-Equilibrium: On Economic Systems Theory and the Task of
   Research*, Amsterdam: North-Holland.
Kregal, J. A. (1976) 'Economic methodology in the face of uncertainty', *Economic
   Journal*, 86.
────── (1980) 'Economic dynamics in the theory of steady growth: an historical
   essay on Harrod's "knife-edge"', *History of Political Economy*, 12(1).
Loasby, B. J. (1991) *Equilibrium and Evolution*, Manchester: Manchester University
   Press.
Robinson, J. (1956) *The Accumulation of Capital*, London: Macmillan.
────── (1962) *Essays in the Theory of Economic Growth*, London: Macmillan.
────── (1974) 'History *versus* equilibrium', *Thames Papers in Economic Analysis*,
   Autumn. Reprinted in Robinson (1978b), *q.v.*
────── (1978a) 'A lecture delivered at Oxford by a Cambridge economist', in
   Robinson (1978b), *q.v.*

——— (1978b) *Contributions to Modern Economics*, Oxford: Blackwell.

Rogers, C. (1989) *Money, Interest and Capital*, Cambridge: Cambridge University Press.

Samuelson, P. A. (1947) *The Foundations of Economic Analysis*, Cambridge, Mass.: Harvard University Press.

Shackle, G. L. S. (1947) 'Probability and uncertainty', reprinted in Shackle, *Uncertainty in Economics*, Cambridge: Cambridge University Press, 1955 and 1968.

19

EQUILIBRIUM, PATH DEPENDENCE AND HYSTERESIS IN POST-KEYNESIAN MODELS

*Amitava Krishna Dutt**

INTRODUCTION

Geoff Harcourt has been a major contributor to, and proponent of, post-Keynesian economics. Within the broad diversity of post-Keynesian economics (see Hamouda and Harcourt 1988) two different approaches can be detected, between which there exists a fair degree of tension. One uses determinate models which in some form or other invoke the concept of equilibrium, and includes the contributions of what Hamouda and Harcourt have called the third strand of post-Keynesianism, that is, the macrodynamics of Kalecki and Robinson and their followers.[1] The other questions the relevance of such models, stressing instead the notion that economic agents live in an environment with an irreversible past and an uncertain future, so that history and expectations play a crucial role in determining economic outcomes, which cannot be captured with determinate equilibrium models. This group includes Shackle, Robinson (when she writes about equilibrium) and several writers in what Hamouda and Harcourt call the first strand of post-Keynesianism. Harcourt himself seems to have considerable sympathy for both these approaches, which is not surprising for one who advocates the 'horses for courses' approach and writes that 'there is no uniform way of tackling all issues in economics ... the various strands in post-Keynesian economics differ from one another, not least because they are concerned with different issues and often different levels of abstraction of analysis' (Hamouda and Harcourt 1988).

However, many of the contributions with the first approach do not appear to provide any role to history – which is a central post-Keynesian idea, while the second approach leads to such dismissive appraisals as '[p]ost Keynesian economics remains an eclectic collection of ideas, not a systematic challenge' (Dornbusch and Fischer (1987); see also Solow (1988)). There clearly seems to be a strong need for overcoming these problems of the two approaches.

The objective of this paper is to argue that these two different approaches to post-Keynesian analysis are not really inconsistent with each other, and that history *and* equilibrium can usefully be incorporated into simple post-Keynesian macroeconomic models. To do so, a distinction is made between standard equilibrium models and those which allow a form of path dependence due to zero roots. Two examples of models with path dependence in post-Keynesian economics, interpreted as zero root models, are then provided. The final section of this paper distinguishes between these types of models and those with hysteresis, and suggests how they can be modified to imply hysteresis.

EQUILIBRIUM MODELS AND ZERO ROOT MODELS

A general dynamic continuous-time model with two-state variables can be expressed in terms of two equations of motion as follows:

$$dx/dt = F(x, y) \tag{1}$$

$$dy/dt = G(x, y) \tag{2}$$

where x and y are two variables which can change over time, t, and F and G are two time-invariant functions. If we assume that the trace of the Jacobian for this system is negative, and that its determinant is positive, for all relevant x and y, the equilibrium at $<x^*, y^*>$, at which $dx/dt=0$ and $dy/dt=0$ in equations (1) and (2), if it exists, is unique and globally stable. An example is shown in Figure 1. Many – indeed most – dynamic economic models are of this type, and we may call them equilibrium models. In these models, history plays no role in determining the final outcome, since wherever the system starts from it will always end up at the same equilibrium.

If post-Keynesians wish to take seriously the idea that history matters for the outcome, equilibrium models of the type just described are inadequate for their purposes. Some role for history can be introduced by bringing in the possibility of a finite number of multiple equilibria. Depending on where it initially starts from, the system may tend to one particular equilibrium. But within the neighbourhood of each equilibrium it still remains true that history or initial condition does not matter.

One route to incorporating history more fully into dynamic models is with zero root dynamic systems for which the characteristic roots of the Jacobian matrix of the system are zero. This will occur if function G can be written in the form $H(F(.))$ in equations (1) and (2). In this case the system has an infinite number of equilibria, and the phase portrait of the system can be illustrated as shown in Figure 2. The slightest change in the path of the system will imply a change in the equilibrium of the system, so that history plays a

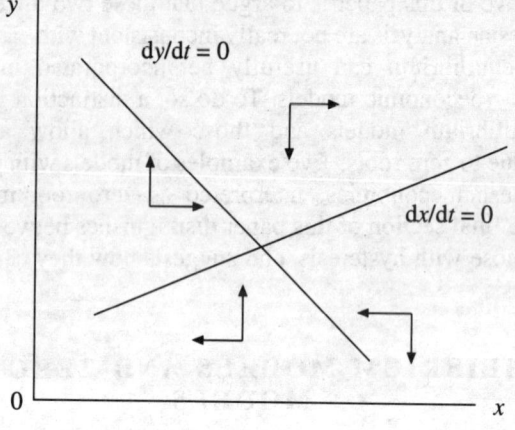

Figure 1

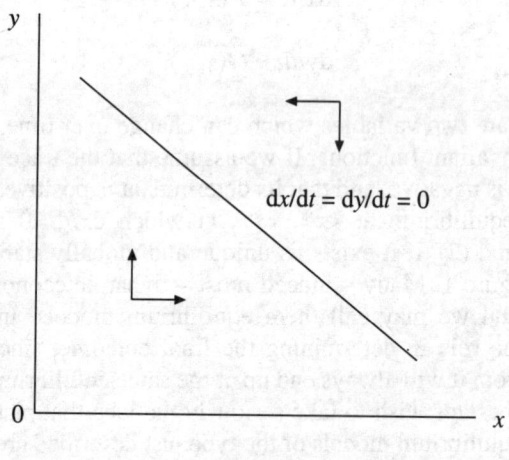

Figure 2

more fundamental role. Systems of this kind can be called path-dependent systems.

There are a number of examples of zero-root systems in economics. One is the case of an endogenous natural rate of unemployment discussed by Sachs (1987), a post-Keynesian version of which is developed by Isaac (1991, 1994). Another is a model of unemployment in which the rate of capacity utilization plays a role in the two simultaneously operating mechanisms of price adjustment and capital formation, due to Van de Klundert and Van Schaik (1990). In the next two sections we examine two examples which are specifically relevant to post-Keynesian economics.

SHORT- AND LONG-PERIOD EXPECTATIONS

Since uncertainty and expectational issues plays a central role in post-Keynesian economics, we start with an example which focuses on how expectations change in an uncertain environment. As is well known, in analysing decision-making by firms, Keynes (1936) distinguished between short-period expectations which are relevant for production and employment decisions, and long-period expectations which are relevant for investment decisions. In Keynes's analysis of the determination of output and employment in the short period in which capital stock is given, *in equilibrium* short-period expectations have to be realized; but since long-period expectations refer to the distant future beyond the short period, the question of their realization does not arise.

Kregel (1976) has distinguished between three models which Keynes used involving alternative assumptions regarding short- and long-period expectations and their interaction: first, a static model which takes long-period expectations to be constant and short-period expectations to be realized (and the two expectations are independent); second, a stationary model which takes long-period expectations to be constant but allows short-period to be disappointed and hence changing (so that the two expectations are independent); and third, a shifting equilibrium model which assumes that long-period expectations can change, and short-period expectations may be disappointed and hence change, *and* that the two expectations are interrelated. Although Keynes used the second and third models in *the General Theory*, and used the first model in his 1937 lecture notes (Keynes 1973) where he wrote that 'if I were writing the book again I should begin by setting forth my theory on the assumption that short-period expectations were always fulfilled',[2] it is the third model which seems to be closest to Keynes's own ideas on the nature of decision-making in an uncertain environment. Keynes (1936) argued that in such an environment economic agents often fall back on conventions, and one such convention is that they extrapolate the present into the future. If this is the case, changes in short-period expectations can be expected to affect long-period expectations. Moreover, according to Keynes, although investors could be thought of as forming probability distributions of future returns on current investment expenditure when making investment decisions, they were aware that such distributions were based on flimsy foundations, so that changes in present circumstances can easily be expected to change their long-period expectations relating to investment.

To analyse the effects of interdependent expectations we can use a simple closed-economy Marshallian model (similar to the model in Dutt (1991–2)) with no government fiscal activity, which draws on some of Keynes's ideas in chapters 3 and 5 of *The General Theory*. Sweeping aggregation issues under the rug we assume that firms have a given production function which relates the flow of output of a single good, Y, to the flow of labour services employed, N, with a given stock of capital goods and technology, so that

$$Y = F(N) \tag{3}$$

with $F' > 0$ and $F'' < 0$ so that marginal product of labour is positive and diminishing with employment. The economy is purely competitive, and firms decide on how much to produce by maximizing expected profits, given their short-period expectation about expected price, e. This implies that

$$W/e = F'(N) \tag{4}$$

where W is the money wage rate, which is assumed to be given. They make investment plans (in real terms) depending on their long-period expectation, E, so that

$$I = I(E), \tag{5}$$

where $I' > 0$. Finally, we assume that real consumption depends on real income or output and the actual price level, P, so that, using a linear form for simplicity, we have

$$C = c_0 + c_1 Y + c_2 P, \tag{6}$$

where $c_0 > 0$, $1 > c_1 > 0$ and $c_2 < 0$. The influence of the price level on consumption can be caused by redistributive effects (according to which a rise in price, given the money wage, reduces the real wage and redistributes income to non-wages from which the propensity to save is higher) or real-balance effects.

We now consider two periods. First, in the market period, firms take e and E as given, and in equilibrium the price, P, clears the goods market. Given e, N is determined from equation (3), and Y from equation (2), and P is determined from the market-clearing condition,

$$Y = c_0 + c_1 Y + c_2 P + I(E)$$

which implies, using equations (2) and (3), that in market-period equilibrium,

$$P = (1/c_2)\{(1 - c_1)[F(F'^{-1}(W/e))] - [c_0 + I(E)]\}. \tag{7}$$

This equation implies $\partial P/\partial e = -(1/c_2)(1 - c_1)F' \, F''^{-1} W/e^2 < 0$ (since a rise in short-period expected price increases employment and output, creates an excess of supply of goods and reduces the equilibrium price and $\partial P/\partial E = -(1/c_2)I' > 0$ (since a rise in long-period expectations raises investment, creates an excess demand for goods and increases the equilibrium price). Curve $P(e)$ in Figure 3 shows the level of P at each level of e for a constant level of E. Note that there is no reason why P, the realized price, should be equal to e, its expectation.

Second, in the short period, if we provisionally consider the case of a stationary model, and assume that E is constant, but that e changes adaptively according to the equation

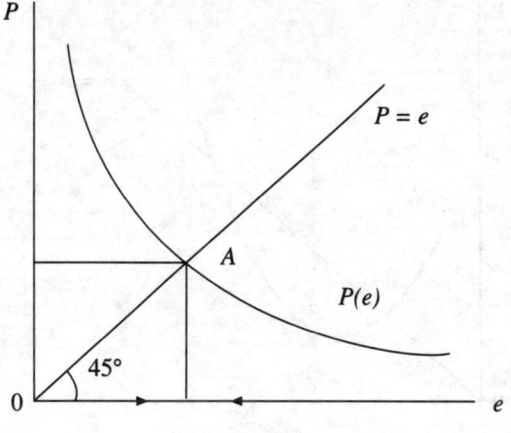

Figure 3

$$de/dt = \alpha(P - e) \qquad (8)$$

where $\alpha' > 0$ and $\alpha(0) = 0$, e will rise (fall) above (below) the 45° line of Figure 3. It is obvious that e will change over time and converge to the short-period equilibrium at A, at which

$$P = e \qquad (9)$$

which implies that the short-period equilibrium is necessarily stable.

If we now interpret the shifting equilibrium model to imply that there is a stable relationship between e and E of the form:

$$E = E(e) \qquad (10)$$

where $E' > 0$, we get, from equations (7) and (10), $dP/de = \partial P/\partial e + (\partial P/\partial E)E'$, which is of ambiguous sign. If $E'' > 0$ and I' is high enough, it is possible for the $P(e)$ curve – now with E given by equation (10) rather than a constant – to take the shape given by the curve in Figure 4. As the figure shows, in this shifting equilibrium model multiple equilibria and an unstable equilibrium may arise (as is the case of the equilibrium at U), but there is no path dependence as defined above. Thus even this version of the shifting equilibrium model cannot make history matter (except to the extent that the initial condition determines whether the system is unstable or stable) unless there is a stretch at which the $P(e)$ curve coincides with the 45° line.

But equation (10) does not provide the only way of allowing for the interaction between short- and long-period expectations. In fact, it can be argued that it is unlikely that a particular level of e will imply a unique level of E at all times. The long-period expectation of firms and hence their investment level is more likely to be affected by *changes* in the level of their short-period expectation rather than just by the *level* of the latter. A simple way of formalizing this is to assume that

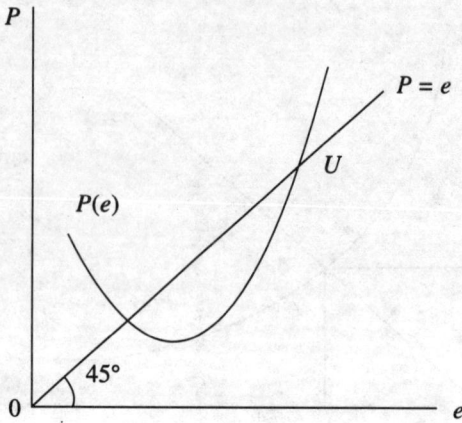

Figure 4

$$dE/dt = \beta(de/dt) \qquad (11)$$

where $\beta' > 0$ and $\beta(0) = 0$, which implies that changes in the level of long-period expectation depend on changes in the level of short-period expectation.

In this case the dynamic system showing short-period adjustments assuming that market-period equilibrium is always satisfied is given by the pair of equations:

$$de/dt = \alpha(\pi(e,E) - e) \qquad (12)$$

$$dE/dt = \beta(\alpha(\pi(e,E) - e)) \qquad (13)$$

where the function π represents the right-hand side of equation (7) and where, as seen above, $\pi_1 < 0$ and $\pi_2 > 0$.

The phase diagram for this system is shown in Figure 5. Since both de/dt

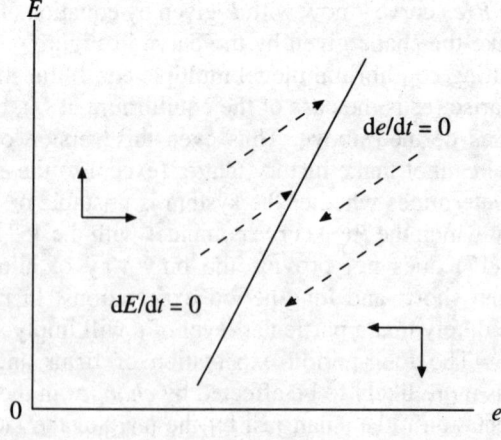

Figure 5

244

$= 0$ and $dE/dt = 0$ imply the same condition, that $\pi(e,E) = e$, the two demarcation curves for the two equations (12) and (13) coincide. The slope of the line is given by $dE/de = -(\pi_1 - 1)/\pi_2$, which is positive. Since dE/dt rises with E and de/dt falls with e, the directions of vertical and horizontal arrows are as shown in the figure by the solid arrows. Possible paths the economy takes are shown by the dashed arrows. The stability of the equilibria require the trace of the Jacobian of the system, given by $\alpha' [(\pi_1 - 1) + \beta'\pi_2]$, to be negative. for stability we therefore require that the product $\beta' I'$ be sufficiently small, to ensure that $(\pi_1 - 1) + \beta'\pi_2 < 0$. The stable case is shown in the figure. The system thus exhibits path dependence; if the relation between short- and long-period expectations can be described by equation (11), history matters.

GROWTH MODELS WITH ENDOGENOUS EXCESS CAPACITY

The second example is that of a Kalecki–Steindl growth model (see Dutt 1990) with unemployed labour, in which firms maintain excess capacity and practise mark-up pricing à la Kalecki and make investment plans taking into account their capacity utilization rates (among other things). A simple one-sector, closed-economy model of this type, following Rowthorn (1982) and Dutt (1984), which assumes that wage-earners consume all their income and profit-recipients save a fraction, s, of theirs, can be represented with the following equations:

$$1 = (W/P)a_0 + (r/u) \tag{14}$$

$$P = (1 + z)Wa_0 \tag{15}$$

$$g^s = s\,r \tag{16}$$

$$g^I = x + \lambda(u - u_n), \tag{17}$$

where W denotes the exogenously fixed money wage, P the price level, a_0 the unit labour requirement assumed to be given for simplicity, u the rate of capacity utilization measured by the ratio of output to real capital, r the rate of profit (the rate of profit to the stock of real capital), z the exogenously given mark-up rate of firms which represents Kalecki's degree of monopoly, g^s the saving–capital ratio, g^I the investment–capital ratio, u_n the 'normal' rate of capacity utilization, and x and λ are additional parameters of the investment function. Equation (14) is the identity showing that a unit of output is distributed between wages and profits, equation (15) is the behavioural mark-up pricing equation, equation (16) represents savings behaviour, and equation (17) represents investment behaviour (where other possible determinants of investment have been dropped for simplicity).

It is assumed that the rate of capacity utilization adjusts to clear the goods market in this model, which implies that

245

$$g^I = g^s. \tag{18}$$

Substituting from equations (14) to (17) into this equation we get

$$x + \lambda(u - u_n) = s\,[z/(1 + z)]u$$

which can be solved for the equilibrium rate of capacity utilization given by

$$u = (x - \lambda u_n)/\{s[z/(1 + z)] - \lambda\}. \tag{19}$$

This equilibrium value is stable if

$$s[z/(1 + z)] > \lambda. \tag{20}$$

For an economically meaningful equilibrium value of u, we also assume that

$$x > \lambda u_n. \tag{21}$$

The resulting equilibrium value of the rate of capital accumulation (assuming away depreciation) is given by

$$g = x + \lambda\{(x - \lambda u_n)/\{s[z/(1 + z)] - \lambda\} - u_n\}. \tag{22}$$

Several striking results follow from this model when there is a rise in z. It follows from equations (19) and (22) that there is a fall in u and in the growth rate as measured by g. Since $g = g^s$, equation (16) implies that there is a fall in r. Finally, equation (15) implies that the real wage, W/P, is equal to $1/a_0(1+z)$, so that there is a fall in the real wage. These results imply that in the absence of technological changes (that is, with a_0 constant), a rise in the real wage must be accompanied by a rise in the rates of growth and profit of the economy.[3]

This type of growth model has been criticized by a number of writers, including Auerbach and Skott (1988) and Committeri (1986), as being internally inconsistent because it implies that the long-run equilibrium u will not, in general, be equal to u_n. Auerbach and Skott (1988), for instance, have argued that in an equation such as (17), x should be interpreted as the rate of growth when u is at its long-run level, which implies that in long-run equilibrium $u = u_n$.

Although it is not the only way, one possible way of defending the Kalecki–Steindl model against this line of criticism is to make u_n and x endogenous, following Lavoie (1995).[4] Considering the case of time-invariant adjustment parameters and writing Lavoie's dynamic equations in a continuous-time formulation, we may write:

$$du_n/dt = \mu(u - u_n) \tag{23}$$

$$dx/dt = \rho(g - x) \tag{24}$$

where μ and ρ are positive constants. Equation (23) implies that firms change u_n adaptively when u is different from u_n. Explanations for this equation can be developed depending on what one takes to be the determinant of u_n at any point in time. If it is taken to be determined simply by the actual experience of firms, if actual utilization exceeds (is less than) what firms previously considered normal, they will adjust what they consider normal upwards (downwards). Alternatively, if it is taken to be determined by strategic considerations, so that firms may reduce their normal (or desired) capacity utilization if they expect a higher rate of entry than at present, and we take entry rates to be proportional to investment rates, then we obtain an equation such as

$$du_n/dt = \mu'(x - g)$$

This equation, using equation (17) and the short-run equilibrium condition, implies equation (23) where $\mu = \mu'\lambda$. Equation (24) is straightforward: if x is interpreted as the expected rate of capital accumulation the dynamics follow from the assumption of adaptive expectations.

Substituting from equation (19) into (23) we get the two equations:

$$du_n/dt = \mu(\{(x - \lambda u_n)/[s[z/(1 + z)] - \lambda]\} - u_n) \tag{25}$$

$$dx/dt = \rho\lambda(\{(x - \lambda u_n)/[s[z/(1 + z)] - \lambda]\} - u_n) \tag{26}$$

The phase diagram for this system is shown in Figure 6. The demarcation curves corresponding to $du_n/dt = 0$ and $dx/dt = 0$ are found from equations (25) and (26) to be the same and the common slope is given by $s[z/(1 + z)]$. The movement of x and u_n are shown by the solid arrows, and possible paths of the economy are shown by the dashed arrows. The stability of the system requires that the sign of the trace of the Jacobian of the dynamic system is negative, for which the necessary and sufficient condition is

$$\mu s[z/(1 + z)] > \rho\lambda. \tag{27}$$

Since condition (20) is already assumed to be satisfied, it is sufficient for

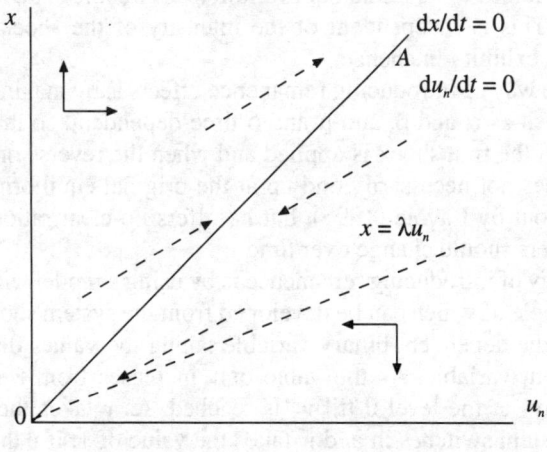

Figure 6

247

stability that $\mu \geq \rho$, that is that the speed of adjustment of expected growth is not larger than the speed of adjustment of the normal level of capacity utilization. The stable case is depicted in the figure.

Assuming that condition (27) is satisfied, so that the system is stable, depending on where the economy starts from, it will end up at a particular equilibrium on the line OA. History thus plays a role in the sense that the starting point (and the path of the economy) determines the final outcome.

Note that in final equilibrium u is equal to u_n, so that the model is absolved of the usual criticism of Kalecki–Steindl models in that they do not require long-run capacity utilization to be at its normal level. Note also that a fall in the mark-up rate, z, will rotate the OA line downwards (since the equation of the demarcation line is given by $x = s[z/(1 + z)]u_n$). Since the path of the economy is shown by north-east pointing arrows above the demarcation line, the economy must end up at a point on the new OA line at a new long-run equilibrium with higher x and u_n. This establishes that a fall in the mark-up rate (and hence a rise in the real wage which is given by $W/P = 1/(1 + z)a_0$) increases the rate of capital accumulation of the economy, g (which is equal to x in equilibrium).[5]

HYSTERESIS

The models discussed above embody the idea of path dependence in the sense that the initial position of the economy determines its final equilibrium. A shock to the system which alters the initial conditions without affecting any of the structural parameters of the model has a permanent impact on the final equilibrium. However, if the economy described by these zero-root models is initially at an equilibrium, and is subjected to a shock, and this is followed by a second shock of the same intensity and in the opposite direction, the economy will return to its initial equilibrium (see Amable et al. (1995: 174–7 for a proof). This is independent of the intensity of the shock. Thus these models do not exhibit remanence.

One simple way of introducing remanence effects is by making adjustment parameters such as α and β, and μ and ρ time-dependent, so that if they are different when the first shock is applied and when the reverse one is applied, the system does not necessarily end up at the original equilibrium. This has been pointed out by Lavoie (1995), but he offers no clear rationale for why these parameters should change over time.

Another way of introducing remanence is by using a model with hysteresis, a simple example of which can be developed from the system shown in Figure 7 where w is the dependent binary variable taking the values 0 or 1 and v is the independent variable. As the value of v increases from zero to v_1 and beyond, w stays at the level 0 till v_2 is reached. As v takes the value v_2 or higher, the system switches in and w takes the value of 1. If v then decreases below v_2 (but stays above v_1) w will stay at 1. It switches out when v goes

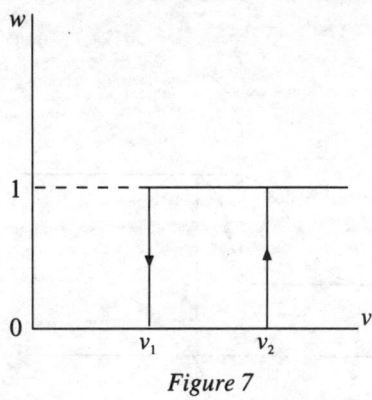

Figure 7

below v_1. Thus, for $v \in [v_1, v_2]$, w can take the value 0 or 1 depending on what the prior values of v were. Thus the history of v, and not just its current level, determines the level of w. Moreover, if the system starts from any point in the interval $[v_1, v_2]$, and it is then shocked to some level outside it and then brought back to the initial level, the value of w may change. If we now introduce a number of such units which can be called hysterons and aggregate over them to get the total value of the dependent variable, given by $W = \Sigma w$, and let the values $<v_1, v_2>$ be different for different units, then history will begin to matter in a more complicated way. The precise time path of v determines exactly how many hysterons are in or out, and hence, the value of W (which will be equal to the number switched in) at any time. The history stored by the system actually consists of the past maxima and minima of the independent variable. There are several examples of this type of model in economics, including that of the effects of exchange rate changes on exports (see Amable *et al.* 1994), of labour markets and unemployment (see Cross 1995) and of investment (Dixit 1992).

This approach can be applied to the models discussed in the previous sections. For the model of the interaction between short- and long-period expectations, assume for a particular firm that when short-period expectation, e_i, increases, at first there is no change in the long-period expectation, E_i (since the disappointment of short-period expectations and its revision need not imply that long-period expectations need to be revised). However, when e_i reaches a particular level – say e_i^* – and beyond, long-period expectation begins to increase with increases in e_i and then presumably stabilize. When e_i is at a high level and begins to fall, at first there will be little change in E_i, but with further reductions in e_i, when it reaches the level say e_i^{**} and below, E_i will drop quite sharply. If increases in e_i can be expected to build up optimism about the future and decreases in it to increase pessimism, it can be expected that $e_i^* < e_i^{**}$. A possible relationship between short- and long-period expectations can then be shown as in Figure 8. If we now allow for many firms, each with possibly different levels of e_i^* and e_i^{**}, that for

249

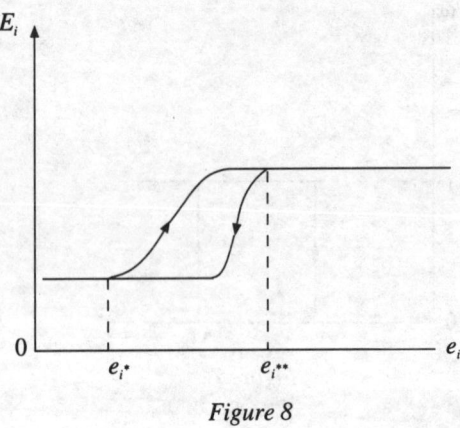

Figure 8

simplicity each firm has the same level of e_i at any point in time (though this assumption can easily be relaxed), and assume that for each firm investment is a function of its long-period expectation (where we now ignore the indivisibilities and irreversibilities of the investment decision), then it follows that aggregate investment and short-period expectation will be related in a hysteretic system. Since the short-run equilibrium level of Y will depend on the level of I, the system involving Y (and hence, employment) will also be hysteretic.

For the model of growth and distribution we can draw on the analysis of Dixit (1992). This analysis invokes three properties of investment decisions: first, it entails some sunk costs which involve expenses that cannot be recouped by reversing the action; second, the economic environment involves uncertainty; and third, since the investment opportunity does not generally vanish, the act can be postponed. If it is assumed that a particular project gives rise to a particular ratio of investment to capital stock for a firm, these assumptions imply that when the variable to which investment responds – the level of capacity utilization in the present model – increases, the firm may initially postpone increasing its investment rate till u increases beyond a certain triggering level u_H, and when u falls it will postpone reversing its decision to reduce the investment rate till u falls below a certain level $u_L <$ u_H. This behaviour for a particular firm is shown in Figure 9 where, for simplicity, discrete jumps in g are considered. When we aggregate over many firms with different u_L and u_H, presumably reflecting different fixed costs and different perceptions of uncertainty (and for simplicity assume that all firms have identical u at any point in time), we get a hysteretic system. Note that this approach not only introduces hysteresis and hence a role for history, but also deflects the criticism of the Kalecki–Steindl models regarding the fact that u need not be equal to u_N in long-run equilibrium by questioning the appropriateness of assuming that there is a unique u_N even at a point in time.

250

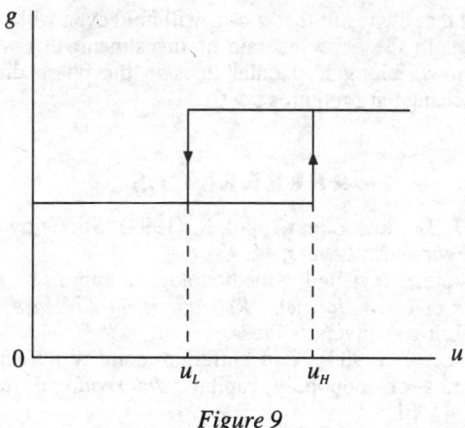

Figure 9

CONCLUSIONS

This paper argues that the two approaches to post-Keynesian economics – one employing equilibrium macroeconomic models and the other emphasizing the role of history – can be synthesized by using models with zero roots or with hysteresis. This argument is illustrated using two examples of models from the post-Keynesian literature, one which examines the relationship between short- and long-period expectations in a short-period Keynesian model, and the other a Kalecki–Steindl growth model with endogenous capacity utilization rates. The analysis suggests that zero root and hysteresis models provide promising ways of modelling the role of history in post-Keynesian economics.

NOTES

* I am grateful to Richard Hule and Marc Lavoie for their comments on an earlier draft.
1 Also included are those in what they call the second – neo-Ricardian – strand, and some contributions from the first – Marshallian – strand, which uses the post-Keynesian aggregate-demand/aggregate-supply framework. Harcourt, especially earlier on in his career, himself made important contributions to this style of post-Keynesian analysis: see, for instance, Harcourt (1965).
2 I have argued elsewhere (see Dutt 1991–92) that this should be seen in the context of the major purpose of *The General Theory*, which was to explain the *qualitative* property of equilibrium – whatever its position – of having unemployed labour.
3 Not all Kalecki–Steindl models – defined as those in which equilibrium u is endogenous – produce these unambiguous results. With different types of investment functions, growth and distribution may not be directly related.
4 The only things that are added to Lavoie's work are: a phase diagram interpretation and zero unit root formulation, which is made possible by the continuous-time modification of his analysis; and the interpretations of why u_n changes adaptively. Otherwise the following discussion makes no claims to originality.

251

5   It may be noted that the result that $u = u_n$ will hold even with $\rho = 0$, so that there is no adjustment in the expected rate of investment; this will imply that the economy will move along horizontal lines in the phase diagram. The result concerning the change in z requires $\rho > 0$.

REFERENCES

Amable, B., Henry, J., Lordon, F. and Topol, R. (1994) 'Strong hysteresis versus unit root dynamics', *Economics Letters*, 44: 43–7.

——— (1995) 'Hysteresis revisited: a methodological approach', in Rod Cross (ed.) *The Natural Rate of Unemployment. Reflections on 25 years of the Hypothesis*, Cambridge: Cambridge University Press.

Auerbach, P. and Skott, P. (1988) 'Concentration, competition and distribution – a critique of theories of monopoly capital', *International Review of Applied Economics*, 2(1): 44–61.

Committeri, M. (1986) 'Some comments on recent contributions on capital accumulation, income distribution and capacity utilization', *Political Economy*, 2(2): 161–86.

Cross, R. (1995) 'Is the natural rate hypothesis consistent with hysteresis?', in Rod Cross (ed.) *The Natural Rate of Unemployment. Reflections on 25 years of the Hypothesis*, Cambridge: Cambridge University Press.

Dixit, A. (1992) 'Investment and hysteresis', *Journal of Economic Perspectives*, 6(1): 107–32.

Dornbusch, R. and Fischer, S. (1984) *Macroeconomics*, 4th edn, New York: McGraw-Hill.

Dutt, A. (1984) 'Stagnation, income distribution and monopoly power', *Cambridge Journal of Economics*, 8(1): 25–40.

——— (1990) *Growth, Distribution and Uneven Development*, Cambridge: Cambridge University Press.

——— (1991–92) 'Expectations and equilibrium: implications for Keynes, the neo-Ricardian Keynesians and the post-Keynesians', *Journal of Post Keynesian Economics*, 14(2): 205–24.

Hamouda, O. and Harcourt, G. (1988) 'Post-Keynesians: from criticism to coherence?', *Bulletin of Economic Research*, 40(January): 1–33.

Harcourt, G. (1965) 'A two-sector model of the distribution of income and the level of employment in the short run', *Economic Record*, 41(March): 103–17.

Isaac, A. (1991) 'Is there a natural rate?', *Journal of Post Keynesian Economics*, 15(4): 453–70.

——— (1994) 'Fiscal policy and the natural rate', in A. K. Dutt (ed.) *New Directions in Analytical Political Economy*, Aldershot: Edward Elgar.

Keynes, J. M. (1936) *The General Theory of Employment, Interest and Money*, London: Macmillan.

——— (1973) *The Collected Writings of John Maynard Keynes*, ed. D. Moggridge, vol. XIV, London: Macmillan.

Kregel, J. (1976) 'Economic methodology in the face of uncertainty: the modeling methods of Keynes and the post-Keynesians', *Economic Journal*, 86(June): 209–25.

Lavoie, M. (1995) 'The Kaleckian model of growth and distribution and its neo-Ricardian and neo-Marxian critiques', *Cambridge Journal of Economics*, 19(6): 789–818.

Rowthorn, R. (1982) 'Demand, real wages and growth', *Studi Economici*, 18: 3–54.

Sachs, J. (1987) 'High unemployment in Europe. Diagnosis and policy implications', in C. Henrie (ed.) *Unemployment in Europe*, Stockholm: Timbro.

Solow, R. M. (1979) 'Alternative approaches to macroeconomic theory: a partial view', *Canadian Journal of Economics*, 12(3).

Van de Klundert, T. C. M. J. and Van Schaik, A. B. T. M. (1990) 'Unemployment persistence and loss of productive capacity: a Keynesian approach', *Journal of Macroeconomics*, 12(3): 363–80.

20

EXPLORING 'THE ORIGINAL KALECKI MODEL T'

Simplifications and generalizations[1]

K. Vela Velupillai

PREAMBLE

After all, not to expect too much from any one line of enquiry and to have an open mind that is tolerant of all lines of enquiry is not a bad working rule for social scientists.

(Harcourt 1977: 22)

My own mentor – 'a twentieth century eclectic', as Geoff Harcourt aptly described Richard Goodwin (Harcourt 1985) – entitled his planned essay in these volumes appropriately: 'Harcourt, Guide and Friend to Young and Old'. This is how I have known Geoff these past twenty-five years: as a guide and friend in my formative years; now, as I reach the end of my innings, he still remains a guide and friend to whom I turn, from time to time, for words of wisdom and advice in personal and professional matters. My own lasting regret in this friendship of a quarter of a century is that due to irrational expectations I missed the opportunity of opening batting with Geoff for Clare Hall.

Geoff Harcourt was instrumental in securing my admission as a graduate student in Cambridge. That one act of kindness changed the whole course of my life. I had, like so many in my generation, been enlightened by Geoff's writings on capital theory and macrodynamics. The lucid exposition of intrinsically difficult material, the imaginative extensions of Cambridge theories of growth and income distribution, the extraction of the simple economics underlying complex analytical edifices – these were the quintessential Harcourt traits. They were instrumental in my education as an economist and in my subsequent years as a teacher of macroeconomics. In choosing my topic for this essay in honour of Geoff Harcourt I have been guided by these characteristics: the Cambridge tradition, to put it succinctly. It is the macroeconomic traditions of Kaldor, Kahn, Robinson, Goodwin and Sraffa, which he, almost more than any other single person, has sought to preserve and extend in important and interesting ways.

It is of course, the Keynesian tradition and Harcourt is *the* post-Keynesian *par excellence.* I have, however, always felt that Harcourt's post-Keynesianism in intellectual content, political commitment and methodological underpinnings is essentially post-Kaleckian. From this perspective I have chosen to pay homage to Harcourt via an attempt to revive some aspects of Kaleckian macrodynamics. Geoff Harcourt's tastes are classic, in every sense of the word (and this applies to his cricket as well). I go back, therefore, to 'the original Kalecki Model T'. It would be entirely within the realm of possibilities to visualize Geoff Harcourt driving a Model T on his daily journey between Sidgwick Avenue and Jesus Lane.

Quite apart from making a case for the plausibility of testing the hypothesis that the owner of the observed 'Model T' at the Sidgwick site is Geoff Harcourt, I also want to make the point that Robertson once made with characteristic wit and claim that it characterizes Geoff's intellectual credo:

> Now, as I have often pointed out to my students, some of whom have been brought up in sporting circles, high-brow opinion is like a hunted hare; if you stand in the same place, or nearly the same place, it can be relied upon to come round to you in a circle.
>
> (Robertson 1956: 80)

Geoff Harcourt has long maintained that the fundamental tenets of classical political economy, modified, extended and interpreted by Keynes, Kalecki and Sraffa, should be the guiding principles in economic analysis and policy prescriptions. This is not for dogmatic reasons; it is because these tenets, in his opinion, form the basis for enlightened liberalism and for an economics that is relevant and applicable in advanced industrial societies. Geoff's point, as I understand it, is that the many high-brow developments in economic theory – meaning increasing and almost indiscriminate use of irrelevant mathematics – return, time and again, like the hunted hare, to the same classical principles. The Kaleckian example I tackle in this essay is an attempt to substantiate this thesis as succinctly as possible.

THE MODEL T

> Using American and German material, Mr. Kalecki has little difficulty in arriving at a major component that shows a 10-year period. This accounts for the business cycle which, according to this model, certainly requires a starting impulse – some trouble, for instance, having occurred in the apple-growing industry at the time Adam and Eve dwelt in paradise – but then might go on forever.
>
> (Schumpeter 1939: 189)

It is possible to show that the particular 'apple-growing industry at the time Adam and Eve dwelt in paradise' is quite unnecessary. Kalecki's 'Model T' is part of the folklore of mathematical business cycle theory – at least on this side of the Atlantic. It is, therefore, slightly superfluous to repeat, somewhat mechanically, that classic model. If I, nevertheless, indulge in being superfluous it is simply for notational convenience and to provide the background for the points I wish to make.

The 'original Model T', as such, was not quite ever seen again. However the elements that went into its making reappeared in other combinations in almost all of Kalecki's subsequent 'macrodynamic theories of business cycles'. One of the points I wish to make in these notes is simple: a consistent and correct economic and mathematical implication of the assumptions underlying the elements that went into the making of the 'Model T' would have resulted in a nonlinear discrete time model,[2] thus obviating the necessity of special assumptions about coefficients or, for that matter, reformulating it along the lines of incorporating 'Slutsky's famous result'.

Beyond the simple – almost simplistic – point there lies the tortured territory of methodological and conceptual issues in modelling strategy: the role of period analysis and the nature of mathematical formalisms of discrete versus continuous equations (or inequalities of mixed systems); the validity of linearizations and the perennial tendency to reason globally. Some of these issues will be taken up in the concluding section.

Kalecki's closed (noncompetitive) private economic system is represented as follows:

1 A 'national' income identity or, better, budget constraint for income from capital:

$$B = C + A \tag{1}$$

where C: consumption from capital income
A: gross capital accumulation
B: total real income of capitalists.

2 A consumption function for income from capital

$$C = C_1 + \lambda B \tag{2}$$

where C_1 = a positive constant.   and: $0 < \lambda < 1$.
From (1) and (2):

$$B = \frac{C_1 + A}{1 - \lambda} \tag{3}$$

3 Whenever investments take place three stages are delineated by Kalecki:[3]
   (a) investment orders: I_t
   (b) production of capital goods: A_t
   (c) deliveries of capital goods: L_t
4 There is an assumption to link (a) and (c):

$$L(t) = I(t - \theta) \tag{4}$$

i.e., there is an average gestation lag of θ, for the economy as a whole, between decisions to invest and deliveries of final (capital) goods.

5　Next, the link between (a) and (b) – i.e., between I_t and A_t; for this denote: $W(t) = sum$ of all orders made in an interval $(t - \theta, t)$.

Assume $\dfrac{1}{\theta}$ of each order is executed per unit of time, i.e.:

$$A(t) = \frac{W(t)}{\theta} \tag{5}$$

Then:

$$W(t) = \frac{1}{\theta} \int_{t-\theta}^{t} I(\tau)d\tau \tag{6}$$

and, therefore:

$$A(t) = \frac{1}{\theta} \int_{t-\theta}^{t} I(\tau)d\tau \tag{7}$$

Equation (7) simply signifies the fact (by assumptions) that the output of capital goods at time t is equal to the average of orders made in the interval $(t - \theta, t) \equiv \theta$.

6　Now, denote by $K(t)$ the capital stock at time t. Then (by assumption):

$$\dot{K} = L(t) - U \tag{8}$$

where $U =$ (constant) depreciation factor.

7　Next an additional behavioural function for investment:

$$I(t) = K(t)f(B / K, \rho) \tag{9}$$

where the 'plausible' reasoning is:
(a)　there are two main determinants of investments:
　　(α)　gross profit rate $= B/K$;
　　(β)　money rate of interest $= \rho$;
(b)　these variables do not influence the absolute level of investments but only its level relative to the capital stock, i.e., I/K;
(c)　on the other hand, ρ varies proportionately to the general business conditions which are, in turn, proxied by B/K;

$$\text{i.e., } \rho = g(B/K) \tag{10}$$

$$\text{and g'>0. Thus: } I(t) = K(t)\phi[(C_1 + A) / K] \tag{11}$$

and $\phi' > 0$.

8 Now, a linear approximation of (11) yields:

$$\frac{I(t)}{K(t)} = m\left[(C_1 + A)/K\right] - n \tag{12}$$

where: $m, n > 0$

i.e.,
$$I(t) = m(C_1 + A) - nK(t). \tag{13}$$

9 The derivation of the reduced form equation, from the above basic elements, is quite simple and straightforward:

$$\dot{I}(t) = \frac{m}{\theta}\left[I(t) - I(t - \theta)\right] - n\left[I(t - \theta)\right]U] \tag{14}$$

which, be redefining:

$$J(t) = I(t) - U$$

can be rewritten as:

$$\dot{J}(t) = \frac{m}{\theta}\left[J(t) - J(t - \theta)\right] - nJ[(t - \theta). \tag{15}$$

This is one form of the famous linear mixed differential-difference equation which has been extensively studied in the mathematical macrodynamic literature ever since the pioneering studies by Tinbergen and Frisch – and has even entered the applied mathematics literature (cf. Minorsky (1974, chapter 21: 537–40) and Bellman and Cooke (1963, chapter 13, #13.7 and pp. 454–5).

10 The final form of (15) or (14) obscures the simple economic underpinnings of a possible cyclical mechanism. The typical economics of fluctuations will be:

(a) Suppose investment orders $I(t)$ increases: $I(t)\uparrow$.

(b) After a time lag, deliveries of capital goods $L(t)$ must increase: $L(t)\uparrow$.

(c) Almost immediately after order increases take place there will be an increase in 'carry-on': $A(t)\uparrow$.

(d) From (13) it is clear that the initial impact of $I(t)\uparrow$ is cumulative.

(e) Eventually the capital stock would have also increased: $K(t)\uparrow$.

(f) The increase in the capital stock diminishes the difference between 'carry-on' and the capital stock (cf. (13)) which in turn drags $I(t)$ and eventually $L(t)$.

11 Some observations on the implicit assumptions before we move on:

(a) There is, potentially, an inelastic credit system lurking in the background (cf. Kalecki 1936), almost reminiscent of Irving Fisher's debt-deflation mechanism.

258

(b) What was the justification for linearizing (9) to lead to (11) – and then reason and discuss as if (14) (equivalently (15)) holds globally?

(c) Having defined $W(t)$ as the sum of all orders made in an interval should it not, on economic grounds, in fact be *summed* rather than integrated?

(d) Why should investment orders suddenly increase? Are these the external shocks? Whims (animal spirits!) of capitalists? And, above all, is it a disturbance to a system in (stable) equilibrium? If so what are the characteristics of the equilibrium (equilibria!).

None of these crucial issues – except for (a) (*cf.* Kalecki 1936: 359–60) – are discussed satisfactorily from either a mathematical or an economic point of view. We take up (b) and (c) in the next section with implications for (d).

SIMPLIFICATIONS AND GENERALIZATIONS

No doubt there are many Kalecki Effects walking about the world, some of them dressed up in such grand mathematical clothes that they are not likely to come my way. But I want to tell you about my meeting, a year or two ago, with one of them who seemed a fairly plain-spoken and approachable person.

(Robertson 1956: 80)

Let me take item 11(c) (above) first. By definition, $W(t)$ 'is equal to the total of orders allocated during the period' $(t - \theta, t)$ (Kalecki 1935: 329). What is the economic logic or necessity of summing continuously? Why not simply:

$$W(t) = \sum_{t-\theta}^{t} I(t) \tag{16}$$

Then:
$$A(t) = \frac{1}{\theta} \sum_{t-\theta+1}^{t} I(\tau) \tag{17}$$

Also, why:
$$\dot{K}(t) = L(t) - U? \tag{18}$$

Why not:
$$K(t) - K(t-1) = L(t) - U? \tag{19}$$

Thus, this variant of Model T would result in the following set of components:

$$L(t) = I(t - \theta) \tag{4}$$

$$W(t) = \sum_{t-\theta}^{t} I(\tau) \tag{16}$$

$$A(t) = \frac{1}{\theta} \sum_{t-\theta+1}^{t} I(\tau) \qquad (17)$$

$$I(t) = m(C_1 + A) - nK(t) \qquad (13)$$

and: $$K(t) - K(t-1) = L(t) - U. \qquad (19)$$

Simple algebraic manipulations lead to the following reduced form equation for $I(t)$:

$$\gamma I(t) - I(t-1) + nI(t-\theta) = nU \qquad (20)$$

where $\gamma \equiv 1 - \left(\dfrac{m}{\theta} \right)$.

This is a perfectly ordinary linear difference equation! Why one wonders, was there so much fuss about the solution of a mixed linear difference-differential system? We shall return to such methodological speculations in the next section.

What about the point raised in item 11(b) about the linearization of the investment equation? Indeed Kalecki's own heuristic reasoning suggests a classic S-shaped curve for global dynamics:

> It is commonly known that, except for financial panic (the so-called crises of confidence), the market money rate rises and falls according to general business conditions. We make on that basis the following simplified assumption: *The money rate ρ is an increasing function of the gross yield B/K. . . . We further assume that [ϕ] is a linear function.*
>
> (1935: 330–1; italics in original)

But in his reply to criticisms by Tinbergen and Frisch, Kalecki notes, *inter alia*:

> the rate of growth of the function [ϕ] is more rapid, the greater the elasticity of the credit system, i.e., the smaller the advance of the interest rate called forth by the given rise of prices and production.
>
> (1936: 359)

And, then, in defending the choice of a particular value for the constant m (this is part of the point raised above in 11(d) and in the observation made by Goodwin (1956)) Kalecki argues, 'counterfactually', that the elasticity of the credit system would be variable if m did not have that particular value:

> Let us suppose that m has a slightly smaller value than that given above; it is easily seen that this results in damped oscillations and in a short time the business cycle will practically disappear. But the requirements of liquidity of banks and enterprises will become less stringent and the

disappearance of cyclical fluctuations will have the effect of an increase in reserves. The credit system will become more elastic and a given rise of price and production will call forth a less marked advance in the rate of interest.

(1936: 360)

There is an infelicity here. The 'Model T' linearized version is made the basis for a justification, in a circular way, for the linearization! The appropriate procedure would have been to linearize around the 'steady state' or 'equilibrium' solution of the system – but the full non-linearized discrete Model T may have resulted in periodic or strange attractors for the long-run 'steady state' solution. It is, in fact, easy to derive the non-linearized reduced form for $I(t)$ or $K(t)$ in the discrete case:

$$I(t) = K(t)\phi\left\{\frac{C_1 + A(t)}{K(t)}\right\}. \tag{11}$$

But
$$K(t) - K(t-1) = L(t) - U = I(t-\theta) - U. \tag{20}$$

Substituting for $I(t-\theta)$ in (20) we get:

$$K(t) - K(t-1) = K(t-\theta)\phi\left\{\frac{C_1 + U + \frac{1}{\theta}K(t) - \frac{1}{\theta}K(t-\theta)}{K(t-\theta)}\right\} - U. \tag{21}$$

What sort of animal is (21)? It is an 'animal of a ferocious character' (*cf.* note 2, below). The nature of the ferocity depends, probably, on the nature of ϕ and the value of θ.

Kalecki himself assumes a value of six months for θ. Even for that value, normalizing the time unit in terms of θ, equation (21) is a nonlinear second-order difference equation. Today we know the pitfalls of reasoning globally by linearizing locally – at least one hopes that we know better today.

What is even more remarkable is that a linearization of the function ϕ, at this point, does not save one from a nonlinear (high)-order difference equation. It becomes clearer when (21) is written as:

$$\frac{K(t) - K(t-1)}{K(t-\theta)} = \phi\left\{\frac{C_1 + U + \frac{1}{\theta}K(t) - \frac{1}{\theta}K(t-\theta)}{K(t-\theta)}\right\} - \frac{U}{K(t-\theta)}. \tag{22}$$

It would surely be interesting to study the possible 'bizarre behaviour' exhibited by the above discrete nonlinear system. This note, however, was not

261

an exercise in the numerical validation of some 'Kalecki effects' – it had more limited aims of possible simplifications without violating the plausible economic assumptions of 'the original Model T'. In this connection it might be useful to remember that Kalecki himself 'sums' rather than 'integrates' when he resorts to numerical exercises (*cf.* Kalecki 1935: 337–40, in particular). And, from (22), it is easy to see that the possible dynamic behaviour of a nonlinearized Model T may exhibit rich dynamics and escape the various strictures of Frisch, Schumpeter and others.

CONCLUDING NOTES

As I recall it, the implication was that a theory that had been around for as long as Kalecki's should have been tested by now and, if found wanting, discarded.

(Harcourt 1977: 16)

Geoff Harcourt was reporting the methodological view expressed by a distinguished mathematical economist. But at the frontiers of business cycle theory we seem to keep returning to issues that were at the core of Kalecki's approach to modelling fluctuations: time to build in real business cycle theories, the importance of imperfect competition in neo-Keynesian theories and, of course, the whole basis for political business cycle theories. This is the Robertsonian 'hunted hare' philosophy that makes a mockery of naive Popperian views of 'progress' in the social and moral science that is economics – as Harcourt, I surmise, would say.

Thus the moral that can be drawn from some of the points made in these pages seems to be greater humility in the possibilities of global reasoning for macrodynamic systems and the dangers of arguing for the acceptance of a theory on the basis of 'confirmation' with facts. Very many years ago Trygve Haavelmo made this latter point with clarity, simplicity and depth (Haavelmo 1940).[4] It has gone completely unheeded in these heady days of modelling in terms of 'mimicking observed covariation in key aggregative variables ' – the hallmark of *newclassical* methodology.

There are other, deeper, questions to be asked that pertain to the nature of the strategy adopted in specifying behavioural equations, determining technical coefficients and characterizing long-run behaviour. Some of these issues lie at the frontiers of research in business cycle-theory – and will remain at the frontiers in whatever way the theory develops. Others, characterizing long-run behaviour, require consideration of timescales. In the older mathematics and some of the newer economics the method of relaxation oscillation was used (fast–slow dynamics). Such issues are implicit in the various economically rich and politically relevant macrodynamic models Kalecki experimented with for almost forty years. Despite the mathematical crudity of his methods he was able to reach profound and quite original economic conclusions. That is a testimony to his economic intuition and the power of his reasoning. The mathematics was almost unnecessary.

The problem, however, arises when ordinary bread-and-butter economists like myself get carried away by the mathematics and reason as if the model is the economy. In this sense Kalecki's models may have misguided generations of well-meaning economists who had neither the master's genius nor his powerful economic intuition.

This is where the guidance of Geoff Harcourt has been supremely effective. He has been indefatigable in his efforts to explain the economic underpinnings and macroeconomic policy implications underlying the genius and intuition in the classic works. This is why the macroeconomic frontiers keep returning to Smith and Ricardo; to Keynes and Pigou; to Kaldor and Kalecki.

ACKNOWLEDGEMENT

I am indebted to Professor Malcolm Sawyer for constructive comments that removed some of the ambiguities in an earlier version. He is not responsible for the remaining infelicities.

NOTES

1   The original Kalecki Model T assumed the coefficients to be such as to give an undamped cycle, on the grounds that in fact cycles do not disappear. This simple error in logic was so severely criticized by Professor Frisch that the model has never been seen again. Now Mr. Kalecki accepts the criticisms and incorporates in his model Slutsky's famous result: that random shocks will give rise to continuing and irregular cycles in an auto-regressive model, and that these cycles look very much like the same sort of thing as trade cycles. This, of course, does not establish that they are trade cycles. There are in fact two ways of explaining the maintenance of oscillation – shocks and nonlinearities.

(Goodwin 1956: 506)

2   Richard Goodwin described the nature of such equations in a colourful way:

Combining the difficulties of difference equations with those of non-linear theory, we get an animal of a ferocious character and it is wise not to place too much confidence in our conclusions as to behaviour.

(1950: 319, n. 6)

3   This particular aspect has come under the critical and imaginative scrutiny of Steindl (1981).

4   The point made in item 11(d), was taken up by Haavelmo with particular reference to Kalecki's audacious methodology:

E.g. M. Kalecki ('A Macrodynamic Theory of Business Cycles,' ... p. 336), goes so far as to impose on his system not only the condition of cyclical solutions, but also the condition of constant amplitude (no damping) in order to produce maintained oscillations which can be directly compared with the observed cycles.

(Haavelmo 1940: 312, n. 1)

REFERENCES

Bellman, R. and Cooke, K. L. (1963) *Differential-Difference Equations*, New York: Academic Press.

Goodwin, R. M. (1950) 'A non-linear theory of the cycle', *The Review of Economics and Statistics*, XXXII (4): 316–20.

—— (1956) Review of the 'theory of economic dynamics' by Kalecki, *Economic Journal*, LXVI (263): 507–10.

Haavelmo, T. (1940) 'The inadequacy of testing dynamic theory by comparing theoretical solutions and observed cycles', *Econometrica*, 8: 312–21.

Harcourt, G. C. (ed.) (1977) *The Microeconomic Foundations of Macroeconomics*, London: Macmillan.

—— (1985) 'A twentieth century eclectic: Richard Goodwin', *Journal of Post Keynesian Economics*, Spring: 410–21.

Kalecki, M. (1935) 'A macrodynamic theory of business cycles', *Econometrics*, 3: 327–44.

—— (1936) 'Comments on the macrodynamic theory of business cycles', *Econometrica*, 4: 356–60.

Minorsky, N. (1974) *Nonlinear Oscillations*, New York: Robert E. Krieger Publishing Co.

Robertson, D. H. (1956) *Economic Commentaries*, London: Staples Press.

Schumpeter, J. A. (1939) *Business Cycles: A Theoretical, Historical and Statistical Analysis of the Capitalist Process*, New York: McGraw-Hill Books Co.

Steindl, J. (1981) 'Some comments on the three versions of Kalecki's theory of the trade cycle', in J. Løs *et al.* (eds) *Studies in Economic Theory and Practice*, Amsterdam: North-Holland.

21

THE T-F-M APPROACH TO PRODUCTION ANALYSIS AND THE ANALYSIS OF STRUCTURAL CHANGE[1]

Michael A. Landesmann

INTRODUCTION

The Cambridge controversies of the late 1960s to which Geoffrey Harcourt prominently contributed were mostly understood at the time as a critique of neoclassical economic theory. However, these debates also gave rise to streams of economic theorizing which attempted to produce alternative theoretical frameworks. One direction of non-neoclassical theory concentrated on the analysis of structural economic dynamics (see, e.g. Pasinetti 1981 and 1993; Lowe 1976; Quadrio-Curzio 1986). The present paper is a short sketch of a contribution to positive production analysis which emphasizes organizational issues and the fact that actual forms of production organization are always compromises in the fulfilment of a range of 'efficiency' criteria. We believe that the framework presented (we call it the 'T-F-M approach to production analysis', combining the analysis of tasks, funds and materials in process) is conducive to the study of structural change in actual economies.

THE PRODUCTION PROCESS AND STRUCTURAL ECONOMIC DYNAMICS

In this paper we consider the interaction over time among three fundamental networks of productive elements; (i) the tasks being performed; (ii) the agents (fund elements) participating in the process; (iii) the materials that enter the process and undergo a transformation in the course of productive activity. Each one of these three networks is associated with the time dimension in terms of either durability or the sequential character of process structures: tasks have to be completed and sequenced, often within given time intervals; agents may utilize one or more capabilities to different degrees in different time intervals; materials may be carried through a sequence of fabrication stages in a continuous or intermittent way. The state of a productive process at any given time reflects the coordination pattern among productive elements within each network, and the coordination of the different networks with each other.

The 'real time' dimension in characterizing productive activity is of particular relevance for the study of change in economic systems: the reason is that production processes which have inherent features of persistence tend to constrain the feasible range of dynamic paths which the economic system may follow. Production processes are generally characterized by the coexistence of features of persistence and features of change: the transformation of materials (essentially, the transformation of raw materials into finished products) is obviously a process of change, whereas the 'persistence' element is associated with the productive apparatus, and with the organizational set-up that 'survives' from one production period to another and ensures that a certain productive potential is maintained over time. 'Structural economic dynamics' may be defined as the analysis of economic transformations that explicitly account for the relative persistence of certain elements of economic structure while other elements are subject to change. The evolution of structures is thus regulated by a principle of relative structural invariance. Structural dynamics is a process in which different elements (or the relationships between such elements) of the existing structure are changing at different speeds (a special case would be that of elements and/or relationships that do not change at all). As a result, the relative position of each element would become modified through time, and the evolution of the economic structure will be characterized by different degrees of resilience with respect to factors of change (such as technical innovation or population growth).

The T-F-M approach exploits the notions of networks (productive inter-relationships) based on 'neighbourhood' and 'similarity' relationships at the level of tasks, fund inputs and material in process flows to study structural economic dynamics. Economic change involves the activation of a sequence of such networks and one can thus speak of an endogenization of the process of economic change. In such a process, 'relative rigidities' play a role leading to a clear hierarchy in the adjustment ability of different networks (these rigidities depend upon the time horizon considered and the nature of the impulse); also 'buffers' (i.e. underutilized capacities and inventories) play a role in 'dynamic network' specification in that they determine whether the impact of a particular impulse could – again, within a given time horizon – be contained within a particular region of the economic system. The notion of 'decomposable dynamics' is thus distinctly related to the analysis of the relative rigidities (structural invariances) of different networks/subsystems and to the organizational or conjunctural availability of buffers.

THE THREE ANALYTICAL DIMENSIONS OF PRODUCTION ANALYSIS

As mentioned above, the distinguishing characteristics of the approach that we shall adopt is that it isolates three levels of analysis of a production process:

- task identification and task arrangement;[2]
- fund factor analysis (the bundling and utilization of capabilities);[3]
- material transformation and the organization of material in process flows.[4]

Production theory has generally avoided a complete description and analysis of the production process in terms of all the three above components which interact in a way that brings about a clearly identifiable pattern of productive activity. Instead, the attention of economists has generally concentrated upon one or another category of productive elements, to the exclusion of others. Thus, for example, the category of 'production factors' is often introduced which pools together 'agents' and 'materials in process', thus losing sight of an important distinction of production processes. Also, the clear dependence of hiring particular sets of agents given the task specification of a process or, reversely, the dependence of task definition and task allocation upon the availability of a particular collection of agents (fund elements[5]) has been insufficiently explored in the recent literature. Thirdly, the fact that the availability of particular materials and knowledge about these materials constrains the set of transformation processes which need to be followed and the tasks which need to be executed has only been emphasized by a rather specialized group of analysts (see, e.g. Cohondet et al. 1988).

Let us explore the analytical components of a production process in more detail.

The structuring of tasks in a process

A production process may be described as an arrangement of tasks. The arrangement (in particular the clustering and sequencing of tasks) is such that the process as a whole may be considered as a purposeful activity, that is as an activity deliberately aimed at a certain result and designed for that purpose (see also Scazzieri 1993). Tasks themselves gain purpose only because they have a particular position in the internal organization of a process. Tasks are made up of primitive operations that describe elementary acts such as particular types of movements, holding operations, and so on. Primitive operations in themselves are not purposeful. They become purposeful only after a certain number of primitive operations are put together into tasks and a structuring of these tasks occurs within a process. In this case, primitive operations become elementary components of a purposeful overall activity.

We shall find that there are various ways of combining primitive operations into tasks. These ways depend upon the physical characteristics of the materials upon which, and the capabilities and capacities of 'actors' (fund factors) with which, such tasks are performed. Tasks thus have to be defined both in relation to the stages in the processes of transformation of specific materials as well as in relation to the activities of fund input elements. The specific skills and capacities of different fund elements constrain the specification of tasks and the type of task arrangement that can be implemented in a productive process.[6]

Some agents may be capable of performing a large set of primitive operations, while other agents may only be able to perform a much narrower set of such operations. On the other hand, primitive operations may (and in many cases will) be complementary to each other (such as 'holding' and 'cutting'). This has an important implication: if a primitive operation complementary to another is not included in the same task, it has to be included in another task and this requires strict coordination in the activities of those who perform these two tasks. It may be that two primitive operations are complementary in the sense that they have to be performed in a sequence. If such operations are not included in the same task, the two tasks in which they are included will have to be sequentially arranged. However, not all precedence patterns of tasks derive from this type of complementarity. As we will see, it might be the nature of the available fund inputs and the issue of capacity (or capability) utilization which requires a particular sequencing of tasks. Or it could lie in the nature of the material in process (for which N. Georgescu-Roegen uses the 'process fund' notion[7]) that tasks have to be performed in a particular sequence.

In general, then, any given production process will require the execution of a number of tasks according to a definite precedence pattern. In many cases, however, there will be options as to the precise sequencing of fabrication stages and in the sequencing of tasks linked to such stages. The choice of task specification and task arrangement defines the organizational issues related to this analytical dimension of a productive process. As we saw, the choice of such arrangements is dependent upon the two other dimensions of the productive activity.

The coordination of productive agents (fund elements)

It is generally possible to identify, within a production process, a set of elements that are responsible for the actual transformation of the material in process, without being in any relevant physical sense embodied in the commodity (commodities) that is (are) being produced. We may call productive elements which are required for the transformation process to take place without themselves getting materially absorbed by it, the active operators of the process under consideration. As a first approximation, the active operators may be identified if we describe that process in terms of the distinction between 'who (or what) is acting' and 'what is acted upon'. When considering the pattern of coordination among active operators that makes any specific productive transformation possible, it may be useful to distinguish between two types of active operators: flow agents and fund agents. This distinction refers to the degree of permanence of such agents in the course of the productive transformation associated with a given process.

Flow agents are active elements (examples could be fuel or chemical catalysts) that are supplied either from other processes or from external sources and which participate in it when they are required for certain stages of that process. Flow agents ought to be distinguished from work-in-process materials, for the latter cannot be considered as active elements of the production process, due to the fact that such materials are the building blocks from which the finished commodities are made. However, the distinction between materials-in-process and flow agents might be rather fluid in a number of cases.

A distinctive feature of fund elements is that their definitional characteristics remain substantially unaltered from the beginning to the end of the production process. It is worth noting that by 'substantially unaltered' we do not mean a complete preservation of the entire set and structure of characteristics. Some degree of change in the bundle of characteristics is allowed as long as the fund element under consideration is structurally preserved.[8] There are tolerance thresholds beyond which a given fund element changes fundamentally its characteristics, at least as far as its usability in particular production processes is concerned (a bridge or machine breaks down, etc.). Within certain limits, the performance characteristics of a given fund element might change without any qualitative difference in its capabilities to perform a particular set of tasks. Fund agents, of which machines and hired workers are examples, are often associated with a particular production process even at times when they do not perform any particular task(s) within that process.

A critical feature in the arrangement of fund inputs within a production process is the way in which fund inputs are allocated to the execution of particular tasks. In this connection, it is generally important to determine the adequate degree of 'task specialization' of the different fund inputs. To this purpose, we may regard fund inputs as bundles of capabilities (see also Landesmann 1986). Each fund input element f^k may be defined in an n-dimensional capability space C as a vector of measurable capabilities:

$$f^k = \{\bar{c}_i^k\} \text{ where } \bar{c}_i^k \text{ are in } R^n.$$

The reason why such a representation is possible is that capabilities have in most cases a clear quantitative expression.[9] For example, capabilities such as speed can be expressed in terms of a certain number of particular types of movements which can be performed over a certain time interval; memory can be expressed as a capacity to store a particular number of pieces of information at a moment in time. Other capabilities, such as accuracy, can be measured by certain quantitative boundaries, such as the ability to distinguish (and work upon) size differences of particular materials down to, say, 0.001 mm. In most circumstances, therefore, it is safe to assume that the capabilities of different fund input elements with respect to particular tasks can be compared in cardinal space.

The performance of fund input elements *vis-à-vis* particular tasks is a multidimensional concept in the same way that capabilities are defined in multidimensional space. In order to arrive at an overall performance indicator, different performance criteria, such as accuracy, speed, etc. have to be weighted. Any ranking of different fund inputs' abilities to perform particular tasks will be a function of the weighting scheme adopted. Given a particular weighting scheme, an ordering of fund inputs in terms of relative task adequacy with respect to particular tasks can be obtained.[10]

Such an ordering of 'task performances' will be taken into account when allocating fund inputs to particular tasks such that all the tasks belonging to a particular process would actually be performed; as we will see, however, this will not be the only criterion which will be taken into account when deciding upon a particular 'job specification programme'. The latter can be defined as a mapping from the set of capabilities (or skills) embodied in the different fund input elements to the set of tasks to be performed in a particular production process (remember that tasks themselves were defined as sets of 'primitive operations') (see Figure 1). C refers to the space of capabilities, P to the space of 'primitive operations'; f^k, f^n, f^r refer to different fund input elements and τ_{ij} refers to tasks i ($i = 1, \ldots, n$) to be executed in a process j.

We may say that a job specification programme is complete if all tasks to be performed in a given process are allocated to particular types of funds. Furthermore, if only the criterion of 'relative task adequacy' were to be applied in deciding upon a particular job specification programme, then this would lead to a particular ranking of such programmes of the type: $J(\alpha) > J(\beta) > J(\gamma) > \ldots$ where each $J(\omega)$ ($\omega = \alpha, \beta, \gamma, \ldots \subset \Omega$) refers to a particular job specification programme. We can see that the job specification programme determines the pattern of coordination between fund input elements. The sequencing of tasks and the contents of these tasks in terms of bundles of primitive operations implies a pattern of coordinated activity of fund input elements; on the other hand, the existing capability structure of fund inputs will affect the appropriate specification and sequencing of tasks to make the best use of available capabilities.

We now come to the crucial issue of fund input utilization. As pointed out above, fund elements are generally available in productive units whether or not they are currently used to execute tasks. This introduces the second relevant criterion in deciding upon a particular fund-task allocation (or job specification) scheme, namely to take account of the problem of utilization of

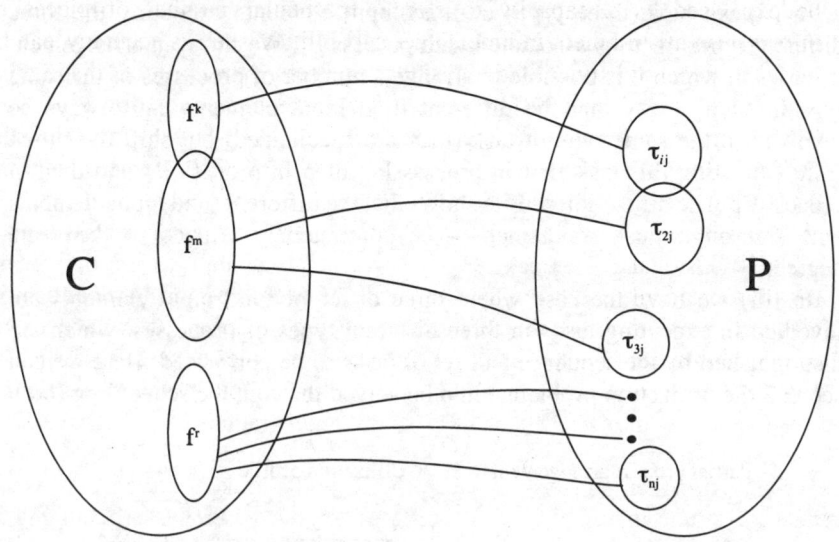

Figure 1 Capabilities, tasks and the job specification programme
Note: C refers to the space of capabilities, P to the space of 'primitive operations'; f^k, f^m, f^r
refer to different fund input elements and τ_{ij} refers to tasks i ($i = 1, \ldots,$ n) to be executed in a
process j.

available fund input elements. As was discussed earlier on, the definition of fund input elements in a multidimensional capability space implies that the problem of 'capacity utilization' must also be seen as a problem with as many dimensions (i.e. whether and to which degree a particular fund input element is utilized in all of its dimensions, speed, accuracy, etc. when executing a particular task or set of tasks). Traditionally, the notion of capacity utilization in production analysis has often been limited to a single dimension, and at times we will also proceed in this way. However, at other times, organizational production analysis will have to consider the multidimensionality of the utilization problem (see the discussion of historical forms of production organization in Landesmann and Scazzieri (forthcoming: chapter 8)).

The issue of fund input utilization leads us to the arrangement of task executions over time and also to the arrangement of different processes of the same or different types over time. Figure 2 shows three such arrangements.

In (i) we have the same type of fund input element involved sequentially in the three tasks which constitute a process P_1. If we look at the utilization profile (right-hand side) we can see that the degree of utilization (here demonstrated in only one dimension) will change over time as the different tasks require different 'capacities' in one or more capability dimensions; the fund input element does not change its own capacities according to these varying needs.

271

In (ii) we have three types of fund input elements executing the three different types of tasks associated with process P_1. We show an arrangement in series in which it is possible to arrange a number of processes of the same type in such a way that the different fund input elements can always be involved in the same type of task (they are specialized) but shift over time from executing this task first in process P_1^1, then in process P_1^2 and then in process P_1^3. The utilization profile shows that the different fund input elements will – through this arrangement – be continuously utilized to the same degree.[11]

In (iii) we have the case where three different fund input elements are involved in executing tasks in three different types of processes, which are distinguished by the sequence and set of tasks to be performed. Here we can see that the utilization problem could be solved through the scheduling (both

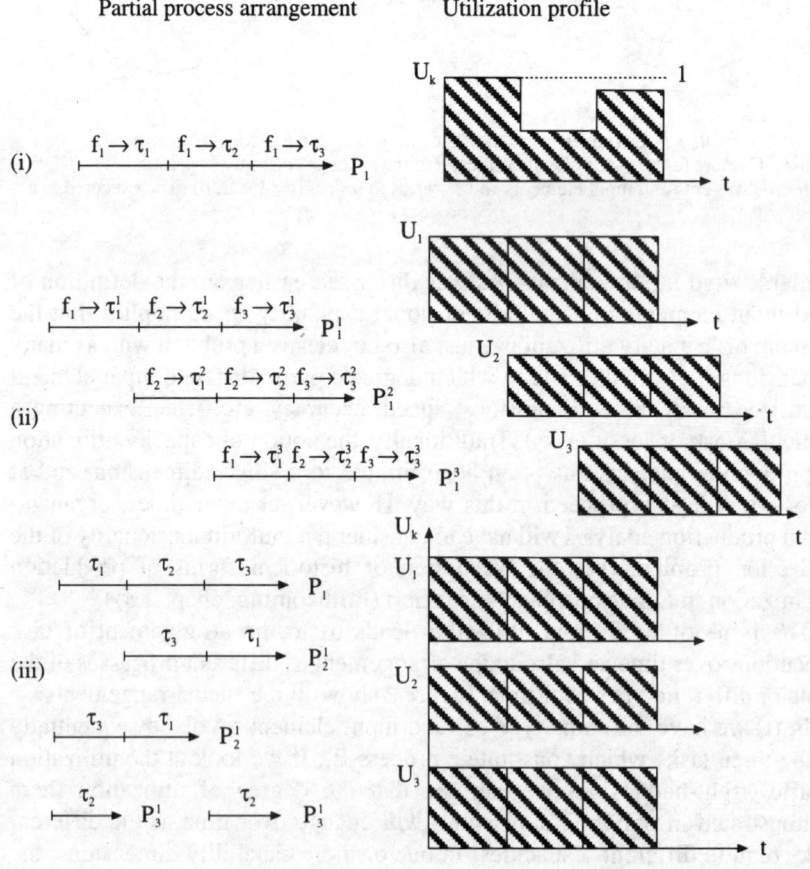

Figure 2 Alternative utilization patterns of fund input elements

272

in time and in scale) of different types of processes which are complementary in their utilization profiles of different funds' available capabilities.

The utilization pattern of fund elements is an important explanatory feature of different forms of production organization and of 'networks' in industrial organization.

Material transformation processes

A critical feature of production processes is that certain materials go through distinct and interrelated stages of fabrication. The sequentiality of such stages, as well as the continuity of the whole transformation process as materials move from one stage to another, is an important characterizing feature of a number of different forms of production organization. An example may be found in Marx's discussion of the factory system, in which material in process in all its stages of fabrication moves continuously through the different lines of production.[12] On the other hand, in other forms of production organization, the continuity aspect is not much stressed, for stoppages of the material in process occur quite often, although there may be a strong emphasis upon a high degree of utilization of certain types of fund inputs.

The sequentiality of fabrication stages may or may not require continuity of the transformation process as well; this depends upon the physical characteristics of the material in process and the process arrangement itself. This may explain different forms of production organization in certain types of production activity. For example, the need of ensuring the continuity of the transformation process is particularly relevant if certain stages of fabrication produce continuous flow outputs such as red-hot iron, rather than units of indivisible output elements, such as a table, a pair of shoes, an automobile, and so on. This could explain why, in medieval craft production, the pressure to move away from the 'job-shop' pattern of fabrication, which was based on stop and go phases of the material transformation process, was particularly strong in those processes in which the continuous flow of half-finished materials was an essential prerequisite of certain intermediate stages, such as the dying process in textile production. Production units in which output emerged in indivisible quantities, such as the carpenter's or blacksmith's workshop, were less exposed to such pressure.

Just as the overall production process can be decomposed into a set of tasks (the arrangement which defines the job programmes to be executed by the different available fund input elements) so does the view of the production process as a process of material transformation allow a decomposition into transformation stages. The scope for such a decomposition and the organizational arrangement of such stages is dependent upon two factors: the knowledge of the properties of the material which is being transformed, and the possibilities which the capabilities/skills of fund factors provide to organize the transformation process in a particular way. The material

273

transformation process can be visualized as a system of pipelines which represents the timing and sequential but also, at times, parallel arrangement of stages in the materials transformation process. It is clear that further decomposition of materials in process into their constituent components and further differentiation or the integration of stages of material transformation do affect such an organizational scheme.

To sum up, the organization of the overall process of material transformation which can be represented as a system of pipelines denoting the timing and the sequential arrangement of the different stages in that transformation process, is strongly dependent on the state of knowledge of the constituent components of the materials being transformed, on the scope to change the methods of transformation at the various stages and upon the capabilities/ skills of fund factors which act upon the decomposed sequences of transformation processes.

FLEXIBILITIES AND RIGIDITIES IN THE PRODUCTION PROCESS

In this section we want to summarize the organizational constraints and possibilities which are associated with the different dimensions of the production process outlined above. We will deal with the following factors:

- input indivisibilities and process indivisibilities – limitations in the bundling and unbundling of capabilities and limitations in the sizes of inputs and processes; this also includes limits to the decomposability of materials in process;
- limited knowledge of the scope for task differentiation and task specification.

Let us discuss features of flexibility and rigidity linked to each of the three dimensions of our analysis of production processes in turn.

Fund inputs

As regards rigidities, the existing technological knowledge restricts the structure of capabilities that can at any point in time be embodied in particular types of fund inputs. Furthermore, there might be an important scale dimension linked to the embodiment of particular capability compositions (e.g. blast furnaces of different sizes have different properties as regards heating efficiency; the same is true for the material throughput to capacity ratio of pipes of any sort, etc.) This scale dimension, which we shall call *fund input indivisibility*, plays an important role in considering the rationale for specific forms of production organization. In addition, there is the rigidity related to the continuous availability of fund input capacities over particular periods of time which poses the utilization issue discussed earlier.

Materials in process and the transformation process

Here again the existing knowledge about materials and the set of feasible transformation processes of such materials constrains at any point in time sequencing possibilities of stages of fabrication and of the particular types of agents (flow and fund agents) required to initiate and carry through the different stages of these transformation processes. As discussed earlier, the potential to interrupt processes of transformation has consequences for the type of production arrangements (and consequent inventory dynamics) which could be implemented. If there are strict continuity requirements the required sequencing arrangements are more rigid. In addition there is also an important scale dimension linked to transformation processes, which Georgescu-Roegen has pointed out:

> Examples of processes that are not indifferent to size are so abundant in natural sciences that one can only wonder how their existence may ever be ignored by other disciplines. At the microscale, organic chemistry offers innumerable examples where new qualities emerge after polymerization, i.e. after a certain scale has been reached ... At the macroscale, in the theory of structures it is almost impossible to find a linear relation between homogenous and perfectibly divisible materials – iron, cement, insulation, etc. – and variables expressing measures of some quality – resistance to strain, elasticity, radiation, and so on.
>
> ... All individual process whether in biology or technology follow exactly the same pattern: beyond a certain scale some collapse, others explode, or melt, or freeze. In a word, they cease to work at all. Below another scale, they do not even exist.
>
> (1976: 288)

This points to the fact that the set of feasible transformation processes is itself scale-dependent, i.e. at certain scale intervals certain transformation processes can take place; at other scale intervals, other transformation processes have to be adopted,

Task specification and task arrangement

Existing process knowledge defines the known 'task anatomy' of a productive process, i.e. the feasible set of task specifications and task arrangements. Advances in process knowledge increase the set of feasible task specifications and thus allow new patterns of task executions to be introduced.

We mentioned earlier that sequentiality and simultaneity requirements in the execution of different tasks result from the complementary nature of different primitive operations which belong to different tasks; however, this is not the only reason for a required sequencing of tasks; the other important reason is that tasks are formulated in response to the logic of particular

275

transformation processes which require a sequence of tasks to be performed and, if there are some degrees of freedom available in such a sequencing, it could be the utilization requirements of available fund elements which requires a particular arrangement of tasks to be executed.

We can thus see that constraints with respect to a particular time structuring of a productive process can arise in all the three dimensions of a production process and, in addition, two of these dimensions (fund inputs, and materials in process and the transformation process) might involve scale requirements with regard to the levels at which activities are to be executed. Constraints with respect to the time structuring and with respect to scale are the two fundamental constraints on the internal organizational structure of a process, and these constraints are of course a function of the state of technological (or process) knowledge in all the three dimensions:

1   knowledge about the possibilities of capabilities (skills) bundling in the development (or training) of fund input elements and knowledge about potential utilization patterns of given capability structures;
2   knowledge about properties of existing materials and the development of new materials and the characteristics of feasible transformation processes of such materials;
3   knowledge about the 'process anatomy' in terms of feasible task specifications and task arrangements.

In all these three dimensions learning processes (expansions of knowledge) affect each other.

DIMENSIONS OF THE PROBLEM OF IMPERFECT SYNCHRONIZATION IN A PRODUCTION PROCESS

In this section it is argued that perfect synchronization of all the three levels of operation of production processes (i.e. of agents, tasks and materials) is a very special case and that, in general, agents are coordinated with each other according to a time pattern different from the one characterizing the coordination of tasks, or the coordination of material-in-process flows. Basically, there are two fundamental reasons why imperfect synchronization would be the rule in actual production organizations: (a) the difficulty of matching the time sequencing requirements of the three distinct analytical dimensions of the production process, i.e. those of task interdependences, agents' coordination and utilization patterns and time sequences of material transformation processes and material flows, and (b) the constraints which input and process indivisibilities impose quite distinctly on the three dimensions of the production process.

The coordination among productive elements (tasks, agents and materials) is essentially coordination among operational tasks, capabilities and agents' performances, and material transformation processes over time. As a result, the time-structure of production emerges as a multi-level network, such that, for example, tasks are coordinated with each other according to a pattern that is distinct from that characterizing the coordination over time of agents' capabilities and of stages in the material transformation processes. For example, tasks a, b, c, and d could be arranged in such a way that a precedes b and c, while b and c are simultaneous and must both precede d; on the other hand, the 'bundling' of capabilities may be such that certain agents are able to perform a and b while other agents are able to perform c and d. Finally, the sequencing of material transformation stages may be such that the first stage requires tasks a and b, the second stage tasks b and c and the third (final) stage tasks c and d. In this case, the coordination over time of different productive elements is characterized by a problem of synchronization. For the pattern of sequentiality or coincidence would be different depending on whether we consider execution of tasks, performance of capabilities or completion of production stages.

A production process may show a pattern of continuity along one particular dimension while showing patterns of discontinuity along other dimensions. For example, continuity of task execution is compatible with the intermittent utilization of capabilities, or the intermittent completion of fabrication stages. The condition on the number of staggered processes that allows for the continuous execution of tasks is not necessarily coincident with the equivalent condition allowing for the uninterrupted utilization of capabilities. In the case above, a sufficient number of staggered processes (as in the serial arrangement of Figure 2) allows for the continuous execution of tasks at the level of the productive unit; however, such an outcome is not necessarily associated with the continuous execution of fabrication stages. Similarly, it is not difficult to imagine cases in which the continuous utilization of capabilities is impossible.

The above distinction between three different layers of coordination within any given production unit highlights the multidimensional character of the time-structure of production. Patterns of simultaneity or sequentiality may coexist, depending on whether we consider tasks, capabilities or transformation processes. For example, tasks may (at least partially) be overlapping in time, even if the corresponding operations have to be performed in a sequence. Or, fabrication stages could be sequential even if the corresponding tasks are executed by agents operating at the same time.

The above discussion has shown that the patterns of required sequentiality and/or simultaneity on each of the analytical dimensions of a production process pose, in the general case, formidable coordination problems which can usually *not* be solved in a manner such that perfect synchronization (which implies perfect continuity of material in process flows, no inventories and no underutilized capacities) at all the three levels could be assured. The constraints on the possible time structuring at the various levels constitute one major problem in the overall synchronization in a productive process; the other problem results from input and process indivisibilities, as mentioned above. Due to limited space we do not want to explore here in detail the relationship between scale and productive organization, but we would like to point out that the different analytical dimensions each pose separate problems of indivisibility and hence overall coordination across the three analytical dimensions will almost certainly lead to compromise arrangements in which some of the phenomena linked to imperfect synchronization (i.e. temporary underutilization of capacities, stop-go phases in transformation processes and inventories) will almost certainly appear.[13] (For details see Landesmann (1986).)

THE EVOLUTIONARY CHARACTER OF PRODUCTIVE ORGANIZATION

The previous section attempted to show that the actual 'functioning' of a production process requires the operation of a complex organizational structure, such that tasks, funds and transformation processes are coordinated with one another both in time and scale. Such a pattern of coordination is often the result of the emergence of a set of interlocking practices, such as those associated with a workshop or an industrial district, but is not necessarily the outcome of deliberate planning by particular agents. As a result, time-coordination takes an evolutionary or historical dimension that is not necessarily linked with a pattern of consistent intertemporal choices. Rather, coordination may often emerge as a result of adjustment but also of inertia in changing existing practices. Observable patterns of industrial coordination are thus compatible with a considerable degree of imperfect synchronization, and perfect synchronization appears to be only an ideal type case in which the utilization patterns, task arrangements, and the continuity of material-in-process flows are perfectly matched. In this particular case, coordination problems of production processes in both time and scale bring into existence a form of production organization that may also be described by ignoring the time-structure of production.[14]

Most other forms of production organization, however, would be insufficiently characterized by a description which ignores the 'time structure' aspect, since this would overlook the compromise nature of the patterns of coordination of tasks, capabilities and fabrication stages which in most cases imply imperfect synchronization. For example, job-shop manufacturing is based upon a relatively loose organization of tasks and capabilities and a precise arrangement of the transformation stages of materials in process up to the point of delivery.[15] A similar pattern is to be found in agricultural forms of production organization, which generally show considerable flexibility of task arrangements and capability utilization but which are otherwise constrained by fixed available times during which certain biological processes have to take place. On the other hand, the time-structure of 'putting out' processes and of most modern forms of production arrangements (such as just-in-time, the various flexible manufacturing systems, etc.) are remarkably different; they are characterized by a more precise identification (and separation) of capabilities but also show a complex pattern of time coordination relative to material in process flows, which covers inventory adjustment and the carry over of stocks of semi-finished goods from one time period to another. For this reason, fully synchronized production can hardly be detected in actual production organizations, and a snapshot description of the production process (i.e. ignoring coordination patterns over time) cannot bring out the characterizing features of most forms of production organization.

NOTES

1 A fuller presentation of the approach outlined in this paper is contained in Landesmann and Scazzieri (forthcoming). This book was jointly written with Professor Roberto Scazzieri from the University of Bologna. The present paper draws heavily on our joint work.

2 The analysis of 'tasks' has its roots in the Smithian analysis of division of labour, as well as in the other numerous contributions of the eighteenth and nineteenth centuries in which the 'advantages' of division of labour had been considered (see, for example, Beccaria 1771; Storch 1815; Gioja 1815–17; Hermann 1832; Babbage 1832, 1835; Dunoyer 1845; Marx 1867; Leroy-Beaulieu 1896). The rich literature on 'time and motion' studies produced mainly in the United States around the beginning of this century made an important contribution to the analysis of the operational structure of productive activity. However, it also considerably narrowed the scope of production analysis by shifting attention away from other dimensions of the production process, and away from a full acknowledgement of the variety of organizational set-ups within which productive activities may take place (see, for example, Taylor 1911; Church 1912–13; and Gantt 1912). The task specification of a production process is a feature that is largely neglected in current production theory. However, there are important insights into this dimension of production processes by some more recent writers in the production organization literature, such as Woodward (1965).

3 The view that the characteristics of productive agents may be associated with their capabilities may also be found in the early literature on the division of labour (see Smith 1776; Gioja 1815–17; Rae 1834; Babbage 1832). Charles Babbage initiated the abstract treatment of the capabilities of tools and machines (Babbage 1826; see also Babbage 1832, and Ampère 1834). Recently, the capability dimension has been emphasized in the management literature (see, for example, Bessant and Haywood 1986) and in the analysis of the anthropological foundations of economic behaviour (see Sen 1985; Dasgupta 1993).

4 The importance of the raw material basis of productive activities has been emphasized by John Rae (1834). Subsequent contributions have considered the materials-in-process dimension of production processes when examining the relationship between production and time (see Menger 1871; Böhm-Bawerk 1889; Clark 1899; Mayer 1925; Hayek 1941; Hicks 1973). Recently, the

influence of materials-in-process flows in decisively shaping adjustment processes in an economy has been explored by Lowe (1976) and Quadrio-Curzio
(1986).

5   Our view of the constitutive elements of a production process has a number of
features in common with the one developed in a number of important
contributions by Nicholas Georgescu-Roegen (see Georgescu-Roegen 1969,
1971), according to whom a critical distinction is that between 'fund elements'
(inputs that enter a process under a certain description and also leave that process
under 'essentially' the same description) and 'flow elements' (inputs that lose
their identity in the course of the production process, for they enter the process
with a certain description and leave the process under a different description).
The above distinction between agents and materials keeps track of the difference
between production elements that get transformed in the course of the production
process and others that do not, in the sense that they may be identified by a set
of characteristics which remain 'essentially' unchanged in the course of their
utilization over a particular time period. As we shall see below, this feature is a
distinctive characteristic of fund elements.

6   We define task specification as the bundling of sets of primitive operations into
tasks; this is distinguished from task arrangement, which refers to the organizational arrangement of tasks in the overall productive process; it defines their
sequential and parallel ordering and thus the functional interrelationships of tasks
in a productive process.

7   We generally do not adopt Georgescu-Roegen's 'process fund' notion since the
analytical distinction between 'funds' which essentially maintain their characteristics in the course of a specified production process and a 'process fund'
(material in process) which undergoes qualitative change in the course of the
process of transformation is too great to employ the same concept. There might
be capital-theoretic reasons to see a commonality between the two types of
elements, but these do not concern us here.

8   An analysis of structural stability can be found in the engineering literature; see,
e.g. Przemieniecki (1985).

9   For a general argument relevant in this connection, see Cartwright (1989:
141–82).

10 Take the case of three types of fund elements f^k, f^m and f^r which are being ordered
in terms of their task-adequacy with respect to two types of tasks τ_i and τ_j.
Denoting by $f^k \rightarrow \tau_j$ the allocation of fund element of type k to undertake task j,
we may have the following orderings:

$$f^k \rightarrow \tau_i > f^m \rightarrow \tau_i > f^r \rightarrow \tau_i$$
$$f^r \rightarrow \tau_j > f^m \rightarrow \tau_j > f^k \rightarrow \tau_j$$

where the symbols > and < denote, respectively, the relations 'more adequate
(task performance) than' and 'less adequate (task performance) than'.

11 The example given here is somewhat special in that the times to execute the
different types of tasks have been assumed to be the same, but the argument can
be generalized to the case where the execution times of different tasks differ. In
that case new processes have to be started at the smallest common denominator
of the fractions $1/t(\tau_1)$, $1/t(\tau_2)$, $1/t(\tau_3)$ where $t(\tau_k)$ $k = 1,2,3$ denotes the execution
time of task τ_k. The number of fund input elements hired in this (integer) case has
to increase accordingly. For a discussion of the general case, see Landesmann
(1986).

12   If we confine our attention to some particular lot of raw materials, of rags,
for instance, in paper manufacture, or of wire in needle manufacture, we

280

perceive that it passes in succession through a series of stages in the hands of the detail workmen until completion. On the other hand, it we look at the workshop as a whole, we see the raw material in all the stages of its production at the same time.... The different detail processes, which were successive in time, have become simultaneous, go on side by side in space. Hence, production of a greater quantum of finished commodities in a given time.

(Marx 1967, edition quoted 1970: 327)

13 E. A. G. Robinson pointed this out long ago in his study *The Structure of Competitive Industry*:

Mechanical units do not arrange themselves easily into groups such that they give their best results with an output, one of one hundred units a day, another of two hundred, a third of four hundred, so that they can be fitted neatly into the industrial jig-saw. There will be several different mechanical bottlenecks in the firm, each requiring to be used, for greater efficiency, up to its fullest capacity, but each requiring a daily output in order that it may be used. The escape from this difficulty may be a compromise, one machine being overdriven, so that it produces slightly more than it can with optimum efficiency, another producing slightly less.

(1958: 25–6 first edn 1931)

14 See also Georgescu-Roegen (1970).
15 Abruzzi gives the following characterization of the job-shop form of production organization:

the process is ... segmented into linked organic work phases, each as functionally unified as is operationally feasible. Also, each of these phases is decomposable into individual work cycles having the same characteristics, which vary in number and quality according to particular job orders. The organic work phases thus have variable contours, which means that they are mutable and elastic. With these properties, there is no necessity for defining separate connecting phases: successive phases, being organic and variable, have internal connecting operations with the quality of being fully sequential in the functional sense. In sum, then, the organic work phases ... are mutually interdependent to the point that their very structures are functionally linked. It follows that the production sequencing order is variable rather than fixed, with linkages based eventually on work content rather than work pace.

(1965: 101–2)

REFERENCES

Abruzzi, A. (1965) 'The production process: operating characteristics', *Management Science*, 11(6): B98–B118.
Ampère, A.-M. (1834) *Essai sur la philosophie des sciences*, Paris: Bachelier.
Babbage, C. (1826) 'On a method of expressing by signs the action of machinery', in *Philosophical Transactions* (Royal Society): 250–65.
——— (1832) *On the Economy of Machinery and Manufactures*, London: Charles Knight.
——— (1835) *On the Economy of Machinery and Manufactures*, fourth edn, London: Charles Knight.

Beccaria, C. (1771) Elementi di economia pubblica', in *Cesare Beccaria. Opere*, ed. S. Romagnoli, Florence: Sansoni, 1958.

Bessant, J. and Haywood, B. (1986) 'Flexibility in manufacturing systems', *Omega: The International Journal of Management Science*, 14(6): 465–73.

Böhm-Bawerk, E. von (1889) *Positive Theorie des Kapitales*, Innsbruck: Wagner (translated as *The Positive Theory of Capital*, London: Macmillan, 1981).

Cartwright, N. (1989) *Nature's Capacities and their Measurement*, Oxford: Clarendon Press.

Church, A. H. (1912–13) 'Practical principles of rational management', *Engineering Magazine*, 44 (1912): 487–94, 673–80, 894–903; 45 (1913): 24–33, 166–73, 405–11.

Clark, J. B. (1899) *The Distribution of Wealth*, New York: Macmillan.

Cohendet, P., Ledoux, M., Zuskovitch, E. (1988) (eds) *New Advanced Materials. Economic Dynamics and European Strategy*, Berlin, Heidelberg, New York: Springer-Verlag.

Dasgupta, P. (1993) *An Inquiry into Well-Being and Destitution*, Oxford: Clarendon Press.

Dunoyer, C. (1845) *De la liberté de travail*, Paris: Guillaumin.

Gantt, H. L. (1912) 'The task and the day's work', in *Addresses and Discussions at the Conference on Scientific Management held October 12–13–14 1911*, The Amos Tuck School of Administration and Finance, Dartmouth College, Hanover, New Haven.

Georgescu-Roegen, N. (1969) 'Process in farming versus process in manufacturing: a problem of balanced development', in *Economic Problems of Agriculture in Industrial Societies*, ed. G. U. Papi and C. Nunn, New York: St Martins Press, pp. 497–528.

—— (1970) 'The economics of production', *American Economic Review*, LX (May): 1–9.

—— (1971) *The Entropy Law and the Economic Process*, Cambridge, Mass.: Harvard University Press.

—— (1976) *Energy and Economic Myths: Institutional and Analytical Essays*, Oxford: Pergamon Press.

Gioja, M. (1815–1817) *Nuovo Prospetto delle Scienze Economiche*, Milan: Pirotta.

Hayek, F. A. von (1941) *The Pure Theory of Capital*, London: Routledge.

Hermann, F. B. W. von (1832) *Staatswirtschaftliche Untersuchungen*, Munich: A. Weber.

Hicks, J. (1939) *Value and Capital. An Inquiry into Some Fundamental Principles of Economic Theory*, Oxford: Clarendon Press.

—— (1973) *Capital and Time, A Neo-Austrian Theory*, Oxford: Clarendon Press.

Landesmann, M. (1986) 'Conceptions of technology and the production process', in M. Baranzini and R. Scazzieri (eds) *Foundations of Economics. Structures of Inquiry and Economic Theory*, Oxford and New York: Basil Blackwell, pp. 281–310.

—— (1996) 'The T-F-M approach to production analysis and the analysis of organisational change'; Working Paper no. 96–2; Johannes Kepler University Linz.

—— and R. Scazzieri (1990) 'Specification of structure and economic dynamics', in M. Baranzini and R. Scazzieri (eds) *The Economic Theory of Structure and Change*, Cambridge: Cambridge University Press, pp. 95–121.

—— (forthcoming) *Production and Economic Dynamics*, Cambridge: Cambridge University Press.

Leroy-Beaulieu, P. (1986) *Traité théorique et pratique d'économie politique*, Paris: Guillaumin.

Lowe, A. (1976) *The Path of Economic Growth*, Cambridge: Cambridge University Press.

Marx, K. (1867; 1970) *Das Kapital*, vol. I, Hamburg: O. Meissner; English edition, London: Lawrence & Wishart.

Mayer, H. (1925) 'Produktion', in L. Elster, A. Weber, F. Wilser (eds), *Handworterbuch der Staatswissenschaften*, vol. 6, Jena: Gustav Fischer, pp. 1108–22.

Menger, C. (1871) *Grundsätze der Volkswirtschaftsleh*, Vienna: Braumüller.

Przemieniecki, J. S. (1985) *Theory of Matrix Structural Analysis*, London: Constable; New York: Dover.

Quadrio Curzio, A. (1986) 'Technological scarcity: an essay on production and structural change', in M. Baranzini and R. Scazzieri (eds), *Foundations of Economics, Structures of Inquiry and Economic Theory*, Oxford and New York: Basil Blackwell, pp. 311–38.

Rae, J. (1834) *Statement of some New Principles on the Subject of Political Economy, exposing the fallacies of the system of the free trade and of some other doctrines maintained in the Wealth of Nations*, Boston, Mass.: Hilliard, Gray.

Robinson, E. A. G. (1931; 1954) *The Structure of Competitive Industry*, Cambridge: Cambridge University Press.

Rosenberg, N. (1969) 'The direction of technological change: inducement mechanisms and focusing devices', *Economic Development and Cultural Change*, 18: 1–24.

—— (1976) *Perspectives on Technology*, Cambridge: Cambridge University Press.

Scazzieri, R. (1993) *A Theory of Production, Tasks, Processes and Technical Practices*, Oxford: Clarendon Press.

Sen, A. (1985) *Commodities and Capabilities*, Amsterdam: North Holland.

Smith, A. (1776) *An Inquiry into the Nature and Causes of the Wealth of Nations*, London: Strahan & Cadell.

Storch, H. F. (1815) *Cours d'économie politique, un exposition des principes qui déterminent la prospérité des nations*, St Petersburg: Pluchart.

Taylor, F. W. (1911) *The Principles of Scientific Management*, New York and London: Harper.

Woodward, J. (1965) *Industrial Organisation: Theory and Practice*, London, New York, Toronto: Oxford University Press.

22

LIMITS TO RELATIVE PRICE MOVEMENTS

Ian Steedman

The various Sraffa-based criticisms of marginalist theory which emerged in the 1960s and 1970s took on many different manifestations – reswitching, capital-reversing, upward sloping relative demand curves for primary inputs, etc., etc. Yet behind these varied forms there always stood one and the same fundamental fact, namely that the relative prices of produced commodities changed (in general) whenever the uniform rate of profit changed, whether or not the technique of production also changed. That fundamental fact also stood, of course, at the root of the notorious 'transformation problem' of Marxian economics. Since Geoff Harcourt has been greatly interested in such questions, it may not be inappropriate to devote this contribution to his Festschrift to a consideration of *how much* relative prices can change as the rate of profit changes. It is very well known that only under very special conditions do they not vary at all. But when they *do* vary, by how much do they vary? This question has received some attention in the context of empirical, input–output studies (see, for example, Bienenfeld (1988) and Ochoa (1989)) but it would, presumably, be desirable to see whether any limits to relative price movement can be established theoretically. For while it is certainly true that *any* degree of relative price sensitivity to the rate of profit is sufficient to undermine many well-known constructions in economic theory, the extent of such sensitivity is still of importance in determining, for example, the probability of reswitching, the likely magnitude of the errors involved in approximating production prices by 'Marxian values', etc. It should perhaps be said at once that what follows does not provide definitive answers to the questions which are implicitly being raised here but it may be hoped that it does provide some suggestions as to how such questions might be dealt with.

PRICE VECTOR INCLUSION

Consider the square price/wage/profit rate system described by

$$pB = mE + (1 + r)pA \qquad (1)$$

where B, E and A are the matrices of outputs, primary inputs and produced inputs, respectively, while p, m and r are the money price vector, the money wage rate vector and the uniform rate of profit. Since we shall not consider changes in relative wage rates here, define the money wage bill vector by $b \equiv mE$ and rewrite (1) as

$$pB = b + (1 + r)pA \qquad (2)$$

Provided that $(B - A)$ is non-singular, we can of course vertically integrate equation (2) to obtain

$$p = v + rpH \qquad (3)$$

where $v \equiv b(B - A)^{-1}$ is the vertically integrated money wage bill vector and $H \equiv A(B - A)^{-1}$ is the vertically integrated matrix of produced input requirements.

Suppose now that A (and hence H) is non-singular. (Or at least that this is so for some part of the system shown in (1) and consider that part.) Using the rows of A as a new basis, write

$$b = tA \qquad (4)$$

From (4)

$$v = tH \qquad (5)$$

and, indeed, (5) also implies (4). If the vector t is semi-positive then (4) states that the row vector b lies 'inside' the convex polyhedral cone defined by the rows of A. (The word 'inside' will be used in the weak sense of 'not outside'.) Denoting that cone by $C(A)$, one can say, from (4) and (5), that b lies inside $C(A)$ if and only if v lies inside $C(H)$. Now we know, of course, that when the profit rate is at its maximum $r = R$ (with $b = v = 0$), the price vector p^* satisfies

$$p^* = Rp^*H \qquad (6)$$

and that, if H is semi-positive and irreducible as will be supposed here, p^* is positive. Hence, from (6), p^* lies inside $C(H)$. But (3) and (5) show that

$$p = (t + rp)H$$

and hence that, if t is semi-positive, p lies inside $C(H)$ *for all* $0 \le r \le R$. Not only does p^* lie inside $C(H)$, but *all* economically relevant price vectors do so. We may thus say that if b lies inside $C(A)$ then $C(H)$ always contains the price vector $(0 \le r \le R)$ and hence that, if $C(H)$ is a 'sharp' cone, with only 'small' angles between the rows of H, the relative prices of produced commodities will vary only to a limited degree as r varies in the relevant range. What determines whether $C(H)$ is 'sharp'?

Suppose now that our economic system involves only single products, so that one may set $B \equiv I$. Define the 'Leontief' matrix $L \equiv (I - A)^{-1}$, so that

$H \equiv LA \equiv AL$. Since A and L are both semi-positive, we see at once that $C(H)$ lies inside both $C(A)$ and $C(L)$. 'How much' does it lie inside them? In the following section we shall consider a special case in which the answer to that question can be stated as, 'It depends on R and the smaller is R, the "sharper" is $C(H)$'.

We may note first, however, that since $[B-(1 + r)A]^{-1} \equiv (B - A)^{-1}$ $(I - rH)^{-1}$, whenever $(B - A)^{-1}$ is semi-positive the (variable) cone formed by the rows of $[B - (1 + r)A]^{-1}$ lies inside the (variable) cone formed by the rows of $(I - rH)^{-1}$. Hence the former cone places a tighter restriction on the angle between $p(r)$ and p^*.

CIRCULANT MATRICES

In order to exemplify the kind of reasoning suggested above, we shall now suppose that $B \equiv I$ and that A is a circulant matrix, i.e., a matrix of the form:

$$A \equiv \begin{bmatrix} a_0 & a_1 & a_2 & & \cdots & a_{n-1} \\ a_{n-1} & a_0 & a_1 & & & a_{n-2} \\ a_{n-2} & a_{n-1} & a_0 & a_1 & & a_{n-3} \\ \vdots & & & & & \\ a_1 & a_2 & a_3 & a_4 & & a_0 \end{bmatrix} \quad \text{(D1)}$$

As will be seen from the definition (D1), each row of A consists of the same n elements, arranged in the same order but always shifted one space to the right as one passes from row i to row $(i+1)$. (For this purpose, $1 = n + 1$.) Consequently, A may be written in the more compact form $A \equiv$ circ $[a_0, a_1, \ldots, a_{n-1}]$, since this expression fully defines A. It need hardly be said that there is no good economic reason for supposing an input–output matrix to be a circulant matrix and that if we make such a supposition here it is for mathematical convenience, in order to illustrate a basic idea in a special case. The convenience of the circulant matrix for our present purpose is as follows. Let s be a row summation vector; it is obvious from (D1) that:

$$sA = \left(\sum_0^{n-1} a_i \right) s$$

so that s is in fact p^* and $(1 + R)^{-1} = (\sum_0^{n-1} a_i)$. (Note that s^t is a right-hand vector of A.) Now, since $p^* = s$, it is clear from (D1) that every row of A makes exactly the same angle with p^*. Moreover, when A is a circulant matrix, L and H must also be circulant matrices[1] so that, again, all the rows of L make a common angle with p^* and all the rows of H make a common angle with p^*. It is thus obvious how to define and measure the 'sharpness' of $C(A)$, $C(L)$ and $C(H)$. The most fundamental circulant matrix is defined by $\Pi \equiv$ circ $[0,1,0,\ldots, 0]$, since any circulant matrix may be written as the weighted sum of powers of Π. We now consider the very special case

$$(1 + R)A = \Pi \quad \text{(7)}$$

which makes $C(A)$ as 'blunt' as possible, since each row of A is orthogonal to every other row. From (7) one can derive:

$$[(1+R)^n-1]\,L = \text{circ}[(1+R)^n, (1+R)^{n-1}, \ldots, (1+R)] \tag{8}$$

and

$$[(1+R)^n-1]\,H = \text{circ}[1, (1+R)^{n-1}, \ldots, (1+R)] \tag{9}$$

Whilst the rows of A are mutually orthogonal, it is clear from (8) and (9) that the rows of L and of H are far from being so and, indeed, that as R is (notionally) decreased towards zero, both the rows of L and the rows of H tend to become proportional to the row summation vector $s = p*$.[2] To be more explicit, let Θ_M be the angle between s and each row of the circulant matrix M. Then, from (7), (8) and (9):

$$\cos\Theta_A = n^{-1/2} \tag{10}$$

$$\cos\Theta_L = \cos\Theta_H = \left\{ \left(\frac{2+R}{nR} \right) \left[\frac{(1+R)^n - 1}{(1+R)^n + 1} \right] \right\}^{1/2} \tag{11}$$

For $n \geq 2$ and $R > 0$, (10) and (11) show that $\cos\Theta_A < \cos\Theta_H$ or $\Theta_H < \Theta_A$. As R tends to zero, in (11), $\cos\Theta_H$ tends to unity or Θ_H tends to zero.

Alternatively, let $\emptyset_M$ be the angle between the adjacent rows of the circulant matrix M. While the rows of A in (7) are mutually orthogonal, it follows from (8) and (9) that:

$$\cos\emptyset_L = \cos\emptyset_H = \left[\frac{(1+R) + (1+R)^{n-1}}{1 + (1+R)^n} \right] \tag{12}$$

From (12), the adjacent rows of L or of H (the top row is 'of course' adjacent to the bottom one) are far from being orthogonal and, indeed, as R is (notionally) decreased towards zero, $\emptyset_L$ and $\emptyset_H$ tend to zero.

Thus even when the rows of A are mutually orthogonal one finds that Θ_H and $\emptyset_H$ are both much smaller than $(\pi/2)$; the most 'blunt' $C(A)$ possible can still generate a reasonably 'sharp' $C(H)$ if R is not too large. Of course, Θ_H and $\emptyset_H$ are both increasing in n; for example, $\cos\emptyset_H$ tends to $(1+R)^{-1}$ as n increases without limit. On the other hand, we have deliberately considered a 'worst case' for the 'sharpness' of $C(H)$ and less extreme cases of the 'bluntness' of $C(A)$ will tend to produce 'sharper' $C(H)$.

(We may note that if A is given by (7) and $(1+R)\rho \equiv (1+r)$ then:

$$(1-\rho^n)[I-(1+r)A]^{-1} = \text{circ}\,[1, \rho, \ldots, \rho^{n-1}]. \tag{13}$$

The interested reader can readily calculate from (13) the cosine of the angle between each row of $[I-(1+r)A]^{-1}$ and $s = p*$. The angle between adjacent rows of that matrix is given by

$$\cos \emptyset = \left(\frac{\rho + \rho^{n-1}}{1 + \rho^n} \right)$$

which generalizes (12).)

The obvious next step is to extend the above to a general circulant matrix A as defined in (D1) but, alas, the inversion of $(I - A)$ seems not to be over-simple, even though A has such a definite structure. One can, of course, obtain results for special circulants; if, for example, $(1 + R)A = \text{circ}(c_0, c_1, 0, \ldots, 0)$ then $[I - (1 + r)A]^{-1} = \text{circ}[1 - c_0\rho)^{n-1}, (1 - c_0\rho)^{n-2}(c_1\rho), \ldots, (c_1\rho)^{n-1}]/[(1 - c_0\rho)^n - (c_1\rho)^n]$, where $(1 + R)\rho \equiv (1 + r)$. L and H follow easily and it is simple – if tedious – to find $\cos \Theta_A$, etc. It is not clear, however, that the extra insights gained justify the volume of calculation required. We therefore turn to another type of A matrix.

SYMMETRIC MATRICES

Consider another very special – and economically implausible – case, that in which $B = I$, A is symmetric and hence L and H are symmetric. Let $A \equiv Q$ $â$ Q^t, where Q is orthogonal with its first column, Q_1, semi-positive and the elements of the diagonal matrix $â$ satisfy $(1+R)a_1 = 1$ and $-a_1 < a_j < a_1$ for all $j \neq 1$. The top row of Q^t is, of course, proportional to p^*. Let $\Theta(M^i)$ be the angle between p^* and the ith row of the symmetric matrix M. It is easily calculated that:

$$\tan^2\theta(A^i) = \sum_{j=2}^{n} (a_j/a_1)^2 \left(\frac{Q_{ij}}{Q_{i1}} \right)^2$$

$$\tan^2\theta(L^i) = \sum_{j=2}^{n} \left(\frac{1 - a_1}{1 - a_j} \right)^2 \left(\frac{Q_{ij}}{Q_{i1}} \right)^2 \qquad (14)$$

$$\tan^2\theta(H^i) = \sum_{j=2}^{n} \left(\frac{a_j}{a_1} \cdot \frac{1 - a_1}{1 - a_j} \right)^2 \left(\frac{Q_{ij}}{Q_{i1}} \right)^2$$

It is readily seen from (14) that $\Theta(H^i)$ is smaller than both $\Theta(L^i)$ and $\Theta(A^i)$ and that, *ceteris paribus*, $\Theta(L^i)$ and $\Theta(H^i)$ both tend to zero as R tends to zero. (How fast $\Theta(L^i)$ and $\Theta(H^i)$ tend to zero depends, of course, on how close to unity are the a_j other than a_1.) How $\Theta(H^i)$, for example, varies with i, will of course depend on the structure of the matrix Q. The reader may wish to consider how more can be said about the conditions under which, A being symmetric, the maximum value of $\Theta(H^i)$ will be 'small', so that $C(H)$ is 'sharp' and relative price variation will be small whenever the direct wage bill vector lies inside $C(A)$.

CONCLUDING REMARKS

The approach to thinking about the limits to relative price movement which was proposed in the section on 'price vector inclusion' was, of course, not limited to any particular structure of the A matrix – it even allowed for joint production. Thus the very special nature of our subsequent illustrations of that approach, supposing single products and a circulant or symmetric A matrix, should not be taken to mean that the approach itself depends on very special assumptions. It is hoped that the reader will be stimulated to apply the approach to more general cases, which can nevertheless yield some 'specific' results.

NOTES

1   For introductory remarks on the properties of circulant matrices see, for example, Aitken (1967: 131–2) and Bellman (1970: 242–3); for a full monograph study, see Davis (1979). Notice that, in (D1), every commodity is a Sraffa-basic provided that at least one a_i other than a_0 is positive.
2   Because $(1 + R)H = \Pi L$ in the very simple case considered here, the ith row of L is simply $(1 + R)$ times the $(i - 1)$th row of H: this is not, of course, true for the more general circulant A matrix, for which $C(H)$ lies inside $C(L)$.

REFERENCES

Aitken, A. C. (1967) *Determinants and Matrices*. Edinburgh: Oliver & Boyd.
Bellman, R. (1970) *Introduction to Matrix Analysis*. New York: McGraw-Hill.
Bienenfeld, M. (1988) 'Regularity in price changes as an effect of changes in distribution', *Cambridge Journal of Economics*, 12: 247–55.
Davis, P. J. (1979) *Circulant Matrices*. New York: Wiley and Sons.
Ochoa, E. M. (1989) 'Values, prices, and wage-profit curves in the US economy', *Cambridge Journal of Economics*, 13: 413–29.

23

THE MYTHS OF FREE
BANKING

Mervyn K. Lewis

It is not often that a lecture is interrupted by an announcement that a bank run is taking place, but this is what happened to me on a Thursday morning in October 1974 at the University of Adelaide. When the message from Geoff Harcourt arrived, I hurriedly disbanded the class – appropriately enough one in monetary economics – and the Economics Department trooped up *en masse* to the city centre to see what was going on. There was quite a hullabaloo, although that was as much from the hundreds of onlookers as from those taking out money. For the most part, those withdrawing funds from the Hindmarsh Building Society were queued in an orderly fashion – Australians also know how to queue – and in that respect, it was a run rather than a panic. Nevertheless, the queue of withdrawing customers stretched for more than a block and numbers seemed to be building up fast. Matters came to a head when the colourful and talented Labor Premier, Don Dunstan, arrived on the scene equipped with loud-hailer to assure people that their money was safe and that the building society was backed by the state government. Mob psychology being what it is, most of the crowd then dissipated, somewhat shamefacedly.

Even so, the withdrawals continued for some time, and the tide was not turned until a special sitting of the South Australian parliament was called, and the government tabled the Building Societies Temporary Assistance Bill 1974, drafted overnight, authorizing the state government to borrow $10 million from the Reserve Bank of Australia in order to provide assistance to the state's building societies. Only much later did it emerge how hard-pressed the societies had been at the time.[1] In total, 10,000 of the 60,000 depositors of the Hindmarsh Building Society withdrew balances. In the space of four days alone at the beginning of October, withdrawals totalled $10 million from a balance sheet of $48 million. Despite being in breach of statutory liquidity ratios as the run unfolded, the Hindmarsh was given special dispensation by the Registrar of Building Societies to continue lending, so allowing the society to maintain the semblance of 'business as usual' – a factor considered important by the management in stemming the tide.

The run on the Hindmarsh soon spread to the state's other leading building society, the Co-operative Building Society, and the withdrawals also sparked runs on building societies in Queensland, where the situation became so serious that the Reserve Bank was forced to intervene and funnel emergency loans to the societies via the trading banks. In the case of the Co-operative Building Society, the appearance of normalcy was maintained, while paying out $5 million, by the simple tactic of not verifying signatures and authorizations, clearing customers so quickly from the chambers that a queue could not form. Clearly, a 'silent run', a term used to describe a run confined to withdrawals of large-valued deposits by wholesale customers, can also take place in retail markets.

Two decades after the event, it is no clearer than it was at the time why the run began and why the Hindmarsh should have been the chosen target. Many of the building societies wiped out in the crash of the 1890s can at least be said to have contributed to their own downfall by channelling depositors' money into speculative property and land developments. (Cannon 1966). The same was true of some of the banks which were forced to close their doors, although there was often little discernible difference between the balance sheets of those banks that failed and those that survived (Pope 1989). In all, fifty-four out of sixty-four banks and thirty-five of the thirty-six para-banking organizations were forced to close or suspend payment in the shake-out which followed the building society and banking scandals of those years.

Admittedly, on the morning of the day when the run on the Hindmarsh began, the local newspaper, *The Adelaide Advertiser*, carried the story of the collapse of Cambridge Credit, a finance company engaged in lending on property development. But, unless the society's depositors happened to have been keen students of nineteenth-century colonial history, there is no obvious reason why this event should have brought the Hindmarsh under suspicion. The society had no connection with Cambridge Credit, nor with any other finance company for that matter. Nor was the Hindmarsh involved in commercial or other real estate developments. Its balance sheet looked exactly how that for a building society ought to have looked. Three-quarters of assets were home mortgage loans to members, secured against residential property. Most of the remaining assets were invested in government bonds and bank deposits. The society had been operating for ninety-six years in a sound manner, and had not been associated (before or since) with any imprudent behaviour.

Experience is a powerful teacher, and witnessing an apparently 'irrational' run with potentially damaging consequences has made me sceptical of the extremes of the free banking position, despite my predisposition towards free market solutions. Free banking is a description which embraces a number of different themes, and in the UK confusion comes from the use of the term 'free banking' to refer to a 1985 marketing campaign by the Midland Bank which resulted in the abolition of charges for keeping a current account (see

291

Llewellyn and Drake 1993).[2] Moreover, what is meant by free banking has changed markedly over time as the financial system has evolved. Free banking in nineteenth-century United States meant a system in which any organization could enter the banking industry so long as it met the statutory requirements for minimum capital and adhered to regulations covering its operations (Dunbar 1992). In this context, 'free' meant that entry to the industry was possible, not that it was unregulated.

Hayek later used the term free banking to describe 'a system ... which not only gives all banks the right of note issue and at the same time makes it necessary for them to rely on their own reserves, but also leaves them free to choose their field of operation and their correspondents without regard to national boundaries' (1937: 77). By 1976, this proposal had become one of allowing banks to take deposits, issue liabilities, make loans in the currency of their choice, including gold coins, and to open branches in each others' territories. Since at that time many banks were already doing these things in the Eurocurrency markets, the suggestion had already been overtaken by events. Only the private currency issue part of the plan was at all radical. Even so, Hayek did not envisage the abolition of government-issued money. Rather the idea was for privately issued currencies to serve as a discipline upon over-issue by governments. Such competition would force the authorities to improve the quality of government money or face extinction by market forces. In fact, Hayek drew a distinction between holding money and using money (essentially Sir Dennis Robertson's (1928) 'money sitting' and 'money on the wing'). He had in mind that people would continue to use government money in transactions but would not be willing to hold it as a store of value in preference to private issue, which he envisaged would be pegged to some commodity basket valued by consumers (Flanders 1994).

Thus is it only relatively recently that free banking has moved beyond currency competition to involve the abolition of the central bank. In its current representation, free banking means unregulated competitive banking in a system operating without a central bank or monetary authority (Dowd 1989; Selgin 1987; White 1984).[3] An immediate question that arises is what constitutes money in such a world. One answer, originating from Fischer Black (1970, 1975), is that an unregulated financial system would not need money. Instead a sophisticated form of barter would operate in which transfers would be effected involving assets of all kinds, with instant commands via computer terminals to sell and buy securities, and transfer credits to other accounts in settlement of debts. Even hand-to-hand transactions could be settled by bearer units, with the prices posted daily in newspapers (or via the Internet) just as the prices of unit trusts are advertised now. There would presumably need to be some commonly agreed-upon *numeraire* in which such prices were denominated, which could be achieved, as Dowd (1988) suggests, by redefining the pound sterling as a certain weight of a particular commodity or basket of commodities.

In effect, under free banking there might be a separation of the means of payment from the unit of account, as envisaged by the 'new monetary economics' school (Harper and Coleman 1992). The difficulty here is that some institutions might be tempted to offer units with a fixed price in terms of the resource unit of account, and it might then become the practice to state prices in terms of the bearer units, in much the same way that contracts written in gold pounds came to be written in paper pounds. The hoped-for stable standard might then dissolve into a purely fiduciary standard, and be subject to Friedman's critique.

In *A Program for Monetary Stability*, Friedman argued that private money would tend to be over-issued, noting that 'this is what happened under so-called 'free-banking' in the United States and under similar circumstances in other countries' (1959: 6). He argued that under free competition, there would be an incentive to issue money until marginal revenue equalled marginal cost. Since the cost of issuing paper money is close to zero, fiduciary currency would tend to degenerate into a commodity standard – in fact a literal paper standard. Advocates of free banking have responded in turn to Friedman's advocacy of government intervention to prevent over-issue by accusing him of having little faith in competition, and of failing to distinguish the issue of money from its maintenance, which would necessitate that banks provide quality services to money-holders, not the least of which is that the value of the currency be kept constant in terms of some basket of commodities.

In practice, most examples of free banking have been against the backdrop of a specie standard of some sort or have been in a system where government paper money circulates. In these circumstances, issues of convertibility and the safety of the banking system arise. Those opposed to public intervention in the business of banking have long recognized that the villain of the piece is fractional reserve banking. This is why the Chicago school has always proposed 100 per cent reserve banking, in which banks must back deposits fully with holdings of cash or specie. ('Narrow' banking, the modern-day equivalent, would extend the range of assets to include interest-bearing government bonds.) Without such a restriction, there would exist an incentive for the 'goldsmith bank' to economize on cash holdings. Balances held in transactions accounts with banks rise and fall with the ebb and flow of payments. Each customer holds a positive balance (ignoring overdrafts) because it is too costly to make deposits of currency coincide with withdrawals or the writing of cheques. To customers, these balances represent funds which cannot profitably be lent out because they are needed for transactions purposes. To the bank, however, the aggregation of such balances does constitute an opportunity for profitable lending. Provided that additions to and withdrawals from customer accounts are random, the banks' currency holdings will not deviate greatly from the average value. Hence, rather than themselves hold idle cash, banks have an incentive to exchange a large part of their currency holdings for interest-bearing assets, and so engage in financial intermediation.

All of this has been known for some time. As long ago as 1888, Edgeworth provided a formal analysis of fractional reserve banking and liquidity management, demonstrating that the random depositing and withdrawal of funds tend to offset each other, enabling a bank to hold substantial earning assets while issuing liabilities payable on demand. He showed that so long as depositors' withdrawals can be treated as a stochastic event, and depositors' actions are independent of each other, then the amount of cash reserves needed by a bank to achieve a certain (low) probability that it would find itself with balances insufficient to meet depositors' demands can be calculated statistically. Maintaining reserves equal to some multiple of the standard deviation of withdrawals will then normally allow the bank to achieve a given probability of not running out of reserves.

But the corollary is that fractional reserve banking can render banks vulnerable to the encashment of deposits which the bank has used as a springboard to make loans to finance longer-term investment projects. Consider the balance sheet structure of banks in the UK and US (Lewis 1992). Holdings of cash represent only 1 to 2% of assets. Two-thirds of assets are held in the form of loans and advances. On the other side of the balance sheet, 80% of liabilities are in the form of deposits, most of which mature either on demand or with less than one week's notice. This transformation of illiquid assets (loans) into liquid liabilities (deposits) can be regarded as a special form of insurance – in essence, 'liquidity insurance'. The bank can be thought of as buying primary securities issued by borrowers of funds and then offering them to lenders of funds with an insurance policy added against the contingency that depositors have unexpected needs for cash. In the normal course of events it will be possible to estimate the fraction of depositors demanding liquidity and to provide for liquidity needs along the lines sketched out by Edgeworth and others. However, should depositors be concerned about the solvency of the bank, they have little to lose but much to gain by withdrawing their funds without delay. In this case, independence of depositors' behaviour and the intermediary's ability to meet deposit withdrawals break down, with those first in line gaining under the 'first come-first served' payout rule of deposit claims.

Some writers (e.g. Calomiris and Kahn 1989) view this sequential service rule as a desirable incentive-compatible feature. Those depositors who actively monitor the institution's performance must invest time and effort in doing so, and receive compensation for their diligence by being 'first in line'. As a result, there is an incentive to invest in monitoring effort, which in itself acts as a market discipline upon the banks concerned. More usually, however, the possibility of a bank run is seen as an unfortunate and undesirable by-product of banks' intermediation activities. This is the essence of Diamond and Dybvig's (1983) model – the first formal analysis of banking instability.

Their analysis is set in a hypothetical economy in which there is a sole, multi-period, productive process operating. People can invest in this process, but they face unexpected consumption shocks and any interruption of the investment prior to maturity is costly. A bank enables people to improve the terms on which their urgent demands to withdraw funds can be made, since the aggregate consumption needs can be predicated accurately even if individuals do not know whether they will have spending requirements. The bank invests deposits in the production process on depositors' behalf and the bank deposit contract provides insurance should a depositor turn out to need to withdraw funds. Those forced to withdraw because of the consumption shock receive a higher return than if they had invested directly, and what remains is distributed to those withdrawing later.

But Diamond and Dybvig's bank has a 'good' and 'bad' equilibrium. The good one occurs when those experiencing a consumption shock withdraw funds, as predicted. The bad equilibrium results when those individuals are joined by the others. In this case, the run on the bank, however triggered, proves to be self-fulfilling, for when everyone seeks to withdraw deposits the promised value of deposits plus interest cannot be met from the liquidation value of bank assets (since the higher return promised relies on only a fraction of depositors withdrawing funds) and the return to a depositor depends instead on his or her place in the queue. One 'solution' (if that is the correct description) canvassed by Diamond and Dybvig is the suspension of convertibility – the bank simply closes its doors and prevents early withdrawals. However, the preferred solution of the authors is government deposit insurance – the near universal system used to protect bank depositors, most notably in the United States.

Although described by Friedman and Schwartz as 'the structural change most conducive to monetary stability since state bank note issues were taxed out of existence immediately after the Civil War' (1963: 434), government deposit insurance is anathema to most free-marketers, and Diamond and Dybvig's conclusions have been subjected to very close theoretical scrutiny by the free bankers (see Dowd (1992) for a survey). Free bankers have also questioned the practical relevance of the Diamond and Dybvig result, and it is this aspect upon which we focus. First, there is the vexed issue of deposit insurance. Deposit insurance prevents bank runs in three ways: it reduces the incentive to run from a suspect institution; bad banks do not fail but are taken over and merged or wound up by the government agency; and since depositors know that they are insured against losses, a run is less likely to spread to sound institutions. Deposit insurance is thus unlike conventional insurance, in that the aim is not so much to recompense people after a loss of deposits, but to maintain confidence in banks so that a major factor causing losses, namely a bank run, does not eventuate. In this particular objective deposit insurance has succeeded admirably, but at a considerable cost, for deposit insurance shares with other types of insurance the problem of moral hazard: the insurer is subject to the moral risk that the policyholders' behaviour can affect the probability of loss. Since banks know that their customers are protected, they have an incentive to sail closer to the wind. The US savings and loan crisis of the 1980s is one manifestation of this risk; so too, perhaps, is the property loan saga of the early 1990s (Lewis 1994). How this moral hazard is controlled is as crucial to the successful operation of deposit insurance as it is for other types of insurance. Insurers have developed methods to overcome moral hazard – premiums related to risk, limiting amounts insured, deductibles, coinsurance and the imposition of preventative and risk reduction measures – and these all have their analogues in banking and deposit insurance (White 1989).

A second issue follows on from the first and revolves around the incentives to safe and sound banking (Dowd 1995). In a system of free banking, banks know that they are vulnerable to a run and must make sure that they retain their customers' confidence by pursuing conservative lending policies and maintaining financial strength. If they don't, then depositors will withdraw balances and the bank will soon run out of cash. Without a central bank to help out, a bank has to be strong and must have the confidence of its customers, or else it won't survive. Here we note that the Hindmarsh had ninety-six years of following conservative policies, but that did not seem to help when the crunch came. Confidence is not the same as absolute certainty. One of the directors of the society recalls talking to an old chap who stayed in the queue despite the Premier's reassurance that the institution was safe:

> The old man said, 'Mate, I couldn't afford to take the chance – it's all I've got.' And he was right. If you've got your last bob in something and there's a rumour that it's unsafe, you have to get it out.
>
> (Sykes 1988: 472)

Another element in the free banking position is to give a large role to the interbank market. The argument is that, when runs occur, people move their funds from weak institutions to strong ones. All that is needed to prevent a crisis from occurring is for deposits to be recycled back via the interbank market to the banks under attack. If a bank is well-capitalized and its balance sheet is strong, it should be able to borrow funds against collateral from the banks which are in receipt of deposit inflows. Again, we note, these assumptions seem to be at variance with Australian experience. In the 1890s crisis, apparently sound colonial banks like the National were unable to borrow from the strong ones, the Anglos. In part this was because the advantaged institutions saw a market opportunity arising from the likely demise of their rivals. But they also feared that they would come under suspicion if it became known that they were lending to the 'unsafe' banks. In addition, the notion that deposit funds are simply recycled from one institution to another does not accord with what happened to the Hindmarsh and the Co-operative. There was a large cash drain from the system. A lot of the cash redeposited after the run was still in the bundles supplied by the banks. Some of the currency smelt of mothballs – it had been kept under the carpet.

Free bankers have a point. Too often in the past the case for public regulation of banking was simply presumed, rather than argued through. More market discipline is needed in banking markets, especially in the area of deposit insurance. Nevertheless, based on my own observations on 'Black Thursday', October 1974, I feel more comfortable with Friedman's stance than that of the free banking movement. Moreover, I suspect that this is one occasion when Geoff Harcourt will be happy to vote with Professor Friedman.

NOTES

1   Much of this information comes from Sykes (1988).
2   Indeed, I was amused to find out that Llewellyn and Drake used much the same title as the present paper, while writing about this quite different meaning of free banking.
3   Laidler (1992) provides an excellent survey of the literature.

REFERENCES

Black, F. (1970) 'Banking and interest rates in a world without money: The effects of uncontrolled banking', *Journal of Bank Research*, 1(3): 9–20.

——— (1975) 'Bank funds management in an efficient market', *Journal of Financial Economics*, 2 (December): 323–39. Reprinted in *Financial Intermediaries. The International Library of Critical Writings in Economics*, 43, ed. M. K. Lewis, Cheltenham: Edward Elgar, 1995.

Calomiris, C. W. and Kahn, C. (1989) 'The role of demandable debt in structuring optimal banking arrangements', Mimeo, Northwestern University.

Cannon, M. (1966) *The Land Boomers*, Melbourne: Melbourne University Press.

Diamond, D. W. and Dybvig, P. H. (1983) 'Bank runs, deposit insurance and liquidity', *Journal of Political Economy*, 91(3): 401–19. Reprinted in *Financial Intermediaries. The International Library of Critical Writings in Economics*, 43, ed. M. K. Lewis, Cheltenham: Edward Elgar, 1995.

Dowd, K. (1988) 'Private money: the path to monetary stability', Hobart Paper 122, London: Institute for Economic Affairs.

——— (1989) *The State and the Monetary System*, Oxford: Philip Allan.

——— (1992) 'Models of banking instability: a partial review of the literature', *Journal of Economic Surveys*, 6(2): 107–32. Reprinted in *Financial Intermediaries. The International Library of Critical Writings in Economics*, 43, ed. M. K. Lewis, Cheltenham: Edward Elgar, 1995.

——— (1995) 'Should we abolish the Bank of England?', Inaugural Lecture, Sheffield Hallam University, April.

Dunbar, C. F. (1992) 'Free banking', *New Palgrave Dictionary of Money and Finance*, Vol. 2, London: Macmillan.

Edgeworth, F. Y. (1888) 'The mathematical theory of banking', *Journal of the Royal Statistical Society*, LI: 113–27. Reprinted in *Financial Intermediaries. The*

International Library of Critical Writings in Economics, 43, ed. M. K. Lewis, Cheltenham: Edward Elgar, 1995.

Flanders, M. J. (1994) 'Hayek and the revival of free banking', Working Paper No. 12–94, The Sackler Institute for Economic Studies, Tel Aviv University, May.

Friedman, M. (1959) *A Program for Monetary Stability*, New York: Fordham University Press.

—— and Schwartz, A. J. (1963) *A Monetary History of the United States 1867–1960*, Princeton, N.J.: Princeton University Press.

Harper, I. R. and Coleman, A. (1992) 'New monetary economics', *New Palgrave Dictionary of Money and Finance*, Vol. 3, London: Macmillan.

Hayek, F. A. (1937) *Monetary Nationalism and International Stability*, London: Longmans, Green; New York: Augustus M. Kelley; reprinted edition 1964.

—— (1976) *Choice in Currency: A Way to Stop Inflation*. Occasional Paper 48, London: Institute of Economic Affairs.

Laidler, D. (1992) 'Free banking: theory', *New Palgrave Dictionary of Money and Finance*, Vol. 2, London: Macmillan.

Lewis, M. K. (1992) 'Balance sheets of financial intermediaries, *New Palgrave Dictionary of Money and Finance*, Vol. 1, London: Macmillan.

—— (1994) 'Banking on real estate', *The Competitiveness of Financial Institutions and Centres in Europe*, ed. D. E. Fair and R. Raymond on behalf of the Société Universitaire Européenne de Recherches Financières, Dordrecht: Kluwer Academic Press: 47–71.

Llewellyn, D. and Drake, L. (1993) 'The myth of free banking', *Banking World*, July: 20–2.

Pope, D. (1989) 'Free banking in Australia before World War I', Working Paper 129, Department of Economic History, Australian National University, Canberra.

Robertson, D. H. (1928) *Money*, Cambridge: Cambridge University Press.

Selgin, G. (1987) *The Theory of Free Banking*, Totowea, N.J.: Rowman and Littlefield.

Sykes, T. (1988) *Two Centuries of Panic: A History of Corporate Collapses in Australia*, Sydney: Allen & Unwin.

White, L. H. (1984) *Free Banking in Britain: Theory, Experience and Debate 1800–1845*, Cambridge: Cambridge University Press.

White, L. J. (1989) 'The reform of federal deposit insurance', *Journal of Economic Perspectives*, 3(4): 11–29. reprinted in *Financial Intermediaries. The International Library of Critical Writings in Economics*, 43, ed. M. K. Lewis, Cheltenham: Edward Elgar, 1995.

24

DEFINING AND MEASURING UNEMPLOYMENT IN THE UNITED KINGDOM

Updating the recent controversy

John Wells

INTRODUCTION

UK unemployment reached a cyclical peak in winter 1992/3, and in the ensuing months the issue moved sharply up the political agenda, with John Smith, then leader of the Labour Party, committing the party when in government to a return to full employment – ableit as a *quid pro quo* to the trade unions for their support for his OMOV (one member, one vote) reform of party democracy. During the course of 1994, unemployment remained at the forefront of political debate, partly through the efforts of John Prescott who, both as Opposition employment spokesperson and during his campaign for the Labour Party leadership, articulated widespread public disquiet about the UK's headline unemployment count: the official claimant count (CC) of those unemployed and receiving unemployment-related benefit.[1] Public confidence had been undermined by the frequent changes – totalling 35 to date, virtually all serving to reduce the count – arising from alterations/ reductions in eligibility for benefit as well as technical statistical changes. Prescott quite courageously, given the strength of official disapproval, insisted that unemployment, properly measured, was at least one million higher than the CC, which stood at that time at just below three million. He thereby endorsed the long-held position of the Unemployment Unit,[2] who have argued that unemployment as measured on the previous 'registrant' basis,[3] would have been one million higher (see also Gregg 1994), as well as the position of other researchers (Wells 1995a, 1995b) who pointed to the one million identified by the household Labour Force Survey as being unemployed (according to the 'search' and 'availability' criteria used by the ILO/ OECD) but who were not claiming benefit.

DEFINING AND MEASURING UNEMPLOYMENT: THE ROYAL STATISTICAL SOCIETY'S REPORT

The Council of the Royal Statistical Society (RSS), concerned by the political controversy and evident lack of public confidence in the headline claimant count, and the possible implications for the professional integrity of its members working in the Government Statistical Service, established a Working Party on the Measurement of Unemployment in the UK, whose membership included the present and immediate past presidents of the RSS. Their report was published on 5 April 1995.

The report begins with a number of useful thoughts about the issues involved in defining and then measuring unemployment.[4]

Involuntary unemployment

The Cambridge economist Pigou was the first, it seems,[5] to introduce the term 'involuntary unemployment' in his 1914 volume *Unemployment*. He defined unemployment as the number of persons without paid work who would like to work in their customary occupation at the going rate for the job.

> The amount of unemployment ... in any industry is measured by the number of hours' work ... by which the employment of the persons attached to or occupied in that industry falls short of the number of hours' work that these persons would have been willing to provide at the current rate of wages under current conditions of employment.
>
> (1914: 16)

The stress on current rate of wages reflected, it appears, the then National Insurance Act whereby a man was still treated as unemployed even if he refused to work at less than the going rate for the job. Equally, the reference to the 'going rate' ensures that those with unrealistic wage expectations are classed as 'voluntarily' unemployed. Pigou, in his 1933 book *Theory of Unemployment*, reiterated the same definition (see Kahn 1976):

> A man is only unemployed when he is *both* not employed and *also* desires to be employed.... The desire to be employed must be taken to be desire to be employed at current rates of wages.
>
> (1933: 3, 4)

Keynes, in his clearest statement on the subject,[6] adopted the same approach to defining 'involuntary unemployment':

> the population generally is seldom doing as much work as it would like to do on the basis of the current wage ... More labour would as a rule be forthcoming at the existing money-wage if it were demanded.
>
> (1936: 7)

In this definition, Keynes excluded voluntary unemployment, frictional unemployment (of the between-jobs variety), seasonal unemployment and the unemployable – which together constituted what he called a 'normal' level of unemployment. But 'involuntary unemployment' included structural unemployment (though Keynes did not use the term) and 'so-called' (his term) cyclical unemployment in addition to demand-deficient unemployment due to a persistent slump.

Operationalizing the concept

In trying to make this definition of involuntary unemployment operational for measurement purposes, the practical problem arises as to how to establish whether people without paid work really want a job or not. The approach adopted by international labour statisticians[7] has been to apply 'search' and 'availability' criteria. And the ILO/OECD guidelines on 'search' and 'availability' criteria for involuntary unemployment are currently interpreted in most countries as being those without work, even for one hour, during the reference period, who are available to start work within two weeks and who have actively sought work during the previous four weeks (White and Leyland 1992). Such a definition, whilst excluding inactives who do not want to work, is unable to distinguish between seasonal, frictional, unemployables (= 'normal' unemployment) and 'involuntary' unemployment.

Nor, self-evidently, does the ILO definition make any reference to the 'going rate for the job'. In the UK, currently, there is ample evidence of pressure being applied to unemployed claimants both to revise downwards their wage aspirations and to accept jobs other than in their previous line of work. One obvious question is whether those who persist in refusing to accept a deterioration in their conditions of employment should cease to be called as 'involuntarily unemployed'; Pigou and Keynes would answer in the negative. But, this is, perhaps, to underestimate the pace of structural change and the need for adaptation in the modern world.

Unemployment as a measure of inflationary pressure

In thinking about unemployment, a second focus of concern of economists, in addition to the unmet demand for paid employment, is the relationship between the labour market and developments in the macroeconomy – particularly wage and price inflation. The focus here is on unemployment as a measure of excess supply or demand for labour and its implications for wage inflation. Keynes's estimates, in the 1930s and 1940s, of the 'normal' level of unemployment consistent with money wage stability (when involuntary unemployment was zero, i.e. full employment) exceeded by a wide margin the rate of unemployment which was consistent with non-accelerating inflation during the post-war full employment era down to the mid-1970s. 'Normal' unemployment evolved, in Friedman's hands, into the 'natural' rate, which he defined as the rate consistent with a stable functional distribution of income:

> At that level of unemployment, real wage rates are tending, on average, to rise at a 'normal' secular rate i.e. at a rate that can be indefinitely maintained so long as capital formation, technological improvements etc. remain on their long-run trends.

$$(1968: 8)$$

Any attempt to hold unemployment below the 'natural' rate would result in accelerating inflation and a shift in the functional distribution against profits. The 'natural' rate developed into the NAIRU (the non-accelerating inflation rate of unemployment) – with all its attendant problems of estimation. Attention focused on the difference between the actual and the NAIRU as a measure of excess demand in the labour market. Of course, estimates of the NAIRU are shrouded in controversy, and the difference between actual and NAIRU cannot be taken as an estimate of 'involuntary unemployment'.

The ILO/OECD measure of 'search' and 'availability' unemployment, i.e. those who demonstrate active participation in the labour market, can be seen as the answer to the search for a measure of excess labour supply which is relevant from the point of view of money wage determination, and, hence, inflation. Most economists, however much they believe in the role of social, institutional and historic factors in wage determination, also accept that market conditions play their part through, for example, influencing the relative bargaining strength of employers *vis-à-vis* employees. However, not all 'search' unemployed, as measured by the ILO, exert an equal influence on wage determination. Layard *et al.* (1994) argue strongly, based on econometric evidence, that the long-term unemployed are extraneous to the wage bargain; they are a non-competing group, either because employers use their long-duration unemployment as a signal of their lack of employability or because of a genuine duration-related deterioration in their skills, productivity, motivation, etc. If the long-term unemployed play little role in bidding down money wages, then their unemployment is 'inefficient' or redundant from the macroeconomic perspective of restraining wage inflation. If this is true, the long-term unemployed should be excluded if we want our unemployment measure to reflect simply the forces bearing on money wage determination and inflation – though they should obviously be included for other purposes.

A social definition of unemployment

Moving beyond 'search' and 'availability' unemployment, it is possible to develop what the RSS report terms a more 'social' approach to defining unemployment, by including, in addition, those without a job and who would like to work, but whose links with the labour market are more tenuous. A more social perspective takes as its starting point the desire for paid work amongst the population, expressed in the form of the number of labour hours which individuals would like to offer, whether or not this is expressed in the form of active job search and availability; and then judges the performance of the economy or society on how far people's aspirations for paid employment can be met by the world of work. This social approach goes beyond Pigou/ Keynes's definition, which implicitly focused on those unemployed who previously held a job – by including, in addition, potential new entrants to the labour force who have never previously been in paid employment and those who may be re-entering the labour force following a long period of absence. These last two groups would include large numbers of female carers. A social approach would also include 'discouraged' workers – those, who, because they do not believe there are any jobs available, have given up active job search and, hence, are treated as 'inactive' and not unemployed according to ILO definitions. A social approach would also include older unemployed workers, close to the retirement age, who in the UK are allowed to 'sign-off' and, hence, no longer appear on the claimant count (CC), despite continuing to receive benefit; relieved of the requirement to engage in active job search as a condition for receiving benefit, such individuals also fail to satisfy the ILO unemployment criteria, being treated as 'inactive'.

Thus, there exist large numbers of people who are without paid employment and would like a job, but are either not actively looking for work and/or not available. Some of these may be included in the CC – despite the increasing strictness with which 'actively seeking' and 'availability' conditions are being applied by the UK benefit authorities – but all will be treated as 'inactives' on the ILO approach. Despite this, data in the household Labour Force Survey, which employs ILO definitions, do enable us to derive a social measure of unemployment for the UK (see below). If a social definition of unemployment is adopted, then, as the RSS report's authors argue, 'it is easy to see how a case could be made for believing that current [headline] figures seriously underestimate the "true" level of unemployment ... once attention is focussed on those at the margins of the workforce, including the prematurely retired, "discouraged" workers, the unskilled, young and part-time workers' (p. 18).

The need for a range of measures

Given the many different possible definitions of unemployment, the RSS report recommends the development of a range of indicators to describe different aspects of the unemployment problem: the number wishing to work (the social measure), the strength of attachment to the labour force (address-ing economists' concern for a measure sensitive to money wage determina-tion), and the numbers of unemployed young people and long-term unemployed. The report's authors, whilst recoiling from the idea of a single measure, on account of the different dimensions of unemployment as outlined above, nevertheless recognize the need for a 'headline' figure to inform, for example, political debate.

The RSS report argues strongly that the choice of which measure or range of measures a country adopts is a political question (p. 21) – which could be derived, ideally, through consensual discussion. The statistician's job, then, is to make the definition operational. This is a far from straightforward activity, however, as a person's employment status cannot always be classified unambiguously. For example: should a part-time worker who wants a full-time job be considered employed, under-employed or unemployed? This is another reason why there can be no single answer to the question: 'how many are unemployed?' The report's authors would also like all labour force accounting to be done in terms of hours, which would certainly be a convenient way of dealing with the problem of e.g. the number of part-time workers who would like to work longer hours (currently treated as employed and not part of the unemployed under any definition) from whom we need to net out the number of those working full-time but wishing to work shorter hours.

One shortcoming of available unemployment measures is that they are essentially a snap-shot of a dynamic system. The labour market can be represented by stocks of individuals in various states (employed, unemployed, inactive) between which flows of people take place over time. At any particular point in time, the stock of, say, the unemployed can be counted – but the system is driven by flows between these categories. Thus, measures of unemployment give a static picture of an essentially dynamic system in a constant state of flux.

Shortcomings of the claimant court (CC)

The RSS report naturally has a lot to say about actual existing UK measures. On the CC, the report argues that, since it is essentially a by-product of an administrative system for paying unemployment-related benefits, changes in the CC inevitably reflect both changes in labour market conditions as well as changes in the administrative rules for paying benefits. This cannot be other than unsatisfactory. Two developments in the UK social security regime – one recent and one forthcoming – illustrate the shortcomings of the CC. The recent introduction of incapacity benefit, with its tightening of eligibility conditions compared with the former invalidity benefit, has already resulted in some recipients being reclassified out of invalidity into unemployment and showing up on the CC. Working in the opposite direction, the forthcoming replacement of unemployment benefit and unemployment-related income support by the JSA (job-seekers' allowance) – which curtails the twelve-months contributory unemployment benefit (UB) to six months – is likely to reduce the CC to the extent that those who have exhausted their right to six-month contributory JSA may find themselves ineligible for means-tested

JSA.[8] The report's critique of the CC is quite devastating: 'The CC is not trusted, is not based on any agreed concept of unemployment, is inconsistent over time due to changes in the claimant system and cannot be used for international comparisons' (p. 36). The report recommends that it should be dropped as the headline figure but retained and renamed as the unemployment benefit count (UBC).

The RSS recommends that the ILO 'search' and 'availability' measure of unemployment, derived from the houschold Labour Force Survey, should replace the CC as the headline unemployment figure. However, in one important respect the report is critical of ILO definitions, namely in respect of 'employment'. To argue, as do current ILO guidelines that *one hour* of work is sufficient for a person to be classed as 'employed' requires modification – as a person working short hours is grossly underemployed, even if not strictly unemployed, whether in relation to the potential number of hours which they could work or their income.[9]

However, it might be asked: since the CC and ILO roughly coincide in their estimates of total unemployment,[10] what is the point of the switch? Figure 1 plots CC and ILO, using seasonally adjusted data for the UK, for the period 1984–95.[11] It confirms that CC and ILO unemployment are roughly similar, although ILO unemployment has generally been higher than CC, and CC has been more cyclically sensitive.[12] However, the RSS report's authors argue that: 'there is no particular reason why they should tally very closely

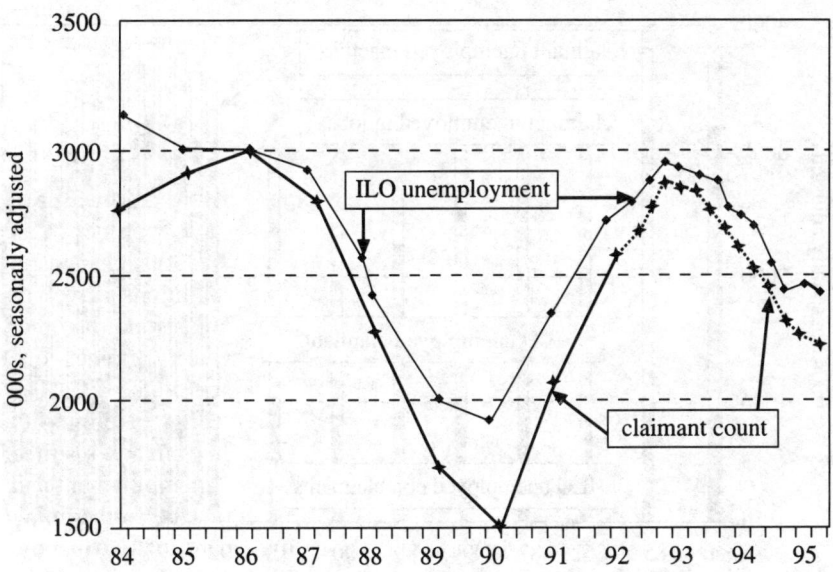

Figure 1 UK unemployment: ILO unemployment and claimant count compared, 1984–95

... it is coincidental that the two figures are roughly the same'[13] – thereby rejecting the argument, frequently deployed in the *Employment Gazette*, that the similarity between the CC and ILO unemployment confirms the validity of the CC. The reason the two measures roughly equate only by coincidence is because: (i) they are defined and measured in quite separate ways, and (ii) the populations to which they refer whilst having a substantial common component (ILO unemployed claimants), also have a large element which is unique to each.

Thus, (see Figure 2), CC and ILO unemployment contain a common core of ILO unemployed claimants – those who are unemployed according to both definitions: claimants who, according to the LFS, are also actively seeking work and available to start. However, ILO unemployment includes, in addition, ILO-unemployed non-claimants – those actively seeking and available for work, but not eligible for benefit.[14] Interestingly, the number of ILO/search unemployed non-claimants has remained remarkably stable over the past decade at between 900,000 and one million, exhibiting little cyclical sensitivity. One explanation for this may be that new labour force entrants or returnees are likely to behave pro-cyclically – replenishing the number of ILO-unemployed claimants as quickly as others leave that status to gain jobs.

The claimant count (CC), on the other hand, includes, in addition to ILO unemployed claimants, individuals who are not classified as unemployed according to ILO definitions: employed claimants and 'inactive' claimants.

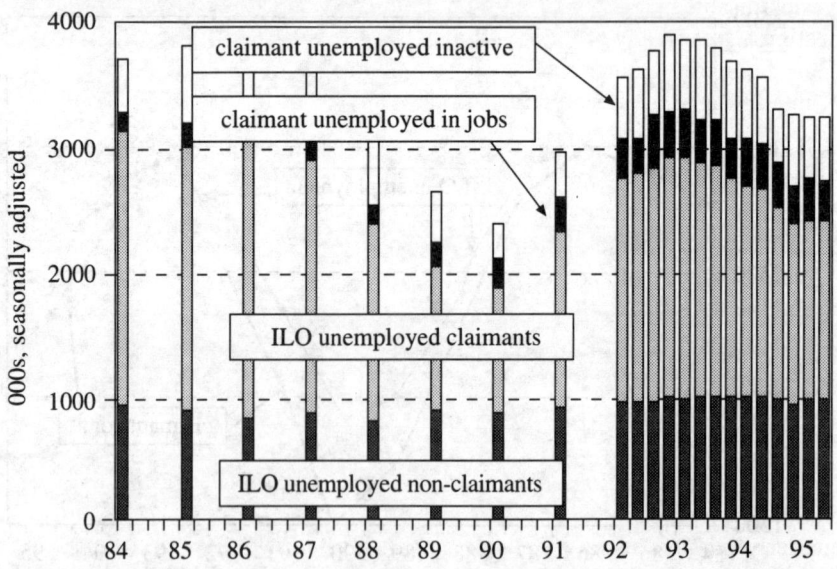

Figure 2 UK unemployment, 1984–95: the union of claimant count and ILO unemployment

306

Employed claimants – currently numbering 300,000 and mainly men – combine benefit with small amounts of paid employment, which is permitted under the UK benefit rules.[15] The numbers in this category, as the *Employment Gazette* is always at pains to stress, 'should not necessarily be regarded as an indication of activity in the "shadow" economy' (October 1993: 462). They reflect, rather, the emergence of mass unemployment and the decline in male employment opportunities. Clearly, employed claimants have a strong claim to be counted amongst the unemployed, since the restrictions on the hours which may be worked and the income earned in combination with benefit mean that such claimants are, at a minimum, grossly underemployed.

The CC includes, in addition, hundreds of thousands of individuals classified as 'inactive' on ILO definitions (ILO 'inactive' claimants) – because they are either not 'available' or not 'searching' or both or because they do not wish to work.[16] The existence of this large group is undoubtedly somewhat of a conundrum, since all claimants have, in theory, satisfied the benefit authorities as to 'search' and 'availability' – criteria which have been more strictly applied in recent years. Moreover, evidence of job search activity required by the LFS questionnaire is fairly undemanding (e.g. studying situations vacant columns in newspapers or journals; asking friends, relatives, colleagues or trade unions about jobs, etc.). Reasons given by ILO 'inactive' claimants for their lack of job search include: retirement, temporarily sick/disabled, looking after family/home, etc. A case can be made for treating a great many of these individuals as unemployed – although some of them should be on other benefits.

Interestingly, the RSS report concludes (p. 25):

if we take a wider definition based on the *union*[17] of the two definitions [CC, ILO unemployment] the figure would rise to [near four million]. This example demonstrates the restrictive nature of the ILO definition of unemployment. However, if the CC measures unemployment of type A and the ILO measure that of type B, the *union* of the CC and the ILO is a valid measure of unemployment.

This is precisely what critics of the CC have been arguing (see Wells 1995a and Employment Policy Institute 1992)[18] – and it lies behind the claim that 'true' unemployment is one million more than the headline CC total.

If the UK is to move to a monthly 'headline' figure, based on the household LFS and ILO definitions, then it faces the choice between: (i) surveying 60,000 households monthly rather than quarterly; (ii) extrapolating between quarterly surveys using claimants – a way of exploiting the information provided by the administrative measure favoured in a number of other countries (White and Leyland 1992); and (iii) basing the monthly figures on a 20,000 household survey – at the cost of greater sampling error. So far, the UK government has not accepted the principle of the need for a switch from

CC to LFS/ILO for the monthly 'headline' figure – although the recently appointed head of the CSO is an academic statistician who almost certainly supports the RSS report's main recommendations.

A SOCIAL MEASURE OF UNEMPLOYMENT TO INCLUDE THOSE 'WITHOUT WORK, WANT A JOB BUT INACTIVE'

In winter 1994/5, the Labour Force Survey recorded a total of 2.4 million people who wanted a job but who were classified as 'inactive' according to ILO definitions and, therefore, not unemployed, because they failed to meet the job 'search' and 'availability' criteria. Some of these individuals – but only a fraction of them – will be included in the CC. The group also includes 'discouraged' workers, i.e. those who have given up searching because they do not believe a job is available. The total of over two million has been pretty much constant over the past few years and is made up as shown in Table 1.

Of the 2.4 million who are not seeking and/or not available, the reasons given for their inactivity were as set out in Table 2.

Clearly, these individuals represent part, in some sense, of the country's labour reserves, although they are only on the margins of the labour market.

Table 1 Great Britain: 'want a job but classified inactive', spring 1995 (millions)

	All	*Male*	*Female*
Total	2.4	0.9	1.5
Not seeking but available	1.0	0.3	0.6
Not seeking and not available	1.1	0.4	0.7
Seeking but not available	0.3	0.1	0.1

Source: *Labour Force Survey Quarterly Bulletin*

Table 2 Great Britain: reasons for inactivity of those who are not seeking and/or not available, spring 1995 (000s)

	All	*Male*	*Female*
(a) Want a job and are not seeking			
Discouraged workers	136	75	61
Long-term sick/disabled	538	331	207
Looking after family/home	752	51	700
Students	250	134	116
Others	417	184	233
(b) Want a job, seeking, not available	276	130	146

Source: *Labour Force Survey Quarterly Bulletin*

A recent study of 'discouraged' workers[19] suggested their numbers are correlated with unemployment overall – suggesting that they are closer to the unemployed than to 'inactives'. Also, long-duration unemployment is a significant precursor of 'discouraged' status.

As for the long-term sick/disabled, rapidly rising numbers in receipt of invalidity benefit in the UK[20] as well as in other industrial countries (Blondal and Pearson 1995) suggests strongly that IVB is frequently used as an alternative to unemployment-related benefits – partly on account of its higher value. Most recipients are probably long-term, structurally unemployed middle-age males. A recent attempt by Beatty and Fothergill (1995) to estimate unemployment levels in Britain's former coal-mining communities, using data from the 1991 population census shows that if 'long-term sickness and disability', and involuntary premature 'retirement' are added to unemployment (census definitions[21]), then unemployment, properly estimated, exceeds the CC by a factor of at least two. Beatty and Fothergill's methodology is the quite unexceptional one of taking the excess sickness and retirement rates in the former coal-mining communities relative to a norm represented by the prosperous South-East region of the country.

Of those wanting a job but inactive, who give 'looking after family/home' as their reason for lack of 'search/availability' – 752,000 in all, principally women – it is clear that they could only be incorporated into the labour market, if there were to be major institutional changes in the way in which care for the young and the old is organized in the UK. Nevertheless, it is a very revealing figure.

YOUTH UNEMPLOYMENT

Youth unemployment has become a controversial issue in the UK – partly because unemployed sixteen- and seventeen-year-olds are, for the most part, not eligible for unemployment-related benefits, because it is assumed by the authorities that they are either in work, in full-time education, or on a training programme. Unemployed sixteen- and seventeen-year-olds do not, therefore, show up in the CC. However, if ILO unemployed (i.e. searching and available), they do show up in the LFS – though a proportion are in full-time education seeking only part-time work. Currently, there are about 120,000 ILO unemployed sixteen- and seventeen-year-olds (of which 70,000 are young men). About 50,000 of these are in full-time education and are looking for part-time work only – but their number are roughly equal to those classed as 'inactive' but not in full-time education.

Youth unemployment is also controversial in the context of the political debate concerning the UK's opt-out from the EU Social Chapter and the Labour Party's proposal to introduce, if elected, a national minimum wage – of some unspecified value. Government ministers claim, on the basis of OECD inter-country data using ILO definitions, that youth unemployment in the UK is lower than in Continental European countries where minimum wage legislation exists.

However, conventional estimates of the percentage unemployed which use the labour force (employed plus unemployed) in their denominator can be quite misleading, when 'inactivity' rates are very high – as in the case of the youth cohort a large proportion of whom is engaged in schooling – and 'activity' rates are low. Where 'activity' rates are low, the unemployed may represent quite a high proportion of the 'active' labour force (employed plus unemployed), albeit they are a small proportion of the total age cohort. Thus, in Belgium and many other Continental European countries (see Table 3), where schooling rates are high and labour force activity rates are low, unemployed 15–19 year-olds, though constituting quite a small share of the total age cohort, show up in the form of very high unemployment rates, when conventionally measured as a percentage of the 'active' labour force. In the UK, by contrast, schooling rates are low and labour force activity rates are correspondingly higher than the European norm (see Table 3). UK youth unemployment, when measured as a percentage of the active labour force, is about average in the European context – but much lower than countries such as France, Italy, Spain and Eire. However, UK male youth unemployment, when measured as a percentage of the total cohort of young men, was higher in 1992 – the latest year for which comparative data currently exist[22] – than in any other EU country. It is, surely, unemployment expressed as a percentage of the population which is the relevant measure – to see, for

Table 3 Male youth (15–19 years) employment, unemployment and inactivity: (a) as % of age cohort and (b) unemployment as % of economically active (employed plus unemployed): EU countries, 1992

	(a)			(b)
				unemployed
	inactive*	employed	unemployed	as % economically
country	as % of total age cohort			active
EU12	67.0	27.1	5.9	17.9
Belgium	91.1	7.3	1.6	18.5
Denmark	36.2	59.3	4.5	7.1
West Germany	59.8	38.4	1.8	4.4
Greece	80.1	16.2	3.7	18.6
Spain	71.7	19.4	8.9	31.4
France	84.7	11.4	3.9	25.3
Eire	73.6	18.6	7.8	29.6
Italy	73.7	18.4	7.9	30.0
Luxembourg	na	na	na	na
Netherlands	56.6	39.2	4.2	9.6
Portugal	57.8	38.4	3.8	9.0
UK	44.7	44.9	10.4	18.9

Note: * 'inactive' 15–19 year-old males are mostly in full-time education or training

example, what proportion of the youth cohort might be prey to criminality as a result of unemployment. Note that, because UK schooling rates are low (an adverse factor from the point of view of its future economic development), youth unemployment, as conventionally measured, appears low – providing a wholly misleading indicator to policy-makers of labour market and overall economic performance.

SUMMARY AND CONCLUSIONS

Unemployment can be defined in a number of different ways, depending on the precise focus of interest – and, to each definition, there corresponds a particular statistical measure. Involuntary unemployment, defined as those without a job, willing to work at the current rate for their skill and actively engaged in job search, is probably best measured by ILO 'search' and 'availability' unemployment. However, if our interest is in the labour market as a possible source of inflationary pressure, then the long-term unemployed, who appear to exert little pressure on wage determination, should probably be excluded. They would, however, figure prominently in any measure which was sensitive to the uneven distribution of the costs of unemployment – a disproportionate share of which is borne by the long-term unemployed. A social measure of unemployment would go beyond 'search' and 'availability' unemployment to include, additionally, those who would like paid work but who, for various reasons, find themselves on the margins of the labour market.

These different concerns suggest strongly the need for a range of statistical measures of unemployment. In the UK case, the claimant count is clearly unsatisfactory as a 'headline' unemployment measure and should be replaced forthwith by the ILO measure (derived from a monthly LFS) – even if the two show little difference in aggregate – since the ILO measure would exhibit greater consistency over time and international comparability. But, attention should also be focused on deriving a social measure on unemployment. The estimates in this paper suggest that the effective labour reserve in the UK economy – containing all those who would like paid employment, whether or not engaged in active job search – could be as high as five million. Further, UK male youth unemployment in 1992 was, when measured as a percentage of the age cohort, the highest in the EU. Satisfying this huge demand for work is certainly a major challenge – but not unrealizable in a society beset by huge unmet needs for goods and services of all kinds.

NOTES

1 i.e. UB (unemployment-insurance benefit), IS (income support) or signing-on for national insurance credits. The CC replaced the previous administrative count of those unemployed and registered at government employment offices – the so-called 'registered' unemployed – in November 1982. Canada is the one other

OECD country whose administrative count is based on benefit recipients. See White and Leyland (1992).

2　See, for example, the Unemployment Unit's monthly publication, *Working Brief.*

3　See N. 1 above.

4　The following remarks, whilst stimulated by my reading of the report, go considerably beyond what can be found therein.

5　See Kahn (1976) and see also the very useful treatment of 'involuntary unemployment' in Taylor (1987).

6　Kahn (1976) criticized Keynes's other well-known formulation ('in the event of a small rise ... etc.) as 'unnecessarily complicated'. Kahn also viewed Keynes's treatment of voluntary unemployment as 'unsatisfactory'.

7　At the thirteenth International Conference of Labour Statisticians held in 1982; see Hussmans (1990).

8　Because, e.g., their partner is working or is already in receipt of means-tested benefit.

9　The reason this is an important issue comes up (see below) in relation to 'employed' claimants – those combining work with benefit – treated as 'active' and employed on ILO definitions – when there is a strong case for including them amongst the unemployed.

10　Although the composition differs considerably, with the CC having more men and ILO unemployment containing more women. This reflects the fact that the two populations do not fully coincide (see text) – despite the existence of a large intersecting set, i.e. people unemployed on both definitions. The differing proportions of men and women in each total reflects the fact that claimants classified as ILO 'inactives' are predominantly male, whereas ILO unemployed non-claimants are predominantly female.

11　I am grateful to Emma Tonks of the CSO for providing me with these hitherto unpublished seasonally-adjusted series.

12　The reason being that the non-claimant component of ILO unemployed has varied little with the economic cycle, whereas claimants classified as non-ILO unemployed (because either 'employed' or 'inactive') have been very cyclically sensitive (for explanation of concepts, see discussion below).

13　See replies to questions by Professors Bartholemew and Moore, Employment Select Committee (1995: 6).

14　The politicians on the Employment Select Committee were quite agitated by the existence of the nearly one million ILO/search unemployed non-claimants – though Professors Bartholemew and Moore did not provide a very satisfactory explanation of who they were, for want of an adequate knowledge of the rules of the UK unemployment benefit regime. In fact, this category consists of, *inter alia*, ILO unemployed sixteen- and seventeen-year-olds who are mostly ineligible for benefit, unemployed persons who are ineligible for unemployment benefit because of, e.g., inadequate contribution record (low pay below the national insurance lower limit, new entrants to the labour force), voluntary quits, those ineligible for means-tested income support after unemployment benefit exhaustion (due to spouse being in employment or on benefit) or failing the means test (a self-employed person with savings) or individuals not bothering to claim benefit.

15　Note that it is sufficient for a person to work just 1 hour for them to be classified on ILO definitions as employed – whether claimant or not.

16　Claimants who say they do not wish to work – the numbers vary between 130 and 250 thousand – cannot be treated as unemployed on any definition.

17　The authors are deploying the notion *union* from set theory.

18 EPI (1992) develops what it calls LFSEXP or expanded LFS/ILO measure –
    which includes, in addition to ILO unemployed, 'inactive' claimants (less those
    who do not want to work) and 'discouraged' workers. Curiously, employed
    claimants are excluded from this measure, despite their possessing in many ways
    a better claim for inclusion than many 'inactive' claimants.

19 OECD (1995: chapter 2): 'Supplementary measures of labour market slackness:
    an analysis of discouraged and involuntary part-time workers'.

20 Thus, the number of male invalidity claimants of working-age in the UK rose
    from 459,000 in 1979/80 to 927,000 in 1992/3 (Social Security Statistics) –
    implausibly the result of a rapid deterioration in health.

21 Unemployed and looking for a job during previous week including those wanting
    a job but prevented from looking by holiday or temporary sickness.

22 Eurostat (1994). The year 1992 was the depth of the UK cycle – but it is not clear
    why the comparative situation should have improved as the economy recovered
    and youth unemployment declined in subsequent years, because the other EU
    economies also recovered.

REFERENCES

Beatty, C. and Fothergill, S. (1995) *Labour Market Adjustment in Areas of Chronic Industrial Decline: the Case of the UK Coalfields*, Sheffield: Sheffield Hallam University, Centre for Regional Economic and Social Research.

Blondal, S. and Pearson, M. (1995) 'Unemployment and other non-employment benefits', *Oxford Review of Economic Policy*, 11(1): 136–69.

CSO, *Labour Force Survey Quarterly Bulletin* (various).

Employment Policy Institute (1992) 'Figuring out unemployment', *Economic Report*, 7(2).

Employment Select Committee (1995) *Unemployment and Employment Statistics: Minutes of Evidence*, 2 May 1995, HC 411-i (Session 1994–95).

Eurostat (1994) *Labour Force Survey: Results 1992*.

Friedman, M. (1968) The role of monetary policy', *The American Economic Review*, LVIII (1).

Gregg, P. (1994) 'Out for the count: a social scientist's analysis of unemployment statistics in the UK', *Journal of the Royal Statistical Society* A, 157, Part 2: 253–70.

Hussmans, R. (1990) 'International standards on the measurement of economic activity, employment, unemployment and under-employment', in R. Turvey (ed.), *Developments in International Labour Statistics*, London: Pinter.

Kahn, R. F. (1976) 'Unemployment as seen by the Keynesians', in G. D. N. Worswick (ed.), *The Concept and Measurement of Involuntary Unemployment*, London: George Allen & Unwin.

Keynes, J. M. (1936) *The General Theory of Employment, Interest and Money*, London: Macmillan (1964).

Layard, R., Nickell, S. and Jackman, R. (1994) *The Unemployment Crisis*, Oxford: Oxford University Press.

OECD (1995) *Employment Outlook*, Paris (July).

Pigou, A. C. (1914) *Unemployment*, London: Williams & Norgate.

—— (1933) *The Theory of Unemployment*, London: Macmillan.

Royal Statistical Society (1995) *Report of the Working Party on the Measurement of Unemployment in the UK*.

Taylor, J. B. (1987) 'Involuntary unemployment', in J. Eatwell *et al.* (eds), *The New Palgrave: A Dictionary of Economics*, Vol. 4, London: Macmillan.

Wells, J. (1995a) 'The missing million', in K. Coates (ed.), *The Right to Work*, Nottingham: Spokesman.

—— (1995b) 'Unemployment, job creation and job destruction in the UK since 1979', in P. Arestis and M. Marshall (eds), *The Political Economy of Full Employment*, Aldershot: Edward Elgar.

White A. and Leyland, J. (1992) 'How unemployment is measured in different countries', *Employment Gazette*, September: 421–31.

Unemployment Unit, *Working Brief*.

25

HIGH YOUTH WAGES CAN GENERATE GENERAL AND PERSISTENT UNEMPLOYMENT

Murray C. Kemp, Ngo Van Long and Koji Shimomura

INTRODUCTION

Nearly all developed countries suffer from unemployment which is acute and entrenched and which, moreover, extends to all age groups. However, modifying this last characteristic, in some countries unemployment is most severe among the young, which suggests that youth wage rates lie above their market-clearing levels.

In the present note we develop a simple macro model, the solution paths of which are consistent with the above facts of life. The essential features of the model are (a) overlapping generations of workers, (b) learning on the job by employed workers and (c) a youth wage rate which exceeds its market-clearing level. How the youth wage rate happens to be at that level will not concern us. It may be set too high by monopoly labour unions which are controlled by older workers; or it may be set too high by wage-fixing authorities which are guided by considerations of inter-generational equity.

Suppose that each individual has a working life of three periods. Given the specification (a)–(c), he might have any of four employment profiles. He might find unskilled employment in his youth then proceed to semi-skilled employment in his middle age and skilled employment in his old age; or he might first find unskilled employment in his middle age then proceed to semi-skilled employment in his old age; or he might first find employment in his old age; or he might never find employment. During any particular time period, therefore, the unskilled work force may contain young, middle-aged and elderly workers; the semi-skilled work force may contain middle-aged and elderly workers; but the skilled work force may contain only elderly workers. In these circumstances, there may be pressure during any period of time for the market-clearing wage for semi-skilled labour to fall below the artificially high wage for unskilled labour; and the same is true of the market-clearing wage for skilled labour. There also may be pressure for the wage for skilled labour to fall below the wage for semi-skilled labour. Whether the wage for more skilled labour can ever fall below the wage for less skilled labour depends on the degree to which labour markets are segregated. We shall examine each of the extreme cases, that of complete segregation and that of complete non-segregation. To model non-segregated labour markets in a context of learning has proved to be something of a challenge. Indeed, our method of handling the problem is, in our opinion, a substantial contribution of our paper.

The disequilibrium youth wage rate generates unemployment among the young. However, combined with the learning process (b), it also causes unemployment among older workers. For the unemployed young of one period become the unskilled middle-aged of the next period and possibly the unskilled old of the following period, competing respectively with the young of the next and following periods. Moreover, given suitable initial conditions, the disequilibrium youth wage generates oscillations of employment and output. Finally, it is noted that widespread and oscillatory unemployment cannot be generated by a minimum wage for any relatively skilled category of labour.

ANALYSIS

As we have specified, each individual lives for three periods of time. During the first period of his life, an individual born in period t is a member of the unskilled work force $V_{1,t}$. As an unskilled worker he is capable of performing only unskilled tasks. He may or may not find work at the given wage rate for unskilled labour. If he succeeds in finding work then, in period $t+1$, he becomes a member of the semi-skilled work force $V_{2,t+1}$. As a semi-skilled worker, he is capable of performing both unskilled and semi-skilled tasks. Since the wage for semi-skilled labour is market-clearing, he succeeds in finding work and, in period $t + 2$, is a member of the skilled work force $V_{3,t+2}$. As a skilled worker, he is capable of performing unskilled, semi-skilled and skilled tasks. Since the wages for skilled and semi-skilled labour are market-clearing, he again succeeds in finding work. If, on the other hand, he fails to find work in period t, he remains unskilled and enters the unskilled work force of period $t + 1$, $V_{1,t+1}$. If he then finds unskilled work in period $t+1$, he enters the semi-skilled work force of period $t + 2$, $V_{2,t+2}$; otherwise, he remains unskilled and enters the unskilled work force of period $t + 2$, $V_{1,t+2}$. We may normalize by equating the number of newborn in each period to one, so that the total population is constant at $V_{1,t} + V_{2,t} + V_{3,t} = 3$.

It should be noted that the learning by employed workers renders them capable of performing a larger class of tasks; it does not render them capable of more efficiently performing a given set of already-feasible tasks.

It will be convenient to begin our analysis under the institutional specification that semi-skilled workers cannot compete for unskilled employment and skilled workers cannot compete for unskilled or semi-skilled employment–that, in other words, the three labour markets are segregated. Under this specification, the market-clearing wages for semi-skilled and skilled labour might drop below the administered wage for unskilled labour and the market-clearing wage for skilled labour might drop below the market-clearing wage for semi-skilled labour. This restrictive specification will be abandoned in due course.

Segregated labour markets

Let $L_{1,t}$ be the level of employment among the unskilled of period t, so that $V_{1,t} - L_{1,t}$ is the level of unemployment. Similarly, let $L_{2,t}$ be the level of employment among the semi-skilled of period t. Since the wage for semi-skilled workers clears the market, the level of employment among the semi-skilled is $L_{2,t} = V_{2,t} = L_{1,t-1}$. Finally, the wage for skilled workers is market-clearing, so that the level of employment among the skilled is $L_{3,t} = V_{3,t} = L_{1,t-2}$.

Homogeneous output depends on the inputs of unskilled, semi-skilled and skilled labour and of given and constant amounts of unspecified other factors. Thus total output is:

$$Y_t = F(L_{1,t}, L_{2,t}, L_{3,t}) = F(L_{1,t}, L_{1,t-1}, L_{1,t-2}).$$ (1a)

It will be assumed that, if all inputs are positive,

$$\frac{\partial}{\partial i} F_t(L_{1,t}, L_{1,t-1}, L_{1,t-2}) \equiv F_i(L_{1,t}, L_{1,t-1}, L_{1,t-2}) > 0$$ (1b)

$$\lim_{i \to 0} F_i(L_{1,t}, L_{1,t-1}, L_{1,t-2}) = \infty$$ (1c)

$$\frac{\partial^2}{\partial i^2} F(L_{1,t}, L_{1,t-1}, L_{1,t-2}) \equiv F_{ii}(L_{1,t}, L_{1,t-1}, L_{1,t-2}) < 0$$ (1d)

where $i, j = L_{1,t}, L_{1,t-1}, L_{1,t-2}$, and that

$$\frac{\partial^2}{\partial i \partial j} F(L_{1,t}, L_{1,t-1}, L_{1,t-2}) \equiv F_{ij}(L_{1,t}, L_{1,t-1}, L_{1,t-2}) \geq 0$$ (1e)

where $i, j = L_{1,t}, L_{1,t-1}, L_{1,t-2}$, $i \neq j$. These are, of course, conventional restrictions on F.

The employment of unskilled workers is determined by the marginal productivity condition

317

$$\frac{\partial}{\partial L_{1,t}} F(L_{1,t},L_{1,t-1},L_{1,t-2}) \equiv F_{ij}(L_{1,t},L_{2,t},L_{3,t}) = w \qquad (2)$$

where w is the given youth wage in terms of output. To help ensure that w binds at all times, it is assumed that w is greater than the full-employment value of the youth wage:

$$w > F_1(1,1,1). \qquad (3)$$

The system is completed by the addition of the initial conditions

$$L_{1,0},L_{1,-1} \text{ given.} \qquad (4)$$

It will be assumed that

$$0 < L_{1,0},L_{1,-1} \leq 1. \qquad (4b)$$

It is a feature of the model (1)–(4) that

$$L_{1,t} < 1 \text{ for all } t > 0. \qquad (5)$$

For

$$F_1(L_{1,1},1,1)$$

$$\geq F_1(L_{1,1},L_{1,0},L_{1,-1}) \text{ (from (1a) and (4b))}$$

$$= w \text{ (from 2))}$$

$$> F_1(1,1,1) \text{ (from (3))}. \qquad (6)$$

From (1d) and (6), $L_{1,1} < 1$. By the same reasoning, if $L_{1,1},L_{1,0} \leq 1$ then $L_{1,2} < 1$; and so on. It then follows from (5) that the system will never bump against the ceiling of full employment. Similarly, from the Inada condition (1c), the system will never touch the floor of unemployment, with $L_{1,t} = 0$.

It is a further feature of the model that if an individual is unemployed in his youth then he will always be unemployed. This is an immediate implication of (5) and the assumption that employers give preference to younger workers.

In the special Cobb–Douglas case,

$$Y_t = L_{1,t}^{\alpha_1} L_{1,t-1}^{\alpha_2} L_{1,t-2}^{\alpha_3} \qquad 1 - \alpha_1 - \alpha_2 - \alpha_3 > 0$$

and (2) and (3) reduce to

$$\alpha_1 L_{1,t}^{\alpha_1-1} L_{1,t-1}^{\alpha_2} L_{1,t-2}^{\alpha_3} = w \qquad (7)$$

and

$$w > \alpha_1 \qquad (8)$$

respectively. Later it will be convenient to work with the logarithmic versions of (7) and (8):

$$(\alpha_1 - 1)u_t + \alpha_2 s_t + \alpha_3 h_t = \ln w - \ln \alpha_1 \qquad (7')$$

and

$$\ln w > \ln \alpha_1 \tag{8'}$$

where $u_t \equiv \ln L_{1,t}$, $s_t \equiv \ln L_{2,t}$, $h_t \equiv \ln L_{3,t}$ and the new variables u, s and h stand for unskilled, semi-skilled and highly skilled.

Evidently there is a unique steady state in which

$$L_{1,t} = L_1 \equiv (w/\alpha_1)^{\frac{1}{\alpha_1+\alpha_2+\alpha_3-1}} \tag{9}$$

and

$$u_t = u \equiv \frac{\ln w - \ln \alpha_1}{\alpha_1 + \alpha_2 + \alpha_3 - 1}. \tag{9'}$$

The steady-state wages for semi-skilled and skilled labour are, respectively,

$$w_{2,t} = w_2 \equiv \alpha_2 L_1^{\alpha_1+\alpha_2+\alpha_3-1} \tag{10a}$$

and

$$w_{3,t} = w_3 \equiv \alpha_3 L_1^{\alpha_1+\alpha_2+\alpha_3-1} \tag{10b}$$

so that

$$\ln w_{2,t} = \ln w_2 = \ln \alpha_2 + (\alpha_1 + \alpha_2 + \alpha_3 - 1)\ln L_1 \tag{10'a}$$

and

$$\ln w_{3,t} = \ln w_3 = \ln \alpha_3 + (\alpha_1 + \alpha_2 + \alpha_3 - 1)\ln L_1. \tag{10'b}$$

It is plausible to assume that

$$\alpha_1 \leq \alpha_2 \leq \alpha_3. \tag{11}$$

Applying (11) to (10), we find that

$$w \leq w_2 \leq w_3 \tag{12}$$

so that, in the steady state, there is no temptation for semi-skilled workers to seek unskilled employment or for skilled workers to seek semi-skilled or unskilled employment.

It remains to consider the behaviour of the economy away from the steady state. The characteristic roots of the basic difference equation (7) in $\log L_{1,t} \equiv u_t$ are λ_1 and λ_2, where

$$-1 < \lambda_1 < 0 \tag{13a}$$

$$-1 > \lambda_2 > 0 \tag{13b}$$

$$\lambda_1 + \lambda_2 = \frac{\alpha_2}{1 - \alpha_1} > 0 \tag{13c}$$

so that

$$-1 < \lambda_1/\lambda_2 < 0. \tag{13d}$$

Let us define

$$x_t = u_t - u_{t-1}. \tag{14}$$

Evidently

$$x_t = A_1\lambda_1^t + A_2\lambda_2^t \tag{15}$$

where A_1 and A_2 are constants determined by the initial conditions (4). If $A_1 \neq 0$, the motion of u_t may be oscillatory, at least for a time. However it follows from (15) that, if $A_2 \neq 0$,

$$x_t x_{t-1} = (Y_t)^2 [\lambda_1 (X_t/Y_t)^2 + (\lambda_1 + \lambda_2)(X_t/Y_t) + \lambda_2] \tag{16}$$

where $X_t \equiv A_1\lambda_1^t$ and $Y_t \equiv A_2\lambda_2^t$. In view of (13d), X_t/Y_t converges to zero. This fact, together with (13b), implies that $x_t x_{t-1}$ is positive for sufficiently large t. Recalling the definition of x_t, we may conclude that, if $A_2 \neq 0$, u_t is eventually monotone.

We now embark on a detailed analysis of the dynamics of segregated labour markets. In the course of the analysis we will develop a diagrammatic technique which will be useful in our later study of unsegregated markets.

From (7'), and bearing in mind that $s_{t+1} = u_t$ and $h_{t+1} = s_t$,

$$
\begin{bmatrix} s_{t+1} \\ h_{t+1} \end{bmatrix}
=
\begin{bmatrix} \dfrac{\alpha_2}{1-\alpha_1} & \dfrac{\alpha_3}{1-\alpha_1} \\ 1 & 0 \end{bmatrix}
\begin{bmatrix} s_t \\ h_t \end{bmatrix}
+
\begin{bmatrix} \dfrac{\ln\alpha_1 - \ln w}{1-\alpha_1} \\ 0 \end{bmatrix}
$$

and

$$
\equiv \mathbf{H}
\begin{bmatrix} s_t \\ h_t \end{bmatrix}
+
\dfrac{\ln\alpha_1 - \ln w}{1-\alpha_1}
\begin{bmatrix} 1 \\ 0 \end{bmatrix}
\tag{17}
$$

and

$$
\begin{bmatrix} s_{t+1} - s_t \\ h_{t+1} - h_t \end{bmatrix}
= (\mathbf{H} - \mathbf{I})
\begin{bmatrix} s_t \\ h_t \end{bmatrix}
+
\dfrac{(\ln\alpha_1 - \ln w)}{1-\alpha_1}
\begin{bmatrix} 1 \\ 0 \end{bmatrix}
\tag{18}
$$

where $\mathbf{I}$ is the identity matrix. The loci $\Delta s_t = 0$ and $\Delta h_t = 0$ are displayed in Figure 1. The point of intersection P represents the steady state of the system. At P, $s_t = s^\infty \equiv (\ln\alpha_1 - \ln w)/(1 - \alpha_1 - \alpha_2 - \alpha_3) = h^\infty = h_t$. In the four regions I–IV, arrows indicate the direction of movement. Notice, however, that, in contrast to the motions of differential equations, trajectories can cross

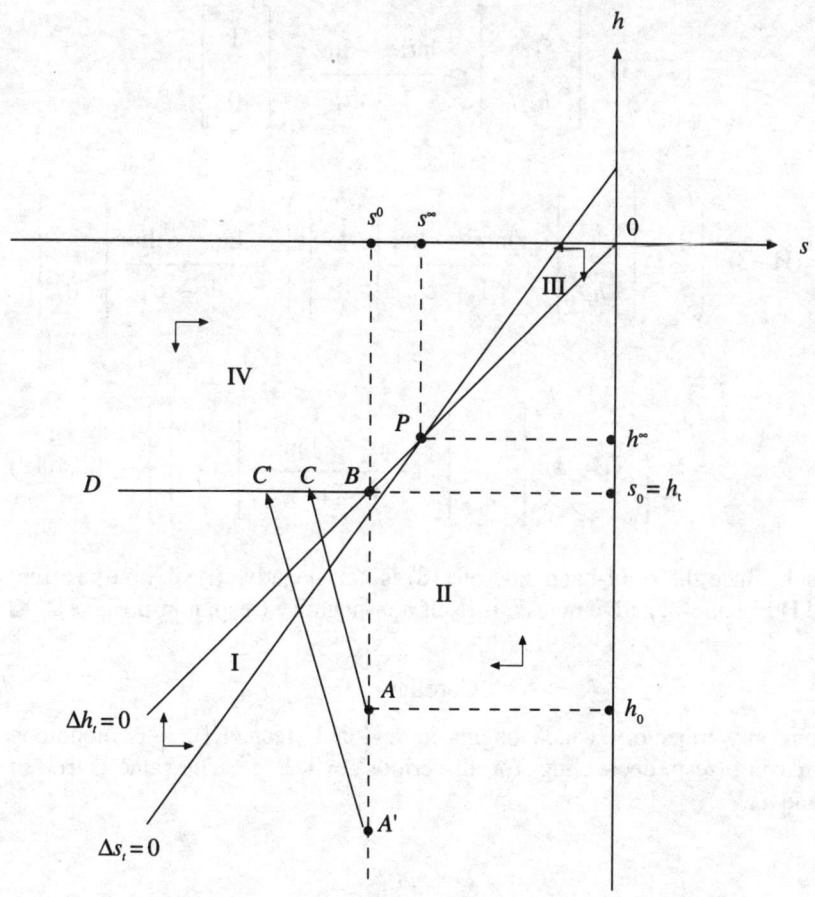

Figure 1

boundaries in discrete steps with the direction of movement determined by the region of origin.

Lemma 1

Any trajectory which begins in region I (resp. III) stays in region I (resp. III).

Proof

If (s_t,h) is in region I (resp. III) then the right-hand side of (18) is a non-negative (resp. non-positive) vector. Making use of (17),

321

$$(\mathbf{H} - \mathbf{I}) \begin{bmatrix} s_{t+1} \\ h_{t+1} \end{bmatrix} + \frac{\ln\alpha_1 - \ln w}{1 - \alpha_1} \begin{bmatrix} 1 \\ 0 \end{bmatrix}$$

$$= (\mathbf{H} - \mathbf{I}) \left\{ \mathbf{H} \begin{bmatrix} s_t \\ h_t \end{bmatrix} + \frac{\ln\alpha_1 - \ln w}{1 - \alpha_1} \begin{bmatrix} 1 \\ 0 \end{bmatrix} \right\} + \frac{\ln\alpha_1 - \ln w}{1 - \alpha_1} \begin{bmatrix} 1 \\ 0 \end{bmatrix}$$

$$= \mathbf{H} \left\{ (\mathbf{H} - \mathbf{I}) \begin{bmatrix} s_t \\ h_t \end{bmatrix} + \frac{\ln\alpha_1 - \ln w}{1 - \alpha_1} \begin{bmatrix} 1 \\ 0 \end{bmatrix} \right\} \qquad (19)$$

which, since the right-hand side of (18) is non-negative (resp. non-positive) and $\mathbf{H}$ is a non-negative matrix, is itself non-negative (resp. non-positive). ■

Corollary

Along any trajectory which begins in region I (resp. III), s_t is monotone increasing (resp. decreasing) for all periods $t = 1, 2, \ldots$. The same is true of h_t and u_t.

Lemma 2

1   Any trajectory which begins in region II (resp. IV) with $s_0 < s^\infty$ (resp. $s_0 > s^\infty$) moves in one period to region IV (resp. II).
2   Any trajectory which begins in region II (resp. IV) with $s_0 > s^\infty$ (resp. $s_0 < s^\infty$) moves in one period to region III (resp. I) or region IV (resp. II).

Proof

Let us focus on the case in which the trajectory begins in region II. The case in which it begins in region IV can be handled in a similar way.

1   Consider Figure 1, with the initial point $\mathbf{A}(s_0, h_0)$. Since $h_1 = s_0$, and in view of the arrow scheme characteristic of region II, the point (s_1, h_1) must lie in the horizontal line BD, to the left of B, say at C. Similarly, the initial point A' moves to C', to the left of C, where, from (17) and by construction, the paths AC and $A'C'$ are parallel.
2   Consider Figure 2.

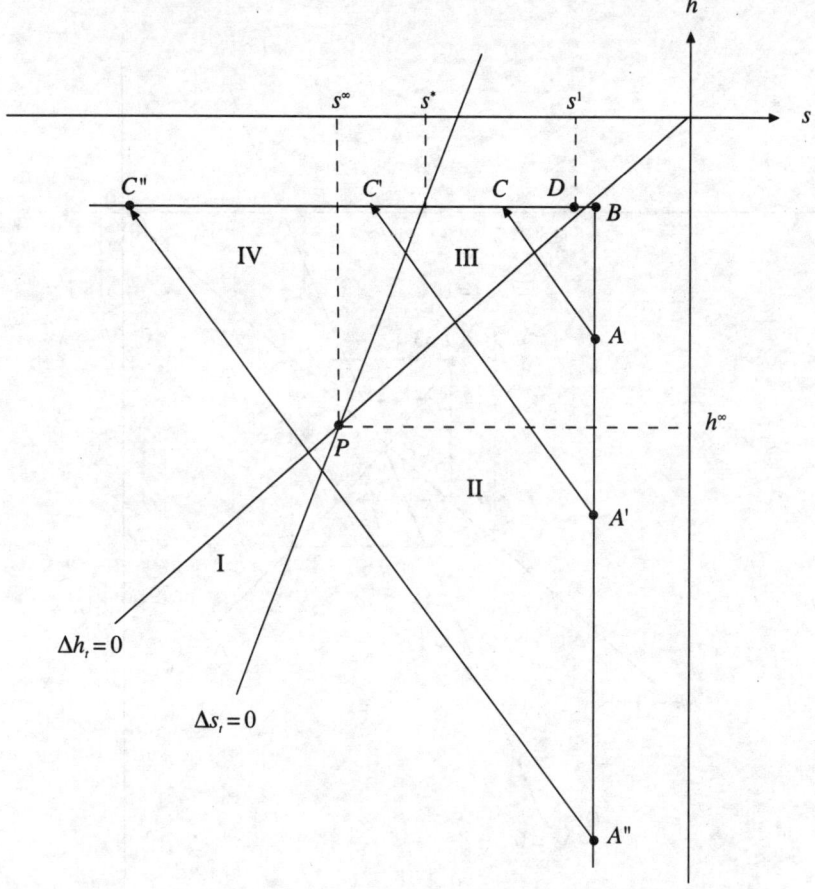

Figure 2

While trajectories which begin in region I or region III are monotone, those which begin in region II or region IV may be oscillatory. Indeed, trajectories which begin in II or IV may oscillate for ever. Thus in Figure 3 there is displayed a one-dimensional manifold on which A_2, the coefficient of λ_2^t in (15), is zero.

Unsegregated labour markets

We have noted the possibility that, at some point along an equilibrium trajectory, $w_{2,t}$ or $w_{3,t}$ may drop below the minimum youth wage w, thus creating an incentive for semi-skilled workers to seek unskilled work, and the further possibility that, at some point, $w_{3,t}$ may fall below $w_{2,t}$, creating an

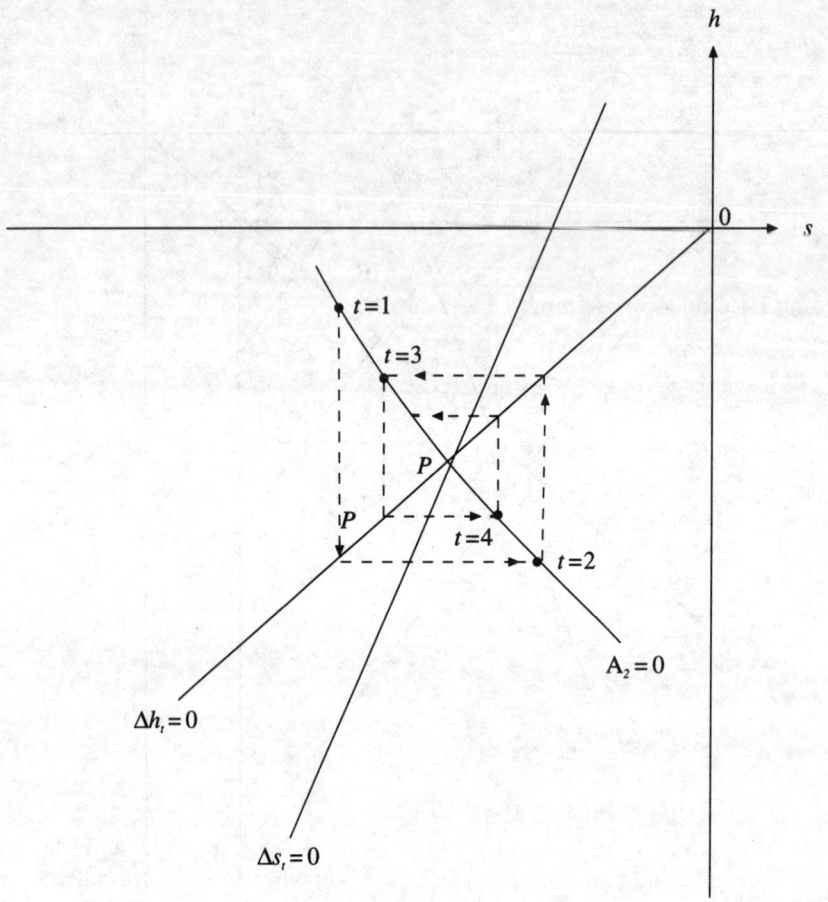

Figure 3

incentive for skilled workers to seek semi-skilled work. Our assumption of market segregation has effectively suppressed those incentives. However we now relax the assumption and incorporate in our analysis the inter-market migration of labour in pursuit of higher wages.

We begin by adding some scaffolding to our diagrams. In labour market equilibrium,

$$\ln w = \ln\alpha_1 - (1 - \alpha_1)u_t + \alpha_2 s_t + \alpha_3 h_t \qquad (20a)$$

$$\ln w_{2,t} = \ln\alpha_2 + \alpha_1 u_t - (1 - \alpha_2)s_t + \alpha_3 h_t \qquad (20b)$$

$$\ln w_{3,t} = \ln\alpha_3 + \alpha_1 u_t + \alpha_2 s_t - (1 - \alpha_3)h_t \qquad (20c)$$

Solving (20a) for u_t and substituting into (20b) and (21c), we obtain

$$\ln w_{2,t} = \ln\alpha_2 + \frac{\alpha_1}{1 - \alpha_1}(\ln \alpha_1 - \ln w) - \frac{1 - \alpha_1 - \alpha_2}{1 - \alpha_1}s_t + \frac{\alpha_3}{1 - \alpha_1}h_t$$

$$(21a)$$

$$\ln w_{3,t} = \ln\alpha_3 + \frac{\alpha_1}{1 - \alpha_1}(\ln \alpha_1 - \ln w) + \frac{\alpha_2}{1 - \alpha_1}s_t - \frac{1 - \alpha_1 - \alpha_3}{1 - \alpha_1}h_t \quad (21b)$$

From (21a) and (21b), in turn,

$$\ln w_{2,t} - \ln w = \ln\alpha_2 + \frac{\alpha_1}{1 - \alpha_1}\ln\alpha_1 - \frac{\ln w}{1 - \alpha_1} - \frac{1 - \alpha_1 - \alpha_2}{1 - \alpha_1}s_t + \frac{\alpha_3}{1 - \alpha_1}h_t$$

$$(22a)$$

$$\ln w_{3,t} - \ln w = \ln\alpha_3 + \frac{\alpha_1}{1 - \alpha_1}\ln\alpha_1 - \frac{\ln w}{1 - \alpha_1} + \frac{\alpha_2}{1 - \alpha_1}s_t - \frac{1 - \alpha_1 - \alpha_3}{1 - \alpha_1}h_t$$

$$(22b)$$

$$\ln w_{3,t} - \ln w_{2,t} = (\ln\alpha_3 - \ln\alpha_2) + s_t - h_t \qquad (22c)$$

From (22) we obtain the three loci $w_{2,t} - w = 0$, $w_{3,t} - w = 0$ and $w_{3,t} - w_{2,t} = 0$ inscribed in Figure 4. The locus $w_{2,t} - w = 0$, represented by the straight line *GEB*, divides the quadrant into two regions - the region above *GEB*, in which $w_{2,t} - w > 0$, and the region below *GEB*, in which $w_{2,t} - w < 0$. Similar interpretations may be given to the other loci. It may then be deduced that, everywhere in the region *AEG* $w \le w_{2,t} \le w_{3,t}$ and there is no incentive for labour to migrate. In other words, everywhere in *AEG*, analysis based on the assumption of market segregation remains valid even in the absence of segregation.

Suppose now that, for some t, $w_{2,t} < w$, so that there is an incentive for semi-skilled workers to seek unskilled work at the minimum wage w. In view of (5), the semi-skilled middle-aged workers will find themselves in competition with the unskilled and underemployed youth. In these circumstances, any fixed hiring cost, applicable to newly employed workers and to workers who transfer to a job for which they are 'overqualified', will induce firms to prefer younger to older workers. Let us introduce such a cost. Then the semi-skilled middle-aged workers will be unable to find unskilled work and of necessity will reconcile themselves to semi-skilled work at wage $w_{2,t}$. The same argument applies *a fortiori* to skilled workers when $w_{3,t} < w$. Hence we may focus on the case in which $w_{3,t} < w_{2,t}$, that is, on the region above the line *AED*. The region within which there is no incentive to migrate has

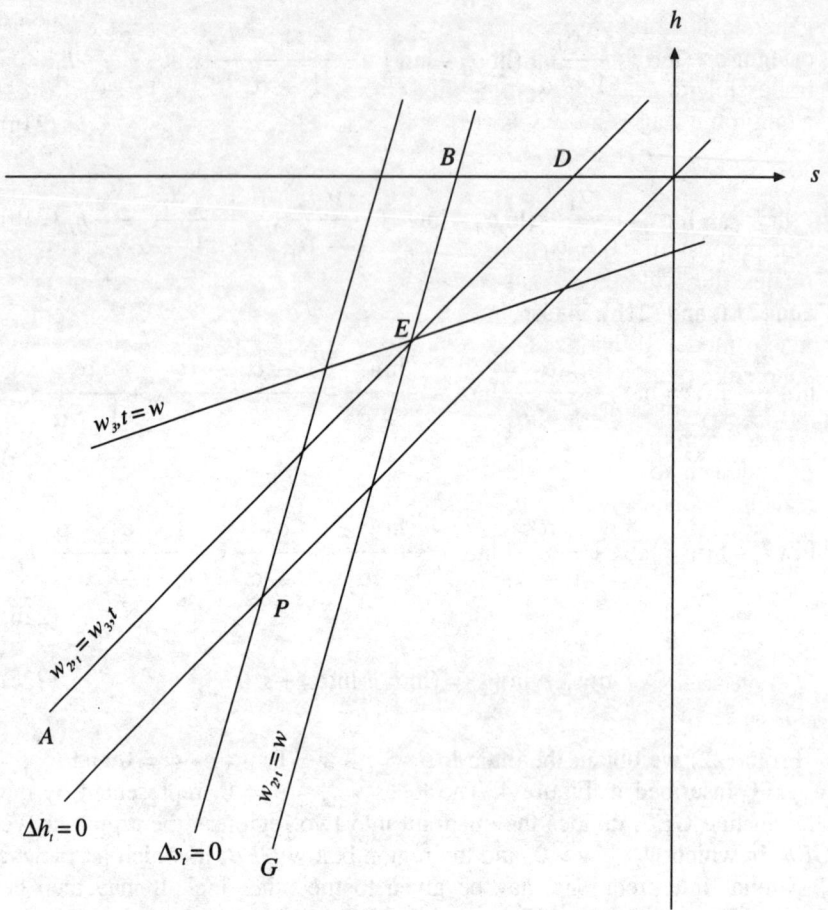

Figure 4

grown to include the whole of the plane below *AED*.

Suppose that, for some t, (s_t, h_t) lies above *AED*. Then some skilled workers take semi-skilled employment; that is, the system jumps from (s_t, h_t) to, say, (s_t', h_t') on *AED*.[1] The motion of the system from (s_t', h_t') can be decomposed into two parts. The first part comprises the segregated motion described by (17) and indicated by the arrow scheme of region III or region IV in earlier diagrams; this part of the motion takes the system from (s_t', h_t') to, say, (s_{t+1}', h_{t+1}'). The second part consists of another jump, from (s_{t+1}', h_{t+1}') to (s_{t+1}, h_{t+1}), where $s_{t+1} = s_{t+1}'$ and $h_{t+1} = s_t$. The new point may lie in any of regions I, II and III but, wherever it lies, $w_{3,t+1} > w_{2,t+1}$.

That completes our account of the implications of an artificially high wage for unskilled labour. As promised, it has been shown that such a wage can

326

generate unemployment which is both widespread, extending to all three categories of labour, and oscillatory. It remains only to note that it is impossible to generate unemployment with these characteristics by imposing a minimum wage for semi-skilled or skilled labour.

FINAL REMARKS

Our purpose in the present paper has been to highlight a mechanism which relates the widespread and persistent character of unemployment to dis-equilibrium youth wages. It has not been our purpose to construct a complete macro-model. If that had been our objective it would have been necessary to supplement our sub-model of the labour market with a further sub-model of saving and investment, which in turn would have required the recognition of a period of retirement. We can report that we have experimented with a model extended in this way, with segregated labour markets, and found that our principal conclusion, that a youth wage imposed at an artificially high level can generate widespread and persistent unemployment, is preserved.

NOTE

1   Recalling that s_t and h_t are logarithms, the point (s'_t, h'_t) is determined as the intersection of AD and the locus of $e^s + e^s = e^{s_t} + e^{h_t}$.

26

LABOUR MARKETS AND COMPETITION AS AN EVOLUTIONARY PROCESS

J. Stan Metcalfe

The development in the past decade of evolutionary models of technological and organizational change has greatly enriched our understanding of the mechanisms by which innovations are absorbed into the economic system. As is by now well understood, technical progress consists not only in the innovations alone but on the process by which they are diffused, superior methods gradually displacing inferior methods. From this absorption or diffusion process follow all the social and economic consequences of innovation. Based upon the fundamental evolutionary notions of variation and selection it has been possible to develop models of creative destruction which enable one to make the link between the innovative behaviours of firms, the idea of competitive advantage and the process of structural change. Beginning with the work of Nelson and Winter (1982) a wide variety of approaches have explored and extended the evolutionary themes with, in more recent years, the development of sophisticated simulation models.[1] A central question in all these approaches is the role of competition in raising the efficiency with which resources are used and this is the general background theme I shall explore in this brief paper. My precise purpose is to extend the familiar discussion of competitive selection in product markets by adding a process of competitive selection in factor markets, i.e. the labour market. I shall then explore how factor market selection influences the 'progressive' nature of the competitive process, that is to say, whether competition results in superior methods of production displacing inferior methods.

As with all evolutionary models of pure selection, I consider a population of *given* behaviours and ask how competition changes the relative importance of those behaviours to create changes in economic structure. We shall find that the fundamental dynamics of change are embodied in what I shall call Fisher's principles, named after the eminent English geneticist (1930). These principles relate summary measures of the rate and direction of evolutionary change to appropriate measures of the variety of behaviour in the population.[2]

My treatment proceeds in two stages. I first deal with product market selection based upon differences in the unit costs of competing firms. Secondly I recognize that unit costs depend upon the given methods of production and the wages paid for labour inputs, which in turn depend upon the properties of the labour market environment. In this way the variety in unit costs which shapes product market selection is premised upon the nature of factor market selection. Moreover, since evolution is a process of change, my approach is inherently concerned with the relative growth and decline of the firms articulating different methods of production.[3] In this way I hope to make a tentative link between the study of evolutionary processes and the concerns of post-Keynesians and other economists with pricing policy and the growth of firms, and the relation between income distribution and variety in behaviour. In this regard I am addressing a major feature of modern capitalism, namely the relationship between its dynamic behaviour and patterns of wages and profits. These are themes which have been central to Geoff Harcourt's work on pricing and distribution, where the emphasis is upon price-setting behaviour in relation to the rate of growth. In essence I am working with a microeconomic model of economic growth in which increases in the efficiency of resource use are contingent upon patterns of structural change shaped by market environments.

That we ignore change in the coefficients of production, technical progress in the narrow sense, is not to admit for once that this is unimportant; rather it is to accept that the treatment of technical progress involves much more than questions of economics, while the consequences of technical progress can be contained more precisely within the economic domain.

PRICES, GROWTH, AND PRODUCT MARKET SELECTION

I begin with a stylized model of product market selection. Consider a population of competing firms producing an identical product with different methods of production; whether these differences are technological or organizational in origin need not concern us. It is a well-established fact that even within the same field of activity, unit costs and labour productivity differs widely across competing firms or establishments. The constant returns to scale methods of production will be given for each of the competing firms. The firms are growing firms, investing a fraction of their profits in capacity expansion. The long-run behaviour of any one firm may then be summarized in terms of three groups of stable routines. The technological and organizational routines which determine its methods of production, unit labour requirements and the capital:output ratio; the financial routines which determine the allocation of funds to capacity expansion; and the routines which determine the normal prices it sets for its products and for labour inputs. In general, the behaviour of firms differs in all these dimensions, if not many more, and, indeed, the characteristic strength of the evolutionary approach is to make sense of this broad variety in behaviour. However, our present purpose is much more limited: we allow the firms to differ in only one dimension – unit labour requirements – and establish on this basis the consequential diversity in growth rates and prices. If g_i, p_i, are defined as the capacity growth rate, and price set by firm i, f as the common propensity to accumulate, dependent on the financial rules of the firms and their capital output ratios; and h_i as unit cost, we can relate these magnitudes as follows:

$$g_i = f[p_i - h_i] > 0, \quad p_i > h_i$$

$$g_i = 0, \quad p_i \leq h_i \tag{1}$$

Notice that the accumulation routine embodies two themes: that investment only takes place if the firm is operating at what it considers to be full capacity; and that the investment is deemed profitable, a judgement which is made in relation to current profitability. If the firm is not profitable its capacity level is at best constant, although its output level may of course vary within the confines of that capacity. Thus at any time the population of firms may be partitioned into three categories: dynamic firms, operating at capacity and accumulating according to the given rules; marginal firms, which just break even and are not accumulating and, in general, operate with spare capacity; and, non-viable firms which are loss-making and could be considered to be out of business. In what follows we shall focus entirely on the behaviour of dynamic firms, the modifications which follow from the existence of marginal and non-viable firms being readily incorporated into the argument as necessary (Metcalfe 1992).

Turning to the pricing behaviour of a firm, each firm posts a price so that the growth of capacity is exactly sufficient to satisfy the growth of demand in its particular market. Thus our concern is with the long-period normal conditions in which investment plans are exactly fulfilled, there being neither shortage of capacity nor surplus capacity at the level of each firm. The foundation for this pricing decision is what the firm considers to be its normal unit cost of production, h_i. I shall take it that h_i is proportional to unit labour requirements and, with the factor of proportionality set the same in each firm, we can simplify matters and write unit costs as the product of the wage rate and marked-up unit labour requirements, thus $h_i = w_i a_i$. The profit margin which is set above unit costs to determine the price depends on the rate of growth of the firm's own market which, of course, depends on how the price it sets compares with the prices set by rival firms in the population. As with any serious mark-up principle, the mark-up is not rigid, it is determined by purposeful rules and it reflects the competitive pressure which a firm faces.[4]

Of course, how this works out depends upon the nature of the market environment as an information system and, in particular, how this influences the relation between the growth of any one firm's market and the entire pattern of prices. Here we follow a method first employed by Phelps and Winter (1970) which turns out to be a natural foundation for an evolutionary discussion. At any point in time, and given the organization of the market, each firm has a customer base, the members of which are assumed to interact with the customers of other firms at random and compare prices. Since the products are identical, customers can be anticipated to shift to a different supplier if they discover that it posts a lower price. From this we can write the rate of growth of demand for the individual firm, g_{di}, as

$$g_{di} = g_D + \delta[\bar{p}_s - p_i] \tag{2}$$

where $\bar{p}_s = \Sigma s_i p_i$ is the average price level formed by weighting each price by the market share, s_i of that firm. The rate of growth of the overall market is g_D and is taken as given from outside with, of course, $\Sigma s_i g_{di} = g_D$. The market selection coefficient, δ, measures the degree of imperfection of the market: if $\delta = \infty$, there is full diffusion of information about prices and there is no consumer inertia; if $\delta = 0$ each firm's market growth rate is completely independent of comparative pricing behaviours. The value of this selection coefficient will reflect the institutions of the market in generating appropriate information and the inertia and decision rules of customers in making their choices about suppliers.

On combining (1) and (2) and equating the growth rate of capacity to the growth rate of demand we find that the normal price is

$$p_i = \frac{g_D}{f} + \frac{\delta}{f + \delta} \bar{h}_s + \frac{f}{f + \delta} h_i \tag{3}$$

from which follows the result that the average price is given by

$$\bar{p}_s = \frac{g_D}{f} + \bar{h}_s.$$

On average, prices are marked up by exactly the amount required to fund a capacity growth rate equal to the growth of the market, this mark-up being greater the smaller is the propensity to accumulate.[5]
For the normal growth rates we find that

$$g_i = g_D + \Delta[\bar{h}_s - h_i]; \quad \Delta = \frac{f\delta}{f + \delta} \tag{4}$$

where $\bar{h}_s = \Sigma s_i h_i$ is the population average unit cost level, and Δ is what we shall call the selection coefficient.

The pricing rule embraced in (3) combines a Kalecki/Steindl normal cost perspective with the need to generate funds to finance the growth of the firm.[6] In setting its price each firm is constrained by the market growth rate, the behaviour of its rivals as reflected in $\bar{h}_s$, and the degree of market

331

imperfection. One immediate consequence of this formulation is that the degree to which a firm can increase its price following an increase in its own unit costs is greater the greater is its market share.[7] In this sense, market power means that higher costs can be reflected to a greater degree in higher prices. If all unit costs increase by the same amount, each firm's profit margin remains unchanged but an increase in any individual firm's unit costs necessarily reduces its margin and increases the margins of its rivals.

Turning now to the growth rate we have in (4) a simple case of a dynamic replicator principle, a firm grows more quickly or more slowly than the population average according to whether its unit costs are smaller or greater than average. Since

$$\frac{d\bar{h}_s}{dt} = \sum \frac{ds_i}{dt} h_i = \sum s_i (g_i - g_D) h_i$$

it follows from the replicator dynamic in (4) that

$$\frac{d\bar{h}_s}{dt} = - \Delta V_s(h) \tag{5}$$

where $V_s(h)$ is the 's' weighted variance in unit costs, $\sum s_i (h_i - \bar{h}_s)^2$.

This fundamental evolutionary proposition tells us that the rate of improvement in average practice unit cost is proportional to the variation of unit cost within the population of dynamic firms. This is Fisher's principle applied to a competitive process in which firms differ in only one dimension, namely unit cost. Variety drives change and gives the improvement in average behaviour an unambiguous direction and rate. Three further points need to be noted before moving to the role of labour markets and wage-setting behaviour. The first is that the moments of the population distribution in (5) are not constructed in an arbitrary fashion. Rather the constituent elements are weighted in a fashion dictated by the economic theory underpinning the dynamics of change. In this simple case the weights are the shares in capacity (output), but more generally this is not so and the underlying theory indicates the appropriate weights, as we see in more complex cases below. Secondly, of all the possible patterns of change in market share that could be imposed on the population of firms, that governed by the replicator principle (4) maximizes the rate of reduction of average unit costs (Metcalfe 1994). Thirdly, the diversity of behaviour in unit costs is associated with diversity in behaviour with respect to growth rates and prices to generate specific patterns of association between these variables. Thus primary variety (unit costs) creates secondary variety in the endogenous variables in the competitive process, so, $V_s(g) = \Delta^2 V_s(h)$, and $V_s(p) = \left(\dfrac{f}{f + \delta} \right)^2 V_s(h)$. Similarly, the covariance between prices and growth rates is given by $C_s(p,g) = \Sigma s_i(g_i - g_D)p_i = -\Delta C_s(h,p) = (\Delta^2/\delta)V_s(h)$.

The way in which primary and secondary variety are related thus reflects the interaction between the market environment and the propensity to accumulate. A more perfect market, for example, implies a smaller variance of prices and a greater variance of growth rates in relation to a given variance in unit costs. An evolutionary framework therefore generates two classes of theoretical propositions: those concerned with patterns of association or covariation between combinations of exogenous and endogenous variables; and a dynamics of change of the endogenous variables, such as market shares.

However, the fact that competitive selection works in favour of lower cost firms does not imply that it works in favour of firms with the more resource-efficient methods of production unless we make some hypothesis about the inter-firm distribution of wage rates. Let us turn therefore to our main theme, the dynamics of competition and the operation of the labour market.[8]

WAGES AND SELECTION

Because the methods of production employed by each firm are fixed, the rate of growth of employment in any firm is equal to its rate of growth of capacity and thus output. Hence the aggregate rate of employment growth in this population of dynamic firms, g_E, is necessarily positive and equal to $\Sigma v_i g_i$, v_i being the share of the ith firm in total employment in the population. Notice that, in general, the employment share weights, v_i, are not equal to the output share weights, s_i, and that these natural weights are linked by the relation $v_i = s_i a_i / \bar{a}_s$, since a_i is employment per unit of output in the ith firm, and $\bar{a}_s = \Sigma s_i a_i$, is average employment per unit of output. That is to say, v_i also measures the proportionate contribution which a firm makes to average employment per unit of output in the population. Whilst there can be no change in labour efficiency at the level of the individual firm, *ex hypothesi*, this is not true for the average labour efficiency in the population of firms, simply because of their changing relative importance as selection operates on their comparative behaviours. Indeed the central issue for us is whether selection improves average efficiency, that is, reduces over time the value of $\bar{a}_s$, the ratio of total employment to total output.

In fact the rate of change of average employment per unit of output is given by

$$\frac{d\bar{a}_s}{dt} = \bar{a}_s(g_E - g_D) = \bar{a}_s \Sigma(v_i - s_i)g_i = C_s(a,g). \tag{6}$$

Again we find a clear example of Fisher's evolutionary principle, the covariation between unit labour requirements and growth rates across the population of firms measures the rate of improvement in average employment per unit of output. If average efficiency is to increase over time it follows that this covariance must be negative, firms with below average values of a_i must have above average values of g_i. Now whether this is the case or not will depend not only on the inter-firm distribution of efficiencies but also on what is assumed about the inter-firm distribution of wage rates.

The simplest place to start is by assuming that all firms pay the same wage rate, w, which is simply a given value. It follows that $h_i = wa_i$, $\bar{h}_s = w\bar{a}_s$, and $V_s(h) = w^2V_s(a)$. In this case Fisher's principle carries through with little difficulty and we find that

$$\frac{d\bar{h}_s}{dt} = -\Delta w^2 V_s(a) < 0$$

and

$$\frac{d\bar{a}_s}{dt} = -\Delta w V_s(a) = C_s(a,g) < 0 \tag{7}$$

The primary source of economic change is not the variance in unit costs, but the variance in employment per unit of output across the population of firms. Selection is efficient in the sense that it works to increase the shares in output and employment of firms with above average efficiency. It follows immediately from (7) that the higher is the money wage, the faster will be the rate of selection. The rationale behind this is not difficult to see, and follows from the effects of a change in the wage rate on the distribution of prices and thus growth rates. If a firm is less efficient than average, the higher wage reduces its growth rate, while the converse is true for firms which are more efficient than average. Thus the distribution of growth rates shifts in favour of more efficient firms, accelerating the process of selection.[9] Notice also that average efficiency increases more rapidly the greater are the coefficients δ and f, reflecting the point that it is the market environment which links together variety and change.

What happens if, instead of the uniform wage, we have an arbitrary inter-firm wage structure – for whatever reason, the labour force is partitioned into non-competing groups. Then, $h_i = w_i a_i$ and $\bar{h}_s = \bar{a}_s \bar{w}_v$, where $\bar{w}_v = \Sigma v_i w_i$ is the average wage constructed using the employment share weights. The consequences for the selection process are considerable, for if wage rates are arbitrary there is no longer any guarantee that firms of above-average efficiency will have below-average unit production costs. While selection will always be to the advantage of firms with lower unit costs, these need not now be the firms with superior methods of production. This means that selection could be perverse with $C_s(a,g) > 0$, and average unit costs falling while at the same time average employment requirements increase.

To explore what is implied by perverse as distinct from efficient selection we begin by observing that

$$- C_s(a,g) = \Delta \, C_s(a,h)$$

and that

$$C_s(a,h) = \bar{a}_s C_v(a,w) + \bar{w}_v V_s(a) \tag{8}$$

when $C_v(a,w)$ is the v_i weighted covariance between a_i and w_i.[10] If selection is to work in favour of more efficient methods of production, it follows that the covariance between unit costs and unit employment requirements must be positive. This would certainly be true if the relation between wages and unit employment requirements were random, for then the covariance $C_v(a,w)$ would be zero. Indeed it would be as if we had uniform wages. Hence, the problem of inefficient selection only arises if the joint distribution between w_i and a_i is not random and $C_v(a,w)$ is sufficiently negative to make $C_s(a,h)$ < 0. Now, if the wage distribution really is arbitrary there is nothing to rule this out on *a priori* grounds, and so perverse selection is certainly possible. On the other hand, it would seem that an arbitrary wage structure is difficult to defend; economic mechanisms are surely such as to impose a wage distribution in relation to the fundamentals of the competitive process.

To proceed further we need an explicit wage-setting mechanism at the level of the firm and a labour market environment from which the pattern of wages is determined endogenously. To this end we assume that firms, as well as setting normal prices, set normal wages. That is, they set wages that attract labour to them at the rate necessary to fulfill their normal expansion plans, this wage being dependent on the wages set by other firms. We further assume that the mechanism for the inter-firm flows of labour mirrors that of the flow of customers in the product market; workers, mixing randomly, compare notes of wage offers, as it were, and choose employers accordingly. To capture this we write the growth rate of employment in the ith firm as

$$g_{Ei} = g_E + \varepsilon[w_i - \bar{w}_v] \tag{9}$$

where $g_E = \Sigma v_i g_{Ei}$, and ε is the selection coefficient measuring the degree of information imperfection or inertia in the labour market. A firm which is increasing employment faster than average must pay a wage higher than average, and conversely. A uniform wage with perfect information follows if $\varepsilon = \infty$, and arbitrary wages if $\varepsilon = 0$. Since this mechanism leaves the general scale of wages undetermined, we fix this by setting $\bar{w}_v = \omega$, a constant.[11]

To solve for the normal wage rates we combine (1) and (9) and eliminate p_i using (3) to obtain

$$w_i = \frac{1}{\varepsilon + \Delta a_i} [(g_D - g_E) + (\varepsilon + \Delta \bar{a}_s)\bar{w}_v]. \tag{10}$$

From this, and setting $\bar{w}_v = \omega$, we can recover the replicator dynamics for s_i and v_i as

$$\frac{ds_i}{dt} = s_i(g_i - g_D) = \frac{\Delta s_i}{\varepsilon + \Delta a_i} [\varepsilon \omega (\bar{a}_s - a_i) - (g_D - g_D) a_i] \tag{11}$$

$$\frac{dv_i}{dt} = v_i(g_i - g_E) = \frac{\varepsilon v_i}{\varepsilon + \Delta a_i} [(g_D - g_E) + \omega \Delta (\bar{a}_s - a_i)] \tag{12}$$

In both expressions we see a distance from mean principle at work in the terms $(\bar{a}_s - a_i)$, but this is also combined with a term which measures the difference between the growth rate of demand and the growth rate of employment. Now (11) and (12) pose a difficulty in that the ratios $\Delta s_i/(\varepsilon + \Delta a_i)$ and $\varepsilon v_i/(\varepsilon + \Delta a_i)$ are no longer natural weights which sum to unity. Yet our evolutionary method depends on the use of proper weighting schemes to define the moments of the relevant distribution of behaviour. To make progress we must define two new weighting schemes in addition to the natural weights defined by s_i and v_i. This technique of defining the appropriate weighting scheme is central to the evolutionary method employed here, for it enables us to recover Fisher's principle even though unit costs are endogenously determined. Let these new weights be u_i and z_i

$$u_i = \frac{\varepsilon + \Delta \bar{a}_u}{\varepsilon + \Delta a_i} s_i \quad \text{and} \quad z_i = \frac{\varepsilon + \Delta \bar{a}_z}{\varepsilon + \Delta a_i} v_i$$

with $\sum u_i = \sum z_i = 1$ and $\bar{a}_u = \sum u_i a_i$, $\bar{a}_z = \sum z_i a_i$. We shall give these new weights an economic interpretation below; for the moment they are just devices to sum expressions (11) and (12). Summing (11) and using the definition of u_i we find

$$\sum s_i(g_i - g_D) = 0 = \frac{\Delta}{\varepsilon + \Delta \bar{a}_u} [\varepsilon \omega (\bar{a}_s - \bar{a}_u) - (g_D - g_E)\bar{a}_u]$$

from which it follows that

$$(g_D - g_E) = \omega \frac{\varepsilon(\bar{a}_s - \bar{a}_u)}{\bar{a}_u}. \tag{13}$$

Similarly, summing (12) using the weights z_i gives

336

$$(g_D - g_E) = \omega \, \Delta(\bar{a}_z - \bar{a}_s).$$

From this it follows that we can express $C_s(a,g)$ in terms of the various weighted averages $\bar{a}_s$, $\bar{a}_z$ etc.,

$$C_s(a, g) = \omega \Delta \frac{(\bar{a}_z - \bar{a}_s)}{\bar{a}_s} = \omega \varepsilon \frac{(\bar{a}_s - \bar{a}_u)}{\bar{a}_s \bar{a}_u}.$$

Using these relations we can establish now a number of characteristics of the selection process. First, we can eliminate $(g_D - g_E)$ from the equations (10) for the individual firm wage rates to obtain

$$w_i = \omega \left[\frac{\varepsilon + \Delta \bar{a}_z}{\varepsilon + \Delta a_i} \right] = \omega \frac{\bar{a}_s}{\bar{a}_u} \left[\frac{\varepsilon + \Delta \bar{a}_u}{\varepsilon + \Delta a_i} \right]. \qquad (14)$$

A firm which pays the average wage has $a_i = \bar{a}_z$, and, comparing any two firms we see that their relative wages rates are given by

$$\frac{w_i}{w_j} = \frac{\varepsilon + \Delta a_j}{\varepsilon + \Delta a_i}. \qquad (15)$$

More productive firms pay higher wages but the relative values of the wage rates do not change during the selection process; they are independent of the patterns of output and employment.[12]

Let us return briefly to the properties of the weights z_i or u_i and show that they do indeed have a simple economic interpretation. In fact it follows directly from (14) and the relation between z_i and v_i that

$$z_i = \frac{v_i w_i}{\omega}.$$

The economic interpretation of z_i is that it measures the proportionate contribution which the wage bill in firm i makes to the total wage bill in the population of firms. Because of the relation between s_i and v_i, it also follows that $z_i = s_i h_i / \bar{h}_s$, which measures the proportionate contribution which the ith firm makes to the average level of unit costs in the population. By a similar argument it follows that

$$u_i = \frac{s_i w_i}{\bar{w}_s}$$

where $\bar{w}_s = \sum s_i w_i$. So the economic interpretation of u_i is that it measures the proportionate contribution which the ith firm makes to the average industry wage constructed by using the output weights s_i, rather than the employment weights v_i.[13]

Figure 1 provides a diagrammatic summary of the wage-setting process in the case of two firms. The ray OW indicates the relative value of the wage rates as given by (15) and firm 1 is assumed to be more efficient, $a_1 < a_2$. The line d–d shows the values w_1, w_2 consistent with the given average wage, $\sum v_i w_i = \omega$ and has a slope equal to the relative employment shares v_1/v_2. This line rotates around point b as employment shares change. The lines F_1 and F_2 respectively for firms 1 and 2, show, for a given wage set by the other firm,

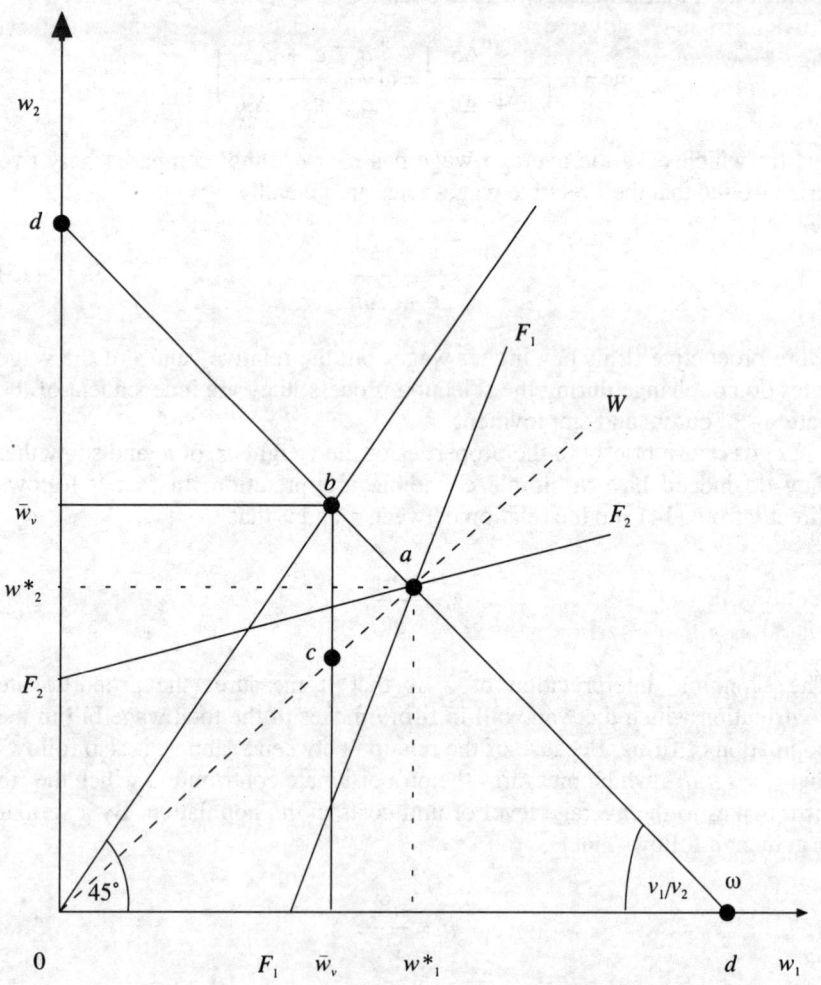

Figure 1 Wages and selection, two firms

what the required normal wage is to put that firm on its path of normal expansion (14).[14] At a particular moment the wage pattern (w_1^*, w_2^*) which is consistent with normal selection is indicated by point a. Both firms set wages which meet their growth objectives, and their values are consistent with the given average wage and the prevailing structure of employment.

Should selection be efficient, firm 1, the more productive firm, would be expected to increase its share of employment over time, and the lines F_1 and F_2 and d–d would move in such a way that point (a) gravitated to point (c), reached when firm 1 accounted for all employment. That selection is efficient follows directly. Notice first that at point a, $w_1^* > \omega$ and $w_2^* < \omega$, so that even though $a_1 < a_2$ we do not know if $h_1 < h_2$. To an as yet undetermined degree, firm 1's efficiency advantage is offset by the fact that it is paying a higher wage. However, $w_1^x > \omega$ implies that employment in firm 1 is growing faster than employment as a whole; conversely for firm 2. This must also imply $g_1 > g_D > g_2$ and $h_1 < h_2$, so that we can conclude that selection in the two firms' case is efficient. The firm with more productive methods outcompetes the other firm and accounts for an increasing share of output and employment over time. Necessarily $\bar{a}_s$ must fall over time.

The more general multi-firm requires more attention. Consider the position of a firm whose share in output is not changing, a firm with $g_i = g_D$. From (11) such a firm would satisfy the condition $\varepsilon\, \omega(\bar{a}_s - a_i) = (g_D - g_E)a_i$ or eliminating ω (from 14) this is equivalent to

$$\bar{a}_s(\bar{a}_u - a_i) = 0.$$

Hence the firm which is average with respect to its performance in the output market is one for which $a_i = \bar{a}_u$ not one for which $a_i = \bar{a}_s$, as would be the case with a uniform wage ($\varepsilon = \infty$). However, such a firm must also satisfy the condition $h_i = \bar{h}_s$ or $w_i a_i = \omega \bar{a}_s$, hence $w_i/\omega = \bar{a}_s/\bar{a}_u > 1$, since $\bar{a}_s > \bar{a}_u$.[15] So for the firm with a constant value of s_i we deduce that $g_i > g_E$ since $w_i > \omega$. Hence it follows that $g_D > g_E$ and so $C_s(a,g) < 0$, and we have established for the general case that selection is progressive. Even though more efficient firms do pay higher wages and the differentials are caused by their greater productivity, they are not so great as to offset their efficiency advantages.[16]

We can now be more precise about the exact value of the covariance $C_s(a,g)$ which we have decreed to be the crucial summary statistic of the efficacy of the selection process. Recall from (8) that the magnitude of $C_s(a,g)$ depends on $V_s(a)$ and $C_v(a,w)$. To derive the latter covariance we employ the weights z_i and find that

$$C_v(a,w) = -\frac{\omega\ \Delta\ V_z(a)}{\varepsilon + \Delta\ \bar{a}_z}, \tag{16}$$

confirming that firms with lower employment per unit of output pay higher wages. This covariance increases with the z_i weighted variance of a_i and declines to zero as the labour market becomes increasingly perfect or the product market becomes less perfect.

Substituting this result into (8) we find that

$$\frac{d\bar{a}_s}{dt} = C_s(a,g) = - \frac{\varepsilon \, \Delta \, \omega \, \bar{a}_s}{(\varepsilon + \Delta \, \bar{a}_u)\bar{a}_u} \, V_u(a) < 0. \tag{17}$$

Selection is indeed progressive, and selection is driven by variety as defined by the u_i weighted variance of unit labour requirements. The greater the variance the greater the rate of improvement in average efficiency. Moreover, the particular theory of selection indicates how variety is to be measured in this case using the weights u_i. Expression (17) is none other than Fisher's principle applied to a world of firms in which wages, prices and growth rates are endogenously determined. The rate of change in average efficiency, suitably defined, is proportional to the variance in efficiency, suitably defined. The only difference with the simple case of a uniform wage is that the factor of proportionality between change of mean and variance is no longer a constant. That it can be uncovered in this complex environment with product market and labour market selection is perhaps surprising, and is one indication of the breadth of application of Fisher's principles. After all, the variance of h_i involves the product of a_i and w_i and the variance of a product is a notoriously difficult quantity with which to work.

Fisher's principle also reflects the logic of a market economy quite precisely in that the nature of the labour and product markets determine how variety is resolved into patterns of change. If both markets are perfect, uniform wages and prices are established and the rate of improvement of average efficiency is maximized. At the other extreme, if the product and labour markets are segmented and specific to each firm, then evolution ceases to operate and the structure is frozen into its existing pattern. Market imperfections have the consequence that they slow down the rate at which market selection operates, while imposing a greater degree of variation in prices and wages and a smaller degree of variation in rates of growth. But this is simply a way of making the familiar point that the more perfect are markets, the greater the competitive pressure faced by firms. Not surprisingly a good deal of business practice is concerned with influencing the degree of market perfection in order to gain competitive advantage.

CONCLUDING REMARKS

That evolutionary thinking provides a natural framework for investigating growth and structural change is now well established: a natural framework because it recognizes that economic change is premised upon variety in behaviour. Nothing could be further from the world of the uniform agent, for in such a world the historical development of modern capitalism becomes impossible to comprehend. I have suggested in this paper that the patterns of change require an understanding of the growth of firms and of the properties of the product and factor market environments in which firms compete. Moreover these patterns of change fit with what I have called Fisher's principles: a precise way of making clear why and how variety directs change. Competition is here a process, not a state of equilibrium. Of course, this leaves aside the other major component in the evolutionary picture, the origins of variety in relation to innovating behaviour of firms. That really is another story.

ACKNOWLEDGEMENTS

I wish to thank Cristiano Antonelli for posing the question which led to this paper. He is of course not responsible for the result of which he may or may not approve. I am also grateful to Peter Swann, and Heinz Kurz and his colleagues at the University of Graz with whom the general ideas in this paper were discussed in the course of my delivering the 1995 Schumpeter Lectures. I also thank Sharon Boardman and Nick Weaver for valuable help in producing this draft.

NOTES

1 On the general theme, see Hodgson (1993), Witt (1992) and Nelson (1995). Interesting examples of simulation models include Silverberg et al. (1988), Silverberg and Verspagen (1994) and Kwasnicki (1994).
2 Extending the analysis to include endogenous changes in behaviour, particularly those induced by the working of competition, is an important part of the argument but not one which can be addressed here, for reasons of space.
3 Cf. Harcourt (1976).
4 Cf. for example, Kaldor (1985: 40–3), and on the general theme of cost-based pricing, Okun (1981: chapter 4) and Harcourt (1976).
5 The space to link this view to other treatments of the growth of the firm is not available here. A fuller discussion would include a comparison with Wood (1975) and Eichner (1976), among others.
6 Recall at this point Kalecki's two coefficients which summarized his concept of the degree of monopoly and which he labelled m and n. In comparison, $m = \delta/f + \delta$, and $n = f/f + \delta$; Kalecki (1954).
7 Note that $\partial p_i/\partial h_i = (f + \delta s_i)/(f + \delta)$, and $\partial p_i/\partial h_j = \delta s_j/(f + \delta)$.
8 Clearly this involves a view of competition as a process far removed from the idea of competitive equilibrium and, indeed, this process would be understood by any businessman as the normal process of competition. On this see Robinson (1954).
9 This follows directly from (4) above, in that

$$\frac{dg_i}{dw} = f\left[\frac{dp_i}{dw} - a_i\right] = \Delta[\bar{a}_s - a_i].$$

341

Of course, the change in the wage is a change relative to the unit price of expanding capacity.

10 The derivation of (8) and the subsequent equations are contained in an appendix available on request from the author. The manner of proof reflects the general method of adopting an appropriate weighting scheme.

11 ω and g_D thus become the two parameters of the evolutionary process. In fact to close the system we are free to choose any two of g_D, and g_E, $\bar{w}_v$ and $\bar{p}_s$ as determined from outside. In a small open economy with a given supply growth of labour one might instead choose $\bar{p}_s$ and g_E as given from outside.

12 The relation between the two measures of the average wage is given by $\bar{a}_s(\bar{w}_v - \bar{w}_s) = C_s(a,w)$. The relation between the four sets of weights we have employed can also be summarized by the expression

$$(\varepsilon + \Delta\bar{a}_z)v_iu_i = (\varepsilon + \Delta\bar{a}_u)z_is_i.$$

Notice that $\bar{a}_u\bar{w}_s = \bar{a}_s\bar{w}_v = \bar{h}_s$.

13 Notice the implied relation between the various definitions of the population means of a_i thus $\varepsilon(\bar{a}_u - \bar{a}_s) = \Delta(\bar{a}_s - \bar{a}_z)\bar{a}_u$. If $\varepsilon = \infty$ or $\Delta = 0$ then $u_i = s_i$ and $z_i = v_i$ and if $\varepsilon = 0$, $s_i = u_ia_i/\bar{a}_u$ and $u_i = z_ia_i/\bar{a}_z$.

14 F_1 and F_2 are derived from (10) by putting $v_1w_1 + v_2w_2 = \omega$ and expressing w_1 in terms of w_2, and vice versa.

15 By a similar argument the firm with a constant share of employment, $g_i = g_E$, satisfies the condition $a_i - \bar{a}_z$.

16 Cf. Mood et al. (1974: 180).

REFERENCES

Downie, J. (1958) *The Competitive Process*, London: Duckworth.

Eichner, S. (1976) *The Megacorp and Oligopoly*, Cambridge: Cambridge University Press.

Fisher, R. A. (1930) *The Genetical Theory of Natural Selection*, Oxford: Oxford University Press.

Harcourt, G. C. (1976) 'Pricing and investment decision', *Kyklos*, 29: 449–71.

Hodgson, G. (1993) *Economics and Evolution: Bringing Life back into Economics*, Ann Arbor, Mich.: University of Michigan Press.

Kaldor, M. (1985) *Economics without Equilibrium*, Cardiff: University of Cardiff Press.

Kalecki, M. (1954) *The Theory of Economic Dynamics*, London: George Allen & Unwin.

Kwasnicki, W. (1994) *Knowledge, Innovation and Economy. An Evolutionary Exploration*, Wroclaw: Oficyna Wydawnicza Politechnika.

Metcalfe, J. S. (1992) 'Variety, structure and change: an evolutionary perspective in the competitive process', *Revue D'Économie Industrielle*, 59: 46–61.

—— (1994) 'Competition, Fisher's principle and increasing returns in the selection process', *Journal of Evolutionary Economics*, 4: 327–46.

Mood, A. M., Graybill, F. and Boes, D.C. (1974) *Introduction to the Theory of Statistics*, 3rd edn, Maidenhead: McGraw-Hill.

Nelson, R. (1995) 'Recent evolutionary thinking about economic change', *Journal of Economic Literature*, 33: 48–98.

—— and Winter, S. (1982) *An Evolutionary Theory of Economic Change*, Boston, Mass.: Harvard University Press.

Okun, A. (1981) *Prices and Quantities: A Macroeconomic Analysis*, Oxford: Basil Blackwell.

Phelps, E. and Winter, S. (1970) 'Optimal price policy under atomistic competition', in E. Phelps (ed.) *Microfoundations of Employment and Inflation Theory*, London: W. W. Norton.

Robinson, J. (1954) 'The impossibility of competition' in E. H. Chamberlin (ed.) *Monopoly and Competition and their Regulation*, London: Macmillan.

Silverberg, G. and Verspagen, B. (1994) 'Collective learning, innovation and growth in a boundedly rationale evolutionary world', *Journal of Evolutionary Economics*, 4: 207–26.

Silverberg, G., Dosi, G. and Orsenigo, L. (1988) 'Innovation, diversity and diffusion: a self-organisation model', *Economic Journal*, 98: 1032–54.

Witt, U. (1992) 'Evolutionary concepts in economics', *Eastern Economic Journal*, 18: 405–19.

Wood, A. (1975) *A Theory of Profits*, Cambridge: Cambridge University Press.

27

THE LABOUR MARKET OF FEAR

Peter Riach

The 'flexible labour market' was a resounding catchphrase of British economic and political life during the 1980s. It was ruthlessly pursued via legislative action to reduce trade union power, with the closed shop and secondary picketing being in the front-line of attack. Regulations protecting the employment rights of workers were weakened and the wages councils, custodians of minimum wages in low-wage industries, were abolished. Public services, such as refuse collection, were contracted out to the private sector. Fixed-term contracts and performance-related pay were introduced into activities as diverse as policing and academic life. All this was done in the conviction that the market paradigm of the neoclassical textbooks was the appropriate instrument for sorting out wage and employment levels. In a brave new world of flexible prices and quantities, *homo economicus* would ensure labour market clearance and productivity growth.

> In a 'flexible' labour market where employment is little regulated (in terms of pay, working hours, restrictions on dismissal, etc.) the creation of low-paid, part-time, short-term or otherwise non-standard jobs is unconstrained, and there is a high level of job turnover, employers screen less intensively before hiring.
>
> (OECD 1992: 207)

This *laissez-faire* perception of labour market performance was not of course confined to Britain. I recall a seminar in Canberra where the speaker, newly returned, and anointed, from Chicago asserted that there were only four things wrong with the Australian labour market: trade unions, unemployment benefits, progressive income tax and minimum wages.

It is my belief that the 'flexible labour market' policy involves both a misunderstanding of employer–employee relations and a misrepresentation of the policy intent.

Geoff Harcourt and I were undergraduates at the University of Melbourne in the 1950s and, as an examination of *Conversations with Post Keynesians* (King 1995) will show, the Faculty of Economics and Commerce offered a quite exceptional education at that time. The Faculty had very close links with

Cambridge, so we read Marshall, Robertson, Keynes, Austin Robinson, Joan Robinson, Shove, Dobb, Kaldor and Sraffa. But we also were set Boulding, Harrod, Kalecki, Lange, Lerner, Rothschild, Phelps Brown and Tarshis. It was in the days before paradigms, and when pluralism was taken for granted. Wilfred Prest would teach us *Value and Capital* and about the magic of the invisible hand, but Don Cochrane and Keith Frearson explained the necessity of Keynesian demand management, whilst Joe Isaac introduced us to Kalecki and Rothschild. It is my express purpose below to demonstrate that this undergraduate education, which Geoff and I shared, was capable of producing economists who would quickly recognize the fallacies in this naive advocacy of 'flexible labour markets'.

MISUNDERSTANDING

The advocates of flexible labour markets have been highly selective in whom they have read and what they read. In a world inhabited by *homo sapiens* with interdependent preferences and some degree of control over their intensity of work effort, inflexibilities in wages and employment can represent quite rational employer behaviour. 'Unlike machines, workers cannot be bolted down. But even if they could be bolted down by contract, they still would be different from machines because they cannot be switched on and off' (Okun 1981: 74).

Those researching wage theory and labour economics have long recognized the benefits employers derive from a degree of stability in wages and employment. 'A reluctance to mistreat workers has long been an important consideration in the minds of businessmen and has been common knowledge among economists willing to work with primary data for half a century' (Cornwall 1983: 31).

One wage theorist writing in the 1930s, who recognized the mutual benefits of stable wages and employment, was J.R. Hicks:

> experience in working for a particular employer makes a man more useful to that employer: he gets to understand the particular sort of work his employer needs and also the personal idiosyncrasies of his employer.... If 'regularity' is associated with, and is largely due to an advantage which accrues to employers if they can maintain the same men in their employment, it also brings about a similar advantage to workmen if they can continue to work for the same employer. If a workman is to continue in the same employment, he will find it convenient to live near his work, and once he has come to live in a place specifically chosen so as to be near some particular employer, he is likely to incur quite significant costs if he moves. On both sides, therefore, there is an economy in maintaining the mutual relationship.... It greatly enhances the stability or 'rigidity' of wage-rates.
>
> (1963: 69–70)

A labour economist also writing in the 1930s was J. T. Dunlop and he identified the detriment to morale and productivity of wage flexibility:

> The employer may judge the decrease in wage rates possible – in view of trade-union strength – to be not worth the loss in 'morale' which would have an adverse effect on output. Wage-earners may be less careful or may even curtail their rate of effort deliberately.
>
> (1938: 428)

Dunlop goes on to quote from the National Society of Painters' *Monthly Journal* (No. 6, February 1922):

> 'Employers have to realise that workmen are human beings and when these unjustified attacks are made for the wholesale cutting down of wages, their attention is directed to some form of retaliation and "ca' canny" is the first one that appeals to the workmen as the most effective instrument to hand'.
>
> (1938: 428)

It is particularly noteworthy that one of the most influential founders of neoclassical market analysis, W. S. Jevons, had the practice of 'ca'canny' recommended to him personally by his businessman father. Jevons senior wrote to Jevons junior when he was an assayer at Sydney's Royal Mint about wage bargaining tactics with Captain Ward, Deputy Master of the Mint: 'I don't think you should *strike* for it but I think you should *teaze* the Cap [Ward] and don't do too much for your £500, work slow and put on your hat at 4 o'clock' (White 1982: 32).

The thesis that inflexible money wage rates can reflect rational employer behaviour, because of this morale effect, has been formalized in recent years as 'efficiency wage theory'. In his survey articles on 'Theoretical foundations for sticky wages', Haley claims that Leibenstein was the first to formulate this theory:

> The basis of the efficiency wage hypothesis is the assumption that worker productivity is a function of the wage paid. The earliest formulation of the theory applied to developing countries where it was argued that higher wages would improve nutritional standards and increase worker productivity (Leibenstein, 1957)
>
> (Haley 1990: 129)

In fact the efficiency wage hypothesis had been formalized three years earlier by Kurt Rothschild in his *Theory of Wages* as 'the economy of high wages':

> The marginal productivity theory states that there is *one* wage, and one wage only, at which a given number of men will be employed, so long as capital supply and productivity (dependent on technical knowledge and the demand for the final commodity) do not change. The wage is

regarded as a function of the number of men, capital supply, and productivity. The theorem of the 'economy of high wages' shows, however, that we cannot assume that productivity is an independent variable uniquely determining a certain wage level. It is itself a function of the wage level, both cause and effect of wage changes. Therefore, there is more than one equilibrium position, and the marginal productivity theory cannot tell us which equilibrium combination of wages and productivity is the 'proper' one.

There is no doubt that the principle of the 'economy of high wages' is of considerable practical importance. Thus, it is widely held that the fixing of minimum wages in the 'sweated' industries so increased the productivity of the workers (by improving their standard of living and by forcing the employers to pay more attention to the proper organization of production) that the large-scale unemployment which had been expected in many circles did not materialize.

(1954: 30–1)

Rothschild adds in a footnote that, over and above this impact via the physical standard of workers, productivity may respond to higher wages because of psychological effects on worker contentment.

Perlman has indicated a difficulty with Rothschild's procedure for analysing this phenomenon. Rothschild shifts the marginal product function to the right in response to a higher real wage rate, which implies that productivity has increased at *all* wage levels, whereas the 'economy of high wages' implies increased productivity only at increased wage levels. 'What is needed is a reconstruction of a single demand curve taking into account improved efficiency at higher wages' (Perlman 1969: 51). This correction, however, does not detract from Rothschild's prior claim to the thesis that labour productivity is a function of the wage level.

The short-run consequence of money wage flexibility can take the form of reduced cooperation or deliberate disruption, within the constraints of delivering 'perfunctory compliance'. The long-run consequence of employment flexibility – fixed-term contracts and ready resort to lay-offs during economic downturns – is a workforce which directs its energies to maximizing its opportunity cost in the external labour market, rather than to the long-term welfare of the employer. In professional and managerial jobs employees have significant discretion over their allocation of time to various tasks. Clearly, in a world of fixed-term contracts and ready resort to demotion and firing, there is a strong disincentive to expend time on tasks which do not enhance external employability. Certainly it would be irrational to transfer any skills to workforce competitors. In academic life, teaching and course development would be neglected in favour of research and publication. In secondary teaching, time would be concentrated on maximizing the grades of A-level students, at the expense of general educational development.

347

The 'implicit contract' literature is the contemporary theoretical formulation of the practices which employers invoke to avoid such worker behaviour and to ensure long-run loyalty. If these implicit contracts are dishonoured, in the quest for wage and employment flexibility, employers can expect to forgo the consideration which was the intent of these implicit arrangements. In withdrawing this consideration, and adopting the tactic of maximizing external employability, workers would merely be manifesting that ruthless self-interest which is so highly regarded by the advocates of flexible labour markets.

Crudely designed incentives and sanctions can do real harm to the objectives they are overtly intended to benefit, as rational individuals seek, commendably, to protect their self-interest. The recent introduction into British higher education of teaching and research assessment, involving crude performance indicators, is a case in point:

> People may adapt their behaviour to reflect the fact that they are not trusted and thereby confirm that they should not be trusted. For example in higher education it has recently been suggested that academics have manipulated examination results to conceal matters from funding council quality assessors, something which they probably would not have done in the absence of an auditing process with funding implications.
>
> (Power 1994: 13)

A couple of years ago, when discussing these issues with an MBA class, I suggested the following *hypothetical* behaviour – a lecturer faced with a 'quality' audit involving a crude performance indicator of pass rates could simply set about delivering carefully prepared model answers to the examination questions in her/his last half-dozen lectures: even the uniquely British system of external examining would find this practice difficult to detect. A student in this MBA class immediately volunteered that that had been exactly what *had* taken place on her bachelor's degree.

The regular research assessment exercises may also harm serious inquiry by acting to inhibit time-consuming projects with lengthy gestation periods. The centenary issue of *The Economic Journal* in 1991 contained several articles lamenting the absence of a tradition of direct data collection in the economics profession. Twenty years earlier, in his Presidential address to the American Economic Association, Leontief had expressed similar concern and criticized the 'undue reliance on indirect statistical inference as the principal method of empirical research' (1971:4). He challenged the reward system which operates in academic economics: 'Devising a new statistical procedure, however tenuous, that makes it possible to squeeze out one more unknown parameter from a given set of data, is judged a greater scientific achievement than the successful search for additional information that would permit us to

348

measure the magnitude of the same parameter in a less ingenuous, but more reliable way' (*ibid.*:3).

Regular research assessment exercises, which emphasize the desirability of a steady output of publications, act to reinforce this reward system. Quite simply, collecting one's own data can be extremely time-consuming, so a system rewarding regularity in publication will divert energy elsewhere: 'The easiest way to avoid perishing by not publishing is to access an existing data base, download a batch of data to your computer, and put the data through the econometric wringer' (Friedman 1991: 36).

The field experiments of sexual and racial discrimination in labour-hiring which I codirected with Judith Rich extended over five years (1983–8) (Riach and Rich 1991 and 1995). Our joint input during that period averaged around two days per week and the data collected in that time cover three pages of an academic journal. The significance of such field experiments, which are now conducted by the Urban Institute in Washington and by the International Labour Office, is that they do provide an *unequivocal* measure of the incidence of discrimination at the time of selection for job interview. One is not relying on 'indirect statistical inference' from 'an existing data base', which is the tradition established by Oaxaca (1973). In contrast to Oaxaca's econometric procedures, there are no specification problems with a field experiment in which all relevant characteristics, except sex or race, are carefully controlled.

We conducted these experiments while employed by Monash University in Australia in an environment free of research assessment exercises. It is difficult to believe that a British academic, concerned about job security and/ or promotion, would be attracted to such a time-consuming research procedure. As Friedman correctly points out, the opportunity cost is far too great.

An additional and predictable oversight by the supply-side exponents of the flexible labour market is the demand-side impact of wage and employment flexibility. Once again the warnings were there decades ago, if only they had been more eclectic in their reading: 'The growth in the rigidity of money wages is, therefore, not in general, as has often been alleged, a major cause of unemployment, but on the contrary an important stabiliser in a world which otherwise might experience violent fluctuations in prices and incomes and all the uncertainty that goes with them' (Rothschild 1954: 135). Workers are also consumers, and consumers will quite rationally be wary of contracting long-term commitments and debt when future income levels are uncertain. Such an obvious and fundamentalist Keynesian point is certainly anathema to those devoted to the neoclassical paradigm and *laissez-faire* policy, but it is clearly consistent with the recent experience of the British economy in general, and the housing market in particular.

349

MISREPRESENTATION

The most cursory examination of any neoclassical textbook reveals that markets have two sides; therefore a policy which goes under the guise of a 'flexible labour market' should carry an obligation to ensure flexibility for sellers as well as buyers. Men over fifty and women over forty are just two obvious groups of sellers who have almost no employment flexibility whatsoever. In other words 'flexible labour' is a cynical euphemism for a policy of shifting the balance of power in the labour market to the employer.

A decade ago Balogh identified monetarism as 'the incomes policy of Karl Marx' (1982: 187).

> [monetarism] amounts to the worst possible kind of 'incomes policy': an attempt to restrain wages by using massive unemployment to weaken the bargaining power of those remaining employed.... Its effects on class feelings and union militancy will make any relaxation of dear money more and more difficult, as the workforce grows more and more determined to compensate for past suffering by turning any such relaxation into higher wages. In thus deliberately setting out to base the viability of the capitalist system on the maintenance of a large 'industrial reserve army', monetarists may validate Marx's analysis.
>
> (*Ibid.*: 177)

Balogh was recognizing here that the policy priority had shifted away from full employment to inflation control, and that the mechanism upon which monetarism relied to check inflation was the deliberate creation of a large pool of labour market 'outsiders'. It soon became apparent, however, that 'outsiders' were composed primarily of a long-term group who posed little threat to the 'insiders'. Consequently a complementary policy of undermining the security of 'insiders' and making for greater substitutability between 'insiders' and 'outsiders' became necessary: a policy which was labelled the 'flexible labour market'. If monetarism is the 'incomes policy of Karl Marx', it is appropriate to invoke Kenneth Boulding and recognize that the 'flexible labour market' is 'the labour market of fear'. 'At the opposite pole from the gift is tribute – that is, a grant made out of fear and under threat. A threat is a statement of the form "you do something that I want or I will do something that you do not want"' (1973: 4). In the 'labour market of fear' this could take the form: 'You accept this deterioration in your working conditions and my capricious management style, or I will sack you.'

These are developments which Kalecki predicted fifty years ago:

> [U]nder a regime of permanent full employment, 'the sack' would cease to play its role as a disciplinary measure. The social position of the boss would be undermined and the self assurance and class consciousness of the working class would grow. Strikes for wages increases and improvements in conditions of work would create political tension ...

discipline in the factories and 'political stability' are more appreciated by the business leaders than profits. Their class instead tells them that lasting full employment is unsound from their point of view and that unemployment is an integral part of the 'normal' capitalist system.

(1943: 326)

If this 'labour market of fear' becomes an entrenched feature of British society it may well be necessary to rethink the 'Last Night of the Proms': there is a certain incongruity in the massed voices singing 'Britons never, never, never shall be slaves' and that Britain is 'Mother of the free'. Napoleon called the English a nation of shopkeepers: nowadays it would be more appropriate to call them a nation of auditors.

CONCLUSION

The political advocates of *laissez faire* – from Norman Tebbit to John Redwood – would do well to heed Joan Robinson's advice:

> The purpose of studying economics is not to acquire a set of ready-made answers to economic questions, but to learn how to avoid being deceived by economists.

(1960: 17)

The New Right has been very selective in its choice of economic prophets and has conveniently overlooked the caveats laid down by its most esteemed prophet: 'whoever imagines that masters rarely combine is as ignorant of the world as of the subject. Masters are always and everywhere in a sort of tacit, but constant and uniform combination, not to raise the wages of labour above its natural rate' (Smith 1976: 84). In view of this recognition of buyer power it is difficult to imagine Adam Smith supporting policies aimed at producing a group of powerless and insecure sellers.

I have deliberately quoted at length from the founding fathers, and founding mother, of the post-Keynesian paradigm to demonstrate that alterative insights into the labour market process have been long available to indicate the fallacies involved in the 'flexible labour market'. This 'labour market of fear' is bad for the employer, it is bad for the consumer and the macro-economy; moreover it does not work – on the admission of one of its initial supporters, David Blanchflower:

> [R]eforms focused directly on the labour market, or were expected to improve the economy by changing the labour market: industrial relations laws that weakened union power; measures to enhance self employment; privatisation of government-run or owned business; reduction on the value of unemployment benefits and other social receipts relative to wages; new training initiatives; lower marginal taxes on individuals; elimination of wage councils that set minimum wages.

351

Blanchflower goes on to report the results of his research with Freeman and Oswald, examining the impact of these reforms. His conclusion is salutary:

> [T]he policies must be seen as largely unsuccessful ... the reforms failed to improve the flow out of unemployment into jobs. Long-term unemployment still remains a major problem ... there has been a devastating loss of full-time jobs for men ... the economy does not appear to be better able to withstand economic shocks. Placing all of one's eggs in the decentralized world of the 'free market' may be far from ideal.
>
> (1995: 11)

It is time for policy-makers of all political persuasions to step outside the narrow world of neoclassical theory and *homo economicus*, to appreciate the benefits bestowed by a degree of wage and employment inflexibility in a dynamic world inhabited by *homo sapiens*.

REFERENCES

Balogh, T. (1982) *The Irrelevance of Conventional Economics*, London: Weidenfeld & Nicolson.

Blanchflower, D. (1995) 'Mrs T's reforms undone by high unemployment', *The Guardian*, 13 February.

Boulding, K. (1973) *The Economy of Love and Fear*, Belmont, Calif. Wadsworth Publishing Company.

Cornwall, J. (1983) *The Conditions of Economic Recovery*, Oxford: Martin Robertson.

Dunlop, J. T. (1938) *The Economic Journal*, September, 48: 413–34.

Friedman, M. (1991) *The Economic Journal*, 101: 33–40.

Haley, J. (1990) 'Theoretical foundations for sticky wages', *Journal of Economic Survey*, 4: 115–55.

Hicks, J. R. (1963) *The Theory of Wages*, London: Macmillan.

Kalecki, M. (1943) 'Political aspects of full employment', *The Political Quarterly*, 14: 322–31.

King, J. (1995) *Conversations with Post Keynesians*, Basingstoke: Macmillan.

Leontief, W. (1971) 'Theoretical assumptions and unobserved facts', *American Economic Review*, 61: 1–7.

Oaxaca, R. (1973) 'Male–female wage differentials in urban labor markets', *International Economic Review*, 14: 693–709.

OECD (1992) *The Job Study, Part II – The Adjustment Potential of the Labour Market*, Paris.

Okun, A. (1981) *Prices and Quantities*, Oxford: Basil Blackwell.

Perlman, R. (1969) *Labor Theory*, New York: John Wiley and Sons.

Power, M. (1994) *The Audit Explosion*, London: Demos.

Riach, P. A., and Rich, J. (1991) 'Testing for racial discrimination in the labour market', *Cambridge Journal of Economics*, 15: 239–56.

—— (1995) 'An investigation of gender discrimination in labor hiring', *Eastern Economic Journal*, 21: 343–56.

Robinson, J. (1960) *Collected Economic Papers*, Vol. 2, Oxford: Basil Blackwell.

Rothschild, K. W. (1954) *The Theory of Wages*, Oxford: Basil Blackwell.

Smith, A. (1976) *An Inquiry into the Nature and Causes of the Wealth of Nations*, eds
R. H. Campbell and A. S. Skinner, Oxford: Clarendon Press.
White, M. V. (1982) 'Jevons in Australia: a reassessment', *The Economic Record*, 58
(March): 115–55.

28

WORKERS' RIGHTS AND ECONOMIC FLEXIBILITY

Ugo Pagano

INTRODUCTION

The years that I spent in England lecturing at the University of Cambridge were characterized by the political strength of Thatcherism and by a certain feeling of impotence of the left.

When Rupert Murdoch fired the printing workers during a strike, not only the workers but the ideas of the left seemed indefensible. Defending the privileges of the printers seemed intellectually difficult; market rigidities were believed to be a fundamental obstacle to economic efficiency and damaged the unemployed workers (were not the unemployed electricians ready to take their job in Murdoch's new plant outside London?).

When, at the end of 1989, I decided to go back to the University of Siena (but to come back every year for one month to continue teaching a course for the M. Phil. paper on the 'Economics of the Institutions'), Thatcherism seemed to be spreading to the entire world. The 1989 revolution was interpreted as the final proof that obstacles to market flexibility could only lead to economic and political disasters.

Geoff's door was always open. I used to come in and discuss the economic and political situation with him. We shared the view that socialist bureaucracies were oppressive and inefficient, and that some flexibility was very desirable. However, we found the Thatcherite attack on all sorts of workers' rights not only morally difficult to digest (if you can have an ethical stomach!) but also undesirable from the point of view of economic efficiency. More cooperative economies could do better and, in many respects, were doing better.

In this essay I will try to synthesize some economic arguments, that can be used to justify our common feelings[1] that some 'rigidities' (that is some workers' rights on their jobs or in their firms) can be good for the economy.

In order to justify these claims I will use a term like 'specificity' that belongs more to the 'New Institutionalist' jargon than to the 'Post-Keynesian'[2] terminology that is associated to the work of Geoff Harcourt. However, the departure from the more traditional terminology is largely illusory: a 'specific investment' involves the development of assets that cannot easily be redeployed for other uses; this does largely overlap with the concept of an 'irreversible investment' or the concept of an 'illiquid' investment. Even if differences in language can cause fierce disputes (sometimes wars), we cannot hide the fact that we are saying similar, or at least related, things.

I

Roughly speaking, the workers can have two types of rights with respect to the work that they perform. On the one hand, they may have the right to some unspecified job in a particular organization for a long time – in some cases, until retirement. On the other hand, a union of workers can have the exclusive right to perform some well-specified jobs in all organizations but the single worker does not have the right to a job in a particular organization; the specification of the contents of these jobs and the relative training is to be agreed by the unions and employers' associations.

In some cases the workers have both types of rights: they have a right to stay in a particular organization and the right to perform a certain well-specified job within this organization. In some other cases they can have only one of these two rights. Finally, in some other cases they lack both the right to a job in a particular organization and the collective power to determine the common contents of their jobs in the different organizations: this is the case under which the management enjoys the full 'right to manage' (a right that was often mentioned during the Thatcher years) and the economy should enjoy the 'marvels' of market flexibility.

These different rights held by the workers correspond to different distributions of physical assets; it can be claimed (and it was claimed) that they 'truncate' some of the 'traditional' rights of owners of physical assets. While this is certainly true, it says nothing about the efficiency of these alternative distributions of assets.

If a worker has the right to be employed for some time in a particular firm, the owners of the asset do not have the right to employ the assets of the firm without that worker. So they do not have a right that employers have under 'classical capitalism'.

Likewise, if only the workers belonging to a certain union can work in a certain trade, the owners of assets do not have the right to employ the asset with other workers that could do a similar job.

From the point of view of the employers, the rights of the employees limit their right to use their assets. Indeed, the entitlement of job rights can be seen as a form of 'asset redistribution'.

'Classical socialism', 'classical capitalism', 'company workers' capitalism' (where workers have the right to a job in a particular organization) and 'unionized capitalism' (where the workers have the right to determine together with the employers' association the contents of the jobs in each particular firm) correspond to alternative distribution of the rights on physical assets.

It is always difficult (and often misleading) to identify an abstract model with a particular country and/or historical period.

However, as a first approximation, one could see 'Taylorism' as an example of 'classical capitalism'. The Taylorist model of capitalism is still very widespread, especially in the secondary sector of some capitalist economies and in the third world.

By contrast, 'company workers' capitalism' can be found in the primary sector of advanced capitalist economies and coincides with the ideal model of the 'Japanese firm'; even if a large sector of the Japanese economy departs from this ideal type, the lifetime right to an unspecified job is a typical feature of many large Japanese companies.

Finally, 'unionized capitalism' can be considered as a typical organizational model of a real national economy: West Germany (and now perhaps the all-German economy). Here, the union and the employer together with the state educational system to determine the standardized division of labour that characterizes each single German firm.

Thus, one can say that there is no single 'model' of capitalism, and that different forms of capitalism exist even when one relates them to the Marxian notion of mode of production based on the distribution of the 'means of production'.

II

What can be said about the relative efficiency of the alternative forms of economic organization that we have considered above? Is the 'rigidity' entailed by workers' rights an impediment to the development of the economy?

We will try to make the argument more precise by considering the different combinations of occupational and organizational rights that we have just considered. Coupling together the cases in which each type of these rights does and does not exist we obtain four possibilities, that are synthetically represented in Table 1.

(a) Workers have both occupational and organizational rights

In a rigid bureaucracy workers have the right to stay in an organization and the right to a specific type of job within this organization.

This form of organization can sometimes be convenient. This may happen when it is important to guarantee the independence of the individual performing these jobs. The independence could be threatened if other agents had the power to remove them from a particular position within a certain organization. It can be argued that for this reason in some countries judges

Table 1 Matrix of organizational rights and occupational rights

	Organizational rights	No organizational rights
Ocupational rights	(a) 'Classic socialism' (rigid bureaucracies) Characteristics: Rigidity of markets and firms Examples: Armies, judiciary, former socialist countries, etc.	(b) 'Unionized capitalism' (occupational labour markets) Characteristics: markets' flexibility and firms' rigidity Examples: Physicians, German-type industrial organization, etc.
No occupational rights	(c) 'Company workers' capitalism' (internal labour markets) Characteristics: Firms' flexibility and market rigidity Examples: Japanese-type firms	(d) 'Classical capitalism' (spot markets for labour) Characteristics: flexibility of markets and firms but rigidity and low level of workers' skills. Examples: Assembly-line workers; Taylorism; Henry Ford's factory, etc.

have these rights and, for similar reasons, 'academic tenure' is usually defended.

Moreover, this form of organization can have the advantage of creating some attachment and identification to a particular role in a certain organization. This can be very important to an organization like the army or the police, and it is not surprising that, in most countries, some of their members not only have long-term employment but also rights to specific positions that can be lost only in cases of serious misbehaviour.

Even if the market has such a limited role for assigning and monitoring the jobs that fall under this category, their existence can be a precondition for the successful working of a market economy: one must rely on independent judges and policemen to enforce contracts and guarantee the respect of all sorts of basic rights on which a market economy is founded. It can be also argued that the independence of teachers and lecturers is a condition for that autonomy of judgement which is a fundamental characteristic of a market economy.

However, this form of organization has severe disadvantages. Extending it to the whole or to even a substantial part of the economy can cause tremendous rigidities and inefficiencies. In this respect the collapse of the socialist economies provides an unlimited number of examples.

At least in the short run such organizations are deprived of two important sources of flexibility. They have only a limited capacity to change the proportions of workers performing the different occupations by hiring and firing. Equally, they cannot move the workers inside the organization from one occupation to another, nor can they change the specification of these occupations.

(b) Workers have neither occupational nor organizational rights

This is a situation that is, sometimes, regarded as a heaven of market flexibility and efficiency. The employers can determine the division of labour within their firms and, at the same time, they have hiring and firing rights.

This arrangement of 'classical capitalism' is also identified with a situation where ownership rights on capital are not truncated. The owners of capital are free to use (or not to use) their capital with the workers and the organization of work that they prefer.

Because of these 'full ownership rights', capitalism is supposed to give the maximum incentive to investment. However, these rights give a full incentive to invest only to owners of physical capital: if the workers make investments that are specific to the other assets of the organization, their rights on their own human capital assets are being 'truncated'.[3]

In other words, in a real-life situation of incomplete markets, there is a trade-off between the incentive to invest of the owners of physical and of human capital. In the Tayloristic firm or under Fordism this trade-off is solved by sacrificing the investments of human capital.[4] Under this model of 'classical capitalism' (classical also in the sense that it fits very well with the 'classical' descriptions of Babbage, Ure and Marx) workers do not make specific investments requiring particular rights.

However, one should not jump to the conclusion that, *given the skills of the workers*, the existing property rights are appropriate or 'efficient'. The opposite is also true! *Given the property rights of classical capitalism* there is little incentive for the workers to invest in their skills.

In other words, classical capitalism may be stuck in a 'vicious circle' of cumulative causation between the rights and the technology that is adopted. Or, to put it in terms of the terminology that I have often used: classical capitalism may be an inefficient organizational equilibrium.[5]

Paradoxically, this inefficiency is related to a rigidity of the organization of classical capitalism. Flexibility of economic organization requires that workers learn a great deal of activities that are specific to the organization. But this would require that workers have incentives that do not exist under classical capitalism.

Of course, under classical capitalism there is some sort of organizational flexibility: the workers can be easily moved among tasks requiring little specific learning. But, insofar as organizational flexibility requires some organization-specific learning, there seems to be a trade-off between the internal flexibility of the organizations and their external market flexibility. The terms of this trade-off are even more evident in the other two sets of organizational and occupational rights that we shall consider.

(c) Workers have organizational rights but they do not have occupational rights

The workers have a right to a job within an organization, but not to a particular well-defined occupation. The employers have the power to decide the division of labour within the organization and to assign the workers to a particular occupation but their power to fire their workers is seriously limited.[6]

In this situation, given the rights that they have in the organization, the workers now have a greater incentive to invest in organization-specific skills and, given the skills that they develop, they now have a greater interest to have some rights on the organization. In other words, we are now in a different 'organizational equilibrium' where there is a virtuous circle of cumulative causation between the rights and the skills of the workers.

Observe that this virtuous circle has been obtained at the cost of there now being less incentive to invest in physical capital. However, the company may enjoy greater internal flexibility. The workers are now ready to make the organization-specific investments that are necessary to undertake different jobs within the same organization.

This internal organizational flexibility is obtained at the cost of some extra degree of market rigidity. Given the specificity of the skills that are developed, changing organization is costly. Moreover, while the rights of the workers are not only a cause but also an effect of this situation, their existence makes these costs very evident.

(d) Workers have no organizational rights but they have occupational rights

The workers do not have a right to a job within the organization but, if they are employed, they have the right to a job of a well-specified quality that has the same characteristics across organizations.

In comparison to the case of 'company workers' capitalism', the employers keep their hiring and firing rights but they lose the power to decide the division of labour and the right to assign the workers to a particular occupation. Under 'unionized capitalism' this right belongs to the employers' association and to the occupational union that, with the support of the educational authorities, decide the common standards that should characterize the different jobs. In these ways the 'specificity' of the jobs is greatly reduced and, sometimes, almost eliminated.

Observe that specificity is *not* an intrinsic characteristic of the skills of workers. It means that these resources are not being demanded and supplied somewhere else in the economy. Thus, in principle, it is possible to create conditions such that these alternative uses for the resources exist. In this case, specific resources are transformed into general purpose resources.

Unions and employers' associations can introduce safeguards which have the effect that each organization introduces occupations requiring similar skills. These safeguards allow the creation of a market for skilled labour.[7] This may sound somewhat paradoxical if 'one does not accept that it is a mistake that the model of the competitive market economy is devoid of institutional content' (Dasgupta 1993: 143). Employers' associations and unions are usually regarded by orthodox economics only as obstacles to the smooth working of the market economy. The present framework shows that they may be (perhaps at the same time) institutional pre-conditions for the existence of some markets.[8]

In spite of its restrictions on 'the management's right to manage', employers may find 'unionized capitalism' a desirable form of organization. Under this institutional arrangement each organization can employ workers, coming from other organizations, who have skills similar to those needed by their own organization. However, it may be in the interest of each individual employer to 'free ride' on this arrangement: each employer can give to its employees jobs that are less general and more specific to the particular needs of the employing firm. In this way each individual employer could save on training costs and relax its own job specification constraints. This would lead to a classic prisoner's dilemma failure of collective action. Therefore, the unions and the employers' associations have not only to bargain the common training and job specification standards. They must also monitor that each particular firm does not deviate from these standards, endangering that market for skilled labour that is a public good for both the employers and the employees.

Thus, the development of general purpose resources, that are necessary to the flourishing of ('external') markets, requires institutions and safeguards that are more complex than those which favour the development of specific resources. Or, in other words, markets may require governance systems that are more complex than those of firms.

In the first case all employers and employees must be involved through their associations in the deal. By contrast, in the second case, a safeguard for firm-specific skills may be agreed by a single employer and its employees.

When both types of safeguards collapse, the result may be a market for 'generic' labour where workers under-invest in both general purpose and specific skills. The worker of a typical assembly-line factory can be easily moved from one firm to another for the simple reason that he does not learn much in any single employment.

The collapse of safeguards and rights may enhance economic flexibility.

However, this flexibility is associated to a deficiency of good quality activities characterized by substantial learning by doing. In this situation, introducing the rigidities entailed by workers' occupational or organizational rights might improve economic efficiency.

III

In real life economic systems, the forms of organizations that we have considered coexist in a very 'impure' way. Still we believe that the 'purity' of the ideal types that we have considered may provide some framework to analyse the institutional complexity of reality.

Two aspects of reality can give us a lot of food for thought. On the one hand, there are activities that are organized in similar ways in the different countries; for instance physicians seem to have strong occupational rights in most of the modern economies. On the other hand, some other activities are organized according to different property rights and technologies in different countries.[9]

In other words, in some cases the interaction between rights and technologies seems to lead to unique organizational equilibria. By contrast, in other cases there are multiple organizational equilibria, one of which (for instance, company workers' capitalism in Japan and unionized capitalism in Germany) seems to characterize large sectors of the economy.

Our task should be to explain both the cases of unique and multiple organizational arrangements, think about their relative efficiency and, after that, make our contributions to the debate concerning the complex institutional choices faced by each country.[10] This complexity was not well understood by the politicians ruling during the Thatcher years. Unfortunately, too many economists outperformed the simplicity and the blindness of the politicians. In 1982 Geoff had already observed that:

> It is one of the ironies of modern economic theory that in the city of Liverpool where unemployment is on average somewhere up near 20 per cent, and among black youths some extraordinarily higher figure, the chief proponent of rational expectations in the UK, who stresses that if people are unemployed it is because of a voluntary decision, is the Professor of Economics at the University of Liverpool. All I can say is that it speaks volumes for the legendary tolerance of the British that he has been allowed to lecture without someone coming in and at least throwing a blackboard duster at him.
>
> (Harcourt 1982: 287)

All I can add is that, in the following ten years, many of us were to be assailed by the need of throwing a blackboard duster. The awareness of this need made some of us very guilty. But the need did not go away.

NOTES

1   A common feeling does not mean sharing an economic argument. Geoff cannot be incriminated for any flaw of my argument.
2   On 'post-Keynesianism' see Harcourt and Hamouda (1988).
3   A very good exposition of the radical critique of this form of organization can be found in the first two chapters of Sawyer (1989).
4   On this point see Barca (1994).
5   The concept and the properties of organizational equilibria are examined in Pagano (1993). Competition may well fail to select efficient organizational equilibria. On this point see Pagano and Rowthorn (1996).
6   On the relative advantages of this form of organization see Wilkinson (1977).
7   On occupational markets, see Marsden (1986), Pagano (1991) and Ryan (1984).
8   Some of these institutional preconditions are similar to those considered by Dasgupta and David (1988) to allow the evaluation and the mobility of scientists. In some ways the world of scientists belongs to 'unionized capitalism' whereas the world of 'technologists' defined by Dasgupta and David belongs to the world of 'company workers' capitalism'. It is rather puzzling that the New Institutional literature (for instance, Williamson (1985) has devoted much attention to the governance problems of the firm and has almost ignored the complexity of the safeguards that are necessary to ensure the viability of occupational markets.
9   We should not be puzzled by the diversity of institutional arrangements. As David (1994) has observed, institutions may be somewhat harder to change than technologies.
10 This view of the role of the economists is not far from that which Hayek believed to be appropriate. Harcourt (1984) quotes (adding emphasis) the following passage from Hayek (p. 442, 1975):

> If man is not to do more harm than good in his efforts to improve the social order, he will have to learn that in this, *as in all other fields where essential complexity of an organised kind prevails*, he cannot acquire the full knowledge which would make mastery of all events possible. He will therefore have to use what knowledge he can achieve, not to shape the results as a craftsman shapes his handiwork, but rather to cultivate a growth by providing the appropriate environment, in the manner in which the gardener does this for his plants.
>
> (Hayek 1975: 442)

Harcourt contrasts this view with that of Keynes:

> Keynes wanted us to be humble folk like dentists – he obviously had good teeth. Hayek now wants us to be gardeners. I prefer Hayek's solution and Keynes' argument.
>
> (Harcourt 1984: 205)

REFERENCES

Barca, F. (1994) *Imprese in cerca di padrone*, Bari: Laterza.
Dasgupta, P. (1993) *An Inquiry into Well-Being and Destitution*, Oxford: Oxford University Press.
—— and David, P. (1988) *Priority, Secrecy, Patents and the Socio-Economics of Science and Technology*, Centre for Economic Policy Research, Stanford University, Publication No. 127.

David, P. A. (1994) 'Why are institutions the "carriers of history?" Path dependence and the evolution of conventions, organisations and institutions', *Structural Change and Economic Dynamics*, 5(2): 205–21.

Harcourt, G. C. (1982) 'Making socialism in your own country', in Sardoni, C. (ed.) (1992) *On Political Economists and Modern Political Economy. Selected Essays of G. C. Harcourt*, London: Routledge.

—— (1984) 'Reflections on the development of economics as a discipline', in Sardoni, C. (ed.) (1992) *On Political Economists and Modern Political Economy. Selected Essays of G. C. Harcourt*, London: Routledge.

—— and Hamouda, O. F. (1988) 'Post-Keynesianism: from criticism to coherence?' in Sardoni, C. (ed.) (1992) *On Political Economists and Modern Political Economy. Selected Essays of G. C. Harcourt*, London: Routledge.

Hayek, F. A. (1975) Nobel Lecture: 'The pretence of knowledge'. *The Swedish Journal of Economics*, 77(4): 433–42.

Marsden, P. (1986) *The End of Economic Man*, Brighton: Wheatsheaf.

Pagano, U. (1991) 'Property rights, asset specificity, and the division of labour under alternative capitalist relations', *Cambridge Journal of Economics*, 15(3): 315–42. Reprinted in Hodgson, G. M. (1993) *The Economics of Institutions*, Cheltenham: Edward Elgar.

—— (1993) 'Organisational equilibria and institutional stability', in Bowles, S., Gintis, H. and Gustafsson, B. (eds.) *Markets and Democracy*, Cambridge: Cambridge University Press.

—— and Rowthorn, R. (1996) 'The competitive selection of democratic firms in a world of self-sustaining institutions', in Pagano, U. and Rowthorn, R. (eds.) *Democracy and Efficiency in the Economic Enterprise*, London: Routledge.

Ryan, P. (1984) 'Job training, employment practices, and the large enterprise: the case of costly transferable skills', in Osterman (1984) *Internal Labor Markets*, Cambridge, Mass.: MIT Press.

Sawyer, M. C. (1989) *The Challenge of Radical Political Economy*, London: Harvester Wheatsheaf.

Wilkinson, F. (1977) 'Collective bargaining in the steel industry in the 1920s', in Briggs, A. and Saville, J. (eds.) *Essays in Labour History 1918–1939*, London: Croom Helm.

Williamson, O. E. (1985) *The Economic Institutions of Capitalism*, New York: The Free Press.

29

CHANGES IN THE NOTIONS OF UNEMPLOYMENT AND WHAT THAT MEANS FOR THE POOR

Frank Wilkinson

CHANGES IN THE NOTIONS OF UNEMPLOYMENT

A central belief in conventional economics is that in capitalist systems, provided workers are prepared to accept the market wage, all who want to work will find employment, so that unemployment is essentially *voluntary*. Underlying this belief is the most resilient notion in economics: with given techniques, if employment is to increase, real wages have to fall. This contention rests primarily on the theory of the diminishing marginal productivity of labour, which states that as the employment of labour increases relative to capital, labour productivity will decline. If, then, firms are to expand output and employment and maintain profitability, wages will need to fall in line with declining productivity. Economists have also traditionally believed that full employment is guaranteed from the demand side by the working of 'Say's Law': supply creates its own demand.

Keynes refuted Say's Law. He argued that as income increases, the proportion saved grows and as no mechanism exists to mobilize savings for investment, the increase in the latter is insufficient to generate sufficient effective demand to secure full employment. The result is *involuntary* unemployment: the inability of workers to find jobs at, or even below, the going wage because of a shortage of demand. The Keynesian revolution thus switched the explanation for unemployment away from too high wages in the labour market towards too low demand in the product market.

Theorizing about persistent inflation in the post-war period re-directed the attention of economists to conditions in the labour market as an explanation for unemployment. Philips (1958) purported to show by historical example an inverse causal relationship between levels of unemployment and rates of wage increase. The importance of Phillips' analysis was that it focused attention on what were increasingly regarded as unacceptable levels of inflation and offered legitimization to what had been previously regarded as an unacceptable level of unemployment, despite its Keynesian assumption that wage movements originated in the state of demand in the product market. However, from the mid-1960s a simple trade-off between unemployment and inflation was increasingly cast in doubt by the tendency for both to rise together. The theoretical response to this new phenomenon was most clearly articulated by Milton Friedman (1977) who argued that inflation is determined by increases in the money supply in excess of the increase in nominal output. Friedman rehabilitated pre-Keynesian orthodoxy by asserting that the level of employment was determined by supply and demand in the labour market. Labour market inflexibilities and imperfections meant that even at full employment there could be a degree of joblessness, and this Friedman called the 'natural' rate of unemployment: that level of unemployment at which the rate of inflation was stable. Friedman's theory was labelled 'adaptive expectations' because he accepted that a monetary stimulus could increase employment in the short term, before workers' inflationary expectations and wage demands adjusted to the reality of rising prices and directed unemployment back to the natural rate. This view was challenged by the rational expectations theorists, who argued that by experiencing inflation, individuals come to understand the inflationary process and what triggers it. This rules out unanticipated inflation and the possibility of any deviation of unemployment from the natural rate. The rational expectations school of monetarists thus fully restored the pre-Keynesian orthodoxy of the primacy of real wages in determining the level of employment.

An alternative explanation for the accelerating inflation of the 1960s was that it resulted from attempts by wage-earners to compensate for the erosive effects of tax and price increases on real take-home pay (Coutts et al. 1976). It was demonstrated that during the late 1960s the combined effects of price and taxes was to so slow down the rate of increase in real after-tax earnings that in some years they fell. The militant response to this, it was argued, caused the wage explosion of the late 1960s (Wilkinson and Turner 1972). Further research[1] suggested that in periods when the pace of real incomes was constrained by slow increases in productivity, adverse movements in the terms of trade, increases in taxation or some combination of these, strongly organized groups on both sides of the labour market could protect their real income by raising wages or prices. This threw the burden of adjustment onto weakly organized groups, who responded by improving their organization and pressing for compensating wage or price increases. As more and more groups effectively indexed their incomes to rising prices, the pace of inflation accelerated. By contrast, when conditions were more conducive to increases in real incomes (when productivity was rising rapidly, the terms of trade were improving, when taxes were falling, or some combinations of these) inflationary pressures subsided. This suggested that inflation is a political process that could be countered by appropriately designed institutions for wage determination. It also followed from this analysis that by lowering productivity, the deflationary response to inflation is counter-productive. However, the insights of what came to be called the 'real wage resistance hypothesis' were diverted into more conventional channels.

The idea of a resistance to real wage reduction as a source of inflationary pressure was modelled together with elements of Marxist and monetarist thought by Rowthorn (1977) to produce the 'conflict' theory of inflation, a model in which unemployment again played a central role in controlling inflationary processes. According to Rowthorn, labour and capital aspire to shares of income which they secure by wage claims and price increases respectively. If these aspired-to shares sum to the total available for distribution, inflation remains constant. But if there is an aspiration gap (i.e. if the total of the shares aspired to sum to more than the total available for distribution), the effect is inflationary. Rowthorn went on to argue for a Marxist reserve army of labour mechanism, triggered by adjustment in the money supply, which by increasing competition between workers in the labour market and by firms in the product market, would reduce wage and price pressure, closing the aspiration gap and reducing inflation. Rowthorn's ideas about the disciplinary role of unemployment were adopted by more orthodox economists in the form of NAIRU (non-accelerating inflation rate of unemployment) (Meade 1982). This notion welded the conflict theory of inflation to the more orthodox theory of the downward-sloping demand curve for labour. However, whereas Rowthorn had regarded unemployment as bringing the combined claims of labour and capital into line with the resources available so as to remove inflationary pressure, in Meade's analysis trade union monopoly bargaining power automatically causes unemployment by pressing the wage share against its limits as determined by the diminishing marginal productivity of labour and/or the degree of monopoly exercised by firms in the product market.

There has been a growing consensus across a broad spectrum of economic schools that some equilibrium level of unemployment exists at which inflation stabilizes, and that this is determined by supply and demand in the labour market. But the relationship between inflation and unemployment has proved far from stable (Michie and Wilkinson 1992) and a continued belief in ISUR (the inflation stability unemployment rate[2]) requires a continuous re-explanation of why the equilibrium level should change so much. Nevertheless, the economics profession has risen to the challenge[3] and the list of reasons included in the next paragraph as to why the level of ISUR varies so much is by no means exhaustive.

ISUR is seen as having shifted for a variety of reasons, operating both from the demand and supply sides of the labour market. In their models, the demand prices for labour – the wage offered – is a residual after the profits and non-labour costs of production are deducted from price. Several factors, in addition to diminishing marginal productivity and imperfections in product markets, have been identified as raising the non-labour costs of production and reducing the demand price for labour. These include increases in real terms (i.e. relative to product prices) of raw materials, capital goods prices, interest rates and exchange rates. These, it is argued, have reduced the demand price for labour, requiring a decline in wages relative to productivity, and the unwillingness of labour to concede this has increased the natural rate of unemployment. Various factors have also been identified as increasing the supply price for labour and hence the natural rate of unemployment. Social welfare benefits, increases in asset values and in interest rates are seen as raising out-of-work income and hence the supply price of labour. Increases in the equilibrium level of unemployment are also attributed to trade unions, legal minimum wages, restrictive labour and employment legislation, and the deskilling of workers by long spells of unemployment or by technical change. Meanwhile, strategically located 'insiders' are seen as taking advantage of the costs of their hiring and firing, their firm-specific skills and their insider knowledge to raise wages above the market clearing rate, to the disadvantage of the unemployed. The size of the labour force is also said to have increased owing to demographic trends, and demand for labour – unskilled labour in particular – has been adversely affected by labour-saving technical progress. The slowness to adjust to external shocks is also said to explain the persistence of unemployment. Joblessness is therefore regarded as resulting from either a failure of real wages to adjust downwards in line with the declining demand price for labour or because, for various reasons mainly related to their skills and attitudes, workers are unemployable. Unemployment is thus voluntary or 'structural' (Phelps 1993), not amenable to macroeconomic stimulus and can only be countered by supply-side measures.

WHAT THIS HAS MEANT FOR POLICY

The idea of a necessary trade-off between wage levels and unemployment has been progressively embraced in macroeconomic policy. In the 1950s, under Keynes's influence, policy was based on the idea that employment was determined by the level of effective demand in the product market. In the 1960s, under the influence of the Philips' curve analysis, policy-makers became more tolerant of unemployment. In the 1970s, ISUR came increasingly to dominate theory and by 1976 the British government had abandoned its commitment to full employment. Since 1979, monetarism has dominated anti-inflationary policy and labour market deregulation has been allotted the task of securing full employment. There can be little doubt that, measured by unemployment levels, these experiments with pre-Keynesian economics have failed. But if, as explained by its apologists, ISUR has shifted because of changes in supply- and demand-side conditions in the labour market, unemployment is not a good indicator of economic performance. However, other indicators give no more support to the claim that the introduction of monetarist macroeconomic or labour market deregulation policies have had their predicted beneficial effect. Between the peak years 1979 and 1990, output per head in manufacturing grew by 3.8% per year but, as manufacturing output increased at less than 1% per year, employment in manufacturing fell at an annual rate in excess of 3%. Investment as a proportion of GDP increased from 17.5% to 19.5% between 1979 and 1990. However, this is explained by a boom in real estate investment in the distribution and financial sectors: manufacturing investment fell from 3.1% of GDP to 2.6%. The failure of manufacturing output to expand at the same pace as the economy (which grew at 2.2% per year) resulted in a surge of imports, so that Britain became a net importer of manufactured goods for the first time since before the Industrial Revolution. As a consequence of this, the balance of payments on current account deteriorated from a surplus of 1.3% of GDP in 1979 to a deficit of 2.8% of GDP in 1990. The scale of the inflow of capital necessary to sustain the high and growing current account deficit without a collapse of sterling forced up real interest rates. The real short-term interest rate (Treasury bill yield adjusted for manufacturing output prices) rose from 2.7% in 1979 to 8.8% in 1990. The only real success of the 1980s was the increase in consumption, which grew in real terms from 57.2% to 63.1% of GDP between 1979 and 1990.

The boom of the late 1980s was brought to an end by a severe credit squeeze. By 1992, GDP was 2.5% below its 1990 level, manufacturing output was 6% lower, manufacturing investment had fallen to 2.2% of GDP, but the balance of payments deficit was still 2.4% of GDP. The economy was stimulated by the British withdrawal from the ERM in September 1992 and the subsequent devaluation and cuts in interest rates; by 1994 GDP was 6% higher than its 1992 level. At very best, however, the latest up-turn in the economy has been weak. Manufacturing output had still to recover its late 1980s peak in 1994, when manufacturing investment was 2% of GDP. Exports responded to the 1992 sterling devaluation, but imports continued to grow strongly, so that the 1994 balance of payments deficit on current account remained as high as 1.6% of GDP. The budget deficit also posed a threat to the recovery. Under the pressure of high levels of unemployment and growing poverty, it proved impossible to contain government expenditure, which increased from 39.1% to 43.3% of GDP between 1990 and 1994, with social security spending alone rising from 11.4% to 14.8% of GDP. In early 1995, the supply constraint began to tighten and price increases in the supply chain began to accelerate. Materials purchased by manufacturing increased in price by 9% between April 1994 and April 1995 and over the same period the prices of metal manufactures, chemicals and man-made fibres, all major industrial inputs, increased by 14%, 7.3% and 9.3% respectively. These price increases and the fall in the official unemployment count were interpreted as signalling a future increase in the general price level, and the government increased interest rates. Higher interest charges were added to increasing costs and the increase in output stalled.

Theoretical explanations of unemployment appear therefore to have been transformed by policy into causes of unemployment, in a regular cycle of increasing joblessness and declining economic performance. The acceptance of the notion of a level of unemployment which stabilizes inflation and which has shifted upwards with changes on the demand and supply side of the labour market has a particular pernicious effect. Central bankers have now embraced this view, so a reduction of unemployment from whatever level triggers amongst them expectations that inflation will accelerate and leads, as recent experience in the US and Britain has shown, to an increase in interest rates which dampens recovery. ISUR can therefore be regarded as a mechanism by which inflation expected by bankers is converted into unemployment caused by policy: in effect, the theoretically postulated causal relationships between unemployment and inflation is reversed by policy practice.

WHAT THIS MEANS FOR THE POOR

The implementation of pre-Keynesian macroeconomic policies and labour market deregulation (Deakin and Wilkinson 1991) have resulted in the re-emergence of mass unemployment of inter-war proportions, a deep restructuring of labour markets away from full-time secure employment and a dramatic increase in the inequality of income. Measuring the unemployment consequences of the policy shifts of the 1980s and 1990s raises major problems. Since 1979, no fewer than twenty-nine changes have been made to the way unemployment is officially counted, all but one of which have reduced recorded unemployment. The official definition of unemployment has also been changed from persons *registered* as unemployed, to the current definition of those out of work *claiming* unemployment benefits of various kinds. Between 1979 and 1993, claimant unemployment increased from around 1 million to 2.8 million. The Unemployment Unit has estimated that on the basis of those *registered* as unemployed, unemployment increased from around 1.4 million in 1979 to more than 4 million in 1993. These estimates receive support from a study by Wells (1994) which shows a level of unemployment in early 1994 'closer to the Unemployment Unit's total of 4 million than to the official claimant count of under 3 million'.

The record of deregulatory policies is no better if employment, rather than unemployment, is taken as the measure of success. It is myth that the policies pursued in the 1980s and 1990s have led to substantial job growth in comparison to previous decades. Official figures show that by 1983 total employment – a figure which includes employees, the self-employed and members of the armed forces – had fallen by 1.7 million from its 1979 peak. It then recovered slowly, but after 1989 a second intense depression again reduced the number of jobs, to 0.6 million below its 1979 level. Employment was also restructured during this period, with a decline in the number of full-time, secure jobs. Between 1979 and 1993, male full-time employment fell by 2.3 million; this was only partly compensated for by an increase of 0.5 million in male part-time jobs. Meanwhile, female employment increased by 1.3 million, although only 196,000 of these jobs were full-time. Overall, in this period the number of employees fell by 1.7 million and self-employment increased by 1.1 million (0.4 million of whom were part-time). Much of the 'new' self-employment resulted from government incentive schemes for the unemployed, and is very low paid (Joseph Rowntree Foundation 1995: 53).

As unemployment has grown and employment has become increasingly part-time and/or casual, pay, and more generally income, have become more unequally distributed. Between 1977 and 1992 the average real wages of the bottom 10% of male earners were static; the median or mid-point increase was 27%; while for the top tenth of earners, the average increase was 44% (Goodman and Webb 1994). During this period the earnings of non-manual workers rose more quickly than those of manual workers, and full-timers' earnings rose more quickly than those of part-time workers. Of the self-employed in 1993, more than 20% had incomes which were below half the average income for all individuals (Department of Social Security 1995). The rise in inequality of earnings, together with cuts in social security provision, has contributed to a sharp increase in household poverty. Official sources show that between 1979 and 1993 the lowest decile of households saw no increase in their income before housing costs are taken into account, whereas the highest decile had a rise of 45%. When housing costs are taken into account, the lowest decile had a drop in real income of 17%, compared to an increase of 62% for the highest decile (*ibid.*).

The degree of job insecurity and dissatisfaction arising from these developments is not easy to measure. Some part-time jobs are stable and secure, and some individuals may welcome the flexibility offered by part-time work and self-employment. Conversely, many full-time jobs pay very low wages and offer only partial guarantees of continuing employment. The essential question here is how insecurity affects different groups and to what extent it is growing. There is little doubt that an ever-growing number of workers are affected by insecurity. One recent assessment (Coutts and Rowthorn 1995) is that 13.5 million workers in the British economy are now in a 'primary' sector of the labour force which, on the whole, enjoys secure and well remunerated full-time employment, with a further 6.5 million in an 'intermediate' category of those who, while not having a full-time job, are nevertheless relatively well-paid and secure. This leaves a further 9 million 'disadvantaged' workers without secure or well-paid employment. Of this 9 million, 4.9 million are in employment and 4.1 million are without employment. Thus 'around seventy per cent of the labour force are financially comfortable and reasonably secure, while thirty per cent live in either insecurity or comparative poverty' (*ibid.*). This analysis, if anything, errs on the side of caution; it does not seek to assess how many of those in the 'primary' segment, who are apparently secure, perceive their position as being under threat, as more firms use redundancy as a measure of first rather than last resort. The important point is that the ratio of disadvantaged to advantaged has increased over the past fifteen years and continues to do so.

One perceived benefit of the change in government policy was that in the 1980s Britain appeared to have achieved a greater degree of political and social stability after the turbulence of the 1970s. This can be explained by the contribution the intensified exploitation of the growing 'underclass' had made to the 'contentment' of the more affluent members of society who hold electoral power (Galbraith 1992). The so-called 'contented classes' are the wealthy; those whose employment is protected from the erosive effects of unregulated competition, from public and private sector 'downsizing' and from government control of pay; and those who benefited from regressive realignments of the tax/benefit systems. The increase in the incomes of the contented class has absorbed the lion's share of the additional resources made available by the increase in productivity, the improved terms of trade, the North Sea oil windfall, the sale of public assets, the cuts in welfare benefits and the reductions in the earnings of the low paid.

However, the political benefits of the new economic order have proved as transient as the economic benefits. There is a growing threat to social stability from unemployment and related poverty and crime, and from the effective exclusion of a growing proportion of the population from any meaningful economic or social prospects. It is also becoming increasingly clear that many of the previously protected white collar and managerial jobs are becoming more precarious as redundancies and casualization penetrate deeper into the primary employment sector. Moreover, the resources for largesse for the contented classes are no longer available whilst economic growth is constrained by the growing balance of payments deficits and erosion of the productive base. Consequently, the government is faced with the alternatives of reducing the income of the contented classes, who are noticeably discontented at the prospect, or accelerating the process of economic and social decline by redistributing to them a greater share of the, at best, slow growing national cake. But that can only be done by adding a further twist to the downward economic and social spiral by cutting ever deeper into the welfare state and further reducing the earnings and job prospects of the lower paid.

WHAT THIS MEANS FOR ECONOMIC AND SOCIAL RE-GENERATION

Present government policies rest on the twin fallacy that the economy tends to full employment and that left to its own devices the labour market will generate economic efficiency. Keynes exposed the first fallacy, but the

371

Keynesian revolution failed to revolutionize thinking about the labour market. There is nothing 'natural' or inevitable about the allocation of income and resources arrived at through the play of market forces. There is no such thing as a 'free' labour market, and the idea that a market equilibrium can be restored through deregulation is an illusion. In particular, relationships in the labour market are permeated by inequalities of bargaining power, by structural barriers to mobility and by institutionalized discrimination, which together lead to the systematic undervaluation of the labour of disadvantaged groups, which has been greatly increased by recent government policy. Whether or not there is an 'ideally' efficient free labour market system which can be theoretically modelled is of little relevance to the formulation of policy in a world where the distribution of income and economic opportunities is largely determined by power relationships and institutional forces.

Britain's cumulative economic decline can only be reversed if full employment policies are coupled with strategies to re-regulate the labour market.[4] Effective labour standards improve efficiency, create a more favourable macro-environment for sustainable growth and help the public purse.

The ability of any one firm to adopt a high-productivity route to competitive success is limited if its rivals are able to compete on the basis of low pay and poor working conditions. This is why labour-market regulation is an essential component of any industrial policy which has enhanced competitiveness as its goal. Basic levels of protection in such areas as wages, working time and conditions of employment aim to forestall destructive competition by setting a floor below which terms and conditions may not fall. Effective labour standards constitute, therefore, a form of discipline for firms, requiring them to engage in continuous improvements to products and techniques in order to stay competitive. The existence of a pool of undervalued labour, on the other hand, offers a means by which firms can compensate for organizational and other managerial inadequacies, for example by delaying the scrapping of obsolete equipment. The survival of the more technologically and managerially backward also helps prevent more progressive firms from expanding their share of the market. The overall effect is a lower average level of productivity and a slower rate of introduction of new techniques and products. In addition, labour standards may be used to promote cooperation between firms in joint product development, the pooling and sharing of resources for gaining access to new markets, and generally improving performance. Co-operation requires minimum levels of stability in social relations, security, and mutual trust. None of these is easy to secure on any broad scale unless there is some form of collective understanding which assures each competitor that undercutting wages and other destructive competition are not to be tolerated.

Labour standards also affect the quality of labour. High standards do not simply permit but also effectively require firms to adopt strategies based on enhancing the quality of labour inputs through improvements to health and safety protection, training and skills development. It is now widely recognized that high-trust work organization is necessary to secure worker cooperation in technical development, product enhancement and continuous quality control. Worker involvement is the key to such development, but this cannot be relied on where there is no long-term commitment by employers to their workforce and no assurance that workers' interests will not be summarily sacrificed to those of other stakeholders in the firm, such as shareholders and creditors. The effectiveness of the modern business enterprise depends on providing workers with rights which give them a voice alongside those of other stakeholders: this involves, at the very least, guarantees of effective collective representation and participation for employees. Participatory standards – standards providing for the collective representation of both employers and workers – enable collective interests to be expressed and mechanisms put in place for the resolution of disputes. Moreover, poor pay and working conditions and the absence of job security also have a negative impact on incentives for training. One orthodox economic explanation for low pay is that it results from lack of training and that higher pay will further discourage employers from investing in training. But experience shows that low-paying employers are the least likely to train; they are more often in the business of exploiting rather than creating human capital. Moreover, jobs with poor terms and conditions of employment are unlikely to be afforded high social status, whatever their skill level, and this will help discourage individuals from acquiring the necessary entry qualifications by undertaking education and training.

The more even distribution of economic opportunities resulting from the imposition of effective labour standards will also improve the prospects for employment generation, by its effect on the level and structure of consumption. The redistribution of income from the rich, who save a high proportion of their income, to the poor, most of whose income is consumed, will raise the level of demand in the economy and generate employment. In the longer term, a more equal distribution of income will make more generally affordable a healthier diet and one which is more environmentally friendly, thereby creating the conditions for improving the quality of life for everyone and for increasing the level of sustainable economic and employment growth. Standards are also needed to ensure that economic opportunities are as widely shared as possible. It is essential to bring about the successful redeployment of workers displaced by technical progress and changing patterns of consumer demand. This requires a macroeconomic policy which incorporates a full-employment target over the medium term; adequate and widely available facilities for retraining; the minimization of artificial barriers to entry into particular occupations; and an effective strategy on working time. Such measures are required both to maintain demand in the labour market and to prevent the establishment and growth of social and economic disadvantage.

Labour standards have the important role of avoiding the use of social security and/or the tax system to subsidize low pay. Such subsidization often succeeds only in transferring income to low-paying employers, thereby exacerbating the problem which the transfers were intended to deal with. Family credit creates a set of perverse incentives: employers are encouraged to pay lower wages, while means-testing discourages workers from pressing for or seeking out higher wages, by imposing a high marginal tax rate on any wage increases which they might secure. At the same time, the taxpayer is faced with a growing burden on public expenditure. In April 1989, for example, there were 285,000 claims for family credit at a monthly cost of around £7 million. By January 1994, the number of claims had risen to 521,000 at a monthly cost of £24 million; annual expenditure on family credit in 1993–94 was over £1 billion (Department of Social Security 1994). This figure can be expected to grow sharply over the next few years if the trend of relative decline in low pay continues and if plans to extend similar benefit payments to single people and childless couples are implemented. The proliferation of part-time work at low rates of pay and self-employment means also that the tax base is being eroded. In construction, which saw a considerable increase in self-employment in the 1980s, both (lawful) tax avoidance and (illegal) tax evasion have become widespread. The resulting loss to government revenues has been estimated at between £2 and £4 billion annually. The tax regime for construction has also contributed to a policy of cut-throat competition over labour-costs which is undermining training and leading to skill shortages.

CONCLUSIONS

The evolution of the notion of the determination of unemployment since Keynes involved a curious voyage back into history. By the late 1970s pre-Keynesian notions of the causes of inflation and unemployment had been reinstated to become the conventional wisdom in economics and had been fully incorporated into economic and social policy in Britain. Monetarism and free market economics have provided government with the justification for concentrating the cost of economic crisis on the have-nots and have salved the conscience of the haves by assuring them that although the income distribution is unequal, it is efficient. To explain the subsequent rise in unemployment and the growth of poverty, economists have supposed poor labour quality and work orientation of the poor and/or their unwillingness to accept the reality of the changing economic situation by accepting lower wages. This revisionism in economic theory, with its emphasis on invisible hands in regulating human affairs and its scapegoating effects, invites comparison with the tendency for fundamental religions to reappear in periods of intense crisis.

But despite the growing reserve army of labour, the continuous decline in the relative wages of the poor, the cuts in social welfare and the intensified coercion of the unemployed to find work, the economy has failed to respond. The growing problem of the twin deficits – budget and balance of payments – and the progressive supply constraint are all evidence of the failure of monetarism and supply-side economics. The imposition of policy rooted in these theories has deepened the political and economic segmentation and further reduced Britain's efficiency. The effect of the deepening political divide is to rule out any alternative economic policies, as both political parties compete for the votes of the erstwhile contented classes by offering tax cuts financed by cuts in welfare provision. Increasingly, the poor have become effectively disenfranchised, as both main parties embrace some version of the monetarist/supply-side story and neither makes any pretence to represent their interests.

Keynesianism was seen as failing because of inflation: reversion to pre-Keynesianism has re-created the unemployment, poverty and social deprivation in which the Keynesian revolution had its roots. This reaffirmation of the intellectual and moral bankruptcy of traditional notions of unemployment invites economists and particularly Keynesian economists back to the drawing board and underlines the central role that fairness and equity must play in any redesign of economic theory and policy.

NOTES

1   See Tarling and Wilkinson (1977, 1982 and 1985) and Wilkinson (1988).
2   A term I have invented to encompass NATUR (Friedman's natural unemployment rate), NAIRU (Meade's non-accelerating inflation rate of unemployment) and AIMRA (Rowthorn's anti-inflation mobilized reserve army) and any other equilibrating mechanism resting on the idea that unemployment is the necessary condition for controlling inflation.
3   For a collection of the reasons for a shift in ISUR, see Layard *et al.* (1991). For some of the reasons they left out, see the review of their book by Phelps (1992).
4   For discussion of the role of labour standards as a precondition for economic efficiency, see Sengenberger and Campbell (1995).

REFERENCES

Coutts, K. and Rowthorn, R. (1995) *Employment in the United Kingdom: Trends and Prospects*, ESRC Centre for Business Research, University of Cambridge, Working Paper No. 3.
——— Tarling, R. and Wilkinson, F. (1976) 'Wage bargaining and the inflation process', *Economic Policy Review*, No. 2, University of Cambridge, Department of Applied Economics.
Deakin, S. and Wilkinson, F. (1991) 'Labour law, social security and economic inequality', *Cambridge Journal of Economics*, 15(2).
Department of Social Security (1994) *Social Security Statistics 1993–1994*, London: HMSO, Tables A1.01, A1.02.
——— (1995) *Households with Below Average Incomes*, London: HMSO.

Friedman, M. (1977) *Unemployment and Inflation*, Institute of Economic Affairs, Occasional Paper 51.

Galbraith, J. K. (1992) *The Culture of Contentment*, New York: Houghton Mifflin.

Goodman, A. and Webb, S. (1994) 'For richer, for poorer: the changing distribution of income in the UK, 1961–1991', *Fiscal Studies*, 28.

Harvey, M. (1995) *Taxed into Self-Employment: The Unique Case of the UK Construction Industry*, Institute of Employment Rights.

Joseph Rowntree Foundation (1995) *Inquiry into Income and Wealth, Vol. 2*.

Layard, R., Nickell, S. and Jackman, R. (1991) *Unemployment, Macroeconomic Performance and the Labour Market*, Oxford: Oxford University Press.

Meade, J. (1982) *Wage Fixing*, London: Allen & Unwin.

Michie, J. and Wilkinson, F. (1992) 'Inflation policy and the restructuring of the labour market', in Michie, J. (ed.), *The Economic Legacy: 1979–1992*, London: Academic Press.

Phelps, E. S. (1992) 'A review of unemployment', *Journal of Economic Literature*, XXX.

Philips, A. W. (1958) 'The relationship between unemployment and the rate of change of money wage rates in the United Kingdom 1861 to 1957', *Economica*, XXV(2).

Rowthorn, R. (1977) 'Conflict, inflation and money', *Cambridge Journal of Economics*, 1(2).

Sengenberger, W. and Campbell, D. (eds) (1995) *The Role of Labour Standards in Industrial Restructuring*, Geneva: International Institute for Labour Studies.

Tarling, R. and Wilkinson, F. (1977) 'The social contract: postwar incomes policies and their inflationary impact', *Cambridge Journal of Economics*, 1(4).

——— (1982) 'The movement of real wages and the development of collective bargaining in the period 1855 to 1920', *Contribution to Political Economy*, 1.

——— (1985) 'Mark-up pricing inflation and distributional shares: a note', *Cambridge Journal of Economics*, 9(1).

Wells, J. (1994) 'The Missing million', *European Labour Forum*, Summer.

Wilkinson, F. (1988) 'Real wages, effective demand and economic development', *Cambridge Journal of Economics*, 12(1).

——— (1991) 'The structuring of economic deprivation and social deprivation and the working of the labour market in industrial countries', *Labour and Society*, 16(2).

——— and Turner, H. A. (1972) 'The wage-tax spiral and labour militancy', in Jackson, D., Turner, H. A. and Wilkinson, F. (eds) *Do Trade Unions Cause Inflation?*, Cambridge: Cambridge University Press, 2nd edn, 1975.

30

UNEMPLOYMENT PROSPECTS FOR MODERN CAPITALISM

John Cornwall and Wendy Cornwall

INTRODUCTION

There has never been any doubt regarding where Geoff Harcourt stands on the employment issue: full employment is a necessary condition for a just and equitable society. This is a view we wholeheartedly share, and an appropriate starting point for this paper, written to honour Geoff and his work.

Since the 1970s, politicians, bankers and business leaders have increasingly measured economic performance in terms of output growth and stock and financial market behaviour, to the virtual exclusion of unemployment, previously a prime indicator. This shift in emphasis coincided with rising unemployment. It also coincided with resurgent neoclassicism in the economics profession, which provided theoretical credentials for the shift.

While there can be no doubt that GDP growth is an essential measure of aggregate economic health, the unemployment rate is equally essential. Where the growth rate measures changes in average economic welfare, the unemployment rate provides insight into the distribution of its benefits. It is evidence of the extent of wasted resources, of an economy failing to function efficiently. Rising unemployment, even if accompanied by output growth, is evidence of deteriorating economic health. The ultimate aim of this study is to forecast general trends in OECD unemployment for the rest of this century.

As economists, we are aware that predicting the future is fraught with danger. It is enough to recall the widespread belief among economists during the closing years of the Second World War that the postwar period would be a repeat of the 1930s. It was held that once the conversion to a peacetime economy had been achieved, mature capitalism would be incapable of generating sufficient aggregate demand to prevent mass unemployment. In fact what followed was the greatest economic boom yet experienced by capitalism.

In spite of the difficulty of forecasting accurately even in the short run, attempts to predict general macroeconomic trends in the medium term can be useful. Such efforts force investigators to look beyond the immediate determinants of economic performance and to concern themselves with some of the underlying structural processes that drive the economy. Clearly the usefulness of understanding the structural forces that constrain and influence macroeconomic performance variables is not confined to medium-term forecasting. For more than two decades the developed capitalist economies have functioned poorly, and in our view the sources of this macro malfunction are structural. While human error and other outside disturbances can cause poor performance, a well-functioning economy has mechanisms that buffer such shocks, reducing both their duration and severity. In advanced industrial economies, these mechanisms are not manifestations of the neoclassical self-regulating properties such as Pigou effects. They are induced or activated by macroeconomic policy, and the feasibility of any policy depends upon the economy's institutional structure. We argue that institutional changes, attributable in large part to actual macroeconomic performance, have created an institutional framework in which certain policy goals, such as full employment, cannot be attained without large real costs. Consequently, the key to influencing future economic performance lies in understanding the structural shifts that have caused the current malfunction.

Structural change, especially institutional change, is usually slow, proceeding by increments until the cumulative effect is strong enough to alter the way the economy works, and to present policy-makers with a new set of constraints. We will argue that the continuing poor macroeconomic performance can be traced to earlier postwar developments, some as early as the 'golden age' of capitalism, approximately the early 1950s to the early 1970s. These historical connections must be made clear if we are to understand the current difficulties.[1]

While our ultimate aim is to examine the future trend of unemployment, the interim goal is to develop an analytical approach that is consistent with the broad feature of macroeconomic development in the OECD economies in the postwar period, one that can be extended to studies of individual economies and enriched by including economy-specific detail. In general terms, our 'model' is Keynesian; the system is demand-driven and, in the absence of government intervention, the economy is given to periods of poor macroeconomic performance, such as high rates of unemployment. Contrary to the assumptions of the new classical macroeconomics, and consistent with empirical investigations of the characteristics of actual unemployment in the past two decades, most of this unemployment is involuntary. In such cases a necessary condition for realizing full employment is intervention by the fiscal and monetary authorities to guarantee sufficient aggregate demand. However, our approach extends traditional Keynesian analysis by emphasizing the impact of institutions on economic performance. The ability and willingness of the authorities to target the full employment goal depends crucially on institutional arrangements, particularly those in the labour market. Even here we retain the interventionist character of Keynesian economics. While institutional change tends to be slow, institutions include not only the customs

378

and norms that define accepted conduct in economic relations, but also the body of law and regulation established by governments. This introduces a conduit for institutional change that raises the possibility that change might be accelerated.

Analysis of the structural determinants of performance allows us to assess trends in unemployment in the OECD economies for the remainder of the 1990s. To briefly anticipate our conclusions, the future would look favourable were it not for the continued existence of certain economic institutions. These define accepted behaviour in economic relations, and in doing so exert a powerful influence on economic outcomes. Unless they undergo radical change in the very near future, the high unemployment conditions which have already plagued the developed capitalist world for over two decades are set to continue, at least through the rest of this century. Because the difficulties are rooted in the fundamental structure of the economy, such as in institutions that change slowly, the only escape from this conclusion lies in the possibility of change accelerated by public policy. An extension of the analysis examines the likelihood that a political solution will be used, and accords it a low probability.

We confine our analysis to eighteen OECD member economies, excluding the smallest and least developed.[2] The next section summarizes events beginning in the 1960s, providing the background for the remainder of the discussion.

POSTWAR DEVELOPMENTS

Before the fall: 1960–73

In the period of sustained growth from 1960–73 these eighteen economies experienced unemployment rates far lower than have been achieved since, the average rate for the group being 2.3%, but without suffering the expense of high inflation. While this group of economies shows relative homogeneity respecting inflation performance, their unemployment rates demonstrate a very marked bimodal distribution. Canada, Ireland, Italy, the United Kingdom and the United States cluster at an average unemployment rate of 4.4%, while the remainder are clearly at (or perhaps above) full employment, their average being 1.4%.[3] In short, the data suggest that these five economies could keep their inflation rates in line with the rest only by accepting rates of unemployment higher than the full employment rate.[4]

The ability to achieve low rates of both inflation *and* unemployment depended to a large extent upon the labour market institutions of a country. These determined which of two types of labour market strategies were adopted by labour to achieve a desired rate of growth of real wages. Depending upon the strategy chosen, full employment was or was not consistent with politically acceptable rates of wage and therefore price inflation.

Under a market power strategy, wage settlements were the outcome of an unrestricted collective bargaining process whereby, through negotiation of the money wage, the bargainers attempted to arrive at a 'fair' real wage. Since labour's market power increased as unemployment fell, this strategy generated a negative relationship between rates of unemployment and money wages, i.e. the Philips curve. The five high-unemployment economies adopted this strategy, and as their record reveals, full employment proved to be inconsistent with politically acceptable rates of inflation; their unemployment rates were allowed to exceed full employment in order to contain inflation. We will refer to such economies as having an inflationary bias.

The majority of the OECD economies adopted in various forms a social bargain strategy. In these cases, labour accepted the need for money wage restraint in the interest of achieving the national goals of wage and price stability and international competitiveness. In return, labour received full employment and, depending upon the country, other rewards such as generous welfare benefits and rising real wages due to growing productivity associated with full employment.

The balance of payments imposes a second constraint on the ability to achieve low rates of unemployment. During the golden age, many of the smaller economies in the full employment group had persistent payments deficits, but these were small relative to GDP and accompanied by rapid export growth. Consequently, foreign lenders were willing to finance these deficits, as were borrowers to accumulate foreign debt. Indeed rapid export growth played an essential role in removing payments constraints for most of the deficit economies (and in allowing others to avoid them entirely). A prime source of this growth was the ability of many economies to borrow technology, largely from the United States. The resulting large productivity bonus generated cost advantages, significantly contributing to export success.

Relieved of payments constraints, and with well-functioning social bargains, most of the OECD economies were free to pursue independent aggregate demand policies during this period. As mentioned, the result was an average unemployment rate of 1.4% for the successful economies. Moreover these economies were in stable low unemployment–low inflation equilibrium. Should a devaluation become necessary to maintain external balance, achievement of the targeted value was assisted by capital controls, and by the coordinated response of central banks and international agencies to perceived exchange rate misalignments. The end of this period of remarkable stability and growth can be traced to the late 1960s. The severity of the emerging problems became very clear in the early 1970s, as the breakdown of Bretton Woods and a series of other shocks radically altered the international economic environment.

The 'Great Inflation' and the policy response

The first sign of the end of the golden age was the accelerating inflation rate in many OECD countries. To explain this, most accounts have emphasized the role of a series of adverse shocks, such as commodity price rises and the establishment of a flexible exchange rate system following the demise of Bretton Woods. There can be no doubt that these external events contributed to the problem, but the lingering nature of their effects suggests that there have also been *internal* changes in these previously stable economies. Of particular and lasting importance are the changes that took place in labour market institutions. In a number of case studies, the acceleration of inflation was traced to an increased unwillingness of labour to support national wage and price stability goals by restraining money wage demands. The result was the collapse of the 'first generation' of social bargains in many of the formerly full employment economies.[5] Underlying this collapse were rising economic aspirations and expectations built up during the 1950s and 1960s, together with a spreading belief by labour that it was not receiving its fair share of income under an income policy. Only by adopting a different labour market strategy, in which it could exert its market power to the full in collective bargaining, did labour feel it could obtain an increased share of income. A critical effect of the breakdown in social bargains was to activate previously latent cost-push inflationary mechanisms.

This change in labour market strategy, and its associated rapid acceleration of rates of wage and price inflation, was shortly followed in the early 1970s by a series of adverse shocks. Among these were the breakdown of the Bretton Woods Agreement and rapid and strong increases of prices in international commodity markets, including oil. These and other common adverse disturbances then fed into the cost-push mechanisms which amplified and prolonged their inflationary impact. The result was a continuing acceleration of inflation rates everywhere in the early 1970s.

This sharp rise in inflation was accompanied by an equally rapid deterioration of payments positions. In response, governments almost every-where imposed severely restrictive aggregate demand policies. Taking the eighteen economies as a group, unemployment rose from its average of 2.3% for 1960–73 to 4.1% for 1974–9. For eight of these economies, the increase in unemployment was great enough to exclude them from the low unemployment group, thus reversing the golden age distribution of good and poor performers; only Austria, Japan, Norway, Sweden and Switzerland were able to maintain the full employment goal. The inflationary bias had now spread to the majority of the OECD economies.

The second oil shock and its aftermath

Some reduction in inflation rates accompanied the relatively high unemployment of 1974–9 in most of these economies. But inflation rates again accelerated in 1979–80, largely due to the impact of the second oil shock, a second run up of commodity prices and the resulting activation of cost-push mechanisms in a now larger number of economies with no social bargains. Governments again responded with restrictive aggregate demand policies, leading to the most serious recession of the postwar period. By the mid-1980s aggregate demand policies were eased, allowing some recovery in growth and unemployment. Nevertheless, for the entire group of eighteen economies over the 1980s decade, the average rate of unemployment was approximately triple the average 1960–73 rate and one and a half times the 1974–9 rate. Although unemployment rates rose only slightly during the 1980s in the five well-performing economies, by the early 1990s even Austria, Japan, Norway, Sweden and Switzerland sacrificed the full employment goal as unemployment rates rose to roughly double their 1980s rates.

THE RISE AND SPREAD OF THE INFLATIONARY BIAS

The underlying factor responsible for the upward trend in unemployment rates has been the rising trend everywhere in the inflation costs of low unemployment.[6] Reversing the inflationary trend has been the dominant goal of aggregate demand policies. Even so, by the 1990s the OECD economies face a very unfavourable trade-off between inflation and unemployment, including a most unacceptable rate of inflation at full employment. The rising inflationary bias in the OECD economies can be attributed to one or more of these institutional changes, depending upon the economy.

First, in many economies an inflationary bias developed following the breakdown in the late 1960s of formerly successful social bargains. There have been no successful attempts to reintroduce these policies. Second, the prevailing labour view since the mid-1970s has been that it has had to bear the main cost of fighting inflation. High unemployment and a failure of real wages to grow are two of these costs, and accelerated money wage demands are the means of redressing the balance and catching up in real wages. Such effects operate with greater force under low unemployment conditions.[7] They have increased the inflationary bias and have made it more difficult to reintroduce social bargains.

Third, beginning in the early 1970s, there was a marked change in the international monetary regime. A system of relatively flexible exchange rates replaced the fixed exchange rate system originating in the Bretton Woods agreement. The early 1970s also marked the beginning of a steady process of deregulating international capital movements. Unregulated international capital markets under a flexible exchange rate system raise the inflation cost of pursuing the full employment goal or of a policy of simply reducing unemployment, if it involves depreciation of the currency to combat a possible payments deficit.[8] In either case, the response of managers of large mobile capital funds to unilateral reflationary policies acts to worsen the inflation–unemployment trade-off both directly and by interacting with the internal institutional changes just discussed. Thus the more credible, persistent and ambitious is the stimulative aggregate demand policy, the greater and more prolonged will be the speculation against the currency because of the policy's impact on expected and actual rates of inflation. Any country that reflates unilaterally can expect to encounter serious difficulties in controlling the extent of the depreciation of its exchange rate, the rate of inflation and the decline in real wages. These developments will soon force the abandonment of the stimulative aggregate demand programme.

Note an important implication of these last remarks. The deregulation of international capital flows introduces an asymmetry in the way in which the world financial community affects the ability of governments to pursue and achieve macroeconomic goals. While stimulative aggregate demand policies will eventually be reversed by market forces, restrictive policies are self-reinforcing. By restricting aggregate demand and moving the current account towards surplus, expected rates of inflation decline and foreign capital is attracted into the country, thereby pushing the exchange rate higher and reinforcing the initial restrictive policy (Stewart 1983: chapters 5 and 6).

SUMMARIZING THE CAUSES OF THE RISING INFLATIONARY BIAS

To a large extent the causes of the greater inflationary bias were common across the OECD economies, followed similar sequential patterns and have had a cumulative and sustained impact. The breakdown of social bargains in the late 1960s came first. It led to a sharp acceleration of inflation rates, restrictive aggregate demand policies and a growing labour resentment and desire to recoup accumulated losses. Reinforcing both influences on the inflationary bias was the spreading deregulation of international capital movements. Initiated in the 1970s, the volume of transactions of speculative funds expanded rapidly during the 1980s and into the 1990s. Together these three forces have been sufficient to generate a strong inflationary bias throughout the OECD, eliciting restrictive aggregate demand policies and a prolonged and widespread period of high unemployment and stagnation. Their continued existence has serious implications for the remainder of the 1990s. Under existing institutional structures, the OECD economies are caught in a high unemployment equilibrium trap.[9]

SUPPLY CONSTRAINTS ON EXPANSIONARY POLICIES

Typically macroeconomic forecasters assume rather uncritically a given set of structural features of the economy fixed over the forecast period, i.e., tastes, technologies and endowments, a model describing the interaction of the economic variables and best-guess estimates of the exogenous variables, especially the policy instruments. Obviously no matter how adequate the model, unanticipated changes in the economic structure or the policy variables (as well as shocks) during the forecast period can lead to deviations from the forecast values. More importantly for our purposes, little if any attempt is made by the forecaster either to include institutions as part of the economic structure that affects performance or to support the assumption of a stable economic structure. Such strategies are assumed to be outside economists' traditional framework of analysis.

Earlier sections have stressed the importance of institutions in influencing macroeconomic outcomes. A theme running throughout the paper has been that to understand differences in macroeconomic performance over time (as well as differences between economies at the same point in time), institutions must be treated as an integral part of the structural features of the economy. Like tastes and technologies, institutions act as constraints on the economic variables and so affect performance. By tracking the effects of the evolving institutional framework on macroeconomic performance (and the effects of performance on institutions) over the postwar period, it is possible to assess which institutions exerted significant constraints on performance and how they did so.

Accurate intermediate-run forecasting requires the same kind of attention to institutions. The conditional forecasts of macroeconomic performance for the remainder of the 1990s assume that those institutions that have given rise to the inflationary bias will be in place throughout the forecast period. It is further assumed that their continued existence will lead to the continuation of restrictive aggregate demand policies, preventing any major improvement in the unemployment picture. The assumption that these institutions will persist for the remainder of this century seems highly plausible. There is little evidence to indicate that governments and the other key participants involved in social bargain policies are willing to enter into a second generation of social bargains. Second, the labour market policies most likely to develop in the near future will be framed in terms of unleashing 'market forces' even further and not in terms of policies promoting greater cooperation and compromise. Current policies, euphemistically referred to as 'deregulation', 'restructuring' and 'responses to globalization', are cases in point. They work to intensify labour's belief in the unfairness of the economic system. Third, there is very little support for reimposing capital controls; indeed, prevailing sentiment is for even more widespread deregulation (Commission of the European Community 1994).

THE DEMAND FOR EXPANSIONARY POLICIES

Much has already been said about the unwillingness of the authorities in the past to supply the aggregate demand needed to significantly reduce unemployment because of the inflation costs. Our forecasts, based on a Keynesian perspective in which aggregate demand determines output and employment, also assume that aggregate demand policies will not be adopted to reduce unemployment substantially, say to rates midway between those prevailing today and golden age levels. The question arises: could the continuation of high unemployment into the forecast period raise sufficient protest that the authorities would, in the interest of political stability, feel compelled to implement stimulative aggregate demand policies?

To answer this question it is necessary to distinguish between two political levels at which the greater demand for policies to reduce unemployment might be voiced. First, for some time electorates have expressed the view that reducing unemployment must be given the highest economic priority. This raises the possibility that electorates (or median voters, in public choice theory) could intensify their demands for action and that governments would comply. According to public choice theory, the aim of politicians is to advocate and implement policies that maximize their chances of re-election. In the case under consideration, this increased demand for lower unemployment leads to the advocacy and implementation of the electorate's desired aggregate demand policies.

However, there are good reasons to believe that this derived demand for stimulative aggregate demand policies is at variance with the political processes of the real world. The first thing to recognize is that these same electorates have reduced the effectiveness of their demands in the past in two ways: political activity in support of their causes has been sporadic, poorly organized or both, and demands for more jobs have been combined often with contradictory demands for deficit and debt reduction as well as for reduced roles for government.

Even ignoring these problems, it can be argued that it is still unlikely that governments will be pressured to reduce unemployment over the forecast period. This brings the discussion to actions at the level of political representation of the electorate. The earlier question is now modified to become: would highly organized, well-focused and greater electorate demand for policies to reduce unemployment be reflected in a shift in policies at this second political level?

Lindblom, among others, argues persuasively that in all private enterprise market-orientated societies corporate business occupies a privileged position compared to other interest groups, for at least three reasons (Lindblom 1977: part V). First, corporate business is not merely a special interest as are, say, labour unions, but is made up of organizations performing what governments believe to be essential functions covering every major aspect of production and distribution. Governments must, therefore, be prepared to continuously provide corporate executives with the inducements to make the key economic decisions needed for the proper functioning of an economy. Second, no other special interest group has comparable funds to spend to influence policy outcomes, nor the organizations in place to further its cause, nor the access to government. Finally, corporate business has the ability to indoctrinate citizens in such a way that the latter often voluntarily agree to serve its interests. Taken together, these factors allow corporate business to gain disproportionate and powerful direct and indirect controls over government policy compared to other organized interests and especially compared to the electorate. More particularly, corporate business attitudes towards the unemployment–inflation dilemma have a disproportionate impact on macro-economic policy outcomes.

Recognition of these findings shifts the focus of political analysis from the preference of the electorate to those of the business sector and the possibility that there are forces, as yet unconsidered, that could lead to a shift in the preferences of business leaders toward lower unemployment at the expense of higher inflation. Kalecki pointed out over a half a century ago that business leaders are likely to be aware that a substantial reduction in unemployment and a rise of aggregate activity is beneficial in one sense, as profits would be higher. However, offsetting this are the effects of the shift in relative political power to labour that tighter labour markets generate. As Kalecki viewed matters, such a shift would lead to a lack of control over the workforce, less discipline on the shop floor, increased strike activity and, certainly of great importance today, accelerated wage demands (Kalecki 1943).

It is true that Kalecki envisaged these adverse political effects as resulting from the maintenance of full employment conditions for some time. Nevertheless there are a number of reasons why any kind of shift in demand by the business sector towards more stimulative aggregate demand policies is highly unlikely. Globalization of competition, and particularly the impact of competition from the low-wage NICs, makes even the most secure corporation concerned about controlling the work place. Loose labour markets are increasingly seen as a means to this end. To this can be added the still fresh memories of the Great Inflation, the near fanatical fear of important international agencies and central bankers of reigniting inflation even in its mildest form and the perception that unilateral stimulation of the economy will lead to the importation of higher inflation rates. We are forced to conclude that our assumption that the overall stance of aggregate demand policy will remain restrictive across the OECD economies is well founded.

THE FORECASTS

In the light of this analysis, our forecasts for the period up to the year 2000 are already clear. First, there is very little probability that there will be institutional change, whether spontaneous or induced by public policy, that will remove the inflation and payments constraints faced by governments. Second, prolonged high unemployment has accentuated the disproportionate influence that corporate and financial interests exert on governments. These will ensure the continued unwillingness of the monetary and fiscal authorities to supply sufficient aggregate demand to significantly reduce unemployment. Third, the demands for political action made by the electorates are contradictory, and other interest groups lack the resources and organization needed to force the authorities to alter their present commitment to restrictive aggregate demand policies.

Under these conditions, we expect the average OECD unemployment rate for the rest of the 1990s to remain close to the average experienced from 1980 to 1994. On a more speculative note, there is unlikely to be any significant improvement in unemployment rates in the individual economies, again compared with the 1980–94 period. The conditions outlined above prevail in all the economies studied here, so that even those which once had successful social bargains show no sign of resolving their problems. As a result, the employment prospects for modern capitalism in the intermediate term present a uniformly dismal outlook.

Our analysis has stressed the importance of economic structure to understanding and forecasting macroeconomic trends in the medium term. It may be alleged that our conclusions are too general to qualify as forecasts. In response, we note that only general trend forecasts were promised, and that our approach applied to case studies of individual economies would provide greater detail. Integrating institutional structure into the analysis highlights the difficulties of achieving recovery in the medium term by clarifying the constraints under which the economy, and governments, operate. In doing so, it counters unjustified optimism in the power of market forces to resolve problems.

ACKNOWLEDGEMENT

This work was supported by grants from the Social Sciences and Humanities Research Council of Canada and the Faculty of Science, Dalhousie University.

NOTES

1   For a fuller account, see Cornwall 1994, chapters 9 and 10.
2   Greece, Iceland, Luxembourg, Mexico, Portugal, Spain and Turkey are excluded.
3   The United Kingdom is excluded from the full employment group because unemployment rates never fell below 3% after 1966 and averaged 3.6% from 1966–73.
4   The full employment rate of unemployment is conservatively set at 3% in the

text. At this rate, involuntary unemployment is assumed to become negligible.

5   See Phelps Brown 1975; Flanagan *et al.* 1983; Goldthorpe 1978; Perry 1975, especially the 'Comments'; and Soskice 1978.

6   This was made especially clear by the behaviour of inflation rates during the 1980s. Even the mild recovery of unemployment during this decade to what would have been considered recession unemployment rates in earlier periods was enough to cause widespread acceleration of inflation rates.

7   See Cornwall (1994: 169) for discussion of additional hysteretic effects of restrictive aggregate demand policies.

8   The current exchange rate system is flexible relative to the Bretton Woods arrangements. The text statement is not meant to deny the existence of managed exchange rates.

9   This is not to imply that a fiscal constraint is unimportant. The point we make is that even in the absence of a fiscal constraint, the institutional developments we emphasize would ensure continuation of the world slump throughout the 1990s.

REFERENCES

Commission of the European Community (1993) *Growth, Competitiveness, Employment: The Challenge and Ways Forward into the 21st Century*, Brussels.

Cornwall, J. (1994) *Economic Breakdown and Recovery: Theory and Policy*, Armonk, N.Y.: M. E. Sharpe.

Flanagan, R., Soskice, D. and Ulman, L. (1983) *Unionism, Economic Stabilization and Incomes Policies: European Experience*, Washington, D.C.: Brookings Institution.

Goldthorpe, J. (1978) 'The current inflation: towards a social account', in F. Hirsch and J. Goldthorpe (eds) *The Political Economy of Inflation*, London: Martin Robertson.

Kalecki, M. (1943) 'Political aspects of full employment', *The Political Quarterly*. October; reprinted in *Selected Essays on the Dynamics of the Capitalist Economy, 1933–1970*, Cambridge: Cambridge University Press, 1971.

Lindblom, C. (1977) *Politics and Markets: the World's Political-Economic-Systems*, New York: Basic Books.

Perry, G. (1975) 'Determinants of wage inflation around the world', *Brookings Papers on Economic Activity*, No. 2: 403–47.

Phelps Brown, H. (1975) 'A non-monetarist view of the pay explosion', *Three Banks Review*, No. 105.

Soskice, D. (1978) 'Strike waves and wage explosions, 1968–1970: an economic interpretation', in C. Crouch and A. Pizzarno (eds) *The Resurgence of Class Conflict in Western Europe since 1969*, New York: Holmes and Meir, vol. 2: 221–46.

Stewart, M. (1983) *Controlling the Economic Future*, Brighton: Wheatsheaf.

31

THE STOCK MARKET AND THE CORPORATE SECTOR

A profit-based approach

Anwar Shaikh

I first got to know Geoff Harcourt's work through his wonderful review essay on the Cambridge Capital Controversy (Harcourt 1969). I had entered graduate school in economics at Columbia University in the Fall of 1967, and helped occupy the buildings in the student strike of 1968, and was generally disrespectful of the neoclassical theory I was being taught. Geoff's essay had an immediate and powerful impact on my thinking. It introduced me to the works of Joan Robinson, Sraffa, Pasinetti, Garegnani, Bhaduri and many others. It showed me that classical and Marxian economics could be rigorous alternatives to neoclassical theory. Its critique of the notion of an aggregate production function led directly to my first seminar paper, which also became my first publication shortly thereafter, entitled 'The Humbug production function'. Its discussion led me directly back to Sraffa's little book, and through it to the classical economists and to Marx. These ideas continue to ground my work to this very day. All in all, Geoff's article became such an important part of my intellectual arsenal that the very sight of this dog-eared and tattered copy frightened my beleaguered professors (most of whom, however, successfully resisted the temptation to read it).

One of the powerful themes to which Geoff's work introduced me is the classical notion of a perpetual oscillation of market rates of profit around one another – i.e. the notion of a turbulent tendency for rates of profit to equalize across spheres of capital investment. In the article which I contribute to this Festschrift, I show that the (incremental) rate of return in the US stock market is indeed equalized, in a surprisingly direct manner, with the corresponding return in the corporate sector, and that it is this fact which explains the gyrations of the US stock market.

INTRODUCTION

This paper shows that the level and volatility of the stock market rate of return can be explained directly by fundamentals – measured by the incremental rate of profit in the corporate sector. It is argued that the two rates are linked by the mobility of capital across sectors.

In a competitive economy, the mobility of capital tends to equalize (risk-adjusted) rates of return across investments and sectors. Various branches of economic theory, such the theory of the firm, the law of one price, the theory of finance, and even the present-value principle, depend directly on this mechanism (Dybvig and Ross 1992: 43; Mueller 1986: 8; Diermeier *et al.* 1984: 74).

The fact that capital can move across various applications implies that the evaluation of any given investment must always be relative to the alternatives forgone in making it. This opportunity cost underlies the notion of a reference ('required') rate of return, to which the actual return on any given investment must be compared at any moment of time, and with which it is equalized over time (Ibbotson Associates 1994: 129–30).

Under certain *additional* assumptions (such as constant or slowly changing required rates of return), one can derive the standard discounted present value (PV), and the dividend-discount (discounted cash flow or DCF) models of asset pricing. But these standard models do not perform well empirically. Our own approach is therefore somewhat different. We begin from the common premise that competitive risk-adjusted rates of return tend to become equalized across sectors. But instead of making the additional assumptions needed to arrive at DCF models of stock prices, we directly compare the annual stock market rate of return to the current rate of return on investment in the real sector. To this end, we develop an appropriate measure of the real sector rate of return on investment, and show that its movements are closely mirrored in those of the stock market rate of return. By implication, the so-called risk premia of the sectors are quite similar. This allows us to demonstrate that the stock market is directly driven by fundamentals, i.e. by the profits of the firms issuing stock. It also allows us to critically assess the standard DCF models.

MODERN FINANCE THEORY

Much of modern finance theory is built around the hypothesis that the mobility of capital equalizes risk-adjusted rates of return (Dybvig and Ross 1992: 48; Cohen *et al.* 1987: 131–48). This includes Markowitz's return-risk trade-off, the approximate equality of risk-adjusted returns in the capital-asset pricing (CAPM) and arbitrage pricing theory (APT) models, and the stochastic equality between expected and actual returns in efficient market theory.[1]

The present-value principle is also based on this same assumption. When applied to the stock market, this leads directly to the ubitiquous dividend-discount model, in which the price of a stock is said to be equal (in equilibrium) to the discounted present value of the expected stream of dividends. Let r_{s_t} = the rate of return on a stock held over period t (i.e. from the beginning of period t to the beginning of period $t + 1$), p_{s_t} = the price of the stock, d_t = the dividend paid by the stock, and r_t = some relevant required rate of return. Then equality of rates of return implies:

$$r_{s_t} = r_t, \text{ where by definition } r_{s_t} \equiv \frac{\Delta p_{s_{t+1}} + d_{t+1}}{p_{s_t}}. \tag{1}$$

Equation (1) can be rewritten in terms of the current opening stock price:

$$p_{s_t} = \frac{d_{t+1}}{1 + r_t} + \frac{p_{s_{t+1}}}{1 + r_t}. \tag{2}$$

We can write a similar equation for $p_{s_{t+1}}$ and substitute it into the right-hand side of equation (2), and then do the same thing for the remainder term involving $p_{s_{t+2}}$, and so on. This yields:

$$p_{s_t} = \frac{d_{t+1}}{(1 + r_t)} + \frac{d_{t+2}}{(1 + r_t)(1 + r_{t+1})} + \frac{p_{s_{t+2}}}{(1 + r_t)(1 + r_{t+1})}$$

$$= \frac{d_{t+1}}{(1 + r_t)} + \frac{d_{t+2}}{(1 + r_t)(1 + r_{t+1})} + \frac{d_{t+3}}{(1 + r_t)(1 + r_{t+1})(1 + r_{t+2})}$$

$$+ \frac{p_{s_{t+3}}}{(1 + r_t)(1 + r_{t+1})(1 + r_{t+2})} \tag{3}$$

If we assume that the remainder term approaches zero as we continue expanding the preceding expression, we are left with a familiar-looking result in which the current stock price is expressed as the discounted present value of (expected) future dividends, where the discount rates are *time-varying* current and (expected) future required rates of return. But as Campbell notes, this restatement of the arbitrage process 'is tractable only if the expected [required] returns are constant, which is one reason why the academic literature has focused for so long on this unlikely special case' (Campbell 1991: 158). Imposing the strong restriction that $r_t = r$ for all t then gives us the familiar dividend-discount model of stock prices (equation 4 below). If in addition dividends are assumed to grow at some constant rate g over time, with $0 \le g < r$ ($g = 0$ being the case of a constant dividend), we get the Gordon model in equation 5 below (Le Roy 1992: 172–4).

$$p_{s_t} = \sum_{k=1}^{\infty} \frac{d_{t+k}}{(1 + r)^k}$$

(dividend-discount model with a constant rate of discount) (4)

$$p_{s_t} = \frac{d_{t+1}}{(r - g)} \text{, for } r > g$$

(Gordon model, constant discount and dividend growth rates) (5)

THE REQUIRED RATE OF RETURN FOR THE AGGREGATE STOCK MARKET

Equations 3–5 are merely alternative ways of expressing the assumption that over time the stock market rates of return will be kept in line with some (as yet unspecified) required rate of return. For this to be meaningful, we also need a theory of the required rate itself.

Most discussions of the required rate of return begin from the assumption of perfect competition and perfect capital markets. In this case, the required rate is assumed to be 'the' rate of interest, since in long-run equilibrium every asset *and* every industry is assumed to earn a rate of return exactly equal to the interest rate. When risk (as opposed to true uncertainty) is introduced into the story, the concept of the required rate is expanded to encompass an economy-wide riskless interest rate and an asset- or industry-specific risk premium. This of course necessitates an independent means of assessing specific risk and the hypothesized risk premium associated with it, so as to construct the required rate.[2]

Empirical models of the aggregate stock market generally assume constant dividend growth rates and constant (or slowly varying) required rate of return, although estimates of these particular rates vary substantially.[3] But while the resulting models are theoretically tractable, their empirical performance is quite poor (Shiller 1989: 88). As Shiller has so graphically demonstrated, actual stock prices are strikingly different from those implied by standard dividend discount models (*ibid.*: 78–82).

The problem stems from the very assumptions that make the models tractable: i.e., the hypothesized constancy of discount and dividend growth rates over time. Figure 1 (data sources and methods are described below in the Data Appendix) displays the actual annual rate of return in the aggregate stock market (r_{st}), and its long-term average ($r_{st})_{avg}$, which can be taken to be an estimate of the corresponding required rate of return.[4] Figure 2 depicts a similar pattern of the actual dividend growth rate. In neither case is it particularly useful to assume constant expected values for these variables.

The persistent empirical problems of standard stock market models have

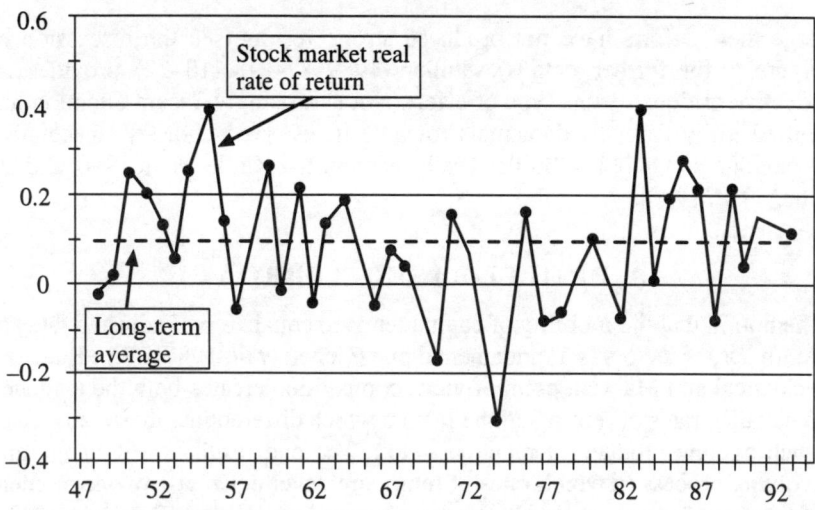

Figure 1 Stock market rates of return

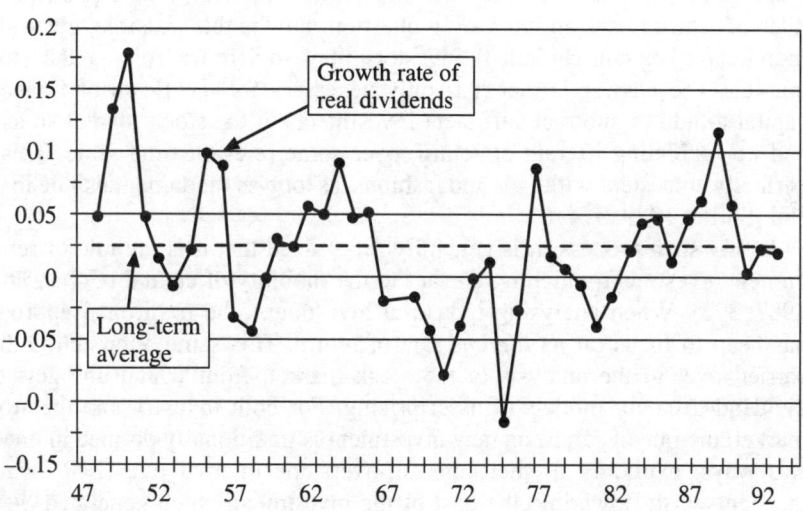

Figure 2 Real dividend growth rates: actual vs. long-term average rates

led several authors to explore alternative formulations. Barsky and De Long (1993: 302) retain the assumption of a constant discount rate but allow the expected dividend growth rate to vary slowly over time. On the other hand, Fama and French (1988), Shiller (1989: 81–2), Fama (1991), and Campbell (1994) experiment with time-varying expected discount rates. But by and large these efforts have not produced strong results (see the discussion of Figure 5 for further details). Shiller (1989: 87–91, 118–32) provides an effective critique of this type of effort. Not surprisingly, recent attention has shifted away from fundamentals towards investor psychology, speculative behaviour, and bubbles (Shiller 1989: chapters 1–2; Cutler *et al.* 1990; and De Long *et al.* 1990).

A PROFIT-BASED APPROACH

The notion that the mobility of capital tends to equalize risk-adjusted rates of return across sectors is a fundamental one (Cohen *et al.* 1987: 375). But from a classical and Marxian point of view, competition creates both the tendency to equalize rates of return and the factors which differentiate these same rates (such as new products, techniques, etc.). The end result is a dynamic and evolving process in which rates of return are never equal at any one moment of time, but rather ceaselessly fluctuate around one another (Botwinick 1993: chapter 5; Mueller 1986: 8; Mueller 1990: 1–3). We will call this process 'turbulent arbitrage', to distinguish it from the more conventional view of a state of equilibrium in which rates of return are exactly equal. The possibility that capital flows between the stock market and the real sector equalize their rates of return raises an interesting question: how is this possible, given that individual (i.e. non-capitalist) investors play so large a role in the stock market? The answer is that it is only necessary for the flows of financial capital to add or subtract sufficient investments in the stock market so as to end up regulating its rate of return, over some relevant time scale. This is perfectly consistent with fads and fashions, as long as fundamentals rule in the end (Shiller 1989: 374–6).

In any such process, it is generally recognized that it is the rate of return on *new* investment which is relevant to the mobility of capital (Cohen *et al.* 1987: 375). When analysing industrial investment, the traditional approach has been to focus on its *lifetime* rate of return. This same approach is then carried over to the analysis of the stock market, from which one gets the dividend-discount models of asset pricing. For both industry and the stock market, the rate of return on new investment is traditionally defined in one of two ways: explicitly as that constant-over-time internal rate (IRR) which discounts cash flows into the cost of the investment which generated them; or implicitly by the excess of present value over investment costs at some *a priori* constant-over-time discount rate.[5] Both methods have well-known problems (Mueller 1990: 9). In addition, as previously discussed, both methods rely on the empirically implausible assumption of a constant (or at least slowly varying) real discount rate.[6]

An alternative approach is to try to directly estimate the lifetime rate of return on new investment. Here, the most common method has been to approximate the return on new investment by means of the average rate of profit on *total* capital invested. The latter is directly observable and may, under certain quite restrictive conditions, be close to the long-run return on new investment. However, the general validity of this approach is a matter of vigorous dispute (Mueller 1990: 9–14).

I will take a somewhat different approach to the problem. To begin with, I would argue that uncertainty and ignorance in real historical time make the short run, as distinct from the long run, of 'signal importance' (Vickers 1993: 25). Current profits reflect many transitory factors, including the effects of short-run disequilibrium dynamics. Nonetheless, abnormally high or low profits alter capital flows, which in turn brings 'new uncertainties and new positions of profits and loss', which feed back on capital flows, and so on. What obtains is a series of ceaseless fluctuations in which near-term (as opposed to lifetime) rates of return on investment play a central signalling role (Geroski and Mueller 1990: 187; Mueller 1986: 8). This is obvious in the case of the stock market, which is inherently short-term because all stocks of a particular company (no matter what their 'vintage') are alike in the market.

The current rate of return in the stock market was defined previously in equation 1. If the relevant variables are expressed in real terms, then it is a real rate. What remains, therefore, is to approximate the corresponding near-term rate of return in the corporate sector.

We begin by recognizing that total current profits P_t can always be expressed as the sum of the current profits on the most recent investment $(r_t I_{t-1})$ and the current profits on all earlier vintages (P'_t). By subtracting past profits P_{t-1} from both sides of this identity, we can write

$$\Delta P_t \equiv P_t - P_{t-1} = r_t I_{t-1} + (P'_t - P_{t-1}). \tag{6}$$

Our aim is to estimate the current rate of return on near-term investment r_t. In equation 6 all other terms are observable except $(P'_t - P_{t-1})$, since P'_t is unknown. But the shorter the evaluation horizon, the closer will be current profit on carried-over vintages (P'_t) to last period's profit on the same capital goods (P_{t-1}). If we can assume that for relevant short-term horizons (say up to a year), the difference $(P'_t - P_{t-1})$ is not large relative to the other terms, we can directly approximate the current rate of return on new investment (Elton and Gruber 1991: 454) as

$$r_t = \left(\frac{\Delta P_t}{I_{t-1}} \right). \tag{7}$$

If real profits P_t and investment I_{t-1} are net magnitudes, then r_t is the (net) incremental rate of return on capital (since net investment = ΔK_{t-1}, where K_t is the real capital stock at the beginning of the period t). When profits and investment are in gross terms, we may think of r_t as either the gross incremental rate of return, or as an approximation to the net rate. Using gross variables confers a considerable advantage, because net rates require adequate measures of depreciation and retirement investment, and there are many well-known problems associated with estimates of these magnitudes (Feldstein and Rothschild 1974; Usher 1980).

In comparing stock market and corporate profitability, it is important to recognize that existing measures of corporate profits are net of all interest payments. The appropriate stock market measure is therefore the *net* (of interest) rate of return, $r'_{st} = r_{st} - i_t$, where i_t = the real prime rate of interest charged by banks (see the Data Appendix for further details).[7]

Figure 3 compares the current real net stock market rate of return r'_{st}, to the (gross of depreciation but net of interest) accounting rate of return $R_t = P_t/K_t$ often used as a proxy for the long-term rate of return (Mueller 1990: 9). Figure 4 then compares r'_{st} to the real gross incremental corporate rate of return r_t. It is immediately apparent that the average rate R_t performs very poorly in explaining the stock market rate of return. The real incremental rate r_t, on the other hand, performs extremely well indeed. The correlation between the stock market rate and the average corporate rate R_t is only 0.048, while that with respect to the incremental rate r_t is almost nine times higher at 0.414.

Since the stock market rate of return is essentially a normalized measure of the change in earnings (net of interest), the parallelism between it and the stock market rate strongly validates the practical concern of stock market investors with interest rates and changes in earnings.[8] It also confirms the general sense of empirical students of the stock market that its 'investors should not expect a much greater or fear a much smaller rate of return than that provided by businesses in the real economy' (Diermeier *et al.* 1984).

The concept of turbulent arbitrage proposed in this paper does not actually

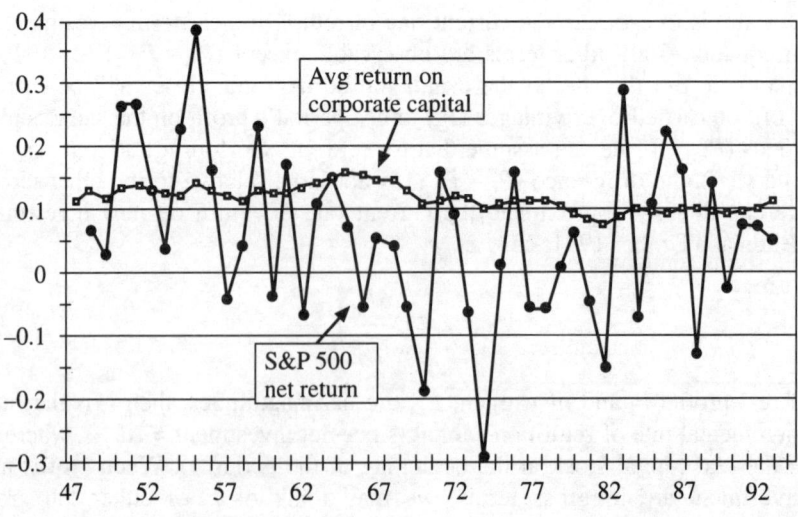

Figure 3 Rates of return: stock market vs. average corporate rate

396

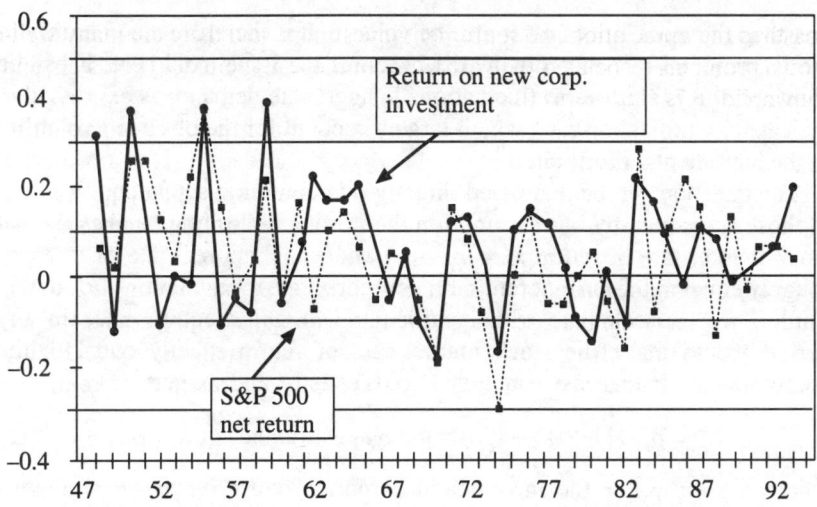

Figure 4 Rates of return: stock market vs. incremental corporate rate

require a close correlation between two variables. It would be possible, for instance, to have two variables fluctuate around each other and yet not be statistically correlated.[9] But they would have to be 'close' in some sense, such as in the mean, or perhaps in terms of percentage mean absolute or squared deviations. But in our case the close visual correspondence between the two rates of return depicted in Figure 4 is also well reflected in the similarity of their means, standard deviations, and coefficients of variation (standard deviation/mean), as shown in Table 1.

A central puzzle in the stock market literature concerns the 'unexplained volatility' of equity prices relative to those predicted by standard models (Shiller 1989: 79; Tease 1993: 42), which as we have seen are predicated on empirically unsupportable assumptions of constant discount rates and dividend growth rates. The preceding findings shed new light on this problem too. Since dividends per share are relatively smooth, it is largely the task of stock prices to vary in such a way as to keep stock market returns on track with the underlying fundamentals. If the fundamentals themselves are volatile, as they

Table 1 Comparative statistics for stock market and corporate real returns

	Mean	*Standard deviation*	*Coeff. of variation*
S&P 500 net rate of return ($r_{st} - i_t$)	0.0603	0.1361	2.2570
Return on new corp. investment ($\Delta P_t / I_{t-1}$)	0.0678	0.1463	2.1578

397

are, then the stock prices must also be volatile. It is therefore the volatility of the incremental rate of profit which becomes the issue. And here, it can be shown that it is short-term fluctuations in aggregate demand, as expressed in the capacity utilization rate, which largely account for the observed volatility of the incremental profit rate.[10]

The question can be addressed directly by comparing actual equity prices to those warranted by our assumption that turbulent arbitrage makes the net stock market rate of return $r'_{st} = r_{st} - i_t$ (where i_t = the real rate of interest) roughly equal to the current return on new corporate investment r_t. Following Shiller, we can calculate which particular *warranted* equity price in any period would make the stock market rate of return exactly equal to the corporate rate. In this case equation 1 holds exactly, and we get

$$p^w_{s_t} = p_{s_{t-1}}[1 + (r^+_t - y_{s_t})] = \text{the real warranted equity price} \qquad (8)$$

where $r^+_t = r_t + i_t$ = the incremental corporate return *inclusive* of interest opportunity cost, and $y_{s_t} = d_t/p_{s_{t-1}}$ = the equity yield. Figure 5 compares the estimated real warranted equity price $p^w_{s_t}$ to the actually observed real equity price p_{s_t}. Again following Shiller, both of them are detrended by dividing them by a thirty-year moving average of real earnings per share. This makes them comparable to his own famous diagrams (Shiller 1989: 78–82).

Several things are striking about this data. First, it is clear that the actual price fluctuates around the warranted price, precisely in the manner one would expect from the the notion of turbulent arbitrage. Second, in sharp contrast to standard results, the actual equity price is less, not more, volatile

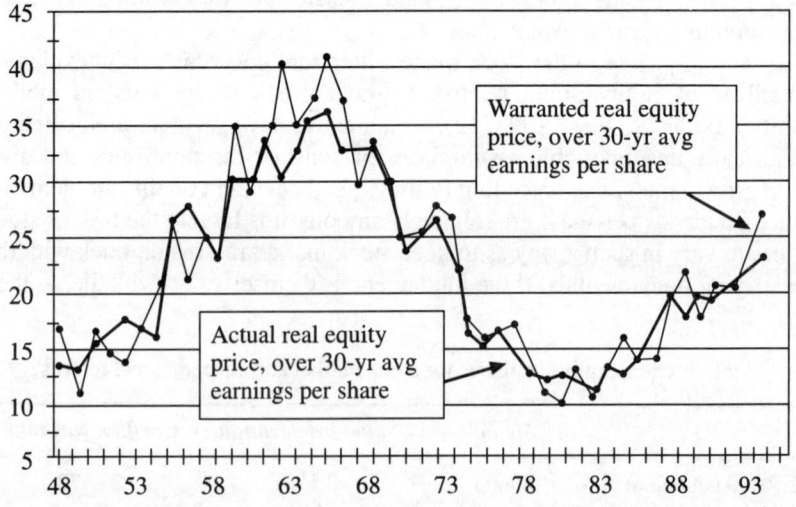

Figure 5 Actual and warranted equity prices, detrended by 30-yr average earnings

than our measure of warranted price. This is of course a reflection of the difference in the models employed. Finally, the simple correlation coefficient between the two series is 0.935 ($R^2 = 0.875$), which compares extremely favourably with typical results for the standard dividend discount model. Shiller (1989: 81–2) gets a simple correlation coefficient of 0.296 ($R^2 = 0.088$) with constant discount rates, and of 0.048 ($R^2 = 0.0023$) with varying discount rates. Barsky and De Long's (1993: 302) *best* estimates based on a varying dividend growth rate only explain 9% of the variance of annual stock price changes. And Campbell's (1990: 46) annual stock return forecasting equation with time-varying interest rates and stock market yields produces an $R^2 = 0.025$ between the two sets of prices.

SUMMARY AND CONCLUSIONS

This paper finds that the empirical movements of stock prices can be explained directly by fundamentals. The connection derives from the fact that the stock market rate of return, which is an intrinsically short-term or contingent rate, is tied to the near-term rate of return on new corporate investment (which we proxy by the incremental corporate rate of profit) by the intersectoral movements of capital between the two sectors. The two rates track each other quite closely (Figure 4), never equal but always fluctuating around each other, displaying similar means and standard deviations (Table 1). The same holds, even more strongly, for the relation between actual equity prices and those warranted by this process of 'turbulent arbitrage' (Figure 5). The correlation between the two is 0.935, which is far higher than (say) Shiller's findings of 0.296 for the conventional dividend-discount model.

The theoretical approach taken in this paper implies that the incremental profit rate in the real sector is the opportunity cost (i.e. the 'required' rate of return) for financial capital invested in the stock market. Since this real sector return is itself highly volatile, driven by short-term fluctuations in aggregate demand, the volatility in returns (Figure 4) and stock prices (Figure 5) is thereby explained by movements originating in the real sector, which are themselves rooted in fluctuations in aggregate demand. It is then easy to see why conventional theoretical models, which typically assume constant required rates of return (discount rates) and constant dividend growth rates, are largely unable to explain the movements in stock prices. On the other hand, since the incremental rate of profit is the change in earnings normalized by investment, the findings of this paper accord well with the experience 'on the street' that stock price movements are driven by interest rates and changes in earnings.

Lastly, it is interesting to note that the approach taken in this paper is consistent with a fixed investment function *identical in general form* to that proposed by Kalecki. In arguing for the equalization of incremental profit rates across sectors, I have explicitly argued that these incremental rates

399

strongly influence relative investment flows across sectors. If we normalize investment decisions D_t relative to (say) the level current profits P_t, one plausible form of the investment function is

$$\frac{D_t}{P_t} = f\left(\frac{\Delta P^e_{t+1}}{I_t}\right). \tag{9}$$

Now, if future rates of return on new investment are projected on the basis of current rates[11] (and current new information, which we ignore here), then we can rewrite equation 9 as

$$D_t = P_t \cdot f\left(\frac{\Delta P_t}{I_{t-1}}\right) = F\left(\underset{+}{P_t}, \underset{+}{\Delta P_t}, \underset{-}{\Delta K_t}\right) \tag{9'}$$

where $I_{t-1} = \Delta K_t =$ the change in the beginning year capital stock.

Kalecki himself arrives at a fixed investment decision function of exactly the same general form. 'When the profitability of new investment projects is being weighed', he writes, 'expected profits are considered in *relation* to the value of the new capital equipment' (1968: 96). One would think that this would lead straight away to a formulation such as in equation 9 above. But in fact Kalecki separately lists the change in current profits ΔP_t as a positive factor in investment decisions because with a given volume of investment a change in profits 'renders attractive certain projects which were previously considered unprofitable and thus permits an extension of the boundaries of investment plans', and then separately lists the change in capital stock ΔK_t as a negative factor 'because an increase in the volume of capital equipment, if profits P, are constant means a reduction in the rate of profit' (Kalecki 1968: 97–8; Sawyer 1985: 50–1). It seems to me that even this is a somewhat roundabout way to arrive at his own starting point, namely that investment decisions are dependent on the ratio of the increment to profits produced by new investment to the value of this investment. Finally, Kalecki also adds a third factor to account for the effect of internally accumulated funds, which he defines as the sum of depreciation, retained earnings, and 'the "personal savings" of the controlling group invested in their own companies through subscription to new share issues' (*ibid.*). This total 'gross savings out of profit' (Sawyer 1985: 49) is obviously a function of aggregate gross profits P_t, although Kalecki chooses to proxy it by total economy-wide gross savings S_t. With this we can immediately see that the general functional form of Kalecki's own investment function[12] is identical to that derived from the premise of the equalization of profit rates across industries and sectors.

$$D_t = f\left(\underset{+}{S_t}, \underset{+}{\Delta P_t}, \underset{-}{\Delta K_t}\right) = F\left(\underset{+}{P_t}, \underset{+}{\Delta P_t}, \underset{-}{\Delta K_t}\right) \tag{10}$$

since $S_t = h(P_t) =$ a function of total gross profits.

The equality of the two general forms of investment decision functions is merely a reflection of their common emphasis on the importance of profitability in the investment decision (*ibid.*: 52). The possible differences in interpretation about the individual components should not be allowed to obscure this important fact.

DATA APPENDIX

The stock market data refers to the S & P 500 index of common stocks (Standard and Poors 1993, and earlier data). Nominal dividends per share d' were derived by multiplying the current yield (d'/p'_s) by the nominal stock price index p'_s. Both were deflated by the implicit price deflator for total gross private domestic fixed investment (1987 = 100) as shown in the *Economic Report of the President* (ERP 1995: Table B-3) and then used to calculate the real stock market rate of return r_{s_t} (equation 1 and Figure 1) and the growth rate of real dividends (Figure 2). Finally, the real rate of interest i_t was calculated as the difference between the nominal prime rate of interest charged by banks (ERP 1995: Table B-72) and the rate of growth of the investment deflator described above, and this was used to calculate the net stock market rate of return $r'_{s_t} = r_{s_t} - i_t$ (Figures 3–4). Average real earnings used to detrend the price series (Figure 5) was constructed from data on long-term earnings per share and on producer prices (1982 = 100) generously provided by Robert Shiller.

The corporate data refer to the domestic US economy. The beginning-of-year capital stock K_t is for total (non-residential and residential) fixed private corporate capital, gross stock, end-of-year, constant-cost valuation, in millions of 1987 dollars, shifted forward one year (BEA 1993: Tables A6, A9, and subsequent updates). Real investment I_t, in 87-$, is the sum of fixed private corporate non-residential and residential investment (BEA 1993: Tables B4, B6, and subsequent updates). Real corporate profits P_t were calculated by deflating nominal total domestic (corporate) profits, gross of capital consumption allowances, by the investment deflator. The former was calculated as the sum of non-financial and financial profits, lines 3+4, Tables 6.16 A-C, *National Income and Product Accounts* (BEA 1992–93, and subsequent updates) and corporate consumption of fixed capital (*ibid.*, Table 8.11, line 2). The average real rate of profit (Figure 3) was calculated as P_t/K_t, and the incremental rate of profit (Figure 4) as $r_t = \Delta P_t/I_{t-1}$.

ACKNOWLEDGEMENTS

I wish to thank Neil Buchanan and Levent Kockesen for helpful comments, Robert Shiller for providing his long-term stock market data, and the Jerome Levy Economics Institute for its generous support.

NOTES

1 'The efficient market hypothesis says that the price of an asset should fully reflect all available information. The intuition behind this hypothesis is that if the price does not fully reflect all available information, then there is a profit opportunity available' which, even if small, 'presumably would be attractive at large scale to many investors' (Dybvig and Ross 1992: 48). On the assumption that arbitrage moves to eliminate discrepancies, actual prices and those expected on the basis of the available information, the remaining 'deviations of actual returns from expected returns should be random – they ought, on average, to be zero and uncorrelated with information to the market' (Tease 1993: 43).

2 Various measures of risk include the familiar variance and standard deviation, as well as less familiar ones such as the mean absolute deviation, the interquartile range, and entropy. But importing such univariate measures into standard economic constructs has proved problematic. Less restricted characterizations of risk, on the other hand, only offer partial orderings of random variables (Machina and Rothschild 1992: 202–3).

3 For instance, in work on the aggregate stock market, Shiller (1989: Figure 4.1, pp. 78–9) and Ibbotson Associates (1994: 136–46) estimate the discount rate from the sample mean of the real rate of return in the stock market; Barsky and De Long (1993: fn. 9, p. 300) assume a real discount rate of 6%; and Campbell uses the long-term average stock market yield as the discount rate (Campbell 1991: 178).

4 Shiller (1989: Figure 4.1, pp. 78–9) and Ibbotson Associates (1994: 136–46) calculate the real rate of discount in this manner.

5 We could define the rate of return on new investment as $r = i + (PV(i) - I)/I$, where i = the rate of discount chosen and the rest represents the excess return (the percentage excess of present value $PV(i)$ over investment I). Then no investment would be chosen unless $r \geq i$.

6 Dumenil and Levy (1990) undertake an interesting attempt to directly estimate the lifetime flows of profits associated with given investments, by making particular assumptions about the time paths of the capital–labour and capital–output ratios associated with a given investment, and about the expected path of the real wage over the lifetime of that investment. However, they use these to estimate the constant discount rate, i.e. the constant internal rate of return which will equate the discounted present value of the lifetime profit flows to the value of the given investment in a given year. They calculate this discount rate for every year's investment, and find that the resulting measure is quite smooth and follows the long-term average of the rate of profit on total capital (Dumenil and Levy 1990: 406–10).

7 The net interest component of corporate income excludes corporate interest payments to the financial sector. One could try to estimate these and add them back into total profits, but the relevant data from the US Internal Revenue *Statistics of Income* appear only after a three-year lag.

8 Peavy argues that 'variations in stock prices can largely be explained by changes

402

in the cash flow [gross profits] of corporations and changes in the discount rate that prices these cash flows ... [which is why] investors carefully monitor movements in corporate profits and interest rates' (1992: 10).

9   A simple case is of two (say) rates of return $r_{2t} = r_{1t} + \varepsilon$, where ε = a small random variable with zero mean, and r_{1t} = a constant. Then r_{1t} and r_{2t} are close to one another, fluctuate around each other, have the same means, but are completely uncorrelated.

10 Although we cannot pursue it here, it is possible to show that changes in corporate real investment can be linked to changes in real profits, and that the sharp fluctuations in the latter reflect changes in capacity utilization.

11 If current investment decisions determine actual investment flows at some point later (Kalecki 1968: 96), there is no contradiction here between the proposition that current investment *decisions* D_t depend on the current rate of return, and the proposition that current investment I_t (based on past investment decisions) helps determine current realized profits P_r.

12 Sawyer (1985: 51) makes it clear that the particular linear form in which Kalecki writes his investment decision function is merely a 'linear approximation' of the general functional form.

REFERENCES

Barsky, R. B. and J. B. De Long (1993) 'Why does the stock market fluctuate?', *Quarterly Journal of Economics* CVIII(2): 291–311.

BEA (1992–93) *National Income and Product Accounts*, 2 Vols. Washington, D.C.: Bureau of Economic Analysis.

Botwinick, H. (1993) *Persistent Inequalities: Wage Disparities under Capitalist Competition*. Princeton, N.J.: Princeton University Press.

Campbell, J. Y. (1990) 'Measuring the persistence of expected returns', *AEA Papers and Proceedings* 80(2): 43–7.

——— (1991) 'A variance decomposition for stock returns', *The Economic Journal* 101 (March): 157–78.

——— (1994) 'What moves the stock market?', *NBER Reporter* (Fall): 8–10.

Cohen, J. B., E. D. Zinbarg, *et al.* (1987) *Investment Analysis and Portfolio Management*, Homewood, Ill.: Irwin.

Cutler, D. M., J. M. Poterba and L. H. Summers (1990) 'Speculative dynamics and the role of feedback traders', NBER Working Paper No. 2385.

De Long, J. B., Andrei Shleifer, L. H. Summers, and R. J. Waldman (1990) 'Noise trader risk and financial markets', *Journal of Political Economy* 98(4): 703–38.

Diermeier, J. J., R. G. Ibbotson and L. B. Siegel (1984) 'The supply of capital market returns', *Financial Analysts Journal* (March–April): 74–80.

Dumenil, D. and D. Levy (1990) 'Post depression trends in the economic rate of return for U.S. manufacturing', *The Review of Economics and Statistics*, LXXII(3): 406–13.

Dybvig, P. H. and S. A. Ross (1992) 'Arbitrage', in J. Eatwell, M. Milgate and P. Newman (eds) *The New Palgrave Dictionary of Money and Finance*, London: Macmillan, 1: 43–50.

Elton, E. J. and M. J. Gruber (1991) *Modern Portfolio Theory and Investment Analysis*, New York, John Wiley & Sons, Inc.

ERP (1995) *Economic Report of the President*, Washington, D.C.: US Govt. Printing Office.

Fama, E. F. (1991) 'Efficient capital markets: II', *Journal of Finance*, 5(December).

——— and K. R. French (1988) 'Permanent and temporary components of stock prices', *Journal of Political Economy* 92(2): 246–73.

Feldstein, M. S. and M. Rothschild (1974) 'Towards an economic theory of replacement investment', *Econometrica* 42(3): 393–423.

Geroski, P. A. and D. C. Mueller (1990) 'The persistence of profits in perspective', in D. C. Mueller (ed.), *The Dynamics of Company Profits: an International Comparison*, Cambridge: Cambridge University Press.

Harcourt, G. C. (1969) 'Some Cambridge controversies in the theory of capital', *Journal of Economic Literature* (June).

Ibbotson Associates (1994) *Stocks, Bonds, and Inflation: 1994 Yearbook*, Chicago, Ill.: Ibbotson Associates.

Kalecki, M. (1968) *Theory of Economic Dynamics*, New York: Monthly Review Press.

Le Roy, S. F. (1992) 'Stock prices and martingales', *The New Palgrave Dictionary of Money and Finance*, 3: 588–91.

Machina, M. J. and M. Rothschild (1992) 'Risk', *The New Palgrave Dictionary of Money and Finance*, 3: 201–5.

Mueller, D. C. (1986) *Profits in the Long Run*, Cambridge: Cambridge University Press.

—— (1990) 'Profits and the process of competition', in D. C. Mueller (ed.), *The Dynamics of Company Profits: an International Comparison*, Cambridge: Cambridge University Press.

Peavy, J. W. (1992) 'Stock prices: do interest rates and earnings really matter?', *Financial Analysts Journal* (6): 10–12.

Sawyer, M. C. (1985) *The Economics of Michal Kalecki*, Armonk, N.Y.: M. E. Sharpe, Inc.

Shiller, R. J. (1989) *Market Volatility*, Cambridge, Mass.: The MIT Press.

Standard and Poors (1993) *Standard and Poors Analysts Handbook: Official Series*, New York.

Tease, W. (1993) 'The stock market and investment', *OECD Economic Studies*, 20 (Spring): 41–63.

Usher, D. (ed.) (1980) *The Measurement of Capital. Studies in Income and Wealth*, Chicago, Ill.: University of Chicago Press.

Vickers, D. (1993) 'The investment function: five propositions in response to Professor Gordon', *Can the Free Market Pick Winners? What Determines Investment*, Armonk, N.Y.: M. E. Sharpe.

32

EXPANDING EMPLOYMENT IN THE GLOBAL ECONOMY
The high road or the low road?[1]
Ajit Singh

INTRODUCTION[2]

A most pressing problem before the world community today is that of
unemployment and underemployment – the existence of mass unemployment
in advanced economies (the North) and the lack of adequate employment
opportunities in many developing countries (the South) for their fast-growing
labour forces. The emergence of a much more integrated and liberal world
economy in the last decade or so as a consequence of globalization and freer
movements of capital and trade, has apparently made little contribution
towards meeting this global employment challenge. Whether or not one
agrees with those who argue that globalization is a part of the problem rather
than its solution, it is quite clear that unless people's legitimate needs for
remunerative jobs and productive work can be met, the new liberal
international economic order will be in serious jeopardy. As Sir John Hicks
observed with respect to the 1930s.

> The main thing which caused so much liberal opinion in England to lose
> faith in Free Trade was the helplessness of the older liberalism in the
> face of massive unemployment, and the possibility of using import
> restriction as an element in an active programme fighting unemploy-
> ment. One is, of course, obliged to associate this line of thought with the
> name of Keynes. It was this, almost alone, which led Keynes to abandon
> his early belief in Free Trade.
>
> (Hicks (1959), quoted in Bhagwati: (1994: 233))

Apart from its implications for the liberal world economic regime, there
are other obvious, but no less important, reasons for the employment question
to head the world economic agenda. These were commented on in an earlier
paper (Singh 1995c) (hereafter referred to as 'Institutional Requirements'), to
which the present paper is a sequel. Institutional Requirements specifically
examined the issue of mass unemployment in the North and argued that new
instruments and policies would be needed if the purpose was to restore full

employment in industrial countries. It departed from much of the literature by adopting an explicitly historical and institutional approach to the analysis of mass unemployment in the North. The present paper complements that analysis by considering also the current and potential underemployment and unemployment problems in the South. This paper will outline the linkages between the employment problems in the two regions, examining them within a common framework in the context of a liberalized world economy. It will advance the following main theses.

1   The first-best solution is for the two regions to cooperate by following positive-sum policies which help to create employment in the North as well as the South in a virtuous circle of cumulative causation. These policies, whose essential core is a trend increase in the rate of growth of real world demand and output, can in principle not only lead to full employment with rising real wages in the North but can also help the South to provide the jobs required for its rapidly expanding labour force.

2   This is the 'high road' and in economic terms it is perfectly feasible. This is in part because, it will be argued here, there exists a backlog of technology represented by the information and communications technology revolution. The full potential of this technological revolution has not been harnessed so far in most parts of the world, owing to an insufficient rate of growth of demand and output.

3   The paper contrasts the demand growth approach to reducing unemployment with that of labour market flexibility, currently recommended by the IMF, the OECD and other international organizations for countries in the North as well as in the South. The latter is, however, regarded here as the 'low road'. Flexible labour markets, it will be suggested, will not be able to provide full employment with rising real wages in the North, nor will they be able to create sufficient job opportunities in the South. With a constant level of aggregate demand, more labour market flexibility will simply lead to greater competition among job-seekers and hence reduce the price of labour, often resulting in an increase in disguised unemployment. Moreover, at the international level, if each country tries to improve its competitive position by reducing wages, the net result may be competitive devaluations of the kind which occurred in the 1930s and hence even greater instability for the international economy.

4   The successful implementation of the high road approach requires important institutional changes which emphasize cooperative relationship between workers, employers and governments in individual countries as well as between nation states in both the North and the South.

UNEMPLOYMENT AND UNDEREMPLOYMENT IN THE NORTH AND THE SOUTH

Mass unemployment in the North

In the 1980s, fifty years after the Great Depression, industrial countries came again to be haunted by the spectre of mass unemployment. The unemployment situation, into the 1990s, continues to be dire in several European Union countries. As the OECD has noted, the 35 million people presently unemployed in the member countries 'represent an enormous waste of human resources, reflects an important amount of inefficiency in economic systems, and causes a disturbing degree of social distress' (1994: 9). The study estimates that unemployment in the form of involuntary part-time work, short-time working and discouragement of job-seekers from looking for new employment could add 40 to 50% to these unemployment figures.

The current mass unemployment stands in striking contrast to the situation which prevailed in the industrial countries in the not too distant past. During the period 1950–73, which has been aptly described as the Golden Age of the world economy, leading industrial countries not only enjoyed full employment but had over-full employment. In addition to being able to employ all their own people, these countries also provided jobs for additional labour from abroad. In countries like France and West Germany nearly 10% of the labour force came from other nations. Most developing countries also participated in and benefited from the worldwide prosperity ushered in by the Golden Age. The Golden Age of simultaneous prosperity for the North and the South evidently came to an end with the first oil shock in 1973. Since then, the rate of growth of the OECD and the world GDP has nearly halved.

EMPLOYMENT CHALLENGE IN THE SOUTH

It may come as a surprise to some that the recorded rates of unemployment in most developing countries tend to be relatively low. This is because in the virtual absence of publicly provided social security systems, people are obliged to engage in any economic activity, however non-remunerative and non-productive it may be. The problem of unemployment in poor countries, therefore, manifests itself generally in the form of what Joan Robinson called 'disguised unemployment', or as 'underemployment'. To illustrate, in 1988–9 in Ghana, the proportion of labour force unemployed was, according to World Bank estimates, only 1.6%. However, nearly a quarter of the workers were 'underemployed', i.e. they worked 'less than full time, not because they choose to but because more work was unavailable' (World Bank 1995).[3]

Nevertheless, the actual employment situation in many Third World countries, particularly in Latin America and Sub-Saharan Africa, is dire. There are not only current high rates of urban, especially youth and 'educated' unemployment, but more importantly, it is necessary to provide productive jobs for a labour force which is growing at approximately 3% a year. On the basis of past relationships between economic variables, to create jobs at this rate in order to meet the employment needs of new entrants to the labour force, the economies of these countries need to grow at a rate of about 6% per annum (UN 1993). Unfortunately, in what has been rightly called the 'lost decade' of the 1980s for the developing continents of Latin America and Africa, the rate of economic growth was considerably less than was required; it was only of the order of 2.1% per annum in Sub-Saharan Africa and 1.6% per annum in Latin America (see Table 1).

In the 1990s, as a consequence of large-scale private capital flows to Latin America, there has been a revival of economic and industrial growth in a number of economies on that continent. However only one or two of them (Chile, and perhaps Argentina) have so far shown signs of reverting back to their previous (i.e. pre-debt crisis) long-term trend rates of growth. For most countries in the region the prospect for faster long-term economic growth has again been put into jeopardy by the recent financial crisis in Mexico. The economic situation in the African countries in the 1990s is if anything even less promising.

To illustrate the implications of this slow long-term economic growth for employment, consider the case of Mexico. Between 1990 and 1992, the economically active population (EAP) in that country is estimated to have increased by 1.2 million persons each year. However, during this period only 339,974 jobs, i.e. 28% of the EAP, was absorbed by the formal labour market. Yet it is important to observe that in the two years before the debt crisis – 1980 and 1981 – the Mexican economy expanded at an average rate of about 7% per annum and created three-quarters of a million new jobs each year in the formal sector.[4]

EMPLOYMENT, POVERTY AND ECONOMIC GROWTH

At the macroeconomic level, there is an important indirect relationship between the employment question and that of the reduction of poverty. Just as the creation of sufficient employment opportunities requires a reasonable rate of economic growth, so does the eradication of poverty and meeting the minimum basic needs of the people.[5] In its influential 1976 report, the ILO estimated that even allowing for some redistribution of incomes, if the minimum basic needs of the poorest 20% of the Third World's population were to be met by the year 2000, their economies would have to grow at an annual average rate of 7% a year. These rates, coincidentally, are not all that different from those required to create sufficient employment opportunities for the South's growing population.

REAL WAGES, EMPLOYMENT AND ECONOMIC GROWTH IN DEVELOPING COUNTRIES DURING THE 1980S

Those economies (mainly in Asia) that were able to achieve high rates of growth have succeeded in significantly reducing poverty, as well as recording fast growth of both real wages and employment. On the other hand, low economic growth in the Latin American and African countries over the recent period has had a serious negative effect both on poverty and on formal sector employment generation in these economies. To illustrate, ILO (1995) provides evidence that in the last decade, in the fast-growing East Asian economies (e.g. Malaysia, Singapore, Taiwan, Korea), labour shortages emerged and there was significant immigration of labour from neighbouring lower-income countries. Manufacturing employment grew at a rate of over 6% per annum during the 1980s for the dynamic economies of the region. Real earnings rose during this decade at an average rate of 5% per annum.

In contrast, in slow-growing Latin America, there was a steady fall in modern-sector employment between 1980 and 1992, with paid employment falling at a rate of about 0.1% per annum during the 1980s. This reversed the trend of the previous three decades, when steady economic growth had led to a significant expansion of modern-sector employment. In most countries, the average real wage fell during the 1980s, recovering in only a few countries towards the end of the decade. Minimum wage fell on average by 24% in real terms across the region, while average earnings in the informal sector declined even more sharply (by 42%).

The question of why Asian countries succeeded and the Latin American and the African countries failed in the 1980s and into the 1990s is the subject of an important debate. The contrast between the Asian and Latin American economic performance in the recent period is particularly striking, as in the previous fifteen years (1965–80), the two groups of economies had been growing at much the same rate, i.e. at an average rate of about 6% per annum (see Table 1). For reasons of space, this debate will not be reviewed here.

Table 1 Rate of growth of GDP, 1965–80 and 1980–90 (average annual % growth)

Country group	1965–80	1980–90
Low-income economies (excl. China & India)	4.8	3.9
Middle-income economies	6.3	2.5
Latin America	6.0	1.6
Sub-Saharan Africa	4.2	2.1
South Asia (incl. India)	3.6	5.2
East Asia (incl. China)	7.3	7.8
All low and middle-income economies	5.9	3.2

Source: World Bank (1992)

Suffice it to note that the Bretton Woods institutions ascribe the Latin American failure in the 'lost decade' of the 1980s essentially to internal causes, e.g., inherent inefficiencies of the Latin American regimes, too pervasive a role of the state.[6] However, in a series of contributions, Banuri (1991), Fishlow (1991) and Singh (1994) have provided detailed analysis to suggest that the reason for those intercontinental differences in economic performance was not the internal economic factors, but rather external shocks. The magnitude of these external shocks and their adverse impact on the balance of payments and on economic growth of the Latin American economies was much greater than that for the Asian countries. The Latin American countries were particularly hard hit by the capital supply shock, which is either ignored or not properly examined in the orthodox analyses of these issues.

THIRD WORLD COMPETITION AND ITS IMPACT ON ADVANCED ECONOMIES

Since 1980, the labour markets of the North's industrial economies have been dominated by three significant tendencies, namely deindustrialization, high overall unemployment and increasing inequality between skilled and unskilled workers, particularly in the US. Popular opinion in industrial countries increasingly blames competition from LDCs for these job losses or for stagnating real wages for unskilled workers. So, unlike the 1950s and 1960s, when free trade with advanced countries was feared by developing countries, today it is the former who are more concerned about the ill-effects of a liberal trading regime.

With a few exceptions, mainstream economists have generally denied these unfavourable consequences of North–South trade. However, Wood (1994) has presented important analyses and evidence to challenge this conventional wisdom. He estimates that Southern competition has reduced manufacturing employment in the North by 12%. Further, to the extent that Southern competition induces labour-saving technical progress in the North, Wood suggests that this may have resulted in additional job losses of equal magnitude. Thus for Wood, the fast growth of imports from the South, despite a sizeable trade balance in favour of the North, is a main cause of both deindustrialization and overall unemployment in industrial countries. He also marshalls impressive evidence to suggest tentatively that the rising inequality between skilled and unskilled workers in the North is due largely to Southern competition rather than technical change.

These conclusions are controversial and have generated a large critical literature.[7] The essential point is that although Wood's analysis may be correct within the terms of his own traditional Hecksher–Ohlin model, the model is rather limited in that it excludes aggregate demand and capital accumulation. If a rise in real global demand (as a result, for instance, of better policy coordination among industrial countries) leads to a higher trend rate of growth of output, the negative impact of Southern competition on unskilled workers in the North may be more than outweighed by what Bhagwati calls the lift-all-boats effect of faster overall growth. Such considerations may also help resolve some of the controversy in this area by explaining why, during the 1950s and 1960s, countries like the US, the UK and West Germany were able to absorb not only fast-growing imports from the then low-income countries (e.g. Japan) but also greater immigration than now, without experiencing mass unemployment or stagnant real wages.[8]

LABOUR MARKET FLEXIBILITY, GROWTH OF DEMAND AND UNEMPLOYMENT IN THE NORTH AND THE SOUTH

There is continuing debate in the North about the causes and remedies for the current mass unemployment. Orthodox economists argue that the main causes are labour market rigidities and the welfare state. Theoretically, this thesis is justified in terms of the concepts of the natural rate of unemployment or that of NAIRU (non-accelerating inflation rate of unemployment). It follows from this analysis that the remedy for unemployment lies in making real wages more flexible, deregulation of the labour market by relaxing restrictions on dismissal of workers, reducing trade union power, and pruning the welfare state. The proponents of this view cite the better unemployment record of the United States, with a less regulated labour market, as evidence in support of the labour market flexibility thesis.

The thesis has been challenged by several analysts. First, it has been pointed out that labour market performance should not be judged in terms of a single variable such as the rate of unemployment. In terms of other relevant indicators such as growth of overall national productivity and per capita income, it turns out that the performance of European economies has been superior to that of the US (CEPR 1995).

Second, as noted in Institutional Requirements, in the absence of an adequate social safety net in the US, people are pushed into disguised unemployment, i.e. they are forced to accept very low-productivity, low-wage jobs in order to survive. Eatwell (1995) and UNCTAD (1995) have formalized the concept of disguised unemployment and estimated its empirical significance for a group of leading advanced countries. They postulate a segmented labour market: in the high-productivity, high-wage sector, the level of employment is determined by aggregate demand, while in the low-productivity, low-wage employment sector, it is determined by the supply of labour to that sector. If there is a fall in aggregate demand leading to lay-offs in the former sector, in the absence of a social safety net, the latter sector would act as a perfect sponge for displaced workers. Measured employment in that case will become independent of aggregate demand. This, UNCTAD

411

(1995: 210) suggests, 'is the full-employment that would be attained with a highly flexible labour market'. Empirical estimates of disguised unemployment indicate that if it is added to open unemployment, 'true' unemployment is much higher than measured underemployment in the US and Japan. These estimates show that corrected for disguised unemployment, true unemployment rates have tended to converge among the leading industrial countries in the 1980s.

The US–European comparison of labour market practices and outcomes also raises other questions about the labour market flexibility thesis. The first point here is that the US labour market was more flexible than the European market, not just in the recent period, but also in the Golden Age. However, the European unemployment record in the Golden Age was much superior to that of the US. Secondly, continuing with this kind of analysis of changes in labour market conditions and performance over time, it may be observed that the European labour market has been much more flexible in the 1980s compared with the 1950s and 1960s, yet there was more or less full employment in the earlier period whilst the later period is characterized by mass unemployment. As noted in Institutional Requirements, the same difficulty with the labour market flexibility hypothesis arises in explaining the fact that the labour market was much more flexible in the 1930s compared with the post-war Golden Age. Matthews and Bowen (1988) show that real product wages rose far more in the 1950s and 1960s in the UK compared with the 1930s, yet the earlier period had the Great Depression and the later period more or less full employment.

At the policy level, the limitations of the labour market flexibility programme were exemplified by the experience of the UK in the 1980s and into the 1990s. During this period, the UK labour market became much more flexible as a result of a sustained attack on the trade unions and the welfare state by the Conservative governments. This, however, has not led to more job creation or less unemployment. On the contrary, there has been a huge trend increase in unemployment in that country compared with the 1970s, let alone the Golden Age. It may be recalled that the average rate of unemployment in the UK between 1960 and 1973 was only 1.9%; in the period 1974–9 it was 4.2%; while between 1980 and 1994 it was 8.9%.

The reason for these empirical failings of the labour market flexibility thesis lies in part in its theoretical limitations. The hypothesis is rooted in micro-economics and is based on a partial equilibrium approach. It assumes that, other things being equal, faced with a cut in wages as a consequence of competition among the unemployed, a profit-maximizing firm will increase employment and output. An alternative view, conceptualized by Keynes, is that the firm will expand its output only if it can be sure that it will be able to sell it. In other words, employment will expand only if there is an increase in demand and output, and not just because there is a cut in wages. A cut in wages could reduce aggregate demand and therefore employment.

412

The reason why there was full employment in the Golden Age in spite of the welfare state and labour market rigidities is to be sought in the much higher rate of growth of real demand and output in that period. As observed in Institutional Requirements, the Golden Age was the outcome of a specific economic regime, a new development model which differed significantly from the one which prevailed in the industrial countries in the inter-war period, or the one which has ruled in the post-1980 period. The Golden Age model involved a social consensus with respect to institutional arrangements regarding the setting of wages and prices, the distribution of wages between income and profits, and with respect to government policies in relation to state fiscal, credit and welfare policies which guaranteed minimum living standards and maintained aggregate demand. Employers agreed to productivity wage bargaining and the trade unions acted with restraint. Whether or not there was a voluntary consensus at the international level, under US hegemony, the international economy worked under stable and orderly monetary and trading arrangements. The net result was a virtuous circle of high rates of growth of demand, investment, productivity growth and real wages which ratified and maintained high rates of accumulation. This enabled trade unions to satisfy the aspirations of their members without inflationary wage demands, which in turn made it possible for employers to continue to have high rates of accumulation.

Strikingly, the experience of the developing countries also does not provide any support for the labour market flexibility thesis. As aggregate data on real earnings in manufacturing for the three developing continents in Table 2 indicates, there were enormous declines in earnings in the 1980s in Latin America and Sub-Saharan Africa. However, as noted earlier, these large reductions in real earning did not lead to any increase in employment growth in these two continents. On the contrary, there was a substantial fall in modern sector job expansion. In sharp contrast, Table 2 shows that in East Asia, earnings rose at a rate of 5.1% per annum over the period 1981–90. However, as suggested earlier, in the East Asian case, this was accompanied by a large rise in employment, particularly in the modern sector.

The essential reason why both real wages and employment expanded in East Asia, whilst both fell in Latin America and Sub-Saharan Africa, lies in the differences in the real rates of growth of demand for countries on the three continents. The Latin American and African economies became severely balance-of-payments constrained during the 1980s as a consequence of the debt crisis and therefore had low rates of growth of real aggregate demand. The East Asian economies escaped the debt crisis and were thereby able to maintain their previous high rates of growth of real demand.

Table 2 Real earnings in manufacturing in Sub-Saharan Africa, Latin America and Asia

Region	Years	Average annual rate of growth (percentage)
Sub-Saharan Africa*	1975–80	−0.6
	1980–88	−12.3
Latin America and the	1971–80	−2.13
Caribbean	1981–92	−3.13
East and South-East Asia	1971–80	5.32
	1981–90	5.12
South Asia		*Index of manufacturing real earnings per employee (1987=100)*
	1971	86.2
	1980	87.4
	1985	91.4

*Real annual earnings per employee in manufacturing, 1987 $.
Source: ILO, *World Employment* 1995: Table 12, p. 64.

TECHNICAL PROGRESS, PRODUCTIVITY, GROWTH AND EMPLOYMENT

It is widely believed that the world is undergoing a new, far-reaching technical revolution as a result of the rise and spread of information technology. Freeman (1989) has argued that the 'information and communication technology (ICT) paradigm' presently sweeping the globe is as important in terms of its spill-over effects and overall economic impact as any of the three major technological revolutions of the past two centuries. This raises the important question of whether high rates of unemployment and under-employment in developed and developing countries are due to the new technology. Has the pace of technological progress become so fast that there is 'jobless growth' – i.e. economic growth does not create any employment at all – or in a less extreme form, the hypothesis would be that a given percentage change in economic growth leads to a smaller increase in employment than was the case in the past.

It is shown in Institutional Requirements that available evidence for advanced economies does not support either of these hypotheses. The data show that productivity growth in these countries has fallen rather than increased since 1973, which suggests that the full potential of the new technology is not being realized. Similarly, there is no evidence of any decline in the recent period in the employment elasticity of output (Boltho and Glyn 1995). The reason why there is mass unemployment in industrial countries today is not that there has been jobless growth, but that these countries have been expanding at a slower rate than before.

Freeman *et al.* (1995) provide evidence of the purposive use of the ICT technology in one part of the world, namely East Asia. The authors show how in that region a virtuous circle of high output and productivity growth, greater international competitiveness, and high growth of employment has been created. This, however, has not happened in other regions because of slow economic growth. Freeman *et al.* note that a revolutionary new technology can only provide the basis for a virtuous circle of growth. Whether this virtuous circle can be realized and sustained depends on macroeconomic, employment and trade policies. They point out that a 'good match between technologies, policies and institutions can result in prolonged periods of full employment.'

SUMMARY AND CONCLUSION

This article has outlined some main issues in analysing mass unemployment in the North and severe underemployment as well as unemployment in the South. It is an urgent task for the international community to find policies which can achieve both full employment in the North and provide jobs for the South's fast-growing labour force.

It is suggested here that the pursuit of labour market flexibility is unlikely to achieve full employment in the North with rising real wages. Moreover, this strategy runs the danger of increasing disguised unemployment and leading to a competitive erosion of labour standards. It will also be socially divisive and pit First World workers against Third World workers. Past history suggests that the net result will be a negative sum *ad-hoc* protectionism in industrial countries.[9]

The goal of full employment in the North, with rising real wages, can only be attained with a substantial trend increase in the rate of growth of real demand and output. That will not only lead to faster growth of employment, but by harnessing the potentialities of the new information and communication technologies revolution, it will also promote productivity growth in a virtuous circle of cumulative causation in accordance with Verdoorn's law.

Faster economic growth in the OECD economies will help developing countries by increasing demand for Southern products; by improvements in the South's terms of trade; by greater capital flows from the North to the South and hopefully also by the governments of the North being able to afford and willing to provide larger aid programmes. This should, *ceteris paribus*, lead to faster employment and output growth in the LDCs. Similarly, greater employment and faster output growth in the South would help the North by a positive feedback through greater Southern imports.

However, as noted in Institutional Requirements, in the present circumstances, the pursuit of these positive-sum policies by Northern governments is not a straightforward proposition. The faster expansion of real aggregate demand and production cannot be achieved simply by the usual Keynesian method of changes in demand management policies of the leading industrial countries. Past evidence would suggest that, in the absence of an appropriate restraining institutional framework at the national and international levels, reliance on such policies would simply result in an excessively sharp rise in commodity prices (as occurred in the early 1970s), an increase in trade union militancy and higher inflation, which in turn would thwart the expansionary process. Instead of the post-1980 labour market flexibility doctrine, the restoration of full employment with only moderate inflation requires more cooperative institutional arrangements involving workers, employers and governments in individual countries. It will also require more cooperative relationships between nation states, within the North (to achieve, *inter alia*, macroeconomic policy coordination), and between the North and the South (in order to obtain for example, more orderly movements in commodity prices).[10]

NOTES

1 I have enjoyed Geoff and Joan Harcourt's generous and warm friendship from the time I first came to Cambridge over thirty years ago and they took me in hand. It is a pleasure to dedicate this essay to Geoff on the occasion of his sixty-fifth birthday. The paper addresses issues which have for long been Geoff's important concerns. For his recent writing in this area, see Harcourt (1992, 1993 and 1995).
2 This paper draws on material in Singh and Zammit (1994) and Singh (1995a).
3 It will be argued below that the concept of disguised unemployment is not only pertinent to developing countries, but also has application today in advanced economies.
4 See further Singh (1988) and Peters (1994).
5 For the relationship between employment, basic needs, poverty and economic growth, see Singh (1979). See also ILO (1976).
6 See further World Bank (1991). See also Sachs (1985), Maddison (1985) and Summers and Thomas (1993).
7 See among others Krugman and Lawrence (1993), Leamer (1994), Sachs and Schatz (1994), and UNCTAD (1995).
8 UNCTAD (1995) observes that between 1958 and 1975 import penetration by Japan, as well as by Italy, both in the United States market and in the national markets of the other five then members of the European Economic Community (EEC) was on a scale comparable to the rise of today's late industrializers.
9 For a fuller discussion of this issue see Singh (1995b).
10 For a fuller analysis of the institutional requirements for full employment in advanced countries, see Institutional Requirements.

REFERENCES

Banuri, T. (1991) *Economic Liberalisation: No Panacea*, Oxford: Clarendon Press.
Bhagwati, J. (1994) 'Free trade: old and new challenges', *Economic Journal*, (Oxford) 5(423).
Boltho, A. and Glyn, A. (1995) 'Can macroeconomic policies raise employment', *International Labour Review*, 134(4–5): 451–70.

CEPR (1995) *Unemployment: Choices for Europe*, London: CEPR.

Eatwell, J. (1995) 'Disguised unemployment: G7 experience', A lecture delivered at South Bank University, Processed.

Fishlow, A. (1991) 'Some reflections on comparative Latin American economic performance and policy', in Banuri (1991) (*op. cit.*).

Freeman, C., (1989) 'New technology and catching up', *The European Journal of Development Research*, 1(1).

——, Soete L. and Efendioglu, U. (1995) 'Diffusion and the employment effects of information and communication technology', *International Labour Review*, 134(4–5): 587–603.

Harcourt, G. (1992) 'Markets, madness and a middle way', the second Donald Horne Address, Melbourne, 1992, also published in *Australian Quarterly*, 64(1): 1–17.

—— (1993) 'A large G&T', *ALR*, 148 (March): 34–6. A longer version was published as 'Macroeconomic policy for Australia in the 1990s', *The Economic and Labour Relations Review*, 4(2): 167–75.

—— (1994) 'Taming speculators and putting the world on course to prosperity: a 'modest proposal', *Economic and Political Weekly*, XXIX (September): 2490–2.

Hicks, J. R. (1959) *Essays in World Economics*, Oxford: Clarendon Press.

ILO (1976) *Employment Growth and Basic Needs: A One-world Problem*, Geneva.

—— (1995) *World Employment Report*, Geneva.

Krugman, P. and Lawrence, R. (1993) *Trade Jobs and Wages*, NBER Working Paper, No. 4478.

Leamer, E. E. (1994) *Trade, Wages and Revolving Door Ideas*, NBER Working Paper, No 4716.

Maddison, A. (1985) *Two Crises: Latin America and Asia 1929–38 and 1973–83*, Paris: OECD.

Matthews, R. C. O. and Bowen, A. (1988) 'Keynesian and other explanations of post-war macroeconomic trends', in Walter Eltis and Peter Sinclair (eds), *Keynes and Economic Policy: The Relevance of the General Theory after Fifty Years*, London: Macmillan Press.

OECD (1994) *The OECD Jobs Study: Facts, Strategies*, Paris: OECD.

Peters, E. (1994) 'Recent developments in Mexican employment (1982–92)', Faculty of Economics, Universidad Nacional Autonoma de Mexico, mimeo.

Sachs, J. D. (1985) 'External debt and macroeconomic performance in Latin America and East Asia', *Brookings Papers on Economic Activity*, 2: 523–64.

—— and Schatz, H. J. II. (1994) 'Trade and jobs in US manufacturing', *Brookings Papers on Economic Activity*, 1.

Singh, A. (1979) 'The basic needs approach to development versus the new international economic order', *World Development*, 7(6): 585–606.

—— (1988) 'Employment and output in a semi-industrial economy: modelling alternative policy options in Mexico', in M. Hopkins (ed.) *Employment Forecasting: The Employment Problem in Industrialising Countries*, London: Pinter Publishers.

—— (1990) 'The actual crisis of economic development in the 1980s: an alternative policy perspective for the future', in A. Krishna Dutt and K. P. Jameson (eds), *New Directions in Development Economics*, Aldershot: Edward Elgar.

—— (1993) 'Asian economic success and Latin American failure in the 1980s: new analyses and future policy implications', *International Review of Applied Economics*, September: 267–89.

—— (1994) 'Growing independently of the world economy: Asian economic development since 1980', *UNCTAD Review*: 91–106.

417

—— (1995a) Review of Wood (1994) (*op. cit.*), *Economic Journal*, 105(432): 1287–9.

—— (1995b) 'Industrial policy in Europe and industrial development in the Third World', in P. Bianchi, K. Cowling and R. Sudden (eds), *Europe's Economic Challenge: Analyses of Industrial Strategy and Agenda for the 1990s*, London: Routledge.

—— (1995c) 'Institutional requirements for full employment in advanced economies', *International Labour Review*, 134(4–5): 471–95.

—— and Zammit, A. (1994) 'Employment and unemployment, North and South', in J. Michie and J. G. Smith (eds), *Managing the Global Economy*, New York: Oxford University Press.

Summers, L. and Thomas, V. (1993) 'Recent lessons of development', paper presented at the UN University/World Bank Symposium on Economic Reform in the Developing Countries, 6 February.

UNCTAD (1995) *Trade and Development Report*, Geneva.

United Nations (1993) *World Social Report*, Geneva.

Wood, A. (1994) *North–South Trade, Employment and Inequality*, Oxford: Oxford University Press.

World Bank (1991) *The Challenge of Development: World Development Report*, Washington, D.C.

—— (1995) *World Development Report*, Oxford: Oxford University Press.

33

WHAT ARE THE CONSTRAINTS ON THE PURSUIT OF KEYNESIAN MACROECONOMIC POLICIES?

Malcolm Sawyer

INTRODUCTION

Amongst his many contributions to economic theory and policy, Geoff Harcourt has recently put forward a range of proposals seeking to secure full employment. In this chapter, the intention is to explore the constraints on the use of Keynesian policies for that purpose, and specifically focus on the constraints posed by the supply-side and the financial markets. In doing so, Geoff's recent concerns over the constraints posed by unregulated financial markets come to the fore.[1]

In this chapter a relatively narrow range of Keynesian macroeconomic policies is considered, namely the use of fiscal and monetary policies in pursuit of high levels of economic activity (notably full employment) which may involve substantial budget deficits. Keynesian policies are broader than that, and specifically can involve the stimulation of investment through, for example, seeking to reduce uncertainty or to lower the cost of finance.[2]

Two major objections which non-Keynesians raise against the effectiveness of expansionary demand policies to secure full employment relate to the existence of a supply-side determined equilibrium level of employment or output (often summarized by the term NAIRU: non-accelerating inflation rate of unemployment) and to problems of funding of any resulting budget deficits, including the reactions of financial markets. In the next section the first of these objections is addressed and then two further sections consider the funding problems, dividing those into the difficulties associated with funding the deficit, and the constraint imposed by the operation of financial markets. In a further section, policies to reduce the influence of the financial markets in ways which may create more possibilities for the pursuit of Keynesian macroeconomic policies and for the achievement of full employment are considered.

A high level of aggregate demand (however generated) is seen here as a *necessary but not sufficient* condition for the achievement of high levels of economic activity (including employment). It is argued that there are at least four other constraints on the achievement of full employment which would also need to be addressed.[3] First, it is possible (indeed, for countries like the UK, virtually certain) that the balance of trade position which would arise at full employment would be one of substantial deficit which might prove unsustainable.[4] Second, shortages of productive capacity may prevent the full employment of labour, and perhaps as a consequence expansions of aggregate demand would tend to be inflationary. Third, a move towards full employment is likely to involve some inflationary pressures, and a fear of inflation may cut short any expansion through political and other pressures to deflate the economy. Fourth, sustained full employment may have adverse effects on productivity in economies which rely upon competition and the threat of unemployment to underpin work effect.

NAIRU AS A CONSTRAINT ON KEYNESIAN POLICIES

The NAIRU concept generally involves three further ideas. It is, first, a supply-side equilibrium position which, as the title suggests, involves non-accelerating inflation with accelerating inflation arising from lower levels of unemployment. Second, the NAIRU supports a classical dichotomy whereby the level of output is set by supply-side considerations alone, leaving demand-side considerations to set the level of prices. Third, there is the strong suggestion that the equilibrium position is unique: the term itself refers to a single rate of unemployment (and this is more clear-cut with the related concept of the natural rate of unemployment).

The unique equilibrium and the complete separation of the supply and demand sides are *not* an inevitable feature of the type of models from which the NAIRU is generated. Manning (1992), for example, provides a model of price and wage-setting which has two equilibrium positions for which he provides some empirical support. Sawyer (1982) provides a model which involves not only multiple equilibria but also is without a clear separation between demand and supply sides. However, these models are very much in the minority, and the popular representation of NAIRU involves a unique equilibrium and the separation of the demand and supply-side considerations. It is, of course, the case that if indeed the economy is characterized by either multiple equilibria or the influence of aggregate demand on the level of economic activity then a role for Keynesian style demand management policies re-emerges.

The NAIRU is clearly a construct of economic theorizing which may (or may not) be helpful in thinking about the economy. But there is no way in which it can be demonstrated to actually exist in the real world and hence using estimates of the NAIRU involves a leap of faith in the existence of some (unique) NAIRU. Estimates of the NAIRU are typically derived from price and wage-setting equations, and the theoretical construct is imposed on the estimation of those equations. In some respects it is the economists' equivalent of the astronomers' black hole: the concept may be useful for thinking about the world, but there is no direct evidence for its existence. The concept only 'works' if observations about the real world are consistent with predictions derived from a theory which makes significant use of the concept. It can be further observed that the price and wage relationships which interact to determine the NAIRU have often proved unstable and subject to shifts, which makes any estimate of the NAIRU also unstable. It is argued here that the estimates of the NAIRU (or related concepts) which have been produced have shown a strong tendency to move in sympathy with actual levels of unemployment. Further the estimates are sensitive to the precise form of equations estimated. Both of these features, which are now illustrated, must cast severe doubt on the existence of any unique and stable NAIRU.

Nickell (1990) estimates the equilibrium rate of unemployment (equivalent to the NAIRU) in the UK as having risen as follows (with actual rates of unemployment given in parenthesis):

- 1956–9: 2.2% (2.24%)

- 1960–8: 2.5% (2.62%)

- 1969–73: 3.6% (3.39%)

- 1974–80: 7.3% (5.23%)

- 1981–7: 8.7% (11.11%)

- 1988–90: 8.7% (7.27%).

Layard et al. (1991: 436) report actual and equilibrium unemployment for nineteen countries for each of three decades and an essentially similar pattern is provided, namely the two types of unemployment move together. Lombard (1995) reports three estimates for the NAIRU in France for the early 1980s (when the actual unemployment rate averaged 8.3%) of 9.0%, 7.7% and 6.9%, which suggests a high level of NAIRU and some sensitivity to methods of estimation. Some further estimates covering a wide range of countries is given in OECD (1994: 22) and a similar picture is given in figures reported in ECE (1992: Table 5.7) (summarized in UNCTAD 1995: 170).

Setterfield et al. 'suggest that estimates of the NAIRU [for Canada] are extremely sensitive to model specification, the definition of variables and the same period used. [Further] ... the final range of all NAIRU estimates ... is about 5.5 percentage points. Indeed, the size of this range is so great that it covers virtually the entire range of male unemployment rates in Canada since 1956' (1992: 134). The Directorate-General for Economic and Financial Affairs of the European Commission concluded that the concept of the

NAIRU is 'unusable operationally' because 'empirical studies on both sides of the Atlantic have shown that large variations in NAIRU may be caused by apparently small differences in sample, retained explanatory variables and analytical formulation. Furthermore, the confidence interval around these estimates is so large that it generally contains the whole historical range of unemployment rates observed in the last 15 to 20 years'.[5] But as UNCTAD (1995: 172) observes, 'natural rate estimates are still used to assess and guide macroeconomic policy, thereby contributing to rising unemployment'.

The NAIRU is an estimate of the level of unemployment at which inflation would not accelerate; this can be alternatively expressed as saying it is the level of unemployment at which the rate of change of wages minus the rate of increase of prices is equal to the rate of increase of (labour) productivity,[6] for otherwise inflation will be tending to accelerate or decelerate. This would mean that real wages rise in line with labour productivity, and hence the distribution of income between wages and profits remains unchanged. The share of wages in national income is fairly stable (though by no means constant). It is perhaps not surprising that if a level of unemployment can be found for which the distribution of income would remain unchanged (and in this model, inflation be non-accelerating) it will lie in the middle of the range of unemployment observed. The calculation of a NAIRU may then merely reflect that the distribution of income is fairly stable (and specifically the shares of wages and of profits do not exhibit any strong trend), rather than confirming the existence of a NAIRU as portrayed in the underlying theory.

The movements in the estimated NAIRU can be ascribed to hysteresis and path-dependence, though this often amounts to little more than putting a label on the phenomenon (for discussion of hysteresis, see Cross (1988)). The significance of the movements in the estimated NAIRU here is twofold. First, the instability of the estimates serves to cast doubts on the existence of the NAIRU (and of course a unique one in particular). Second, even if there is at any point in time a level of unemployment consistent with constant inflation, that level can be changed over time. Theoretical constructs in economics are unlikely to be neutral in their policy implications or more generally in guiding the way in which economists think about policy issues, and the notion of the NAIRU (even when described in different terms) forms a significant constraint on policy discussions even though there is little evidence for the existence of a stable unique NAIRU.

BUDGET DEFICITS

Even with significant levels of unemployment, most western governments are running budget deficits (and have been doing so for the past two decades) though in many cases the deficit can be attributed to a combination of interest payments on government debt and capital expenditure. Thus full employment achieved through some combination of higher public expenditure and lower

422

taxation would involve a substantial budget deficit in most industrialized countries. Hence it is relevant to consider the constraints placed on such reflationary policies by the prospective budget deficit.

There are two possible (though to some degree related) limits on the ability of governments to run a budget deficit sufficient to underpin full employment. The first arises from the argument that continuing budget deficits are unsustainable, and the second from the reaction of the financial markets. A budget deficit may be seen as unsustainable in a variety of ways, but it is suggested here that two are particularly significant: namely a budget deficit would be seen as unsustainable if it led to a spiralling national debt to GDP ratio (and hence to rising interest payments on the debt relative to GDP), or that the level of interest payments whilst not rising (relative to GDP) might nevertheless constitute what was seen as too heavy a burden on taxpayers (through adverse incentives from the tax rates and from the general transfer from the relatively poor to the relatively rich which the interest payments on national debt often represent).

It is well-known that the debt to GDP ratio will not rise provided that $g \geq r$, with g the growth rates of the economy and r the (post-tax) rate of interest (with the primary deficit to GDP ratio being held constant).[7] The difficulty for budget deficits which has arisen in recent years is simply that real rates of interest have been at unprecedently high levels, whilst economic growth has been sluggish.[8] The higher interest rates can be attributed to the pursuit of tight monetary policies in the belief that tight money and high interest rates will (eventually) dampen down inflation.

In so far as governments, like individuals, face the 'principle of increasing risk' (Kalecki 1937) then higher deficits (relative to GDP) would entail higher interest rates and hence the maximum sustainable budget deficit would be determined by $g = r(d)$, where d is the debt to GDP ratio. Since if $(g - r)$ is positive it is likely to be rather small, i.e. of the order of 0.01 or 0.02, the debt to GDP ratio will stabilize at a large multiple of the primary budget deficit to GDP ratio (clearly with numbers given previously, at multiples of 100 or 50). But perhaps more significantly, the interest payments would stabilize at $(r/(g - r))$ B/Y. This would mean that the overall budget deficit (including interest payments) would be much larger than the primary deficit and that those payments would appear to constitute a large transfer of income to the holders of government debt. The transfer may be made on the basis of further borrowing, and in that way it is a transfer within the rentier class. Further, it should be noted that the government is in effect permitting the savings to occur by running a deficit and absorbing those savings. If investment were higher, thereby reducing the need for public expenditure, savings would again occur and profits flow to the wealthy.

The national accounts identity would provide $S = I + (G - T) + (X - M)$, where S is savings, I investment, G government expenditure (in total), T taxation, X exports and M imports. Applying the identity at full employment makes the obvious point that a budget deficit corresponds to some combination of excess of private savings over investment and foreign trade deficit. Insofar as the budget deficit is in effect mopping up the excess of private savings over investment, then the Keynesian alternative to running a deficit would be the stimulus of investment and the discouragement of savings. But the Keynesian position is clear: budget deficits are the counterpart of net private savings. If it is considered politically or otherwise infeasible to run budget deficits, action should be taken on (i.e. reduce) net private savings.

The arguments against raising public expenditure and stimulating demand will often be wrapped up in semi-moralistic arguments on the need to balance the budget, not to live beyond one's means and the need for 'sound money'. But 'the social function of the doctrine of "sound finance" is to make the level of employment dependent on the "state of confidence"' (Kalecki 1971: 139). The restrictive policies find particular support amongst the financial community. 'Our basic observation is that such restrictive policies have always been supported by banks and financiers (the City, Wall Street) more than any other group in the economy. It is they who have consistently clamoured for high interest rates and for restrictive budgetary measures' (Bhaduri and Steindl 1983).

FINANCIAL MARKETS

The financial markets are often viewed as placing limits on the use of fiscal policy (notably budget deficits) and to do so through two channels. First, interest rates (particularly on bonds) rise with a budget deficit thereby limiting the government's ability to borrow. This is clearly a possibility with the government faced, like any other borrower, with a rising cost of borrowing (as noted above). It can here first be noted that in the international financial markets any government is still a relatively small borrower. Thus the bidding up of price against oneself, which can arise when there is a dominant buyer, may not arise here. But the operation of the 'principle of increasing risk' may still arise. It could be argued that the high interest rates arose from high levels of government borrowing. But the evidence linking budget deficits and interest rates is weak. For example, in a paper which is generally hostile in Keynesian macroeconomic policies (in effect answering 'no' to the question posed in the title of their paper), Cunningham and Vilasuso have to concede that '[u]nfortunately, empirical studies examining the relationship between interest rates and fiscal deficits are far from conclusive' (1994/5: 190) and that 'whether fiscal deficits are associated with higher interest rates has yet to be resolved in the economics literature' (ibid.: 191).

Second, there is the danger of adverse reactions (or the threat of such) by the foreign exchange markets to particular policies, leading to a fall in the value of the currency. The distinction made by Sayer (1992) in his discussion of the power of the City of London as to 'whether market prices are based on economic fundamentals or bubbles, fads and herd behaviour' is useful here. There is the complication here that even if the actions of the financial markets are based on bubbles, fads etc., they may nevertheless influence the economic fundamentals. Clearly, if the fad raises interest rates, investment may be thereby affected and hence the fundamentals of the economy changed. Similarly, a falling exchange rate would stimulate domestic inflation, which would change the fundamental value of the (nominal) exchange rate. Clearly, if it is the former then the financial markets may perform a useful service by providing early signals that an economic policy is unsustainable in the longer term. As Sayer argues, fundamentally unsustainable 'policy strategies [include those] that give rise to accelerating inflation, a worsening balance of trade or rapidly growing public sector deficit ... would have to be abandoned in response to underlying fundamental constraints such as the disruption caused by hyperinflation, balance of payments constraints and the "fiscal crisis of the state"' (1992: 141). A further difficulty arises here: namely any fiscal expansion of the economy is likely to involve some elements of rising inflation, worsening balance of trade and growing budget deficit. The advocates of fiscal expansion would argue that such effects may be short-lived, or 'a price worth paying' and do not lead to hyperinflation, etc. In such a case, the financial markets do not pose any threat to the range of policies (Keynesian or otherwise) which we would wish to advocate (but no one is going to admit to advocating unsustainable policies).

However, even when financial asset prices reflect fundamentals, the operation of financial markets may still pose a constraint on the economic policies pursued. The 'fundamentals' of interest to the financial markets may be quite different from the 'fundamentals' of concern to others: for example, the financial markets may focus more on the rate of inflation whilst others may feel that unemployment is of more importance. Market participants will be concerned over the rate of inflation (in foreign exchange markets, specifically expectations on the differential inflation rates between countries, in domestic financial markets expectations over domestic inflation relative to the nominal rate of interest). Inflation affects the returns which participants in financial markets receive. Unemployment and the level of economic activity are of no immediate concern to operators in financial markets, since they do not directly affect the financial returns in the way in which inflation does (and indeed if some form of Phillips' curve analysis is accepted, reductions in unemployment, which are associated with higher inflation, are unwelcome to financial markets).

The use of the term 'fundamentals' carries two implicit suggestions. First, the fundamentals give rise to a unique set of (equilibrium) prices, whereas there are theoretical reasons for thinking that there may be multiple equilibria (e.g. Allingham 1987). The reasons are, in general, theoretical (rather than empirical) since the conditions for equilibria (unique or multiple) are properties of particular theoretical models. If there were to be multiple equilibria, then the expectations of the financial markets may be an important element in which equilibrium is selected, even though the chosen equilibrium may not be the socially preferred one. Second, the term suggests a separation between the real side of the economy ('the fundamentals') and the financial side akin to the classical dichotomy. In contrast, our view would be that of mutual interdependence.

The financial markets pose a different type of constraint on the pursuit of sustainable fiscal policies when the 'bubbles, fads and herd behaviour' come to determine movements in prices (notably interest rates and exchange rates). There is now an extensive literature which indicates that financial market prices are 'excessively volatile' (and casual observation of the movements in the exchange rates in the past twenty years would be supportive of that view).[9] Further, there are theoretical literatures (surveyed by, for example, Camerer (1989)) which provide models in which individual rational behaviour can generate 'bubbles'. In a world of uncertainty, where knowledge of the economic fundamentals is given to few, it is perhaps inevitable that asset prices will fluctuate and follow fads and fashions. The significant question here is whether the adoption of a Keynesian demand reflation (especially if pursued by a left-of-centre government) would set off adverse reactions in the financial markets, and whether those reactions undermine the reflation. The reactions are likely to create an air of crisis and strong political pressures to abort the reflation.

The history of sterling in recent years and specifically its membership of and then departure from the Exchange Rate Mechanism (ERM) is instructive. It could be argued that the departure of sterling from the ERM and its associated fall in value from *circa* DM 2.80 (in August 1992) to *circa* DM 2.45 (by the end of 1992) reflected the correction by financial markets of attempts by governments to impose an exchange rate which did not reflect 'fundamentals'.[10] However, this would raise the question as to why the market-determined value of sterling had been around DM 2.90 prior to sterling's entry into the ERM, a value which effectively determined sterling's entry value into the ERM. Further, there is the question as to why the financial markets took two years before asserting the role of the 'fundamentals' (which could not be said to have changed significantly over the previous two years).

If financial markets behave closer to the 'bubbles' representation than the 'fundamentals', then financial asset prices are essentially unpredictable, and further, the way in which markets react to particular information or policies may also be unpredictable. This has two implications for our line of argument. First, it enables those opposed to a particular policy to pontificate that if that policy is followed, the financial markets will react in an adverse manner. A recent notable example of this arose in the dispute between the Chancellor of the Exchequer and the Governor of the Bank of England in May 1995 over interest rate changes. The Governor argued that there would be 'retribution by the markets' if interest rates did not rise: rates were held constant and nothing of the sort happened (see *Financial Times*, 22 June 1995). Second, significant changes in asset prices (and here of particular concern in interest rates and exchange rates) occur for essentially random reasons, and any government, whatever policies it pursues, faces the prospect of a 'run on the pound'. For example, Coakley and Harris (1983: 193) report a fall in the value of sterling against the dollar of 5.6% in a fortnight in November 1982, despite the monetarist policies being pursued by the Thatcher government. The sterling crisis of 1976 which led to the IMF visit to the UK and the imposition of conditions on public expenditure is a further example of an exchange rate crisis which owed more to 'fads and bubbles' than to 'fundamentals'. For

> there is also evidence to support the view that the convulsion in the foreign exchange market [during 1976] was in part a 'confidence crisis' unrelated to the 'fundamentals'. For, indeed, all the obvious funda-mentals – the inflation rate, the money supply, the current account – were moving in a favourable direction at the time and there were the additional factors that by 1976 the prospective value of North Sea oil to the exchanges was understood and the government's hand had been strengthened politically by the results of the Common Market entry referendum.
>
> (Artis and Cobham 1991: 271)

Financial markets are only one set of markets amongst many others, but in one sense there is no compelling reason why the judgements of the participants in the financial markets should be given precedence over the judgements of participants in other markets. For example, interest rates affect participants in product and labour markets as well as financial markets, but typically financial markets 'rule the roost' in influencing changes in interest rates. But in another sense, given the central role of finance in capitalist economies the dominance of the financial markets is not so surprising. If financial markets operated in a benign fashion *vis-à-vis* other markets and economic policy, this dominance would not be harmful. However, we view the financial markets as a source of instability which can be transmitted to other sectors of the economy and the participants in those markets as able to impose their objectives (which we do not share) on economic policy-making. The pursuit of Keynesian policies (and more generally the achievement of full employ-ment) require restraint on the power and influence of the financial markets, and elsewhere we have made some 'modest proposals' in this regard in respect of European monetary institutions and the imposition of a tax on financial transactions (Arestis and Sawyer 1996).

CONCLUSIONS

We would draw three conclusions. First, there is not a unique equilibrium supply-side-determined level of employment (or of unemployment or of output) which prevents the achievement of full employment. It follows that the classical dichotomy must also be rejected. Second, a necessary though not sufficient condition for the achievement of full employment is the creation of an appropriate level of aggregate demand, whether through expansionary fiscal policy or through the stimulus of investment and the discouragement of savings. Third, the operation of financial markets may be a major obstacle to the creation of sufficient aggregate demand, and hence policies are required to control financial markets.

ACKNOWLEDGEMENT

I am grateful to Philip Arestis for comments on a draft of this paper, which arose from joint work which we are undertaking.

NOTES

1 See, for example, Harcourt (1992) and Harcourt (1994).
2 For discussion on possibilities for Keynesian policies, see 'Symposium of Keynesian policies', *International Review of Applied Economics*, 10 (1). For some Keynesian policy proposals see Arestis (1996).
3 For further discussion, see Sawyer (1995b).
4 It is, of course, the case that if most or all countries were at full employment then whilst some would face a trade deficit, others would not, since the sum of balance of trade positions must be zero. Further, as discussed in the context of budget deficits, a trade deficit may be sustainable (in the sense of maintaining a constant relationship to GDP) provided that the rate of growth exceeds the rate of interest on foreign borrowing (see Sawyer 1995a).
5 Quote is from *European Economy*, Supplement A, January 1995, p. 2 as reported in UNCTAD (1995: 172).
6 It would also be necessary to make some assumptions about the rate of change of foreign prices, the exchange rate and indirect taxation.
7 See Sawyer (1995a) for the relevant algebra. Pasinetti (1996) also discusses the conditions for a sustainable budget deficit.
8 'Since modern capital markets came into existence, there have never been such high long-term rates as we recently have had all over the world' (Homer and Sylla 1983: 1, quoted in Pasinetti 1996). The recent high levels of real interest rates are indicated by the estimates of Tease *et al.* (1991). They estimate the long-term real rate of interest for the UK as 2.86% in the 1960s, −1.34% in the 1970s and 5.00% in the 1980s: corresponding figures for France were 1.72%, −3.79% and 4.07%; for Germany, 3.85%, 3.16% and 5.00%, and for the United States, 2.60% 1.31% and 6.20%.
9 The work of Shiller (e.g. Shiller 1981, 1984, 1990, and the papers collected together in Shiller 1989) has strongly suggested that there is excessive volatility in the stock and bond markets.
10 The use of the term 'fundamentals' here begs the question of what is the 'fundamental' value: it could refer to, for example, the exchange rate which would bring purchasing power parity, or that which would be consistent with trade balance. In the early 1990s on the first criteria sterling was probably undervalued, whilst it was overvalued on the second.

REFERENCES

Allingham, M. (1987) 'Uniqueness of equilibrium' in J. Eatwell, M. Milgate and P. Newman (eds) *The New Palgrave*, London: Macmillan.

Arestis, P. (1996), 'Post-Keynesian economic policies for "world prosperity"', this volume.

—— and Sawyer, M. (1996) 'European monetary integration: a post-Keynesian critique and some proposals' in P. Arestis (ed.), *Keynes, Money and the Open Economy: Essays in Honour of Paul Davidson*, volume 1, Aldershot: Edward Elgar.

Artis, M. and Cobham, D. (1991) 'Summary and appraisal' in M. Artis and D. Cobham (eds), *Labour's Economic Policies, 1974–79*, Manchester: Manchester University Press.

Bhaduri, A. and Steindl, J. (1983) 'The rise of monetarism as a social doctrine', *Thames Papers in Political Economy*.

Camerer, C. (1989) 'Bubbles and fads in asset prices', *Journal of Economic Surveys*, 3.

Coakley, J. and Harris, L. (1983) *The City of Capital*, Oxford: Basil Blackwell.

Cross, R. (ed.) (1988) *Unemployment, Hysteresis and the Natural Rate Hypothesis*, Oxford: Blackwell.

Cunningham, S. R. and Vilasuso, J. (1994/5) 'Is Keynesian demand management policy still viable?', *Journal of Post Keynesian Economics* 17.

ECE (1992) *Economic Survey of Europe in 1990–1991* (United Nations publications, Sales No. E.92.II.E.1).

Harcourt, G. C. (1992) 'Markets, madness and a middle way', *Australian Quarterly*, 64 (Autumn: 1–17: reprinted in G. C. Harcourt (ed.), *Capitalism, Socialism and Post-Keynesianism: Selected Essays of G. C. Harcourt*, Aldershot: Edward Elgar.

—— (1994), 'A "modest proposal" for taming speculators and putting the world on course to prosperity', *Economic and Political Weekly*, XXIX (38): 2490–2; reprinted in G. C. Harcourt (ed.), *Capitalism, Socialism and Post-Keynesianism: Selected Essays of G. C. Harcourt*, Aldershot: Edward Elgar.

Homer, S. and Sylla, R. (1983) *A History of Interest Rates* (3rd edn), New Brunswick, NJ: Rutgers University Press.

Kalecki, M. (1937) 'The principle of increasing risk', *Economica* 3.

—— (1971) *Selected Essays on the Dynamics of the Capitalist Economy*, Cambridge: Cambridge University Press.

Layard, R., Nickell, S. and Jackman, R. (1991) *Unemployment: Macroeconomic Performance and the Labour Market*, Oxford: Oxford University Press.

Manning, A. (1992) 'Multiple equilibria in the British labour market: some empirical evidence', *European Economic Review*, 36.

OECD (1994) *Economic Outlook*, 58 (December).

Pasinetti, L. (1996) 'The social "burden" of high interest rates' in P. Arestis, G. Palma and M. Sawyer (eds) *Capital Controversy, Post-Keynesian Economics and the History of Economic Theory: Essays in Honour of Geoff Harcourt*, London: Routledge.

Sawyer, M. (1982) 'Collective bargaining, oligopoly and macro economics', *Oxford Economic Papers*, 34.

—— (1983) *Business Pricing and Inflation*, London: Macmillan.

—— (1995a) 'Obstacles to the achievement of full employment in capitalist economies' in P. Arestis and M. Marshall (eds), *The Political Economy of Full Employment: Conservatism, Corporatism and Institutional Change*, Aldershot: Edward Elgar.

—— (1995b) 'Overcoming the barriers to full employment in capitalist economies', *Economie Appliquée*, 48: 185–218.

Sayer, S. (1992) 'The city, power and economic policy in Britain', *International Review of Applied Economics*, 6.

Setterfield, M., Gordon, D. V. and Osberg, L. (1992) 'Searching for a will o' the wisp: an empirical study of the Nairu in Canada', *European Economic Review* 36.

Shiller, R. J. (1981) 'Do stock prices move too much to be justified by subsequent changes in dividends', *American Economic Review*, 71: 421–35.

—— (1984) 'Stock prices and social dynamics', *Brookings Papers on Economic Activity* 2: 457–98.

—— (1989) *Market Volatility*, Cambridge, Mass.: MIT Press.

—— (1990) 'Speculative prices and popular models', *Journal of Economic Perspectives*, 4: 55–66.

Tease, W., Dean, P., Elmeskov, J. and Hoeller, P. (1991) 'Real interest rate trends: the influence of saving, investment and other factors', *OECD Economic Studies* 17:

UNCTAD (1995) *Trade and Development Report, 1995*, New York and Geneva: UN.

34

POST-KEYNESIAN ECONOMIC POLICIES FOR 'WORLD PROSPERITY'

Philip Arestis

INTRODUCTION

In a number of recent contributions, Geoff Harcourt (for example, 1992, 1993) has advocated a set of proposals with the specific aim to 'to put the world on course to prosperity' (Harcourt 1994). The purpose of this paper is to support his main arguments strongly, and embrace in the main analytical framework Keynes's socialization of investment.

At the heart of Geoff's analysis and economic policy proposals, is the objective of full employment. This contribution, too, begins with the full-employment premise and also suggests, as Geoff did in an early paper (1965), that full employment cannot be the only objective of post-Keynesian economic policy. Governments should also strive to promote a more equal distribution of market power and, thus, income and wealth. A common thread that runs through post-Keynesian economic policies is that the capitalist economic system, based on free market principles, is inherently cyclical and unstable. Left to itself, it cannot achieve and maintain full employment of resources. It is also marred with inequalities in the distribution of market power and, therefore, of income and wealth. Forces of cumulative causation are thought to be operative, accentuating inequalities which are structurally inherent.[1]

It may be helpful to summarize the essence of what is proposed here at the outset. Government intervention is necessary in principle to achieve and maintain full employment. The increased power of trade unions and workers at full employment, along with the resulting inflationary pressures, must be addressed. Social consensus on the distribution of income along with wage and price setting mechanisms which are 'friendly' to low inflation should be considered seriously. There could very well arise a serious balance-of-payments constraint well before full employment is reached. Policies to enhance the supply side of the economy may be necessary to alleviate this problem. Even with sufficient demand, full employment might still be difficult, if not impossible, to maintain, if there is inadequate or unbalanced supply potential. Consequently, control of capital accumulation, in the form of socialization of investment, may be necessary to remove these constraints. The rest of the paper will be devoted to demonstrating the potential of these economic policies and briefly touch on the constraints and obstacles that may be present in their implementation.

ECONOMIC POLICY IMPLICATIONS

We may begin by referring to the standard income identities from which the following can be derived:

$$(G-T) = (S_o - I_o) + (S_r - I_r) + (Q - X) \tag{1}$$

where the symbols have the following meaning: G = government expenditure, T = taxes S_o = savings of the oligopolistic sector, I_o = investment expenditure of the oligopolistic sector, S_r = savings of the rest of the economy, I_r = investment expenditure of the rest of the economy, X = exports, Q = imports.

Next, assume that expansion is initiated through government deficit to achieve full employment.[2] The deficit faced by the government sector implies a surplus in either the business sector or in the other sectors, or a deficit in the foreign sector. We may concentrate on the surplus sectors to begin with. The surplus is likely to be conspicuous in the oligopolistic business sector: for the high levels of aggregate demand will lead to increasing rates of capacity utilization and a disproportionate increase in cash flow. This surplus will tend to constrain the growth rate of the economy, a consequence which can only be avoided if the government initiates further deficits. We thus have a situation where the government sector must be prepared to tolerate a mounting deficit and debt, if the economy is to remain on the higher output growth rate, a situation not likely to persist for very long.[3] If, however, the surplus sectors are prepared to increase their investment/output ratio, or, indeed, reduce their saving/income ratio or some combination of both, then the higher growth rate could be maintained. The surplus sectors might be separated into three parts: the oligopolistic sector, the non-oligopolistic sector and the personal sector.

The required increase in the investment/output could conceivably material-ize if the oligopolistic sector perceives the deficit as causing favourable long-lasting effects on their sales. For if the oligopolistic sector believes that any increase in government deficit completely crowds out business investment, then, there would be no revision of expectations, and the effect could be the reverse of what is required. When it comes to affecting the volatile business expectations, it would be more appropriate for a continuous presence of the government than periodic pump-priming action. This is 'both ... the only practicable means of avoiding the destruction of existing economic forms in their entirety and ... the condition of the successful functioning of individual initiative' (Keynes 1936: 380). In fact, policy-makers may be able to play on growth expectations and thereby influence investment. That would obviously be difficult, but in the past attempts were made which could be viewed as aiming at influencing growth expectations, as for example the National Plan of the UK government in the 1960s, and the French Indicative Planning of the 1950s and 1960s.

The obvious question to ask is whether there are any policy instruments which might be used to stimulate investment in the oligopolistic sector. The message here is that there is very little that policy-makers can do, since investment in this sector is insensitive to policy instruments, given the way prices are determined in this sector (Harcourt and Kenyon 1976; Eichner 1976). Oligopolist investment is relatively immune to monetary policy changes, given the self-financing nature of this sector and thus its insensitivity to interest rate movements, although it is true to say that some external financing occurs. Given growth expectations, oligopolists will expand their plant and equipment to maintain their market share, regardless of the going rate of interest. The capital funds market can be avoided entirely, given that pricing is used to finance investment (although it must be conceded that high and rising interest rates are bound to have an impact sooner or later; and the experience of high interest rates in the 1980s and 1990s is relevant here). Fiscal measures are equally ineffective, given the power and ability of corporations to shift taxes which limit the capacity of taxation increases to absorb surpluses (see also Asimakopulos and Burbidge 1974).

The possibility of reducing the saving/income ratio of the oligopolistic sector raises three cases. The first is price controls. Price controls have been objected to as being unworkable and ineffective. The main objection to price controls is that firms will come, sooner or later, to anticipate policies of controlling price increases to redistribute the surplus, so that unless these policies refer to both incomes and prices, they are likely to have an adverse effect on business confidence and investment. Price controls have also been shown to be ineffective in that their impact is shown to be 'temporary' and 'sporadic' (Coutts et al. 1978: 24). There are, of course, the associated problems of changes in the quality and nature of products which are difficult to take into account when price controls prevail.

Equally problematic is the second case where the corporate tax rate may be employed to shift the savings curve downward. Increases in the tax burden on oligopolists are, of course, passed on to the household sector in the form of higher prices. The empirical evidence tends to support a great deal of 'shifting', but on the question of full 'tax shifting' it is rather inconclusive. Coutts et al. (1978: 96) suggest that within roughly three years, two-thirds of direct tax adjustments get passed on to price-changes (see also Asimakopulos and Burbidge 1974). King (1975) and Beath (1979) argue that the full 'tax shifting' hypothesis is confirmed.

Similar problems exist in the case of the third possibility, i.e. the wage rate. Most crucially, the enigma in this case is how to ascertain that wage rate which would be consistent with an acceptable governmental deficit and business sector surplus as well as with a particular growth rate and price level. There is absolutely no guarantee that such a unique wage rate can conceivably be achieved. However, if it does not come about, then certain severe problems could very well appear. A too-low average wage rate would not sustain the desired growth rate, while a too-high wage rate would cause a wage–price inflation spiral. A too-high wage rate would leave the oligopolistic business sector short of funds to undertake the necessary amount of investment, in which case prices would be forced to increase. In addition to the problems this increase itself would create, it could also kick off a wage–price inflation spiral. Such a sequence of events clearly implies that market forces cannot be relied upon to avoid the problems just referred to. It would appear that some form of control of wages and prices may be necessary.

We may turn our attention now to the other surplus sectors, and consider first the non-oligopolistic sector. The sensitivity of investment and savings to aggregate demand in this sector is rather different from what it is in the oligopolistic business sector. The savings relationship is expected to be less sensitive to fluctuations in the income growth rate than in the oligopolistic case. This is so since the savings generated as a result of fluctuations in the income growth rate are likely to be transferred at an increasing rate to the owner(s) of the firm and thus to the household sub-sector – and perhaps returned to the firm if required. The savings relationship for this sector is thus expected to be practically horizontal. The investment relationship is expected to be more sensitive to changes in the growth rate of output in the non-oligopolistic than in the oligopolist case. The rationale for this difference is the single-plant operation that is one of the distinguishing characteristics of the non-oligopolistic sector. The absence of multi-plant operation suggests that any expansion of the growth rate of output may be associated with price-level increases, on the assumption that single plants do not have much excess capacity. In the personal sector, both savings and investment (consumer durables and residential construction) are essentially determined by the growth of income and output. Under these conditions, whenever the government sector sustains a deficit, the personal sector may behave in such a way as to alleviate it. But by itself it is unlikely to succeed in the absence of the required stimulus of investment and capacity in the other two sectors. This may very well produce balance-of-payments worries, as argued below.

We are thus led to conclude that mounting deficits, initiated by the government in an attempt to push the economy onto a higher growth rate, cannot be alleviated by the behaviour of the three sectors. However, the wage–price inflation spiral referred to above is of paramount importance for the personal sector. For when it sets in, it could create a further surplus in this sector on top of the one in the oligopolistic business sector. This takes us straight back to the need for control of wages and prices in the shape of an incomes policy, and in the form of a social consensus arrived at by collaboration between trade unions, government and industry. Such policy is not meant to hold down money wages in the way incomes policies were applied in the UK in the 1960s and 1970s, for example, which required lower real wages throughout the duration of the policy. But real wages cannot be held below the desired level (or trend) for long periods. It thus follows that although some modicum of success may be possible in the short term, a permanent or long-run incomes policy is impracticable in that in the long-run there is a full catching-up effect in the level of money wages. Nor is it meant to be TIP (tax-based incomes policy), whereby incentives to firms are intended to hold money-wage increases in line with productivity (Weintraub and Wallich 1973). This is an interesting proposition, in that it also provides an in-built incentive for growth. By allowing firms to increase price faster than money wages, TIP provides the environment whereby real wages are dampened so that the mark-up over costs is widened, thus establishing a crucial financial condition for investment growth. Clearly, though, the success of these policies depends crucially on whether the growth of money wages is sufficiently contained. This observation raises the important consideration of the income distribution effects of TIP, which hit workers particularly hard (Appelbaum 1982).

An incomes policy which might have a reasonable chance of success is one that is applied to all forms of incomes, and it gains acceptance by all affected by it, rather than being imposed. It should also have the support of not just the trade unions but of the various other economic groups. Such a policy, therefore, implies that the non-governmental representatives would have a substantial role to play in the formation of overall governmental economic strategy (see also Harcourt 1993).

Turning now to the foreign sector, expression (1) above clearly states that a budget deficit will sooner rather than later result in a deficit in the balance of trade, if the surplus in the sectors discussed above is in general small and changes slowly and predictably. Unless capital inflows are attracted by growth prospects, a balance of payments crisis could very well ensue which implies that expansionary policies would have to be reversed, producing the familiar scenario of 'stop-go' policies. This difficulty may very well arise from the inability of the economy to respond to the increased demand well before full employment of labour is reached, due to a number of obstacles such as poor research and development, inadequate excess capacity, lack of trained and skilled labour force, poor educational standards and consequently lack of skill and talent amongst economic agents and thus absence of innovation which is so vital to boost investment.

Consequently, expansionary policies cannot be effective for long unless they are accompanied by policies to tackle the balance of trade deficit. Manipulating the exchange rate for this purpose may not always work, since devaluation can raise the level of output, employment and income and lead to a rise in imports that may very well be equal to the increase in exports resulting from devaluation.[4] Whether or not import controls could be effectively employed without undesirable repercussions, there is still the real possibility of investment not being sufficiently stimulated to sustain full employment. The usual argument is that the manufacturing sector needs some sort of 'sheltering', which would increase productivity and thus investment. However, there is nothing to guarantee that this investment will in fact materialize, particularly given the political uncertainty that would attend any such radical development (see also Harcourt 1992). This argument supports and strengthens the policy implication that attempts to stimulate the economy through fiscal and monetary policies cannot be successful unless they are accompanied by some form of control of investment. But control of investment by itself may not be effective if cooperation from the trade union movement is not forthcoming. Trade unions would be far more likely to cooperate if they were to be involved in the decision-making mechanism. Consequently, the type of investment control envisaged here is socialization of investment which, unlike Keynes's (1936), would actually involve the trade unions in the process.

Wood (1975) argues for a policy of 'profit-sharing' whereby every company would be obliged by law to transfer each year a fixed proportion of its retained profits in the form of ordinary shares into the ownership of its employees. There is the Swedish wage-earners funds model, which is based on the notion of transferring to the workers both ownership and control of firms – with due compensation to the owners for the loss of their assets. The fundamental assumption of this thesis is that workers' performance would be enhanced due to stronger incentives and motivation on the part of workers. Thus firms, in this view, would provide a superior mechanism for tackling working conditions and thus productivity. The danger with this scheme, though, is that it could potentially create divisions between workers in the oligopolistic and in the competitive sectors and amongst workers themselves when their performance differs. It might be better, therefore, to consider the possibility of transferring partial ownership of capital to an organization representing the political and economic interests of all workers, an aspect which is actually embedded in the Swedish wage-earners fund case. In this way there is direct involvement of the trade union movement in the process of capital accumulation (Arestis 1986).

Socialization of investment alongside trade union participation would also remove the obstacles to achieving full employment that so concerned Kalecki (1943), especially as the dislike of the captains of industry for the socio-political change normally associated with attempts to sustain full-employment dissipitates to some extent. Changes of this nature would be welcomed by the trade unions, and they might be more willing to engage in healthy collective bargaining. Such policies, however, would have to be accompanied by active labour market and manpower policies to encourage labour mobility and thus facilitate labour market adjustments for the unemployed. It is also important to note that tackling unemployment would have to be top priority for this set of policies, since if these policies were not pursued with a firm commitment to full employment, their chances of success would be seriously threatened. Glyn and Rowthorne (1988) argue that unemployment has been lower in those countries (Sweden, Norway and Austria) where commitment to full employment has been part of a broad social consensus between trade unions, industry and the state, which also involved economic restructuring and incomes policies.

We may, therefore, suggest that a combination of fiscal and monetary as well as exchange rate policies, commitment to full employment on the part of the policy-makers, active labour market and manpower policies, social consensus policies over the distribution of income, and socialization of investment, stand a good chance of success. A very important implication of this set of policies is that they go a long way towards meeting the Marxist critique of post-Keynesian economics that it 'cannot resolve the struggle over the distribution of factor shares between capital and labour, nor over control of the labour process that gives rise to profits' (Chernomas 1982: 139). It clearly can, within the parameters set by the socialization of investment process.

CONSTRAINTS AND OBSTACLES TO POST-KEYNESIAN ECONOMIC POLICY

This policy 'menu' is by no means problem-free. Post-Keynesian economic policy analysis recognizes that there are obstacles to an interventionist policy of the type just referred to. Political and social pressures are thought to impose significant constraints on the achievement of these objectives. Kalecki (1943) argues that although governments are able to influence economic developments, this prerogative will not be utilized to its full potential. According to Kalecki (*ibid.*), this is entirely due to the 'power of vested interests'[5] which finds expression in the objections to full employment by the 'industrial leaders' who dislike government interference in the private sector.

A further problem is that since the policies rely heavily on social cooperation and social consensus between the state, industry and labour, experiments which failed in the past, especially in the UK, there is nothing to suggest that they will not fail again. The short answer is to say that social cooperation and social consensus would have to be created by involving people in the process itself (Cowling 1987). There is, of course, the experience of some other countries which have been conspicuously successful with economic policies that relied on social consensus (Sweden, Norway, Australia and Austria are the best examples in this respect). Indeed, there exists overwhelming evidence which suggests that increased participation is one of the dominant determinants of productivity and that those firms that adopt 'workers' participation' type policies experience superior sales, growth, profitability and better performance overall than similar firms which do not pursue policies of this nature (Hodgson 1984).

There is still the problem of the serious constraint imposed on these policies by the operation of transnational corporations and international financial capital. The operations of transnationals in the short run could very well jeopardize expansion. In the long run it is expected that these firms would undertake a greater volume of investment once the economy had achieved a sustained expansionary path. In the short run, however, control over the operations of transnational corporations would have to be established. Fiscal measures could be used to promote domestic rather than foreign investment, although the evidence here is that transnationals could easily overcome this type of measure. There is also the experience of other countries we should consider, which is very revealing indeed. Japan, the USA, France, Canada and most notably a number of developing countries, have all adopted policies towards transnationals. These policies have ranged from monitoring their activities and taking positive steps to discriminate in favour of domestic firms where there were fears of multinational dominance, to tighter and more direct regulation on their activities.

Similarly, policy-makers can, and should, attempt to have an impact on the sphere of regulation of international financial capital and trade flows. The degree of success in this respect for countries like the UK is enhanced when such measures are taken at the European level as part of the European Union's measures. Keynes (1980: 52) envisaged strict capital controls to deal with situations when the centres of international financial capital became untameable. Indeed, he argued that capital controls, both inward and outward, should be permanent. Also permanent, in his view, should be the control of the entire financial system. Keynes even propounded the idea of planning to embrace the whole of the international economic system. Hicks (1985) reinforces this view by advocating concerted action by a number of the more 'important' countries. An interesting idea in the same spirit has been put forward by Tinbergen (1989) who proposes close cooperation between the European Union and Japan. Cooperation of this type may enhance the chances of success of the proposal that relies on the imposition of a transactions tax to tame speculators (for a summary and a critique, see Arestis and Sawyer 1996). Similar proposals to tame speculators and lead the world to prosperity have been put forward by Harcourt (1994).

These measures, especially those taken in collaboration with other countries or groups of countries, have assumed even more significance and importance recently in view of the internationalization of capital. The problem of controlling the activities of international capital, both industrial and financial, in the new environment becomes even more awkward when attempted in isolation. The inevitable conclusion emanating from these developments and the analysis pursued in this study is that there may be no alternative to policies being explicitly and firmly 'internationalist' (Radice 1989). Harcourt argues along similar lines when he suggests that

> the advanced countries should give a lead in creating institutions which have aims which are similar to those of Bretton Woods, especially the set of proposals that Keynes argued for ... we need measures which make both deficit and surplus countries react to their situations in such a way as to allow employment to be sustained and growth to continue, individually and collectively.
>
> (1994: 36)

Davidson (1992–3) has propagated specific proposals for the creation of suitable international institutions with the full-employment objective being at the heart of his proposals, while Arestis (1993) and Arestis and Sawyer (1996) have proposed similar institutions and objectives for the European Union.

SUMMARY AND CONCLUSIONS

The major policy implication of post-Keynesian thinking as exemplified above would appear to be some form of socialization of investment. But socialization ought to be accompanied by explicit and permanent social consensus on the distribution of income under the umbrella of a 'social contract' among the three groups – trade unions, industry and the state – which are generally recognized as being all-important in any economic system. In this environment, wage pressures that damage profitability and accumulation can be avoided, especially so if there is a commitment to full employment by governments. These policies should also be accompanied by appropriate industrial policies which would promote participation of the workforce in decision-making.

In fact, some of these ideas have been successfully implemented in certain 'capitalist' economies. There are, in particular two well-documented examples of socialization of investment: Sweden, which is probably the best-known example (Arestis 1986) and Austria, where a successful form of 'social control' of investment has been implemented (Tichy 1984). The example of Japan could be added (Cowling 1987) and, to a lesser extent, those of France and Germany. As it happens, these economies belong to that group of countries which have been doing particularly well in terms of economic performance in the turbulent recent, and not so recent, past. Interestingly enough, Harcourt's (1994) economic policy proposals sit very comfortably with the experiences of these countries, and as such they are as relevant today as they have always been.

ACKNOWLEDGEMENTS

I am grateful, as always, to Geoff Harcourt and Malcolm Sawyer for very helpful comments, and for numerous discussions on the theme of this paper and many other topics.

NOTES

1 There is a great deal of evidence on the persistence of economic disparities and the role of markets in perpetuating inequality; see Sawyer (1989) for a recent contribution.
2 The direction of budget deficits should always be considered, to avoid peculiar results. Robinson puts it very aptly when she argues that 'It was the so-called Keynesians who persuaded successive presidents that there is no harm in a budget deficit and left the military-industrial complex to take advantage of it. So it has come about that Keynes' pleasant daydream was turned into a nightmare of terror' (1972: 7).
3 However, so long as the growth rate of the economy exceeds the post-tax rate of interest (in either nominal or real terms), budget deficits do not lead to a rising debt to GDP ratio (Arestis and Sawyer 1996).
4 The view has been put forward (for example, Cripps and Godley 1978) that the authorities should impose import controls in an environment of 'managed' international trade. In view of the recent global and European developments in particular, the policy of import controls has lost a great deal of its early attraction. It can be argued, however, that managed international trade can easily be initiated by the whole European Community, rather than by a single member country. Indeed, the supporters of import controls favour the notion that some form of managed international trade should be in place.
5 There is an interesting contrast here between Kalecki and Keynes. Kalecki's 'power of vested interests' is different from Keynes's faith in the 'power of ideas' (Sawyer 1985: chapter 9).

REFERENCES

Appelbaum, E. (1982) 'The incomplete incomes policy vision', *Journal of Post Keynesian Economics*, Summer.
Arestis, P. (1986) 'Post-Keynesian economic policies: the case of Sweden', *Journal of Economic Issues*, XX (3): 709–23.
—— (1993) 'An independent European central blank: a post-Keynesian perspective', paper delivered at the 11th Keynes Conference, University of Kent, 19 November. Forthcoming in V. Chick (ed.), *Keynes and the Post Keynesians*, London: Macmillan.
—— and Sawyer, M. C. (1996) 'European monetary integration: a post Keynesian critique and some proposals', in P. Arestis (ed.), *Keynes, Money and the Open Economy: Essays in Honour of Paul Davidson*, Volume 1, Aldershot: Edward Elgar Publishing (forthcoming).
Asimakopulos, A. and Burbidge, J. B. (1974) 'The short-period incidence of taxation', *Economic Journal*, 334(84): 267–88.
Beath, J. (1979) 'Target profits, cost expectations and incidence of the corporate income tax', *Review of Economic Studies*, July.
Chernomas, B. (1982) 'Keynesian, Marxist and post-Keynesian policy: a Marxist

analysis', *Studies in Political Economy*, 10.

Coutts, K., Godley, W. and Nordhaus, W. (1978) *Industrial Pricing in the United Kingdom*, Cambridge: Cambridge University Press.

Cowling, K. (1987) 'An industrial strategy for Britain: the nature and role of planning', *International Review of Applied Economics*, November.

Cripps, T. F. and Godley, W. A. H. (1978) 'Control of imports as a means to full employment and the expansion of world trade: the UK's case', *Cambridge Journal of Economics*, 2.

Crotty, J. R. (1983) 'On Keynes and capital flight', *Journal of Economic Literature*, 21(1): 59–65.

Davidson, P. (1992–3) 'Reforming the world's money', *Journal of Post Keynesian Economics*, 15(2): 153–79.

Eichner, A. S. (1976) *The Megacorp and Oligopoly: Micro Foundations of Macro Dynamics*, Cambridge: Cambridge University Press.

Glyn, A. and Rowthorne, R. (1988) 'West European unemployment: corporatism and structural change', *American Economic Review*, Papers and Proceedings, 78(2): 194–9.

Harcourt, G. C. (1965) 'A two-sector model of the distribution of income and the level of employment in the short run', *Economic Record*, March: 103–17.

—— (1992) 'Markets, madness and a middle way', *Australian Quarterly*, 64 (Autumn): 1–17. Reprinted in G. C. Harcourt (ed.) (1995) *Capitalism, Socialism and Post-Keynesianism: Selected Essays of G. C. Harcourt*, Aldershot: Edward Elgar.

—— (1993) 'Macroeconomic policy for Australia in the 1990s', *Economic and Labour Relations Review*, 4(2): 167–75. Reprinted in G. C. Harcourt (ed.) (1995) *Capitalism, Socialism and Post-Keynesianism: Selected Essays of G. C. Harcourt*, Aldershot: Edward Elgar.

—— (1994) 'A "modest proposal" for taming speculators and putting the world on course to prosperity', *Economic and Political Weekly*, XXIX (38): 2490–2. Reprinted in G. C. Harcourt (ed.) (1995) *Capitalism, Socialism and Post-Keynesianism: Selected Essays of G. C. Harcourt*, Aldershot: Edward Elgar.

—— and Kenyon, P. (1976) 'Pricing and the investment decision', *Kyklos*, 29(3): 449–77.

Hicks, J. R. (1985) 'Keynes and the world economy', in F. Vicarelli (ed.), *Keynes's Relevance Today*, London: Macmillan.

Hodgson, G. M. (1984) *The Democratic Economy*, Harmondsworth: Penguin.

Kalecki, M. (1943) 'Political aspects of full employment', *Political Quarterly*, October–December.

Keynes, J. M. (1936) *The General Theory of Employment, Interest and Money*, London: Macmillan.

—— (1980) *Activities, 1940–46: Shaping the Post-War World: Employment, Collected Writings, Vol. XXVII*, London: Macmillan.

King, M. (1975) 'The UK profits crisis: myth or reality?', *Economic Journal*, March.

Radice, H. (1989) 'British capitalism in a changing global economy', in A. MacEwan and N. T. Tabb (eds), *Instability and Change in the World Economy*, New York: Monthly Review.

Robinson, J. (1972) 'The second crisis of economic theory', *American Economic Review*, Papers and Proceedings, May.

Sawyer, M. C. (1985) *The Economics of Michal Kalecki*, London: Macmillan.

—— (1989) *The Challenge of Radical Political Economy: An Introduction to the Alternatives to Neo-Classical Economics*, Hemel Hempstead: Harvester Wheatsheaf.

441

Tichy, G. (1984) 'Strategy and implementation of employment policy in Austria: successful experiments with unconventional assignment of instruments to goals', *Kyklos*, 3(37).

Tinbergen, J. (1989) 'How to reduce unemployment', *Review of Political Economy*, 1(1): 1–6.

Weintraub, S. and Wallich, H. (1973) 'A tax-based incomes policy' in S. Weintraub (ed.) *Keynes and the Monetarists*, New Brunswick, NJ: Rutgers University Press.

Wood, A. (1975) *A Theory of Profits*, Cambridge: Cambridge University Press.

35

CORPORATE RESTRUCTURING IN EUROPE AND THE REGULATION OF COMPETITION

Andy Cosh and Alan Hughes

INTRODUCTION

This paper[1] is concerned with the interrelationship between two of the most significant developments in European industrial organization in the 1980s. The first of these was the emergence on a large scale of cross-border merger activity. The second was the apparent resurgence in the numbers of small- and medium-sized enterprises in the European Community. Both of these developments have been the subject of detailed study, especially in the context of completion of the internal market. The implications of the former for the latter have, however, not been the subject of systematic analysis. It is true that students of merger activity have been concerned with its impact upon industrial concentration and economies of scale. This has implications for the changing role of small business, but only as a by-product of the analysis of mergers between the giants. Discussion of merger policy has also focused on its role in regulating the strategic behaviour of giant firms and multinational corporations (Neven *et al.* 1993). Discussion has become focused on the merits and demerits of large firms as such, rather than upon the optimal structure of industry as a whole, and upon the patterns of interrelationships between large and small firms as customers and suppliers as much as competitors.

Whilst it is inevitable that competition policy concentrates its focus on the upper tail of the size distribution of firms, we believe that this neglects the important role of small firms both as acquirers and as the object of attention by other larger acquirers. Patterns of acquisition involving smaller firms may have profound implications for the long-run evolution of competitive structure and patterns of buyer/supplier relationships and may yet never be within the reach of merger policy which by its nature is confined to the regulation of the creation and abuse of dominant positions by the very largest businesses. Our object in this paper is to start to redress this balance. In the next section we sketch out a model of competition as a dynamic process which enables us to highlight the ways in which large and small firms may interact, the role of merger in that interaction and the possible impact upon that interaction of the completion of the internal market. The following section looks at the significance of smaller acquisitions in the context of the UK economy and the internationalization of its takeover activity. This is followed by an analysis of the scale, cross-country pattern and broad sectoral spread of merger activity within the EC and across its boundaries. A final section draws upon the results of the previous sections to sketch out a policy agenda which focuses on the wide range of industrial and financial policies within which competition policy must be located if the impact of merger upon the size distribution and performance of businesses to be properly regulated.

MERGERS, SMALL FIRMS AND THE COMPETITIVE PROCESS

We regard competition not as a state of affairs but as a dynamic process linking structural change with market behaviour. Competition is seen as a process of rivalry between producers, taking the form of contests within existing markets and potential entry into new areas. Competitive rivalry is conducted in terms of price, and product and process characteristics. It affects the rate of growth of technical change in products and processes, the rate of diffusion of new ideas across firms, as well as the allocation of resources between markets, and the evolution of market structures themselves.

In any given product market, at any given time, the size distribution of firms and the spread of efficiency across them will reflect past investment and growth, and will condition future growth and efficiency improvements. Firms with the lowest cost structures will have, *ceteris paribus*, the highest profits to finance competitive expansion, and will attempt to set a price which promises to attract customers and provide sufficient funds to pay for capacity expansion (either via retentions or attracting outside finance). Thus low-cost production will go with a competitive transfer of market share away from the least, towards the most efficient, producers. Those threatened with an ever-diminishing market share must either innovate to get back into the competitive process by improving their efficiency, or gradually be driven out of business in their existing line of activity.

The transfer and innovation mechanisms are beneficial in the sense that they serve to improve the allocation of output between firms of differing efficiencies and spur the inefficient to improve their performance. Unless there are systematic tendencies leading to a loss of efficiency as firms expand or there is a very powerful innovation mechanism, then the competitive process will lead to increasing concentration and the gradual demise of unsuccessful and hence relatively small firms.

In so far as the completion of the internal market is concerned, the clear implication is that there will be, *ceteris paribus*, a reinforcement of the transfer mechanism as restrictions on market entry are removed, and an increase in the size of markets, favouring scale economies and large firms. The competition policy response is then traditionally a trade-off between the latter gains and the abuse of dominant positions which are created. The completion of the market may equally, however, provoke strategic reactions by existing firms, in the form of cross-border mergers with existing businesses. Merger policy may then come to play a particularly central role in regulating the competitive process. Although there is some evidence to suggest that the structure of industries evolves over their life cycle with the transfer mechanism dominant it is obviously a highly stylized description. Moreover it is not necessarily the case that the completion of the internal market need be associated with rising concentration. The pace of the transfer mechanism and the survival of small firms in the face of it, vary considerably across markets.

In recent decades there has been a resurgence in the small-firm sector, with employment shares of smaller firms (e.g. employing less than 50, 100 or 200 workers) rising in most industrial economies (Sengenberger *et al.* 1990; Dunne and Hughes 1992; ENSR 1995). How may we account for this in principle? (For a thorough review of the relevant theoretical literature see You (1995)). Forces on the supply side making it more likely that small firms will prosper are: the absence of significant technical and other scale effects; insignificant learning effects; high transport costs; low capital intensity of production; rapid technical change and the importance of flexible response to it; high exit and low entry barriers. On the demand side, the position of small firms is enhanced by specialist customer requirements; unstable demand coupled with high storage or inventory costs; and high personal service content. Small firm birth and survival accordingly tends to be more significant in services as opposed to goods. These influences, however, also affect the cross-sectional distribution of small firms within manufacturing (Porter 1980; White 1982; Acs and Audretsch 1987; Mills and Schumann 1985; Beesley and Hamilton 1984).

Other forces, too, may affect the pace of structural change and the relative shares of small and large firms as time unfolds. Organizational and motivational issues internal to businesses may condition their ability or desire to innovate, and hence their competitive strength (McEachern and Romeo 1978; Williamson 1970, 1975). There are, moreover, influences arising from the 'social organization' of industry which interact with technical supply side changes and demand patterns and may influence the scope for small-firm growth and survival. These depend as much upon questions of inter-firm relationships and patterns of vertical integration as upon given technical conditions of production and conditions of demand in a given product market

(Best 1990). Thus vertical disintegration and increased, or changed, patterns of subcontracting by large firms as a response to the risks of growing market uncertainty; rigidities and high costs of internal sourcing as a result of trade union organization within larger plants; and the possibility of exerting increased pressure on suppliers with access to cheap labour, may all lead to small-firm creation and growth.

Equally new forms of industrial organization in which close and direct inter-firm links and associations of small businesses play a central role may emerge in part as a response to technical change. These may include networks of subcontracting around large firms (of which the Japanese subcontracting system provides the most notable example), as well as the industrial districts epitomized by the close geographical grouping of large numbers of small firms in Northern Italy. These could be regarded as a collective innovative response to the rules of the competitive process outlined above (Segal *et al.* 1988; Russo 1985; Brusco 1982; Pyke and Sengenberger 1992). It is clear that the cultural, legal, and historical factors which determine the nature of these patterns of inter-firm relationships and of changes in them over time may lead to important differences in the impact of small firms on the competitive process between countries. Moreover to the extent that changed techniques of production facilitate such arrangements, differences may emerge between industries, and in given industries, over time.

The impact of mergers involving small firms on their performance and on the competitive process is in principle ambiguous. Where a negative impact is assumed it is either based on the proposition that a horizontal merger between two firms in an industry will raise their joint market share (and thus by implication increase their desire and ability to indulge in anti-competitive behaviour) or is based on the view that large firms suppress rivalry from and end the growth prospects of small firms as independent units by acquiring them, with deleterious effects on their subsequent performance. Against this is usually set the possible benefits to be had from economies of scale or superior management abilities in the larger businesses created by merger. This is not, however, the whole of the story. Merger between small and medium-sized firms may raise, rather than lower, the tempo of the competitive process if for example they produce efficiency gains through the avoidance of duplicated R&D efforts (Ordover and Willig 1995). In more general terms, merger offers an alternative to growth by internal investment for small as well as for large firms. Given external growth possibilities, merger, by reducing managerial services per unit of expansion, offers a way of pushing outwards the limits to growth arising from shortages of management resources (Pensore 1959)). Merger may, of course, also enhance the external possibilities themselves if it offers scale or scope economies and enhances the competitive power of the firms involved. This may be especially significant if the scale curve is steepest in its early stages. It must be noted, however, that the effects, for instance, of scale itself cannot be a sufficient motive for merger, since that is merely one way of achieving scale; internal growth is also possible. Thus auxiliary arguments in favour of a merger are required, stressing the speed and cost of the merger process compared with internal growth.

There are a number of reasons, however, for expecting that the merger opportunities may differ between large and small firms. Thus, for instance, acquisition-intensive strategies may be easier for larger quoted as opposed to smaller unquoted companies, since the targets of the latter will generally have to be willing to be absorbed. Takeover bids for unwilling targets with dispersed share ownership are a less available option than for larger companies. However, selling out may be an attractive way of realizing capital gains or of overcoming management succession problems. The opportunity to sell out is then an important element in the overall context in which entrepreneurs evaluate the advantages and disadvantages of funding and developing a business. Where the pressure of the competitive process leads to decline through inefficient management, then selling out to allow new management to take over may be a 'civilized alternative' to bankruptcy. Finally, it may be argued that for the largest companies with potential market power it is in fact the prospect of takeover that replaces product market discipline in keeping management on its toes and ensuring that technical efficiency (if not allocative efficiency) is maintained. Thus even where the transfer mechanism leads to dominant product market positions, the capital market keeps up the pressure to perform. Herein lies an apparent competition policy paradox. How can the disciplinary potential of the takeover mechanism be maintained if constraints are placed upon larger merges in the desire to keep product market concentration low? Whether these are serious problems or not depends upon the impact of merger in practice.

Much of the literature on the impact of merger on the competitive process pays little attention to the positive small firm aspects outlined above and has instead merely pointed to a link between merger activity and increased concentration at the market level. Even here, however, a pattern of large firms acquiring small ones may not be deleterious to the opportunities for small firm growth generally, nor for the rate of innovation in the industry as a whole. The sequential nature of the innovation process, for instance, from R&D through invention and innovation to the diffusion of new products and processes, imposes differing organizational and incentive requirements at different stages in the process and for different scales of firm (Burns and Stalker 1961; Rosenberg 1973; Freeman 1982; Williamson 1985). Thus within a given industry, or group of industries, there may be a complementarity between firms of different sizes specializing in different stages, and the optimal relationships between them may include a spectrum ranging from arm's-length commercial transactions, through joint ventures, to minority share-holdings and ultimately majority ownership acquired by merger. The coexistence of firms of different sizes with differing interrelationships may therefore represent a mix of market and hierarchy suitable for particular

447

technical conditions. Equally, once past an initial stage of development in an independent, small, flexible, informally structured organization, a new product or process may most effectively be taken further by the acquisition or integration of the smaller organization within a larger firm. There the continued involvement of the originators can be combined with access to the financial and marketing skills of the larger unit. Much will depend here, however, upon the ability of the larger organization to achieve its own input without adversely affecting creativity in the acquired enterprise. From the point of view of the larger firm, the possibility of forming looser relationships with small firms, with a view to subsequently closer ownership ties, acts as stimulant to venture capital provision by the large firm. In that sense the possibility of merger could stimulate small, innovative, firm growth opportunities. Essentially, large firms come to play a second-best role in filling a capital market gap, with merger and consequent ownership an inducement to them to behave in this way. Merger in this optimistic scenario is then best seen as one element in a spectrum of institutional possibilities open to small firms with a desire to maintain their development, and to large firms seeking ways of maintaining their vitality and expanding their corporate portfolio. Whether this optimism is justified, however, is an empirical question, but we first indicate the scale of cross-border mergers and show that the place of small firms within them is significant enough to merit the emphasis we have placed upon it. In doing so we must, however, reiterate that merger alone is just one facet of the institutional arrangements possible and that a proper understanding of the large-firm/small-firm interface requires further work on informal and formal alliances and patterns of subcontracting relationships. Mergers, however, remain as good a starting point as any.

CROSS-BORDER MERGER ACTIVITY AND THE ROLE OF SMALL FIRMS

As far as takeover and merger is concerned, after a period of quiescence in the 1970s there has been an explosion of global takeover activity in the 1980s, reaching a peak at the end of the decade. In contrast to earlier periods this has involved a substantial increase in cross-border activity. For example, it has been estimated that in the twelve-month period ending in September 1989, 2,600 cross-border acquisitions, worth nearly $120bn, took place. The typical deal was relatively small, with over 90% costing less than $100m. Of the total, 754 acquisitions, worth around $17bn, took place within the European Community. In addition, EC-based companies bought up over 750 companies abroad worth over $50bn, the vast majority in North America (Cosh and Hughes 1991). European involvement in cross-border acquisition activity is clearly now very big business indeed. To gauge the importance of this activity relative to *intra*national trends, we can look first at the UK, which has the most detailed and consistent data series on domestic and overseas acquisition activities, and then proceed to a direct analysis of the mainland European economies, where the evidence is, however, more fragmentary and based more on commercial sources. The discussion which follows draws upon Cosh and Hughes (1991) and (1994a), to which the reader is referred for a more detailed analysis of the data on international acquisition activity.

Table 1 reveals a boom in overall UK acquisition activity in the 1980s. It also shows that acquisition activity overseas by UK companies has risen faster than foreign acquisitions in the UK market. Tables 2 and 3 provide a more detailed geographical breakdown of foreign acquisitions of, and by, UK companies. The high levels of acquisition activity in the second half of the 1980s were accompanied both by a rise in the average size of deal (whether deflated by consumer or stock market prices) and in the scale though *not* the numbers of cross-border acquisitions. Table 2 shows that acquisitions by foreign companies in the UK increased in significance in the 1980s compared with the 1970s. Moreover, it appears that in the course of the 1980s itself, European acquisitions in the UK increased in importance. In the years 1980–85 about one-eighth of inward acquisitions originated in Europe. This has risen to around one-third by the years 1986–91. There was also a dramatic increase in the relative value of these acquisitions. In 1986–91, for instance, EC-based acquirers purchased more than twice the value of UK companies as US acquirers did, and almost half as much as all other foreign acquirers (including the Australian, Japanese, Scandinavian and Swiss) put together. By contrast, in the early 1980s, the value of EC-based bids had accounted for only one-tenth of the value of inward acquisitions.

This rise in inward acquisition activity, however, was dwarfed by the scale and rate of increase of UK acquisition activity abroad. The relevant data are shown in Table 3. Over the years 1986–89 UK companies acquired six times as many foreign companies, for around three times as much cash, as was represented by overseas acquisition activity in the UK. In the US alone, UK companies spent almost £17.5bn on acquisitions in 1989; and during the 1980s, the balance of acquisition activity between the UK and US was heavily in favour of the UK. These imbalances appear to have narrowed markedly at the start of the 1990s.

Throughout the 1970s, UK acquisitions in the EC economies had greatly exceeded activity flowing in the other direction. The gap narrowed considerably even in the last decade in terms of the values of acquisitions. Thus during 1989–91 UK companies spent £10bn on acquiring 695 EC-based concerns. The flow in the other direction was £9.3bn, but only 176 acquisitions were involved. Evidently EC acquirers find UK targets or partners about four times as large on average, as UK firms find in mainland Europe. The typical UK deal in Europe is uncontested and small with 56% of such acquisitions worth less than £5m and 70% worth less than £10m in 1989 (*Acquisitions Monthly*, December 1989). It is apparent that whilst contested megabids catch the headlines and attract the most regulatory attention, the

Table 1 United Kingdom acquisition activity, 1969–91 (annual averages)

Years	Number of acquisitions	Total expenditure (£m)			UK acquisitions of foreign companies			Foreign acquisitions of UK companies		
		Current prices	Consumer prices[1]	Stock market prices	No.	£m current prices	1988 consumer prices[1]	No.	£m current prices	1988 consumer prices[1]
1969–71	841	1034	5943	6648	52	69.3	391	24	49.4	286
1972–75	809	1159	5306	6420	61	107.7	462	11	84.5	338
1976–79	484	1017	2168	4434	32	225.4	476	10	59.5	138
1980–83	458	1792	2461	4899	89	706.2	1011	37	270.1	379
1984–87	716	10716	11751	12740	86	2321.2	2520	26	546.9	603
1988–91	1028	17270	15917	14956	n.a.	n.a.	n.a.	n.a.	n.a.	n.a.

Source: Cosh and Hughes (1991); Business Monitor MQ7, Business Bulletin, *Acquisition & Mergers Within the UK*
Notes: 1 The current price series has been converted to constant 1988 prices using the retail prices index.
2 The current price series has been converted to 1988 stock market values using the FT All Share index.

Table 2 Foreign acquisitions of UK companies, 1969–91

(a) Business Monitor MQ7 Series (Annual Averages)

Years	Total		EEC countries		Other countries	
	No.	Value £m	No.	Value £m	No.	Value £m
1969–71	24	49.4	2	0.6	22	48.8
1972–75	11	84.5	2	5.1	9	79.4
1976–79	10	59.5	3	6.8	7	52.7
1980–83	37	270.1	6	45.6	31	224.5
1984–85	25	367.9	2	17.2	23	350.7
1986	22	485.9	5	238.9	17	247.0
1986[1]	27	584.0	–	–	–	–
1987	42	1161.0	–	–	–	–
1988	76	2484.0	–	–	–	–

(b) CSO Bulletin

Years	Total		EEC countries		USA		Other countries	
	No.	Value £m	No.	Value £m	No.	Value £m	No.	Value £m
1986[2]	52	2874	14	1098	16	263	22	1513
1987	58	2701	12	979	189	225	27	1497
1988	94	5690	31	1158	23	1158	40	3630
1989	162	10861	58	3830	37	4804	67	2227
1990	143	10958	53	3409	32	1820	58	5729
1991	151	6997	65	2077	38	3062	48	1658

Source: Cosh and Hughes (1991); Business Monitor MQ7, Business Bulletin, *Cross Border Mergers and Acquisitions*
Notes: 1 The break in the MQ7 series in 1986 is caused by a change in the method of identification. Until 1986 the data are based on financial press reports, but thereafter are based on information collected to produce the balance of payments.
2 The principal difference between the MQ7 and CSO Bulletin series for 1986–91 are that the latter includes indirect acquisitions through existing group companies (which are excluded from the MQ7 series). A less important difference is that the CSO series includes financial companies.

Table 3 Foreign acquisitions by UK companies, 1969–91

(a) Business Monitor MQ7 Series (annual averages)

Years	Total		EEC countries		Other countries	
	No.	Value £m	No.	Value £m	No.	Value £m
1969–71	52	69.3	18	23.3	34	46.0
1972–75	61	107.7	36	54.8	25	52.9
1976–79	32	225.4	8	20.1	24	205.3
1980–83	89	706.2	16	53.8	73	652.4
1984–85	69	874.0	14	44.5	55	829.5
1986	89	3333.1	13	69.6	76	3263.5
1986[1]	212	4735.0	–	–	–	–
1987	282	5972.0	–	–	–	–
1988	444	5547.0	–	–	–	–

(b) CSO Bulletin cross border mergers and acquisitions

Years	Total		EEC countries		USA		Other countries	
	No.	Value £m	No.	Value £m	No.	Value £m	No.	Value £m
1986[2]	317	8940	62	643	176	7127	79	1170
1987	431	12059	124	1615	195	9141	112	1303
1988	606	17317	191	1764	290	13728	125	1825
1989	681	22621	284	2730	266	17543	131	2349
1990	586	12592	249	4026	183	7168	154	1758
1991	443	7542	162	3289	124	2824	159	1430

Source: Cosh and Hughes (1991); Business Monitor MQ7, Business Bulletin, *Cross Border Mergers and Acquisitions*
Notes: See notes to Table 2.

typical cross-border acquisition is a non-contested mini-deal involving a private or non-quoted company.

We have so far provided an analysis of European acquisition activity only in so far as it is reflected in the acquisition data of the UK. For an intra-European dimension we have to turn to commercial data sources. The first arises from the databank prepared by *Acquisitions Monthly*, which is based on the financial press supplemented by information from financial institutions and other agencies involved in the acquisitions process. Analysis of this data source for the years 1984–88 reveals a number of interesting inter-country patterns. The importance of the UK as a European acquirer in North America is confirmed, with around 60% of inward acquisitions into North America accounted for by UK businesses. Inward acquisitions *into Europe*, according to this source, have, however, been located primarily in Germany, which accounted for nearly 33% of activity into Europe from North America compared with around 20% each accounted for by the UK and France. West Germany also emerges as the most important destination for cross-border bids by other European countries, accounting for over 20% in total. West Germany was the single most important location for acquirers from the UK, Switzerland and Austria, Scandinavia and the Netherlands. West Germany and the UK were ranked almost equally in terms of acquisitions emanating from France. Only the Southern European countries of Italy and Spain deviated from this Northern emphasis by acquiring most frequently in their nearest neighbour, France. (For a fuller discussion, see Cosh and Hughes (1991).) This analysis of numbers of acquisitions can be updated and supplemented by values, and this is shown in Table 4. The table concerns itself only with the cross-border acquisition of an EC company and the upper half shows the nationality of the acquired company. Thus the scale of foreign acquisitions of UK companies can be set in context. In addition, the lower half of the table shows the distribution of these acquisitions by value and number by origin of the acquirors. It shows the importance of intra-EC acquisition activity and that United States companies typically select larger targets. Large deals are also the exception when considering cross-border acquisitions, with only an estimated 7% costing more than $100 million dollars to effect (*KPMG Dealwatch*, March 1990).

European Commission information for the period 1982–9 also suggests that acquisitions and joint ventures involving the largest European firms increased both absolutely and relatively to purely domestic activity (which also increased) in the course of the 1980s (*European Commission Annual Reports on Competition Policy* 1982 onwards).

There is little systematic evidence as to the industrial direction of the international merger activity we have described. For mergers involving the largest European firms it does appear that horizontal activity is dominant. Table 5, which covers both intra- and international mergers and acquisitions, shows diversifying motives as relatively important. It also reveals a substantial shift away from rationalization and restructuring motives towards expansion and a strengthening of market position as 1992 grew closer.

In interpreting the data we have provided it is important to bear in mind its limitations. First, as interest in international activity has grown, so have the financial rewards in collecting and disseminating information about it. Upward trends in identified acquisitions may therefore simply reflect improved reporting. This may bias comparative data over time for European and cross-border merger data, compared with that for the UK and the US which have runs of data based on official or longer-established commercial databases. On the other hand, the growth in commercial activity in this area is itself a reflection of a phenomenon which is growing in importance. Second, even given the increased efforts put into data collection by private agencies, the amount of public domain information which can be analysed by them varies enormously between countries. One particular problem to which

Table 4 Cross-border acquisitions of EC companies

(a) The sellers

Target country	1989		1990		1991	
	No.	Value £m	No.	Value £m	No.	Value £m
France	258	2678	295	4239	228	2397
Germany	452	2589	463	3717	500	2107
Italy	151	2329	158	2363	93	773
Netherlands	119	1040	174	3641	118	1546
UK	236	17248	316	14145	276	6474
Other EC	311	3932	511	6760	363	6017
Total	1527	29816	1917	34865	1578	19314

(b) The acquirors

Buyer country	1989		1990		1991	
	No.	Value £m	No.	Value £m	No.	Value £m
France	220	5470	330	6270	261	3328
Germany	116	3152	125	1085	138	1635
Italy	54	762	73	886	73	1153
Netherlands	57	458	121	603	94	1217
UK	342	2615	298	4894	185	1536
Sweden	86	680	159	6486	86	683
USA	198	10040	199	2257	214	2755
Japan	45	515	55	1768	66	559
Others	409	6124	557	10616	461	6448
Total	1527	29816	1917	34865	1578	19314

Source: *Acquisitions Monthly*, July 1990 and February 1992

Table 5 Main motives for mergers and acquisition by major EC businesses
1985/6–1989/90

Motive	%		
	1985/6	*1988/9*	*1989/90*
Rationalization restructuring	35.0	3.8	12.2
Expansion	18.1	31.3	26.9
Complementarity	14.4	10.6	5.6
Strengthening market position	11.3	42.4	45.3
Diversification	12.5	7.2	3.0
Other	8.8	4.9	7.1
Total	100.0	100.0	100.0

Source: European Commission: Reports on Competititon Policy
Note: Analysis is based on all merger cases for which precise information about motives was available.

this gives rise is the lack of data on values as opposed to numbers of acquisitions, which may lead to a misleading interpretation of variation in acquisition intensity both over time and between countries. Even allowing for these caveats, it seems clear that cross-border acquisition has become a significant feature of the European scene. It also seems to be the case that its incidence has been uneven across countries within the EC, although here we must be especially cautious in view of reporting difficulties.

CONCLUSION: AN AGENDA FOR CROSS-BORDER MERGER REGULATION

The scale of takeover activity that we have described, and its increasingly international character, may be regarded as basically virtuous for the broad sets of reasons outlined earlier. The first of these emphasizes the positive role of mergers in the competitive process, via increasing the scale of output of plants and especially firms, and leading through economies of scale and scope, enhanced ability to innovate and carry out R&D, and industrial rationalization, to lower costs and greater efficiency. The second broad reason for taking a relaxed, or positive, attitude towards heightened levels of takeover activity, is that they represent the workings of an efficient market for corporate control and its extension in geographical coverage to Europe as a whole.

Arguments for taking a more circumspect or hostile view may be counterpoised against these two strands of thought. In contrast to the scale and efficiency arguments, opponents of merger point to anti-competitive effects. Takeovers have a direct impact on the relative size of firms, and in the case of horizontal mergers have a direct impact on market shares, and hence potentially upon market power. There is thus a possible trade-off between efficiency gains and monopoly power. There may also be important distributional implications. One important category of distributional effects for cross-border mergers are geographic. To the extent that the claimed efficiency gains from merger depend on the reallocation of employment or management functions between regions or countries, then there may be important multiplier effects on regional employment opportunities and indigenous innovative activity. These go beyond the effects picked up in terms of each company's individual accounts, or indices of market power, and we return to this below.

This is not the place to review the evidence bearing on these issues (for a discussion, see Carty *et al.* (1991), Hughes (1992)). Instead, the point which we wish to make is that whether the verdict on small- and larger-scale acquisitions is good or bad, a system of cross-border merger regulation which focuses only upon mergers where both parties are of a large given minimum size and high degree of multinational spread leaves much of the role of mergers in the competitive process unregulated.

In view of our emphasis upon smaller mergers, the first point to note about merger policy is its scope. In the case of the UK, by the late 1980s around 22% of all industrial and commercial company mergers were large enough to be referrable for investigation, though only a handful in each year were actually investigated. The great bulk of acquisition activity was untouched. In the EC the coverage is designed to result in about fifty cases being examined each year (EC *Nineteenth Report on Competition Policy*, p. 34) – once again, a small number in relation to the magnitude of the merger activity described earlier in this paper. Such coverage makes perfectly good sense from an administrative point of view, and it can be argued that only the most substantial cases of potential abuse warrant the cost of intervention. It does mean, however, that policy effects are limited to mergers involving large firms. As we have seen, there are good reasons for believing that a major impact on the competitive process may arise from large companies acquiring smaller businesses. Whilst the limited evidence we have suggests that this may yield private benefits to the firms involved, the implication for market structure is that new entrants, especially innovative ones, may regularly end up in the control of existing giants. In this way dominant firms may maintain their position not necessarily through any superior internal efficiency but because capital market failures inhibit the ability of smaller firms to play an independent role in the competitive process. An important adjunct to merger policy must therefore be industrial and financial policies aimed at the amelioration of disadvantages experienced by smaller growing businesses in the capital market (Hughes and Storey 1994; Cosh and Hughes 1994b). As far as competition policy itself is involved, it is also important that restrictive trade practices policy should be flexible enough to permit cooperative arrangements between small businesses in the pursuit of specialization, rationalization or R&D programmes which will improve their competitive position. European policy in this respect is in advance of that in the UK. Thus block exemptions for certain kinds of agreements covering the areas outlined above have been granted by the Commission. Recently suggested reforms to the UK system of RTP policy which will move it nearer to that in the EC generally are therefore to be welcomed (see the discussion in Hughes (1989b) and Jacquemin (1988)).

In addition to policies aimed at improving financial flows to smaller businesses, it will be necessary for attention to be paid to the role of capital market changes in furthering acquisition activity. European policy like that in the UK is reactive once merger events have been proposed or have occurred. If as we have suggested the increased integration of capital markets in Europe leads to the emergence of more open equity-based systems of company finance, then the possibility of intensified merger activity arises. There are already pressures from the UK for the creation of a 'level playing field' for takeover along US/UK lines. Serious consideration therefore needs to be given to the standardization of company law so as to reduce the worst excesses of both the open shareholder-dominated US/UK systems, in which non-equity stakeholders are virtually ignored, and the closed finance-group dominated holding company systems which are more prevalent in Europe. A more pluralistic representative form of corporate governance would be both more democratic and likely to curb the excesses of merger mania that characterize the stock markets of the US and the UK. A more open system of reporting and accountability would assist both in identifying the incompetence of incumbent management and the extent of group holding company influence in European industrial structure. There is increasing evidence to suggest that changes in industrial organization at the enterprise level are less driven by changes in technology and scale of production than by questions of business organization and finance. It follows that increasing attention needs to be paid to these factors in regulating the competitive process where inter-enterprise rivalry takes place.

The second major point to note about merger policy is the terms upon which investigations are justified, and then decisions to allow or disallow are made. In the UK at present there is an illogical mismatch between the criteria for referral, and the criteria upon which, once referred, a decision is based. This is because as a matter of policy, only mergers which pose a clear threat to competition are referred for investigation. On the other hand the legislation requires a wide range of issues to be assessed in deciding whether merger is or is not likely to act against the public interest. Thus, to take a specific example, a major merger thought to have consequences on the regional balance of employment or industry could not be referred on those grounds. They could only become relevant once a reference on competition criteria had been announced. This emphasis in the UK legislation on competition is echoed in the EC regulation. In both cases this raises serious issues in relation to cross-borders mergers. It is perfectly possible and increasingly likely that very large mergers, with potentially significant local employment and sourcing effects, will not be investigated by either national or EC legislation systems focusing solely on 'competition' because of appeals to the increased size of the EC internal market as the relevant one for market share tests. Moreover, a merger once approved by the Commission cannot be held up by a national authority except on very limited grounds arising from questions of national security, prudential regulation or the freedom of the press. Consideration should therefore be given to derogation from the exclusivity of EC merger regulation in those cases where a national government believes an objective of an EC-consistent industrial policy is threatened by the outcome of a merger. This may be particularly relevant in the case of regional policy, and may have an important bearing on policies to encourage integrated systems of small firm development which depend heavily upon stable vertical supplier/customer relationships. This is an area where a potential conflict arises between the desire to pursue an appropriate exclusive community level system of regulation, and a national or local system of industrial policy based on a detailed knowledge of local needs and resources.

In sum, the emergence of European cross-border mergers on a significant scale raises major problems of regulation. These arise not only in the area of merger policy itself. It is necessary that competition policy towards mergers be seen as part of an overall industrial policy designed to improve economic efficiency. That itself will require policies towards the development of capital markets more able to meet the needs of smaller innovative businesses than is at present the case. The scale and incidence of merger activity is also susceptible to policy measures aimed at developing a more pluralistic system of corporate governance, so that reliance on the blunt instrument of takeover to discipline inefficient management may be reduced.

ACKNOWLEDGEMENT

The authors acknowledge the support of the ESRC Centre for Business Research, University of Cambridge in conducting the research on which this paper is based.

NOTE

1   This paper draws upon and updates data and arguments contained in two previous papers by the current authors. These are Cosh and Hughes (1991) and Hughes (1992), to which the interested reader is referred for further details of international cross-border activity and European competition policy. An earlier version of this paper appeared in 1992 as 'Corporate restructuring in Europe in the 1980's', Small Business Research Centre Working Paper No.21, Cambridge.

REFERENCES

Acs, Z. J. and Audretsch, D. B. (1987) 'The determinants of small-firm growth in US manufacturing', International Institute of Management Berlin Discussion Paper, April.

Barber, J., Metcalfe, J. S. and Porteous, M. (eds) (1992) *Barriers to Growth in Small Firms*, London: Routledge.

Beesley, M. E. and Hamilton, R. T. (1984) 'Small firms seedbed role and the concept of turbulence', *Journal of Industrial Economics*, 33 (December): 217–32.

Best, M. H. (1990) *The New Competition*, Oxford: Polity Press.

Brusco, S. (1982) 'The Emilian model: productive decentralisation and social integration', *Cambridge Journal of Economics*, 6: 167–84.

Burns, T. and Stalker, E. M. (1961) *The Management of Innovation*, London: Tavistock.

Carty, J., Cosh, A. D., Hughes, A., Plender, J. and Singh, A. (1990) *Takeovers and Short-Termism in the UK*, London: Institute for Public Policy Research.

Cosh, A. D. and Hughes, A. (1991) *Megabids and Minideals: A Profile of Global Acquisition Activities in the 1980s*, Cambridge: Small Business Research Centre.

—— (1994a) 'Acquisition activity in the small business sector', in Hughes, A. and Storey, D. (eds) *Finance and the Small Firm*, London: Routledge.

—— (1994b) 'Size, financial structure and profitability: UK companies in the 1980s', in Hughes, A. and Storey, D. (eds) *Finance and the Small Firm*, London: Routledge.

Dunne, J. P. and Hughes, A. (1992) 'The changing structure of competitive industry in the 1980s' in Dunne, J. P. and Driver, C. (eds) *Structural Change in the UK Economy*, DAE Occasional Paper No. 58, Cambridge: CUP.

ENSR (1995) *The European Observatory for SMEs*. Third Annual Report, Zoetermeer, Netherlands: European Network for SME Research.

Freeman, C. (1982) The Economics of Industrial Innovation, London: Frances Pinter.

Hughes, A. (1989a) 'The impact of merger: a survey of empirical evidence for the UK', in Fairburn, J. and Kay, J. A. (eds), *Merger and Merger Policy*, Oxford: Oxford University Press.

—— (1989b) 'Small firms merger activity and competition policy', in Barber, J., Metcalfe, J. S. and Porteous, M. (eds) *Barriers to Growth in Small Firms*, London: Routledge.

—— (1992) 'Competition policy and the competitive process: Europe in the 1990s', *Metroeconomica* 43(2): 1–50.

—— and Storey, D. J. (eds) (1994) *Finance and the Small Firm*, London: Routledge.

Jacquemin, A. (1988) 'Cooperative agreements in R & D and European antitrust policy', *European Economic Review*, 32: 551–60.

McEachern, W. A. and Romeo, A. (1978) 'Stockholder control, uncertainty and the allocation of resources to research and development', *Journal of Industrial Economics* XXVI: 135–62.

Mills, D. E. and Schumann, L. (1985) 'Industry structures with fluctuating demand', *American Economic Review*, 75 (September): 758–67.

Neven, D., Nuttall, R. and Seabright, P. (1993) *Merger in Daylight: The Economics and Politics of European Merger Control*, London: Centre for Economic and Policy Research.

Ordover, J. A. and Willig, R. D. (1995) 'Antitrust for high-technology industries: assessing research, joint ventures, and mergers', *Journal of Law and Economics*, XXVIII (May).

Penrose, E. T. (1959) *The Theory of the Growth of the Firm*, Oxford: Blackwell.

Porter, M. (1980) *Competitive Strategy*, New York: Free Press.

Pyke, F. and Sengenberger, W. (eds) (1992) *Industrial Districts and Local Economic Regeneration*, Geneva: International Institute for Labour Studies.

Rosenberg, N. (ed.) (1973) *The Economics of Technological Change*, Harmondsworth: Penguin.

Russo, M. (1985) 'Technical change and industrial districts: the role of inter-firm relations in the growth and transformation of ceramic tile production in Italy', *Research Policy*.

Segal, Quince and Wicksteed (1988) 'Strategic partnerships and local employment initiatives.' A report of the EEC Task Force on medium and small businesses (unpublished).

Sengenberger, W., Loveman, G. W. and Piore, M. J. (eds) (1990) *The Re-emergence of Small Enterprises*, Geneva: International Institute for Labour Studies.

White, L. J. (1982) 'The determinants of the relative importance of small business', *Review of Economics and Statistics*, February.

Williamson, O. E. (1975) *Markets and Hierarchies: Analysis and Anti-Trust Implications*, New York: Free Press.

—— (1985) *The Economic Institutions of Capitalism*, New York: Free Press.

You, Jong-il (1995) 'Small firms in economic theory: a survey', *Cambridge Journal of Economics*, 19(3): 441–62.

36

WHEN WORKERS SAVE NOTHING AND CAPITALISTS CONSUME EVERYTHING

Was Kaldor right about why Latin America had such poor savings performance?

Gabriel Palma

GROSS NATIONAL SAVINGS IN LATIN AMERICA

One of the most striking phenomena of post-Second World War economic development in Latin America – and one of the many issues which I have discussed with my friend Geoff Harcourt, to whom I dedicate this chapter (a fellow post-Keynesian who also thinks that savings matter!) – is Latin America's systematic poor savings performance. In fact, one of the main economic arguments in favour of the neoliberal economic reforms recently implemented in the region was that (mainly through financial 'deepening' and the liberalization of the capital account) these reforms should be able to lift the savings performance of the region significantly. However, with the exception of Chile (and even in this case, only since the late 1980s, over a decade after the beginning of the reforms, and after the implementation of drastic tax reforms), savings, particularly private savings, have been particularly 'sticky' in Latin America (ending up, if anything, even lower after the first wave of neoliberal reforms).

Latin America's savings efforts have been particularly poor when compared with those in East Asia. It is well known that there has for a long time been a contrasting economic performance between Latin America and East Asia, and in particular between Latin America and the four 'first-tier' newly industrializing countries (NICs).[1] The different economic performances between these two groups of countries can be traced to many different economic, political and institutional variables, but probably none more important than their respective national savings and investment rates.

Figure 1 shows that while in the 1950s and early 1960s the share of national savings in GNP was substantially higher in Latin America than in the NICs, in the late 1980s and early 1990s in Latin America this rate was less

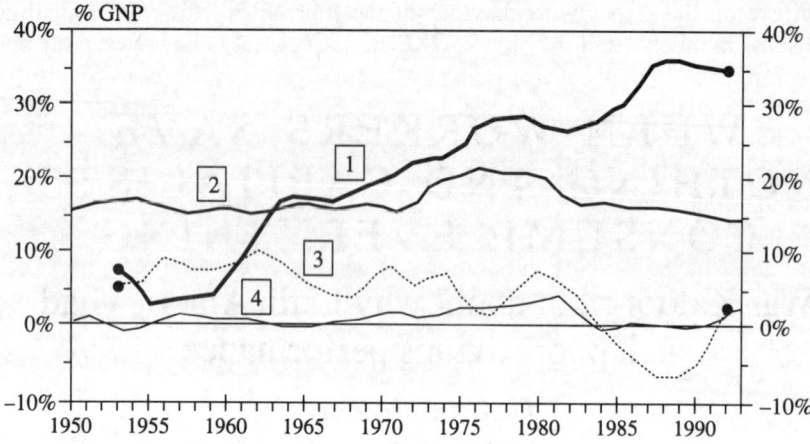

Figure 1 Latin America and NICs: gross national and foreign savings, 1950–93
(constant 1980 prices, 3-yr moving averages, % GNP)

[1] Gross national savings rates in the NICs.
[2] Gross national savings rates in Latin America.
[3] Foreign savings rates in the NICs.
[4] Foreign savings rates in Latin America.

National savings for the NICs are data for Korea between 1953 and 1960, and for Korea and Hong Kong thereafter; the World Bank does not provide these data for Taiwan or Singapore.[2] Foreign savings for the NICs are data for Korea between 1953 and 1960, and for Korea, Hong Kong and Singapore thereafter. The figures for the NICs are unweighted averages, and those for Latin America are weighted averages (unless otherwise stated, this will be the case throughout this paper for all averages of both regions).

Sources: Data on Latin America: the Statistical Division of the United Nations Economic Commission for Latin America and the Caribbean (ECLAC); data on the NICs: Korea's National Accounts, for Korea between 1953 and 1960, and for all countries thereafter, the World Bank database. Unless otherwise stated, these are the sources for all data in this paper.

than half that of the NICs. Figure 1 also shows that in GNP terms both groups of countries had a substantial degree of access to external resources; for the NICs this was much higher in the 1950s, 1960s and 1970s, while Latin America had a substantially larger one in the 1980s and early 1990s (although part of it was simply forced rescheduling of existing foreign debt).

In terms of gross fixed investment one also finds a similar comparative picture between these two groups of countries. As in gross national savings, Latin America's investment figure in 1993 was only half that of the NICs, having been substantially higher in the 1950s and early 1960s. The 1980s and 1990s investment figures for Latin America are particularly poor for machinery, equipment and infrastructure (the 'capacity building' investment), and substantially better for residential construction. The net investment figures for Latin America are even more disappointing.[3]

The main aim of this chapter is to study some issues related to the growth (or lack of it) and the structure of Latin America's savings, always keeping an eye on the respective behaviour of the four NICs. However, I shall not discuss in much detail the obvious (Keynesian) causal links between the poor performance of both savings and investment in Latin America (other than when discussing the corporate profit-savings-investment nexus), nor the traditional set of variables which are inevitably included in studies of savings behaviour of the region (such as the roles of slow economic growth, demographic variables related to the life-cycle hypothesis, the 'depth' of the financial sector, interest rates, inflation and political instability). These variables have normally appeared significant but still unable to 'explain' a substantial amount of savings behaviour in Latin America.[4] From this point of view, the aim of this paper is more restricted than that of a comprehensive macroeconomic analysis of these issues, trying (following Kaldor's writing on the subject) simply to look at what I believe to be some of the key 'stylized facts' of Latin America's savings, which are often missing from other studies on the subject. In order to do this, I shall study the different behaviour of household and corporate savings, look at the role of income distribution on savings, that of the consumption pattern of the elite, the effects of the post-1982 neoliberal reforms, and the apparently growing degree of 'crowding-out' between different components of savings (not just between private and public savings). Finally, I shall discuss the recent increase of savings in Chile, which followed a 'Kaldorian' type of fiscal reforms implemented in 1984 aimed at improving the country's extremely poor corporate savings performance.

WHAT HAPPENED TO SAVINGS IN LATIN AMERICA?

The main problem of most studies on savings in Latin America is the unreliable nature of the savings data. The basic issue is that savings are inevitably calculated as a residual, and as such, inherit all the statistical problems of other components of national income, in particular of investment.[5] One example of these problems is shown by what happened recently in Chile. In 1992 the Central Bank published a new set of national accounts. One of the consequences of these changes was that the share of gross fixed capital investment in GDP at current prices jumped, on average, by about 30% in the eight years in which both national accounts overlap (1985–92). As gross domestic savings are assumed by definition to be equal to gross domestic investment (gross fixed investment plus changes in stocks), domestic savings increased proportionately. Furthermore, as the new savings and investment figures were only recalculated back to 1985, and the old accounts were stopped in 1992, at the moment there are no consistent data for a meaningful study of Chile's medium- or long-term savings and investment performance. For this reason, I have not included Chile's official data in the household and corporate savings figures below, and have discussed this country separately

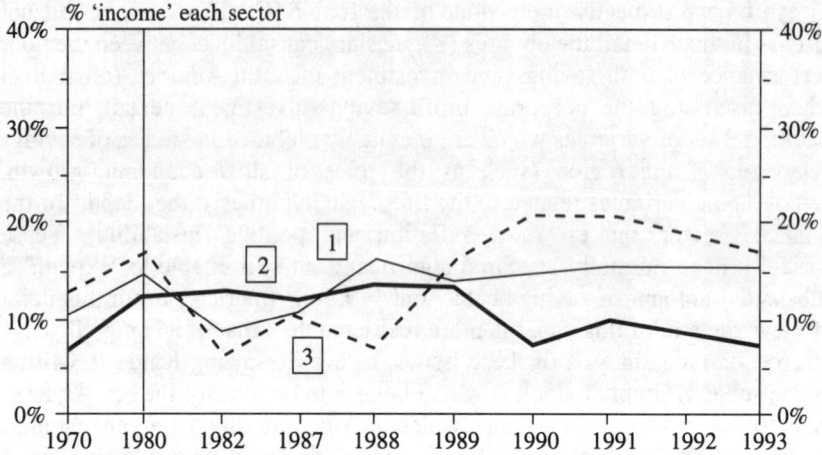

Figure 2 Latin America (6): corporate, household and government gross savings as percentages of respective 'incomes', 1970–93 (current prices, median values)

[1] Corporate savings as a proportion of after-tax profits.
[2] Household savings as a proportion of households' disposable income.
[3] Government savings as a proportion of government revenues. After-tax profits were calculated by adding corporate savings to 'net property and entrepreneurial income' of the household sector (this is a proxy for distributed profits); corporate sector includes all the business sector. Household income is defined as household consumption plus household savings (i.e., it is a measure of household disposable income). Finally, government income is total government revenues. As two of the six countries are oil-exporters with large economic fluctuations during this period, I have chosen throughout this paper, median values as the most representative statistics for the region.

(using, when possible, additional information, mainly of a microeconomic nature).

The changing structure of Latin America's savings

One issue that it is important to discuss is whether the low national savings rate of Latin America is the result of low savings propensities of *all* sectors of the economy (households, corporations and governments), or whether there are important differences between them. Figure 2 illustrates this issue, showing the savings propensity (out of respective 'incomes') of each of these three sectors in 1970 and in the period between 1980 and 1993 in the six Latin American economies in which I have been able to disaggregate private savings between households and corporations (Colombia, Ecuador, Paraguay, Peru, Uruguay and Venezuela).

The crucial issue shown by Figure 2 is the collapse of household savings in the 1990s (to about half their relative levels through most of the 1980s, both before and after the debt crisis, to a level similar to their 1970 level).

464

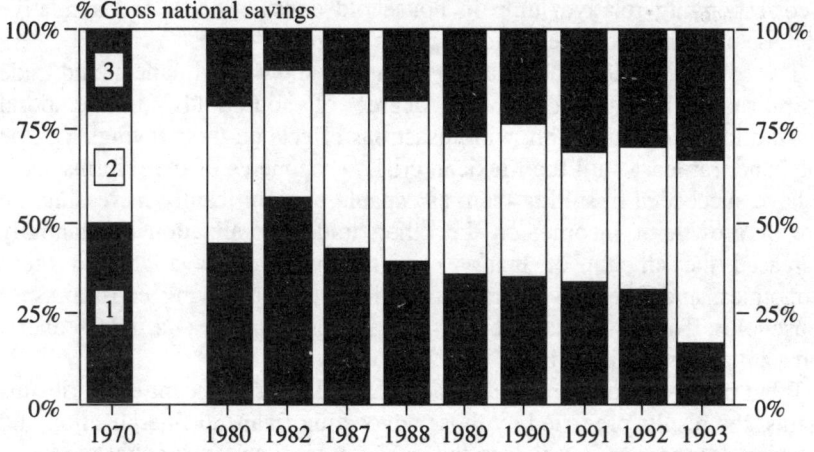

Figure 3 Latin America (6): shares of gross corporate, household and government savings in gross national savings, 1970–93 (current prices, median values)
[1] Household savings.
[2] Corporate savings.
[3] Government savings.
The countries included are the same as in Figure 2.

Corporate savings, in turn, returned in the 1990s to their (pre-crisis) 1980 level, and government savings had a substantial improvement in the late 1980s. This is a curious picture, because so far the neoliberal reforms do not seem to have made much of an impact on corporate savings, they have brought down significantly the savings propensity of the household sector, and have made (in relative terms) the government the key saving agent of these economies.

Partial evidence of other Latin American countries seems to corroborate this picture which, as we shall see below, is very different from the one found in the NICs. Figure 2 also shows the necessity of having to disaggregate private savings between its two components (households and corporations) due to the growing differences in their savings behaviour. Failing to do this has been one of the main reasons why most econometric studies on private savings in Latin America have only been able to 'explain' a small proportion of its (aggregate) variance. This issue becomes even more obvious in Figure 3, which shows the structure of Latin America's savings that emerges from these different savings propensities.

In the case of Latin America, between 1970 and 1980 the share of both household and government savings decreased relative to corporate savings. This pattern changed significantly with the debt crisis of 1982, but in 1987 the structure of national savings had returned roughly to the pattern of 1980. However, thereafter, there is a collapse of household savings (and, obviously, a corresponding relative jump in household consumption), and a relative increase of both government and corporate savings.

The collapse of household savings seems to show that financial and trade liberalization have increased the degree of households' intertemporal substitution in consumption, with disastrous effects on their savings. On the one hand, (at least until the Mexican crisis) proponents of the reforms seem to have succeeded in selling them as capable of significantly increasing the rate of growth of income; on the other, trade liberalization substantially increased the amount of luxury consumption goods available in these economies, and financial liberalization lifted the borrowing constraints of households. The result was a boom in their consumption and indebtedness, and a collapse in their savings.

What makes the above phenomenon particularly significant is that it runs against the results predicted by those advocating financial liberalization and financial 'deepening' ever since the publication of the influential works of McKinnon and Shaw in the early 1970s. In fact, by making credit too easily available for consumption purposes in the household sector (and increasing expectations of future incomes unrealistically), these reforms seems to have reduced household savings to such an extent that in many countries investment and economic growth have been seriously affected.[6]

An extreme case of low household savings in Latin America is found in (of all countries) Chile, where this figure has in fact been systematically negative. However, the peculiar case of Chile is that this phenomenon does not seem to have been a major constraint on investment and growth since the late 1980s (although there is ample evidence that it had a negative effect on investment and growth in the first decade of the reforms).

In the case of Chile, trade and financial liberalization (and an overvalued rate of exchange) brought down household (and corporate) savings to such an extent in the 1970s that private savings (household plus corporate savings) became negative even *before* the 1982 debt crisis (−3.2% of GDP in 1981, falling to −6.5% of GDP in 1982). The post-debt-crisis period has been characterized both by a substantial recovery of corporate sector savings (if these data were correct, corporate savings in Chile today would be at East Asian levels), and by the fact that household savings were still negative in 1994 (not a very East Asian phenomenon). Furthermore, household savings were still negative in 1994, despite the fact that these data include contributions to the new private pension funds (equivalent to approximately 4% of GDP).

Data from the NICs show that not only have all three sectors of the economy substantially increased their level of savings, but that the key difference with respect to Latin America (and particularly to Chile) in terms of national savings is in the household sector. This does not mean that there is not also a substantial difference in the role of corporate savings in economic growth in both regions (through a very different profit-savings-investment

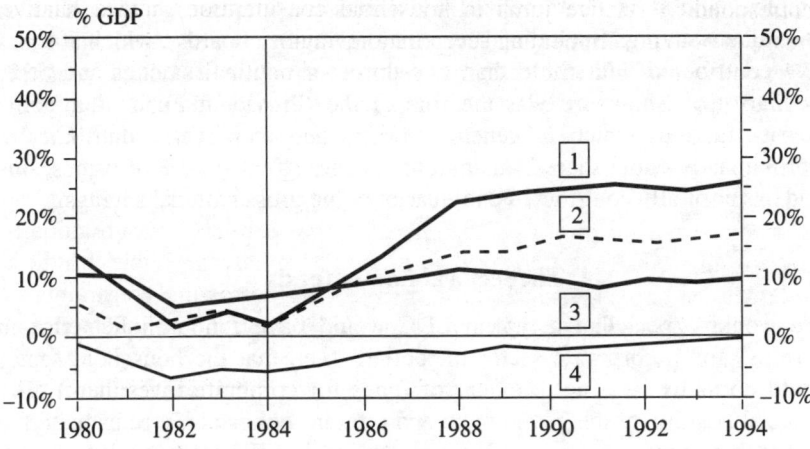

Figure 4 Chile: gross national, corporate, household and government gross savings, 1980–94 (current prices, % GDP)

[1] Gross national savings.
[2] Corporate savings.
[3] Government savings.
[4] Household savings.
Source: P. Arrau (1995). Figures from 1980 to 1984 are taken from the old national accounts, while those from 1985 to 1994 are from the new national accounts; as a result, the two sets of figures are not comparable, particularly for corporate savings.

nexus), but that at least in terms of magnitude, the largest difference is in household savings. In the case of Korea, for example, household savings represented a relatively low share of national savings in 1970 (less than 20% of the total), but ended up providing almost half of total national savings in the 1990s. This is exactly the opposite case of the six Latin American countries discussed above (where, in 1970, household savings represented nearly half of total savings but in 1993 contributed hardly more than one-tenth of the total). As is well known, the increase in the NICs' household savings propensities often came hand in hand with 'forced savings', in the form of increased social security contributions, (price) restrictions on luxury consumption, and credit rationing for consumption and mortgages lending. However, the Korean government also encouraged 'voluntary' savings of the household sector by developing attractive long-term savings schemes. The increase in the savings of the corporate sector also came about with different forms of incentives and pressures from the government.[7]

The changes in the savings structure of Taiwan are similar to those of Korea. The special characteristics of the Taiwanese financial sector (as in Korea) seem to have had a large responsibility for this phenomenon of a large increase in the share of household savings.[8] The case of Singapore is more complex, and it is characterized by a massive increase of the share of government savings (including seven major statutory boards), which at times have contributed with more than two-thirds of national savings.[9] Another peculiarity of Singapore was the role of the 'Provident Fund' – a social security fund to which in general workers and employers contribute, in approximately equal shares, an amount between 40% to 50% of wages; this fund has normally contributed one-quarter of the gross national savings.

The sectoral flow of funds

One would expect that a typical LDC would have a household sector in 'surplus' and a corporate sector in 'deficit' (i.e., that the household sector would normally be a net provider of funds for corporate investment). The financial position of the government and foreign sectors could be expected to change between countries and along the cycle. The case of Korea, for example, is an extreme case of this 'normal' situation, with the household

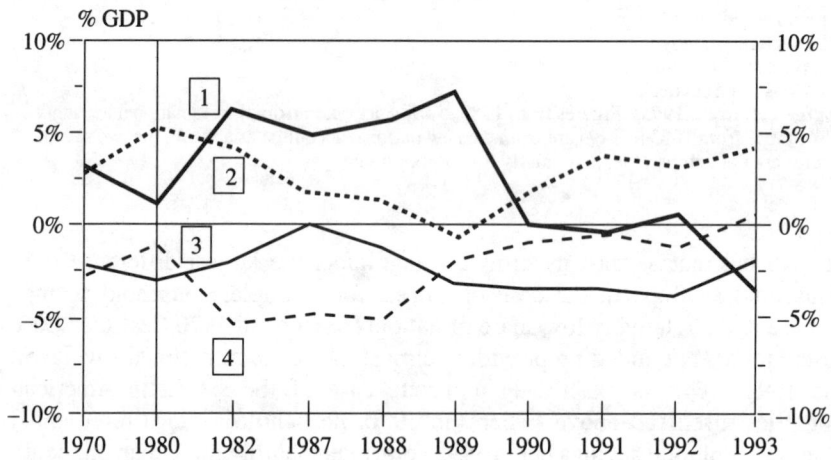

Figure 5 Latin America (6): sectoral surpluses of the corporate, household, public and foreign sectors, 1970–93 (current prices, median values, % GNP)

[1] Household sector.
[2] Foreign sector.
[3] Corporate sector.
[4] Government sector.

The 'surplus' of each sector is its savings minus investment, expressed as a percentage of GNP; that of the foreign sector is the share of foreign savings in GNP. Stocks are not included in investment, therefore all four 'surpluses' do not add up to zero. When the figures for residential construction were not available, the private sector investment figures were disaggregated (following the evidence of the countries where these data were available and the advice of national account experts of ECLAC) into 30% coming from the household sector and 70% from the corporate sector.

sector at a substantial surplus (about 7% of GNP in the second half of the 1980s and early 1990s), the government also being in surplus (at about 3% of GNP in this period), and a corporate sector being a large user of funds from the other sectors (with a deficit of approximately 10% of GNP in this period).[10] Latin America, however, is a weaker case of this 'normal' situation.

When the economies of Latin America started to recover from the debt crisis in 1987, all seemed to go back to pre-crisis trends. This crisis had had the effect of reducing both the foreign surplus and the small deficit of the corporate sector (this deficit actually disappeared), and of substantially increasing both the deficit of the government sector and the surplus of the household sector. With the recovery, the corporate sector deficit grew again (although not by very much), the government deficit began to close rapidly, and the foreign sector surplus began to increase as foreign capital returned to the region. However, the surplus of the household sector not only declined, but it actually disappeared altogether, to end up with a clear deficit in 1993. In fact, by then, an amount equal to *all* the surplus of the foreign sector was being absorbed by the deficit of the household sector.[11]

In terms of flow of funds, Chile presents a different picture from the rest

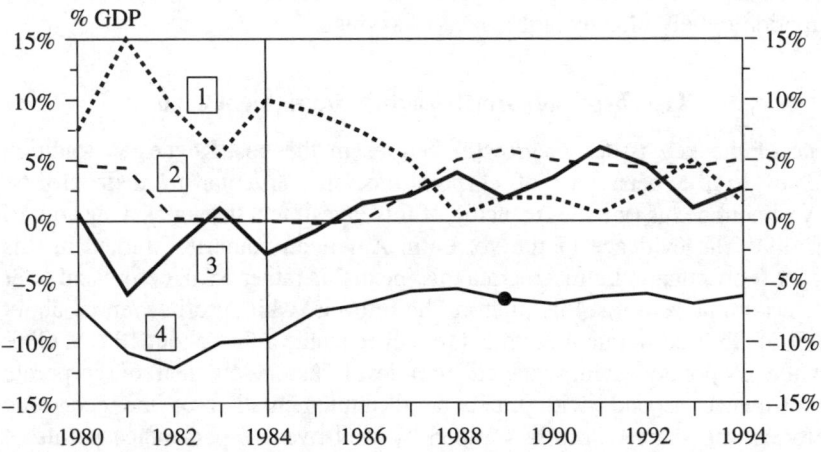

Figure 6 Chile: sectoral surpluses of the corporate, household, public and foreign sectors, 1980–94 (current prices, % GDP)

[1] Foreign sector.
[2] Government sector.
[3] Corporate sector.
[4] Household sector.
Until 1987 household investment was equal to residential construction; after this date, as this information was no longer available any more, it was assumed (as in the case of the other Latin American countries above) to be equal to 30% of private investment (approximately equal to the share of residential construction in private investment before that date).

of Latin America and, particularly, from the NICs.

One of the most peculiar characteristics of the Chilean economy during the second half of the 1980s and early 1990s was that in terms of flow of funds, the household sector behaved in a way which one would have expected of the corporate sector, while the corporate sector did the opposite. As Figure 6 shows, it is the household sector which has a substantial deficit, while the corporate sector moved progressively into a substantial surplus! As there are problems with the corporate savings figures in Chile (mentioned above), I have also looked at this issue using the information which I have gathered from balance sheets of the fifty-eight largest private national corporations.[12] These data show that although this group of large corporations was actually in deficit when all their investment expenditures were taken into account (as opposed to the surplus shown in Figure 6), from the point of view of investment in *own* firm, there was a trend for them to be in surplus; i.e., their savings tended to be more than sufficient to finance the investment made in their own corporations. However, this emerging surplus was being used to finance their takeovers and investments in other firms. In any case, their overall deficits were not significant from the point of view of GNP (or even from the point of view of their output). This behaviour contrasts with that of the NICs, where the large corporations had levels of investment largely superior to their (already high) levels of savings.[13]

The corporate profits-savings-investment nexus

One of the key issues in growth theories in the post-Keynesian tradition relates to the behaviour of corporations, in particular to their profits-investment nexus (via the financing of this investment through savings out of profits). The evidence of the six Latin American countries studied in this paper shows that in Latin America this 'nexus' is rather weak before and after the economic reforms. First, before the reforms, while profits were at about 50% of GNP, corporate investment remained stable at just about 10% of GNP (while corporate savings stayed at a level just below that of corporate investment); second, with the general implementation of the economic reforms, the share of profits jumped by well over 10 percentage points of GNP, but corporate savings and investment hardly increased at all. This is not much evidence of a strong corporate profit-savings-investment nexus in either period. The evidence from the NICs shows a different picture, with a strong profit-savings-investment nexus.[14]

Chile's case since the late 1980s is different from that of the rest of Latin America, and in a way closer to that of the NICs. The same sample of large national private corporations mentioned above shows a much larger share of savings out of profits in the 1990s, when the trend (following substantial fiscal reforms in 1984 to encourage corporate savings) was towards saving almost half the profits in this sector. This was substantially higher than the savings rate of corporations in Chile before – for example, Figure 4 shows that in 1980 and 1981 (i.e., before the debt crisis) the corporate sector made practically no contribution to national savings – and higher than the median figure for all the business sectors in the six Latin American countries discussed above (in which only about 15% of profits were saved). This is probably one of the most important differences (if not the most important) between Chile and the rest of Latin America, and helps to explain both the recent better economic performance of Chile within Latin America, and the effectiveness of fiscal reforms (along Kaldorian lines, which will be discussed below) devised to encourage corporate savings.

The 'crowdings-out'

One of the characteristics of savings in Latin America after financial liberalization is that all sorts of 'crowdings-out' have emerged (or became stronger) between different components of domestic savings – 'crowding-out' understood here simply as negative correlations between different components of savings. Of course, these correlations do not necessarily imply causality, but they are so strong that more research is needed to explain them.

The most famous crowding-out of them all in the recent economic literature is that between private and public savings – the famous 'Ricardian equivalence'. Data on Chile since the beginning of the neoliberal economic reforms, for example, show a clear negative correlation between these two components of national savings.[15] Another, and often forgotten, crowding-out is that between private and foreign savings; this was particularly strong in the late 1980s and 1990s in Latin America, but in Chile commenced with the beginning of the reforms in the early 1970s. As is well known, foreign savings can have a positive effect on national savings via a positive income effect: by lifting a possible foreign exchange constraint on growth, the resulting increase in income can encourage national savings. However, it can also have a negative 'substitution effect' on national savings, as in Latin America after the economic reforms; the case of Mexico is a telling one.

Mexico, like most of Latin America, has had two major periods of inflow of foreign capital, 1973–81 and 1987–94. Figure 7 suggests that during the 1970s the positive income effects of foreign savings on growth and national savings seem to have dominated (a time of foreign exchange constraints), while after trade and financial liberalization, the negative substitution effects seem to have become very strong. This phenomenon is reflected in the fact that during the first period of inflow of foreign capital, national savings also increased (a phenomenon that did not take place in Chile, which was already embarked on its economic reforms), while in the second period they collapsed, especially private savings. This phenomenon was already evident above with a strong negative correlation between the surplus of the household sector and that of the foreign sector in the 1980s (see Figure 5 above).

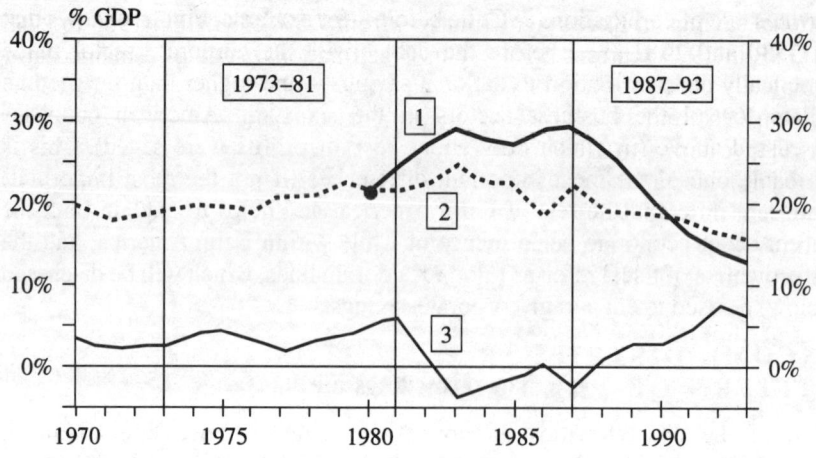

Figure 7 Mexico: gross national, private and foreign savings, 1970–93 (current prices, 3-yr moving averages, % GNP

[1] Private savings.
[2] National savings.
[3] Foreign savings.
Figures for private savings are only available from 1980.

As Figure 1 above shows, apparently a relatively similar crowding-out is found in the NICs before and after 1980. Before this date, the positive income effect of foreign savings seems to have dominated, while after 1980, a clear negative correlation also developed between national and foreign savings (i.e., a strong substitution effect), although in the case of the NICs (as opposed to Latin America) this negative correlation in the latter period was between a rapidly *rising* national savings and a *declining* foreign savings.

Savings and income growth

For a long time, savings studies of Latin America have expressed surprise at the fact that income does not appear to be as significant a variable as might have been expected, and that the marginal propensity to save in Latin America is very small. Also, per capita GDP growth tends to be positive and significant in most private savings equations, but when a Latin American dummy is included in panel data, its coefficient is negative. This implies that in Latin America income growth does not positively affect private savings as strongly as in other regions of the world. The corresponding studies for the NICs show the opposite phenomena.[16]

The most revealing comparison in this respect is between Brazil and Korea during the period 1965–80. During this decade and a half Brazil grew at a rate similar to Korea (8.3% per year); however, while fast rates of growth lifted national savings in Korea significantly – from 7.5% of GNP in 1965 to 27% of GNP in 1979 (current prices) – in Brazil national savings remained at a completely constant share of GNP during this high growth period (20.2% of GNP in 1965 and 19.2% of GNP in 1980, current prices). In fact, in Brazil (in relative terms to GNP) it was foreign savings alone which during this period provided all the additional requirements of investable resources needed to sustain this rapid rate of growth. That is, the share of savings in GNP in Latin America does not seem to be able to rise even when these economies are growing at the NICs' rate.[17]

INCOME DISTRIBUTION AND THE CONSUMPTION PATTERN OF THE PROPERTY-OWNING CLASS; AN ANALYSIS ALONG KALDORIAN LINES

Probably the first major economist to argue that there was something peculiarly wrong with savings and investment in Latin America was Nicholas Kaldor in the 1950s.[18] He first discusses this issue in an article on the economic problems of Chile, which he wrote during a visit to that country in 1956, as a consultant to ECLAC. The essence of his analysis of the obstacles to Chile's economic development can be summarized in two propositions. First, Chile's low rate of accumulation was not the result of an insufficient capacity to generate investable resources, but of the peculiar consumption, savings and investment behaviour of the local property-owning class. Second, Chile's persistent inflation had not provided the economic environment conducive to fast and sustained economic growth.

The study of the Chilean economy raised some new hypotheses that became central in Kaldor's work on developing countries concerning the violation in the LDCs of the traditional post-Keynesian assumptions of the savings behaviour of the capitalist class. In particular he stressed the contrast between the disproportionately high share of profits in Chile's national income and the strikingly low level of private saving.

> [The] high propensity to consume of the capitalist class [can be found in the fact that they] appear to have spent on personal consumption more than two-thirds of their gross income, or three-quarters of their net income after tax. In comparison to other countries, the luxury consumption of the property-owning classes appears to take up an altogether disproportionate share of national resources, part of which would be automatically released for investment purposes if a more efficient system of progressive taxation were introduced and/or if effective measures were taken to encourage the retention of profits by enterprises.
>
> (1956: 266)

These measures could boost savings without the need to reduce workers' income, or requiring large capital inflows from abroad. According to Kaldor, therefore, the Chilean capital class was the weakest link in the country's economic structure and the productive mobilization of the resources wasted by this sector deserved to be a first priority in the formulation of economic policy. This phenomenon of a low propensity to save on the part of the Chilean capitalist class in a context of an increasingly unequal income distribution clearly contradicted the popular view that (through its supposedly positive effect on saving) worsening income distribution was a necessary condition for growth in LDCs.

To put Chile's income distribution and the consumption pattern of the capitalist elite into the perspective of the experience of developed countries, Kaldor compared it with the corresponding figures for the US and the UK. He concluded that

> The most important difference is that in Chile the personal consumption of property owners appears to take up 21.2% of national resources, [but] in Great Britain it appears to take up only 7.4%. Since in Britain the category of property owners includes a relatively large number of small rentiers (which does not appear to be the case in Chile) the implication is that the proportion of national resources engaged in producing goods and services for the luxury consumption of the well-to-do is at least three to four times as high in Chile as Britain.
>
> (*Ibid.*: 26)

This finding convinced Kaldor that for developing countries with these characteristics he had to use a different theoretical framework than the one he had hitherto used in his work on growth and income distribution in industrial economies.[19] In Latin America, government intervention, particularly through taxation of distributed profits and an effective investment policy by the public sector, was the most appropriate way to achieve a dynamic equilibrium. In other words, what Kaldor proposed were institutional changes that would both force Chile's business sector to increase its savings, and make the Chilean public sector both a high-saving (through higher taxation) *and* a high-investing affair.

In relation to the first issue raised by Kaldor, I have shown elsewhere that there is no evidence whatsoever that high inequality has been an incentive for savings in LDCs.[20]

The second issue discussed by Kaldor on Latin America's savings was the high propensity to consume of the region's capitalist class. Figure 8 shows that during this period Latin America had by far the highest income elasticity to consume (and the lowest to invest) in the Third World.

Keynes had stated in 1936: 'The fundamental psychological law [...] is that men are disposed, as a rule and on average, to increase their

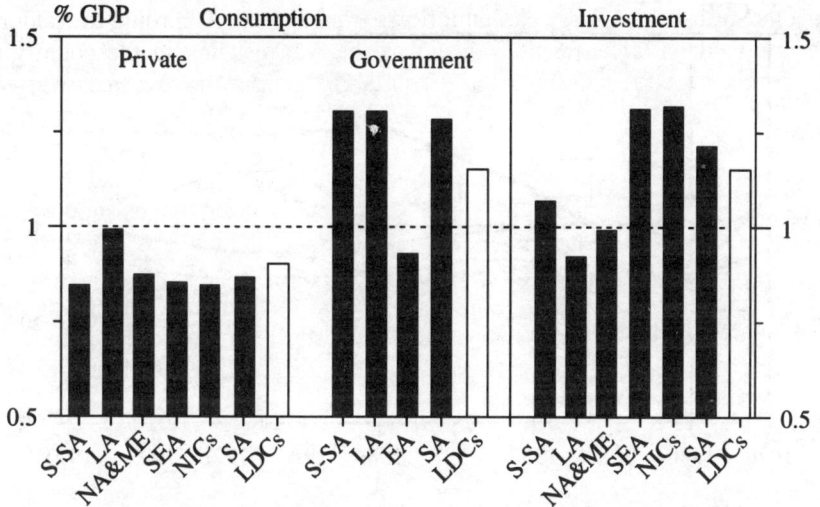

Figure 8 LDCs: income elasticities to consume and to invest, 1965–90 (ratios of average annual growth rates of private consumption and gross domestic investment to GDP)

S-S A = Sub-Saharan Africa; LA = Latin America; NA&ME = North Africa and the non-oil Middle East; SEA = South East Asia excluding the four 'first-tier' NICs; NICs = South Korea, Taiwan, Singapore and Hong Kong; and SA = South Asia, including China. The groups of countries are grouped according to their level of inequality in the 1960s.

Sources: Income distribution data from Palma (1994); this paper uses ECLAC sources for Latin America and mainly World Bank data for the rest of the LDCs. (There are no data on income distribution for the oil-Middle East.) Data on consumption and investment are from the World Bank database.

consumption as their income increases, but not as much as the increase in their income'.

Well, maybe he was not properly acquainted with Latin America!

However, Kaldor's point concerned not just the high propensity to consume in general in Latin America, but that of the capitalist class in particular. As mentioned above, he was concerned that in Chile (in the 1950s) the capitalist class consumed about two-thirds of their gross income. This share was substantially higher than in OECD countries. However, data on the six Latin American economies studied in this chapter show that only in Colombia and Uruguay did the capitalists consume less than 90% of their gross income – but even in these, this share was rising towards the 90% level of the capitalist classes of Ecuador, Peru and Paraguay. In Venezuela, as household savings were negative in 1993, given our assumption that only capitalists save (and dis-save), their consumption in 1993 was 10% greater than their gross income. The data that are available for a comparison with

475

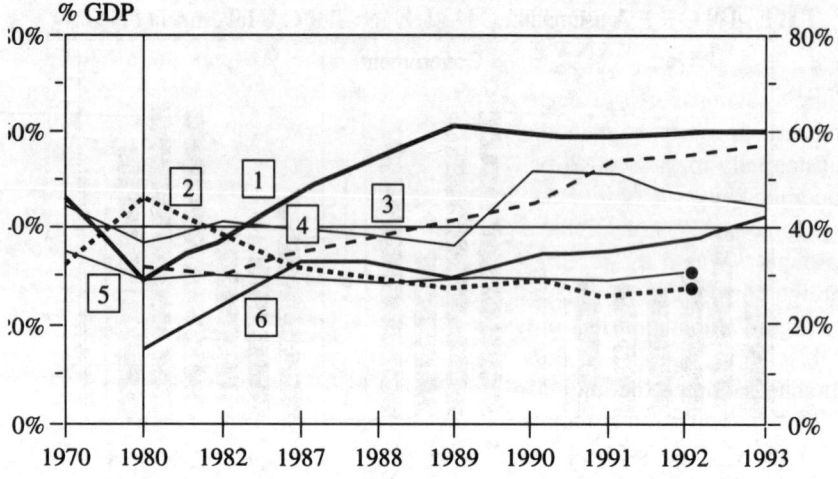

Figure 9 Latin America (6): share of consumption of recipients of property and entrepreneurial income in GNP, 1970–93

[1] Ecuador.
[2] Uruguay.
[3] Peru.
[4] Paraguay.
[5] Colombia.
[6] Venezuela.

Consumption of recipients of property and entrepreneurial income is defined as total 'net property and entrepreneurial income' in the household accounts, minus *all* household savings (that is, it is assumed that only capitalists save in the household sector; therefore, these figures, if anything, would tend to underestimate the share of consumption in GNP of the capitalist group in these countries). Their income is defined as 'net' in national accounts in the sense that the income that they receive after their corporation or other business has paid capital gains taxes, but before they have paid their direct income tax as households; in other words, it is the gross income received by property owners and entrepreneurs from their business.
Source: Each country's national accounts, and ECLAC Statistical Division

NICs and OECD countries show that the corresponding ratios are only a fraction of those in Latin America. Figure 9 looks at the shares of consumption of the capitalist elite in terms of GNP.

Kaldor was concerned that in Chile capitalists used 21% of GNP for their consumption. (The corresponding figure for the UK at that time was 7.4%.) At the end of this period, in Ecuador and Peru, this group was using around 60% of GNP for this purpose, and in Paraguay and Venezuela over 40% of GNP. In the two more moderate cases, Colombia and Uruguay, this ratio was about 30% of GNP. Furthermore, in three economies, Ecuador, Peru and Venezuela, consumption by capitalists doubled in terms of its share of GNP between 1980 and 1993 (when these three economies had fully embarked on their neoliberal reforms).

THE INCREASE IN CHILE'S PROFIT-SAVINGS-INVESTMENT NEXUS

Chile's savings performance continued to be poor after Kaldor's visit, but, in contrast to what happened in the rest of Latin America, it improved substantially in the second half of the 1980s. From the point of view of this paper the key issue of interest is what was it that brought the national savings rate to about 25% of GNP (in the definition of savings of the new national accounts)? Was it the rapid economic recovery (helped enormously by high foreign borrowing *after* the debt crisis, when national savings were so low), the high 'animal spirits' prevailing in the country (particularly after the plebiscite in which the democratic opposition, in order to bring down Pinochet, adopted the main aspects of the economic reforms; this resulted in a large consensus on economic policy, unprecedented in the country), or the 1984 and 1993 tax reforms along 'Kaldorian' lines? I shall concentrate on the analysis of the latter issue.

No major tax reforms took place between Kaldor's visit in 1956 and the mid-1970s. The orthodox economic team of the military regime, which had taken power after the *coup d'état* of 1973, attempted to integrate the many reforms which had been introduced piecemeal in the previous twenty years, and introduced some new ones. As a result, a general reform of taxation took place in 1975. Among other measures, the wealth tax was eliminated, and the wholesale tax was replaced by a VAT of wide coverage. However, from the point of view of savings, the most significant reform was one that actually gave tax incentives to corporations *to distribute all profits*. The idea was twofold; on the one hand, following the letter and the spirit of the Modigliani–Miller theorem, they believed that a reduction in corporate savings would not affect corporate investment; on the other, if corporations distributed all their profits, the stock exchange would be strengthened and become an attractive place for savings from the household sector. However, the effect of this measure was a massive reduction in corporate savings and investment, and a massive increase in corporate debt (which left this sector in a very vulnerable position during the 1982 debt crisis).

After the 1975 reform, the public sector and public enterprises were incorporated as taxpayers into the system and, in 1981, the government began to reduce direct taxes. Nevertheless, these cuts had to be reversed in 1983 owing to the severity of the economic crisis which had started the year before, the worst since the 1930s. At the same time, the social security system was privatized, adding an enormous weight to the budget during the long transition period. However, as the crisis that had started in 1982 deepened, and as private sector savings collapsed even further (as mentioned above, private savings had already become negative before the 1982 crisis; see Figure 4 above), in 1984 the military regime was forced to implement a new tax reform – quoting (of all people) Kaldor's authority[21] – that contradicted most of its original rigid monetarist conceptions. This was done through the partial transformation of the current income tax into an expenditure tax. The main 'Kaldorian' way through which the 1984 reform attempted to encourage savings was a new mechanism by which, if the recipients of distributed profits left these funds in the company (in a special account), they would not be taxed on them. The same procedure applied if these funds were invested in another company. There were many tax advantages for individuals and for firms, under this scheme.[22]

The 1984 reform dramatically increased the amount saved from corporation profits (and on top of their own savings, corporations helped to make additional savings from their 'undistributed–distributed profits' accounts). However, household savings continued to be negative. The new democratic regime continued this Kaldorian policy and made a similar reform in 1993 trying to lift household savings, which still remained negative; the main instrument was also to switch part of income tax of non-profit income from income to expenditure.[23] By 1994 household dis-savings had been reduced to just 0.5% of GNP.

The Chilean tax system today looks, therefore, substantially different from the one that prevailed at the time of Kaldor's visit, and the main 'Kaldorian' tax reforms to encourage savings have been a great success, first increasing savings out of profits, and then out of other types of income. It took thirty years for this key issue of Kaldor's recommendations to be implemented, but he has been fully vindicated. However, the realization that it took so long for his key (and most obvious) policy proposal to be implemented is rather depressing – particularly when similar policies had already proved so successful in the NICs for much of this period.

The key issue is that the property-owning classes of Latin America do not appear to be satisfied with having for their own consumption the same *relative* amount of resources as their counterparts in the industrial countries: they persist in trying to have the same *absolute* amount, even if this means having to use up to 60% of GNP for this purpose! While they have proved to be unsophisticated in their forms of production – and certainly in their politics – they obviously like to be very sophisticated in their pattern of consumption. It has proved very difficult, taken a long time, and it has required a Kaldorian tax reform just to start changing this aspect of the Latin American bourgeoisie.

SOME CONCLUDING REMARKS

Basically, as the NICs have shown since the 1960s, and Chile after the Kaldorian tax reforms implemented in the mid-1980s, in terms of savings, policy matters. Savings do not seem to increase very much 'voluntarily' or 'spontaneously': they need both the whip and the carrot. In the NICs these have taken the form of forced household savings (particularly through increased social security contributions and restrictions on mortgage lending), price and credit restrictions on luxury consumption, attractive long-term returns on savings, tax incentives for corporate savings and high government savings.

This experience of the NICs has not only shown that in order to achieve fast and sustained rates of economic growth, national savings should increase significantly, but also that there are alternative ways of achieving this goal; for example, in Korea and Taiwan the emphasis of increasing the quantity of savings has been placed on the household sector, while in Singapore it has been on central government and public corporations.

In the case of Latin America, only in Chile have savings increased after the implementation of economic reforms, but it took over a decade for this to happen. It also required a massive economic crisis for the authorities to realize that something drastic needed to be done to increase corporate savings (by then, practically non-existent), and that the way forward was a Kaldorian type of tax incentive on corporate savings.[24] In the rest of Latin America, on the whole still stuck in the original version of the neoliberal reforms, savings performance is in most cases extremely poor, particularly household savings. The effects of rigid trade and financial liberalization has proved to be a significant step backwards in this respect, as the figures above show.

This paper has also shown that there are variables that seem to affect savings significantly which have been ignored by most savings studies so far. First, by attempting to explain private savings as a whole, they have ignored the fact that household and corporate savings have had almost opposite behaviours in Latin America. Second, they have also not taken sufficiently into account (if at all) variables such as the consumption pattern of the elite, income distribution, the weakness of the corporate profit-savings-investment nexus, and other 'crowdings-out' than the traditional private–public savings one; there seems to be ample evidence that these variables have influenced savings significantly. Third, normally, the effects of the neoliberal reforms (particularly on household savings) have not been properly isolated.

It has also become evident that there are so many problems with data on savings and other relevant variables in Latin America that priority should be given to both improving traditional savings statistics and obtaining new micro-data (like balance sheets information for corporations) to complement them; until then, the econometrics of Latin America's savings will inevitably be seriously impeded (with the added risk of actually being misleading).

Finally, the main positive lesson from Latin America so far comes from Chile over the last decade: a switch from income tax towards some form of expenditure tax à la Kaldor seems to be able both to lift corporate savings rates, and to make the corporate profits-savings-investment nexus a more dynamic engine of growth. However, the household sector has proved to be a much more difficult sector to tackle, and financial and trade liberalization have not helped in this respect either. Not even the development of private pension schemes, as the Chilean data show, has been able to increase household savings by a substantial amount; in fact, so far it has been more effective in lifting government savings (to pay for the transition period from one pension scheme to another). In terms of household savings, as long as the consumption pattern of the Latin American bourgeoisie continues to have a 'discreet charm' which is income and price inelastic, the NICs' forced savings solutions may be the only way forward.

NOTES

1 Republic of Korea, Taiwan, Hong Kong and Singapore. On average, Latin America started the postwar period with a substantial advantage over the NICs in terms of income per capita (approximately 50% larger), but ended up in the 1990s with one only about one-third that of the NICs – i.e., in these four decades the NICs increased their relative income per capita *vis-à-vis* Latin America by a factor of 4.5. However, there were important differences within Latin America in their relative performance *vis-à-vis* the NICs; for example, Brazil and Mexico had a better performance (with a relative GDP per capita drop *vis-à-vis* the NICs of a factor of about 2.5), while Argentina had an abysmal one (a relative drop by a factor of almost 7; from an income per capita 3.3 times larger to one just about half that of the average NIC).

2 However, other sources show a similar, if not faster, rate of growth of national savings for Taiwan and Singapore; see for example Liang (1981) and Huff (1995), respectively.

3 For a detailed study of Latin America's investment performance during this period, see Palma (1995). See also Agosín (1995).

4 See, for example, Held and Uthoff (1995) and Edwards (1995).

5 For a comprehensive methodological discussion on savings, see Held and Uthoff (1995); see also Palma (1996).

6 Two recent econometric studies support this view; see Japelli and Pagano (1994) and Schmidt-Hebbel *et al.* (1992).

7 See, for example, Wade (1990); World Bank (1993); and Chang (1994).

8 See, for example, Liang (1981); and Wade (1990).

9 Huff (1995).

10 See, for example, Palma (1996).

11 Figure 5 also shows that there has been a clear negative correlation between the household and foreign surpluses (a phenomenon that does not occur in the NICs). This phenomenon is particularly marked in the Latin American countries which applied extreme forms of financial liberalization, like Argentina, Mexico and Peru.

12 For a detailed analysis of these data see Palma (1996).

13 See, for example, Jang (1995).

14 See, for example, Jang (1995); Singh (1995); and Akyüz and Gore (1994).

15 See Palma (1996).

16 See, for example, Liang (1981); and Edwards (1995).

17 Chile needed 'Kaldorian' tax reforms in the mid-1980s to break this savings 'barrier'. See below.

18 Kaldor (1956).

19 Particularly his most extreme assumption of his model – 'workers save nothing

and capitalists consume nothing' – had to be drastically changed to 'workers save (almost) nothing and capitalist consume (almost) everything'.

20 See Palma (1994).

21 Kaldor was amused when he learned from his old Chilean friend Alfonso Santa Cruz that the military dictatorship (quoting his name) was attempting to introduce a form of expenditure tax to encourage savings by corporations: 'It is ironical [Kaldor wrote to Santa Cruz] that a government such as yours should take up my ideas from 25 years ago. When I elaborated them I certainly thought that it would be a very left wing reform which could only be carried out by a left wing government' (Kaldor to Santa Cruz, 29 May 1982).

22 One of the obvious advantages for individuals was that since the marginal rate of taxation was still progressive (up to 45%), there was an incentive to make deposits of this kind in years of high levels of income, and to withdraw funds in years of lower levels of income. In the case of firms, one advantage was that, as these funds had to be adjusted for inflation, such adjustments could be deducted as an operating cost.

23 For example, if part of any type of income was saved under certain conditions, it would be taxed only when withdrawn from these savings schemes. Also, there were new tax incentives to delay the withdrawal of funds from pension funds.

24 In Mexico, it was only after the December 1994 débâcle that the government finally decided to implement a policy package to lift private savings rates, which at the time of the crisis were at only one-third of their pre-reform levels.

REFERENCES

Agosín, M. (1995) 'A tale of two regions: investment in Latin America and East Asia', *Estudios de Economía*, June.

Akyüz, Y. and Gore, C. (1994) 'The investment–profits nexus in East Asian industrialisation', UNCTAD Discussion Papers No. 91.

Arrau, P. (1995) 'Evolución de la tasa de ahorro nacional en Chile: 1980–94', mimeo, Santiago.

Chang, H.-J. (1994) *The Political Economy of Industrial Policy*, New York: St. Martin's Press.

Edwards, S. (1995) 'Why are savings rates so different across countries?: An international comparative analysis', *NBER*, April.

Ffrench-Davis, R., Muñoz, O. and Palma, G. (1994) 'The Latin American economies, c.1950–c.1990', *Cambridge History of Latin America*, Vol. 6, Cambridge: Cambridge University Press.

Held, G. and Uthoff, A. (1995) 'Indicators and determinants of savings for Latin America and the Caribbean', ECLAC Working Papers, No. 25.

Huff, W. (1995) 'What is the Singapore model of economic development?', *Cambridge Journal of Economics*, 19 (November).

Jang, H.-W. (1995) 'Phases of capitalist accumulation in Korea and evolution of government strategy, 1963–1990', unpublished D. Phil. thesis, Oxford University.

Japelli, T. and Pagano, M. (1994) 'Savings, growth and liquidity constraints', *Quarterly Journal of Economics*, February.

Kaldor, N. (1956) 'Economic problems of Chile', ECLAC, mimeo; also in *El Trimestre Económico*, April–June 1959; reprinted in *Essays on Economic Policy II*, London: Duckworth.

Lawson, T., Palma, G. and Sender, J. (eds) (1989) *Kaldor's Contribution to Political Economy*, London: Academic Press. (Also in *Cambridge Journal of Economics*, Kaldor's Memorial Issue, April 1989).

Liang, M. (1981) 'Savings in Taiwan: an empirical investigation', *Journal of Economic Development*, Vol. 6.

Marcel, M. (1987) *Social Security, the Consumption Function and Macroeconomic Analysis*, Cambridge: Cambridge University Press.

—— and Palma, J. G. (1988) 'Third World debt and its effects on the British economy: a southern view on economic mismanagement in the North', *Cambridge Journal of Economics*, September.

Palma, G. (1994) 'Income distribution and growth: a false dichotomy', mimeo.

—— (1995) 'Savings and investment in Latin America since the neo-liberal economic reforms', UNCTAD Discussion Papers, forthcoming.

—— (1996) 'Whatever happened to Latin American savings?: Comparing Latin American and East Asian savings performances', UNCTAD Discussion Papers, forthcoming.

—— and Marcel, M. (1989) 'Kaldor on the "discreet charm" of the Chilean bourgeoisie', *Cambridge Journal of Economics*, Kaldor Memorial Issue, April. Also in T. Lawson, G. Palma and J. Sender (1989) *Kaldor's Contribution to Political Economy*, London: Academic Press; *El Trimestre Económico*, October 1989 and *Colección Estudios*, CIEPLAN, March 1990.

Schmidt-Hebbel, K. *et al.* (1992) 'Household savings in developing countries', *World Bank Economic Review*, September.

Singh, A. (1995) 'How did East Asia grow so fast?', UNCTAD Discussion Papers No. 97.

Wade, R. (1990) *Governing the Market*, Princeton, N.J.: Princeton University Press.

World Bank (1993) *The East Asian Miracle: Economic Growth and Public Policy*, Oxford: Oxford University Press.

37

GROWTH AND EMPLOYMENT

An interpretation of some fundamental transformations in the OECD countries

Ferdinando Targetti

GROWTH AND EMPLOYMENT IN THE CAMBRIDGE OF THE 1970S AND IN THE GROWTH MODELS

I arrived in Cambridge in 1972 armed with a degree from Bocconi, where for two years my economics had been Walras and Pareto in their reinterpretation by Professor De Maria, and an examination course in Keynesian economics during which Professor Lunghini conducted a seminar on the theory of capital. It was this seminar that prompted me to depart for Cambridge, where I had the good fortune to be taught by Geoff Harcourt who was in Cambridge on sabbatical. Thanks to him I gradually absorbed 'Cambridge economics'. I also had the fortune to converse with Piero Sraffa and to attend the lectures of Joan Robinson, Maurice Dobb, Dick Goodwin, Luigi Pasinetti, Pierangelo Garegnani, Mario Nuti, Frank Hahn, Bob Rowthorn, John Eatwell, Ajit Singh and especially Nicholas Kaldor, whom I gradually realized had the most to teach me, with his incomparable ability to grasp the salient facts of economic and social reality and to use theory in their interpretation.

I remember that the 'young' lecturers, and Harcourt at that time was among them, were not sparing in their criticisms of Kaldor's theory of growth with distribution and technical progress, despite their admiration for him personally. One of his ideas that even then aroused criticism concerned employment, and specifically that in a Keynesian model of growth, equilibrium was full employment equilibrium. In Kaldor's various models, full employment was sometimes hypothesized, sometimes explained, but it always appeared in the result. However, debate on the issue was not particulary intense because this was still the golden age of the growth of the developed countries, though it was now drawing to a close (unbeknown to us, however). One of the stylized facts of this period consisted in evidence that, except during downturns in the cycle, output growth proceeded *pari passu* with employment growth, and that this, in the long period, seemingly absorbed the large increase in the labour supply. Only with the passage of time was it realized that growth without employment was not a transitory cyclical phenomenon; it had become a constant feature in the bulk of the industrially developed countries. As early as the early 1980s, before the OECD recognized the phenomenon of 'jobless growth', Kaldor confided in me that the main flaw in his growth models was their (unnecessary) hypothesis of full employment.

Modern growth models, of course, derive from Harrod's pioneering work. In his model, full employment is one possible case among many. In Joan Robinson's models there is a whole range of situations in which growth is stable or unstable, and even when steady, with or without full employment. Disequilibrium in the labour market (overemployment or underemployment) triggers a set of backwash effects on the growth of capital, none of which is determined *a priori* because it may happen that no significant feedback occurs and growth remains stable in underemployment.

Unlike the approach of Harrod and Robinson, which identifies a series of growth paths and which I would therefore call 'open and non-determinate', the Solow–Swan neoclassical growth model is what I would term 'closed and determinate', because it envisages a single stationary state equilibrium growth rate over the long period: i.e. a full employment growth rate. Full employment is not hypothesized *à la* Kaldor, but is a necessary consequence of the working of the model. The most recent vintage of growth models (see Targetti 1993) contests the Solow model (though deriving from it) in its result that the propensity to save does not determine the rate of income growth. The idea underlying this new approach is that the accumulation of capital, whether physical or human, generates positive externalities, and that technical progress is endogenous and depends on accumulation itself. The problem of the relationship between growth and employment does not explicitly arise in these new models. In Solow's model, an accumulation of capital at rates higher (lower) than the rate of growth of the labour supply gives rise to decreasing (increasing) returns on capital and to a slowdown (acceleration) of economic growth. If, instead, the accumulation of capital exhibits positive externalities, decreasing returns on capital are reduced or eliminated, and in this case the economy may grow without being constrained by the labour supply, on account of endogenous technical progress. But what happens if the accumulation rate is lower than the rate of growth of the labour supply? Whether in this case the feedback mechanism is that imagined by Solow or whether it is some other mechanism, these authors, to my knowledge, do not tell us. However, it is my impression that this new approach envisages a range of returns to scale which contrast more or less markedly with the decrease in factor returns. They can therefore be identified as 'open' models which, like the Cambridge models, may incorporate cases of growth without full employment.

A recent example of this is provided by Aghion and Howitt's (1994) neo-Schumpeterian model. According to these two authors, technical progress performs a role of creative destruction: the higher it is (because of investments in R&D), the greater is economic growth, but also the greater is the obsolescence of human capital. Since skilled workers cannot be employed in the sector which produces using unskilled labour, an inverse relation is created between growth and employment, and steady state growth may be greater than is socially optimal. This is an interesting line of inquiry, although at its present stage of development it is unsuitable for explanation of one of the principal stylized facts of the growth of industrialized economies: namely that the last twenty years have seen a fall in both the rate of employment growth and the rate of output growth compared with the previous twenty-year period.

Mention should also be made of a recent contribution by Pasinetti (Pasinetti 1993) which also belongs, I believe, to what I have called the 'open and non-determinate' approach. Pasinetti develops a model of multisectoral economic growth with technical progress, variability over time in the composition of final demand and growth in the labour supply. He identifies a function which represents the macroeconomic condition for equilibrium full-employment growth. Maintaining full employment depends on the relationship among four functions expressing population growth (demographic aspect), the growth of the level of demand (macroeconomic aspect), change over time in the composition of consumption (structural aspect), and the variation in labour inputs per unit of output (technical progress aspect). Pasinetti does not explore – deliberately – the feedback mechanisms on final demand and on production techniques (and on their evolution) engendered by situations of over- or under-employment. His model sets out, in fact, the conditions that must hold for 'balanced' growth to come about, leaving it open as to whether or not they actually arise.

We have therefore seen that there are 'open and non-determinate' theories of growth which employ models yielding a wide range of interweavings between employment and growth, and others which are more 'closed and non-determinate' in nature and which give priority to a growth-determining factor and a re-equilibrium mechanism which leads to the disappearance of unemployment from the growth process. These latter models advance the claim typical of scientism that they possess predictive power, albeit in the long (or extremely long) period. However, since the phenomenon of growth-with-unemployment has arisen and arises in the industrialized countries with an intensity which varies greatly in time and space, one may conclude that 'deterministic' theories are unable to handle it. I believe that growth models should more modestly seek to provide an array of historico-interpretative tools for use by the analyst; tools which can be validly used in a certain period but not in those that preceded or followed it. Analytical effort thus shifts to a search for the factors that account for transition between historical phases.

This is essentially the goal set itself by the French regulation school (Boyer and Saillard 1995), which investigates the phenomena of long-term growth and the crises that mark the passage between the historical phases of the developed capitalist economies. These authors have been closely influenced by Kaldor's theories; and, for my part, many of the arguments set out in this article have in turn been influenced by them.

GROWTH AND STRUCTURAL CHANGE

More than twenty years have passed since the first oil shock; an event, with its indubitable importance, which has long attracted the attention of observers; observers, however, who only subsequently realized that events much more profound than a temporary alteration in the form of the energy sector market were changing the economy of the developed countries. Three brief factual statements highlight the reversal of tendency of the last twenty years. In the OECD countries the long-period growth of output and productivity has decreased by 50% and this applies, though to differing extents, to every macro-area of the OECD: the USA, the EC and Japan (Table 1). And if instead of considering the economy as a whole, one examines only the industrial sector, the phenomenon is even more striking. Simultaneously, unemployment has arisen from an average value of 10 million (in the period 1950–73) to almost 35 million people (1994).

Table 1

	Growth of output (% p.a.)			Growth of productivity (% p.a.)		
	1960–73	1973–83	1983–93	1960–73	1973–83	1983–93
OECD	4.8	2.2	2.8	3.6	1.4	1.9
USA	3.9	1.8	2.7	1.9	0.1	1.2
Japan	9.6	3.5	3.6	8.2	2.6	2.5
EC	4.5	1.8	2.3	4.1	1.9	1.8

Source: OECD, *Employment Outlook*, various years

The unemployment rate has grown principally in Europe. In the period 1950–73 European unemployment was steadily around two million and American unemployment oscillated around five million. In the subsequent twenty years European unemployment grew steadily from two to twelve million; USA employment oscillated around seven million. Therefore an interpretation of the phenomenon has been put forward which, to my mind, is highly reductive, though it predominates in academia and the international agencies. I refer to the claim that the increase in the average unemployment rate has been caused by a structural upturn in the NAIRU (whereby more unemployment is required to curb inflationary wage demands by workers), and that the widening gap between Europe and the USA in the unemployment rate is due to the greater rigidity of the European labour market compared with the American one.

The alternative interpretation that I wish to propose has other theoretical foundations, ones which reflect what I have called 'Cambridge economics'. The 'model' is based on three forces:

- The productivity function, according to which the rate of growth of labour productivity may be broadly divided into two parts: one induced by the growth of output (the parameter linking these two magnitudes is the well-known Kaldor–Verdoorn coefficient); and another, separate from it, attributable to inventions or technical–organizational innovations and independent of the growth of production.
- The demand function which reflects in Keynesian fashion the relation between growth of output and the growth of effective demand which, in its turn, is a function of income distribution.
- Sectoral change – i.e. the variation over time in the relative weights of the three great production sectors (agriculture, industry and services) – which depends on the change over time in the composition of demand and on the differing impact of technical progress on each sector.

TWO HISTORICAL PHASES

Prior to 1973, the forces stylized in the model operated in the industrially developed countries as set out below.

The first period

The productivity function in the first period

In the period considered, goods were highly standardized, and so too were production methods. Firms set themselves the goal of reducing costs rather than improving the quality of the goods produced. Hence derived marked economies of scale, both dynamic and of size in the economic system, and a pronounced increase in productivity generated by learning by doing the same goods on an increasing scale. Under these circumstances the induced component was especially important: roughly speaking, in this period the Kaldor–Verdoorn coefficient for the OECD countries was higher than 50% (Kaldor 1966).

The demand function in the first period

A form of income distribution arose during the period considered which remained steady because productivity increases were translated into higher real wages by those employment-regulating institutions that sociologists call 'neo-corporative'. Higher wages gave rise to stable and high final demand for

consumption goods, and this engendered a proportional growth of investments according to the accelerator principle: under oligopolist competition
(competition for market shares) firms invested so that their productive
capacity could keep pace with the growth in demand.

These forces operated at the level of the countries as a whole. Explanation of
the differing growth performances of individual OECD countries lay instead in
the diverse distance between the country considered and the technological
leader country (Targetti and Foti 1996) and in the differing effects in each
country of the balance of payments constraint (Thirlwall 1979; Targetti 1991).

Sectoral change

In the early postwar period, the OECD area saw increased employment in the
services sector and also – owing to the strong growth of industrial output –
increased employment in the industrial sector itself (Figure 1 for the USA and
the EC). Employment growth (in absolute value and in percentage share) in
the industrial and falling employment in the agricultural sector helped to
induce the high average productivity growth of the countries considered.

The share of the labour force employed in the services sector was
constantly in growth, because of three factors. The first was the growth of
demand for services with respect to goods (Engel's law in the proper sense).

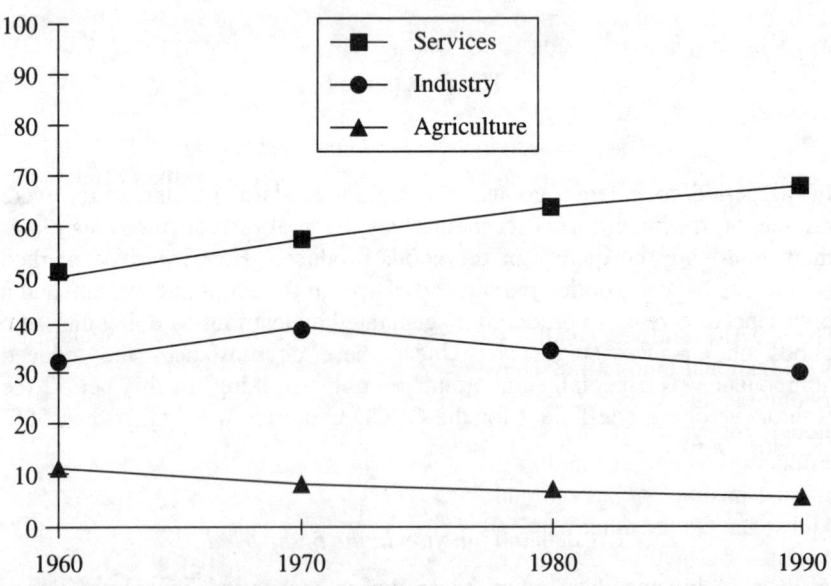

Figure 1 Variation in employment in the three sectors (average percentages of the
labour forces in the United States and the EC), 1960–90
Source: Elaboration of data from OECD, *Employmnt Outlook*, various years

The second factor was that, while the growth of output in the industrial sector created little extra employment, because it brought a considerable increase in productivity, output growth in the services sector largely resolved itself into employment growth. The third factor was the growth of value added, and therefore of employment, produced by the public sector because of the spread, in all the OECD countries, of welfare state services financed out of only slightly increasing fiscal pressure on a rapidly expanding GDP.

In the 1950s and 1960s, therefore, these forces interwove to generate a virtuous circle (especially in the European countries and Japan) which brought world capitalism to its maximum rate of multi-decade expansion in the presence of almost full employment. Indeed, the growth in labour supply due to demographic growth (the baby boom), to the increased activity rate (labour-market entry by women), to the expulsion of labour from agriculture, and to indeed technical progress, was matched in this period by a corresponding growth of labour demand not only in the sector of private and public services but also in the industrial sector, which, though generating labour-saving technical progress, also generated net labour demand because of the high increase in the production of goods.

The second period

I now turn to the last twenty years, a period which has witnessed sustained change in the forms assumed by growth in the OECD countries. The long-term rate of income growth has fallen by more than half compared with the previous period, and so too has the average rate of growth of labour productivity, while the average unemployment rate has tripled.

What is the interpretation offered by this model? I shall consider first the interweaving of forces activated by the productivity and demand functions, and then discuss sectoral change.

The productivity function in the second period

The 1970s, and especially the 1980s, were years of great technical-organizational innovation. They were the years of the electronic information revolution; the years of firms' organizational innovation called the Toyota model; the years of the search for 'total quality', meaning a change in production techniques and in quality controls on goods produced; the years of 'just in time' organizational techniques to keep stocks to the minimum. And so on. On the other hand, as we have seen, they were also years in which the rate of growth of total average productivity declined in all the economic areas considered, compared with the previous twenty-year period. This contradiction takes the name of 'Solow's Paradox' but it is a paradox which can be explained in terms of this model. In fact, all the innovations considered above take largely the form of an exogenous growth of productivity.

Therefore the autonomous component of technical progress has grown while the induced component has simultaneously shrunk, owing to the fact that the Kaldor–Verdoorn coefficient, as well as the rate of output growth itself, has decreased.

The demand function in the second period

The rate of output growth has fallen because, in the 1970s, the mass production/mass consumption equilibrium broke down. Two important macro-phenomena emerged, the first being the dwindling of the wage share. As OECD data clearly show, since 1973 in all the OECD areas, although to different extents, wage shares have tended inexorably downwards (North America 1973–94 from 69% to 67%; EC 1975–94 from 71% to 63%; EFTA 1978–94 from 74% to 68%) (OECD 1994). This is not to imply that real wages have not increased, only that they have increased less than the growth of labour productivity. There has thus come about a breakdown in the dynamic equilibrium established in the golden age of growth and which conveyed an increase in productivity (via wage increases and extensive investments) into an increase in output.

The second phenomenon is the changed form assumed by the investment function. In the golden age of growth, as said, the accelerator mechanism predominated. Firms saw profit not as an objective to maximize but as a financial constraint to respect. In the more recent period the degree of national and international competitiveness has increased. Very probably the changed exchange rate regime since the collapse, in 1971, of the Bretton Woods fixed exchange system, increasing international capital mobility and the lifting of customs barriers, are the main causes of this different competitive regime. The fact is that investment decisions have changed: the maximization of profit has now become the principal goal of investment, which is undertaken less to adjust productive capacity (extensive investment) than to introduce techniques which cut costs, in particular labour costs (intensive investment).

The circle has thus closed: in the golden age, output growth brought productivity growth with it, but also wage and therefore demand growth, and this induced extensive investments which sustained the high level of growth. More recently, increased competitiveness has induced firms to undertake intensive investments which increase productivity and profits; the wage share has diminished and with it demand; extensive investments and the growth of output have fallen, and so too has the rate of growth of labour productivity induced by output growth.

The two functions of technical progress and of demand can be graphically represented on a Cartesian plane, with the rate of growth of output on the horizontal axis and the rate of growth of productivity on the vertical axis. With the passage from the first to the second period the curves shift and change their slope: the demand function becomes steeper because the same increase in productivity translates into a lower increase in demand; the productivity function increases the intercept, representing autonomous technical progress, but it reduces the slope (the Kaldor–Verdoorn coefficient diminishes). The dynamic equilibrium point is at a lower rate of growth of output and productivity despite a higher rate of autonomous technical progress: the Solow paradox is thus explained, and the basis is laid for explanation of increased unemployment.

Sectoral change in the second period

In the most recent twenty-year period, therefore, because of the changed interweaving of forces, there has been a fall in the rate of growth of both output and productivity; but the former rate has declined more than the latter, the result being that the capacity of economic expansion to create work has declined not only because of a fall in the rate of output growth but also because of the lesser capacity of output growth to create jobs. This is especially true of the industrial sector, where one notes a cyclical asymmetry: in the lower phases of the cycle industrial employment is reduced by a lack of demand; in the higher phases, it is not increased, on account of the introduction of labour-saving technical progress (Lunghini 1995). It is this phenomenon that the OECD calls 'jobless growth' (OECD 1986).

One therefore has a rate of growth of labour supply which is positive because of demographic causes and because of the higher rate of female activity. But, on the other hand, labour demand continues to fall in the agricultural sector, stagnates in the industrial sector and is absorbed mainly in the tertiary sector (Figure 1).

THE DIFFERENT MODELS OF THE USA AND EUROPE

The phenomenon of jobless growth differs from one area to another. One finds differing trends in Europe and the USA as regards not only the unemployment rate but also and especially the rate of employment growth: taking the level of employment in 1960 = 100 in both areas, in 1973 North America was 130 and the EC 105; in 1993 respectively 180 and 110. The first finding to stress is that, in the United States, despite the fact that the 1980s were years in which the rate of productivity growth revived after a period in which it came close to zero, productivity continued to grow at rates lower than European ones (Table 1). This was less the case in the industrial sector, but it holds especially true at the level of the economy as a whole.

The explanation for the diverse growth of productivity and employment in the two areas lies, I believe, in the different operation of sectoral change and of tertiarization in each (Petit 1993). Employment in the tertiary sector has increased more in the United States than in Europe (taking 1970 = 100, employment in the tertiary sector in 1990 was over 160 in the USA and 140 in the EC) (OECD various years), but in the United States this sector displays much lower growth of per-capita income and productivity than it does in Europe (Figure 2). Therefore, compared with Europe, tertiarization the United States acts more as a sponge which absorbs labour expelled from the industrial sector, but it widens the gap among wages. In Europe, by contrast, the services sector exhibits an income and productivity growth which is much higher than in the USA and less distant from industrial growth.

Considering that in Figure 2 'tertiary sector' refers to the sum of the private and public service sectors, we may therefore say that the more rapid growth of the tertiary sector in the USA in the last twenty years has taken place despite the lower growth of social services in this country in comparison with Europe, where they have been mainly supplied by the public sector.

In this restricted setting one may accept the contention of orthodox economists that the different unemployment rates in Europe and the USA are due to greater wage elasticity on the other side of the Atlantic. This elasticity entails, however, a wider differential between higher- and lower-paid workers in the USA than in Europe: in the USA high wages are nearly seven times higher than low wages; in the EC they are nearly three times higher (OECD 1993). This elasticity also implies that lower-paid workers will suffer a long-period cutback in their pay, as happened in the USA in the 1980s (in the 1980s

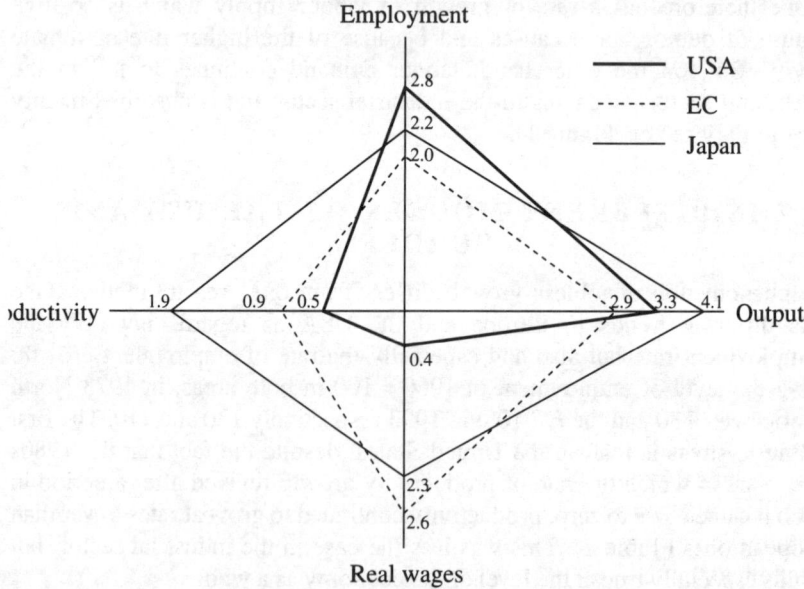

Figure 2 National dynamics in the growth of the tertiary sector, 1973–90 (yearly growth rates)
Source: Elaboration of data from OECD, *Labour Force Statistics*, 1991

pay fell at a rate of more than 1% per year in the USA, while it rose at a rate between 1% and 3% in the various European countries) (*ibid*). Given the importance of labour income in the national income, inequality in labour incomes signifies a more unequal distribution of incomes in the overall economy (Freeman 1994).

Thus delineated is a comparative USA/Europe picture in which the American economic area has higher employment and greater disparities in the distribution of incomes, while Europe has lower employment and less inequality. Another factor responsible for this dichotomy is the foreign trade relationships between the two areas and the developing countries (DCs).

THE DCS AND EMPLOYMENT IN THE INDUSTRIALIZED COUNTRIES

Between 1970 and 1993 the share of world's exports of manufactures by the DCs rose – mainly on account of the growing industrialization of the Asiatic countries – from 5% to 22% with increasing marginal rates from 1975 onwards. This suggests that this progressive competitive encroachment by the DCs on the rich and industrialized countries is bound to continue. The increased penetration of our markets by goods from the DCs, and the greater attractiveness of the DCs' markets for investments by firms of the rich countries, has aroused fears that the phenomenon will bring high unemployment in the developed countries and widening wage disparities between highly skilled and unskilled workers.

The issue is widely debated. On the one hand the free-traders argue as follows: (a) the export of manufactures is the main route to the industrialization of the DCs, and trade barriers erected by the rich countries would be an intolerable betrayal by the rich of the poor; (b) the process will slacken when strong labour demand in the DCs causes wages in those countries to grow and to converge on decreasing wages in the rich countries (the Stoppler–Samuelson theorem); (c) although driven by exports, income growth in the DCs, especially in large countries like India or China with enormous internal markets, will engender analogous growth in their imports from the rich countries, so that, because of this international multiplier, income and employment should increase in the latter as well; (d) in the rich countries, the importing of cheap goods from the DCs produces the same effects as labour-saving technical progress; consumers in the rich countries will buy cheaper labour-intensive goods, and the workers in the rich countries thus 'freed' from the production of these goods can be used to produce goods requiring greater capital input in the sense of physical, organizational and human capital (Ricardo's thesis of the advantages of international trade).

For all these reasons, many economists and many institutions, the World Bank for instance, predict that the acceleration of economic growth in the DCs will place the entire world economy, including the OECD countries, on a growth path higher than it was in the last twenty-year period (the World Bank estimates this differential at a one-half decimal point per year).

By contrast, there are economists and politicians who argue exactly the opposite. Celebrated economists like Maurice Allais in France, Nobel prize-winner for economics in 1988, trade unionists and politicians like Ross Perot, opposed the signing of the NAFTA treatment for free trade among the USA, Canada and Mexico and view free trade between the developed countries and the developing countries – where labour is underpaid, non-unionized and without welfare state guarantees – as an 'unequal exchange' (the reverse of that feared by the third-worldist economists of the 1960s) which will deprive workers in the rich countries of jobs, trade-union protection and welfare guarantees.

Each of these positions captures one aspect of a complex problem. In the long period the change will be to the benefit of both parties to the exchange: China will industrialize thanks to the production of highly labour-intensive goods, and the OECD countries will profit from having trained and employed a labour force specialized in industrial production with high technological content. In the short period, however, the adjustment costs may be consider-able, and in some countries they may outweigh the benefits (although in these cases calculations in terms of social welfare are always difficult). Adjustment costs affect many social categories: those entrepreneurs who must close firms or even abandon entire production sectors; those redundant workers who remain unemployed because labour demand is for different and generally more specialized skills than they possess. They also affect those workers who, though still in employment, find their position worsening in terms of income with respect to better-skilled workers. (Note also that, in some developed countries, low-skilled workers will lose income and/or employment not only to higher-skilled workers in other developed countries, but also to Asian workers, who are both much cheaper – in China and India the hourly cost of labour in manufacturing industry is approximately 1 dollar as compared to 25 in Germany – and who also demonstrate an ability to learn new technologies in no way inferior to that of workers in the areas of earlier industrialization.)

Adrian Wood (1994) has estimated a negative occupational impact amounting to 20% of the unskilled jobs lost in the rich countries over the last thirty years. Internally to this group of countries, adjustment costs will take different forms: trade with the DCs will produce more unemployment or more wage disparity according to the greater (Europe) or lesser (United States and United Kingdom) rigidity of the labour market. As the importing of manufactures from the DCs increases in ratio to GDP, the share of manufacturing employment declines (Figure 3a). As we saw in the previous section, in the USA this phenomenon has generated sizeable occupational absorption in the services sector and a widening of wage disparities (Figure 3b); in Europe it has produced greater unemployment.

494

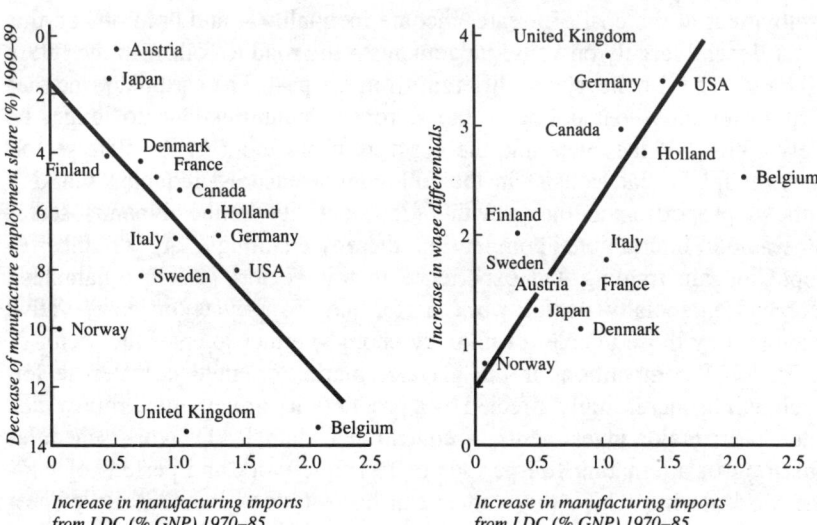

Figure 3 Imports from the developing counries, employment and wage differentials
Source: Wood (1994)

EMPLOYMENT PROSPECTS AND EMPLOYMENT POLICIES

It emerges from the foregoing argument that unemployment is not caused, *à la* Keynes, by a cyclical lack of effective demand; nor is it neoclassically due to a simple raising of the NAIRU. It is a complex phenomenon, the outcome of several causes which manifest themselves differently in the dynamics of different economies. In the past twenty years, the main reason for the onset of the problem of unemployment in Europe and of disparities in the distribution of income in the United States has been interweaving of four factors:

1   a slowdown in the economic growth of the OECD countries as a whole;
2   labour-saving technical progress, which has given rise to a growth of labour productivity more independent, compared with the previous period, from the growth of output;
3   different growths in the two macro-areas of productivity, of employment and of labour incomes in the services sector (which has grown into the economically most important sector in all countries);
4   diverse responses by the two macro-areas to penetration by goods from the DCs.

495

If a country does not wish to pursue the American path of higher employment at the cost of greater income inequality – and opinions on this matter depend largely on value-judgements – the road to follow in the future will have to be, I believe, one different from the past. The cardinal principles of future employment policy in the European countries can no longer be solely control of the cycle and the absorption of labour in the state sector. They should instead consist in the following measures: reducing working hours in proportion to the growth of productivity in the dynamic sector vulnerable to international competition, thereby enabling a larger number of people to gain training and experience in this sector; socially guaranteed incomes for socially useful work performed (in private or co-operative structures) by those unable (or unlucky enough) either to enter the sector of international competition or the private, market-oriented services sector, which will be increasingly affected by a productivity growth more robust than in the past; major investments in education and in R&D; work schedules consisting of alternating life periods of full-time work and periods of part-time work during which the worker can be re-trained into the use of new technologies; investments in infrastructures supporting the high-tech development of firms, along the lines suggested by the Delors Plan (European Commission 1994).

Once separate, growth theory and employment policies should in the future be much more closely interwoven.

REFERENCES

Aghion, P. and Howitt, P. (1994) 'Growth and Unemployment', *Review of Economic Studies*, 61.

Boyer, R. and Saillard, Y. (eds) (1995) *Théorie de la régulation. L'état des savoirs*, Paris: La Découverte.

European Commission (1994) *Growth, Competitivity and Employment*, Brussels.

Freeman, R. B. (1994) 'Jobs in the USA', *New Economy*, Spring: 20–4.

Kaldor, N. (1966) *Causes of the Slow Rate of Economic Growth of the United Kingdom*, Cambridge: Cambridge University Press.

Lunghini, G. (1995) *L'età dello spreco*, Turin: Bollati Boringhieri.

OECD (1986) (1993) (1994) *Employment Outlook*, Paris.

—— (1991) *Labour Force Statistics*, Paris.

Pasinetti, L. (1993) *Dinamica economica strutturale*, Bologna: il Mulino.

Petit, P. (1993) 'Competitivité et employe: les nouvelles dimensions sectorielles de la croissance', in Gazier, B. (ed.) *Employ, nouvelles donnés*, Paris: Economica.

Targetti, F. (1991) 'The economic instabilities of the 1980s', in J. Michie (ed.), *The Economics of Restructuring and Intervention*, Cheltenham: Edward Elgar.

—— (1993) 'Vecchie e nuove teorie della crescita: una rassegna', *Economica Politica*, 2 (August): 261–349.

—— and Foti, A. (1996) 'Growth and productivity. A model of cumulative growth and catching up', *Cambridge Journal of Economics*, forthcoming.

Thirlwall, A. P. (1979) 'The balance of payments constraint as an explanation of international growth rates differences', *Banca Nazionale del Lavoro Quarterly Review*, March.

Wood, A. (1994), *North–South Trade, Employment and Inequality*, Oxford: Oxford University Press.

38

ECONOMIC GROWTH AND THE BALANCE-OF-PAYMENTS CONSTRAINT REVISITED

John McCombie and Tony Thirlwall

INTRODUCTION

Solow (1983) once remarked that members of other academic disciplines regard economics with a certain degree of perplexity. While there are always disagreements at the frontiers of research, they are puzzled by the way schools of thought in macroeconomics describe alternative approaches as 'wrong from the ground up'. Growth theory provides a good example of this point, as there is still no consensus as to why growth rates differ, as evidenced by the antithetical neoclassical and Keynesian approaches.

On the one hand, neoclassical growth theory (whether of the 'old' or 'new' variety) places the emphasis on the growth of the exogenously given labour force, technical progress and capital accumulation (including human capital) as the determinants of economic growth. In this sense, it is a supply-orientated approach. Nations, or regions, are never restricted in their growth by a lack of demand, which is automatically created by the growth of supply. Most of the modelling in this tradition is within the context of a closed economy, and, when the interrelationship between regions or countries is acknowledged, it is simply to allow for capital and labour mobility. Under constant returns to scale this merely accelerates the rate of convergence in per capita incomes. Differences in per capita growth rates result from the eradication of an initial misallocation of resources, reflected in spatial disparities in the capital–labour ratios. (The theory is remarkably silent on why these misallocations arose in the first place.) Borts and Stein (1964) and Barro and Sala-i-Martin (1992) are representative examples of this approach. When increasing returns to scale are introduced, convergence does not occur and growth becomes polarized (Faini 1984; Romer 1986). Nevertheless, the emphasis remains firmly on the supply side.

On the other hand, the Keynesian approach argues that growth for a large number of advanced and less-developed countries is essentially demand or balance-of-payments constrained. Factor inputs are not seen as the exogenous determinants of growth, as in the neoclassical schema. In the advanced countries prior to 1973, labour responded endogenously to the growth of demand for it, either through the inter-sectoral transfer of labour from agriculture or through migration (the so-called 'guest workers'). (See Kindleberger 1967; Cornwall 1977; Kaldor 1978, and Van der Wee 1987.) The rate of capital accumulation is as much a result of the growth process as it is a cause of it, a result that is similar to the steady state growth of the neoclassical model. Since 1973, the slowdown in the growth of output across all the advanced countries has led to a marked increase in both recorded and disguised unemployment, so it is hardly plausible to give a causal role to the growth of the labour supply.

The answer given by the Keynesian approach to the question of why there are differences in growth rates is that a country's economic performance depends ultimately on its performance in the overseas markets. In other words, growth is export-led and the balance of payments can limit a country to a rate of growth well below that of its productive potential (Beckerman 1962; Thirlwall 1979).

In this paper, we present a brief overview of this explanation together with the empirical evidence which, we conclude, provides strong support for the model.

ECONOMIC GROWTH AND THE DYNAMIC HARROD FOREIGN TRADE MULTIPLIER

In this section we briefly outline a simple Keynesian model of long-run economic growth, where the balance of payments plays a crucial role (see Thirlwall (1979) and McCombie and Thirlwall (1994, especially chapter 3) for further elaboration).

We begin with the balance-of-payments accounting identity:

$$P_d X + F = E P_f M \tag{1}$$

where P_d, P_f and E are the price of exports in the domestic currency, the price of imports in the foreign currency, and the domestic price of foreign currency (the exchange rate); F is the value of nominal net capital flows; X and M are the volume of exports and imports. Equation (1) should include a term for interest payments on the net stock of overseas debt (and remitted profits and dividends). For the moment, we shall ignore this for expositional ease, but interest payments will be discussed below when the role of capital flows in relaxing the balance-of-payments constraint is considered.

The demand functions for exports and imports are given by

$$X = k_1 W^\varepsilon (P_d / E P_f)^\eta \tag{2}$$

and

499

$$M = k_2 Y^\pi (EP_f/P_d)^\psi \tag{3}$$

where W is 'world income' (excluding that of the country under considera-. tion), Y is domestic income, ε and π are the income elasticities of demand for exports and imports, and η and ψ are the appropriate price elasticities (η, ψ < 0). k_1 and k_2 are constants.

Taking natural logarithms of equations (1), (2), and (3), differentiating them with respect to time and substituting equations (2) and (3) into equation (1) gives:

$$y = [\varphi\varepsilon w + (1 + \varphi\eta + \psi)(p_d - e - p_f) + (1 - \varphi)(f - p_d)]/\pi. \tag{4}$$

The lower-case variables represent exponential growth rates. φ is the proportion of total foreign receipts accounted for by sales of exports (i.e., φ = $P_d X/(P_d X + F)$).

The growth of a country's income is a function of three components divided by the income elasticity of demand for imports. The first is the effect of world income on a country's growth rate; the second is the combined effect of the price elasticities and the rate of change of the terms of trade, and the third is the effect of the growth of real capital flows.

For economic growth to be potentially balance-of-payments constrained, the combined effect of the second two components must be quantitatively small. Under these circumstances, equation (4) (assuming no initial balance-of-payments disequilibrium) reduces to

$$y_B = \frac{\varepsilon w}{\pi} \quad \text{or} \quad y_B = \frac{x}{\pi} \tag{5}$$

where y_B is the balance-of-payments equilibrium growth rate.

Equation (5) may be interpreted as reflecting the working of the dynamic Harrod foreign trade multiplier or the Hicks super-multiplier (McCombie and Thirlwall 1994: chapter 6).

It may be seen from equation (5) that the growth of a country's income is determined solely by the ratio of the world income elasticity of demand for its exports to its income elasticity of demand for imports multiplied by the growth of world income. (Since the growth of the terms of trade are assumed to be unimportant, $\varepsilon w \simeq x$.) Estimates of ε show considerable inter-country variation and these disparities should be interpreted as reflecting differences in non-price competitiveness. Hence, although this approach is sometimes termed a 'demand-orientated' approach, it can be seen that the supply side, in the sense of the quality, reliability, and all the other factors crucial for non-price competitiveness, are of central importance in explaining economic performance. How may the balance-of-payments constrained growth model be evaluated? There are essentially two complementary approaches.

The first is to consider the available evidence as to whether or not changes in the exchange rate have any marked impact on the growth of exports and imports. Also, how important is non-price competition *vis-à-vis* price competition in international trade? This approach would also need to assess the evidence on the magnitude of capital flows between countries. Are they large enough and persistent enough to offset a lagging country's slow growth of foreign exchange earnings from exports?

The second approach is to test the model directly. This can be done by testing how well equation (5) explains the observed growth of income, using a cross-section of countries. Alternatively, equation (4) could be estimated by regression analysis using time-series data for countries individually.

We commence with the first method and a consideration of the role of price and non-price competition in international trade.

EXPORT PERFORMANCE AND PRICE VERSUS NON-PRICE COMPETITION

We do not argue that changes in relative prices, when measured in a common currency, have *no* effect on the balance of payments. Indeed, there are cases where a devaluation has undoubtedly improved the current account, for a given trend rate of growth, as, for example, in the case of the franc in 1957 and 1958 and of sterling in 1967 and 1992. However, to raise the rate of growth of income consistent with the balance of payments being in equilibrium requires an increase in the growth of exports or a reduction in the growth of imports, or both. Given the conventional export and import demand functions, this requires a *continuous* improvement in price competitiveness, expressed in a common currency. What is denied is that, for a number of reasons discussed below, this is a feasible option.

The first problem is that it may be difficult for a nominal depreciation to be converted into a real depreciation if there is inflationary feedback from higher import prices to higher domestic prices. This may occur because of real wage resistance as workers increase their money wage claims to prevent a cut in the real wage caused by the higher import prices. If they are successful, domestic prices will eventually increase to the same extent as import prices and there will be no gain in price competitiveness. In a number of forecasting models of the UK economy, it is assumed that the advantage of a once-and-for-all nominal depreciation would progressively diminish until, after five years or so, it would be entirely lost (McCombie and Thirlwall (1994: chapter 10); see Wilson (1976) for a theoretical model of this process).[1]

It is true that the 1980s did see swings in real exchange rates that made the devaluations of the 1960s and the 1970s seem small by comparison, and this would seem to confirm that real wage resistance may now be unimportant for many countries. But as Krugman (1989) concedes: 'One of the most puzzling, and therefore one of the most important, aspects of floating exchange rates has been the huge swings in exchange rates that have had only muted effects on anything real.' Consequently, even in the absence of any inflationary feedback, trade flows still appear unresponsive to changes in real exchange rates.

One early hypothesis as to why exchange rate depreciations may be ineffective was put forward by Balogh and Streeten (1951). They were amongst the first to stress the importance of oligopolistic competition in manufacturing and to suggest that this might lead to a resistance on the part of exporters to see their market shares decline. It is surprising just how long it has taken for international trade theory, with the development of the 'new' trade theory based on the Chamberlin–Robinson imperfect competition model, to recognize that product markets are not perfect. Exporters to the UK, for example, will try for as long as possible to maintain market share in the face of a decline in sterling, absorbing changes in the exchange rate in their price–cost margins. This policy is sometimes known as 'pricing to market', and a possible theoretical basis for it has been put forward by, *inter alios*, Dornbusch (1987).

There is increasing empirical evidence of the importance of this oligopolistic response to exchange rate changes. Cowling and Sugden (1989) develop a general model in which the reaction of prices to changes in costs is analysed within asymmetric oligopolistic markets. They argue that 'contrary to the usual assumption, the implication of this [market] structure is that exchange rate changes may leave prices unaltered.' They find that the pricing policy in the European car market is compatible with this model. The substantial appreciation of sterling in 1979/80 led neither to a fall in the relative price of imported cars in the UK nor to an increase in the relative price of UK car exports. They conclude that 'adjustments are more likely to appear via non-price mechanisms such as advertising and product policies and also via the sourcing policies of the transnational corporations'. Strong support for the pricing to market hypothesis is also found by Marston (1990) with respect to Japanese manufacturing.

Firms are unlikely to increase their efforts in exporting if they believe that a depreciation of a currency, even though it may be substantial, is likely to be short-lived. The huge swings of the real exchange rate in the 1980s were more likely to have been interpreted by firms as the consequences of temporary capital flows and speculative bubbles than were earlier exchange rate changes.

Furthermore, with a high degree of product differentiation, price elasticities are likely to be low, so that even a large change in relative prices has little effect on the volume of imports and exports demanded. The early elasticity pessimism, where a change in the exchange rate was thought to have had no effect on the current account during the 1950s, is now considered to have been unfounded. (If trade is balanced and the sum of the absolute values of the price elasticities equals unity, equation (4) demonstrates that changes in the terms of trade will have no effect on economic growth.) But there are two points to note concerning this. First, even if the traditional Marshall–Lerner conditions are satisfied, what is important is the *size* of the elasticities, as these determine the quantitative response of exports and imports to a change in the exchange rate. Secondly, with the development of greater product differentiation over the postwar period in both manufactured goods and services, the size of the price elasticities is likely to have declined over time.[2] Low price elasticities are especially true of the capital goods industries, where technical specifications are often of greater importance than the price.

CAPITAL FLOWS AND THE BALANCE-OF-PAYMENTS EQUILIBRIUM GROWTH RATE

The question then arises to what extent can capital flows (or, strictly speaking, their growth) relax, or indeed eliminate, the balance-of-payments constraint on economic growth. The late 1970s and 1980s saw the progressive deregulation and liberalization of the international financial markets, and an assumption often made is that a country can now borrow as much as it requires on the international capital markets at the going world rate of interest. The ready accessibility to international capital, it is held, has greatly reduced, if not completely eliminated, the balance-of-payments constraint. Deficit countries can now borrow to give themselves the necessary breathing space before a depreciation of the exchange rate putatively works.

There are problems with this argument. First, it overlooks the serious difficulties posed by the accumulation of excessive foreign debt. Secondly, the portfolio approach to the balance of payments shows that foreigners' portfolios will eventually adjust fully to, for example, an increase in a country's interest rate that takes it above the world interest rate. Investors will be unwilling to increase indefinitely the share of their portfolios devoted to overseas assets, notwithstanding this positive interest rate differential. Consequently, with stock equilibrium, there will not be persistent capital flows, even with sustained differences in interest rates.

We shall show that, under plausible assumptions, the growth of capital flows is likely to have only a quantitatively small effect in raising the balance-of-payments equilibrium growth rate.

A more detailed breakdown of the balance-of-payments identity in nominal values than that given by equation (1) is:

$$P_d X + F = P_f E M + i^* k D + i(1 - k)D + ekD \tag{6}$$

where i^* is the nominal interest rate paid on the foreign currency component of the net stock of overseas debt, D, with the latter denominated in the domestic currency; i is the interest rate paid on the domestic currency component of the debt; k is the proportion of the stock of debt denominated in foreign currency; and e is the rate of change of the exchange rate. Rearranging equation (6), and assuming that uncovered interest rate parity holds, so that $i^* = i - e$, we obtain

$$\Delta D = F = -TB + iD = F_1 + F_2 \tag{7}$$

where ΔD is the increase in the debt; F, as noted above, is net capital inflows which comprise borrowings from abroad to cover the deficit on the trade balance ($P_f EM - P_d X = -TB = F_1$) and the interest repayments (F_2). It is useful to term F_1 'active' debt accumulation, since it involves a real resource transfer into the country. F_2 may be regarded as 'passive' debt accumulation as it merely represents the increase in debt due to past trade deficits. (We assume for convenience that there is no amortization of the debt.) Over time, as a country runs a persistent balance-of-payments deficit, the passive contribution is likely to become progressively more important and to increasingly dominate the active debt accumulation. For example, one indicator of the capacity of a country to service and repay its debt that is commonly used by the financial markets is the debt to GDP ratio, namely, $\gamma \equiv D/\text{GDP}$. It will need only a few years of current account deficits of, say, 4% for a country, which is initially neither an overseas debtor nor creditor, to accumulate a debt to GDP ratio of, for example, 20%. If the interest rate is 10%, the interest payments (increase in passive debt) will be 2% of GDP, or about half of a current account deficit of 4% of GDP, which would normally be considered to be substantial.

The growth of the debt to GDP ratio (denoted by $\hat{\gamma}$) is given by

$$\hat{\gamma} = d - gdp = F/D - gdp = -TB/D + i - gdp \tag{8}$$

where d and gdp are the rates of growth of D and GDP, both measured in nominal terms.

For sustainability, the debt ratio has eventually to stabilize, so that $d = 0$. Consequently, this implies that

$$-TB/D = gdp - i. \tag{9}$$

From equation (9), it may be seen that if the nominal rate of interest equals the growth of nominal GDP, a deficit on the trade balance is not sustainable – the trade balance must be in equilibrium. If the nominal interest rate exceeds the growth of GDP, the trade balance must be in surplus for the debt to GDP ratio not to increase indefinitely. It is only when the growth of nominal GDP exceeds the nominal interest rate that a permanent deficit trade balance is sustainable (Howard 1989). These results follow through for the case of real values, as $y \equiv gdp - p$ and $r \equiv i - p$, where p and r are the rate of inflation and the real rate of interest. Thus, the condition for sustainability is $-TB/D = y - r$.

If it is assumed that the maximum sustainable level of debt to GDP is γ^*, then in real terms we have from the relation that $\Delta(D/P_d)/Y = \gamma^* y$, where it will be recalled Y is the level of real income, the condition that

504

$$\frac{(-TB + rD)/P_d}{Y} = \frac{-CAB/P_d}{Y} = \gamma^* y. \tag{10}$$

From equation (10), it can be seen that, if the real interest rate equals the growth of real income, the trade balance must be in equilibrium confirming the analysis couched in nominal terms. Thus, while a country may run a temporary trade deficit while the debt to GDP ratio increases, this is not sustainable if the debt to GDP ratio is eventually to stabilize. A country can, however, run a current account deficit equivalent to the 'passive' debt accumulation multiplied by the maximum debt to GDP ratio, γ^*. While there is no hard and fast rule as to the maximum value of γ, the financial markets usually become increasingly nervous if it exceeds about 0.4% for any length of time (Coutts *et al.* 1990). Thus, if the rate of growth of income is 2% per annum, the maximum sustainable current account deficit as a proportion of GDP is about 0.8%. If γ^* is lower, say 0.25, then the maximum current account deficit is also smaller, in this case 0.5% of GDP. Thus, only a relatively small current account deficit is likely to be sustainable in the long run.[3]

We may consider the implications of these arguments in terms of the balance-of-payments equilibrium growth rate. Consider first the case where the accumulation of debt has occurred to such an extent that the financial markets dictate that there can be no further increase in the debt to GDP ratio. This implies that $d' = y$ (where the superscript $'$ denotes measurement in real terms). Since $\Delta D' = F'$, it follows that $\gamma^* = F'/D' = y$. If we assume that the growth of income is constant, then it follows that the growth of capital flows, measured in real terms, must also equal the growth of income. Hence, the balance-of-payments equilibrium growth rate becomes

$$y = \frac{\theta x}{\pi - (1-\theta)} \tag{11}$$

which will give a reasonably close approximation to the simple rule, $y_B = x/\pi$. This may be shown as follows. Consider a relatively open economy where the proportion of output exported is 30% of GDP. Suppose this country persistently runs a relatively large current account deficit of 4% of GDP, i.e. $F/Y = 0.04$, and that π takes a value of 1.5. Consequently, since $\theta = X/(X + F) = (X/Y)/[X/Y) + (F/Y)]$, it follows that $[\theta/(\pi - (1 - \theta))]x$ equals $0.64x$ compared with the value of x/π of $0.67x$. If, for example, 50% and 15% of GDP are exported, then the equilibrium growth rates are $0.65x$ and $0.61x$, respectively, and these are again close to the values given by the simple dynamic Harrod foreign trade multiplier.

It is important to make a distinction between long-term capital flows and short-run speculative capital flows. The former will be beneficial if they are used for productive investment that will eventually generate increased export earnings and the foreign exchange necessary to cover the interest and amortization payments. Indeed, an alternative definition of the balance-of-payments equilibrium growth rate would be where the 'basic balance' (current account plus long-term capital flows) is in equilibrium.

The problem with short-term capital flows is that they are highly volatile. They respond rapidly to small changes in international interest rate differentials and the exchange rate, especially as the latter may lead to substantial capital gains or losses. The danger of a capital flight is that it may lead to a rapid depreciation of a currency and initiate a vicious depreciation–inflation circle. With a current account deficit and the possibility of an exchange rate depreciation that will bring a capital loss to foreign investors, the interest rate is likely to have to be increased in an attempt to prevent a capital flight. This, in turn, is likely to have an adverse effect on investment and, hence, reduce the growth rate. Moreover, there are limits to the extent to which interest rates can be raised to defend the currency.

To summarize, the implication is that capital flows cannot permit an individual country to increase its growth rate above y_B by very much or for very long.

DIRECT TESTS OF THE MODEL

There are basically two strategies that have been adopted to test the model directly. The first is to test how closely either of the expressions for y_B in equation (5) approximates to the actual growth rates.[4] If a close fit is found, this implies that the quantitative impact of the rate of change of relative prices and the growth of capital flows are small, or, less likely, offsetting.

The second approach is to estimate equation (4), using time series data, and to test the hypothesis that the last two terms are statistically insignificant, or at least have a quantitatively small effect on growth. If it were found, for example, that the coefficient of the growth of world income term was statistically insignificant and the estimates of the price term suggested high price elasticities, then this would serve to provide a refutation of the model in the sense that the country could not be said to be even potentially balance-of-payments constrained. This method has been adopted by Atesoglu (1993, 1993–4, 1994, 1995) for the US, Germany, and Canada. His results provide empirical support for the model. On the other hand, Riedel (1988) found that, for Hong Kong, if the export demand function was normalized with respect to prices, the world income elasticity of demand for Hong Kong's exports was not statistically significant, confirming the neoclassical 'law of one price'. However, Muscatelli et al. (1992) show that, when a more appropriate estimation technique is used, the income elasticity takes a value of over 4.0 and is highly statistically significant. (See also Athukorala and Riedel (1994) and Muscatelli (1994)).

There are four variants of the first strategy. The first test using equation (5) is to calculate the Spearman rank correlation coefficient between y and y_B (Thirlwall 1979; Perraton 1990). The results show that there is a statistically significant relation, but the approach can be criticized on the grounds that it does not show how close the model fits the data.

A second test is to calculate the absolute value of the average deviation of the observed from the predicted growth rate. The results suggests that the average deviation of y from y_B is small, lying between 0.2 and 0.7 percentage points (Thirlwall 1979; Bairam and Dempster 1991; Atesoglu 1993, 1994, 1995; Andersen 1993).

A third test is to regress y on y_B, or preferably y_B on y, and test whether the slope coefficient differs significantly from unity (Andersen 1993; Bairam 1988, 1990, 1993a and 1993b; and Bairam and Dempster 1991). Regressing y on y_B is an inappropriate method of normalization since y_B is derived using estimates of the income elasticities, each with an attached standard error; y, and not y_B, should be the regressor. Generally, the result of regressing y_B on y is that the slope coefficient does not differ significantly from unity, thereby not refuting the hypothesis that growth is balance-of-payments constrained (McCombie 1992). On the other hand, McGregor and Swales (1986) find that (inappropriately) regressing y on y_B does refute the hypothesis as, although there is a high correlation, the slope coefficient is significantly less than unity. However, this result should be discounted for the reasons outlined above.

The regression of y_B on y suffers from two shortcomings. First, an incomplete sample of countries may be taken in which balance-of-payments surpluses and deficits do not cancel out (i.e. there is a systematic tendency for $y_B > y$ or $y > y_B$). Secondly, if there are significant outliers where the observed and predicted growth rates are not equal, the inclusion of such countries in the sample may lead to a rejection of the growth 'law' for all the countries. Japan, for example, proves to be an outlier. For nearly all of the postwar period, Japan has run large balance-of-payments surpluses and its actual growth rate has been significantly below y_B. Japan has had a very rapid growth rate of GDP, averaging around 9% per annum before the 1973 slowdown. Thus, its rate of growth may well have been constrained by the growth of factor inputs. In other words, there was a limit to the speed with which labour could be transferred from agriculture to manufacturing and to the rate of capital accumulation. In this sense, Japan could be said to have been resource-constrained. But we are not back in the neoclassical schema where the growth rate is determined by the growth of labour and technical progress, independent of demand. It was only because of Japan's very fast rate of growth of exports that the country's GDP could grow as fast as it actually did. The problem of outliers may be potentially serious since *all* countries cannot be simultaneously balance-of-payments constrained. (See McCombie (1993) for an extension of the model that allows for this.)

A fourth test which avoids all of these difficulties is to take each country separately and, using the expression $y = x/\pi$, to calculate the implied income elasticity of demand for imports that makes $y = y_B$. This elasticity π^* is then compared with the estimated π obtained from time-series regression. If π and π^* do not differ significantly, then neither will y and y_B. It is found that the vast majority of countries pass this test (McCombie 1989). Perraton (1990), though, finds that of a sample of fifty-nine developing countries, about half fail the test. This suggests that terms-of-trade movements and capital flows are important for many developing countries, as found by Thirlwall and Hussain (1982).

CONCLUSION

In this paper, we have reconsidered the proposition that long-run growth may be constrained by the balance of payments and have argued that there is substantial empirical evidence in support of this contention. Neither changes in the exchange rate nor capital flows are effective in obviating balance-of-payments problems in a growth context. This is confirmed by statistical tests involving the simple rule $y_B = x/\pi = \varepsilon w/\pi$, and by regression analysis using equation (4). It is our contention that explanations of economic growth that ignore the demand side and international variations in the quality of goods etc. produced by an individual country and sold on world markets, are both inadequate and misleading.

NOTES

1   This mechanism should not be confused with the monetarist 'law of one price' and the associated purchasing power parity doctrine, which likewise predicts that the domestic price level will increase by the same amount as import prices. The monetarist explanation is that arbitrage will equalize prices, measured in a common currency, of identical internationally trade goods, subject to transport costs and tariffs. To make this theory operational, and not just a tautology, it has to be assumed that countries export products that are homogeneous. The small country assumption implies an infinite price elasticity of demand for exports and, in this approach, the concept of the balance-of-payments constraint has no meaning. Economies are always at, or near, their full employment level.

2   It is instructive that Andersen (1993) and Bairam (1988), using data from the 1960s to the 1990s, find that for a large number of countries the Marshall–Lerner conditions are not, in fact, met.

3   Howard (1989) expresses equation (10) in nominal terms: $viz.$, $-CAB/GNP = \gamma^* gnp$, in our notation. (Howard uses GNP rather than GDP.) From this, he calculates the possible range of sustainable current account deficits for any γ^* and rate of growth of nominal GNP. For example, he calculates that plausible maximum sustainable CAB ratios, given $\gamma^* = 0.25$, lie between 2.5% and 1.25% assuming the growth of nominal income to be between 10% and 5% per annum. He concludes that 'this longer-run sustainable value of the U.S. current account balance may be quite large.' This may seem a counter-intuitive result, since it implies that one way for a country to relax its balance-of-payments constraint (by

increasing its sustainable current account deficit) is to increase its rate of inflation. However, if we make the plausible assumption that the nominal rate of interest also increases, *pari passu*, with the rate of inflation, then an increase in the rate of inflation will increase the current account deficit only to the extent that the nominal interest payable on the stock of debt increases. The balance of trade must still be zero.

4　The studies covering the early postwar period have used in calculating y_B either Houthakker and Magee's (1969) OLS estimates of π and ε, or Goldstein and Khan's (1978) estimates using a simultaneous equation framework. In practice, there is very little difference in the results of the two approaches. However, in both cases the demand functions were estimated using the logarithms of the levels. Bairam (1993a) found that the data were I(1) and were not cointegrated. This suggests that the appropriate procedure would be to use growth rates in estimating the elasticities. However, when this is done, he finds there is little difference from the estimates obtained from the log-linear regressions.

REFERENCES

Andersen, P. S. (1993) 'The 45°-rule revisited', *Applied Economics*, 25: 1279–84.

Atesoglu, H. S. (1993) 'Balance-of-payments constrained growth: evidence from the United States', *Journal of Post Keynesian Economics*, 15: 507–14.

——— (1993–4) 'Exports, capital flows, relative prices and economic growth in Canada', *Journal of Post Keynesian Economics*, 15: 289–97.

——— (1994) 'Balance-of-payments determined growth in Germany', *Applied Economics Letters*, 1: 89–91.

——— (1995) 'An explanation of the slowdown in US economic growth', *Applied Economic Letters*, 2: 91–4.

Athukorala, P. and Riedel, J. (1994) 'Demand and supply factors in the determination of NIE exports: a simultaneous error-correction model for Hong Kong: a comment', *Economic Journal*, 104: 1411–14.

Bairam, E. (1988) 'Balance-of-payments, the Harrod foreign trade multiplier and economic growth: the European and North American experience, 1970–85', *Applied Economics*, 20: 1635–42.

——— (1990) 'The Harrod foreign trade multiplier revisited', *Applied Economics*, 22: 711–18.

——— (1993a) 'Static versus dynamic specifications and the Harrod foreign trade multiplier', *Applied Economics*, 25: 739–42.

——— (1993b) 'Income elasticities of exports and imports: a re-examination of the empirical evidence', *Applied Economics*, 25: 71–4.

——— and Dempster, G. J. (1991) 'The Harrod foreign trade multiplier and economic growth in Asian countries', *Applied Economics*, 23: 1719–24.

Balogh, T. and Streeten, P. P. (1951) 'The inappropriateness of simple "elasticity" concepts in the analysis of international trade', *Bulletin of the Oxford University Institute of Statistics*, 13: 65–77.

Barro R. J. and Sala-i-Martin, X. (1992) 'Convergence', *Journal of Political Economy*, 100: 223–51.

Beckerman, W. (1962) 'Projecting Europe's growth', *Economic Journal*, 72: 912–25.

Borts, G. H. and Stein, J. L. (1964) *Economic Growth in a Free Market*, New York: Columbia University Press.

Cornwall, J. (1977) *Modern Capitalism: Its Growth and Transformation*, London: Martin Robertson.

Coutts, K., Godley, W., Rowthorn, R., and Zessa, G. (1990) *Britain's Economic*

Problems and Policies for the 1990s, Institute for Public Policy Research, Economic Study, 6.

Cowling, K. and Sugden, R. (1989) 'Exchange rate behaviour and oligopoly pricing behaviour', *Cambridge Journal of Economics* 13: 373–93.

Dornbusch, R. (1987) 'Exchange rates and prices', *American Economic Review*, 77: 93–106.

Faini, R. (1984) 'Increasing returns, non-traded inputs and regional development', *Economic Journal*, 94: 304–23.

Houthakker, H. and Magee, S. (1969) 'Income and price elasticities in world trade', *Review of Economics and Statistics*, 51: 111–25.

Howard, D. H. (1989) 'Implications of the U.S. current account deficit', *Journal of Economic Perspectives*, 3: 153–65.

Goldstein, M. and Khan, M. S. (1978) 'The supply and demand for exports: a simultaneous approach', *Review of Economics and Statistics*, 60: 275–86.

Kaldor, N. (1978) 'Introduction' in N. Kaldor (ed.), *Further Essays on Economic Theory*, London: Duckworth.

Kindleberger, C. P. (1967) *Europe's Postwar Growth: The Role of Labour Supply*, Cambridge, Mass.: Harvard University Press.

Krugman, P. (1989) *Exchange Rate Instability*, Cambridge, Mass.: MIT Press.

McCombie, J. S. L. (1985) 'Economic growth, the Harrod foreign trade multiplier and the Hicks super-multiplier', *Applied Economics*, 17: 55–72.

—— (1989) '"Thirlwall's Law" and balance of payments constrained growth – a comment on the debate', *Applied Economics*, 21: 611–29.

—— (1992) '"Thirlwall's Law" and balance of payments constrained growth: more on the debate', *Applied Economics*, 24: 493–512.

—— (1993) 'Economic growth, trade interlinkages, and the balance-of-payments constraint', *Journal of Post Keynesian Economics*, 15: 471–505.

—— and Thirlwall, A. P. (1994) *Economic Growth and the Balance-of-Payments Constraint*, Basingstoke: Macmillan.

McGregor, P. G. and Swales, J. K. (1985) 'Professor Thirlwall and balance of payments constrained growth', *Applied Economics*, 17 (February): 17–32.

Marston, R. C. (1990) 'Pricing to market in Japanese manufacturing', *Journal of International Economics*, 29 (November): 217–36.

Muscatelli, V. A. (1994) 'Demand and supply factors in a determination of NIE exports: a reply', *Economic Journal*, 104: 1415–17.

——, Srinivasan, T. G. and Vines, D. (1992) 'Demand and supply factors in the determination of NIE exports: a simultaneous error-correction model for Hong Kong', *Economic Journal*, 102: 1467–77.

Perraton, J. (1990) 'Balance-of-payments constrained growth and the developing countries: an examination of Thirlwall's hypothesis', (mimeo), University of Nottingham.

Riedel, J. (1988) 'The demand for LDC exports of manufactures: estimates from Hong Kong', *Economic Journal*, 98: 138–48.

Romer, P. M. (1986) 'Increasing returns and long-run growth', *Journal of Political Economy*, 94: 1002–37.

Solow, R. M. (1983) 'Comment' [on Nordhaus, W. D., 'Macroconfusion: the dilemmas of economic policy'] in Tobin, J. (ed.), *Macroeconomics, Prices and Quantities*, Oxford: Basil Blackwell.

Thirlwall, A. P. (1979) 'The balance of payments constraint as an explanation of international growth rate differences', *Banca Nazionale del Lavoro Quarterly Review*, 128: 45–53.

—— and Hussain M. N. (1982) 'The balance-of-payments constraint, capital flows and growth rate differences between developing countries', *Oxford Economic Papers*, 34: 498–510.

Van der Wee, H. (1987) *Prosperity and Upheaval: The World Economy 1945–1980*, Harmondsworth: Penguin Books.

Wilson, T. (1976) 'Effective devaluation and inflation', *Oxford Economic Papers*, 28: 1–24.

39

ECONOMIC POLICY IN POST-APARTHEID SOUTH AFRICA

Jonathan Michie

Geoff Harcourt's room in Cambridge's Faculty of Economics and Politics is easy to find and to give directions for: it is the one with the poster of Nelson Mandela on the outside of the door. The poster did not just appear once Mandela had become respectable in polite company; it was there when Mandela was a prisoner on Robben Island, refusing offers of release which were dependent on his renouncing violence – the path of violence which Mandela had personally decided on and had pushed through the ANC.[1]

Now that Mandela has moved from Robben Island to the office of President, the huge social, economic and political task of reconstructing and developing a country still suffering under the legacy of apartheid is having to be faced. South Africa requires a major programme of house-building, of electrification and of other public works, along with a diversification from its strength in the minerals and energy sectors into other closely related sectors of the economy. It is from this starting point that we need to consider the reconstruction and development of the South African economy and society.[2]

To start with the state of the South African economy itself, prior to the election of the Government of National Unity (GNU), the government's own 'Normative Economic Model' in 1993 identified several structural defects in the political, economic and social system which would clearly require far more than just economic growth itself. These problems were listed as including: inappropriate education and training; costly functional and physical separation of people; inadequate access to economic opportunities; unsettled community life; inadequate entrepreneurship; and ineffective financial intermediation between savings and development investment. On the neglect of training, the share of GDP devoted to this was reported at only 2%, which the outgoing government acknowledged to be inadequate.

As detailed in MERG (1993) – the report published from South Africa's Macro-Economic Research Group – the South African economy also suffers from a weakness in the capital-goods and intermediate-goods manufacturing sectors. Some sectors have of course been successful, such as mining and energy. But overall, this weakness means that growth tends to lead to imports and hence to balance of payments deficits, and this inevitably leads to a brake on the growth itself.

The starting point for the reconstruction and development of the South African economy should, then, be to recognize that South Africa does have a minerals–energy complex which is very strong in its own area, including in transportation, engineering and construction, and that this could lay the basis for developing other closely related parts of the economy. This therefore gives South Africa a head-start in terms of experience for the sort of construction and development projects which are needed in other economic areas, such as housing and electrification.

But there is no inevitability about these prospects being actually realized. That will require a number of conditions to be satisfied, such as the restoration and maintenance of business confidence. And this itself may require state intervention to ensure the necessary restructuring of the economy.

The purpose of the present chapter is to consider what sort of institutional framework is being – or might be – developed to see through the reconstruction and development of the economy. The first section presents an analysis of South Africa's economic and developmental needs. The paper then considers an alternative view – that of the South African government prior to the 1994 election; the argument in their Normative Economic Model, that wage bargaining should be decentralized, is then considered in light of the literature around 'corporatism'. The paper then focuses on two particular debates around different state–market arrangements: on the role of the civil service, and on the independence of the central bank.

STATE INTERVENTION

South Africa's social and economic structure compels an examination of issues of ownership and control: there is a tremendous concentration of wealth in the hand of the big conglomerates, with just five of these giant corporations controlling more than 80% of the shares on the Johannesburg Stock Exchange. South Africa has the world's most unequal distribution of income (with a Gini-coefficient of 0.6).[3] To address such disparities requires bold policies for economic renewal as well as a heavy legislative programme, aimed not least at making the market function in line with principles of social and economic justice.

State intervention has of course been used in the past to see through structural change, and in particular to effect a change in the distribution of income towards the Afrikaners, and to alleviate the balance of payments constraints arising from the isolation of South Africa. It is unlikely that either of these objectives could have been realized without this degree of state involvement.

The size of the structural changes facing a new South Africa will be still greater than those seen through to date. It will therefore be vital that the public sector is used actively to promote, facilitate and deliver such changes in order to achieve the goals of gender and racial equality, to overcome the dual threats of capital flight on the one hand and social unrest on the other, and to satisfy the very different constituencies that now make up the new South African polity, while still ensuring growth and a redistribution of wealth.

However, the idea of pursuing the sort of industrial strategy which would be required to achieve these aims has been criticized on a number of grounds. First, because of the inefficiency and corruption associated with what was seen as an industrial policy in the past. And second, because the term has been used in the past to describe little more than just trade policy plus 'decentralization', with the latter referring to the homelands policy.

The starting point needs to be to look at what needs to be done, and then to consider whether or not private capital is likely to do it – if this were to appear unlikely, then there is a case for the public sector intervening to ensure that the job is done. The key reason, then, for a democratic government to intervene in the 'free working' of the economy would be if the private sector appeared incapable or unwilling to undertake the huge reconstruction and development tasks facing the country, in terms say of house-building and the balanced development of the housing supply and other associated industries, along with the upgrading of other aspects of the social and productive infrastructure.

South Africa already has a substantial public sector. Eskom, the electricity utility, and the transport enterprise Transnet, for example, are both massive undertakings. The precise status of many of these bodies is subject to interpretation, particularly as many of them have been undergoing changes designed to prepare them for privatization; but they are nevertheless, to all intents and purposes, still state-owned enterprises.

Even the most orthodox of free market economics recognizes the need for state intervention in cases of 'market failure'. The transition to a new South Africa is likely to suffer from all sorts of market failure. In addition, there are many areas of potential economic strengths such as tourism, which to flourish will require a reduction in the level of general criminal violence.[4] The question is, how can such a reduction be brought about? Certainly not by monetary and fiscal prudence alone. Rather, it will require dramatic public action to bring hope and a sense of purpose to the townships and communities most affected by the present levels of unemployment, illiteracy and economic hardship; it is just such a role which the government's Reconstruction and Development Programme (RDP) is attempting to play.

Thus the real 'constraints' should not be seen in terms of the factors usually associated with that phrase – of the foreign exchange constraint or the inflation constraint. Such factors are of course important, but equally it needs to be appreciated that the government will also be constrained to actually pursue the reconstruction and development of the country, or else court political and economic disaster. Such policies would in this sense be in the long-term interests of private sector business itself, regardless of the negative attitude they might display to the idea of policies seen as too interventionist (although, of course, lip-service to the RDP is paid by all).

This distinction between the interests of business in general, on the one hand, and the perceived interests of the individual firm on the other, has been recognized before now: for example, individual firms may want to pay their own workers less to increase profits, while wanting workers in other firms to be paid more, to boost their own firm's sales. The attitudes of individual firms do not necessarily represent the best long-term interests of business collectively.

THE PRE-APRIL 1994 SOUTH AFRICAN GOVERNMENT'S ECONOMIC MODEL

The pre-election government's 'Normative Economic Model' correctly identified a number of defects in the country's political, economic and social system, as detailed above. However, the model, along with its accompanying published commentary, also included a number of naive assumptions and assertions, and some of these appear to have been carried over into the approach and policies of the present government.

First, central to the pre-election government's strategy was 'the need for the government sector to free national resources for more investment, mainly by the private sector'. But there is no automatic mechanism whereby resources 'freed' by the government will reappear as private investment; those resources risk instead lying idle, thereby reducing national income. The approach of the government's published model was static, implying a given national cake, so that if the public sector takes a smaller slice, a larger piece will be left for the private sector. Instead, the size of the national cake is itself a product of public as well as of private spending and investment. Reducing the size of the public sector's 'slice' may simply result in a smaller cake being generated. And since much private sector activity is linked to public sector spending, such cuts may hit private sector production, leading to the cake shrinking yet further. The private sector's increased share of the cake may turn out to be smaller in absolute terms than its present share.

Secondly, rising unit labour costs were identified as harming competitiveness, with wages seen as the culprit – a theme repeated by the Reserve Bank Governor in August 1995. But the rising costs identified were due not to wage increases – real wages fell between 1985 and 1991 – but to falling productivity. Hence the real need is to upgrade and modernize – and these tasks are likely to be undermined by a wage-cutting strategy.

Thirdly, the pre-April 1994 government's model correctly identified increased investment as playing a key role. However, in listing five determinants of investment it ignored the crucial role of demand (and

515

expected demand). It also ignored the vitally important role played by having access to an efficient productive infrastructure. Investment is unlikely to be forthcoming unless there is a demand for the resulting output. And even then, investment may fail to deliver without the necessary productive infrastructure being in place, in terms of transport and communications, education and training, and strong links between the private and public sectors.

Fourthly, the criticism of centralized collective bargaining ignores international experience, where decentralized bargaining loses the pressure on inefficient firms which a centralized system can deliver (see below).

Fifthly, the prescription of financial deregulation as a mechanism for creating new institutional arrangements to provide increased investment in domestic capital formation flies in the face of international experience throughout the 1980s and 1990s. Increased property prices would be a more likely outcome, with any real investment being diverted to yet more shopping malls, or whatever else promised short-term returns.

And finally, globalization is interpreted in a one-sided way, in terms only of weakening the efficacy of national economic policy levers. But the other side of the globalization coin is that gains in national competitive advantage are then magnified in international markets.[5] Economic policy may be more difficult, but it also becomes more important.

WAGE BARGAINING AND 'SOCIAL CORPORATISM'

Should wage bargaining be centralized or decentralized? And should other issues – such as investment and pricing policies – be included in the bargaining process? Should government be involved? These questions have been disputed in policy debates throughout the world, including in South Africa where some attempt at corporatist-type arrangements is being pursued through the National Economic, Development and Labour Council (NEDLAC).

Various claims have been made in the economics, industrial relations and politics literatures regarding the effects of 'corporatism' or 'social corporatism' on economic performance. Many contributors have focused on the case of Sweden and that country's relative success in preventing mass unemployment in the 1970s and 1980s.[6] In the neoclassical economics literature Calmfors and Driffill (1988) make generalized claims about the comparative performance of weakly, strongly and mediumly corporatist economies, finding a U-shaped relationship between employment and centralization of wage bargaining.[7]

The more centralized the bargaining structure, the lower tends to be the country's wage dispersion; Rowthorn (1992), for example, reports a significant coefficient on the Calmfors–Driffill ranking when countries' degree of wage dispersion was the dependent variable. Nevertheless, such an attempt at ranking countries is clearly an extremely complex process and may be misleading; for example the British labour market might appear corporatist because of having a single trade union centre (the TUC), although in reality that body has extremely weak links with the individual trade unions; Japan has a high degree of participation and integration of interests between government and business, but labour interests are fragmented; and so on.

Indeed, it is even hard to pin down the definitions of the terms 'corporatism' and 'social corporatism'. The *New Palgrave Dictionary of Economics*, for example, has no entry under 'social corporatism' and the entry under 'corporatism' does not get much beyond Mussolini's fascism (see Eatwell *et al.* 1987). The expression 'social corporatism' has emerged in the literature, then, as stressing the social democratic and trade union component of the Scandinavian version of corporatism as a more or less coherent system.[8]

The key to the theory of how social corporatist institutions might deliver improved economic performance lies in the idea, first, of their being able to produce different outcomes in the wage bargaining process than would otherwise occur, and second, that these wage outcomes will have beneficial macroeconomic consequences. The argument can be made with regard to either nominal or real wages, and each is dealt with in turn below.

Wage-bargaining and inflation

Wage agreements are made in money terms. But the aim for the workers is to improve living standards, taking account of inflation. Success in reducing the rate of money wage increases will not necessarily reduce the rate of real wage increases, provided inflation – the rate of output price increases – falls fully in line. The difficulty comes in ensuring that a reduction in the rate of money wage rises does indeed result in inflation falling to the same degree, rather than feeding through into higher profits or stagnant productivity instead, which in turn would allow firms to continue using outdated equipment which would otherwise have to be replaced.

This issue can also be thought of in terms of productivity growth being taken out in increased dividend payments and/or increased share price values rather than in reduced output prices. It is only if such issues are faced up to, and realistic solutions to them implemented, that wage bargaining reforms could be expected to deliver what is often promised, namely maintained growth of real wages despite a slower growth of money wages. Fundamentally it would require a bargaining strategy capable of delivering increased real wages across the economy, forcing inefficient firms to upgrade through investment.

517

Wage bargaining and employment

However, a separate argument is sometimes made, that the growth of real wages should indeed be reduced – that this should actually be an aim of restraining money wage growth. This argument is usually made with regard to unemployment, to the effect that workers price themselves out of jobs and that restraining real wage growth would improve competitiveness, allowing increased production and hence increased employment.

The idea that real wages and employment are negatively correlated in the cyclical upturn, with workers being priced back into work, has a long history in economic theory and a negative wage–employment correlation can certainly be found from statistical tests which are carried out on the assumption of 'other things being equal'. But of course, cutting wages would itself prevent other things being equal: consumer demand would also be cut and lower wages might induce firms to postpone productivity-raising investment. Empirical research reveals that there is no consistent correlation between wages and employment over the business cycle: wages are just as likely to be positively correlated with employment as negatively.[9]

Thus, reducing the rate of growth of real wages has a two-way relationship with employment. In the short term it might encourage individual firms to take on more workers because their wage costs are lower. But low wage dependency has two long-term costs to the national economy. In the first place, it redistributes income towards the relatively better off, who consume a higher proportion of imported goods, reducing demand and causing unemployment. In the second place, it eases pressure on firms to replace their outdated equipment and managerial methods, with the result that innovation slows and international competitiveness is lost.

Centralized bargaining

Centralized bargaining exists in countries where the national federations of trade unions and employers, while not necessarily able to impose a uniform settlement upon their members by force of law, nevertheless exert a predominant influence over the bargaining process and its outcome. Countries which have used centralized wage bargaining to bring about a high level of wage equalization have had a comparatively successful record on employ-ment growth since the early 1970s. The Nordic countries come into this category, in contrast to most of the European Union countries, which rely on a combination of national-level and local-level bargaining. The EU countries are characterized by a reasonably high level of wage equality for those in work, but by a poor employment record, resulting in greater inequality between employed and unemployed. Countries with, by contrast, highly decentralized systems of wage bargaining and higher levels of inequality in earnings levels, such as the USA and Japan, have also enjoyed better than average employment growth over this period. However, much of the growth of jobs in the USA (and to a lesser extent in Japan) has taken the form of poorly paid and low-productivity employment. It is only in the North European countries, and in particular Sweden, that a high level of employment growth has been combined with comparative wage equality between occupational groups.

In the Calmfors and Driffill model, the best outcomes are achieved therefore either by what might be termed a 'free market capitalist' approach, or else by what might be termed the 'social corporatist' approach. The worst of all worlds is to fall between the two stools. The non-corporatist end of their U-shaped finding might be thought to deliver high employment either because workers then identify only with their own firm and hence will take wage-cuts in the belief that they will gain from their own firm's resulting competitive advantage, or else because the lack of corporatist institutions leaves workers powerless to prevent wages being driven down to their market-clearing levels (which deliver full employment).

The corporatist approach is said to allow high employment by overcoming the prisoner's dilemma whereby no group of workers will agree to the necessary degree of wage restraint for fear that others might not; hence they fail to achieve the optimal outcome (which would result from all cooperating), albeit they avoid an even worse fate which befalls those who follow a cooperative strategy which is not reciprocated. This is as far as the story goes in much of the literature, stopping at the level of wage bargaining.

However, this does not answer either of the objections made above, against attempting to pursue a strategy of employment creation through wage restraint. These objections can be countered, but only by expanding the nature of the bargaining system, to allow commitments to be made by employers and government. This allows the employers to make commitments on investment levels, and more generally on the use of profits. It also allows the government to make commitments about future levels of aggregate demand in the economy.

NEDLAC and other institutional developments could be seen as providing a potential mechanism for organized labour to advance policy demands which could force through the reconstruction and development of the South African economy. But so far any such potential has remained untapped. Business interests have by and large continued to pursue their own agenda unconstrained. On the other hand, it could be objected that in a country like South Africa, with a relatively small percentage of the population organized in trade unions, the mass of unemployed and poorly organized workers would lose out if organized labour was guiding policy.[10] The opposite is more likely to be the case: with organized labour limited to negotiating wage levels, there is little scope for the interests of the unorganized to be encompassed; it is only if labour is able to secure action on a broader policy front that the interests of the unemployed – and the poorly organized – can meaningfully be represented. Thus, in his analysis of manufacturing wages, Falkov (1994) finds powerful worker organization to have succeeded in placing upward pressure on real wages in the 'upper' segment of that labour market, while falling living standards and growing job insecurity was found amongst unskilled manufacturing workers; thus, 'Policies that focus on accelerating the rate of output growth in the manufacturing sector, the establishment of appropriate collective bargaining institutions, and increasing coverage for unskilled workers, are the only basis for securing both rising employment levels and standards of living in the future' (Falkov 1994: 26).

STATE–MARKET RELATIONS

International experience of various state–market relations has naturally varied tremendously; some of the issues arising from alternative experiences and possibilities as regards the labour market are discussed above. Reading off lessons for South Africa would not be straightforward. Britain, for example, has experimented with a number of labour market policies over the past few decades, but has never succeeded in using centralized bargaining to force through modernization, as happened in Sweden. Other countries have varied their institutional arrangements in face of the global changes, including now Sweden. Australia's 'Accord', for example, was launched as one component of an ambitious programme of economic and social reform, but when the other elements in the reform programme faltered, the wages policy alone was left to bear the brunt, and suffered accordingly.

The key to achieving full employment combined with low inflation requires improved productivity and competitiveness. The focus of any labour market policy should therefore be on how to force firms and industries to match best practice through investment, and to ensure that the resulting productivity gains are passed on in reduced output prices, if necessary through the use of price controls. The ability of governments to manage this will depend in part on the country's institutional structures.

But the argument that independent national governments either have had, or should have, their powers to act limited, has crystallized recently in South Africa as elsewhere around the issues firstly, of whether the responsibilities of the state need to be rolled back, in favour of private enterprise, and secondly and more specifically, over whether the Reserve Bank should be independent. The above general considerations of the state–market relation are now focused on these specific points, below.

The state and its public administration

The development of public administration has in South Africa, as elsewhere, reflected economic developments; and again as elsewhere, the public administration has itself shaped these economic developments themselves.

The case of South Africa is interesting, of course, because of the peculiar nature of the economic, political and administrative developments under the policy of apartheid. Thus the term 'decentralization', when applied to economic policy, meant in the South African context the peculiar construction of the 'homelands' – notionally independent nation states. Political decentralization remains, though, a live political issue both because of the Afrikaner Weerstandbeweging (AWB) demands for an independent homeland and because of the demands for independence for the Zulu Natal region.

Both the state and the market came therefore to have rather peculiar constructions. Huge commuting distances to work, for example, were one consequence of the settlement arrangements. And the political response of the international community in imposing economic sanctions led to still further public interventions in the economy to encourage import substitution, for example.

The pre-election government spent the last couple of years leading up to the first democratic election trying to dismantle as many of these powers, which public administration had come to wield, as possible. This has left democratic South Africa struggling under a double legacy: first, the peculiar construction of an apartheid economy and society, and secondly, an enfeebled public sector incapable of wielding the influence required to force through a change of direction on the economy and society. Left to itself, the free market is likely to develop the economy along its existing lines to a great extent. To dismantle apartheid and reconstruct a new economy and society will require an active public administration, diversifying the economy to build up a capital goods sector, to provide public services to the mass of the population, to monitor public purchasing, contract compliance and other mechanisms for overcoming the legacy of apartheid, and so on.

Equally, public administration itself will need to be rejuvenated, breaking out of its own apartheid straitjacket, developing affirmative action programmes for its own development, and so on. It is generally recognized that South Africa has a bloated bureaucracy, in part a legacy of the apartheid structures. The problem of this unproductive public service has to be tackled, but in doing this it is important that the role of the civil service is linked conceptually to the country's economic, social and political developments, promoting those developments, but renewing itself in the process. It needs to play an active development role, rather than a mere regulatory one.[11]

Independence of the Reserve Bank

There is strong pressure to make central banks independent of elected governments, including the proposals in the Maastricht Treaty for the European Union's new central bank to be independent. In South Africa, the Reserve Bank is supposedly independent, and there is strong pressure for it to continue to be independent in the new South Africa.

The economic and political logic of this is questionable, to say the least; the Reserve Bank should instead be accountable to a democratic government. Indeed, this may well prove to be a necessary condition for a post-1999 ANC government to be able to pursue a balanced programme, as well as for building confidence in the democratic process.

Being 'independent' means in effect being unaccountable to any elected authority. The electorate therefore have no mechanism for influencing the policies of the Reserve Bank. The direct policies are monetary and interest rate, but the Reserve Bank also has influence over exchange rate policies, and interest rate policy has repercussions for fiscal and industrial policies, as well as for the state of the economy and popular wellbeing more generally. This lack of democratic accountability therefore has widespread implications for the whole of economic policy.

It would be possible for an incoming government to attempt to implement the programme on which it was elected, using the remaining economic instruments at its disposal, as for example in America in the 1980s when a fiscal expansion led to rapid economic growth and employment, with a dramatic fall in unemployment. But since monetary policy was independent from this, the conflicting monetary and fiscal policies led to increased interest rates, an overvaluation of the currency, a loss of competitiveness in international markets as well as in the home market, and a huge balance of payments deficit.

An independent Reserve Bank would spell grave dangers politically as well as economically. If the sort of reconstruction and development programmes which are vital to the economy – and vital for defusing the level of violence, introducing some degree of hope and sense of purpose and progress into communities – are made impossible by the actions of an unaccountable Reserve Bank, then the democratic political process will lose all legitimacy. South Africa needs a coherent economic programme with all its elements – fiscal, monetary, industrial, regional, international – kept in balance. That requires an accountable Reserve Bank.

CONCLUSION

The success with which the South African government breaks with the deeply ingrained structures of apartheid within the economy and society will depend to a large extent on the role of the new public administration and the type of state which is developed: whether it can become an active developmental state or else is limited to playing a passive regulatory role. One test will be when the inevitable pressure comes for government to intervene in labour markets: will it respond by limiting itself to incomes policy type reactions, in effect leaving the free market to decide the inflation, investment and employment response, or will it intervene more proactively to expand investment, productivity and output?[12] The development of NEDLAC shows a desire to develop structures – which might be characterized as social corporatist – to pursue the more developmental approach. One particular problem will be how corporatism can be developed in South Africa with its high rates of unemployment. Corporatist structures may be good at preventing unemployment rather than solving it, and have not before been developed in a country already characterized by high unemployment. What still needs to be worked out in practice is how the interests of some of the largest constituencies in South Africa (such as the unemployed and those in the informal economy) will be represented in the system which is developing.

ACKNOWLEDGEMENTS

This chapter draws on work done with Zunaid Moolla of South Africa's National Institute for Economic Policy (NIEP) and I am grateful both to him and to the Institute. The chapter was completed in 1995 while I was a Visiting Professor in the Economics Department of the University of the Witwatersrand and I am grateful to the staff both for their comments and their hospitality.

NOTES

1   That morning in a safe flat in a white suburb I met various members of the local and foreign press ... I said, 'If the government reaction is to crush by naked force our non-violent struggle, we will have to reconsider our tactics. In my mind we are closing a chapter on this question of a non-violent policy.' It was a grave declaration, and I knew it. I was criticized by our Executive for making that remark before it was discussed by the organization ...

    The debate on the use of violence had been going on among us since early 1960. I had first discussed the armed struggle as far back as 1952 with Walter Sisulu. Now, I again conferred with him and we agreed that the organization had to set out on a new course. The Communist Party had secretly reconstituted itself underground and was now considering forming its own military wing. We decided that I should raise the issue of the armed struggle ... and I did so in a meeting in June of 1961.

                                                           (Mandela 1994: 258–9)

2   This general proposition was backed up and enunciated in detail by South Africa's Macro-Economic Research Group (see MERG 1993), the precursor to NIEP.

3   This compares with an average of 0.3–0.4 for the main industrialized countries, reported in Sawyer (1976), with only Brazil approaching South Africa's degree of inequality according to current World Bank data.

4   South Africa's tourism industry currently contributes 3.6% of GDP, as against an international average figure of 7%.

5   See Archibugi and Michie (1995), where the patenting activity of transnational corporations is analysed and the 'globalization' of this is found to be largely a reflection of firms attempting to exploit their technological advantages in foreign markets, rather than representing 'the end of the nation state'.

523

6 See, for example, Glyn and Rowthorn (1988), Rowthorn and Glyn (1990), Henley and Tsakalotos (1992, 1993), Deakin *et al.* (1992), Pekkarinen *et al.* (1992), and Michie (1994).

7 For a development of Calmfors and Driffill's work along more realistic lines, see Rowthorn (1992), and for a critical survey of the literature, see Pohjola (1992).

8 Pekkarinen *et al.* (1992) define social corporatism as an economic system whose labour market is characterized by two basic features: first, centralized bargaining – primarily wage bargaining but also possibly bargaining over government economic and social policies, in which case the state is either formally or informally involved in the process; and second, a non-exclusive and egalitarian approach to such bargaining.

9 For the theoretical and empirical evidence, see Michie (1987).

10 This is argued, for example, by Nattrass and Seekings (1995).

11 As Mandela said on the opening of the Graduate School of Public and Development Management:

> A new public service will bear the enormous task of implementing new development-oriented policies and practically transforming previous apart-heid administrative cultures, practices and habits. The more accessible a new civil service is seen to be ... the sooner the public service will manifest itself as a valuable nation-building asset in the times ahead.

12 Local investment in factories, plant and equipment needs to rise to around 25% of GDP, from the present levels of only 16%, as even Derek Keys has admitted. (See the interview reported in *Business Report* of 17 August 1995.)

REFERENCES

Archibugi, D. and Michie, J. (1995) 'The globalisation of technology: a new taxonomy', *Cambridge Journal of Economics*, 19 (1): 121–40.

Calmfors, L. and Driffill, J. (1988) 'Bargaining structure, corporatism and macro-economic performance', *Economic Policy*, 6 (April): 13–61.

Deakin, S., Michie, J. and Wilkinson, F. (1992) *Inflation, Employment, Wage-bargaining and the Law*, London: Institute of Employment Rights.

Eatwell, J., Milgate, M. and Newman, P. (eds) (1987) *The New Palgrave Dictionary of Economics*, London: Macmillan.

Falkov, L. (1994) 'African wages in the manufacturing sector – 1975 to 1990: an alternative perspective', Masters Dissertation: University of the Witwatersrand.

Glyn, A. and Rowthorn, B. (1988) 'West European unemployment: corporatism and structural change', *American Economic Review Papers and Proceedings*, 78: 194–9.

Henley, A. and Tsakalotos, E. (1992) 'Corporatism and the European labour market after 1992', *British Journal of Industrial Relations*, December.

—— (1993) *Corporatism and Economic Performance: A Comparative Analysis of Market Economies*, Aldershot: Edward Elgar.

Macro-Economic Research Group (MERG) (1993) *Making Democracy Work: A Framework for Macroeconomic Policy in South Africa*, Cape Town: Oxford University Press.

Mandela, N. (1993) 'Message to the Graduate School of Public and Development Management', University of the Witwatersrand.

—— (1994) *Long Walk to Freedom*, Randburg: Macdonald Purnell.

Michie, J. (1987) *Wages in the Business Cycle. An Empirical and Methodological Analysis*, London: Frances Pinter Publishers.

—— (1994) 'Global shocks and corporatism', in R. Delorme and K. Dopfer (eds), *The Political Economy of Complexity: Evolutionary Approaches to Economic Order and Disorder*, Aldershot: Edward Elgar.

Nattrass, N. and Seekings, J. (1995) 'And the jobless?', *Mail and Guardian*, 8–14 September.

Pekkarinen, J., Pohjola, M. and Rowthorn, R. (eds) (1992) *Social Corporatism: A Superior Economic System?*, Oxford: Oxford University Press.

Pohjola, M. (1992) 'Corporatism and wage bargaining', in J. Pekkarinen, M. Pohjola and R. Rowthorn (eds), *Social Corporatism: A Superior Economic System?*, Oxford: Oxford University Press.

Rowthorn, R. (1992) 'Centralisation, employment and wage dispersion', *Economic Journal*, 102 (412): 506–23.

—— and Glyn, A. (1990) 'The diversity of unemployment experience since 1973', in S. Marglin and J. Schor (eds), *The Golden Age of Capitalism*, Oxford: Oxford University Press.

Sawyer, M. (1976) 'Income distribution in OECD countries', *OECD Economic Outlook Occasional Studies*, July, Paris: OECD.

Geoff Harcourt: A Bibliography

ARTICLES, NOTES AND CHAPTERS IN BOOKS

1 (with D. Ironmonger) 'A pilot survey of personal savings', *Economic Record*, vol. 32, May 1956, pp. 106–18.

2 'The quantitative effect of basing company taxation on replacement costs', *Accounting Research*, vol. 9, January 1958, pp. 1–16.

3 'Pricing policies and inflation', *Economic Record*, vol. 35, April 1959, pp. 133–6.

4 (with A. D. Barton) 'Investment allowances for primary producers' *Australian Journal of Agricultural Economics*, vol. 3, December 1959, pp. 12–18.

5 (with J. W. Bennett) 'Taxation and business surplus', *Economic Record*, vol. 36, August 1960, pp. 425–8.

6 'Pricing policies and earning rates', *Economic Record*, vol. 37, June 1961, pp. 217–24.

7 'The payment of prisoners', *Australian Quarterly*, December 1961, pp. 86–9.

8 Review of W. E. G. Salter, *Productivity and Technical Change*, *Economic Record*, vol. 38, September 1962, pp. 388–94.

9 'Investment and initial allowances as fiscal devices', *Australian Accountant*, September 1962, pp. 473–7.

10 (with D. H. Whitehead) 'The world textile industry', ch. 13 of A. Hunter (ed.) *The Economics of Australian Industry*, Melbourne: Melbourne University Press, 1963, pp. 419–59.

11 'A simple Joan Robinson model of accumulation with one technique: a comment', *Osaka Economic Papers*, January 1963, pp. 24–8.

12 'Taxation and primary production', *Farm Policy*, March 1963, pp. 101–5.

13 'A critique of Mr Kaldor's model of income distribution and economic growth', *Australian Economic Papers*, vol. 2, June 1963, pp. 20–36.

14 (with R. L. Matthews) 'Company finance', ch. 9 of R. R. Hirst and R. H. Wallace (eds) *Studies in the Australian Capital Market*, Melbourne: F. W. Cheshire, 1964, pp. 377–424.

15 (with V. G. Massaro) 'A note on Mr Sraffa's sub-systems', *Economic Journal*, vol. 74, September 1964, pp. 715–22. Reprinted in French in G. Farcarello and P. de Cavergne (eds) *Une nouvelle approche en économie politique? Essais sur Sraffa*, Paris: Economica, 1977, pp. 53–61.

16 (with V. G. Massaro) 'Mr Sraffa's *Production of Commodities*', *Economic Record*, vol. 40, September 1964, pp. 442–54.

17 'Incomes policy and the measurement of profits', *Banker's Magazine*, December 1964, pp. 361–4.

18 'The accountant in a golden age', *Oxford Economic Papers*, vol. 17, March 1965, pp.66–80. Reprinted in R. H. Parker and G. C. Harcourt (eds) *Readings in the Concept and Measurement of Income*, Cambridge: Cambridge University Press, 1969, pp. 310–25.

19 'A two-sector model of the distribution of income and the level of employment in the short run', *Economic Record*, vol. 41, March 1965, pp. 103–17.

20 (with G. Whittington) 'The irrelevancy of the British differential profits tax: a comment', *Economic Journal*, vol. 75, June 1965, pp. 373–8.

21 'The measurement of the rate of profit and the bonus scheme for managers in the Soviet Union', *Oxford Economic Papers*, vol. 18, March 1966, pp. 58–63.

22 'Biases in empirical estimates of the elasticities of substitution of CES production functions', *Review of Economic Studies*, vol. 33, July 1966, pp. 227–33.

23 'Cash investment grants, corporation tax and pay-out ratios', *Bulletin of the Oxford University Institute of Economics and Statistics*, vol. 28, August 1966, pp. 163–79 and vol. 29, February 1967, pp. 87–93.

24 'Investment-decision criteria, capital-intensity and the choice of techniques', *Czechoslovak Economic Papers*, no. 9, 1967, pp. 65–91, and ch. 14 of J. T. Dunlop and N. P. Federenko (eds) *Planning and Markets*, New York: McGraw-Hill, 1969, pp. 190–216.

25 'Investment-decision criteria, investment incentives and the choice of technique', *Economic Journal*, vol. 78, March 1968, pp. 77–95.

26 'The macroeconomic implications of Christie Kurien's core sector model', in *The Relevance of the Social Sciences in Contemporary Asia*, World Student Christian Fellowship Federation, 1968, pp. 126–9.

27 'Some Cambridge controversies in the theory of capital', *Journal of Economic Literature*, vol. 7, June 1969, pp. 369–405. Reprinted in Italian in G. Nardozzi and V. Valli (eds) *Teori dello Sviluppo Economico*, Etas Kompass, 1971.

28 'A teaching model of the "Keynesian" system', *Keio Economic Studies*, vol. 6, no. 2, 1969, pp. 23–46.

29 'G. C. Harcourt's reply to Nell', *Journal of Economic Literature*, vol. 8, March 1970, pp. 44–5.

30 (with A. S. Watson and P. D. Praetz) 'The CET production frontier and estimates of supply response in Australian agriculture', *Economic Record*, vol. 46, December 1970, pp. 553–63.

31 (with A. S. Watson and P. D. Praetz) 'Reply to Powell and Gruen, and Byron', *Economic Record*, vol. 46, December 1970, pp. 574–5.

32 'G. C. Harcourt's reply to Ng', *Journal of Economic Literature*, vol. 9, March 1971, pp. 69–70.

33 'Las parábolos neoclásicas y la función agregade de producción', *Cuadernos de Económica*, June 1973, pp. 46–62.

34 'The rate of profits in equilibrium growth models', *Journal of Political Economy*, vol. 81, September–October 1973, pp. 1261–77. Reprinted in French in C. Berthomieu and J. Cartelier (eds) *Ricardians, Keynesians et Marxistes*, Nice: CORDES, 1974, pp. 51–75.

35 (with A. Asimakopulos) 'Proportionality and the neoclassical parables', *Southern Economic Journal*, vol. 40, March 1974, pp. 481–3.

36 'The Cambridge controversies: the afterglow', in M. Parkin and A. R. Nobay (eds) *Contemporary Issues in Economics*, Manchester: Manchester University Press, 1975, pp. 305–34. Reprinted in French as 'Les controverses cambridgiennes: après la tourmente', in G. Grellet (ed.) *Nouvelle critique de l'économie politique*, Paris: Calman, Levy, 1976, pp. 35–76.

37 'The social consequences of inflation', *Australian Accountant*, October 1974, pp. 520–8.

38 'Capital theory: much ado about something', *Thames Papers in Political Economy*, Autumn 1975, pp. 1–16. Spanish version, 'Las controversias de los economistas i un mar de irrelevancias?', *Económica*, 1974, pp. 27–53.

39 'Decline and rise: the revival of (classical) political economy', *Economic Record*, vol. 51, September 1975, pp. 339–56.

40 'Revival of political economy: a further comment', *Economic Record*, vol. 51, September 1975, pp. 368–71.

41 'The Cambridge controversies: old ways and new horizons – or dead end?' *Oxford Economic Papers*, vol. 28, March 1976, pp. 25–65.

42 (with P. Kenyon) 'Pricing and the investment decision', *Kyklos*, vol. 29, 29, fasc. 3, 1976, pp. 449–77.

43 'The theoretical and social significance of the Cambridge controversies in the theory of capital: an evaluation', *Revue d'Économie Politique*, vol. 87, 1977, pp. 191–215 Reprinted in J. Schwartz (ed.) *The Subtle Anatomy of Capitalism*, California: Goodyear, 1977, pp. 285–303.

44 'Eric Russell, 1921–77: a great Australian political economist' (the 1977 Newcastle Lecture in Political Economy) Research Report no. 36, pp. iii + 26.

45 'On theories and policies', ch. 4 of J. P. Nieuwenhuysen and P. J. Drake (eds) *Australian Economic Policy*, Melbourne: Melbourne University Press, 1977, pp. 40–52.

46 'Maurice Dobb 1900–1976', *Economic Record*, vol. 52, 1976, pp. 395–6.

47 'Eric Russell, 1921–77: a memoir', *Economic Record*, vol. 53, December 1977, pp. 467–74.

48 'Policy and responses for Australia', *Economic Papers*, No. 60, December 1978, pp. 61–69.

49 'The social science imperialists' (the 1978 Academy Lecture, November 1978), *Politics*, vol. 14, November 1979, pp. 243–51.

50 'Non-neoclassical capital theory', *World Development*, vol. 7, October 1979, pp. 923–32.

51 'Robinson, Joan', in David L. Sills (ed.) *International Encyclopedia of the Social Sciences, Biographical Supplement*, vol. 18, New York: The Free Press, 1979, pp. 663–71.

52 (with P. M. Kerr) 'The mixed economy', ch. 14 in J. North and P. Weller (eds) *Labor*, Sydney: Ian Novak, 1979, pp. 184–95.

53 'Discussion', *American Economic Review*, vol. 70, May 1980, pp. 27–8.

54 'A post-Keynesian development of the "Keynesian model"', ch. 9 of E. J. Nell (ed.) *Growth, Profits and Property: Essays in the Revival of Political Economy*, Cambridge: Cambridge University Press, 1980, pp. 151–64.

55 'Introduction to Symposium on Income Distribution', *Journal of Post Keynesian Economics*, vol. 4, Winter 1980–1, pp. 155–7.

56 'Marshall, Sraffa and Keynes: incompatible bedfellows?', *Eastern Economic Journal*, vol. 5, January 1981, pp. 39–50.

57 'Notes on an economic querist: G. L. S. Shackle', *Journal of Post Keynesian Economics*, vol. 4, Fall 1981, pp. 136–44. A longer version is the introduction to S. F. Frowen (ed.) *Unknowledge and Choice in Economics*, London: Macmillan, 1990, pp. xvii–xxvi.

58 'The Sraffian contribution: an evaluation', in I. Bradley and M. Howard (eds) *Classical and Marxian Political Economy: Essays in Honour of Ronald L. Meek*, London: Macmillan, 1982, pp. 255–75.

59 'Notes on the social limits to growth', *Economic Forum*, Summer 1981, pp. 1–8.

60 'An early post Keynesian: Lorie Tarshis (or: Tarshis on Tarshis by Harcourt), *Journal of Post Keynesian Economics*, vol. 4, Summer 1982, pp. 609–19.

61 'Reflections on the development of economics as a discipline' (the 1982 G. L. Wood Memorial Lecture, June 1982), published in *History of Political Economy*, vol. 14, no. 4, 1984, pp. 489–517.

62 'Making socialism in your own country' (the 1982 John Curtin Memorial Lecture, August 1982), pp. 28.

63 'Post Keynesianism: quite wrong and/or nothing new?', *Thames Papers in Political Economy*, Summer 1982, pp. 1–19, Reprinted as ch. 6 in P. Arestis and T. Skouras (eds) *Post Keynesian Economic Theory: A Challenge to Neo-classical Economics*, Brighton: Wheatsheaf, 1985.

64 Review of T. Balogh, *The Irrelevance of Conventional Economics*, *Social Alternatives*, vol. 3, March 1983, pp. 61–2.

65 'A man for all systems: talking to Kenneth Boulding', *Journal of Post Keynesian Economics*, vol. 5, Fall 1983, pp. 143–54.

66 'On Piero Sraffa's contributions to economics', in P. Groenewegen and J. Halevi (eds) *Altro Polo Italian Economics Past and Present*, Frederick May Foundation for Italian Studies, University of Sydney, 1983, pp. 117–28.

67 'Harcourt on Robinson', in H. W. Spiegel and W. J. Samuels (eds) *Contemporary Economists in Perspective*, Greenwich, CT: JAI Press, 1984, pp. 639–58.

68 'Keynes's college bursar view of investment', in J. A. Kregel (ed.) *Distribution, Effective Demand and International Economic Relations*, London: Macmillan, 1983, pp. 81–4.

69 Summary of discussion in G. D. N. Worswick and J. Trevithick (eds) *Keynes and the Modern World*, Cambridge: Cambridge University Press, 1983.

70 'The end of an era: Joan Robinson (1903–83) and Piero Sraffa (1898–1983)', *Journal of Post Keynesian Economics*, vol. 6, Spring 1984, pp. 466–9.

71 'John Hicks', in A. Kuper and J. Kuper (eds) *The Social Science Encyclopedia*, London: Routledge & Kegan Paul, 1985, pp. 355–6.

72 'Nicholas Kaldor', in A. Kuper and J. Kuper (eds) *The Social Science Encyclopedia*, London: Routledge & Kegan Paul, 1985, pp. 422–3.

73 'James Meade', in A. Kuper and J. Kuper (eds) *The Social Science Encyclopedia*, London: Routledge & Kegan Paul, 1985, pp. 422–3.

74 'Joan Robinson (1903–83)', in A. Kuper and J. Kuper (eds) *The Social Science Encyclopedia*, London: Routledge & Kegan Paul, 1985, p. 713.

75 'Piero Sraffa (1898–83)', in A. Kuper and J. Kuper (eds) *The Social Science Encyclopedia*, London: Routledge & Kegan Paul, 1985, p. 816.

76 'Foreword', *Cambridge Journal of Economics*, vol. 7, no. 3/4, September/December 1983, p. 209.

77 'A twentieth century eclectic: Richard Goodwin', *Journal of Post Keynesian Economics*, vol. 7, Spring 1985, pp. 410–21.

78 (with T. J. O'Shaughnessy) 'Keynes's unemployment equilibrium: some insights from Joan Robinson, Piero Sraffa and Richard Kahn', in G. C. Harcourt (ed.) *Keynes and His contemporaries: The Sixth and Centennial Keynes Seminar Held at the University of Kent at Canterbury 1983*, London: Macmillan, 1985, pp. 3–4.

79 'The influence of Piero Sraffa on the contributions of Joan Robinson to economic theory', *Supplement to the Economic Journal*, vol. 96, 1986, pp. 96–108.

80 (with M. H. I. Dore) 'A note on the taxation of exhaustible resources under oligopoly', *Economic Letters*, vol. 21, no. 1, May 1986, pp. 81–4.

81 'Bastard Keynesianism', in J. Eatwell, M. Milgate and P. Newman (eds) *The New Palgrave: A Dictionary of Economics*, vol. 1, London: Macmillan, 1987, pp. 203–4.

82 'Post-Keynesian Economics', in J. Eatwell, M. Milgate and P. Newman (eds) *The New Palgrave: A Dictionary of Economics*, vol. 3, London: Macmillan, 1987, pp. 924–8.

83 'Smithies, Arthur (1907–81)', in J. Eatwell, M. Milgate and P. Newman (eds) *The*

New Palgrave: A Dictionary of Economics, vol. 4, London: Macmillan, 1987, pp. 375–6.

84 'Reddaway, William Brian (born 1913)', *The New Palgrave: A Dictionary of Economics*, vol. 4, London: Macmillan, 1987, pp. 108–9.

85 'Theoretical methods and unfinished business', in D. A. Reese (ed.) *The Legacy of Keynes*, Nobel Conference XXII, San Francisco: Harper & Row 1987, pp. 1–22. Also in Portuguese, 'O legado de Keynes: métodos teóricos e assustos incabados', ch. 4 of E. J. Amedeo (ed.) *John M. Keynes: cinqüenta anos da teoria geral*, Rio de Janeiro: INPES/IPEA, 1989, pp. 45–62. A shorter version is reprinted as 'On Keynes's method in economic theory', in M. Sabastiani (ed.) *The Notion of Equilibrium in the Keynesian Theory*, Basingstoke: Macmillan, 1992), pp. 99–105.

86 'Comment arcos sobre o ensaio do Prof. Marglin', in E. J. Amadeo (ed.), *John M. Keynes: cinqüenta anos da teoria geral*, Rio de Janeiro: INPES/IPEA, 1989, pp. 119–22.

87 'Comment on Garegnani', in K. Bharadwaj and B. Schefold (eds) *Essays on Piero Sraffa*, London: Unwin Hyman, 1990, pp. 141–4.

88 (with O. F. Hamouda) 'Post Keynesianism: from criticism to coherence?', *Bulletin of Economic Research*, vol. 40, January 1988, pp. 1–33.

89 'Introduction', *Cambridge Journal of Economics*, vol. 12, 1988, pp. 1–5.

90 'Nicholas Kaldor, 12 May 1908–30 September 1986', *Economica*, vol. 55, May 1988, pp. 159–70.

91 'Robinson, Joan Violet (1903–1983)', in Lord Blake and C. S. Nichols (eds), *The Dictionary of National Biography, 1981–1985*, Oxford: Oxford University Press, 1990, pp. 346–7.

92 'Sraffa, Piero (1898–1983)', in Lord Blake and C. S. Nichols (eds) *The Dictionary of National Biography, 1981–1985*, Oxford: Oxford University Press, 1990, pp. 381–2.

93 (with G. Whittington) 'Income and capital', ch. 7 of J. Creedy (ed.) *Foundations of Economic Thought*, Oxford, Blackwell, 1990, pp. 186–211.

94 'On the contributions of Joan Robinson and Piero Sraffa to economic theory', ch. 3 of M. Berg (ed.) *Political Economy in the Twentieth Century*, New York and London, Philip Allan, 1990, pp. 35–67.

95 'Different approaches and uncomfortable critiques: Joan Robinson and the economics profession', *Cambridge Review*, vol. 111, no. 2308, March 1990, pp. 27–32.

96 'Joan Robinson's early views on method', *History of Political Economy*, vol. 22, no. 3, 1990, pp. 411–27.

97 (with B. McFarlane) 'Economic planning and democracy', *Australian Journal of Political Science*, vol. 25, November 1990, pp. 326–32.

98 'R. F. Kahn: a tribute', *Banco Nazionale del Lavoro Quarterly Review*, vol. 176, March 1991, pp. 15–30.

99 Review of Turner, M. S., *Joan Robinson and the Americans*, and Feiwel, G.R. (ed.) *Joan Robinson and Modern Economic Theory* vol. 1 and *The Economics of Imperfect Competition and Employment: Joan Robinson and Beyond* (vol. 2), *History of Political Economy*, vol. 23, Spring 1991, pp. 158–64.

100 'Marshall's *Principles* as seen at Cambridge through the eyes of Gerald Shove, Dennis Robertson and Joan Robinson', in M. Dardi, M. Callegati and E. Pesciarelli (eds) *Alfred Marshall's 'Principles of Economics'*, 1890–1990: vol. 1, *Quaderni di storia dell economia politica*, vol. 9, 1991, pp. 355–72.

101 'Athanasios (Tom) Asimakopulos, 28 May 1930 – 25 May 1990: a memoir', *Journal of Post Keynesian Economics*, vol. 14, no. 1, Fall 1991, pp. 39–48.

102 'Joan Robinson', in T. Bottomore (ed.) *A Dictionary of Marxist Thought*, 2nd edition, Oxford: Blackwell, 1991, pp. 483–4.

103 'G. C. Harcourt (born 1931)', in P. Arestis and M. Sawyer (eds) *A biographical Dictionary of Dissenting Economists*, Aldershot: Edward Elgar, 1992, pp. 232–41.

104 'Joan Robinson (1903–1983)', in P. Arestis and M. Sawyer (eds), *A Biographical Dictionary of Dissenting Economists*, Aldershot: Edward Elgar, 1992, pp. 454–63.

105 (with A. Singh) 'Sukhamoy Chakravarty, 26 July, 1934 – 22 August 1990', *Cambridge Journal of Economics*, vol. 15, 1991, pp. 1–3.

106 (with B. J. McFarlane) 'A reply to Osiatynski', *Australian Journal of Political Science*, vol. 26, no. 3, November 1991, pp. 355–6.

107 'Markets, madness and a middle way', *The Second Annual Donald Horne Address*, Melbourne, 1992, also published in *Australian Quarterly*, vol. 64, no. 1, pp. 1–17 and, in a revised edition, in 'Viewpoint', *Cambridge Review*, vol. 14, no. 2320, February 1993, pp. 40–5.

108 'Kahn, Richard [Ferdinand], Baron Kahn of Hampstead (1905–1989)', *DNB* (forthcoming).

109 'A post Keynesian comment', *Methodus*, vol. 4, no. 1, June 1992, p. 30.

110 'Kahn and Keynes and the making of *The General Theory*', *Cambridge Journal of Economics*, vol. 17, February 1994, pp. 11–23.

111 'Is Keynes dead?', *History of Economics Review*, no. 18, Summer 1992, pp. 1–9.

112 'George Shackle: a tribute', *Review of Political Economy*, vol. 5, no. 2, 1993, pp. 272–3.

113 (with J. A. T. R. Araujo) 'Maurice Dobb, Joan Robinson and Gerald Shove on accumulation and the rate of profits', *Journal of the History of Economic Thought*, 15, Spring 1993, pp. 1–30.

114 'A Large G & T', *ALR*, no. 148, March 1993, pp. 34–6. A longer version was published as 'Macroeconomic policy for Australia in the 1990s', in *Economic and Labour Relations Review*, vol. 4, no. 2, December 1993, pp. 167–75.

115 'Reply to Gerard Henderson and Ross Gittins', *Australian Quarterly*, vol. 64, no. 4, Summer 1992, pp. 463–4.

116 'The Harcourt plan to "save" the world', *At the Margin*, issue 1, Lent 1993, pp. 2–5.

117 'John Maynard Keynes, 1883–1946', ch. 6 of R. V. Mason (ed) *Cambridge Minds*, Cambridge: Cambridge University Press, 1994, pp. 72–85.

118 'On mathematics and economics', to be published in a volume of the Science and Human Dimension Conference, 'Mathematics: what should non-mathematicians know?' to be edited by J. Cornwell and published by Cambridge University Press. Published in Harcourt, G. C., *Capitalism, Socialism and Post-Keynesianism: Selected Essays of G. C. Harcourt*, Cheltenham: Edward Elgar, 1995, pp. 201–17.

119 'What Adam Smith really said', *Economic Review*, vol. 12, no. 2, November 1994, pp. 24–7.

120 (with A. Hughes and A. Singh) 'Austin Robinson, 20 November 1897 – 1 June 1993: an appreciation', *Cambridge Journal of Economics*, vol. 17, no. 4, December 1993, pp. 365–8.

121 (with M. Kitson) 'Fifty years of measurements: a Cambridge view', *Review of Income and Wealth*, series 39, no. 4, December 1993, pp. 435–47.

122 'What Josef Steindl means to my generation', *Review of Political Economy, Josef Steindl Memorial Issue*, vol. 6, no. 4, 1994, pp. 459–63.

123 'Krishna Bharadwaj, 21 August 1935 – 8 March 1992: a memoir', *Journal of Post*

Keynesian Economics, Winter 1993–4, vol. 16, no. 2, pp. 299–311.

124 'Josef Steindl, 14 April 1912–7 March 1993: a tribute', *Journal of Post Keynesian Economics*, Summer 1994, vol. 16, no. 4, pp. 627–42.

125 'The capital theory controversies', in P. Arestis and M. Sawyer (eds) *The Elgar Companion to Radical Political Economy*, Aldershot: Edward Elgar, 1994, pp. 29–34.

126 'The structure of Tom Asimakopulos's later writings', in G. Harcourt, A. Roncaglia and R. Rowley (eds) *Income and Employment in Theory and Practice*, London: Macmillan, 1994, pp. 1–16.

127 (with C. Sardoni) 'George Shackle and post Keynesianism', to be published in S. Boehm, S. F. Frowen and J. Pheby (eds) *Economics as the Art of Thought: Essays in Memory of G. L. S. Shackle*, (London: Routledge, forthcoming).

128 (with Claudio Sardoni) 'Keynes's vision: method, analysis and "Tactics"', in J. Davis (ed.) *The State of Interpretation of Keynes*, Norwell, MA: Kluwer, pp. 131–52.

129 (with Gabriel Palma) 'Introduction', *Cambridge Journal of Economics*, vol. 18, February 1994, pp. 1–2.

130 "Keynes, John Maynard', in G. Hodgson, W. J. Samuels and M. R. Tool (eds) *The Elgar Companion to Institutional and Evolutionary Economics A–K*, Aldershot: Edward Elgar, 1994, pp. 442–4.

131 'Robinson, Joan', in G. Hodgson, W. J. Samuels and M. R. tool (eds) *The Elgar Companion to Institutional and Evolutionary Economics L–Z*, Aldershot: Edward Elgar, 1994, pp. 442–6.

132 'Comment', in H. G. Brennan and A. M. C. Waterman (eds) *Economics and Religion: Are They Distinct?*, Boston, Dordrecht and London: Kluwer, 1994, pp. 205–12.

133 'Taming speculators and putting the world on course to prosperity: a "Modest Proposal"', *Economic and Political Weekly*, vol. 29, 17 September, 1994, pp. 2490–2.

134 'Joan Robinson, 1903–83', *Economic Journal*, vol. 105, September 1995, pp. 1228–43.

135 'Lorie Tarshis, 1911–1993: in appreciation', *Economic Journal*, vol. 105, September 1995, pp. 1244–55.

136 'Recollections and reflections of an Australian patriot and a Cambridge economist', *Banco Nazionale del Lavoro Quarterly Review*, vol. 48, September 1995, pp. 225–54. (Also in Italian: *Moneto e Credito*, vol. 48, September 1995, pp. 299–329).

137 'Some reflections on Joan Robinson's changes of mind and their relationship to post-Keynesianism and the economics profession', ch. 26 of M. C. Marcuzzo, L. L. Pasinetti and A. Roncaglia (eds) *The Economics of Joan Robinson*, London: Routledge, 1996, pp. 317–29.

BOOKS

1 (with P. H. Karmel and R. H. Wallace) *Economic Activity*, Cambridge: Cambridge University Press, 1967. Italian edition 1969.

2 (With R. H. Parker, eds) *Readings in the Concept and Measurement of Income*, Cambridge: Cambridge University Press, 1969. Second edition, with G. Whittington, Oxford: Philip Allan, 1986.

3 (with N. F. Laing, eds) *Capital and Growth: Selected Readings*, London: Penguin, 1971, reprinted 1973. Spanish edition 1977.

4 *Some Cambridge Controversies in the Theory of Capital*, Cambridge: Cambridge University Press, 1972. Italian edition 1973: Polish edition 1975; Spanish edition 1975; Japanese edition 1980. Reprinted, Gregg Revivals Series, ed. M. Blaug, 1991.

5 *Theoretical Controversy and Social Significance: An Evaluation of the Cambridge Controversies*, Edward Shann Memorial Lecture. University of Western Australian Press, 1975.

6 (ed.) *The Microeconomic Foundations of Macroeconomics*, London: Macmillan, 1977.

7 *The Social Science Imperialists. Selected Essays by G. C. Harcourt*, Ed. P. Kerr, London: Routledge & Kegan Paul, 1982.

8 (ed.) *Keynes and His Contemporaries: The Sixth and Centennial Keynes Seminar Held in the University of Kent at Canterbury 1983*, London: Macmillan, 1985, vi + 195 pp.

9 (with R. H. Parker and G. Whittington, eds) *Readings in the Concept and Measurement of Income*, 2nd edition, Oxford: Philip Allan, 1986, vii + 371 pp.

10 (with Jon Cohen, eds) *International Monetary Problems and Supply-Side Economics: Essays in Honour of Lorie Tarshis*, London: Macmillan, 1986, viii + 162 pp.
Controversies in Political Economy: Selected Essays by G. C. Harcourt, edited O. F. Hamouda, Brighton: Wheatsheaf, 1986, 293 pp.

12 *On Political Economists and Modern Political Economy: Selected Essays of G. C. Harcourt*, ed. C. Sardoni, London: Routledge, 1992.

13 *Post-Keynesian Essays in Biography: Portraits of Twentieth Century Political Economists*, Basingstoke: Macmillan, 1993.

14 (with M. Baranzini, eds) *The Dynamics of the Wealth of Nations: Growth, Distribution and Structural Change. Essays in Honour of Luigi Pasinetti*, Basingstoke: Macmillan, 1993.

15 (with A. Roncaglia and R. Rowley, eds) *Income and Employment in Theory and Practice*, Basingstoke: Macmillan, 1994.

16 *Capitalism, Socialism and Post Keynesianism: Selected Essays of G. C. Harcourt*, Cheltenham: Edward Elgar, 1995.

FORTHCOMING

1 (with C. Sardoni) 'George Shackle and post Keynesianism', in S. Boehm, S. F. Fowen and J. Pheby (eds) *Economics as the Art of Thought: Essays in Memory of G. L. S. Shackle*, London: Routledge.

2 (with P. Riach (eds)) *A 'Second Edition' of The General Theory*, London: Routledge.

3 (with P. M. Kerr) 'Marx, Karl Heinrich (1818–1883)', in M. Warner (ed.) *International Encyclopedia of Business and Management*, London: Routledge.

4 (with W. Bradford) 'Units and definitions', chapter in G. C. Harcourt and P. Riach (eds) *A 'Second Edition' of The General Theory*, London: Routledge.

5 (with P. Riach) 'Introduction' to G. C. Harcourt an P. Riach (eds) *A 'Second Edition' of The General Theory*, London: Routledge.

6 'How I do economics', chapter in S. G. Medema and W. G. Samuels (eds) *Exploring the Foundations of Research in Economics: How Should Economists Do Economics?*, Cheltenham: Edward Elgar.

7 Entry on 'John Maynard Keynes', in T. Cate *et al.* (eds) *The Encyclopedia of Keynesian Economics*, Cheltenham: Edward Elgar.

8   (with D. Spajic) 'The post-Keynesian school' in C. Sardoni (ed.) volume on Economics in *Storia de XX Secolo*, rome: Istituto della Enciclopedia Italiana, 40 pp.

Index